PSYCHOLOGY
FOR
EFFECTIVE
TEACHING

SECOND EDITION

GEORGE J. MOULY

University of Miami

HOLT, RINEHART AND WINSTON, INC.
Atlanta Dallas Montreal Toronto London
New York Chicago San Francisco

122771

Preface

A number of developments of major psychological significance have occurred since the publication of the first edition. Although some of these are still in the "proving" stages, many are bound to have considerable impact upon educational theory and practice. The newer concept of capacity as something one develops through interaction with the environment, for example, as evidenced by the McGill studies and Harlow's "learning how to learn," presents a totally new picture of human potential, a picture of relatively unlimited educational, psychological, and sociological import. The realization of the crucial role of early experience upon every aspect of development is particularly important. Guilford's multi-dimensional structure of the intellect provides a broader perspective of human capacity, particularly as it relates to the current interest in creativity. The greater emphasis on the self-concept and self-actualization provides an equally positive complementary view of human potentiality for growth; along with the newer stimulation theories of motivation, they provide a challenging view of human striving, especially for an affluent society where freedom from hunger and threat of physical harm makes self-fulfillment evermore possible and necessary. Also of direct relevance are the recent advances in the clarification of the mechanism of heredity, the greater recognition of the work of Piaget, and newer emphasis on proactive inhibition as a factor in forgetting, and further progress in the implementation of "experimental" curricula and in the development and use of various technological instructional media.

These recent developments have focused on the need for a reconsideration of all aspects of the education of the modern child. The greater realization of the crucial role of environmental influences on development, for example, places greater responsibility upon the shoulders of parents and teachers and emphasizes the need to consider the dynamic totality of the situation in which the child operates. A course in educational psychology must reflect these newer viewpoints; it must provide an introduction to the new frontiers which the greater orientation of psychologists and educators toward research and the greater availability of research monies are bound to promote.

The school is undergoing significant changes. Along with the current emphasis on quality education, we are at last recognizing, for example, that intellectual and academic retardation are not inevitable concomitants of membership in the lower socioeconomic classes. We are also recognizing that, with our rapidly moving world, knowledge in the traditional sense of so much content is no longer enough—that the goals of the modern school might better be defined in terms of the development of efficient modes of attack, the cultivation of resourcefulness, and "learning how to learn" than in terms of the accumulation of facts for examination purposes. All aspects of the school's operation must reflect this new orientation. If the modern school aspires to promote the maximum development of children, it must not forget that the true worth of the individual is measured not so much by what he knows as by the kind of person he is. If we believe that [a] knowledge comes easy to the child whose security permits full openness to experience, [b] his most fundamental characteristic is an inborn capacity for growth, and [c] he always acts in his best interest *as he perceives the situation,* then perhaps our task is primarily that of promoting his security so as to allow for more adequate perception of reality. The child's personal and social adjustment then becomes both a goal in itself and an essential condition for the achievement of the many objectives of the school and of the society the school is to serve.

The purpose of a course in educational psychology as part of the teacher-education sequence is to provide the student with insights into those psychological principles upon which effective classroom practice can be based. Indeed, the effectiveness of American education revolves in considerable measure upon the adequacy of the teaching of educational psychology, a point recognized by Conant in his recent analysis of teacher-education. If it is to contribute to this end, educational psychology must provide the prospective teacher with a thorough grasp of the basic facts, principles, theories, and viewpoints of psychology having a bearing on the successful operation of the classroom in all its implications. These, in turn, must have a sound basis in research, logic, and other systematic approaches to dependable knowledge.

A text in educational psychology must orient the student toward this knowledge while, at the same time, emphasizing its empirical and theoretical origin as a means of clarifying its validity status and the theoretical perspective from which it is to be appraised. It must introduce research as the primary source of answers to classroom problems and science as the process of the evolvement of evermore precise and dependable answers. However, it must also emphasize the tentativeness of scientific generalizations—especially those of psychology where the complexity of human nature makes for numerous gaps, inconsistencies, and the possibility of alternative interpretations—and especially the fact that even rigorous research findings do not lead directly to unequivocal pedagogical prescriptions. At the same time, while avoiding the frills and the fantastic, it must boldly orient itself toward the novel and the unproven in a spirit of innovation.

A certain degree of simplicity is in order in any introductory text. Certainly a deliberate attempt should be made to keep the style of writing clear and direct and to minimize complex discussion of the finer points of distinction which have no functional relationship to the work of the school. On the other hand, the treatment must not do violence to the natural complexity of human behavior. Rather it must provide a sound basis for effective operation in the classroom and a firm foundation for more advanced work in the field.

The vastness of the amount of psychological material bearing upon the work of the teacher makes it imperative that one be highly selective in choosing the content to be included in an introductory text. The primary criterion in this selectivity should undoubtedly be its functionality from the standpoint of dealing with youngsters in dynamic interaction with their environment—at school, at home, in their community. On the other hand, functionality is not to be equated with practicality at the level of rules of thumb to be applied mechanically and routinely; neither can it be conceived as a matter of providing a specific answer for each specific problem to be encountered in the classroom. On the contrary, the prospective teacher must be provided with broad principles and an overall theoretical perspective which will not only educe meaningfulness out of the confusion of otherwise unorganized facts but will also enable the teacher to deal with insight with the myriad situations which inevitably characterize imaginative teaching.

The question of theoretical orientation can also be troublesome. The matter is one of preference in which bias in the interpretation of content and the perspective from which it is presented cannot be avoided. Whereas a single-channel approach, if one were available, might be comfortable, the present lack of unanimity in theoretical position makes the choice of one theory over the others ill-advised, especially in an introductory (and presumably exploratory) text. None of the present theories commands obvious priority over the others, nor can a single theoretical formulation, as presently developed, be considered adequate to cope with the diversity of situations arising in the classroom. As a consequence, an eclectic position might compensate through greater functionality and perhaps through greater accuracy in the picture it presents for whatever anguish its lack of theoretical consistency might cause the theoretical purist. The question is of greater concern to the psychologist than to the teacher who is more likely to wonder why we should deprive ourselves of the insights provided by Skinner or Rogers just because they are not derived from identical premises; who might question the price to be paid by sacrificing one or the other at the altar of monistically defined consistency. This is not to deny the desirability of the eventual resolution of differences among theories and the derivation of definitive educational implications. A brief overview of the various theories has been presented; the clarification of issues and points of conflict can be pursued further in a more advanced course. In the meantime, the instructor might wish to suggest alternative interpretations as well as emphasize the premises and assumptions from which the presentation of the text has been undertaken.

The author believes that no theoretical position can be more functional from the standpoint of the classroom teacher than that emphasizing the purposiveness of behavior. Not only does such a position appear sound from an empirical as well as a theoretical point of view but it also puts vitality and meaning into the task of guiding the growth and development of children. It is a position which is challenging and interesting to prospective teachers who see its applicability in both the classroom and everyday living. The present text is organized around the dynamics of human behavior as its central theme; one of its major aims is to provide, not specific rules and prescriptions, but rather viewpoints and professional insights into the motivational structure of children, individually and collectively, within the framework of the field forces of the situation in which they operate and into the procedures by means of which maximum self-realization and self-fulfillment can be promoted. The book has evolved from the author's teaching of undergraduate and graduate classes in educational psychology over the past eighteen years. His experience in dealing with teachers and prospective teachers both in college classes and in the field, as well as his own experience in teaching at every level of public school and college, has convinced him of the need for giving teachers a better understanding of the *why* of human behavior.

Each chapter contains a list of exercises and supplementary readings selected to complement the material presented. These, for the most part, have been tried in actual classes and found effective in rounding out the student's grasp of educational psychology. It is expected that the student will use the reference material in keeping with his individual needs and goals. It is also expected that the textbook material will be supplemented by classroom visits, films, and other direct and indirect contacts with children.

Although the text is the work of a single author, many persons have contributed directly or indirectly to its completion. Many have been cited in the references; to them and their publishers, the author expresses his appreciation. Special thanks go to colleagues, former students, and others whose criticisms of the first edition have been most helpful.

G. J. M.

December 1967
Coral Gables, Florida

Contents

PSYCHOLOGY
FOR
EFFECTIVE
TEACHING

PART I

Psychology: The Science of Behavior

Presents the scientific foundation upon which educational practice must rest and the perspective from which the child is to be approached if educators are to be effective in guiding him toward self-fulfillment. The motivation of human behavior—as introduced in Chapters 3 and 4—constitutes the heart of the book.

CHAPTER 1

Emphasizes the importance of psychological insights to effectiveness of educational practice and provides an orientation to promising possibilities highlighted by recent advances in psychology.

CHAPTER 2

Provides a number of theoretical perspectives from which psychological data can be interpreted as the basis for devising promising classroom procedures and for evaluating pedagogical practice.

CHAPTER 3

Presents the all-important concept of motivation from the standpoint of both drive-reduction and stimulation theories and gives consideration to relevant research evidence and its interpretation; emphasizes the fact that behavior is purposive and that the individual learns to satisfy his needs in a given way; pays special attention to early experiences (especially child-rearing experiences) in the development of the individual's basic personality.

CHAPTER 4

Introduces the self-concept as the focus of just who and what the individual is and emphasizes the phenomenological nature of perception through which the individual maintains and protects the self. The basic premise is that behavior is consistent with the individual's perception of the situation and that any attempt to change behavior must, therefore, operate through the development of more adequate insight.

Presents openness to experience as the key to self-actualization; describes how, under conditions of stress, the individual closes off his experiences and consequently becomes incapable of constructive action. In contrast, the self-actualizing person makes optimal utilization of his potentialities and environmental opportunities.

CHAPTER I

Psychology
and the Teacher

The purpose of educational psychology is to help teachers and prospective teachers develop a better understanding of educational processes.

Lindgren, 1962, p. 3

The status of any profession is determined in large measure by the quality of the professional services it provides. These services, in turn, depend upon the quality of the insights and understandings on which professional decisions are based. Teaching has come a long way in establishing itself as a profession, but if its true importance and dignity is to be recognized, teachers must continue to improve the professional skills with which they guide student growth and development. They can do this only if they have a thorough understanding of the principles of educational psychology, for these principles provide the only sound basis for effective teaching.

EDUCATIONAL PSYCHOLOGY:
A BRANCH OF PSYCHOLOGY

To the extent that psychology deals with the study of behavior, it must necessarily supply the major part of the scientific foundation for educational practice. In fact, psychology can contribute to every aspect of educational practice through the clarification of the nature of the learner, of the learning process, and of the role of the teacher. Fortunately, psychologists in recent years have discovered much information which has a specific as well as a general bearing on the broad field of education. Rogers (1956, 1961), for example, points to the implications of recent advances in the prediction and control of behavior. We know how to provide in the classroom the psychological conditions that will promote not only efficient learning of academic content but improved personal adjustment as well. We can predict that Home A, in all probability, will produce children who, intellectually, will grow somewhat brighter over the years, who will be emotionally secure, original, and relatively unexcitable, who will be popular with their peers and likely to be leaders; at the same time, we can predict that Home B is likely to produce excitable children who will be relatively lacking in emotional control and originality. We also know how to set up conditions under which people will report judgments that are contrary to the evidence of their senses. Furthermore, these phenomena make psychological sense: Individuals whose perceptions are swayed by majority opinion tend to be persons who have little understanding of themselves, who are defensive, who have to put up a good front, who are rigid and moralistic, and who have a great respect for authority. They are somewhat anxious, guilty, suggestible, and lacking in ability to tolerate ambiguity; they lack self-confidence, are vacillating, and tend to get confused under stress. Rogers sounds the optimistic note that, in the near future, knowledge in psychology will be exploited as fully as knowledge in the physical sciences is today. In fact, psychology has so many diverse possibilities for the control and prediction of behavior that Oppenheimer (1956) suggests that the powerful control that will be made available will pose far graver problems than any with which physicists have had to cope.

Educational psychology is only one of many branches of applied psychology, each attempting to pinpoint the applications of psychology to a specific area. Educational psychology is concerned with the application of the principles, techniques, and other resources of psychology to the solution of the problems confronting the teacher as he attempts to direct the growth of children toward worthy objectives. It selects from the total field of psychology those facts, those principles, and those techniques which relate to aspects of child growth and development as they operate both in and out of the classroom. Its contribution to teacher education is directly proportional to the extent to which it maintains contact with both the general field of psychology and educational practice. More specifically, educational psychology is concerned with an understanding of [a] the child—his development, his needs, and his individual peculiarities; [b] the learning situation—including group dynamics as they affect learning; and [c] the process by which learning can be made more effective. Stated differently, the central theme of educational psychology is the psychology of learning, with the term *learning* used in the broad sense of change in behavior.

The boundaries of educational psychology are constantly undergoing modification as newer emphases are placed on the various aspects of teacher preparation and the role it is expected to play in teacher-education programs. Furthermore, because boundaries are loosely defined, there is considerable overlapping between what might be considered educational psychology, on the one hand, and what is generally thought of as clinical psychology, social psychology, experimental psychology, and even sociology, human relations, anthropology, physiology, neurology, genetics, and psychiatry, on the other. This lack of clear-cut boundaries among the various areas of psychology and its related fields has also resulted in considerable disparity as to what is generally included in educational psychology. Most modern writers concentrate on such topics as growth and development, learning, and adjustment, but there is wide variation in the relative emphasis and treatment given such topics, and even greater variation in the relative inclusion (or exclusion) of such fringe topics as grading and reporting, statistics, and individual differences.

This lack of agreement is both understandable and desirable, for educational psychology is concerned with the utilization of whatever resources psychology and related disciplines have to contribute to the solution of educational problems. It cannot afford to refrain from stepping into what might be considered the province of other disciplines. Matters of boundary become relatively inconsequential in the light of the task of acquainting prospective teachers with whatever will help them most in understanding and in dealing with children—in and out of the classroom. In practice it is impossible to cover all that is important, and it becomes necessary for instructors and authors to select those phases of the total which, in their judgment, will be most helpful. That they do not agree entirely is to be expected in view of what they want to accomplish and of what they feel can be covered in other courses.

SOURCES OF DATA
OF EDUCATIONAL PSYCHOLOGY

Educational psychology derives its data from sources that range from the relatively objective and scientific to the highly subjective, if not intuitive. Unfortunately, except for the latter category, too little of the educational psychology data has been discovered by the classroom teacher who is in actual contact with the youngsters to whom these data are to apply.

Too often, the teacher's preparation has been oriented toward *methods*, to the neglect of training in child psychology and research methods, to such an extent that he has neither a theoretical nor a procedural framework from which to investigate better ways of dealing with children. Besides, his busy schedule often allows for nothing more than routine teaching. Too frequently the classroom teacher goes on solving vital problems on the basis of common sense while, at higher levels, college professors write articles in professional journals (which teachers do not read) on problems teachers do not have.

Educational Experimentation

Foremost among the sources of the data of educational psychology is experimentation; many of the current classroom practices, e.g., the emphasis on periodic review to promote retention, have a relatively sound empirical basis in scientific experimentation either carried out in the actual classroom setting or under conditions of strict control in the laboratory. Experimentation, whether in education or in any other field, rests on the assumption that there exist invariant relationships between certain antecedents and certain consequents so that, provided a given set of conditions prevails, if one does *this, that* will follow.

Thus, if an object is thrown out of the window of a tall building it will fall down with accelerating speed. This would be as true today and tomorrow as it was yesterday, as true in Brooklyn as in Kalamazoo or Timbuctu. That such invariance in time and space should exist seems logical since denying its existence would mean subscribing to a view that all is chaotic and unpredictable. Yet at times exceptions occur: many a farmer has seen his hat fly upward in a twister and been thankful it was not his barn. In such cases, it is obvious that certain unusual conditions have acted to overcome the law of gravity, and that the law of gravity still expresses a relationship which is quite valid provided we state the conditions to which its validity is restricted. Experimentation in education has likewise produced a number of generalizations, principles, and laws which are valid *under certain stated conditions.* The beginning student in educational psychology who looks for quick answers is likely to be frustrated at the number of contradictions he will find in regard to a given problem. Thus, one investigator finds Method A superior to Method B with regard to a given outcome while a second investigator finds Method B superior to Method A. The apparent contradiction can, of course, be explained in terms of differences in the conditions under which each of the conclusions was reached. Whereas a certain method of study might be superior to another for children in the primary grades, for instance, the reverse might be true for high school seniors. Similarly, one needs to be cautious about applying to the classroom the results of laboratory experimentation and, for that matter, about transplanting any educational results from one situation to another.

In its simplest case, experimentation as a scientific procedure revolves around the fulfillment of the conditions of Mill's Canon of Difference (1873):

> If an instance in which the phenomenon under investigation occurs, and an instance in which it does not occur have every circumstance in common save one, that one occurring only in the former, the circumstance in which alone the two instances differ is the effect, or the cause, or an indispensable part of the cause, of the phenomenon. [p. 452]

Thus, in an experiment, the investigator tries to have a *control* group which is identical in all relevant respects to the *experimental* group except for the one factor under study. Failure to establish equivalence between the two groups would, of course, tend to make for erroneous conclusions. If Group A is more highly motivated than Group B, for example, it might make greater progress even while using an inferior method of study.

Because educational psychology has to deal with children and material infinitely more complex from the standpoint of interaction than that studied by the chemist, for example, it is often difficult to establish rigorous equivalence of the two groups—hence, the correspondingly greater danger of erroneous conclusions and greater likelihood of conflict. For that reason, psychologists sometimes prefer the laboratory where they can exert greater control on the variables of the situation. However, to the extent that this greater control represents a departure from the actual situation to be found in the classroom, the conclusions may apply only to the situation in which they were derived—the laboratory setting. They may provide the investigator with hypotheses as to what is likely to occur in the classroom, but these would have to be verified under actual classroom conditions before they could be accepted with confidence by the teacher.

Probably none of the variables is more troublesome from the standpoint of scientific control than the interaction of teacher characteristics and the "inherent" effectiveness of a given method. Thus, a teacher may find a certain method suited to his personality, his style of teaching, and/or the nature of his classes, even though it may have serious limitations for the average teacher. In other words, the teacher's personality, his competencies, etc., as well as the nature of the students being taught and the objectives being sought, constitute variables that have to be considered in generalizing about whether one method or another is more effective. The question to be answered is not, "Which is the more effective of two methods?" but rather, "Which is more effective for whom and under what conditions?" Thus, even though method is subject to scientific law, the choice among methods must often be made on a personal rather than a general basis. In fact, often the teacher will not really know what is best and need not be ashamed to admit it. There is probably not a single best method. The important thing is that we continue to make progress in our search for more effective ways of fulfilling our many responsibilities.

OTHER SOURCES OF DATA

Not only has experimentation in the field of education produced conflicting results, but it is also true that many problems the teacher faces are of such a nature that they cannot, at least for the present, be subjected to experimentation. As a consequence, much of what goes on in the classroom is based on nothing more substantial than general consensus or even personal experience and opinion that such a procedure is generally effective or that such and such is taking place. Much of our knowledge of the child has likewise been derived through methods that are essentially *clinical*, if not casual, in nature.

One of the most subjective of the sources of data in educational psychology, and also one of the most frequently used, is observation; in fact, it is often the only means whereby certain information can be obtained. The alert teacher, for instance, is bound to notice that certain techniques are generally effective, that children of a certain age display certain behavioral tendencies. As a result of their experience, teachers often adopt a personal framework on the basis of which they attempt to understand children and their behavior. A teacher may believe, for example, that acceleration—or retardation, or ability grouping—is detrimental to the maximum growth of the child. Unfortunately, observation is subject to considerable error, and unless he is trained to make his observations objective and scientific, a person may be led to erroneous generalizations. There is, for instance, a danger of slanting observations to fit preconceived theories and to note only those instances which are in agreement with one's viewpoint.

Another important source of the data of educational psychology involves questionnaires, inventories, scales (including sociometric techniques), tests, and other instruments by means of which the status, and often the growth, of children can be determined. Some of these, such as measures of height and weight used in establishing physical growth norms, can be very accurate. Others, such as questionnaires relating to attitudes or motivation are less dependable, although nevertheless still useful in providing insights into human behavior. Somewhere between these two extremes lie tests of intelligence and achievement which, despite their imperfections, not only yield information useful in dealing with children as individuals, but also permit research on a variety of educational and psychological problems; intelligence tests, for example, besides having served as the basis for identifying the pattern of mental growth and clarifying some of the problems involved in other phases of child development, e.g., academic progress, have also enabled us to carry out experimentation in the relative effectiveness of teaching methods.

These are the major sources from which we have accumulated the creditable body of data which provides the psychological foundation for educational practice. There are still gaps in our knowledge; in fact, we are lacking not only the answers to many of our problems, but also the techniques and tools whereby the answers can be obtained. Particularly lacking in the establishment of education as a science is a unifying theory, such as that found in the physical and biological sciences, which would provide both the basis for interpreting the data obtained from research and a framework to guide our efforts in the discovery of new data. Actually, a number of relatively complete and self-consistent theories have been advanced, each attempting to provide a theoretical framework from which the empirical data of educational psychology can be placed into meaningful perspective. Whereas some theories appear to provide a more logical explanation of some of the data than others, none in its present form is completely satisfactory. Chapter 2 will present a brief overview of the major theories to provide perspective for the position from which the various topics have been approached in the present text.

GAINS TO BE EXPECTED FROM THE COURSE

PURPOSE OF EDUCATIONAL PSYCHOLOGY

The placement of any learning experience in the curriculum implies that such an experience can be of major benefit to the student. Consequently, although it might be difficult to list the specific gains to be derived from a course in educational psychology, considering the lack of uniformity in nature, content, and scope, it would nevertheless be well to explore its potential role in the preparation of teachers—and indirectly in the education of children.[1]

The school is often blamed for whatever goes wrong in society—delinquency, divorce, and even a failure in the national space program. Whatever their validity, these criticisms are not aimed primarily at educational psychology; it is not the function of educational psychology to define the goals for which we ought to strive. Thus, whether the goal of the school is to indoctrinate children into various social ideologies, to turn them into small adults, or to let them be carefree youngsters, this is an issue to be resolved on the basis of the philosophical viewpoint of the social order. And from the time of Plato and, later, Rousseau, we

---

[1] The most adequate formulations of educational objectives are probably those of Bloom (ed.) (cognitive domain, 1956) and Krathwohl et al. (affective domain, 1964). See also Gagné (1965) and Lindvall (1964).

have had people expound philosophical positions to which they insisted the education of youth should subscribe.

Educational psychology is concerned more with the discovery of techniques by means of which we can attain most effectively whatever educational goals we have selected than with their actual selection. It can, of course, lead to a reconsideration of specific goals by demonstrating that they are impractical or unattainable, or that the procedures and techniques by means of which they are allegedly to be attained are based on theoretical considerations that violate accepted psychological principles. For example, whereas most people agree on academic excellence as a worthy educational objective, educators would question whether excellence is to be attained by a return to the classical curriculum of yesteryear or to stiffer grading (with presumably a higher rate of student failure) as advocated by the hard-core proponents of "excellence" in education. Excellence is too often defined in the narrow terms of high test scores, apparently on the assumption that ability to repeat the thoughts of others is adequate evidence that the child is an independent thinker. As Hullfish and Smith (1961) point out, our schools are intimidated by the dual tyranny of the right answer and of efficiency; apparently educators need to get things done in a hurry and the quickest way to get things done is to tell the student the answer. The school's curriculum is frequently oriented toward the wrong objectives: we emphasize the date and the participants of the Treaty of Versailles when the real question is what lesson we should have learned from the Treaty of Versailles. We need to be sure we have a usable answer to the question, "What knowledge is of most worth?"

By the same token, educators frequently resort to clichés as pat solutions to complex problems, clichés that parry questions but do not give answers. Perhaps, as educators, we need to be more concerned with answers that do not get questioned than with questions that do not get answered. Teachers are often unaware of the assumptions underlying their various pedagogical views and practices; saying that Tommy is not ready for school, for example, implies a considerable belief in the role and the nonaccelerability of the maturational components of readiness. Opposing acceleration for the gifted on the ground that they should remain with their age-mates is likewise making crucial assumptions about the relative importance of the factors involved in the optimal grade placement of children.

More pertinent to the area of educational psychology is the criticism that our schools are relatively ineffective, that children sit by the day working at half-steam, being led under duress toward goals that have been made neither meaningful nor desirable and being subjected to competition and examinations which serve only to debase their sense of worth. Unfortunately, these criticisms are partly true for a number of our classrooms. As Lindgren (1962) points out:

> The sad part of it is that most of teaching and educational planning that takes place in educational institutions throughout the world is based on outmoded and ineffective concepts of the teaching-learning process. Consequently, a great deal of progress students make takes place *in spite of* the educational program, rather than because of it. [p. 201]

Lindgren points out further that some teachers have a propensity for getting themselves in difficulty, for violating the principles of educational psychology, and for otherwise negating rather than facilitating the process of education.

The purpose of a course in educational psychology is to promote a greater understanding of the principles underlying the task of guiding children toward maximum self-realization. Accordingly, the course is as crucial to a teacher-education program as physics is to engineering or anatomy is to medicine. Specifically, its function, as we have seen, is to promote greater understanding of the learning process, of the learning situation, and of the learner, not singly but rather in dynamic interaction for they cannot have meaning apart from such interaction. Knowledge of educational psychology will not guarantee good teaching, but, without it, teaching is simply a case of rules of thumb, routine habits, and trial-and-error procedures, many of which can be detrimental to the child. In the area of discipline, for example, a teacher untrained in educational psychology may deal with pupil misbehavior on the basis of such an expedient as autocratic control and probably worsen the situation by promoting apathy, hostility, and even personality damage. Tradition and custom give stability and security, but unless we apply them judiciously and reexamine them periodically they become straitjackets. The role of educational psychology is not to provide rules of thumb but rather scientific and practical insights into the various aspects of the teaching-learning process.

An understanding of educational psychology will put the teacher in a better position to decide what can be done and how, what will not work and why. It will give him a clearer perspective of what constitutes realistic goals for the child in his present state of development and how he can be helped to achieve these goals. It should enable the teacher to do a more effective job of gearing the curriculum to the needs, goals, and purposes of individual children in his class, and to avoid much of the difficulty experienced by teachers who operate on the premise that children should adapt their needs and goals to the curriculum set by the teacher. In short, an understanding of educational psychology should increase the effectiveness with which the teacher helps the child make maximum progress toward the realization of his capacities and, no less important, should result in a reduction of frustration for teacher and pupil alike.

Unfortunately, procedures that are psychologically sound are sometimes difficult for the beginner to use effectively. Just as the student learning to type without guidance often settles for the hunt-and-peck approach, so the beginning teacher is often tempted to use threats of detention, failing grades, and other forms of punishment instead of something more constructive from a long-term point of view. Furthermore, there are times when the best procedure for a given situation is not clear. As a result, the new teacher is often so befuddled he is willing to grasp at any method regardless of its effectiveness.

Actually, psychology is better at telling what not to do than it is at telling what to do. Laymen are often annoyed at what they consider the psychologist's evasiveness when he answers, "It depends" to their questions as to what should be done about a given child or what is the most opportune age to introduce a certain academic task. Educational psychology does not provide the teacher with a Geiger counter to advise him when the child is ripe for a given activity; it can only alert him to the principles on the basis of which sound decisions can be made.

Objectives of a Course in Educational Psychology

An overview of the possible benefits to accrue from a course in educational psychology may be obtained by considering its objectives. Obviously, the objectives vary from college to college, from instructor to instructor, and even from year to year. Nevertheless, since teacher-education programs almost invariably include a course in educational psychology as part of the sequence of professional courses, we may logically expect a certain degree of agreement as to what is hoped will be accomplished by requiring such a course. Thus, despite the variance to be expected in the specific objectives and the content and approach through which these objectives are to be attained, there is agreement as to such objectives as the promotion of insight into the principles of growth and development and into the dynamics of human behavior. In fact, even though the exact formulation and the relative emphasis may vary, there is probably considerable agreement on such specific objectives as:

[a] Functional information and understanding
1. Insight into the psychodynamics of human behavior, including one's own dynamics as a prerequisite to understanding children
2. Insight into the full meaning of the principles of educational

psychology not as rules to be committed to memory but as tools for dealing more effectively with children

3. Understanding of the various aspects of growth and development in their interrelationships and an understanding of the implications of environmental influences on child growth

4. Familiarity with technical vocabulary, leading to increased ability to understand the professional literature, to communicate with other members of the profession, and to reason more effectively concerning professional problems by virtue of improved language tools

[b] Skills and abilities

1. Ability to integrate the facts and principles of educational psychology into a functional program at the performance level, thereby leading to a gradual increase in the proficiency of the prospective teacher in implementing his learning into effective techniques for dealing with children and co-workers

2. Ability to inspire children to their best effort by relating desirable goals to their purposes and needs and by translating curricular content into realistic and challenging opportunities for growth

3. Ability to create and maintain a classroom atmosphere conducive to maximum self-realization for both his pupils and himself

4. Ability to coordinate the efforts of the school with the principles of maturation in order to promote the maximum growth of the child

5. Skill in the selection, construction, and/or utilization of whatever instruments and techniques are appropriate for the appraisal and understanding of the child and his all-round growth

6. Skill in reading the professional literature as a means of maintaining professional growth, thereby leading to ever-increasing effectiveness in dealing with children

[c] Attitudes, interests, and appreciations

1. An appreciation of the child as a growing organism coupled with a deep conviction of his worth and dignity and an unlimited faith in his capacity for growth

2. An appreciation of the uniqueness of the individual and a willingness to make whatever adaptation in curriculum and methodology seems called for in "his best interest"

3. A sense of responsibility for the all-round growth of the child and an appreciation of the effect of various educational influences—including the teacher's own personality—in promoting or impeding such growth

4. Pride in the teaching profession and dedication to the principle that "the child comes first"
5. An attitude of professional alertness leading to a constant quest for better ways of serving children and to a refusal to be guided by routine and expediency at the expense of their welfare
6. An increased interest in the psychology of the child and its application to the classroom
7. A critical and open-minded attitude toward methodology and an appreciation of the role of research in the improvement of education

These objectives can, of course, be formulated differently; others can be added. It is also true that appraisal of progress toward some of them may be difficult, if not relatively impossible. Since the prospective teacher may not have access to a classroom, it may be difficult to appraise how well he can translate what he learns into effective ways of dealing with children. Whether or not progress toward these objectives can be measured, it is nevertheless a worthy (and valid) aim of such a course: a student who has a course in educational psychology must be able to deal with children more effectively during his internship and in the years ahead, or the course has been a failure. In the same way, it is difficult to appraise progress in the area of attitudes, interests, and appreciations; yet these are among the important objectives of a course in educational psychology, and although the prospective teacher is not expected to achieve a complete realization of these objectives, he can at least be expected to make some progress toward them.

WHAT IS TEACHING?

EMPHASIS UPON GROWTH

Among the more significant changes in educational thought concerning teacher education, brought about as a result of recent advances in educational psychology, are the shifts in emphasis from learning as the acquisition of subject matter to learning as a dynamic process of change in behavior, and from techniques of presenting subject matter to techniques of directing child growth. The most important, if not the only, thing that goes on in the classroom is learning. Teaching is useful only to the extent that it facilitates learning, for as Dewey has suggested, a teacher can no more teach unless someone learns than a seller can sell unless someone buys.

Psychology makes very clear that the child must do his own learning; no one can do it for him. Thus, all education is *self-education*. This does not mean that teachers have outlived their usefulness and that their only *raison d'être* is to act as custodians while children learn. Teachers have a very definite function to perform: theirs is the task of stimulating and guiding the child's learning to assure his attainment of socially approved goals in the most efficient way possible.

This new concept of teaching has made the work of the teacher more challenging but also more difficult; instead of having to concern himself only with a few patterns of effective presentation of subject matter, the modern teacher's responsibility is to see that everything that goes on in the classroom is of maximum benefit in promoting the child's all-round development. According to our modern concept of teaching, techniques of presentation are still essential—and any attempt to minimize their importance would obviously be misguided—but, because learning is now recognized as a dynamic and continuous process involving all phases of child growth and development, other considerations have become equally, if not more, fundamental.

Briefly stated, the teacher's task centers on: [a] orienting the child from the standpoint of direction and motivation toward desirable goals, both immediate and long-range; [b] facilitating his attainment of these goals through the introduction of suitable learning experiences; and [c] attending to the more personal aspects of his total growth, e.g., attitudes, values, and personal adjustment. These tasks are highly interrelated; none can be considered apart from the others. Modern education is based on the tenet that it is impossible to affect one aspect of the child's growth without affecting him as a whole. Any attempt to restrict education to the promotion of academic and intellectual growth can only be ineffective and perhaps harmful.

Who Should Teach?

Because of the importance of the teacher in promoting the child's maximum development, the question of who should teach has received considerable attention in recent years. Although the problem is far from solved, it is generally agreed that the basic ingredients of effectiveness in dealing with children are certain personality characteristics and specific training along lines that will enable the teacher to make efficacious use of his capacities in directing pupil growth. Teachers are both *born* and *made*. It is a matter of first selecting students of high ability and sound personality orientation who have an interest in children, then of providing them, through course work and practice, with a knowledge of subject matter and an understanding of children and of the techniques by which they can be helped to attain the highest degree of self-realization.

Teaching, however, is a complex phenomenon, involving teachers, pupils, and subject matter in dynamic interaction. Studies of teacher effectiveness have failed to identify a single pattern of effective teaching.

Although certain teaching patterns are undoubtedly better than others, there probably is not one kind of good teaching that fits universally all teaching situations, all teachers, and all pupils. And up to a point, the prospective teacher might concern himself with the question: "Whom and what can I teach, being the person that I am?" Brookover (1945), for example, found no advantage for either authoritarian or nonauthoritarian teachers in their effectiveness as teachers as judged by pupils, parents, and supervisors.

A great deal concerning teacher effectiveness centers on the choice of a criterion. Unfortunately, the emphasis is often on immediate goals, e.g., student progress as revealed in end-of-year standardized tests, at the expense of more nebulous but more personally profitable and psychologically sound long-range goals. What has the student really gained from passing tests in Shakespeare if he never reads Shakespeare again? To the extent that immediate goals are often false goals, they can, by their very tangibility and immediacy, distort the overall educational process. Overemphasis on the demonstration of teacher effectiveness can lead to such a distortion.

Teachers are human and nobody expects them to be perfect. But society has the right to expect a certain effectiveness in promoting the purposes and objectives for which teachers and schools exist. Certainly, there will always be teachers who are more effective than others. There are some teachers whose overall effect upon the children placed in their care is essentially negative—or at least, the growth they promote in some children or in some aspects of the development of certain children is, it appears, outweighed by the harm they do in other respects. The prospective teacher should thoroughly consider the question: "What makes me think I will make a good teacher? Or even an average teacher?" Or more specifically, "What assets, what personality characteristics, what training do I bring to the teaching situation that will enable me to do an effective job?" These questions are not raised with the idea of creating doubts in the minds of teachers-in-training, but rather of having them appraise their suitability for the teaching field. It is in the best interests of all concerned that those unsuited to teaching be guided away from the profession.

Although it is easy to insist that children deserve good teachers, it is considerably more difficult to pinpoint the characteristics that make for effectiveness in teaching. First, it might be repeated that knowledge of subject and proficiency in teaching, although essential, are not generally the prime determinants of teacher efficiency and success. In such studies as that of Witty (1947), proficiency in teaching was listed twelfth among the traits mentioned by 12,000 children in describing the teacher who had helped them most. This and other studies suggest that the type of person the teacher is and his effectiveness in dealing with children on a personal and group basis are generally more crucial in determining teacher success than is knowledge of subject matter or ability to follow a lesson plan.[2] From a negative point of view, inability to promote a healthy and enthusiastic classroom atmosphere might be considered a more serious shortcoming than inability to solve a problem in algebra or to recall the capital of Switzerland. On the other hand, competence in subject matter and teaching skill must not be minimized; not only are they of first importance in and of themselves but, since teaching cannot be broken down into independent compartments, failure in these areas will inevitably reflect itself in frustration on the part of both pupils and teacher.

It is impossible to enumerate the characteristics and competencies that make a teacher effective: effectiveness is an aspect of the total personality that characterizes a good teacher. Empirical evidence as well as everyday observation places emphasis on such characteristics as emotional stability, a good disposition, democratic and cooperative attitudes, kindliness, consideration, patience, humor, and fairness. In addition, there is a need for professional competence, for ability to make effective use of sound personality patterns and professional insights in relating to children and in promoting their all-round growth—goodwill is not enough. The teacher must be conversant with the principles of educational psychology and proficient in the use of his assets for the benefit of his students. Together they imply understanding of and respect for children as the foundation for establishing meaningful teacher-pupil relationships in a productive program of education. Ability to establish good personal relationships with pupils and a good grasp of subject matter and teaching methods are necessary conditions for good teaching; interpreted broadly, they might constitute *sufficient* conditions. More detailed lists of desirable teacher characteristics have been prepared (e.g., Commission on Teacher Education, 1944), but none is complete. Teacher effectiveness calls for more than a summation of desirable traits. Nevertheless, the following are probably sufficiently fundamental to warrant specific mention: [a] a satisfactory level of intelligence and scholarship; [b] adequate facility in expression; [c] a good background in the psychological, sociological, and philosophical principles underlying education; [d] a sound character, including a sense of trust and responsibility; [e] a good level of general culture; [f] a general democratic orientation; and [g] professional alertness and interest in self-improvement.

Research into the characteristics of student-teachers (Labue, 1954; Schultz and Ohlsen, 1955; Jantzen, 1959) suggests that the number

---

[2] This may simply reflect the greater ability of colleges to screen out students on the basis of academic knowledge and ability to teach than on the basis of personality adjustment.

one motive underlying the desire to teach is interest in young people. Nonpersisters and poor students in teacher education tend to be more interested in occupations offering greater financial gain, for example. Women tend to persist more than men and to make their choice to become teachers at an earlier age. On the other hand, we have yet to devise a dependable system for the identification of good prospective teachers.

TEACHING AS A SCIENCE

There are two basic points of view concerning the nature of teaching. Some see it as a science; they advocate the systematic application of carefully defined procedures designed to yield relatively uniform and consistent results. This view is best demonstrated by experiments in conditioning, for example those of Pavlov and, more recently, Skinner. The opposing viewpoint is that teaching is an art, that although the educative process is subject to scientific law, teaching is so complex as to be essentially unique to each teaching situation. These views are a matter of degree and are not necessarily conflicting. If one accepts as the criterion the definition of science as a body of knowledge derived through the scientific method, teaching would be a science to the extent that the teacher approaches in a scientific way the problems he encounters in the despatch of his responsibilities, i.e., the extent to which he is conversant with psychological principles as they apply to his work and is willing to analyze classroom problems in the light of these principles. According to this definition, teaching is nothing more than a trade for many teachers who have nothing but rules of thumb which they use over and over again regardless of their appropriateness to the situation.

The term *art* used to describe teaching has two shades of meaning. One is art in the sense of artisanship or craftsmanship, where reliance on stock methods enables the craftsman to do acceptable work on a standard job. This is the very antithesis of science; it can never be satisfactory in teaching, since there are no "standard" jobs in teaching. Yet many teachers operate like craftsmen, and not very crafty craftsmen at that. They simply teach as they were taught some 20 years ago by a teacher who, in turn, copied the techniques of *his* teacher. In this, there is stability and, for some teachers, security. But it smells of stagnation. If psychological science has brought to light new facts and new approaches, these ought to be reflected in improvement in classroom procedures. The other meaning is art in the sense of creation, in the sense of the artist who is familiar with many techniques and who knows how to produce the desired results in the most effective manner. Applied to teaching, this implies a number of effective techniques used judiciously and appropriately after careful consideration of the individual case.

Good teaching must be both a science and an art in this sense of the word. It calls for the skillful use of appropriate pedagogical procedures selected on the basis of an intelligent understanding of their strengths and limitations and of the scientific principles underlying problems at hand.

SIGNIFICANT EDUCATIONAL STUDIES

The literature contains a vast number of research studies which are of prime concern to the teaching profession. As an orientation to the nature of research as well as to some of the more significant areas toward which modern educational and psychological research has been directed, a few of the more educationally meaningful studies are reviewed here.[3] Many more will be mentioned in connection with the various topics covered in the text. Space limitations unavoidably cause the discussion to be in various degrees inadequate, and the student is strongly urged to consult the original reports for a more complete presentation.

PROJECT HIGHER HORIZONS

New York City's Project Higher Horizons (September 1959–June 1962) began operations as an outgrowth of the Demonstration Guidance Project launched three years earlier as a pilot study for the identification and stimulation of able students in a single junior high school in a culturally deprived area of Harlem. Success with this pilot study led to its expansion to other junior high schools in similarly deprived areas, and to their feeder elementary schools and the senior high schools in which the junior high school students enrolled upon graduation. It was also extended to cover the dull and average children as well as the more able so that, in a sense, it became a total school program, rather than a special project for the few.

On the premise that the conventional academic program was not meeting the needs of culturally deprived youths, the project was oriented toward providing a concentrated program of experiences more vitally related to their background and their needs. The actual program varied from school to school but was alike in its underlying philosophy of all-out commitment of school and community resources to the task of the full development of the academic potential of its youth. The project was predicated on the premise that academic success depends on the coordinated efforts of the child, his teachers, his parents, and the community. It involved first raising the child's educational and vocational aspirations and then helping him make these aspirations a matter of reality. Special efforts were made to help the children develop pride in

[3] These studies are simply typical of the many studies of major significance from the standpoint of the content of the text. No implication is made that these are the only or even necessarily the best studies that could have been reviewed.

their school and in themselves, to capitalize on their various talents, but especially to value academic endeavors.

The program's basic feature was compensatory education; equal education is just not enough. The education of the handicapped child in the special education program entails a higher per-pupil outlay than that of the child in the regular classroom; the culturally disadvantaged youth is also handicapped (by adverse environmental conditions) and he too needs superior educational opportunities if he is to survive. Involved was the assignment of extra teachers specially trained for dealing with disadvantaged youth, remedial and developmental instruction particularly in the areas of reading and English in order to overcome their language deficit, extra guidance and counseling services, and other facilities beyond those generally offered in public schools.

The teachers play an especially important role in the success of a program of this kind. They must first be convinced that these children can learn, that high school graduation is a reasonable goal for the majority of them, and that blind faith in the traditional IQ as an index of the potential of culturally deprived youth is unwarranted. It is equally important to provide these teachers with improved techniques for identifying and for actualizing the potential lying dormant in these children. Prospective teachers from various New York colleges and universities were encouraged to participate in the program as volunteer helpers and to undergo special preparation for teaching in the Higher Horizons schools.

For these children, cultural enrichment is not simply a fringe benefit; it must be made an integral part of the total program if it is to compensate for their cultural disadvantages and to broaden their cultural horizons to the point where they can see themselves as part of the main culture. The program emphasized visits to community centers ranging from railroad stations and industrial plants to parks, museums, nearby colleges, ballet, and even opera and symphony. Strenuous efforts were made to make the parents aware of the educational and cultural opportunities available to their children (and to them) and to involve them in the enrichment aspects of the program. The project capitalized on the parents' interest in the welfare of their children and attempted to overcome their apathy and discouragement over the education of their children. It stressed the parents' belief in the ability of their children to succeed in an academic program and the reasonableness of higher vocational aspirations for them. The project also involved the cooperation of the whole community. This meant the systematic exposure of the children to the community's educational and cultural resources and revealed itself in such efforts as the development of study centers in churches, civic centers, etc., supervised by volunteer college students, teachers, ministers, and parents.

The earlier Guidance Project demonstrated rather convincingly that supposedly uneducable lower-class children can learn when provided with a concentrated program of meaningful experiences geared to their needs. It pointed to their previous lack of success as a reflection of unrealized potentialities rather than lack of ability; theirs was simply a vast untapped potential waiting to be discovered and developed. A preliminary report of the pilot study (Shaw, 1963) showed that 74 percent of the first class that entered high school under the project graduated in June 1962, almost 50 percent more than in preproject years. Three times as many went on to some form of higher education. Similar results were reported by Schreiber (1963); in a parallel study, he notes that 40 percent more students than before were finishing high school, two-and-a-half times as many were completing academic courses, and three-and-a-half times as many were going on to postsecondary education. Landers (1963), Coordinator of Higher Horizons, while acknowledging that the project was not meant as a panacea, presents circumstantial evidence of higher academic gains, improved pupil and teacher morale, and increased parental and community cooperation. Unfortunately, the final results did not fulfill the early promise of the Guidance Demonstration Project; Wrightstone et al. (1964) attribute this less spectacular performance, at least in part, to such factors as the cutback in financial support along with the relative youth, inexperience, and turnover of the teachers.[4] In essence, the final evaluation provides no substantial evidence of greater gains in IQ, reading, arithmetic, or school attitudes. The project students did maintain a slightly better attendance record than their controls. On the other hand, participating principals and teachers were unanimous in recommending the continuation of the program, largely on the basis of its contribution to cultural as well as remedial and guidance goals.

The Higher Horizons Project, along with its earlier pilot program, has made a significant contribution to the cause of education in general, and of the education of the children from the culturally disadvantaged areas, in particular. It has served as a blueprint for a number of similar programs in cities throughout the country and for the NEA Project Drop-Out. More specifically, it has focused attention on the critical nationwide problem of wasted potential among the culturally disadvantaged, a waste we can ill afford. It provides a clear challenge to the current pessimistic conviction of the inevitability of intellectual, academic, and cultural inadequacy of children from the lower classes. It has awakened American educators and community leaders to the vast human resources lying untapped because of the unsuitability of our present approach.

---

[4] See Riessman (1962) for an appraisal of the project.

THE McGILL STUDIES IN SENSORY DEPRIVATION

A concept getting progressively greater acceptance is that of the individual's need for a certain degree of stimulation for both optimal well-being and maximal development. Both aspects of this problem have been the subject of extensive study by Hebb and his co-workers at McGill University (Hebb, 1958; Heron, 1957; Melzack and Scott, 1957; Melzack and Thompson, 1956; Thompson and Heron, 1954).

In one series of studies, college students paid to lie comfortably in a sound-proof cubicle under conditions of relative sensory isolation found the monotony so intolerable that few could stand more than a couple of days of it. It is especially interesting to note that the intolerable nature of the situation stemmed largely from the deterioration of their ability to think systematically, a breakdown apparently resulting from stimulus deprivation. Even though the subjects had anticipated reviewing lessons, preparing assignments, etc., they found it impossible to concentrate and gradually drifted into daydreaming, which, in turn, also became too exhausting and they just lay there in a state of semivegetation. They found themselves highly susceptible to arguments concerning the existence of ghosts and other bits of "preposterous nonsense." Vivid hallucinations occurred. Their EEG in the waking state corresponded to the normal sleep pattern, suggesting that normal brain operation requires a relatively continuous sensory bombardment. Similar results were obtained by Lilly (1958) in a study involving more drastic sensory isolation.

In another series of experiments, puppies were reared in relatively stimulus-free cages from the time of weaning to the age of maturity, at which time they were exposed to normal living conditions. The results again were dramatic. The deprived puppies displayed irretrievable stupidity in almost all aspects of development, even in such basic matters as avoidance of pain; they bumped repeatedly into an ice pick or a lighted match, apparently unable to associate the pain with its obvious source. They were equally inept from the standpoint of all aspects of intellectual as well as emotional and social behavior. Even after a year of living under normal conditions, they still showed definite evidence of the detrimental effects of their early deprivation of normal stimulation. These findings have empirical and theoretical support from varied sources ranging from Hebb's neurophysiological theory of learning and its underlying empirical foundation to the large number of parallel studies of developmental retardation resulting from stimulus deprivation noted in studies with rats and other animals.

The discovery of the deleterious effects of sensory deprivation has fundamental implications for all aspects of human functioning. It is conceivable, for example, that the nonproductivity of people in the slums or on relief reflects a similar case of drifting into a state of semivegetation.

The irretrievable losses incurred from early deprivation may also be involved in the lesser intellectual and academic status of children from the lower classes whose early environment is typically lacking in stimulus value. A basic implication here is the crucial need to provide young children with a relatively stimulating environment with emphasis on preschool, nursery school, and kindergarten where a considerable systematic intellectual-academic orientation can be provided. This is consistent with the modern view of intelligence as something that is developed through experience.

THREE-YEAR-OLDS LEARN TO READ

An exciting study still in the exploratory stages is that being conducted by O. K. Moore, a Yale sociologist, in teaching two- to five-year-old children to read, to write, to type, and to take dictation (Moore, 1963; Pines, 1963). The key to the experiment is what Moore refers to as a properly responsive environment. The young child sits in a cubicle with a "talking" (i.e., a computerized electric) typewriter. As he strikes a key, the letter or numeral appears in jumbo type on a screen and a soft voice names the symbol. After a period of free playing with the keys, the child may find a red arrow pointing to a letter on the screen; he must then press the corresponding key, for all other keys are locked. Soon he finds himself typing CAT or DOG and he realizes that series of letters and sounds actually represent words or names of things. He also learns to touch-type and spell words on call. Attendance is voluntary; the machine is simply there for him to play with for as long as he wants. He is completely on his own, although a teacher, watching from behind a one-way screen, can step in if needed. The results have been dramatic: within the period of a year, children of three are learning to read, to type, to compose and dictate their own stories, and to transcribe back to the typewriter what they have dictated.

The implications of Moore's work are exciting from both a practical and a theoretical point of view. Apparently, we have not even begun to tap human potential. Moore seems to bear out the views expressed by Gates in 1937 that, with a proper modification of teaching methods, children can read much earlier than the traditional age six and a half. Our current difficulties in teaching young children apparently stem not so much from their immaturity as from our failure to devise more productive teaching methods.

This view is consistent with Hebb's conception of neurophysiological development (1949), Ausubel's objection to the fixed maturation concept (1959), the newer view of intelligence as something one develops (or fails to develop) as a result of experience (Hebb, and co-workers), the importance of early stimulation, and Bruner's conviction that any subject can be taught to any child at virtually any age in some form that is honest and useful (Bruner, 1960). Actually, children are learning to read before the conventional age of six. Durkin (1966) found that 2 percent of her sample in California had learned to read by the age of three, 6 percent by the age of four, and 20 percent by the age of five. It even appears that preschool experience in the sense of an academically and intellectually oriented early environment (e.g., having been read to) is a more important determinant of early reading than the IQ as such.

It is Moore's contention that the early years of life are the most creative and intellectually productive years of our lives—years which are normally wasted academically, perhaps never to be retrieved. Moore is convinced that, in a properly responsive environment, the young child is capable of outstanding feats of inductive reasoning. It is his hope that through a more adequate approach we can produce a new breed of highly imaginative youngsters far better prepared to cope with our unpredictable and complex world. He feels that modern society is evolving so dynamically that we can no longer depend on child-rearing methods that were adequate before (Pines, 1963).

> A new kind of person is needed to handle the present rate of change. This is our chief trouble today: Technological changes but intransigent behavior. It's too late for us—our generation can't make it. At best, we are just the transition group. [p. 64]

His investigation bears directly on the question of policies on admission to first grade and the special importance of a systematic program of early preschool education going back to infancy.

Moore's project constitutes a significant contribution to the field of child development and the cause of education. Along with a number of parallel developments, it is causing a major reconsideration of our present concept of what constitutes human capacity and the limits imposed thereon. It has particular significance from the standpoint of the allegedly "inevitable" intellectual and academic inadequacy of a sizable fraction of our students, characteristic of our present system of operations.

THE NATURE OF LOVE

An important series of investigations (Harry F. Harlow, 1958, 1962) was concerned with the role of contact comfort in the development of love in infant Macaque monkeys, selected as subjects because their basic affectional response patterns are essentially the same as those of human infants. Taking their cue from the close attachment infant monkeys display for a blanket or other soft material, the investigators replaced the regular mother with two artificial mothers—one covered with sponge rubber and terry cloth, the other of identical proportions presenting simply a wire mesh surface. Both mothers were freely accessible to the infant monkeys and both provided warmth through a light bulb installed in the frame. Half the young monkeys could get milk from the soft mother; the other half from the wire mother.

The monkey infants developed an immediate preference for the soft mother—here was a mother, soft, warm, available 24 hours a day. In fact, they showed definite preference for the soft mother even when she did not provide milk and the wire mother did. The young monkeys used the soft mother as a home base from which to explore their environment and, in times of fear, they invariably rushed to the soft mother rather than to the wire mother.

The investigators were not surprised to find contact comfort an important determinant of affection but they did not expect it to overshadow so completely the variable of nursing. Psychologists had previously held that the initial love responses of the infant to its mother resulted largely from her association with the reduction of such primary drives as hunger, thirst, and pain, from which generalized affectional responses were then established. Harlow's findings suggest that, if affection stems from secondary reinforcement associated with the satisfaction of a primary need, that primary need may be contact comfort rather than hunger-thirst as previously postulated. These studies establish, at least for monkeys, the significance of frequent and intimate body contact between mother and infant, a position bearing on the relatively discounted view of the need for cutaneous and tactile stimulation as postulated by Ribble (1943) and Montagu (1950). (See Pinneau, 1950.) It is also related to the evidence that gentled rats thrive better than nonhandled rats (W. J. McClelland, 1956).

The investigators also experimented with hostile and inconsistent wire mother surrogates; one rejecting mother, for example, would blast the baby monkey off her or would shake it with such violence that its teeth clattered. The infant would in its moment of desperation cling all the more tightly; where else can a baby go in times of agony?

However, the monkeys that had been raised under artificial mothering conditions where they could see, hear, and call other infant monkeys, but could not contact them, began to appear less and less normal; they would sit in their cages, mute, staring into space, relatively indifferent to people and other monkeys. Some would go into violent frenzies of rage. Apparently as a result of their lack of normal interaction with their peers, they had developed into neurotic monkeys. The investigators also found that the monkeys raised on the artificial mothers, never having known normal affection, were completely incapable of love. When they reached adulthood, not only did the females reject normal sexual advances, for example, but even those that became mothers turned out to be hopeless and heartless mothers who either ignored their babies or brutally abused them. However, when the investigators allowed the babies brought up on cloth mothers to have contact with one another in a playroom, normal sexual and affectional development did take place. It is interesting to note that beginning around the third month, real monkey mothers frequently push their babies away from them and thereby, intentionally or not, force them to interact with their peers. In contrast, the cloth mother was too good: she never rejected. It is also important to note that monkey babies kept with their mothers for about ten months and then placed for the first time with their peers did not react with them. Apparently mothering can be bypassed if opportunities are provided for early interaction with peers, but mothering without opportunity for early infant interaction is not sufficient. This is in contradition to the current psychiatric view stressing the importance of mother-infant contact rather than interaction with peers as the basic ingredient in the promotion of normal human affectional and social development.

CHARACTERISTICS OF TEACHERS

The question of teacher competence is fundamental to any consideration of the school's effectiveness in fulfilling its responsibilities, because unquestionably the teacher, more than any other component of the educative machinery, determines the "quality" of the "education" the child receives. Unfortunately, despite our prime concern in the matter, reflected in considerable discussion concerning the psychology of the teaching-learning process and vast amounts of empirical research (e.g., Barr, 1961), our knowledge of the complex multidimensional entity called "teacher competence" is relatively limited. Frankly, every aspect of the definition, description, and understanding of teacher effectiveness is more a matter of controversy than of consensus.

David G. Ryans' Teacher Characteristics Study, a vast undertaking involving the participation of over 6000 teachers in 1700 schools in 450 school systems, was designed to be of use to school systems in identifying desirable teacher characteristics for purposes of employment and promotion, and to teacher-preparation institutions in selecting and training teacher candidates (Ryans, 1960).

Factor analysis of classroom observation data yielded three basic teacher behavior patterns:

X_o: Warm, understanding, friendly *versus* aloof, egocentric, restricted;
Y_o: Responsible, businesslike, systematic *versus* evading, unplanned, slipshod; and
Z_o: Stimulating, imaginative, surgent *versus* dull, routine.

A parallel factor analysis of pupil behavior yielded such dimensions as alert versus apathetic; responsible versus obstructive; confident versus uncertain; and initiating versus dependent pupil behavior.

The study attempted to devise indirect measures of the pencil-and-paper variety which would reflect the various components of teacher classroom behavior and the resulting pupil behavior patterns, so as to bypass the practical difficulties involved in actual classroom observation. The outcome was the *Teacher Characteristics Schedule*, a 300-item self-report inventory concerning such matters as self-judgments, educational viewpoints, and personal preferences, from which factor analysis extracted such measures as verbal intelligence, emotional adjustment, and attitudes toward classroom practices and toward school personnel.

The last phase of the study involved a comparison with respect to the above patterns of the various teacher groups classified according to sex, marital status, age, experience, and so forth. The results of these comparisons are too detailed to be presented.[5] The following are typical: Teachers with extended experience tended to score lower than average on all scales except Y_0 (Responsible, businesslike, systematic classroom behavior) and traditional educational orientation. Secondary teachers were more permissive. Male teachers of English were found to be low on Y_0, while female teachers of English were low on Z_0 (Stimulating, imaginative, surgent classroom behavior). Male teachers at both the elementary and the secondary level were markedly more emotionally stable than their female counterparts. Few overall differences were found because of conflicting trends between males and females, elementary and secondary, or other dimensions of teacher classification.

Ryans' study is a major contribution to the field of teacher education; among other things it delineates some of the characteristics distinguishing superior from inferior teachers. For example, teachers found superior on the three basic teacher behavior patterns, X_0, Y_0, and Z_0 (as well as from the standpoint of other criteria of teacher superiority) tended to be extremely generous in their appraisal of the behavior and motives of others; to manifest superior verbal intelligence; to possess a record of above-average school achievement; to display strong interest in reading, literature, music, and the arts; to participate in social groups, to enjoy pupil relationships; to prefer permissive classroom procedures; to have had early experience in caring for children; and to be superior in emotional adjustment. On the other hand, the investigation should be considered only exploratory; additional study is needed to provide further clarification of teacher effectiveness and to identify usable predictors of teaching success. To the extent that, along with John Adams, we believe that a teacher affects eternity, there is urgent need for the definition and the prediction of teacher effectiveness as a prerequisite to the selection of those who will mold the present and thereby direct the future.

[5] See Ryans for complete data or Getzels and Jackson (1963) for a summary of the principal findings.

In a similar study, Heil et al. (1960) attempted to relate pupil achievement to teacher-pupil interaction by classifying teachers and students into various personality types and appraising the growth-promoting effects of each combination. They found, for example, that the self-controlling (well-integrated) teacher was most effective with all types of students, while the fearful teacher was essentially ineffective with all pupils except the strivers. The turbulent teacher was effective with the conformers and strivers, particularly in mathematics and science, but was ineffective with the "opposers" and the "waiverers," the two groups requiring special interpersonal skills to handle. There also appeared to be an interaction between teacher personality and the children's emotional adjustment. Heil's study points to the fallacy of seeking the *ideal* teacher; it makes an important contribution in recognizing that teacher effectiveness is not a unitary concept independent of the learner who is to do the learning.

HIGHLIGHTS OF THE CHAPTER

This chapter serves as an orientation to the field of educational psychology. The major ideas presented can be summarized as follows:

[a]

Educational psychology is that branch of psychology which is concerned with the applications of the principles, techniques, and other resources of psychology to the solution of classroom problems. It is of such fundamental importance to the work of the teacher that teacher-education programs, almost without exception, incorporate some credits in educational psychology as part of the professional preparation of teachers.

[b]

Although the boundaries of educational psychology are not clearly demarcated, most courses on the subject are oriented toward promoting in the prospective teacher greater insight into the psychodynamics of human behavior, greater understanding of the principles of growth and development, and the skills necessary to translate his learning into effective teaching.

[c]

An important change which has taken place in teacher education during recent decades, namely a change in emphasis from merely teaching subject matter to directing pupil growth, has made the role of the teacher more crucial as well as more complex than ever. Hence, the need for care in the selection and training of prospective teachers.

[d]

In view of the special importance of the personal aspects of pupil-teacher relations, it is highly desirable that teachers be emotionally stable, that they understand and respect children, and that they be democratically oriented. This is not to minimize the importance of academic and professional qualifications which are also essential.

[e]

Teaching can be a trade, a science, or an art, depending on whether the teacher operates at the routine level or uses imagination and ingenuity based on a thorough grasp of scientific principles and procedures.

SOURCES OF RELATED MATERIAL

American Association of College Teachers of Education, *Roles and Relationships in Teacher Education*. Washington, D.C.: The Association, 1963.

Bereday, G. Z., and J. A. Lauwerys (eds.), *The Education and Training of Teachers. The Yearbook of Education*. New York: Harcourt, Brace & World, Inc., 1963.

Carlile, A. B., "Predicting performance in the teaching profession," *J. educ. Res.*, 47: 641–668, 1954.

Cartwright, William H., "The teacher in 2065," *Teach. Coll. Rec.*, 66: 295–304, 1965.

Englander, M. E. A., "A psychological analysis of vocational choice: Teaching," *J. counsel. Psychol.*, 7: 257–264, 1960.

Gagné, Robert M., "Educational objectives and human performance," in John D. Krumboltz (ed.), *Learning and the Educational Process*. Skokie, Ill.: Rand McNally & Company, 1965. Pp. 1–24.

Getzels, Jacob W., and P. W. Jackson, "The teacher's personality and characteristics," in N. L. Gage (ed.), *Handbook of Research on Teaching*. Skokie, Ill.: Rand McNally & Company, 1963. Pp. 506–582.

Guba, E. G., et al., "Occupational choice and the teaching career," *Educ. Res. Bull.*, 38: 1–12, 57, 1959.

Haubrick, V. F., "The motives of prospective teachers," *J. teach. Educ.*, 11: 381–386, 1960.

Lindvall, C. M. (ed.), *Defining Educational Objectives*. Pittsburgh: University of Pittsburgh Press, 1964.

Masomer, Paul H., *A Design for Teacher Education*. Pittsburgh: University of Pittsburgh Press, 1964.

Rivlin, H. N., et al., *The Contributions of Educational Psychology to Education*. Washington, D.C.: American Psychological Association, 1948.

Rogers, Carl R., "Persons or science: A philosophical question," *Amer. Psychol.*, 10: 267–278, 1955.

Sharp, D. Louise (ed.), *Why Teach?* New York: Holt, Rinehart and Winston, Inc., 1957.

Smith, E. R., *Teacher Education: A Reappraisal*. New York: Harper & Row, Publishers, 1962.

Stern, G. G., et al., "Two scales for the assessment of unconscious motivation for teaching," *Educ. psychol. Measmt.*, 20: 9–29, 1960.

Stinnett, T. M., and L. D. Haskew, *Teaching in American Schools: A Hand-*

book for the Future Teacher. New York: Harcourt, Brace & World, Inc., 1962.

Turner, R. L., and N. A. Fattu, "Skill in teaching: A reappraisal of the concepts and strategies in teacher effectiveness research," *Bull. sch. Educ.,* Indiana University, 36, No. 3, 1960.

Tyler, Ralph, "The knowledge explosion: Implications for secondary education," *Educ. Forum,* 29: 145–153, 1965.

Wiggins, Samuel P., *Battlefields in Teacher Education.* Nashville, Tenn.: Peabody College for Teachers, 1964.

Withalls, John, "Note on the teacher-education research project," *Psychol. Rep.,* 15, No. 2, 1964.

QUESTIONS AND PROJECTS

1

Get acquainted with the library as it relates to educational psychology by locating the books listed under *Supplementary Readings* in the following pages. Also locate in the *Education Index* recent articles dealing with educational psychology and familiarize yourself with some of the professional journals and with the names of current educational leaders.

2

If you have access to children—in a recreation center or a camp—observe a couple of youngsters who seem to present problems and follow them through the various topics of educational psychology discussed in the text. Thus, with regard to Chapters 3 and 4, attempt to understand the psychodynamics of their behavior; with regard to Chapter 5, make a study of their general growth patterns. As you go through the various chapters, attempt to relate each bit of information to the child as a whole. Not only will you find such a project interesting, but it will also be extremely valuable preparation in understanding children and give the course continuity and meaning.

3

[a] What characteristics distinguish a good from a poor teacher?
Evaluate your suitability as a prospective teacher in the light of the characteristics you listed above. What led you to consider teaching as your life work?
[b] Evaluate the various suggestions for promoting teacher competence.
What are the issues involved in merit pay for teachers? Specifically what might be accomplished by making satisfactory performance on the National Teachers' Examinations a condition for tenure and promotion?

4

The school often experiences difficulty in maintaining a proper balance among its major objectives because of the confusion resulting from perpetually shifting pressures, both external and internal, and from shifting emphases. Identify some of these forces and appraise the effect they have had upon American education. How can the school maintain sensitivity to the demands of the society it serves without, at the same time, losing its focus on the essentials?

5

Every teacher has a philosophy of teaching. What are some of the things in which you believe? What are your present views toward the child who loafs in school? who violates regulations? toward "social" promotion?

SUPPLEMENTARY READINGS

Inasmuch as no single textbook can ever hope to provide a complete coverage of a given course area at the college level, the conscientious student will want to consult one or more of the many excellent texts in educational psychology listed in the card catalog of the library. Also, to the extent that he should have direct contact with the basic literature from which educational psychology is derived, he should make frequent reference to periodicals and other primary sources. A convenient source of the latter is the extensive array of books of readings covering the various aspects of educational psychology. A few of the more pertinent are listed below:

Berelson, Bernard, and Gary A. Steiner, *Human Behavior: An Inventory of Scientific Findings.* New York: Harcourt, Brace & World, Inc., 1964.

De Cecco, John P. (ed.), *Human Learning in the School.* New York: Holt, Rinehart and Winston, Inc., 1963.

Fullagar, William A., et al. (eds.), *Readings in Educational Psychology.* New York: Thomas Y. Crowell, 1964.

Gordon, Ira J., *Human Development: Readings and Research.* Chicago: Scott, Foresman and Company, 1965.

Morse, W. C., and G. M. Wingo, *Readings in Educational Psychology.* New York: Scott, Foresman and Company, 1962.

Noll, Victor H., and R. P. Noll (eds.), *Readings in Educational Psychology.* New York: Crowell Collier and Macmillan, Inc., 1962.

Page, E. G. (ed.), *Readings in Educational Psychology.* New York: Harcourt, Brace & World, Inc., 1964.

Ripple, Richard E. (ed.), *Readings in Learning and Human Abilities.* New York: Harper & Row, Publishers, 1964.

Rosenblith, J. D., and W. Allinsmith (eds.), *The Cause of Behavior.* Boston: Allyn and Bacon, Inc., 1962.

Seidman, Jerome M. (ed.), *Readings in Educational Psychology.* Boston: Houghton Mifflin Company, 1965.

Staats, Arthur W. (ed.), *Human Learning.* New York: Holt, Rinehart and Winston, Inc., 1965.

CHAPTER 2

Psychology
as a Science[1]

It seems abundantly clear that the science of learning and the technology of educational methods at one time prospered in a climate of mutual support, that this has not been the case for some years past, and that such a climate of mutual support should be reinstated in the best interest of both.

Melton, 1959; p. 98

The task confronting the scientist is to formulate laws and principles that express functional relationships among phenomena. The purpose of research in psychology is to identify the factors that affect behavior and the conditions under which modification of behavior occurs, so that desirable behavioral changes can be effected by controlling these conditions in the child's in-school and out-of-school environment. At a higher level of science, the theorist attempts to synthesize into theoretical structure the various empirical findings derived from research. The ultimate

[1] This chapter deals with content of considerable complexity, background for which should have been provided by the course in general psychology. Although a reasonable grasp of this content is of major significance for overall perspective and introduction to basic terminology, its complete mastery at this time is probably not essential. The student might want to restrict his first coverage of this material to a general orientation with periodic reviews of relevant sections as he proceeds through related chapters of the text.

goal is the relatively complete understanding of the learning process and its antecedents so as to permit the prediction, and eventually the control, of the occurrence of the behavioral changes in question.

In an experiment, the investigator is interested in the effect that a certain (independent) variable, e. g., reward, has upon some aspect of the response, such as speed of occurrence or resistance to extinction. The latter is called a dependent variable, since its operation is dependent upon that of the independent variable, the reward in this case. The experimenter's task is to discover functional relations between dependent variables in which he is interested and certain independent variables which he can manipulate. If he is to discover these relationships, he must exercise sufficient control to ensure that whatever effect is noted in the dependent variable can be logically attributed to the operation of the independent variable under study. This is often difficult to do in the natural setting of the classroom, where a multitude of factors interact with the dependent variable and with each other to the point where interpretation as to the cause of the phenomenon may be in doubt. An experiment, therefore, generally calls for a simplification of the natural situation in order to isolate the influence of the variable under investigation. The choice of a criterion is crucial and contradictory results can be obtained with respect to different criteria. Psychologists are primarily concerned with learning, but learning can be inferred only through some aspect of performance such as accuracy of response, resistance to forgetting, or, perhaps, some combination of criteria.

The operation of the independent variable with respect to the dependent variable is not a matter of a one-to-one direct-line operation; rather, scientific explanations involve postulating *hypothetical constructs* to account for the relationships noted among the variables in the situation under observation. Chemists, for example, postulated the existence of molecules long before their existence was verified under a microscope. They simply found that chemical relationships were more logically and meaningfully explained when matter was assumed to be made of molecules. Chemists also postulated the concept of valence to account for the attraction of atoms in a chemical reaction. Such hypothetical constructs are used in all sciences—valence in chemistry, genes in genetics, cell assemblies in physiology, habits and attitudes in psychology. The scientist's task is to discover laws that govern the operation of these hypothetical constructs. The psychologist, for example, has to specify the factors that determine the behavior changes that occur, say, with practice, and to formulate laws pertaining to the relationships existing among such variables.

Learning itself is a hypothetical construct. We speak loosely when we say that practice causes learning. Practice is simply related in a functional way to performance, the adequacy of which is affected by numerous other variables operating in the situation. Performance is a measurable empirical concept, but learning is not; we postulate that learning has taken place as a way of accounting for the change in performance. That the child has learned to read is assumed from the fact that he can now read, which he could not do before. On the other hand, psychology makes learning a central concept and views performance simply as its external manifestation.

Hypothetical constructs can be conceived as *intervening* variables since they are assumed to intervene between independent and dependent variables. Motives, for example, are intervening variables whose existence we infer from observable behavior. We see motivation as a set of conditions, encompassing a wide range of behavior from food-seeking to striving for a grade, which predispose the organism to seek a certain goal with relative persistence. We recognize certain symptoms which lead us to believe that a person is hungry, and we assume he is feeling as we feel when we are hungry. However, this is completely unsupported by public evidence and is "scientifically" irrelevant since it is unverifiable in a strict scientific sense.

Intervening variables can be categorized as experiential or background variables (relating to the extent to which one has the prerequisites for acquiring the behavior in question); transfer variables (including motivation, attitudes and learning sets); and various process variables (such as the ability to make associations and discriminations or to generalize). The latter, dealing with the capacity to perform certain internal processes are known as *mediating factors* because they mediate between stimulus and response.

A special class of mediating factors are the perceptual processes, where *perception* is taken in its broad psychological sense with emphasis on the selectivity with which the individual attends to certain variables (and not to others) and emphasizes certain factors and minimizes others in his interpretation of a situation. Actually, the individual does not respond to a simple stimulus or even the situation as it is, but rather to the overall phenomenon as he visualizes it in the light of his interpretation of the totality of the situation, including his potentialities, the social and physical setting, his motivational status, his past experiences, etc. It is possible, for example, for an experience to be rewarding and pleasant to some people and unpleasant to others, depending on their perception of the situation. Furthermore, this is an area in which only the individual can give a report; the world of personal experiences (labeled the *phenomenal* field by such writers as Combs and Snygg, 1959) is not accessible to outsiders except by inference.

All behavior involves mediating factors; in fact, learning refers to changes taking place in the mediating processes and a major objective of teaching is the development of effective mediating processes. As learning proceeds, many of the mediating processes necessary in the early stages are discarded in the interest of a more efficient operation. The scientist's task is to identify the conditions (e.g., the pattern of teacher behavior) which are likely to be effective in this connection and, of course, the conditions to be avoided.

CONTEMPORARY THEORIES OF LEARNING[2]

Attempts to provide theoretical perspective for the empirical findings of modern psychology have led to the formulation of a number of competing theories, two major categories of which have had an important influence on modern educational and psychological thought and practice. These theories are simply systematic attempts to synthesize empirical results into meaningful structure in order to explain the various aspects of behavior; all fall relatively short of providing a completely systematic, conclusive, and convincing framework comparable to those of the physical sciences. They simply represent reasonably consistent statements of basic psychological perspective which can be used to advantage in dealing with psychological and pedagogical problems.

Contemporary theories of learning can be classified into two major systems: [a] associative theories, and [b] field or cognitive theories. Under each in turn can be categorized several somewhat different and yet basically similar subsystems. This classification is somewhat arbitrary and subject to considerable overlapping. In addition, the agreements and disagreements among the subsystems frequently run across system lines. There is, however, an underlying logic that permits learning theories to be grouped in two major systems with contrasting common ground; there is, for example, a relative difference in outlook and orientation as well as in emphasis. The following discussion presents a brief overview of the better-known theories.

ASSOCIATIONISM

Associationism dates back to Aristotle's concept of association of ideas based on similarity, contrast, and contiguity. Associationism continued to be the only doctrine concerning the nature of learning accepted in the early days of psychology as a science. The standard approach was introspection; the subject simply observed the working of his own mind. A reaction soon set in, however, as psychologists, realizing the highly sub-

---

[2] Learning must be interpreted in the broad sense of a change in behavior. These theories are more appropriately conceived as theories of behavior, or theories of psychology, or even schools of psychology, i.e., viewpoints from which the empirical data of psychology is structured into theoretical perspective.

jective nature of introspection, turned to the examination of overt behavior on the premise that psychology could be a true science only if it switched its focus to bodily processes whose occurrence could be verified, and a new version, known as *behaviorism*, developed from the older associationistic position.

Behaviorism was overtly mechanistic. Watson (1930), for instance, objected to the concept of satisfaction and annoyance as factors in learning on the grounds that these were subjective terms which had no place in a truly scientific psychology modeled after the physical sciences. He confined his study to those aspects of behavior which were sufficiently overt to permit objective observations. This extreme emphasis on overt and verifiable evidence led psychology to a relatively sterile position inasmuch as significant psychological phenomena are not amenable to this sort of verification. Behaviorism had particular difficulty in explaining purposive behavior. The position has been largely abandoned, although its influence is still felt in the orientation of some contemporary psychologists.

Two major versions of associationism are currently in vogue: connectionism (often referred to as the Bond Theory, or S-R psychology) and conditioning. The latter is divided further into classical and instrumental conditioning.

CONNECTIONISM

The foundations of modern associationism were established around 1900 by Thorndike, whose work over a period of 50 years probably constitutes the most significant single contribution to the psychology of learning, especially from the standpoint of its influence upon educational practice in America. As a result of his experiments involving a variety of animals, he came to see learning as a process of developing neural connections between stimuli and responses. Thorndike was impressed by the characteristic trial-and-error nature of the behavior displayed by his experimental subjects, and he concluded that learning was largely a matter of stamping in correct responses and stamping out incorrect responses as a result of their rewarding or annoying consequences.

Thorndike postulated the Law of Effect as the fundamental principle underlying the formation of bonds between stimulus and response; the animal when placed in a given situation would tend to repeat those responses that on previous occasions had been followed by satisfying aftereffects. Learning was a matter of having the learner try various approaches to the problem until, perhaps by accident, the desired response occurred and was stamped in as a consequence of its satisfying aftereffects. Thorndike's contribution to the psychology of learning is of major significance. Although it no longer commands the monopoly it once held and although some of the pedagogical practices to which it lent theoretical support, for example, overemphasis on drill, are now considered out of date, the influence of connectionism is still felt at both the practical and the theoretical levels.[3]

CLASSICAL CONDITIONING

Classical conditioning is best represented by Pavlov's well-known experiment demonstrating the formation and strengthening of an association between salivation in a dog (the conditioned response) and the sound of a bell (the conditioned stimulus) through the repeated simultaneous presentation of the bell with the natural (unconditioned) stimulus for salivation, namely food, serving to reinforce the association. In a way, conditioning represents the simplest form of learning; it relies on the relatively mechanistic process of reinforcement for the formation and strengthening of associations between stimulus and response. It accounts for much of the incidental learning that goes on in everyday life, e.g., the development of attitudes.

GUTHRIE'S CONTIGUOUS CONDITIONING Although based on the classical conditioning model, Guthrie's contiguous conditioning theory (Guthrie, 1959) differs from classical conditioning in that it makes contiguity of a particular stimulus and response the only factor necessary for the two to become associated. It is Guthrie's position that:

[a] The only necessary and sufficient condition for conditioning to take place is that the response occur in the presence of a particular stimulus, regardless of why it occurred.

[b] A given association is established at full strength on an all-or-none basis on the first pairing of stimulus and response, and it remains at full strength until displaced by an incompatible association.[4]

Motivation has no formal place in Guthrie's theory. It is important only to the extent that it keeps the organism active until the goal is attained, during the course of which an adequate response can be conditioned to the desired stimulus, and, further, that upon the attainment of the goal it removes the organism from the field and thus protects the most recent (presumably the successful) association from becoming unlearned. The teacher's task, according to Guthrie, is simply to induce the organism, by whatever means he can contrive, to make the desired

---

[3] A modern connectionist position is that of Miller (1959).

[4] If this seems contrary to common sense, it must be remembered that the response is conditioned to a relatively complex stimulus, not all components of which are essential, and it may be necessary to present the stimulus repeatedly to permit the discrimination between the trivial and the essential aspects of the situation. Pavlov's dogs, for example, did not learn to salivate at the sound of the bell alone but to a multitude of concomitant elements of the bell-ringing situation, and the irrelevant aspects gradually had to be isolated.

response when the stimulus is presented. Guthrie's contiguous conditioning theory is felt to be an oversimplification. The most damaging criticism is that despite new experimental findings Guthrie's system remains
unchanged. According to Hilgard (1956): "Either the system is a mi-
raculously inspired one or it is not stated very precisely, and hence it is
not very sensitive to experimental data."

HULL'S BEHAVIORISTIC REINFORCEMENT THEORY Hull's theory (Hull,
1943; Logan, 1959) is probably the most elaborate from the standpoint of
scientific development, having as its basis a structure of theorems and
postulates from which Hull attempted to deduce the fundamental laws of
learning. In contrast to Guthrie, Hull subscribed to the view that reinforcement is both necessary and sufficient for associations to be formed. Practice alone does nothing; it is all a matter of reinforcement in the sense of
the reduction of tension associated with the frustration of a drive. In fact,
the concept of tension or drive reduction might be considered the most fundamental aspect of Hull's theoretical position. His theory is not particularly
integrated and there is no central concept. It is, however, most comprehensive and detailed, and thus vulnerable to minute criticism from the
standpoint of errors, inconsistencies, and gaps. It is nevertheless a major
achievement, especially as a model of the systematic and quantitative approach to the psychology of learning.[5]

INSTRUMENTAL CONDITIONING

Somewhat more complicated is instrumental conditioning, so-called because here the animal's response is instrumental in accomplishing a
given purpose; e.g., it presses the bar to get a pellet. Instrumental conditioning differs from classical conditioning in that it is goal-directed or
purposive in nature.

[a] Whereas in classical conditioning, the behavior to be conditioned is elicited by a known stimulus (e.g., food), behavior in instrumental conditioning is simply emitted by the organism—undoubtedly as
the result of some antecedent, but the stimulus is neither so readily
identifiable nor under the same degree of control by the investigator.

The nature of the stimulus is really irrelevant: all that is necessary
is for the response to occur—generally as part of the spontaneous activity of the organism—so that it can be rewarded and brought under the
control of its consequence.

[b] In contrast to classical conditioning where a given response is
associated with a new but constant stimulus, the response in instrumental learning undergoes continuous modification as a consequence of
feedback from the reinforcing stimulus to the previous response.

It is not a matter of forming the association of a given response and

[5] See Spence (1960) for an updated and simplified formulation of Hull's basic theory.

a given stimulus with greater strength, greater precision, and greater probability of occurrence, but rather of gradually modifying, or "shaping" the response toward greater adequacy through successive approximations geared to a schedule of differential reinforcement. In this sense, instrumental learning is more realistically similar to learning as it takes place in the classroom, where the task is to promote progressively more adequate behavior.

SKINNER'S OPERANT CONDITIONING   Instrumental conditioning (Skinner, 1959) has come into considerable prominence in recent years as a result of Skinner's success in training animals and, more recently, in shaping academic behavior through programed instruction. Skinner uses the term *operant behavior* to refer to the fact that, to get a reward, the organism must do something, i.e., it must operate upon its environment. Although most of Skinner's work has been with animals, he has been equally successful with children and even psychotic patients, all of whom, he claims, show amazing similarities in their learning processes. His basic premise is that the subject tends to repeat what it was doing at the time its behavior was reinforced; the task is a matter of baiting each step of the way and thus gradually leading the subject to the required performance.

His procedures are designed to shape behavior through selective reinforcement of progressively more adequate approximations to the desired behavior, and, of course, the extinction through nonreinforcement of inadequate behavior. If the experimenter wants the pigeon to peck at a given disk, he places the pigeon in a relatively restricted area in the presence of the disk. As the pigeon, in its spontaneous activity, moves closer to the disk, it gets a bit of food; it will get its next morsel when it gets still closer. In time, just being close is no longer good enough: it must get its head next to the disk and eventually it will get the reward only when it pecks at the disk. A sophisticated pigeon can learn this rather quickly. This differential reinforcement of the subject's successive approximations to the required behavior is both necessary and sufficient for shaping its behavior. Although he accepts both positive and negative reinforcement, Skinner believes that learning must be based on positive reinforcement and he strongly opposes any form of aversive control.

Skinner has no interest in physiological explanations: that the rat should learn a certain association is all that matters, not how this is accomplished. To look inside the organism is simply to obscure what lies outside immediately available for observation. Neither has he any room for the concept that behavior is under the control of a goal. He leans strongly toward a mechanistic approach as the only hope for psychology to achieve in regard to human behavior the degree of precision and control achieved in the physical sciences. He objects to the connectionist concept of satisfying and annoying aftereffects, and he replaces the concepts of goals, motivation, etc. with a simple statement of conditioning; the subject does not respond in a given way because of the consequences that will follow behavior, but rather because of the consequences which *have followed* similar behavior in the past.

Field or Cognitive Theories

The second major family of contemporary learning theories originated in Germany around 1912 with Wertheimer's presentation of what is essentially the present Gestalt theory of psychological thought. As suggested by the term *Gestalt* (i.e., configuration), it emphasizes the global aspects of the situation. Gestalt psychology has consistently emphasized the study of behavior as a totality, and, in a sense, represents a reaction against the mechanistic and atomistic orientation of associationism. Köhler (1927), for example, observed that apes displayed considerable insight and concluded that Thorndike's emphasis on trial and error and the stamping in of responses as the basis for learning was essentially inadequate.

Gestalt psychology has become known as *field* or *cognitive*[6] theory, within which, as in the case of associationism, there are a number of subgroups. Although these subgroups vary in emphasis and viewpoint on some of the more peripheral aspects, they subscribe to the basic concept that human experiences have certain field properties which make the total phenomenon more than the sum of the separate parts. Field theories are an extension of the Gestalt principle; the term *field* is used in the same sense as electrostatic, electromagnetic, or gravitational *field* is used in physics or astronomy, to imply that the forces surrounding an object actually determine its physical properties. Just as the individual note has no meaning apart from the other notes in the melody, so behavior cannot be considered in isolation. To analyze experience as the accumulation of elementary associations, according to field theorists, is to lose sight of their true properties. The field psychologist, for example, points out that color does not have physical existence but, rather, is determined by the field in which it occurs; gray appears blue in a yellow field, and a given shade of gray seems darker on a white background than on a darker background. In contrast to association theories, the field approach is based on the principle of relativism; nothing is perceived as a thing-in-itself but rather in relation to other things in the sense of a *figure-and-ground* arrangement. Learning is part of the larger problem of organizing perceptions into a more complex structure exhibiting increasingly adequate field properties.

[6] Cognitive refers to the intellectual grasping of the meaning or significance of a given phenomenon.

Field psychologists interpret the term *field* as the total psychological world in which the person operates at a given moment; the individual does not react to the environment as it is but rather to the situation as he perceives or interprets it at the moment of behavior. What is important from a behavioral point of view is the meaning the situation has for him. Learning involves structuring the cognitive field and formulating cognitive patterns corresponding to the stimuli relations in the environment. However, cognitive theorists are especially concerned with what the subject is experiencing; they place major emphasis on the selectivity of perception. We are aware of only certain aspects of the total environment; i.e., as we face a given situation, certain aspects come into focus while others remain in the background of a Gestalt *figure-and-ground* arrangement. What the individual sees in a given situation depends on his needs, his purposes, his insights, his past experiences, his potentialities, as well as what is really "out there"; in other words, things are experienced in terms of the psychological makeup of the individual so that reality is psychological (i.e., *phenomenological*) rather than objective and physical.

A second point of emphasis in field psychology is the purposiveness of behavior. The individual sets his goals on the basis of his insights into the meaning of the situation, and his behavior will be intelligent or shortsighted depending on the adequacy of his grasp of the situation. He may have false or vague insights and, as a result, engage in behavior that is misguided or inadequate. Learning involves the development of insight, that is, the development of a more adequate cognitive structure of the total situation, enabling the individual to perceive more effective ways of utilizing its elements in order to achieve his purposes. Practice is important in that it provides repeated exposures from which a more adequate cognitive structure can emerge.

Learning involves the reorganization of experience into systematic and meaningful patterns. According to field theorists, learning is not additive; it is more than the accumulation of simpler elements into a complex and integrated sequence. On the contrary, mental life begins with undifferentiated wholes out of which the parts are gradually differentiated. The learner begins by perceiving the overall configuration, at first imperfectly, but by gradual and progressive differentiation of the components he gets a progressively clearer picture of the whole. The whole is primary; the function and meaning of the parts are determined by the whole in which they appear. The process of learning is not a matter of building simple perceptions into a complex pattern, but one of proceeding from a complex unit which is partially understood to a gradual clarification of the totality of the situation. The emphasis is on organization, relationships, meaningfulness, and cognitive clarity.

Lewin's Vector (Topological) Theory   Lewin's vector psychology (See Cartwright, 1959.), one of the better known of the cognitive theories, is closely related to such fields as physics and geometry from which he has borrowed a number of concepts. It is particularly attractive to people interested in group dynamics. A major concept in Lewin's theory is that of the "life-space," which is the psychological world in which the individual lives. It includes every person, every object, every concept and idea with which the person has psychological contact. The person himself occupies a central position in his life-space. At first, it is relatively unexplored and the individual has only a superficial understanding of his world; in fact, there are within the life-space at all times areas of various degrees of differentiation and organizational clarity. The objective is an ever greater clarification of the life-space, uncovering layer after layer and pushing its boundaries further and further back while, at the same time, attaining greater and greater contact with reality. A problem situation is simply an unstructured region in the life-space so that the individual does not know how to get from point to point. Learning, then, is a matter of differentiating one's life-space so as to connect more of its subregions by defined paths as, for example, deriving interrelationships among heretofore isolated aspects.

Another important concept in Lewin's theory is that of valence, a term borrowed from chemistry to refer to the strength of attraction and repulsion of the elements of the situation. The outcome of a given situation is the result of the various vector forces[7] of attraction and repulsion of the overall system as experienced by the learner. Of course, what repels one person may attract another so that vector forces reside in the meaning of the situation to the individual, and not in the physical environment.

Of special importance are the changes in the valence value of the components of the life-space. As a need is fulfilled, a reassessment is made to incorporate the changes in the various aspects of the situation so as to provide new direction to the individual's psychological locomotion. An important aspect of learning is the change in the valence value of the various goals as a result of the further clarification of the life-space. As the person meditates or matures, he may get insights into the shortsightedness of his present goals, for example. It must also be noted that the individual's life-space is of a moment's duration, even though there tends to be some basic continuity as one experience

---

[7] To the extent that a force acting upon an object is applied at an angle to the desired direction of movement, only part of its magnitude is effective in producing the desired movement; in other words, a given force usually has two components (or vectors), one contributing directly to the desired movement, the other operating at right angles to it, thus adding nothing (except a need for its neutralization). A strong motive which is only remotely related to a given action may actually provide less "net" motivational force for that particular task than a lesser but more pertinent motive.

shades into another. We might compare this to the need for the football player carrying the ball down the field to make continual reappraisal of the situation. In other words, the life-space is continually undergoing reinterpretation as a result of changes in cognitive structure. Reinforcement is not a central concept in Lewin's vector theory; the more his motives lead the person to explore his environment, however, the more likely he is to restructure his perceptual field, and the more likely he is to see new and more effective approaches to the attainment of his purposes.

TOLMAN'S PURPOSIVE BEHAVIORISM   Another major cognitive theory is Tolman's purposive behaviorism, also known as the sign-Gestalt or expectancy theory (Tolman, 1959). It appeals to a number of people in that it is scientifically objective and behavioristic while, at the same time, it emphasizes the cognitive nature of experience and, in a sense, combines the advantages of the cognitive and association theories. According to Tolman, learning involves the establishment of certain relationships between the perception of one stimulus and the perception of another so that a response made to a given stimulus leads to the development of certain expectancies or "means-end readiness." Tolman's major point is that behavior is goal-oriented. It is both cognitive and purposive in the sense that the development of cognitive structure is oriented to making use of the various aspects of the environment as tools or means-objects in the attainment of one's goals. Behavior is initiated by environmental stimuli and psychological states, but there is more than one way of attaining a given goal. The rat in the maze is really learning its way about; it is developing a maplike representation of the situation (i.e., expectancies), and not a sequence of running and turning habits. Once this cognitive structure is attained, it can make use of cognitive signs to guide itself to the goal, not necessarily by the route to which it is accustomed but by the route it sees will get it there most effectively under the present circumstances.

The motivational state of the organism determines what feature of the environment he will attend to, so that motivation is influential in perceptual acquisition, but Tolman is strongly against the Law of Effect and the principle of reinforcement. When drives are aroused, the state of tension leads to a demand for goal objects. These tensions lead to activity that is guided by expectancies, which the subject attributes to the various aspects of his environment, but he is neither pulled nor pushed by external or internal stimuli; he is following a path to a goal looking for the signs, that is, learning relationships. Motivation is not a factor in learning, although it is a factor in performance, and Tolman points out that learning may take place even though in, say, latent learning, it is not demonstrated in performance (Tolman and Honzik,

1930). The principle that, in Tolman's language, is most equivalent to reinforcement is confirmation. A correct response confirms the expectation and thus increases the probability of its occurrence; nonconfirmation, on the other hand, decreases the probability value so that reward regulates performance, not acquisition—at least not directly.

PHENOMENOLOGICAL PSYCHOLOGY   In even greater contrast with the rather atomistic and mechanistic position of the association theories is the phenomenological version of field psychology (Combs and Snygg, 1959; Combs, 1962), a position whose possibilities, while perhaps greatest in a clinical setting, are getting progressively greater recognition in other areas of human development. Educators, for example, are becoming more aware of its implications with regard to the various aspects of classroom operation. It represents a systematic attempt to deal with the world of phenomena in the psychological reality of its essential characteristics. Like other field theories, it views the individual in a state of dynamic equilibrium within the field in which he operates, but it places special emphasis on the phenomenological nature of perception. Perception is defined relativistically; what determines behavior is not objective, but rather psychological or phenomenological, reality. This world of personal experience is accessible to outsiders only through inference, and although this might make such data questionable as scientific evidence, to the phenomenologist the raw data of experience as recorded by the individual is legitimate and meaningful. This is the environment which has psychological significance, since this is what the individual is reacting to. In a real psychological sense, this is "what's out there," without regard to why, when, and wherefore.

OTHER THEORIES

A number of other theories can be mentioned. Functionalism, for example, is an eclectic approach which has considerable appeal for classroom teachers and psychologists who cannot subscribe totally to one or the other of the more theoretically consistent viewpoints. It is a relatively free and flexible attempt to draw from various theoretical positions the explanations having greatest meaning from the standpoint of the practical situation. The emphasis is upon the individual's adjustment to his environment. Its primary interest is on the functionality of relationships rather than on their explanation.

A theory of long standing in the clinical field is psychoanalysis. Freud's emphasis on the influence of early experience on personality development, for example, has found support in such findings as those of Hunt (1941) of the effects of infant frustration on adult hoarding in rats, and of Wolf (1943) on the effects of early sensory deprivation on the later functioning of rats under stress. The Freudian concepts of anxiety, fixation, and repression also have considerable significance for educational practice and will be presented in the various sections of the text without further reference to their psychoanalytic origin.

EVALUATION OF LEARNING THEORIES

Major Issues

The progress of a given discipline is as dependent upon theoretical advances as upon experimental productivity, for, without theoretical orientation, empiricism constitutes a mere accumulation of semirelated facts and laws. The end result of scientific investigation is the discovery of functional relationships among phenomena; however, only through the organization of these relationships into theoretical structure can we attain a broad understanding of their true nature. For a science to develop, facts must be organized into principles, and principles into theories, which will, in turn, suggest hypotheses; these hypotheses can then be tested and lead to further facts and principles. Although there are those who hold contrary views—Skinner (1950), for example, questions the need for learning theories—most psychologists agree on the value of theoretical structure in providing perspective in the investigation of psychological phenomena.

We have a number of theories, each with its specific orientation; all theories agree that learning is the acquisition of responses, but they disagree as to how the acquisition takes place. More generally, they all agree on the basic facts but disagree on their interpretation. Actually, the task of reconciling these positions is the concern of psychology rather than education, and only a brief overview can be provided here. That none of the theories postulated to date is acceptable to all is abundantly clear from the divergent views and the many objections raised against any one theory by subscribers to the opposite views. In fact, in the words of Melton (1956): "It has become fashionable to curse both S-R and the cognitive houses and all their little ones." The same point is made by Olds (1956), who notes that modern psychology sometimes seems more of a quasireligious battleground than a cooperative scientific venture, that proponents engage in vigorous defense of their own position in opposition to that of their colleagues, sometimes to the neglect of their own advancement or the advancement of psychology as a science. As he points out, we need to look for the contribution each theory can make and to orient ourselves toward progress rather than toward violations of one's preconceived canons of science.

Both association and field investigators have been accused of basing their premises on experiments whose results were relatively predetermined by the experimental design. Thorndike, for example, apparently set up his experiments so that the only way the animal could operate was on a trial-and-error basis, with reinforcement as the only possible determinant of learning. Russell (1927) makes the same accusation against both camps.

Many critics object to psychology's overorientation toward animal subjects. Melton views the large amount of experimentation done as a fine example of the application of the scientific method to the study of behavior, but he objects to the domination of learning by the rat. He suggests that to concentrate so much energy and scientific eloquence on an animal with limited symbolic capabilities and nonexistent verbal capabilities seems too high an intellectual price to pay for ease of procurement, maintainability, and reproduction of kind. He hopes for a social revolution among students of learning, wherein man will reestablish his dominance over the rat. Maier (1960) goes a step further. He suggests that psychologists often use theory to supersede rather than to synthesize the facts. A common example is to give the facts a new name. Since it is no longer fashionable to speak of instincts, psychologists now use the term *imprinting*, which apparently means essentially the same thing; they simply make the conflict disappear through word magic. Another common way of dealing with a difficult situation is to give circular answers. Frequently, scientific "explanations" simply restate the problem. To say that people enjoy being with one another because of a gregarious instinct is saying nothing more than people enjoy being with one another because they enjoy being with one another; it is simply describing at a different level of language the phenomenon it alleges to explain. Along the same lines, Spence (1951) feels that the concept of insight is particularly inadequate. To say that a subject suddenly responds correctly because he, suddenly and for the first time, perceives a situation in a new way simply displaces the question. We still need to know what made the subject perceive it in a new way and what are some of the factors that are responsible for this perceptual reorganization.

The criticism of oversimplification is often heard. Whereas it is true that one of the distinguishing features of science is maximal parsimony consistent with the facts, nothing can be gained by theoretical simplicity obtained at the expense of the distortion of the facts or sterility of implication. As Green (1963) points out, Procrustean assumptions designed to twist Euclidean geometry to fit the facts would be neither simple nor elegant, and simplicity in this case would dictate that we adopt the more complex mathematics. A mathematical model, for example, could be mathematically parsimonious but not necessarily psychologically parsimonious or even meaningful. To be of value, a learning theory must encompass a broad variety of learning patterns and learning materials; it must, for example, deal with problem solving, character formation, attitudes, adjustment, as well as skill development and concept formation. To be of value to education and psychology, learning theory must: [a] cover all aspects of learning; [b] extend our understanding of the conditions and forces that affect learning; [c] permit reasonably accurate predictions of behavior; [d] act as a source of hypotheses that can be tested through experimental research to extend our understanding of the teaching-learning process; and [e] permit implications at the operational level.

The extent to which some theories are mechanistic is also a point of issue. Gage (1963) not only questions the adequacy of conditioning as a theory for teaching, but also points out that conditioning is, in a sense, a blind, irrational process which, regardless of how powerful it may be in shaping the behavior of pigeons or of children, is essentially alien to the dignity of man as a thinking animal. He feels that despite its scientific appeal, and even its extension to deal with the formation of complex habits and skills through the building of a chain of conditioned reflexes, conditioning as a theory is too narrow in scope to explain adequately the more significant aspects of behavior, e.g., problem solving and creativity. This is perhaps a point of unavoidable weakness in the associationist position, which, in order to be scientific, has had to sacrifice the more subjective aspects of phenomena; there is always a danger of buying scientific rigor and precision at the expense of psychological significance and meaningfulness. On the other hand, the phenomenological theories have been criticized as too vague, subjective, and unverifiable to be of scientific value. Kendler (1961), for example, charges that the phenomenological flavor of "intervening variables" suggests a level of theoretical explanation which is, in fact, no explanation at all, and which gives no practical basis for operation: If the phenomenal self is not open to appraisal except by inference, how does one proceed to change the child's behavior, or even to understand it?

Most criticisms are leveled at the relatively extreme positions of the theories in question. Many of the criticisms of associationism, for example, are oriented toward the accentuation of its weaknesses particularly as they appeared in its original statement. More recently, a growing flexibility in associationism has enabled it to overcome its alleged weaknesses. The criticisms invariably relate to matters of degree and emphasis and often to misunderstanding and misrepresentation. Gates (1942), for example, rejects the charge that connectionism is mechanistic; he feels that to say that connectionism places the learner in the position of a relatively helpless victim of the external forces bearing upon him is a falsification of the S-R position. He points to the Law of Effect and the Law of Readiness as evidence of Thorndike's insistence on the individual being the captain of his own soul, with the characteristics of the organism—his structure, his emotional states, his drives, his background—rather than the stimulus alone as determining factors of behavior.

Points of Contrast

Some of the basic differences between association and field theories have been noted. The accompanying table shows the major points of disagreement in condensed form. It must be remembered that many of the points of issue are matters of emphasis and degree, and that any such summary inevitably must do violence to the facts. The student should consult more comprehensive sources for a more adequate picture.

MAJOR POINTS OF CONTRAST

ASSOCIATION THEORIES	FIELD THEORIES
Views of Learning	
1. Learning is a matter of association (or bond) between stimulus and response. The organism is set in motion by a stimulus.	1. Learning is the organization of experience into cognitive structure exhibiting field properties.
2. Learning is conceived as a matter of the formation and strengthening of associations.	2. Learning is a matter of meaningful dynamic structure in which relationships are identified. It involves a restructuring of the individual's cognitive field.
3. Learning (under conditions of reinforcement) is the key concept.	3. Perception is the key concept. The central idea is the perception of relationships between parts and wholes, means and consequences, etc. A problem is solved when the learner has restructured the field, i.e., gained insight into its essential relationships.
Part versus Whole	
1. A whole is made up of separate parts; a complex action is the additive combinations of simple acts. Parts are fundamental.	1. The parts emerge from the whole; the whole is primary; the parts have meaning only because of the field in which they exist.
2. A divide-and-conquer attack is made upon isolated parts which can later be added together into an integrated performance.	2. Learning is not additive: it is not a matter of separate elements joined together until the whole is built up. Meaningfulness resides in the totality of the situation or field.
3. Analysis is stressed. It is often accused of being atomistic and molecular.	3. The orientation is toward organization and integration. The opposition is not to analysis but to dissecting the whole into meaningless parts.

MAJOR POINTS OF CONTRAST (*continued*)

ASSOCIATION THEORIES	FIELD THEORIES

Part versus Whole

4. Learning proceeds from simple to complex; operant conditioning stresses organization of responses into progressively more complex behavior patterns (it does not deny understanding but puts emphasis on other features).

4. The individual begins by perceiving the whole (albeit imperfectly). Progressive differentiation of the component provides a clearer picture of the whole and of the parts in relation to the whole.
Learning begins with primary undifferentiated wholes out of which specialized aspects are progressively differentiated.

Views of Reality

1. The environment is real; it is both physical and psychological. Things are seen as they are; the physical environment is sensed, meaning is attained, and a response is made.

1. The environment is phenomenological and relativistic. Objects are looked upon, not as they actually exist, but rather in terms of their psychological significance. Absolute reality exists but does not coincide with psychological reality; things exist in *figure-and-ground* relation to other things, not in isolation.

2. Environment is distorted through selective perception; perception is relative to the individual's purposes at the time of perception. The basis of behavior is not reality but the world as perceived.

Mechanistic versus Dynamic

1. In their attempt to be scientific, association theories tend to be mechanistic. "Psychology's only hope of remaining scientific is to assume man is basically a mechanism." (Hebb)

1. Behavior involves a dynamic interaction between organism and environment. The individual is, in a sense, in dynamic suspension in the field.

2. Represented by a physical machine model with parts, gears and levers; perhaps like a computer doing what it is programmed to do. The learner is essentially a machine operating according to a schedule of reinforcement.

2. Represented by a dynamic system such as a whirlpool, or a hurricane.

MAJOR POINTS OF CONTRAST (continued)

ASSOCIATION THEORIES

FIELD THEORIES

Mechanistic versus Dynamic

3. Accused of involving blind, irrational shaping of the learner's behavior. The pigeon does not have to *want* to learn; he simply has to be induced to respond.
Skinner feels that to assume a purpose constitutes some supernatural guiding force beyond the scope of science (Gates rejects this position.

3. All behavior is cognitive and purposive. Behavior derives its peculiar characteristics from the learner's knowledge of how to use his environment and his potentialities as means-objects for attaining his purposes. Behavior must be interpreted in the light of the goal it is designed to achieve.

4. Associationism is oriented toward objective measurements, quantitative data, reinforcement schedules, etc., all of which are relatively scientific in nature.
Emphasis is on overt behavior—i.e., publicly observable activity of muscles, glands, etc.—which can be measured (especially behaviorism). Association theories are reaction-type theories.

4. Psychological behavior involves purposes, insights, etc., rather than mere physical movements.
Behavior is phenomenological. Cognitive theories have been accused of being subjective, vague and unscientific.

5. Emphasis is on trial and error, drill, reinforcement. The strength of an association is a function of its consequence.
Practice under conditions of reinforcement is fundamental.

5. Emphasis is on insight. Drill must be preceded by insight.
Practice permits the restructuring of the situation, i.e., the development of insight. The strength of a response stems from the degree of perceptual clarity.

6. The learner is the victim of reinforcement.

6. The learner is purposive, interacting within the field.

Historical versus Situational Perspective

1. Emphasis is on the past. (This is a matter of degree; association theories do not ignore the present any more than the field theories ignore the past.)

1. Emphasis is on the present as perceived. The field is contemporary: its psychological existence is of the moment of reaction.

2. Man is a purposive organism interacting with the many factors in the field having psychological meaning at the moment.

MAJOR POINTS OF CONTRAST (*continued*)

ASSOCIATION THEORIES	FIELD THEORIES
Applicability	
1. Probably best for the reaction-type learnings, e.g., habit formation.	1. Probably most suited for concept formation, problem solving, and other higher processes involving a dynamic interaction among the various elements of the learning situation.
Transfer of Training	
1. Transfer through the concept of common elements; generally pessimistic about transfer possibilities.	1. Emphasis on insight, meaningfulness, cognitive structure, etc., is conducive to transfer; dynamic relationships discovered and understood in one situation have maximum applicability to other situations.

The disagreement among the various theories does not imply that we really know very little about the nature of the learning process. On the contrary, we have a large store of knowledge; it is in the ordering of this knowledge that we do not agree—because we are looking at learning phenomena from different perspectives.

The theories differ from the standpoint of the material to which they appear to be oriented; habit formation may well call for a different approach and a different interpretation of learning than creativity, for example. We might question whether all behavior is purposive: certain types of learning, e.g., salivating in Pavlov's dogs, may involve a simple mechanistic association rather than a complex process of dynamic interaction among the various elements of the learning situation. Psychologists are not agreed as to whether all forms of learning can be accounted for by a single theory. It might be argued, for example, that contiguity may represent the significant determinant of the learning of habits, attitudes, emotions, and other relatively involuntary reactions. The development of skills, on the other hand, might be most effectively promoted by a stimulus-response approach, while the solution of problems, the mastery of concepts, and the acquisition of complicated insights, differentiations, and integrations, requiring mediation through the higher mental processes, might be most adequately viewed from the standpoint of cognitive theory. The issue is beyond the scope of the present discussion.

We must avoid the dogmatism of a premature systematization and close-minded adherence to a single point of view; at the same time, we must also avoid superficial naive eclecticism with regard to conflicting positions. Premature standardization of learning theories will achieve a solution at too great a cost. We need to remember that no matter how annoying the diffusion of present theories is, these theories are serving a very definite purpose. For the time being, perhaps a wise eclectic position is justified. Teachers, for instance, need to formulate a consistent set of principles as the basis for teaching if they are to avoid the confusion likely to result from the contradictory implications of the uncritical combination of different frames of reference. We need to work for an increasingly coherent and systematic core of operational principles. For the present, whether to subscribe to one theory or to a mixture of theories is essentially a matter of preference. Various objections to the eclectic position have been raised. The more theoretically oriented psychologists prefer to commit themselves to one theory and to work toward the resolution of its weaknesses. Others hold that a theory is useful or useless, rather than simply correct or incorrect, and feel that at the practical level a fair use of different viewpoints is to be preferred to subscribing to a single theory on the basis of consistency for consistency's sake.

As to validity, it must be clearly understood that neither of the two major positions, nor their subtheories, is obviously false, obsolete, inadequate, or useless. No one experiment will demolish any of the theories, nor, on the other hand, will it prove one theory at the expense of its competitors, whether from the standpoint of its overall formulation or its basic implications and interpretations. Any and all these positions find fervent adherents among psychologists. Each theory represents an honest attempt to deal with some aspect of behavior, and each is capable of making a contribution to the meaningful interpretation of evidence. Not only do they help us to think about behavior, but they also help us to plan research that can lead to further clarification of the field. In the meantime, dogmatic loyalty to any one system to the relative rejection of others seems unwarranted. Any dogmatic pronouncement as to how learning takes place is also unwarranted.

CURRICULAR IMPLICATIONS

What is perhaps more important is the extent to which the various theories provide a consistent and dependable foundation for educational practice. McConnell (1942) in his synthesis of the various theories finds that, despite their differences, they point to the same practical consequences and support essentially the same educational practices. In a sense, the number of issues on which there is complete agreement among the various theories is relatively limited; on the other hand, there is greater agreement on the fundamentals than would appear at first hand.

Gates (1942), himself a connectionist, accepts the bulk of the basic pedagogical implications of field theory as presented by Hartmann (1942), except perhaps for slight differences in emphasis and rationalization. McConnell (1942), Burton (1958), and Hilgard (1956), all present lists of the points of relative agreement on basic issues. It is likely that, as the field becomes more adequately established, it will become progressively more possible to translate one viewpoint into another.

On the other hand, it must also be recognized that learning theories cannot be expected to give the teacher definitive rules of thumb to apply in the classroom. As Hartmann points out:

> Because the reference frame of the educator tends to be the world of the school and the classroom, he is easily led to forget that no single system of psychology was ever developed with the problems of the teacher and the pupil as its primary source of inspiration. . . . [p. 203]

The interpretation of a theoretical position and its translation into a set of functional rules is bound to be a subjective matter. As Gagné and Bolles (1959) point out, despite the rather large amount of information regarding learning, there is still relatively little of a systematic nature that is known to promote efficient learning in the classroom situation. As Melton (1959) observes, just as the discoveries of the physicist made television possible, yet the actual creation of television was the work of engineering technologists, so it is the educational technologists who must design the curriculum and the teaching methods to exploit the psychologists' discoveries concerning the learning process.[8] On the other hand, teachers tend to be impatient with conflicting points of view; they want unequivocal answers which, of course, no psychologist can provide and which no good teacher really wants. Unquestionably, the diversity of classroom operations and the relative fluidity of educational objectives in relation to the individual child demand a high level of flexibility and ingenuity in the use of diverse methods. The maintenance of theoretical orientation under such circumstances is difficult.

A curriculum based on associationism would be characterized by simplicity. In its extreme form, it would call for identifying the responses that mark the educated man, identifying the stimuli which lead to these responses, and presenting these stimuli in order to associate them with the desired responses, either through contiguous presentation or through reinforcement. The desired associations could thus be formed and, if necessary, sequenced one to the other to form whatever behavior pattern is required. At a relatively mechanistic level, connectionists would emphasize having the learner, in a state of readiness, attack a given

[8] Gage (1964) emphasizes the need for theories of teaching concerned with explaining, predicting, and controlling the ways teacher behavior affects pupil learning.

problem with variable and multiple response and rely on the Law of Effect to reward correct responses. The desired connections would be strengthened through properly motivated practice; they would be generalized to similar stimuli and transferred to related situations. Understanding and meaningfulness would be emphasized where appropriate.

Associationism cautions us to be careful as to what we reinforce. If the child is teased until he cries and then his crying leads his tormentors to stop teasing, then, according to Guthrie, the reinforcement of the crying as the most recently occurring response through the withdrawal of the noxious stimulus is actually teaching the child to cry. Children are taught to act competitively by the rewarding of competitive behavior to the point where competition frequently becomes a way of life. Skinner notes that placing two children in a situation with a limited number of toys creates an almost ideal condition for shaping selfish and aggressive behavior. Skinner would also counsel the teacher not to dismiss his class while the children are being rowdy; he would insist that they be quiet and then reward them through dismissal.

The curriculum based on operant conditioning is specific and definitive. The key to successful teaching is to analyze the nature of the task to be learned, to design techniques which manipulate the process with persistence and consistency, and to set up definite and specific reinforcing contingencies so that behavior can be brought under the precise control of its consequences. Teaching here is a matter of a carefully designed program of gradual changes in the contingencies involved and in the skillful use of schedules to maintain behavioral strength. This relatively simple and mechanistic approach is apparently capable of shaping complex behavioral patterns—whether in pigeons, in rats, or in humans. For the kind of learning toward which operant conditioning is oriented, Skinner has been eminently successful:

> It is dangerous to assert that an organism of a given species or age cannot solve a given problem. As a result of careful scheduling, pigeons, rats and monkeys have done things during the past five years which members of their species have never done before. It is not that their forebears were incapable of such behavior; nature simply never arranged effective sequences of schedules. (Skinner, 1958b; p. 96)

The curriculum devised according to cognitive specifications would stress the structuring of the learner's perceptual and cognitive field. The focus would be on insight, meaningfulness, and organization, and the teacher would emphasize understanding and structure both in his presentation of subject matter and in the learning he would have the children do. Classroom procedures would be oriented toward the clarification of issues, the discovery of interrelationships, and the differentiation of relatively unstructured problem situations into situations having greater clarity and focus. Cognitive theorists recognize that understandings, meanings, and attitudes once achieved through insight need to be further clarified through experience and application; they are not opposed to repetition but they insist that insight precede practice. Lewin, for example, sees repetition as necessary to clarify one's life-space, to structure it more adequately, and to develop new relationships and new differentiations of formerly undifferentiated areas as the basis for more adequate behavior.

The cognitive theorist would stress the dominant role played by the *field* in which phenomena occur, as for example, the influence of the total concept on the meaning of the parts, the role of the family or the classroom in the behavior of the child, etc. He would emphasize the development of meaningful relationships within the overall field and would strive to ensure that the student grasp clearly what he is attempting to learn in proper *figure-and-ground* perspective so as to have the phenomenon under discussion properly integrated in the total situation. He would condemn teaching material out of relation to the total situation in which it occurs, or teaching skills in isolation from their use, e.g., the rules for grammar apart from their use in effective communication.

Lewin's concepts of the life-space, valence, field forces, psychological locomotion, and conflict have definite implications for adjustment, character formation, and especially for group dynamics. The teacher needs to be concerned with the personal involvement of the child in his structuring of the present situation. Personal goals are always present, but the child may need to think through his goals in order to discard those that are relatively capricious. Lewin's concept of level of aspiration also has very definite meaning for the classroom.

The phenomenological approach is not so much oriented toward the curriculum and the learning process as it is toward the learner who is to do the learning. Its orientation, although having crucial bearing upon learning in the classroom, is primarily toward the development of the individual as a self-actualizing organism. Only recently have educators begun to appreciate the extent to which the child's perception of himself in relation to his schoolwork and the totality of the school situation has significance upon his operation in the classroom, both academically and personally. It has considerable appeal to those interested in the overall development of the child in interaction with the totality of his environment. The concept of the individual in dynamic suspension in an atmosphere of field forces—whether considered from the standpoint of personal adjustment, group dynamics, or concept formation—has both a scientific flavor and a certain air of common sense and meaningful perspective. Unfortunately, by contrast to the 1-2-3 precision of Skinnerian conditioning, field theories are rather vague as to how the various objectives are to be attained; specifically how is cognitive structure to be effected in one's students? How does one go about effecting changes in the phenomenal field of another person? The phenomenological approach may be particularly useful in the hands of the experts and in certain settings—as attested to by the success of nondirective counseling, for example—but despite its appeal, perhaps the lack of specific recommendations for its implementation may constitute a limitation to its use in the classroom. Its vagueness also raises a question as to its adequacy as a scientific theory.

PHYSIOLOGICAL BASES OF LEARNING

Although learning may be considered a neurobiological phenomenon, we have yet to solve the basic problem of identifying the changes in the nervous system that accompany learning or the process through which learning takes place. Earlier theories assumed a neurological basis. Locke, for example, saw the brain of the infant as a blank sheet on which experiences were to be recorded. At the turn of the century, Thorndike conceived of the nervous system as a giant telephone switchboard in which learning was largely a question of connecting certain input to certain output; every response was the resultant of a connection between stimulus and response effected through the nervous system. With the refutation of Thorndike's neurological position, psychologists, although acknowledging that learning must have a neurological foundation, have restricted themselves to an explanation of behavior at the functional level without commitment to physiological explanation. Most psychologists today simply avoid the issue.

An important exception is the central position given to neurophysiological hypotheses in Hebb's theory of behavior (1949). Hebb's emphasis on the physiological basis of the perceptual processes stems from experiments involving chimps reared in darkness, for example, or congenitally blind human beings who see for the first time as a result of a corneal transplant or the removal of cataracts. He noted that perception of the nature of an object comes slowly after what seems to be a long and tedious process of attentiveness to separate details. He postulates: [a] the organization of sensory and motor-neural elements (which he calls *cell assemblies*), and [b] temporarily organized phase sequences consisting of reverberating circuits through which the momentary perception of the whole alternates with the perception of its parts. The first stage of learning is the establishment of cell assemblies and related phase sequences. This comes very slowly; grasping such basic concepts as squareness or triangularity, for example—which we assume everyone knows—is really a slow, gradual proposition. The first stage then provides the foundation for more rapid subsequent learning. This theory is, of course, speculative but it is consistent with the concept of readiness and with Harlow's concept of learning sets to be discussed in later sections.

HIGHLIGHTS OF THE CHAPTER

Chapter 2 presents a brief overview of psychology as a science. It attempts to give the student a perspective for understanding psychological phenomena. Periodic review of pertinent points should be made as the student progresses through the content of the text. For the time being, the student should be oriented toward the following major ideas:

[a]

Science attempts to identify functional relationships among phenomena and to organize these relationships into theoretical structure.

[b]

In the attempt to account for the relationships noted between dependent variables and the independent variables under study, scientists postulate hypothetical constructs, an important subgroup of which are the perceptual processes; the individual does not respond to the environment as it actually exists but to the situation *as he sees it*. Learning itself is a hypothetical construct.

[c]

Theories of learning can be categorized into two broad categories: the association and the cognitive (field) theories with a number of semi-independent theories under each. Association theories, for example, include connectionism and conditioning, the latter further broken down into classical and instrumental conditioning. Field theories likewise include a number of subtheories, an important category of which are the phenomenological theories.

[d]

None of the theories of learning, as presently constituted is completely acceptable; a number of criticisms of various degrees of validity and of severity have been leveled at each and all of them. The major differences among them are essentially a matter of perspective and of emphasis. They tend to support the same pedagogical practices, although generally for different reasons.

[e]

Learning theorists tend to avoid discussing the neurophysiological changes that occur with learning. A significant exception is Hebb's theory which, among other things, postulates primary learnings that are slow and tedious to acquire but which set the foundation for more rapid learnings later.

SOURCES OF RELATED MATERIALS

Bellack, A. A., *Theory and Research in Teaching*. New York: Teachers College, Columbia University, 1963.

Bigge, Morris L., *Learning Theories for Teachers*. New York: Harper & Row, Publishers, 1964.

Burton, William H., "Basic principles in a good teaching-learning situation," *Phi Delta Kappan*, 39: 242–248, 1958.

Eysenck, H. J., "The contribution of learning theory," *J. educ. Psychol.*, 30: 11–21, 1960.

Gage, N. L., "Theories of teaching," in E. R. Hilgard (ed.), *Theories of Learning and Instruction*. 63rd Yearbook, National Society for the Study of Education, Pt. I. Chicago: University of Chicago Press, 1964. Pp. 268–285.

Gowin, D. B., "Can educational theory guide practice?" *Educ. Theor.*, 13: 6–12, 1963.

Hilgard, E. R., and G. H. Bower, *Theories of Learning*. New York: Appleton-Century-Crofts, 1966.

————, *Theories of Learning and Instruction*. 63rd Yearbook, National Society for the Study of Education, Pt. I. Chicago: University of Chicago Press, 1964. (See Hilgard, "A perspective on the relationship between learning theory and educational practice," pp. 402–415.)

Hill, W. F., *Learning: A Survey of Psychological Interpretation*. San Francisco: Chandler Publishing Company, 1963.

Israel, M. L., "Educational redesign: A proposal," *Sch. Rev.*, 67: 292–304, 1959.

Kramer, Samuel A., "Are theories of learning helpful?" *Educ. Forum*, 19: 227–235, 1955.

Marx, Melvin H., *Theories in Contemporary Psychology*. New York: Crowell-Collier and Macmillan, Inc., 1963.

Melton, Arthur W., "The science of learning and the technology of educational methods," *Harv. Educ. Rev.*, 29: 96–105, 1959.

————, *Categories of Human Learning*. New York: Academic Press, Inc., 1964.

Mowrer, O. H., "Learning theory: Historical review and reinterpretation," *Harv. Educ. Rev.*, 24: 37–58, 1954.

Skinner, B. F., "Reinforcement today," *Amer. Psychol.*, 13: 94–99, 1958.

Spence, Kenneth W., "Relation of learning theory to the technology of education," *Harv. Educ. Rev.*, 29: 84–95, 1959.

Woodworth, R. S., and M. R. Sheehan, *Contemporary Schools of Psychology*. New York: The Ronald Press Company, 1964.

QUESTIONS AND PROJECTS

1

Plan a lesson, say, in the social studies, according to contrasting associationistic and cognitive specifications. What differences might exist in the objectives which the two approaches would emphasize? How might the relative effectiveness of the two approaches be evaluated?

2

Collect a series of statements expressing various theoretical orientations on key issues, e.g., the definition of learning, the role of motivation, etc. Survey the members of the faculty of the departments of education and of psychology as to the position to which they subscribe on these matters.

3

Evaluate: To the extent that teaching is an art, theories of learning contribute nothing to the practical job of teaching. What benefits might a teacher derive from knowledge of psychological theories? What theoretical considerations do you see as of value from the standpoint of educational practice?

4

What is the point of distinction between theories of "learning" and theories of "teaching?" (See Gage in 63d Yearbook, National Society for the Study of Education, Pt. I.)

CHAPTER 3

The Determinants
of Human Behavior

> The individual is a purposive, striving, selective, adjusting, animated organism. He does not spring to life just because stimuli from the outside fall upon him, nor does he lapse back into passivity and desuetude at their termination.
>
> *Hall, 1951; p. 328*

Psychology is the science of behavior. The primary benefit to be derived by prospective teachers from a course in educational psychology is, therefore, a greater understanding of what causes people in general, and children in particular, to behave as they do. This chapter is devoted to a discussion of this especially important problem.

THE CONCEPT OF NEEDS

Behavior, whether desirable or undesirable, does not just occur; it arises in response to some form of internal or external stimulation and is directed toward the attainment of a goal; i.e., behavior is purposive. In fact, as we have seen in Chapter 2, the view of behavior as purposive or goal-oriented is a fundamental premise in a number of the theories of learning, especially that of Tolman (1932). Hall (1951) presents a simi-

lar view when he says that the individual is purposive, striving, and selective. Field psychologists see the individual in dynamic suspension in
psychological space, impelled, propelled, as well as repelled by field
forces in complex and simultaneous interaction with one another and
with the individual. Some of these forces are powerful, others weak;
some are innate, others learned; some are brief, others long-enduring.

Despite the fact that almost all phases of the interpretation of behavior are characterized more by controversy than by unanimity, there
is a general consensus among psychologists that behavior is, in a sense,
an attempt to satisfy some need. A somewhat restricted version of this
position is that behavior stems from the tension resulting from the frustration of a need and is oriented toward the reduction of this tension.
This view has been subjected to criticism, and more recently the concept
of needs has been broadened to include such needs as the need to explore and to manipulate, where the element of tension resulting from
frustration is not readily apparent.

The fact that behavior occurs in response to a need does not restrict the *amount* of one's behavior, since one is besieged at all times
with a multiplicity of needs, only a few of which can be satisfied. It does
restrict the *range* and *direction* of behavior; only the most pressing needs
can be considered and behavior will be oriented toward their satisfaction.
Thus, in the Minnesota semistarvation study (Keys et al., 1945), the
responses of the subjects were oriented primarily toward food while
whatever other needs they may have had were relegated to a position of
secondary priority.

The importance of this concept cannot be overestimated. The concept of needs, drives, goals—or more generally, motivation—can be
considered the key to understanding behavior. It underlies every phase
of human relations, whether these relations involve dealing with a spouse
or children at home, students in the classroom, or associates on the job.
In fact, every aspect of behavior—in the home, school, or community—
can be understood only in terms of motives and their satisfaction in relation to the demands of the situation in which the individual finds himself. Only when the teacher is fully aware of this fact can he provide
effective guidance of the child's growth.

THE NATURE OF NEEDS

Considerable ambiguity is to be found in psychological literature in the
use of terms to refer to various conditions within the organism that determine its behavior. There is not complete agreement among psychologists as to the use of the term *need*, for example. Some refer to the
actual organic deficit or requirement of the body as a physiological need;
Brown (1961) relates needs to bodily imbalance or disequilibrium produced by any one of a number of conditions, such as the withholding of

food. Hilgard (1956) defines needs as physiological states of deprivation or tissue injury. There is a similar lack of agreement as to the meaning of *drive*, although it is generally used as relatively synonymous with *need*, to refer to bodily states of the organism that are experienced as restlessness and that initiate tendencies toward some kind of activity.

In the general case, the energizing aspects of a need are roughly proportional to the degree of deprivation of the need; the activity level of the rat, for example, as measured by the squirrel-cage method, is roughly proportional to the number of hours of deprivation of food, at least to the point where continued deprivation results in physical weakness. Feeding is followed by a period of relative inactivity as far as hunger is concerned. On the other hand, this relationship is only relative. Learning and various mental and physiological conditions, e.g., the presence of more potent needs, affect the extent to which a person is activated by the deprivation of a given need. Furthermore, it would be difficult to establish an exact relationship between the degree of deprivation and its energizing strength in the social needs where the biological aspects are relatively less crucial.

MOTIVATION

The determination of behavior implies not only the energizing of the organism, as might be implied in our definition of *need* or *drive*, but also the direction of its behavior toward certain aspects of the environment capable of overcoming the deprivation the need implies. The energizing phase occurs through the operation of internal stimuli, but the establishment of a behavior pattern capable of satisfying the need, involving aspects external to the organism, is essentially a matter of learning since the organism would not generally know at first how to satisfy its needs. A distinction might therefore be made between the inner stimuli, such as the contractions of the stomach walls in the case of hunger (the energizing aspect), and the learned behavior patterns by means of which it strives to satisfy its hunger (the directional aspect). Implied is the existence of a goal, i.e., a state or condition that the organism seeks to attain in order to satisfy some need. Food would be a goal to a hungry individual. Goals do not exist apart from the person whose behavior is being directed toward them as a result of some inner need.

The term *motive*—in contrast to *need* and *drive*—is generally used to refer to certain conditions within the organism which, besides arousing and sustaining activity, actually predispose it to behave in ways appropriate from the standpoint of the need in question. In other words, although needs continue to be appropriate antecedent conditions for activity, it is the directing of this activity toward the goal that ties down the definition of a motive. Consequently, it is probably more correct to speak of hunger or sex as motives rather than simply as needs or drives.

This is especially true of social needs which are even more obviously affected by learning; the individual does not seek affection or social approval but, because of previous experiences, seeks the affection or approval of certain persons, so that again it is probably better to think of affection and social approval as they influence behavior as motives rather than as needs. On the other hand, as Hall (1961) points out, it would be misleading to suggest consensus on the use of these terms. Actually, because in practice most "needs" or "drives" are so strongly affected by learning that they cannot exist in the original or narrow meaning of the terms, no confusion is likely to result from the use of the term sex *drive* rather than the perhaps more correct term sex *motive*, for example, and many psychologists use the terms interchangeably under the broad designation of motivation. In keeping with the general usage in the psychological literature, the present text will use these terms synonymously even though *motives* would generally be more precise.

Both internal and external stimuli are involved in the motivation of behavior. We need to distinguish, for example, between: [a] the inner stimuli, e.g., physiological stimuli of hunger which arouse the individual to activity and sensitize him to certain aspects of his environment having hunger-reducing properties, and [b] the external stimuli such as the odor and sight of food which arouse and promote food-seeking behavior. Actually, motivated behavior is frequently triggered more by external stimuli than by internal need. Teachers frequently use verbal cues to stimulate children to do things, and certainly suggestions have energized individuals with respect to hunger, sex, and almost any other need. It is also possible for human beings to stimulate themselves with regard to certain needs: a person can whet his appetite by simply thinking of food.

The determinants of human behavior—whether called needs, drives, motives, or purposes—are generally encompassed under the broad heading of motivation which has, therefore, at least two fundamental components: a need state and an external goal. We might then say that motivation refers to a state of the organism in which its energies are mobilized selectively toward the attainment of a given goal. More specifically, motives serve three important functions:

[a] They energize, i.e., activate and sensitize the organism toward certain stimuli.
[b] They direct its behavior toward certain goals.
[c] They reinforce behavior that is effective in the attainment of desired goals.

MOTIVES AS DETERMINANTS OF BEHAVIOR

Motivation is not directly observable; it is a hypothetical construct postulated by psychologists to explain certain behavior. The strength of an individual's motivation must be inferred from his activities, i.e., from the extent to which he exerts himself in order to satisfy an alleged deprivation or to attain a given goal. Whenever learning is efficient, when it is characterized by persistence and seems to result in satisfaction upon the attainment of the goal, we assume the presence of motivation. The identification of the particular motive or motives in operation is, of course, precarious since motives are generally complex and often disguised.

Everyone accepts the concept of motivation or its equivalent but considerable disagreement exists as to its origin, its essential nature, and its role as the determinant of behavior. As we have seen, theories of learning range from those in which motivation occupies a central position to those in which it is relatively incidental. Tolman makes the purposive nature of behavior the central theme of his theory. Field theorists emphasize perception, not motivation; however, since perception is not treated as a static correspondence between stimulus and behavior, they have had to concern themselves with tendencies, tensions, directing forces, and other concepts relating to motivational phenomena. Motivation was given a prominent role by Lewin, whose system is concerned with sources of energy, tensions and stresses, and dynamically organized vector forces operating within the field, implying thereby both direction and strength in the tendencies of the organism to change its life-space. The particular tensions within the organism induce reorganization in the valence system of its subjective environment, thus guiding its behavior toward a given goal in accordance with the properties of the overall field.

Whether motivation is essential to learning is a point of controversy. Hull (1943) postulated the reduction of the tension associated with the frustration of a need as the crucial factor in determining what responses would be learned. Guthrie (1959), on the other hand, does not make motivation directly essential to learning, but he relates motivation to performance from which learning can occur. Motivation may simply maintain the subject in a situation where the factors responsible for learning can operate on him. To the extent that motivation promotes vigorous and variable activity, it increases the likelihood that some adequate aspect of his behavior will be learned. A similar position underlies the shaping of behavior through selective reinforcement in operant conditioning. The distinction between performance and learning as it relates to motivation is also noted in latent learning in which learning apparently takes place without its being reflected in improved performance until the organism is motivated to display such improvement.

It seems logical to assume that the more complex forms of behavior are a function of motivational control, and motivation is generally accepted as one of the conditions on which meaningful learning in the classroom depends. In fact, that learning results from the goal-seeking behavior of the organism is essentially the central theme of present-day psychology. The view that behavior is purposive rather than accidental, although simply a theory, is supported by considerable data suggesting its adequacy, and it has proven productive in the study of human and animal behavior alike.

CLASSIFICATION OF MOTIVES

Classification is unavoidably an arbitrary process governed by such factors as the author's purpose and even personal preference. The classification of motives is no exception; they are so complex and interacting that their classification into neat, clear-cut categories is obviously impossible. Not only does the expression of a given motive vary from person to person (especially between cultural groups) but some motives can be expressed through different behavior, and similar behavior may represent the expression of different motives. What is more, the behavior displayed by a person at a given time is not the outcome of a single motive, but rather the resultant vector of the multiplicity of motives operative at the moment in his motivational space. Even the operation of physiological motives entails complications as a result of social and cultural pressures that obscure their true nature. We can, for instance, separate survival motives as involved in hunger and thirst from social needs, but in civilized society, food-taking is often as much a social as it is a biological act.

Various authors have classified needs or motives according to different systems ranging from a single dual breakdown into viscerogenic and psychogenic to others that are quite elaborate; Murray (1947), for example, lists twenty basic needs. The present discussion will be organized around the relatively fundamental distinction between physiological and psychological needs.

PHYSIOLOGICAL NEEDS

A number of the needs which underlie human behavior are organically induced. These needs are sometimes considered primary in the sense that not only are they basic to the sustenance of life, but, in cases of severe frustration, they also tend to take precedence over such nonorganic needs as affection and self-esteem. On the other hand, experience can modify this relationship, and people have been known to starve themselves to death in order to hoard money—suggesting that what begins as a relatively minor want can grow in importance to the point of overshadowing what was once a more basic need. Also to be remembered is that, if a need is satisfied in everyone, it becomes a common demoninator which no longer functions as the basis for different behavior in different people. Thus, since most people have adequate sleep, rarely is it an important determinant of behavior. As a result, because the physiological needs tend to be satisfied to a greater degree than the the psychological, at least in our culture, they are often less influential in determining behavior than are the latter which are theoretically less basic.

The following is a partial list of the many physiological needs that could be mentioned:

NEED FOR FOOD   Hunger is one of the needs whose importance as the cause of behavior in present-day America is minimized by the ready availability of food. However, teachers find that children sometimes become restless and irritable just before lunch, especially if they have not had an adequate breakfast; in the Minnesota semistarvation studies (Keys et al., 1945), for instance, the subjects were highly irritable and "blew up" at the slightest provocation. It is probable that a certain amount of fidgeting in school and even misbehavior is connected with the tension resulting from hunger pangs. A carton of milk in mid morning, as often provided in kindergarten, might help. The teacher too may find that a cup of coffee during his free period improves his disposition as well as restores his vitality.

A problem in this area is that of the child who concentrates on candy bars and desserts generally as a compensation for feelings of loneliness and insecurity rather than an attempt to satisfy hunger. Occasionally a vicious circle sets in, as in the case of the adolescent girl who, feeling unaccepted, comforts herself by eating sweets; the resultant acne and obesity aggravate her feelings of rejection and often cause her to feel guilty over her inability to exercise self-control, thereby increasing her need for sweets. Education on the importance of a balanced diet, together with diagnostic and remedial work in the area of personal adjustment, may help, but where a basic personality problem exists, improvement is usually slow.

NEED FOR WATER   The need for water can be of tremendous moment in determining the behavior of a person lost in the desert, but it tends to be of minor consequence in the classroom because it can readily be satisfied. Teachers sometimes run into a problem when allowing one child to go out for a drink brings up the problem of everyone else wanting a drink too. Actually, when such a mass exodus occurs, it probably reflects restlessness on the part of the class rather than a real need for water and must be considered from that standpoint. Where teachers make provision for children to move around and to do interesting things, they can be reasonably assured that the latter will run to the water fountain only when they are really thirsty.

When children come into the classroom after hard play, it is understandable that they will actually be thirsty. The teacher can, of course, refuse to let them out of the room. But, if the need is really present, the children will display various signs of restlessness from fidgeting to mischief as they attempt to work off the tension arising from this unsatisfied need—unless, of course, the teacher provides another need (e.g., avoidance of punishment) strong enough to overcome the first. A more constructive way of handling the situation is to call the children in from the playground a minute early and allow them to get drinks before returning to the classroom. The unwise teacher tries to ignore or to operate in defiance of such psychological realities as needs; the wise teacher makes provision for their satisfaction, thus contributing to the peace and quiet as well as to the effectiveness of all concerned.

NEED FOR SLEEP AND REST   Occasionally a child will fall asleep in the classroom. This is most likely to occur when the task is of limited interest; it is correspondingly less likely to occur when classwork calls for active student participation. Generally, there is little that can be done about the symptoms of inadequate sleep: the problem has to be handled from the standpoint of its specific cause. It might help, for instance, to revitalize classroom activities and bring them into line with student goals and purposes. There are times when the child is hardly to blame; some youngsters are lacking in vitality, perhaps as a result of having to rise early in order to take care of a paper route or to get the bus to school. At times, the fault lies with the parents who allow their children to stay up late to watch television or who permit teen-agers to have parties during the week. Unless parental or community cooperation is secured, there is little that can be done. Although actual fatigue resulting from schoolwork is probably rare, it may nevertheless underlie the problem behavior, noncooperation, inattention, irritability, and even the defiance sometimes encountered in the classroom. Mental fatigue or boredom, on the other hand, is common, especially with younger children who may find it difficult to concentrate for long periods and who therefore need short periods and a variety of activities.

NEED FOR ACTIVITY   Youngsters need rest but they also need opportunities to release energy. Just watching the preschool child when he is on his own shows clearly the unnaturalness of keeping him quiet for hours at a time. Even the older child—and for that matter, the adult— has to release excess energy once in a while. Again the unwise teacher tries to enforce quiet; the wise teacher builds his program around the needs of the child and aims for a fair balance between exercise and rest.

NEED FOR SEX   Probably no other need creates as much difficulty in our culture as sex. While the other physiological needs tend to be reasonably well taken care of, the satisfaction of sex needs in present-day America is not only controlled by social taboos, but is, in effect, denied young people for an extended period between the advent of puberty and marriage at the very time when the sex drive is at its peak. The problem is made even more difficult by the fact that there is no substitute gratification as there is for other needs. As a result, the possibilities of guidance are restricted to inhibition and the internalization of taboos.

Furthermore, the taboos and the secretiveness which often accompany the child's legitimate questions only serve to make the subject a mystery and thereby to increase his interest. When he finally gets the information (or misinformation), it is usually from some other youngster under conditions that may well warp his outlook on the subject. One need not accept the Freudian emphasis on sex as the cause of maladjustment to see the validity of this viewpoint: attempts to ignore sex needs will tend to lead to warping of attitudes in exactly the same way as the persistent frustration of any other powerful need. The effect of our present way of dealing with the problem of sex can be seen in the unusual interest in sex stories, in the prudity of many adults when sex is discussed, as well as in the high incidence of sexual delinquency, marital infidelity, and other social ills. It might also be pointed out that, just as in the case of the person who overeats or who eats sweets to excess, the person who is sexually promiscuous often acts so because of feelings of loneliness and rejection rather than because of an excessively strong sex drive. It seems fair to suspect that the various escapades of the middle-aged Don Juan (male or female) probably stem from feelings of insecurity over whether he or she has any sex left rather than from excessive virility. Sexual misbehavior is frequently the expression of a more basic difficulty; i.e., it becomes the vehicle through which personality problems, e.g., hostility toward authority, express themselves.

The need for more realistic sex education is fully accepted by psychologists, clergymen, marriage counselors, and juvenile court officials. But practice lags behind, while youngsters suffer the consequences. As the Kinsey reports (1948, 1953) indicated, most children manage to get considerable information about sex and, perhaps, even more misinformation. Sex education in our culture, actually is not so much neglected as it is actively and deliberately avoided. What is needed are frank answers to questions in a planned sequence of instruction begun at home and early in grade school and continued throughout high school. Such instruction should fit the level of the child. The fifth-grader may be more interested in sex as an aspect of science, whereas in high school a discussion of this subject should be slanted toward family living. As Arbuckle (1962) points out, by the time the child is a teen-ager, his sexual problems are no longer intellectual problems to be solved with facts; rather they are emotional tensions. Actually sex education needs no apology nor subterfuge in name or intent; there is, however, need to go beyond the biological aspects to the moral and ethical questions involved if it is to accomplish its purposes.

The school must also provide for the sublimation of the sex drive. The coeducational setting of the high school, besides promoting heterosexual adjustment which is perhaps the major developmental task of adolescence, also tends to decrease the severity of the problems associated with the sex drive. Boy-girl friendships under supervision help to relieve sexual tensions, particularly if the school sponsors a positive program of guidance designed to promote a greater understanding of sex in its personal, social, and moral aspects. In view of the effects of the sex drive on the personal and social life of the individual, the school must consider the development of sound attitudes toward sex one of its major responsibilities. There is need for a certain repression of the sex drive, but there is especially need for its integration as a positive driving force within the framework of a self-concept where sexual morality is a dominant value. The school also needs to concern itself with the personal and social aspects of sex. To the extent that these are important aspects of the total growth of teen-agers, very often involving them much more critically than the academic menu, the school cannot afford to overlook their existence.

PSYCHOLOGICAL NEEDS

By contrast with the physiological needs, which are generally sufficiently satisfied as to be of comparative unimportance in determining what a person does, psychological needs are important determinants of behavior because they are incapable of complete satisfaction. A person may eat to the point where he cannot touch another bite, but he can never have all the love, security, or social recognition he would like. No sooner is the person happy over being promoted to branch manager than he is unhappy until he becomes president of the company. Again, the breakdown of these needs is essentially a matter of personal preference.

NEED FOR AFFECTION Everyone wants to live in a relationship of reciprocal warm regard with one or more persons, and the average child has at least minimal insurance against the total frustration of this need in the love of his parents and siblings. Later he tries to extend his domain to include a few close friends, then a sweetheart, and eventually a spouse and family of his own. However, it must be realized that many children, including a good number living with their parents, lack even a home base and feel totally unloved.

NEED FOR BELONGING   Closely related to his need for affection is the child's need to feel that he is an acceptable and accepted member of a group. Most children find satisfaction for this need at home and at school, both in the classroom and on the playground. However, the child can satisfy this need just as easily by belonging to a group of ruffians as by belonging to a troop of boy scouts. In view of the important bearing the choice of friends is likely to have upon their later personal and social adjustment, we must be especially careful to place acceptance by desirable groups within reach of all children.

The needs for affection and belonging are often grouped together under the heading of emotional security, the importance of which—particularly in infancy—is universally recognized. Psychologists are increasingly convinced that emotional security in the first year or two of life is crucial in determining later adjustment. The infant, for instance, has no way of knowing why he is not picked up when he cries; he can only fear the worst. He must be able to depend upon his world, to know that the people upon whom he depends will not let him down. Of primary importance in this connection are the child-rearing practices of the home. The child must also find security in the classroom situation. There is need for a carefully planned (although not rigid) schedule in which every child has a place, and for reasonably consistent limits within which he can chart his course.

NEED FOR ACHIEVEMENT   Everyone likes to accomplish what he sets out to do and to feel that his accomplishments are worthwhile. This need is closely related to such other needs as social recognition and self-esteem, and it probably derives much of its potency through conditioning as a consequence of the fuss parents make over the child's early achievements. It will receive special consideration in a later section under the heading of the *achievement motive.*

Schools make it difficult for certain children to satisfy their need for achievement. For the dull child, the likelihood of solving all the problems, getting good grades, or turning out a masterpiece in English is relatively remote. It is equally true that schools often make it difficult for the gifted child to obtain a sense of accomplishment; ordinary schoolwork is often so infantile that he gets no more sense of success from getting it done than the housewife gets from hanging out the family laundry. What he wants is something to challenge his abilities. Our schools need to—and can—be made more vital and dynamic to the bright, the dull, and the average child. Teachers need to pay closer attention to the diversification of instruction and assignments so that every single child is challenged to his level of ability and experience; they need to provide a fair balance between ease that conveys no challenge and difficulty that frustrates.

NEED FOR INDEPENDENCE   People want to govern their own lives, to set their own purposes, without interference and compulsion. This is probably a relatively basic need. The young child wants to eat by himself; even the baby stiffens when held too firmly. Adolescents, particularly, resent being pushed around. And so do adults, but they often forget this when dealing with children; then they wonder why so many children rebel either openly or more subtly through noncooperation or delinquency. Schools tend to be overregimented: children must not arrive before a certain time, but also they must not arrive late; all day they must change activity on command; even the play period is often organized so that there, too, children do what the teacher says. Certainly schools cannot tolerate chaos but children do need a chance to grow! This calls for freedom from overprotection and undue regimentation as well as for increasing responsibility in making and carrying out their own plans.

NEED FOR SOCIAL RECOGNITION   This need, also called the need for status or approval, concerns the apparently universal desire to feel that what we are and what we do is looked upon favorably by others. Since so much of their lives centers on the work of the school, the satisfaction of this need in children is largely in the hands of the teacher, who needs to be aware of his responsibility in this connection, especially because, besides being essentially the sole dispenser of social recognition, he also sets the pattern for other children to follow.

The need for social recognition probably results in large measure from conditioning through the praise his parents confer upon the child when he meets their expectations. It is of primary importance in character formation and in the orientation of the individual toward socially acceptable behavior. On the other hand, too strong a need for social recognition is likely to result in enslavement to the point where not only can he not make his best contribution but he thereby increases the likelihood of his rejection and the need for further slavish conformity as a means of obtaining approval. This is particularly true of adolescents to whom peer approval is of such importance as to cause almost complete conformity in matters of dress, customs, and speech, etc., and the more insecure they are, the more concerned they must be with the reactions of others. Excessive need for approval is also involved in the compulsion of the average person to keep up with the Joneses. On the other hand, persistent failure to achieve recognition and acceptance by the "desirable elements" of society may lead the individual to cease striving for their approval and to show his resentment through delinquency and other forms of unacceptable behavior.

NEED FOR SELF-ESTEEM   The need to feel that what we are and what we do comes up to our own standard is closely related not only to the other psychological needs just discussed but also to the self-concept and the level of aspiration to be mentioned later. What we think of ourselves revolves around our standards of what is right and what is wrong, what is adequate and what is inadequate. Thus, if past experience has led us to prize scholarship, morality, or the social graces, to fail in these respects causes frustration of our need for self-esteem. This need revolves primarily around the values acquired during the process of socialization by means of which society perpetuates its way of life. To the extent that society is successful in having the child internalize its values and standards, he becomes unable to violate the social code without automatically frustrating his own sense of self-approval and suffering guilt feelings. On the other hand, if society is not successful, he can violate the social code without guilt: his only concern is not getting caught and he may actually feel a sense of self-esteem at his cleverness at avoiding detection.

SATISFACTION OF NEEDS

PROBLEMS IN SATISFYING NEEDS

Needs are relatively specific, but the goals the individual seeks in order to satisfy these needs vary from person to person and even from time to time. Thus, whether hunger causes a person to seek bread, meat, or cake depends to as great an extent on the particular tastes he has developed as on their availability and their adequacy relative to his need. In this connection, habits play a major role in the goals selected, even to the point where the individual continues to seek goals that are detrimental to his welfare.

Behavior is not a simple matter of satisfying a single need. The child is at all times besieged by a multitude of needs, on the one hand, and of goals through which these needs can be satisfied, on the other. Since he cannot attend to all these needs nor attempt to reach all goals at once, he must be selective; he may have to choose between the approval of his peers and the approval of his teachers, for example. He often has to choose between satisfying his needs through achievement in schoolwork or outside activities. Social values often run counter to basic needs, e.g., the ideal of sexual morality in relation to the sex drive; in fact, one's own values may be self-contradictory, e.g., the middle-class disapproval of both fighting and cowardice. The individual usually resolves these conflicts on the basis of the relative dominance of the values involved and of his ability to rationalize the violation of his other values. He may suffer from guilt in the process.

Maslow (1943) proposes an interesting hierarchy in the prepotency of needs. Starting with a classification of needs into [a] physiological, [b] safety (including routine, consistency, and security), [c] love, [d] esteem, and [e] self-actualization, he suggests that normally the individual cannot consider a given need unless those of higher priority are reasonably satisfied. Although certain reversals in the hierarchy may occur as a result of past experiences, he usually will not attend to his love needs until his physiological and safety needs are adequately met. It follows from this arrangement that, whereas the physiological needs may be met nearly 100 percent, each successive level will be satisfied to a lesser degree and the last on the list, the need for self-actualization, may go relatively unsatisfied.

Satisfying one's needs is bound to involve a certain amount of difficulty. If there were enough satisfiers for all—if everyone could be president, rich, and married to the most wonderful person in the world—then even the poor would have a million and all that goes with it. But reality is such that the satisfaction of one's needs is far from automatic and assured. We are constantly being frustrated by the elements, by personal limitations, by social regulations, by prejudices. Even the taking of food is governed by numerous restrictions ranging from the unavailability of certain foods to regulations dictating what, when, where, and how they are to be eaten.

Some individuals have considerable difficulty in satisfying their needs. Some have limited assets; others have learned ineffective need-satisfaction patterns and are unable to graduate to more effective procedures. Furthermore, needs have to be satisfied within the framework of the situation and some people find themselves in environments which are particularly severe or perhaps simply incompatible with their makeup. Generally, the more a person deviates from the average, the more likely he is to have difficulty satisfying his needs. The child who is too fat, too tall, too short, too bright, or too dull, who matures early or late, tends to have special problems.

The dull child is particularly likely to have difficulty in satisfying his needs. From the day he comes to school, he finds endless frustration. The teacher may show disappointment and annoyance at his lack of achievement, leading him to feel unloved and unaccepted; his parents may compare him unfavorably with his siblings or with the boy down the street. Tension resulting from the frustration of these needs will force him to look for other ways in which they can be satisfied. If he has assets in other areas, if he is physically superior or possesses some skill which will give him a sense of achievement and of self-esteem as well as promote his acceptance by his peers, all may yet be well. By thinking of himself as an athlete, for instance, and rationalizing that academic work is unimportant, he can shrug off his failure in schoolwork. However, to the extent that he may be relatively lacking in ability in most areas, he will find it more and more difficult to locate a means of satisfying his needs, and he may resort to obnoxious behavior or even delinquency. Certain conditions such as poverty, extended illness, and physical handicaps constitute obstacles in the path of the normal satisfaction of the child's needs which, by cutting off the usual avenues through which needs are met, may cause him to resort to self-defeating behavior. Nevertheless, it must be emphasized that these conditions are only indirectly responsible for unacceptable behavior and many individuals with equally severe impediments achieve excellent adjustment.

The School and the Child's Needs

The school has a definite responsibility to see that every child achieves at least minimum satisfaction of his needs. Not only is pupil adjustment a primary objective of modern education but, in addition, failure to provide for need satisfaction soon results in disruption of classroom activities and harm to other children. Furthermore, it must be noted that the school is perpetually bringing into focus the degree to which children are meeting the demands made upon them. The child may not know he is dull until he enters first grade but, once he enrolls, the school does not let him forget it. So much of his life revolves around the work of the classroom that serious harm can be done if the school is not conscious of its effects upon him.

Teachers must provide each child with the opportunity to satisfy his needs in socially desirable ways. The child who boasts to gain social recognition needs to be shown how he can gratify this need more constructively. Teachers must be alert to opportunities for children with special limitations to gain status; the over-age boy might be made custodian of the baseball equipment or appointed to the safety patrol, for example. A good teacher should be able to find a dozen ways within the framework of the activities of the school in which this can be done. A well-organized cocurricular program of diversified group activities has tremendous possibilities in providing need satisfaction for children who find this difficult within the more restricted phases of classroom operation.

Sympathetic understanding by the teacher is essential. He should realize that children misbehave not to annoy him but because they do not know of better ways of satisfying their needs; they are simply calling for help, and he should consider it a challenge, not an affront. When children seem tense, he should be particularly careful not to aggravate the situation but, rather, to provide the security and understanding they need. It is important that they be able to count on him when all others have deserted them. He should by his behavior convince his pupils that they are wanted and accepted for what they are, because they need this security if they are to experiment in better ways of need satisfaction. This is especially true of children with an unhappy home background who have to depend that much more on the teacher's understanding and acceptance. It is sometimes hard to understand why certain children should have to behave as they do, but, apparently, they have learned through past experiences to gain some gratification through their behavior, and they may be too insecure to explore better ways; even punishment may be rewarding if it is the only way to gain attention!

The teacher is only human. He too has needs to satisfy, and he is in a position to attempt to satisfy them at the expense of his pupils. His need for status, for example, may make it rough on children with a similar problem. This is especially so in the case of the maladjusted teacher. Actually, in view of the mutual interdependence of teacher and pupils, an enlightened attempt at satisfying each other's needs would be advantageous to both; in this the teacher must set the pattern.

THE DRIVE-REDUCTION THEORY

Until recently psychologists subscribed exclusively to the drive-reduction theory of motivation, which postulates that behavior stems from the frustration of a need and is oriented toward attaining relief from the resulting tension. According to this theory (Hull, 1943), behavior becomes goal-oriented by virtue of the fact that certain responses are selectively reinforced through tension reduction resulting from the attainment of the goal. This selective reinforcement leads to an increase in the probability of occurrence of effective responses so that they develop into an integrated goal-directed behavior pattern. Behavior that does not lead to the goal, on the other hand, does not lead to the removal of tension, and is therefore avoided.

The concept of reinforcement through drive reduction appears quite plausible and until recently was accepted as *the* explanation of motivated behavior. However, organisms learn to attach reinforcement value to objects that cannot have need-reduction properties. Money, for example, can provide reinforcement for a variety of behavior patterns even though it cannot constitute primary reinforcement for basic needs. In the study by Wolfe (1936), chimps were trained to accept, in payment for performing certain tasks, poker chips which they could then exchange in a vending machine for primary rewards such as a raisin. They learned relatively complicated tasks such as using a red chip to get food, a blue chip to get water, and a white chip to get out of the cage.

In order to deal with this problem, reinforcement psychologists postulated the principle of secondary reinforcement, which assumes that reinforcement properties can be transferred to neutral stimuli through their repeated simultaneous presentation with a primary reward. In other words, the fact that chimps work for poker chips does not imply a new poker-chip drive characteristic of monkeys; their behavior is simply based on secondary reinforcement of the hunger drive. In fact, the response will soon be lost if not given periodic primary reinforcement. The number and variety of secondary rewards deriving their reinforcement value from association with primary rewards is relatively unlimited. Actually, even primary rewards rarely exist in their natural state. As we examine behavior, we often find it difficult to disentangle the reinforcing conditions that are simply the result of the associative learning from those which are more directly rooted in basic needs.

DELAYED REINFORCEMENT

Reinforcement should follow immediately upon the performance of the response; research has shown that the effectiveness of reinforcement diminishes sharply as the period of delay increases to the point that, as shown in Figure 3-1, it has practically no effect on the learning of rats

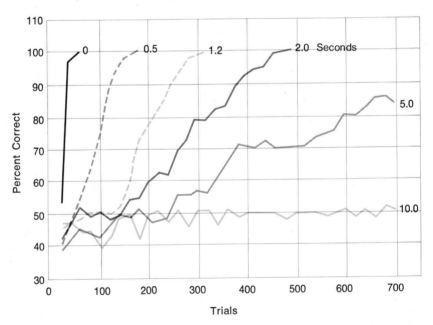

FIGURE 3-1   Learning curves for each of the six different delay groups. (Reprinted by permission from *Psychology of Motivation* by John F. Hall, published by J. B. Lippincott Company. Copyright © 1961 by J. B. Lippincott Company. Adapted from Grice, 1949.)

if the delay is of more than ten seconds (Spence, 1947; Grice, 1948). However, reinforcement tends to remain effective despite the delay if the subject maintains orientation toward both the task and the reward, or, as in the case of human beings with language possibilities, if he can re-activate the connection between a response and its consequence when the reinforcement occurs. Furthermore, human beings often get imme-diate reinforcement in the knowledge that, since they have made the correct response, they have only to wait and the reward will be forth-coming. Children can get adequate reinforcement from the promise of a candy bar next week. On the other hand, it is characteristic of us all to lose sight of remote goals, and the younger the child the greater the need for immediate reinforcement through the establishment of short-term as well as intermediate subgoals. The question of immediate feed-back is, of course, a vital issue in the rationale underlying teaching machines.

PARTIAL REINFORCEMENT

It is not necessary for the rewarding situation to occur at every in-stance of a given response. Partial (or intermittent) reinforcement is gen-erally not as effective from the standpoint of acquisition, but it tends to promote a response highly resistant to extinction. Grant el al. (1951), for example, found that 25 percent reinforcement led to greater persist-ence of response than did 50 percent, 75 percent, or 100 percent rein-forcement. Lawrence and Festinger (1962) in a series of interesting experiments also found small intermittent rewards to yield responses more resistant to extinction than large and regular rewards. Experimen-tal findings in the area of partial reinforcement have obvious implications for child training. The fact that children, when they cry, are generally comforted on a partial reinforcement schedule may explain why some children are so persistent in their crying. Partial reinforcement may also explain why bad habits are so hard to break; it may also explain the persistence of the gambling response—and of cheating in the classroom[1]

FUNCTIONAL ANATOMY

The concept of functional autonomy of motives, as presented by All-port (1937), refers to the persistence of habits, even after the motives that led to their acquisition have ceased to operate. It seems that with increases in habit strength, a response becomes partially autonomous, or functionally independent of its historical antecedents. Earl (1957), for example, trained mice to dig sand to obtain food and found that after a while the very act of digging had become self-demanding. This could be even more pronounced in the case of human beings whose habits are

[1] See Jenkins and Stanley (1950) for an excellent review of partial reinforcement.

infinitely more varied and self-sustaining. A person may be expected, as a result of experience, to have acquired a vast system of habits which exert a strong governing influence upon his behavior. Thus, a person accustomed to smoking has a *need* to smoke and is likely to feel uncomfortable if he is prevented from doing so. In other words, the habit which had a basis in some need at one time now supersedes the original need and becomes a need in its own right. It has become what might be labeled a habit motive, a concept of major educational significance. If the teacher can encourage children to develop habits of persistence, hard work, and honesty, these habits will act as motives in furthering certain types of behavior. Bad habits are equally self-sustaining, of course.

Attractive as the theory may be in accounting for the complex motivational structure of man, it has been subjected to mounting criticism. The theory of functional autonomy has a certain plausibility, but it is by no means accepted as the best way to account for the persistence of motives seemingly far removed from primitive biological urgency, nor does it make clear the process whereby motives become functionally autonomous. It may be that certain activities become self-sustaining by providing rewards relatively inherent in the activity itself—perhaps rewards for a different need; for instance, high quality work done to please someone may eventually lead to work done for the purpose of satisfying one's own need for self-esteem. What is probably involved is a substitution of drives; a person who at one time worked to feed himself finds, by the time he has enough money for food, that money has become a symbol of status so he continues to work, not to get food, which is no longer the primary need, but rather to attain the status which money implies.

OBJECTIONS TO THE DRIVE-REDUCTION THEORY

A number of objections have been raised to what appear to be weaknesses in the drive-reduction theory. Harlow (1953), for example, argues that, even though drive reduction is not completely unrelated to learning, it is a relatively unimportant factor. On the other hand, it is rather difficult to document all the objections which have been raised; the present discussion is simply an overview, and more adequate sources (e.g., Harlow, 1953; Hunt, 1960; and White, 1959) should be consulted for a more complete coverage.

[a] The basic premise of the drive-reduction theory is that behavior stems from tension resulting from the frustration of a need; it is based on Cannon's concept of homeostasis (Cannon, 1939) erroneously interpreted as representing an optimal level of body equilibrium. Actually, Cannon held that homeostasis was merely necessary so that the organism could go about the pursuit of its more significant goals without having to concern itself with the maintenance of equilibrium within the body processes. It would follow from the drive-reduction theory that the

satisfaction of a need would lead to a period of inactivity as far as that need is concerned, although other needs would then become dominant. However, when the organism appears to be completely satisfied, it does not generally become inactive, but rather it seeks activity such as manipulation, exploration, or even sheer exercise. It is active at all times; even in sleep, EEG patterns show that the brain cells are continually active. Children play without apparent need; monkeys explore, manipulate, and otherwise resort to various activities. Hunt (1960), for example, visualizes living matter not as an inert substance to which motion must be imparted by extrinsic forces, but rather as open systems of energy exchange which exhibit activity intrinsically and upon which stimuli may have a modulating, but not an initiating, effect. A similar position is taken by Smith and Smith (1966) who argue that, since the organism is naturally and normally active as long as it is alive, the real problem is not to account for activity through a series of motives but rather to account for inactivity should it occur.

[b] A second premise of the drive-reduction theory is that the organism is running away from tension, a position not only essentially negative but also contrary to fact. Certainly man is activated by something more fundamental and more constructive than the mere avoidance of pain and discomfort. Actually, the individual is often seeking, not a state of equilibrium but rather a state of disequilibrium: much of his behavior is need-producing rather than need-reducing. The fact that boredom is tension-arousing was particularly evident in the studies by Hebb and Lilly presented in Chapter 1.

[c] Behavior frequently occurs in situations where need reduction is clearly not attained or where it cannot take place for some time after the behavior it is supposed to reward, so that we have to postulate the satisfaction of some secondary drive, perhaps through the anticipation of the satisfaction of a primary need. Rats can be made to learn with a reward of saccharine which, having no food value, cannot reduce hunger, for example. The same is true of experiments involving the injection of a saline solution or the self-administration of electrical shocks which apparently serve as motives but which cannot be need reducing. Learning takes place when the food pellets are so infinitesimal that they can hardly have significant need-reducing properties. Animals also learn in situations where food is not allowed to reach the stomach; they learn when food is injected directly into the stomach, and when the stomach is inflated by means of a balloon. Hypnosis can also serve in a motivational capacity even though it is not directly related to the satisfaction of primary needs.

Learning takes place before the food reward is digested to effect need reduction. One can, of course, postulate consummatory behavior as a form of secondary reinforcement. This may be true in certain instances but not in all cases (Sheffield et al., 1954). Hebb (1946, 1949), for example, notes that infant chimps show spontaneous fear of the skull of a monkey even on first exposure where the observed behavior cannot be accounted for on the basis of secondary reinforcement. He proposed a concept of dissonance as a more adequate explanation.

Other questions might be raised about the drive-reduction theory. As Lawson suggests (1960, p. 345): "Currently such a theory of reinforcement is not regarded by most psychologists as consistent with most of the facts. Nevertheless, it cannot be considered a bankrupt idea nor has it been an unproductive hypothesis."[2] In a sense, the theory appears rather naïve and there ought to be a more fruitful approach to the rationale underlying the nature and control of behavior. It is generally easier to find fault, however, than it is to devise a criticism-free theory and, as a result, the need-reduction theory—with certain reservations—is still held by many and is perhaps still essentially true in its main arguments. Recent criticisms simply represent a reluctance to accept the need-reduction theory as the only theory of motivation.

THE STIMULATION THEORIES
OF MOTIVATION

A more positive orientation to motivational phenomena is that of the so-called stimulation theories, whose basic premise is that the organism seeks not equilibrium but, rather, disequilibrium. Leuba (1955) and Hebb (1955) speak of an organism seeking an optimal level of stimulation. Glanzer (1958), in an excellent review of the literature, suggests that the organism requires a certain amount of stimulation per unit of time; if too little stimulation is present in the environment, it will seek stimulation; if too much stimulation is present, it tries to reduce it. Strong support for this view comes from the deprivation studies previously mentioned (Hebb, 1958; Lilly, 1956), suggesting that, far from being an ideal condition which the organism seeks, homeostasis soon becomes completely unbearable.

Among the more commonly accepted stimulation theories are those based on curiosity (Berlyne, 1950; Butler and Harlow, 1957), exploration (Montgomery, 1953), activity (Hill, 1956), manipulation (Harlow, 1953; Terrell, 1959), and competence (White, 1959). They overlap in their basic premise that novel stimuli function as motivational agents. In other words, these drives are evoked exteroceptively by the presentation of a novel stimulus object and incorporate both the behavior-energizing (or activating) and the behavior-directing functions of motives.

[2] See Bolles (1958) for a summary of the literature on drive reduction.

They apparently represent a need for mastering the environment or perhaps part of an overall need for new experiences. The young child very early in life demonstrates the need to explore; he is attracted by bright objects, he wants to see what is on the other side of the street, he has an almost compulsive desire to touch everything from the stove to the electric socket. This is closely related to the need for achievement; the child wants to ride a bicycle, he wants to know what makes a watch work. The adolescent wants to tinker with an old jalopy. Adults, too, are curious; they travel and they ask questions.

THE CURIOSITY, EXPLORATORY, AND MANIPULATORY DRIVES

A number of experiments have shown that animals and human beings display behavior that is essentially exploratory in nature, that is motivated by no "need" other than to explore the environment. A rat free to make successive choice of the arms of a T maze displays a marked tendency to choose different arms on different trials (Glanzer, 1958). When given a choice, rats prefer a pathway with the greatest stimulus complexity to the one to which they have been accustomed (Dember et al., 1957; Havelka, 1956). It is also noted that, when animals are presented with a set of stimulus objects and have responded to them and another set of stimulus objects is presented, they will spend more time with the new objects. Berlyne suggests a *curiosity* drive as an explanation of this phenomenon, while Montgomery refers to an *exploratory* drive. Harlow postulates a *manipulatory* drive to refer to a relatively similar phenomenon. Montgomery and Segall (1955) found that rats learned to solve a discrimination problem when the reward was simply the opportunity to run for a minute in a situation new to them, thus displaying a combined need for activity and exploration. In the Butler and Harlow study, monkeys learned to discriminate between two opaque doors, one of which was unlocked permitting the animal to look into the laboratory. The other was locked and so arranged that, if the monkey selected it, a screen would fall which would prevent it from exploring for a 30-second waiting period. Not only did the monkeys learn the discrimination problem, but they continued opening the door by the hour and by the day without extinction with no reward other than a one-minute peek into the laboratory, suggesting that visual exploration (curiosity) is a primary rather than a secondary drive.

Relatively similar is the manipulatory drive postulated by Harlow as a result of experiments in which monkeys disassembled a complicated set of hasps. Their behavior was characterized by persistence and a high level of efficiency despite the absence of external reward. In fact, Harlow found that placing a raisin under the hasps disrupted the performance by diverting the monkeys' attention. Terrell (1959), in a study of the manipulatory drive in children also found that the manipulatory group learned a task more quickly than did the group promised candy (the control group). Again, the manipulatory drive appeared to be primary in that continued practice without primary rewards did not lead to its extinction, as it would have had it been a case of secondary reinforcement.

It is significant to note that these drives are externally determined and that they are as effective in promoting learning as those based on primary rewards; in Harlow's experiment, the big difference was that the food-rewarded monkeys dropped the puzzle the minute they had obtained the reward. One of the fundamental features of these drives is that they show increasing motivational strength with repeated elicitation, suggesting that they are as basic, innate, and self-sustaining as their internally initiated counterparts. They are particularly significant in that the more readily the individual can take care of his primary survival requirements, the more energy and attention he can devote to the exploration and extension of his world through maximizing stimulation. These drives are, therefore, fundamental in an affluent society where primary needs are generally fulfilled and concern centers on exploring the environment and seeking new experiences. Apparently, as suggested by Maslow's hierarchy of needs, the individual can afford the luxury of exploration only after he has achieved the necessities of life. The curiosity, exploratory, and manipulatory drives perhaps are not crucial for survival, but by promoting contact with the environment, they provide increased opportunity for self-fulfillment. The fact that a desire to learn and to know is as fundamental as any drive based on need reduction is especially important in the light of the quest for truth as the ultimate educational goal, the quest for truth in a realm that knows no limitation and no satiation.

THE COMPETENCE DRIVE

A more elaborate formulation of the stimulation view of motivation is White's concept of competence (White, 1959) in which he explains exploratory, manipulatory, and general activity behavior as part of the process by which the individual learns to interact effectively with his environment. He uses the word *competence* in the broad sense of ability to carry on a successful transaction with the environment and thus grow and flourish, rather than simply maintain oneself. As defined by White, the competence drive encompasses the drives of activity, curiosity, exploration, and manipulation, which he feels are simply aspects of competence. This concept of competence also borders on the achievement motive postulated by McClelland et al. (1953), and, perhaps, even more significantly on the concept of the phenomenological field as postulated by Combs and Snygg (1959), who see the individual's single drive as that of maintaining and enhancing the self. An extension of this view is presented by Combs et al. (Combs, 1962) in the concept of self-actualization, i.e., the need to discover and develop evermore effective and adequate ways of realizing one's potentialities. Sears and Hilgard (1964) discuss, under the term *ego-integrative motives*, achievement and such unconscious motives as self-actualization and self-expansion, all of which have some sort of self-reference and imply some degree of mastery over the environment beyond bare survival.

THE ACHIEVEMENT MOTIVE

Closely related to competence is the need for achievement (*N Ach*) (McClelland et al., 1953; Atkinson, 1958), which may be thought of as a widely generalized level of aspiration. A person with a high need for achievement sees problems and obstacles as challenges to be met; he seeks success. It is also related to actual achievement; Lowell (1952) and French and Thomas (1958) found individuals high in *N Ach* more likely to solve problems related to achievement goals than those low in *N Ach*, largely because of greater persistence.

Achievement is a particular avenue toward self-respect in American society, where some degree of mastery over the environment beyond minimal survival needs tends to be expected. It is especially characteristic of our middle-class orientation as reflected, for example, in the present emphasis on the pursuit of academic excellence. It is interesting to note that achievement striving is so highly internalized in middle-class children that, in contrast to their working-class counterparts, they tend to maintain a high production output even in the absence of external rewards (Douvan, 1956). A considerably greater orientation of boys toward *N Ach* has also been noted, presumably because of the greater social expectations for boys to get ahead (Phillips, 1962).[3]

Achievement motivation tends to develop in homes that emphasize achievement. The home of the child high in *N Ach* tends to insist that he develop on his own rather than remain a subordinate part of the family unit to which he must sacrifice his individual interest. Whether this occurs because the child is neglected or because he is rewarded for developing independence, achievement motivation is fostered by parents who set high expectations for their children, do not maintain emotional ties that are too tight, and encourage the child to master his environment, while at the same time providing some degree of support. Winterbottom (1953) found that the influence most likely to develop strong need for achievement in boys was the mother's encouragement of in-

[3] After a period of general acceptance, the concept of achievement motivation is now being questioned as to validity (Lazarus, 1957; Blake and Mouton, 1959). Birney (1959), for example, feels that the need for achievement is largely situational in character.

dependent activity. These mothers expected boys to try new things, to do well in competition, and to make their own friends. Actually, they tended to demand less at an early age in the way of independent achievement and to impose more restriction on their children's initial freedom, thereby saving them from undue failure and frustration. They rewarded their children both for meeting the demands for independence made on them and also for abiding by the restrictions initially placed upon their independence. Once a home base of dependency and security had been established, however, they encouraged independent behavior. The mothers of sons low in achievement motivation, on the contrary, tended to continue restricting their children beyond the age at which the other mothers had relaxed their restrictions. High N Ach is generally found in homes dominated by a mother who is achievement-oriented, strong, supportive, and strict rather than tender; often the father is inept, thereby preventing the child from identifying with his father and causing him to look to achievement for his rewards (Strotbeck, 1958). McClelland et al. (1953), for example, reported that American college men who scored high in N Ach tended to rate their parents, especially their fathers, as unfriendly, unhelpful, and nonsuccessful, while those who viewed their parents as clever, successful, and self-confident tended to be low in need for achievement.

SENSORY DEPRIVATION

Of considerable support to the stimulation view of motivation is the substantial evidence concerning the unbearable effects of sensory deprivation noted in the studies by Hebb and Lilly reported in Chapter 1. Subjects paid to lie in a relative stimulation-free environment soon found the reduced sensory input so completely intolerable that they had to be relieved. It is interesting to note that boredom was aggravated by the impairment of the subjects' ability to think systematically and productively. Also of interest are the parallel McGill studies (also reported in Chapter 1) showing irretrievable impairment in the intellectual and personality development of dogs resulting from early sensory deprivation.

These studies have obvious implications not only from the standpoint of the individual's adjustment but also, and especially, from the standpoint of his overall social, emotional, and intellectual development. They suggest that one of the primary prerequisites for human (and apparently animal) welfare is the impact of a considerable amount of environmental stimulation, especially in the early period of development. They also raise the possibility that an organism accustomed to a high level of stimulation will have a higher stimulation requirement than one from an impoverished environmental situation. This would again emphasize the differential effects of early experiences and may well have a significant bearing on the success of children from the lower class and their readiness for school, for example. In fact, it might account for the nonproductivity of people from the lower class who have been accustomed to a low level of stimulation and achievement. This is true of people on relief, for example. People unemployed for extended periods of time seem to lose all zest for activity; they have more time for sports, for reading, and for leisure pursuits, but they actually engage in them less. There is a general deterioration of meaningful living as well as a narrowing of outlook on life.

OTHER THEORIES OF MOTIVATION

A number of other theories of motivation could be mentioned, some of which are simply offshoots of those previously discussed. Probably the oldest theoretical formulation is that of Freud, whose theory attempts to relate various stages of motivational orientation to developmental stages. His views are based largely on unconscious motives and have their greatest application in pathology and the clinical interpretation of behavior.

A more recent view of motivation is Hebb's theory of dissonance (Hebb, 1946, 1949) in which he explains fear (and anxiety), not as a result of traumatic experiences but rather as a result of the incongruity that arises when something previously familiar suddenly takes on an air of unfamiliarity. In his experiments, infant chimps displayed spontaneous fear of the plaster cast of a monkey's skull or the deflated rubber figure of a monkey being dragged across the floor. In keeping with his physiological orientation, Hebb postulates that it is the sequential organization of past experiences (See Chapter 2) which, by providing the subjective phenomenon of expectation, forms the basis of fear; a markedly incongruous receptor input, by disrupting the sequential organization, causes the process to have an unpleasant emotional tone, that is, to evoke fear.[4]

MOTIVATION AS A SCIENTIFIC CONCEPT

Useful as it may be in understanding behavior, motivation as a scientific concept is vulnerable to criticism from both a theoretical and a practical point of view. Not only is there confusion as to terminology, but even the basic concepts are open to question. This does not deny that motivation is valuable as a point of departure in clarifying the bases upon which effective behavior might be promoted. A number of interesting but unresolved issues in modern psychology revolve around

[4] Festinger makes the motivational value of the discrepancy between expectation concerning a given situation and perceptions of that situation the basis of his *Theory of Cognitive Dissonance*. (1957).

the conditions under which motives are learned and maintained. As we have noted, motives are simply hypothetical constructs; motivation is postulated when the individual is energized and his behavior is expedited toward a given goal. But the fact is that we have never seen motivation; all we see is behavior which suggests certain restlessness and seeking for food, from which we infer the operation of a hunger motive. The significant feature of hypothetical constructs is not their reality but rather their usefulness in explaining phenomena. We need to know whether this is the simplest or the most adequate explanation of the data we have, realizing that no single hypothetical construct can explain everything. As Festinger (1958) points out, we might postulate an achievement motive to explain the fact that people frequently expend considerable energy to do something well. Another psychologist trying to explain the same phenomenon might postulate the existence of an ego-extension need, while still another, more ambitious, might postulate a survival need. All three would be hypothetical constructs; the choice among them would have to be made on the basis of which one explains the available data most convincingly and effectively.

There is serious danger in inventing a new drive for each new behavioral tendency. This is what we did years ago with instincts. We could end up saying every act is its own motivation, thereby depriving the concept of motivation of any distinctive value it might have. We run the risk of *word-magic*, of deluding ourselves into thinking that we have explained an event when we have assigned it a name, when according to Marx (1960), all we have achieved is the substitution of one kind of ignorance for another. In other words, we have supplied a redundant *description* of the behavior we were supposed to *explain*. As Festinger points out, postulating the existence of an affiliation need means nothing unless we know what this need is supposed to do, i.e., how this need, as an independent variable, is related to some dependent variable; we cannot define an affiliation need in terms of the display of affiliative behavior.

The stimulation theories have a certain appeal; they are positively oriented and the fact that the drives in question tend to be relatively insatiable is of considerable importance. However, any discussion of their basic nature must necessarily be incomplete and tentative; the mechanism of exploratory behavior, for instance, according to Bindra (1959), remains to be convincingly demonstrated. Any number of questions need to be answered. For instance, by what deprivation operation does one increase the manipulatory drive and what is its origin? If a monkey manipulates a puzzle, to what do we attribute the arousal or energizing function? Myers and Miller (1954) question Harlow's position that stimuli not only elicit the drive but also serve as a reward, which puts us in the difficult position of viewing the manipulatory response as its own reinforcement.

Hall (1961) and Brown (1961) raise questions concerning the exploratory drive. In all the experiments, the investigator has a choice between postulating a curiosity, an exploratory, or an activity drive. Because the monkey undergoes no apparent need reduction—and consequently no specified reinforcement—the exploratory drive is posited to account for the behavior. But the presence of the exploratory drive is not announced until the behavior has been observed to occur. Thus, the presence of a drive to explore is postulated and at the same time used to explain the behavior of exploring whenever there is no apparent reason for the activity. This is in violation of the principle that a hypothesis cannot be substantiated on the basis of the data which led to its postulation. If a strange object were to be avoided, the existence of a fear drive—or of conflict induced by incompatible needs—could just as easily be postulated. In other words, the specific drives are seldom found in terms of observable events other than those of the particular action which they are alleged to produce.

Glaser (1962) questions the usefulness of the present views of motivation in that its empirical and theoretical outcomes are not readily applicable to educational practice. In fact, many leading theorists have avoided the term in an attempt to account for learning phenomena in more operational terms. For example, much of the research on motivation has centered on the deprivation of biological needs or the use of punishment, variables which, for obvious practical considerations, are difficult to use effectively in the instructional setting of the classroom. Reliance on the drive-reduction theory, therefore, must automatically be restricted to the manipulation of secondary reinforcement. It is equally difficult for the teacher to engineer a systematic approach that will capitalize on the manipulatory or the exploratory drive.

THE EFFECTS OF CHILD-REARING PRACTICES ON MOTIVATION

The home plays a crucial role in the development of personality in that it sets the basic pattern along the lines of which the later personality will be differentiated. The child will learn many behavioral routines but the basic orientation is determined in large part by the personality laid down in early childhood. Aggressive trends, for example, may lead to delinquency or to socially constructive efforts, but the aggressive trends themselves may date back to treatment received in infancy. It follows that the main responsibility for structuring this basic personality must inevitably fall on the home, with the school and other social agencies playing a significant role in the determination of the direction this personality will take.

Research into the effects of various home situations on child development has yet to produce conclusive results. The home is obviously too complex a variable for it to yield simple unequivocal answers. A given practice produces different effects depending on the strength of the bond of affection between parent and child, the socioeconomic membership of the home, and numerous other factors whose influence is difficult to control. As a result, the determination of the psychological impact of the various components of the home situation on the development of the child has to be tentative.

One of the most comprehensive studies of the effects of child-rearing practices upon child development is that of Sears et al. (1957), in which a series of carefully standardized interviews were conducted with the mothers of 379 five-year-old children concerning such matters as disciplinary techniques, permissiveness, temperamental qualities, etc. Factor analysis of these ratings pointed to eight child-rearing dimensions, the first five of which are considered relatively crucial: [a] permissiveness-restrictiveness; [b] general family adjustment; [c] warmth of mother-child relationship; [d] responsible child-training orientation; and [e] aggressiveness-punitiveness. Essentially equivalent results have been obtained in similar studies by Radke (1946), Baldwin (1948), Becker (1960, 1964), Crandall et al. (1960), and others. There is not complete agreement as to which components are most productive in structuring the effects of child-rearing practices upon child development, but most studies emphasize the significance of such continua as permissiveness-control, autocratic-democratic, punitiveness-nonpunitiveness, maternal warmth-coldness, and dependence-independence.

PERMISSIVENESS-CONTROL

Research suggests that the best emotional climate of the home is one of warm democratic permissiveness in which love is freely given, particularly by the mother; mothers who are warm and affectionate and who reward dependence have children who tend to display a high degree of dependency behavior necessary for adequate socialization.

Emotional stability, cooperativeness, self-control, and general maturity develop best in a family atmosphere where the parents treat the child with affection, are solicitous of his welfare, and exercise control that is sympathetic and understanding. Baldwin et al. (1945), for example, found that children from homes characterized as warm and democratic were active, assertive, socially outgoing, and especially high in originality, planfulness, intellectual curiosity, and imagination, while the children from homes characterized by a high degree of control with low democracy were well-behaved but somewhat lacking in aggressiveness and originality. These findings were corroborated by Symonds (1936) who found children from strict homes to be more courteous, obedient, neat, and dependable, but also more shy, timid, inhibited, submissive, withdrawing, docile, and more troubled with feelings of insecurity and inferiority. The children of the more permissive parents were more aggressive and disobedient, but they were also more self-confident and self-assertive, better at self-expression, freer, more independent, and more spontaneous in behavior.

Similar findings were reported by Watson (1957) who found home permissiveness to be associated with greater initiative and independence, better socialization and cooperation, less inner hostility, more friendly feelings toward others, and a higher level of spontaneity, originality, and creativity. He found children from strict homes to be either extremely persistent or easily discouraged. It must be noted, however, that the findings did not apply to all cases; apparently subtle differences do exist and the overall pattern is too complicated to be summarized easily. Those differences that did emerge, however, were consistently to the credit of the more permissive upbringing. None of these studies supports the contention that children given permissive upbringing are any less capable of withstanding frustration than children given firm control.

Some people have the mistaken notion that giving an infant what he wants will spoil him. Such an idea is illogical; it is like fearing that the child who is given all the food he needs will turn into a glutton. Experience tells us that it is the child who never knows when and how much he is going to have for his next meal who gorges himself. It is the insecure child who is spoiled; he is desperate and demanding because he cannot depend upon his needs being satisfied.

Rather than making the child spoiled and unable to withstand difficulty, raising him in an atmosphere of emotional security and acceptance increases his frustration tolerance. Moloney (1945), for instance, points to the amazing stability of the Okinawan natives who, on the one hand, are indulged as children to an extent entirely unknown in our culture, but who, on the other hand, were able to withstand the hardships of war (including starvation), as well as typhoons and such dread diseases as leprosy and elephantiasis, with a complete absence of psychosis. Before the child can afford to explore, to assume responsibility, to make a contribution, he must be secure in his feeling that failure will not jeopardize his status. Once security is developed, he can be open and unafraid of failure and therefore unafraid of extending his circumference. Only then can he face his conflicts squarely and use his full capacity to overcome them, rather than to suppress them only to have them haunt him and interfere with his efforts.

Parental pressure in the form of nagging, punishment, and undue restrictions, rather than leading to conformity and independent behavior, serves to heighten emotional tension which may express itself in show-off, rebellious, immature, and emotionally unstable behavior. Anderson (1940) found a definite association between parental behavior which the child characterizes as unsympathetic, restrictive, severe, lacking in affection, and pupil behavior which was rated as aggressive, rebellious, attention-getting, and emotionally unstable.

PUNITIVENESS

An important component of child-rearing practices is the gradual "shaping" of the individual's behavior through various forms of "punishment" for transgressions. Contrary to the previous emphasis on complete permissiveness, psychologists now recognize that control is essential to the child's security and maximal development. Bandura and Walters (1963) reject the idea that parents should provide their children with unconditional acceptance and love; such a condition is both impossible to achieve and undesirable. What is important is the nature of the punishment; punitiveness, for example, is associated with aggression and retarded conscience development. Bandura and Walters found parents of aggressive boys to be those who consistently punished aggressive behavior directed toward them, but who encouraged and intermittently reinforced aggression expressed outside the home; these parents habitually used punitive rather than guilt-producing disciplinary measures. On the other hand, mothers who use withdrawal of love as the preferred disciplinary technique tend to have children who have well-developed self-control, provided the mother is warm and affectionate (Crandall et al., 1960) and, of course, maternal reward for compliance is more effective in promoting the child's compliance than is punishment for noncompliance.

Punitiveness has negative consequences; it promotes a desire in the child to be punitive in return. This is clearly seen in the doll play of children. The more punitive the mother, the more aggressive is the child (Chasdi and Lawrence, 1951). Bandura and Walters found that boys whose parents used punitive methods of discipline displayed little aggression toward or in the presence of their parents but were highly aggressive in interaction with their peers and with adults outside the home. When he has to cope with the behavior of others, the child apparently models his behavior after the treatment he himself has received. The least effective way of stopping aggression is for the parent to resort to aggression himself. Such counteraggression usually generates more hostility than it cures. Unfortunately, counterattack by adults works for a while and is often used more and more as it becomes progressively more ineffective and harmful.

A significant outcome of punishment is anxiety. As the punishment is repeated throughout the period of childhood, situations that provoke aggressive feelings come to arouse anxiety over the danger of being punished for aggression, so that eventually aggressive impulses alone become sufficient to arouse what we call aggression anxiety. This is desirable, provided punishment is given in a setting of warmth and affection. A different consequence of punishment, however, is the development by the child of techniques for avoiding punishment. He will not necessarily refrain from aggression because punishment alone seems to have rather localized inhibitive effects. Rather, the total impulse to aggression is made stronger than ever; punishment itself is an additional frustration, and the more severe the punishment, the more aggression it generates. On the contrary, the more nonpermissive but nonpunitive the parent is, the more likely he is to have nonaggressive children; the least aggressive children in the Sears study were found in homes where there was a clear disapproval of aggression, but where it was discouraged through means other than physical punishment.

MATERNAL WARMTH

Probably no factor has greater detrimental effect on the child's development than maternal coldness; it tends to be associated with feeding problems and aggression, and appears to be a significant background condition in emotional upsets related to toilet training. Maternal coldness also retards conscience development. It seems clear that various child-care practices—breast or bottle feeding, the age of weaning, and other overt aspects of such care—are of much less significance in determining present and subsequent personality development than maternal attitudes of warmth, acceptance, and security, which are communicated to the baby in every contact with the mother. Rejection of the baby is easily communicated by minimal cues of muscular tension, tone of voice, or other expressions of which the mother is frequently unaware. As Davis and Havighurst (1946) suggest, the true essence of the parent-child relationship lies more in how the parent feels than in what he does or says. Breast feeding by a rejecting mother who does it only because it is expected of her probably promotes anxiety rather than security.

Of interest here is the report by Sontag (1941, 1957) that the babies of emotionally upset mothers were essentially neurotic at birth. (See Chapter 5.) Further, inasmuch as the mother who is emotionally upset during pregnancy usually continues to be upset after delivery, she is much more likely to have a problem baby than one who is more positive in her attitudes. Also of interest is Harlow's study of love in monkeys. (See Chapter 1.) The infant monkeys reared on mother-surrogates later become neurotic adults even though the emotional attachment and security provided by the cloth mother was no less than that provided by the real mother. Apparently something was missing—all of which raises interesting questions as to what constitutes adequate mothering.

The general consensus of a number of thorough studies of the effects of the mother's employment on her children's development (Herzog, 1960; Stolz, 1960; Nye, 1959; Casler, 1961; Siegel and Haas, 1963) is that the mother's employment *per se* is not an important determinant of the quality of the mother-child relationship. The mother who works may actually provide greater stimulus value to her children as a result of the broadened interest and experience leading to greater self-fulfillment, provided she responds positively to the opportunity to work. In both the Nye and Stolz studies, surprisingly few differences were noted in the children of mothers who worked and those who did not work, from the standpoint of personality adjustment, adjustment and achievement at school, delinquency, and other aspects of development. Again, the important variables seem to be the warmth and attitudes of the mother, the family atmosphere, and the general satisfaction of the mother with whatever role she occupies (Yarrow et al., 1962). It is also important to note that the mother who finds it possible to work is frequently more efficient and more capable than the one who does not. As a result, no generalization seems to hold true for all mothers and all children.

The importance of emotional security has led to considerable concern over the effects of broken homes. The White House Conference on Children and Youth of 1950 noted that one child in 20 lived with neither parent and nearly one in ten lived with only one parent. It is logical to suspect that the broken home itself is not as devastating to the child's emotional security as the atmosphere of emotional tension and animosity which often attends the dismemberment of the home. It also appears that the home in which parents are not so much married as simply undivorced may have as bad an effect, if not worse, on the child (Nye, 1957). Even the stable home does not necessarily provide a secure base; frequently, the child's need for security is frustrated by sibling rivalry, poor family relationships (e.g., authoritarianism; overstrict, overindulgent or inconsistent discipline; overprotection), and other undesirable conditions.

DEPENDENCE VERSUS INDEPENDENCE

Without question *the* developmental task of infancy is the evolvement of dependency as a prerequisite to emotional security. The young child must be secure in the feeling that he can depend on others. Later his fundamental need to grow will cause him to forsake dependence for the greater privileges of independence, but he must develop a sense of trust and security before he can develop a sense of autonomy. Dependence is also essential to social development; failure to develop dependency, and thus anxiety over the possible withdrawal of parental love and affection in the event of misbehavior, makes the young child completely inaccessible from the standpoint of conscience development. He needs an emotionally stable and consistent environment in which he experiences love and acceptance, for only then can he afford to express his feelings without fear or guilt, only then can he be free from evasiveness, repression, hostility, or resentment. Eventually he will become more independent of adults and more dependent upon himself and his peers.

It is necessary for the child to experience over and over again freedom to display independence, to make choices, to accept or to reject food, to do some of the things he wants to do. Firmness may be necessary, for the child must be guided, but he must also be allowed to stand on his own two feet. He must be allowed to defy, to resist, and to exercise initiative; this is the only way he can learn that he is a person in his own right, and the only way he can find out what kind of person he really is. Parents should encourage him to try things for himself, while at the same time they should discourage him from tackling impossible tasks; they also should be prepared to give him their support in the event of failure. As we have noted, Winterbottom (1963) found that the mothers of sons with high need for achievement tended to demand less from their sons in the way of independent behavior at an early age, but, once a home base of dependency and security had been established, they encouraged as much independence as the child could assume.

The young child learns to depend on his mother, to seek her approval, and to avoid her disapproval. He voluntarily restrains himself in his demands for independence in exchange for whatever rewards he considers adequate. The rejected child, on the other hand, has nothing to lose and thus no cause for developing dependency needs. The indulged child likewise has nothing to lose since he can eat his cake and have it too; he can do what he wants to do without forfeiting the love and approval of his parents. He is likely to have trouble in school, however, where he can no longer get things for nothing. Both the overindulged and the rejected child frequently become overstrivers in their attempts to gain the necessary rewards; or, on the other hand, they may give up entirely. Institutionalized children frequently fail to develop dependence and are therefore difficult to socialize. Once they have given up the attempt to gain the approval of others, they tend to respond to inner needs and to insist on immediate satisfactions. Sometimes they alternate between highly demanding and clinging behavior, on the one hand, and highly independent behavior, on the other hand (Bowlby, 1953).[5]

Maternal warmth and demonstrativeness of affection are the best guarantees of the development of dependency. The mother of the most adequately dependent children is one who sets a fairly consistent pattern, who has acceptant attitudes toward dependent behavior, and who is

---

[5] We need to distinguish between normal and neurotic dependency. The latter generally develops from rejection of the child by significant persons in his environment.

warm and affectionate, gentle in toilet training, and opposed to physical punishment. She is also likely to manifest a higher esteem for herself and for her husband. On the contary, overdependent children belong to mothers who irritably reject the dependency demands of their children for a while, but eventually give in and thus provide partial reinforcement of their demands. The overprotective maternal pattern also exerts a detrimental effect upon development in that it tends to promote hostility through the frustration of the child's need for autonomous action.

ORDER OF BIRTH

Also of direct significance in the course of the child's development is the order of birth and spacing of the children. Davis and Havighurst (1946) found the firstborn to tend toward greater selfishness and self-centeredness, to be more emotionally intense, and more easily upset by defeat. He also tends to have a strong conscience, to be more responsible, less aggressive, more intellectually curious, and more likely to articulate clearly than his younger siblings (Koch, 1955). The youngest child, on the other hand, is more likely to be babied, and he may become a pleasant, likable, and dependent person who goes through life leaning on others. He may learn to use other people for his own ends; he may learn that discipline generally breaks down as he uses his personal charm to control adults. The oldest tends to be more serious, shy, and adult-centered, while, by contrast, the youngest tends to be cheerful, plastic, easygoing, and nonstudious (McArthur, 1956). The spacing of children is important. If the firstborn is only a year old when the new sibling arrives, his self-image is still so diffuse that he is not likely to see the baby as a major threat or competitor for his parents' affection. Or if he is seven or eight, he is more independent of his parents and again less threatened. On the other hand, these findings simply represent general trends and undoubtedly what is most important is the way each child is accepted.

SOCIAL CLASS

Differences in expectation connected with differences in social class have a direct bearing on child development. Middle-class parents tend to be more permissive and follow more closely the practices advocated by the experts; they rely more on reasoning, isolation, appeal to guilt, and methods involving the threat of loss of parental love and approval. As a result, they are generally more successful in bringing about self-control through the internalization of the values of the social group. Middle-class families are more rigorous than lower-class families in training their children in feeding and cleanliness habits. They generally begin training earlier and are more likely to emphasize achievement, responsibility, self-reliance, initiative, independence, and self-improvement through education. Lower-class parents, on the other hand, are more likely to train their children in responsibility only after the children are old enough to make the effort pay substantial returns. The home can present difficulties when it subscribes to values and customs different from the rest of the dominant society; the bilingual home, for example, often presents a conglomeration of factors more correctly characterized as biculturalism.

THE EFFECTS OF EARLY EXPERIENCES

Psychologists have always placed particular emphasis on the effects of early experiences upon child development. Freud, for example, felt that the basic personality was established in the child's early years. Of special importance are the effects of early traumatic experiences; it is often claimed that the emotional wounds of infancy are never completely healed and, although they may be forgotten, later stress may reopen them. Many adult problems can be traced to relatively forgotten or repressed experiences. Anthropologists have noted, for instance, that the Arapesch of New Guinea are friendly and optimistic; they share generously even though they live in a land where food is relatively scarce. Other tribes of the same racial stock, on the other hand, are arrogant, aggressive, and quarrelsome. Anthropologists attribute these differences to differences in child-rearing practices in promoting security or insecurity in children (Mead, 1937). As we have seen, Moloney (1945) also attributed the amazing stability of the Okinawan native to the high level of indulgence which he receives as a child.

MATERNAL DEPRIVATION

The problem of maternal deprivation has attracted international attention with the report by Spitz in 1945 that the institutionalization of young children under conditions of drastic emotional deprivation resulted in what he called anaclytic depression, a condition characterized by mourning, negative emotions, loss of appetite, and general wasting away. A similar claim of the adverse effects the deprivation of love had on children kept in hospitals for extended periods was made by Bakwin (1949) who noted that prolonged hospital residence caused infants to fail to gain weight despite adequate diet; they ate less and rarely smiled or babbled spontaneously; they were listless, apathetic, and unresponsive to stimuli. Respiratory infections that would normally last a day or two persisted for a week but cleared up almost immediately when the children returned home. Apparently the emotional deprivation attending hospitalization did far more damage than the physical conditions which brought it about.

Bowlby (1953), in his review of the literature on maternal deprivation, concluded that severe deprivation of maternal care before the age of two—whether deprivation is based on physical absence or psychological rejection—has detrimental effects on personality development. However, the evidence of Bowlby's second report (Bowlby, et al., 1956), while still supporting the proposition that institutionalization in infancy is damaging to child development, was less clear-cut. A stronger position was taken by Ribble (1943) and Montagu (1955) who argued that mothering comfort and skin contact such as might be involved in bathing, fondling, dressing, and rocking the child are essential to his emotional and physical welfare.

Among the more significant studies in this area is that of Goldfarb (1943, 1945) who found children brought up in institutions for three years and then placed in foster homes to be inferior in intelligence, in school achievement, and in ability to conceptualize to similar children placed in foster homes from early infancy. Fourteen years later, they were retarded in a number of areas and displayed various ill effects from their early institutionalization. They continued to be different; they were less well adjusted to the demands of the school and the community, they were more simple in mental organization, less capable of making reflective and practical adjustments, and less capable of normal human relations. They seemed underdeveloped rather than maldeveloped.

In summary, the general consensus derived from research on the extended institutionalization of children in infancy is that:

[a] They display retardation in all aspects of development (especially language) and also in school achievement.

[b] They tend to be apathetic, listless, and unhappy. They display signs of insecurity, emotional hunger, and craving for affection, and make excessive demands for attention. Yet, they are cold, isolated, and have difficulty in entering into meaningful social relationships. They tend to be so hard to reach that even the most well-intentioned foster parent is likely to give up, thus compounding their difficulties. Teachers likewise have little patience with children who are cold and resistant and finally reject them in return for their rejecting attitudes.

[c] Many show physiologic disturbances; as babies, they sleep less, eat less, and are prone to infection.

[d] Their behavior is typically intolerable; they have not developed dependency needs and are, therefore, governed by insistence on immediate gratification. Their behavior is characterized by temper tantrums, aggression, unmanageability, hyperactivity, and a failure to develop normal inhibitions and controls.

After a period of uncritical acceptance, these studies have been subjected to increasingly critical reviews. Criticism culminated in highly documented articles by Pinneau (1950, 1955) who virtually demolished their dramatic claims. His arguments do not erase the evidence concerning the blunting effects of early emotional deprivation, but its implications are best construed from the standpoint of hypothesis rather than of established fact, especially in view of the less drastic findings obtained by other studies and the possibility of more parsimonious explanation. Perhaps all we can say is that such stresses are not good for children and should be prevented to the limit of our capacity, but we cannot make dogmatic statements about the extent and permanence of the damage done in the individual case. Physiological and psychological deprivation of sufficient severity and duration can result in relatively permanent personality damage; nevertheless, children are resilient creatures and many brought up under the worst of circumstances have thrived and others have recovered, again pointing to the human capacity to resist damage and to the ability of the body and mind for self-repair, especially in youth.

The evidence is not conclusive: institutionalization is too complex a variable to provide a simple answer. Dennis and Najarian (1957) found that children institutionalized shortly after birth showed some signs of retardation but no evidence of emotional damage even though they enjoyed little mothering care. Orgel (1941) likewise found the institutionalized children he studied to be rather well-adjusted and basically capable of meeting the demands of family living. Similar results were obtained among the children raised in the kibbutzim of Israel (Faigin, 1958; Rabin, 1957); in fact, some of these children showed greater personal maturity than did the controls. Yarrow's comprehensive study (1961) also failed to show that multiple mothering results in personality damage; as he points out, the factors involved are highly complex, interacting, and relatively unknown.

In a comprehensive critique of the literature, Casler (1961) points out that virtually without exception the studies on maternal deprivation have failed to take into account a number of critical variables, such as the age of separation. For example, a secure bond with the mother must exist before "separation" can take place, and this can occur only after the infant is approximately six months of age because he is essentially incapable of specific reponsiveness before that age. Bakwin (1949) also noted that the effects of separation were most severe in children who, up to the time of separation at six to nine months of age, had experienced a happy relationship with their mothers. Perhaps the age of six to nine months is the age of the struggle between trusting and distrusting the world, and this is why the children who have had a happy relationship up to this point respond so badly to separation. A second variable is the institution itself; certainly all institutions cannot be classified as one. The reason for the separation must also be considered; if the child is ill, this must be taken into account; if, on the other hand, the child is unwanted and essentially abandoned, this factor alone may be responsible for the damage.

According to Casler, the evidence at both the human and the animal level suggests that the damage is more likely to stem from sensory deprivation, i.e., the relative absence of external stimulation. In Spitz' study, for example, the sides of the cribs were often covered with blankets, no toys were provided, and the total visual experience was largely restricted to staring at the ceiling. In addition, the wards were typically quiet so that the children received little auditory stimulation. They were rarely handled and they were relatively inactive so that they had practically no tactile or kinesthetic stimulation. Such circumstances of relatively complete deprivation seem capable of producing in children a syndrome marked by developmental retardation, apathy, absence of normal emotions, and indifference to people. The ill effects of institutionalization on personality development may likewise stem from the lack of opportunity to learn dependency. It would seem that any institution serving babies should take special pains to provide environmental stimulation and close, intimate personal relationships with adults, and further that adoption should be effected early.

HIGHLIGHTS OF THE CHAPTER

Prospective teachers should be familiar with the following concepts:
[a]
Behavior is purposive. It does not just happen; rather, it occurs as part of the individual's attempt to reach his goals and attain his purposes. The question of whether motivation is essential to learning is a point of theoretical dispute, although it would seem that most, if not all, the behavior with which the school is concerned has some degree of motivational origin.
[b]
The child learns to satisfy his needs *in a given way*. To the extent that there is agreement in the use of terms, therefore, the basic determinants of behavior are not needs, which simply energize the organism, but rather motives, which also direct the energized organism toward the attainment of relevant goals.
[c]
The satisfaction of needs is not an optional matter. Although the individual cannot satisfy all his needs, a reasonable degree of satisfaction for his major needs is essential to his welfare. Certain individuals experience difficulty in deriving satisfaction for their needs and may resort

to deviant behavior in a desperate attempt to deal with a frustrating situation.

[d]

Although physiological needs are more fundamental, psychological needs, because of their relative unsatiability, tend to be of greater importance in determing behavior in an affluent society.

[e]

Although questioned as the sole explanation of motivated behavior, the drive-reduction theory is still of definite usefulness. The more recent stimulation theories, e.g., White's competency drive, are more positive in outlook. Actually, objections can be raised against motivation as a scientific concept; it is simply a hypothetical construct of importance in understanding the dynamics of both human and animal behavior.

[f]

Child-rearing practices play a major role in the development of motivational structure. Dependency in early childhood promoted through maternal warmth and love-oriented techniques in a democratic and permissive atmosphere is essential to socialization. Punitiveness is particularly self-defeating.

[g]

Early experiences have a fundamental influence on later personality development. It now seems that the dire effects of institutionalization on young children, once attributed to maternal deprivation, are more logically the result of sensory deprivation.

SOURCES OF RELATED MATERIAL

Archambault, R. D., "The concept of needs and its relation to certain aspects of educational theory," *Harv. Educ. Rev.*, 27: 38–62, 1957.

Bolles, R. C., "The usefulness of the drive concept," in M. R. Jones (ed.), *Nebraska Symposium on Motivation*. Lincoln, Neb.: University of Nebraska Press, 1958. Pp.1–33.

Carnegie, Dale, *How to Win Friends and Influence People*. New York: Simon and Schuster, Inc., 1936.

Fowler, H., *Curiosity and Exploratory Behavior*. New York: Crowell-Collier and Macmillan, Inc., 1965.

Glanzer, Murray, "Curiosity, exploratory drive and stimulus satiation," *Psychol. Bull.*, 55: 302–315, 1958.

Haas, K., *Understanding Ourselves and Others*. Englewood Cliffs, N. J.: Prentice-Hall, Inc., 1965.

Harlow, Harry F., "Mice, monkeys, men, and motives," *Psychol. Rev.*, 60: 23–32, 1953.

———, and C. N. Woolsey, *Biological and Biochemical Bases of Behavior*. Madison, Wis.: University of Wisconsin Press, 1965.

Hebb, Donald O., "The mammal and his environment," *Amer. J. Psychol.*, 91: 826–831, 1955.

———, "The motivating effects of exteroceptive stimulation," *Amer. Psychol.*, 13: 109–13, 1958.

Hunt, J. McV., "Experience and the development of motivation: Some reinterpretations," *Child Develpm.*, 31: 489–504, 1960.

Leuba, C., "Toward some integration of learning theories: The concept of optimal stimulation," *Psychol. Rev.*, 1: 27–33, 1955.

Marx, Melvin H., "Motivation," in C. W. Harris (ed.), *Encyclopedia of Educational Research*. New York: Crowell-Collier and Macmillan, Inc., 1960. Pp. 888–901.

Maslow, Abraham H., "A theory of human motivation," *Psychol. Rev.*, 50: 370–396, 1943.

Rosen, Bernard C., and R. D'Andrade, "The psychosocial origins of achievement motivation," *Sociometry*, 22: 185–218, 1959.

Schafter, E. F., and N. Bayley, "Maternal behavior, child behavior, and their inter-correlation from infancy to adolescence." *Monogr. soc. Res. child Develpm.*, 28: 1–127, 1963.

Sontag, Lester W., and Jerome Kagan, "The emergence of intellectual achievement motives," *Amer. J. Orthopsychiat.*, 33: 532–535, 1963.

QUESTIONS AND PROJECTS

1

Why is it essential for prospective teachers to understand the dynamics underlying the behavior of others? How important is it that teachers be relatively free from an accumulation of unresolved tensions?

2

Discuss the role of needs in the promotion of self-realization. When might the individual's needs lead to self-destruction rather than self-realization? What might be done to ensure proper orientation in this regard?

3

Discuss the role of clothes, cars, and other material possessions in the satisfaction of needs. When might such externals become a liability?

4

Analyze Dale Carnegie's *How to Win Friends and Influence People* from the standpoint of the psychology of motivation. Does this approach imply a certain degree of insincerity, i.e., of manipulation and exploitation of others?

5

Society generally emphasizes normative requirements, e.g., children need to be quiet in school, rather than individual needs. How legitimate are such requirements in a democracy and to what extent should these be enforced? Discuss specific ways in which the two might be synchronized in practice.

CHAPTER 4

The Self-actualizing Person

> Two essential aspects of living organisms are the need to change, to grow, and differentiate toward greater complexity, and the need to integrate and to maintain equilibrium and wholeness, to consolidate our gains.
>
> *Tryon and Henry, 1950, p. 156*

THE SELF-CONCEPT

NATURE AND IMPORTANCE

An idea which has received considerable emphasis in modern psychological writings, and whose significance is now receiving increasing recognition from the classroom teacher, is that of the self-concept. Originally proposed by Lecky (1945) and adopted by Rogers (1951) as the keystone of his system of nondirective counseling, this concept is of major importance in education, particularly in the more personal aspects such as motivation and adjustment which, in the final analysis, are the foundations upon which school and out-of-school success must ultimately rest.

Lecky's basic premise is that all of an individual's values are organized into a single system, the nucleus of which is his valuation of himself

As he undergoes new experiences he accepts or rejects them in terms of their compatibility with his present evaluation of himself. He thereby maintains his individuality and avoids conflict. Thus, the individual's one fundamental need is to develop and to maintain a unified mental organization. The self-concept is best conceived as a system of attitudes toward oneself. Just as a person, as a result of experience, forms attitudes which he organizes into a self-consistent system and defends against attack even if it calls for disregard or falsification of the evidence, so the person, also as a result of his experiences, forms attitudes toward himself. All attitudes are important determinants of behavior, but attitudes concerning the self are much more basic than those in which the individual is less ego-involved and are, therefore, correspondingly more potent in determining behavior.

Building the self-concept involves a slow process of differentiation in which the individual gradually emerges into focus out of his total world of awareness and defines progressively more clearly just who and what he is.

> A person's self is the sum-total of all that he can call his. The self includes, among other things a system of ideas, attitudes, values, and commitments. The self is a person's total subjective environment; it is the distinctive center of experience and significance. The self constitutes a person's inner world as distinguished from the outer world consisting of all other people and things. [Jersild, 1952, p. 9]

Since the self is differentiated as a result of the experiences one undergoes, it follows that underlying the development of the self-concept are the individual's assets and liabilities in relation to the various components of his environment. A major aspect of this development concerns identification with significant persons in his life; the boy's self-concept may be modeled on the image he has formed of his father. The body is a major point of reference in the self-concept of many persons; the athlete, the movie star, and the belle of the ball would be different persons were they to have different physiques. People spend hundreds of dollars on clothes and beauty treatments in a deliberate attempt to capitalize on their physical assets. Others who are less well endowed physically may minimize the body and emphasize other personal characteristics, such as intelligence or musical talent, as the foundation for their self-concept. A physical defect may also serve as the focus around which the self-concept is centered.

The orientation and adequacy of the self-concept which the individual develops out of his interactions with his environment are, to a large extent, a function of the quality of early parent-child relationships. If the mother is constantly angry at the baby, punishes him for wrong doings, rejects him, and emphasizes the "bad baby" aspects, he begins to conceive of himself as bad. As new experiences follow, he tends more and more to evaluate each new situation in the light of his previous generalizations. The school child who fails to learn to read and who is berated by his teacher for his stupidity sees the school as an unpleasant place and himself as stupid. He then interprets future school occurrences in this light, and rejects new material on the prejudgment that because he is stupid, he could not learn even if he tried. As he becomes convinced of this, he gives his environment less and less of a chance to treat him differently; as his self-concept gradually becomes generalized to include more and more of the same confirming events, he forces himself deeper and deeper into the same groove. Once he is convinced of his adequacy (or inadequacy) in a given area, the individual schedules himself, by his expectations, for a continuation of the success (or failure) he has experienced in the past.

In apparent contradiction to the idea of the self are the findings of the Hartshorne and May study of deceit (1928) that a child who cheated in one situation did not always cheat in another, although an outside observer might have expected him to. They concluded that there is no general factor of honesty, that honesty is specific and situational, a position which is contrary to the behavioral consistency postulated by Lecky. It is also a position that is difficult to accept. The key to the contradiction lies in the fact that it is only to the outside observer that the child's behavior is unpredictable. As for the child, his behavior stems from and is governed by a set of values arranged in a definite hierarchy of prepotency. An individual might pocket money dropped on the sidewalk by a stranger but would not think of keeping money that he knew had been lost by a friend. The explanation of this inconsistency in behavior lies in the fact that loyalty is an important value for the individual in question; he behaves in an honest fashion because he is loyal, not because he is honest.

Since most situations to which the individual must react are complex, they bring into play a multiplicity of motives and value-continua in n-dimensional space, reinforcing and interfering with each other in varying degrees. In every case, the dominant value system prevails and this system is logical from the standpoint of the individual. But the outside observer, attempting to predict the behavior without understanding the values by which it is governed, may well see nothing but chaos and haphazardness. And the more different the systems of values to which two individuals subscribe, the less they can make sense out of each other's behavior. The average citizen, for example, has difficulty in appreciating the code of honor among criminals.

Behavior is far too complex to be understood in terms of such superficial traits as honesty which is the product of multiple causation; it must be considered from the standpoint of its underlying foundation. Individuals are *self*-consistent but not necessarily socially consistent. The child who cheats at one time and not at another may be self-consistent. If his dominant values center on the attainment of a good scholastic record, he *has* to cheat whenever his grades are in jeopardy. If in his system of values, he placed honesty above a high scholastic record, he would sooner fail than cheat, although he might cheat in other situations where the choice is between honesty and some other value which he treasures more or where a number of values paired together might outweigh the value he places upon honesty. In such a case, he would have to rationalize his dishonesty or suffer feelings of guilt. In general, the individual will act in accordance with his dominant values, even if he has to pay a price for his transgressions of the social code. But when inconsistencies in his self-concept lead him to violate one of his own dominant values while acting in accord with some of his other values, he is in trouble from a psychiatric point of view. That is, he is in need of help in integrating his system of values so as to avoid internal conflict.

The young child is relatively neutral at first as to the kind of self-concept he develops, but he becomes progressively less free in his choice of the experiences he assimilates or of the interpretation he places upon them in order that they may be assimilated without conflict. As he begins to perceive order in his environment, the most important thing he discovers is himself. At first, he cannot distinguish between himself and the rest of his environment. Soon he discovers his nose and the rest of his body; eventually he recognizes his voice. But he also recognizes that the words *good, bad, cute,* etc., are attributed to him as a person. Gradually he develops a picture of himself which he then strives to maintain and protect by ordering his behavior accordingly. Because the individual's image of himself tends to continue developing in the direction in which it started, early childhood is the critical period in the development of the self-structure. Each new experience is important both in itself and as the basis for accepting or rejecting future experiences. As a result, the individual's behavior is governed not by the physical aspects of the situation in which he finds himself but by his perceptions as altered in terms of his previous experiences, and he relies more and more upon past patterns of behavior.

The self-concept has crucial implications for the individual's development. In fact, it stands at the core of what he does and does not do as can be attested to by clinicians who, day after day, deal with people who, in a desperate attempt to maintain a unified self, continue in short-sighted modes of behavior. The usefulness of this concept is not restricted to abnormal cases; the boy who conceives of himself as a good student cannot do poor work just as the child who has built an ideal of himself as moral and righteous can be depended upon to try to live up to that ideal. To violate these values would lead to feelings of worthlessness and guilt. By the same token, the person who views himself as a slick operator has to live up to that reputation, and the jailing of youthful offenders, for example, often does nothing more than give them a view of themselves as tough, by which standard they then proceed to live even though it will lead to ultimate disaster. The point is well stated by Anderson (1952):

> . . . the need to maintain the structure . . . intact, produces the consistency of behavior with which we are familiar in all people. *The pattern of life of every individual is a living-out of his self-image*; it is his road map for living. People can be counted on to behave according to their own patterns. This consistency is not voluntary or deliberate, but compulsive, and generally is outside of awareness. [p. 236]

Of interest in this connection is the concept of will power often used to explain behavior as it relates to the values of the social order. The righteous person is said to exercise will power while the person who fails to live up to expectations is said to be lacking in will power. Actually, as Jones (1951) points out, to attribute differences in moral conduct to differences in will power is to "do little more than restate the problem." Moral conduct, like all behavior, is governed according to the prepotency of motives and values. Different people have different dominant values and, therefore, different goals, which they strive to attain with equal compulsion, be they in the area of sex or self-respect. It is possible to change dominant values to the point of avoiding previous failings, but that is not increasing will power; it is simply substituting new values of a higher level of acceptability. The child, the teacher, the civic leader, and the thief, all have essentially the same needs, and each is striving to maintain his self-image intact; they display different behavior because they have different dominant values.

THE SCHOOL AND THE SELF-CONCEPT

The school plays a significant role in determining the quality of the child's self-concept, especially with respect to academic materials and other contents with which he has had only limited previous experience. It provides the child with an opportunity for systematically measuring himself against his peers in a variety of situations ranging from intellectual and physical competence to being attractive to members of the opposite sex. It must provide each and every child with the opportunity for productive achievement and maximum utilization of his potentialities. The school can also do harm: indiscriminate grading and reporting to parents followed by condemnation at home may be a significant factor in the development of a negative self-concept. Too frequently, the school is instrumental in inflicting upon certain children the view that they are inadequate, undependable, or unworthy. Society likewise often provides children with false criteria against which to evaluate themselves in developing their self-concept. Too frequently one's worth is measured in terms of the wealth or status of one's family, the car one drives, the clothes one wears, or the academic or athletic record one accumulates.

Whenever learning incorporates self-involvement, the learner has to learn if he is to avoid conflict. On the other hand, as Lecky points out, to the nonspeller, to misspell becomes a moral issue: "He misspells for the same reason he refuses to become a thief." Lecky noted that poor spellers seemed to make the same number of errors per page in their written work irrespective of the difficulty of the material. When the test was cut in half, there were about the same number of mistakes in each half, again regardless of the difficulty of the material. They were apparently misspelling in terms of the concept they held about their competence as spellers. Reading clinicians note the same factors operating in the nonreader; he has a reputation to maintain. To make matters worse, society confirms his concept of inadequacy by making his evaluation of himself a matter of official record. It is a sad truth that many people sell themselves on the idea that they are incompetent, thereby cheating themselves of the success that could be theirs under conditions of more positive thinking.

The necessity of helping the child build a positive self-concept is obvious from its role in determining what he will be and what he will do. Furthermore, since the self-concept he develops depends directly on the way his experiences enhance his self-esteem, the reactions of adults in authority toward him are of special importance. Yet, apparently on the assumption that the more vigorously they bat him down the higher he will bounce, adults often go out of their way to destroy the child's confidence in himself. By constantly nagging and failing him they succeed in convincing him that he is stupid and worthless, and lead him to confirm that viewpoint by his behavior. Parents, with the best of intentions, frequently set up such high goals for their child that they give him a feeling of inadequacy and unacceptability, a feeling that he can never meet the standards they have set for him. Cultural groups also may lead to the formation of a self-concept that interferes with the work of the classroom and, at times, with development of behavior that is in line with the general code of society. Children from the lower class tend to develop a self-concept relatively antagonistic to the "silly stuff" required in school, for instance.

There is a need to set the curriculum in line with the self-concept of students. The fact that boys in our schools tend to have a rougher time than girls is probably caused, at least in part, by conflict with a masculine self-concept. As early as 1909, Ayres pointed to the over-feminization of our schools and the resulting difficulties it created for boys. Boys are expected to be he-men; yet, as pointed out by Lecky, the boy in the first grade must stand before his companions and read in a loud voice, "The little red hen goes cluck, cluck, cluck," or something equally inconsistent with his views of masculine values. We expect boys to be rugged individualists, but schools are identified with the feminine pattern of conformity and, in fact, often conformity to the habits and values which women—since many teachers are women—have found satisfying. McNeil (1964) found that boys outperform girls when beginning reading is introduced through teaching machines but do more poorly in a regular classroom under female first-grade teachers, for example. Even certain subjects (e.g., poetry, typing, shorthand, and drama) may well have an annoying tone of femininity to some boys.

Along the same line, Davis and his colleagues (Davis, 1948; Eells, 1953; Eells et al., 1951) argue that we do the child from the lower classes a great deal of harm by continually assigning to him tasks which are far removed from his experiences and inconsistent with the values of his culture; by failing him when, as a consequence of the unsuitability of our demands, his work is not up to par, we lead him to believe that he is a failure. Once he is convinced of this, a vicious circle sets in which makes it impossible for him to succeed. It is also likely that grades followed by nagging actually reduce rather than increase academic output on the part of the below-average student. This is especially true for the child from the lower class for whom underachievement in school often stems from the conflict between being academically competent and yet not being a sissy—a conflict which he can resolve rather readily by not trying.

It is a safe bet that we, as teachers, can get more out of a student —and lead him to get more out of himself—by building him up through encouragement than by destroying him. We need to stress the positive, stress the fact that we expect him to succeed rather than give him the impression we would be surprised if he did. It is particularly important that the child's first attempts at a task be successful. Success in learning to read, for example, should be among his early experiences in school. Some degree of failure is inevitable, but it should not be introduced too soon, nor too often. The child faced with unrealistic goals or impossible demands will either have to incorporate failure as a part of his self-image or avoid conflict by being "uninterested." This pattern is far too common in our schools. Many students who might not be able to set the world on fire but who could do respectable work if they were encouraged are forced by repeated failure to adopt an "I-can-but-I-don't-want-to" attitude. They cannot allow themselves to try because they could be involved in a self-conflict if they failed after having tried. Thus, a rigid "maintenance of standards" policy is often self-defeating and damaging.

Rarely do people concede that they are complete failures; generally, they give in on some front while emphasizing all the more their adequacy in other areas in order to maintain self-respect. A child may cease trying to be a scholar and concentrate on being an athlete; he may rationalize that only sissies do well in school. What he is doing is building a somewhat different concept of himself to fit in with what he can do. Of course, this is possible only when the self-concept is relatively unformed and the shift is such that it can be assimilated within the current self.

The child's self-image does not always agree with reality. Distortion of reality is a potential danger in the case of all attitudes but the danger is correspondingly greater when the attitudes relate to the self. Thus, in order to defend himself against conflict, the child may blame the teacher for his poor grades and continue thinking of himself as academically competent. He may even project his inadequacies onto others and despise them while he feels superior as a result. Or he may become a chronic, compulsive, overachiever in a determined attempt to maintain his self-image. By forcing the child into numerous activities by which he can evaluate himself, the school plays an important part in the formation of his self-image and it ought to make sure his self-concept is realistic, for not only must there be consistency within the self but there must be consistency with external reality. As Combs and Snygg (1959) point out, an accurate and realistic acceptance of self is essential to effective living; people who are unable to accept themselves as they are operate under serious handicaps because they must necessarily deal with life from false and inadequate premises. Every year hundreds of people die from overexertion, for example; they pay with their lives for their failure to have shifted their self-concept to the reality of aging.

RELATION TO PERCEPTION

Perceptions from the external world are the basic ingredient from which the self is developed and maintained. In an attempt to avoid conflict with incompatible ideas, however, we see only what we want to see and hear only what we want to hear. More specifically, we perceive only those things which are consistent with our motives and goals and interpret our experiences to make them compatible with our present self-concept. Not only is perception selective; it is often definitely erroneous as a result of the distortions brought about by our motives and our self-image; our enemies are seen as sneaky connivers when, by objective standards, they may be of the highest integrity. The more hostile a person is the more likely he is to see hostility in others. In the same way, our perception of the student's misbehavior is colored to a considerable extent by our like or dislike of him just as one's views of the

Kremlin varies according to whether he was born in Leningrad or in Brooklyn. All of which suggests that the old adage "seeing is believing" might be closer to the truth stated in reverse, "believing is seeing."

The self acts as a selective screen, the permeability of which is determined by the nature of the environment relative to the self. Under conditions of stress, this screen becomes a barrier which isolates the individual and he becomes a prisoner of his own defenses, for eventual inadequacy is the inevitable consequence of closing off one's avenues of communication with the outside world. To the extent that extended or intense fear occurs, rigidity in approach known as tunnel vision or, in Gestalt terminology, narrowing of the perceptual field, sets in, which makes him incapable of seeing or trying anything new (Lazarus et al., 1952). The child whose needs for belonging are severely frustrated, for example, persists in antisocial behavior which only serves to accentuate his rejection; he is so busy warding off anxiety that he has no time or energy left to devote to constructive attempts to solve his problem. But since he cannot stand doing nothing, he continues in a way which, even though it provides temporary and partial satisfaction, is not in his best interest from the standpoint of long-term adjustment. As Jersild (1952) points out, whenever a person resists learning that would be beneficial to him, we may suspect he is trying to safeguard his picture of himself. His self-picture may be false and unhealthy, but it is the only one he knows. Only under conditions of security can he afford to release the barriers so that access to experience can be reestablished.

SELECTIVE PERCEPTION AND ACCENTUATION

A basic premise of cognitive psychology is that behavior is the resultant of the individual's perception of the situation, not as it actually exists but, rather, as it appears to him at the moment of behavior. What we perceive is more than what is physically out there. Two persons looking at the same phenomenon may see very different things. Yet what each sees is "reality" to him, the only reality by which he can guide his behavior.

Three aspects of perceptual selectivity are involved:

[a] We are selective in the stimuli to which we attend; we cannot apprehend the total physical environment but can attend only to selective aspects of it. The direction in which our perceptions are oriented is not the exclusive function of the relative arousal value of available stimuli, i.e., their physical properties, but, rather, a function of those properties in relation to the total situation as perceived in the light of our current psychological makeup. What stands out as *figure* from the *ground* of the total perceptual field is a matter of considerable psychological complexity.

The direction of our perceptions is crucially affected by numerous motivational factors, each contributing to perceptual sensitization toward certain valued stimuli and perceptual defense against others. Needs may cause the lowering of the threshold of perception so that the person who is hungry reacts to the odor of food. What one perceives is affected by his mental set. (A person expecting a friend is likely to mistake a stranger for his friend.) We read words in context and do not notice the misspellings. Vinacke (1952) reports that students presented with PASRORT tend to see PARROT or PASSPORT, depending on their mental sets.

[b] Not only do we give preferential attention to certain aspects of our environment, but we also interpret sensory inputs in terms of their meaning in our self-structure. Perception is more than simply sensing. Stimuli cannot be apprehended as they actually exist; nor can they be simply accumulated. Rather, they have to be interpreted so that they can be fitted into the individual's present mental organization. This process is fundamental to all mental life; it involves determining the significance of what we perceive so that it can be assimilated into the existing structure and often slanting its interpretation in order to avoid conflict in the present self.

In shaping sensory inputs to fit existing structure, the individual organizes his perceptions according to a personal frame of reference.[1] Judson and Cofer (1956), for example, found that subjects with strong religious orientation used a religious pattern in selecting the unrelated word in the sequence TEMPLE, CATHEDRAL, SKYSCRAPER, and PRAYER. They chose SKYSCRAPER, while the less religious subjects, apparently oriented toward an architectural structure, chose PRAYER. One's phenomenological goals also play a major role in the interpretation of his perceptions. To the crook, money is something to steal; to the miser, something to hoard; to the drunk, something with which he can buy liquor. Each interprets things in relation to the self and present motives.

[c] Distortion also occurs as a result of selective retention, so that, because of the distortion that accompanies the selective orientation of sensory processes, the biased interpretation of what he actually perceives, and the preferential nature of what he retains, the individual's experiences may depart a considerable distance from the objective reality of the total environment available to him.

The distortion of perception is clearly shown in the phenomenon of accentuation where the individual's needs lead to the magnification of certain aspects of the environment having a bearing on the need state. In the study by Bruner and Goodman (1947), socially valued objects such as coins were perceived as larger than actual size. The greater the value of the coin, the greater the accentuation. The poorer subjects

---

[1] A good review of the literature on this topic is given by Jenkin, 1957.

tended to overestimate the size of the coin to a greater extent than did the wealthier group. Furthermore, they tended to overestimate the size of the coin to a greater extent when the coin belonged to them than when it did not. Lambert et al. (1949) found that the size of a poker chip was consistently overestimated while it served as a token to obtain a reward but that overestimation ceased as soon as the poker chip no longer had redemption value.

Probably the most conclusive study of accentuation is that of Ashley et al. (1951), who had students believe under hypnosis that they were rich or that they were poor. Each subject was asked to adjust a spot of light of variable size to agree with the *remembered* size of a penny, a nickel, a dime, or a quarter, and with the actual size of these coins as present. Each subject made settings in each of the "poor," "rich," and "normal" phases. The subjects in the "normal" state adjusted the spot of light approximately equal to the physical size of the coin; in the "poor" stage, however, the adjusted spot was consistently larger than the actual coin, and in the "rich" state the setting was considerably smaller. The subjects were also shown a slug from an electric terminal box and, in both the "rich" and the "poor" states, estimated its size when made to believe the slug was made of lead, silver, white gold, and finally platinum. There was a definite trend toward overestimation of the size of the slug as the value of the metal supposedly increased, again showing how one's perceptions are slanted in the direction of his needs and values.

THE SELF-IDEAL

We have to make a distinction between what the person feels he is (the self-concept) and what he feels he ought to be. The latter is the self-ideal; in a sense, it represents his standards of conduct based upon his interpretations of the role prescriptions relayed to him by his parents and other significant figures in his environment. Most people would like to be a little better than they actually are; thus there is generally a slight positive discrepancy between the ideal self and the actual self. The individual with a small discrepancy score tends to have a rather comfortable view of himself; the discrepancy provides a positive and attainable goal toward which to strive. This is the self-accepting person. If, from infancy the individual's life history has been one of adequacy and security so that he perceives himself as loved and lovable as well as capable of doing what others expect of him and what he expects of himself, then he develops self-acceptance. Frequently he is a person who has been helped to set realistic goals so that he was able to succeed rather consistently.

Persons with a marked discrepancy between the self-ideal and the self-concept apparently feel they are not up to their own standards and some, at least, may be said to be self-rejecting. These people tend to be self-centered, anxious and insecure; they are frequently compulsive over-strivers who cannot permit inadequacy and who often set impossible goals as a means of protecting themselves when they fail. On the other hand, some are simply people with high aspirations; a large discrepancy between self-ideal and actual self-rating is characteristic of subjects with a high need for achievement (Martire, 1956). Although there are exceptions, self-acceptance tends to be related to the acceptance of others (Berger, 1952). The self-accepting person tends to see his world as friendly and accepting. Fey (1957) found that college students high in acceptance of self and of others were healthiest in their positive con-fidence in themselves and in others, while those low in the acceptance of self and others distrusted themselves and others, were more anxious and impulsive, had lower morale, were overdependent, and showed a marked tendency toward conformity.

THE LEVEL OF ASPIRATION

The discrepancy between the self-concept and the self-ideal can also be considered from the standpoint of the level of aspiration, a concept which has attained considerable acceptance among psychologists. Its importance can readily be seen from the fact that the level of expecta-tion which the individual sets for himself determines his relative success not only in the performance of a given task, but also as a person, and thus determines the kind of self-concept he is likely to develop. The need for a realistic level of aspiration follows directly from the need for the self-concept to maintain contact with reality. "Success" and "failure" are not to be interpreted on the basis of actual performance measured on an absolute scale; rather they are meaningful only with reference to the target toward which the individual was aiming. For the student to get a *B* when he was shooting for an A is a matter of "failure" while to get a *C* when all he was looking for was a *pass* is really a form of success. No matter how adequate from an objective point of view, performance on a task that is felt to be too easy does not yield a feeling of success, while inadequate performance will not result in a feeling of failure if it is in an area in which the individual makes no claim to competence. To have significance from the standpoint of success and failure, performance must be within the narrow range of the individual's aspirations.

The level of aspiration is a function of experience, an important component of which is one's balance of past successes and failures. Sears (1940) found that success tends to induce the individual to raise his level of aspiration, whereas failure generally causes him to lower it. Under conditions of continued failure, however, he may actually raise his aspirations, or perhaps become erratic in the level of the goals he sets, sometimes aiming too low, sometimes too high. Continued failure also leads to a reluctance on the part of the individual to commit himself to a specific goal and to make an earnest attempt to attain it; it is common for students who have not been too successful to refuse to set a goal of a given grade; they simply coast along, somehow hoping for the best and in the meantime, keeping their perceptual field at a low level of differentiation.

Too large a discrepancy between one's level of aspiration and one's actual competence is generally considered unhealthy since it often leads to self-disappointment and eventual self-rejection. To the extent that it results in chronic feelings of guilt, it promotes perceptual distortion as a means of avoiding conflict and sooner or later leads to the closing of the avenues for growth. Whereas research findings are complex and not easily reconciled (Wylie, 1961), it would seem that a comfortable view of one's self is necessary for personal effectiveness. It also follows that, inasmuch as the level of aspiration depends upon past successes and failure, the child should be encouraged to set his aspirations in line with reality and, further that he should be assisted in attaining certain successes in order to develop an adequate level of aspiration.

Inability to set realistic goals is characteristic of the insecure person. The secure individual sets his goals in keeping with his potentialities; he expects slight but regular improvement and is willing to take a certain element of risk. The insecure person, on the other hand, because he cannot tolerate failure or admit inadequacy, becomes either the compulsive overstriver who sets impossible goals which he attempts desperately to attain or which he uses as an alibi to avoid feelings of inadequacy in the event of failure, or he becomes the underachiever who sets such easy goals that he "just can't miss." It is characteristic of the inadequate person to be lacking in both motivation and achievement. Which is the cause and which is the effect is, of course, not clear; they probably act as complementary parts of a vicious circle.

CHANGING THE SELF-CONCEPT

Despite the tendency of the self-image to perpetuate itself through the selectivity it exercises over the experiences it integrates or rejects, a person's ideas concerning himself and the meaning the environment has for him are constantly undergoing revision and reorganization. Whereas older views tend to cause the rejection of incompatible ideas, the new gradually erodes and causes a shift in the old. In the adjusted person, this process is harmonious and gradual but, for the insecure, it may lead to a disorganization of behavior which makes an integrated attack on problems relatively impossible.

The individual as a unified system is faced with two sets of problems:

that of maintaining harmony within himself and that of maintaining harmony with the environment. In order to understand the environment, he must keep his interpretation consistent with his experiences, but in order to maintain his individuality he must organize these interpretations to form a system which is internally consistent. The learner perceives, interprets, and accepts or rejects whatever he meets in the light of the self-system he has developed. Experiences that, if assimilated, would force a reorganization of the self tend to be resisted through denial and distortion or, under conditions of threat, through a closing of communication with the threatening conditions.

Stability however, implies a gradual evolution through the assimilation and integration of one's experiences rather than the maintenance of the *status quo*. The individual is continually engaged in the process of self-discovery, the insights from which have to be incorporated into a new and more adequate self-image. But this reorganization must be gradual and deliberate, consolidating itself as it goes along and must occur within the framework of the current self-image. It takes time to change a self-concept that has taken years to develop; the delinquent, for example, cannot be expected to change to socially acceptable behavior overnight, especially since he frequently rejects any offer of help because experience has led him to believe that people cannot be trusted. There is also need for reasonable stability in the perceptual field; chaos in the environment can lead to confusion and perhaps to a disorganization of the self.

The first step in improvement is to identify the incompatible ideas and to integrate them under conditions where the ensuing anxiety can be kept within tolerable limits. The issue, therefore, concerns the conditions under which a person can change his self-concept. The answer to this question lies in the concept of permissiveness, i.e., freedom from threat, upon which Rogers (1947) bases his nondirective counseling. In a permissive atmosphere, the individual can afford to reconsider previously rejected perceptions and to integrate them, for under such conditions, he is free from having to cling to his values lest he be caught defenseless in the middle of a crisis.

ANXIETY

Meaning of Anxiety

Bearing directly on the question of change in the self-image is the concept of anxiety whose full significance can be appreciated only in relation to a wide variety of topics to be discussed throughout the text. Thus, although even the layman is aware of the connection between anxiety and maladjustment, it is equally obvious that anxiety relates to every phase of human behavior—the self-concept, emotions, socialization, motivation, efficiency in learning, flexibility in problem solving, and creativity. The student therefore should keep this concept constantly in mind as he proceeds through the course, and especially as he tries to understand children and adults whose behavior deviates from the expected.

Tension is generated whenever the individual faces a situation where an obstacle prevents the ready satisfaction of his needs. This tension is usually mild and quickly dissipated as equilibrium is restored through the attainment of suitable goals. In the case of intense or long-continued frustration of important needs, however, the tension may reach such drastic proportions as to interfere with the effective attainment of the goals through which the needs can be satisfied. The term *anxiety* is generally used to refer to tension of this sort although, to be sure, there is no sharp dividing line separating anxiety from the more normal levels of tension, and many writers refer to all levels of tension as degrees of anxiety.

Anxiety is a conscious experience of relatively intense dread and foreboding which is not directly related to external threat; it differs from fear in that it is conceived as being a vague, diffuse, objectless state of tension while fear is temporary, more directly related to a given threatening situation and preparatory to appropriate behavior. Fears that are relatively undifferentiated with respect to the object of threat are known as anxiety states, and clinicians use the term *free-floating anxiety* to characterize fears that are relatively detached from any specific frightening object or situation. Fear can be conceived as a state of apprehension which has a focus on a recognizable danger; in anxiety, on the other hand, it is the security pattern which the individual has developed to deal with threatening situations which is itself being threatened. Because anxiety attacks the very foundation of personality, the individual cannot stand outside the threat, cannot objectify it, and is, therefore, powerless to take steps to meet it, especially in the case of neurotic anxiety where the threat is repressed into unconsciousness. Horney (1937) advances the concept of basic anxiety as consisting of a feeling of helplessness in the face of a potentially hostile world and leading to the development of neurotic defenses and unhealthy strategies for coping with the world. As long as his strategy meets the requirements of the situation, the individual remains functional; anxiety occurs when his system of defenses is so pressed that he fears it will break down under environmental attack.

To the extent that anxiety implies a relative lack of perceptual clarity concerning the nature of the threat, the reaction to anxiety tends to be more chronic and disproportionate than in the case of fear. The complicated system of defense the individual develops against such threat to the self is frequently abnormal and harmful from the standpoint of his long-range welfare. Yet, we must remember that whatever the anxieties he may be experiencing in an attempt to protect his neurotic self, these are presumably less—at least for the moment—than he would experience if he behaved in any other way. In therapy, the counselor helps the client explore his feelings until the latter is able to pinpoint the cause of his distress, for only when it is differentiated can it be approached constructively. This is painful, for the more clearly he perceives the real problem, the greater the threat and, for such a clarification to occur, it is necessary for the person to convince himself that the benefits to be gained in moving ahead are greater than those to be gained in escaping.

REACTIONS TO ANXIETY

The normal reaction to stress is a more determined effort to deal with the situation. Under conditions of inadequate tension (i.e., motivation), the individual tends to be apathetic. As tension increases, he becomes more alert and reaches a higher level of efficiency. With further increase in tension to the level at which the term *anxiety* might be applied, however, the stress becomes such that it is disruptive rather than facilitating. It can result in a deterioration of performance, especially in the finer areas of creativity, problem solving, and subtle human relations.

An authoritative statement on the influence of anxiety on behavior is that of Basovitz et al. (1955), who summarized a number of studies ranging from those of soldiers in combat to clinical investigation of human beings and animals. At low levels of anxiety, there is a general alerting of the organism and an increase in vigilance. The individual is more sensitive to outside events and is better able to cope with danger. This sensitivity continues with higher levels of anxiety, but the ability to differentiate the dangerous from the trivial is gradually impaired. At low levels of anxiety, there is an increase in the ability for productive performance, but as anxiety mounts, the subject becomes less capable of mastery behavior, he loses spontaneity and flexibility, he becomes more rigid, and he responds in terms of habitual and favored response tendencies. He has difficulty in improvising. At higher levels still, he undergoes behavioral disorganization and/or regression to more primitive modes of response. His cognitive field is narrowed so that he focuses his attention so completely on the barrier and the inaccessibility of the goal that he is completely blind to alternative pathways and substitute goals. There is difficulty with coordination and integration, a point which is manifest clinically in the distractability, generalized irritability, and random-appearing behavior of the anxiety patient. High tension interferes with the rational processes of deliberation and choice, eventually reaching a state of panic which seriously mitigates against both effective actions and long-range adjustment.

The individual's reactions to severe anxiety may take on different forms, but they tend to be similar from the standpoint of being ineffectual, stereotyped, and generally compulsive. A very common way of dealing with anxiety is to keep threatening experiences at a low level of differentiation, i.e., to prevent them from coming into focus. Rationalization and denial are common ways of distorting a situation to protect the self. The clearest example of denial is amnesia, where threatening experiences are simply blocked out or disguised as a means of eliminating conflict. Another common reaction to anxiety is the nervous breakdown, a common example of which is the "semester-end neurosis" (Combs and Snygg, 1959). The student who has been going along precariously may see the final examination looming rather large in his perceptual horizon. As the pressure begins bearing down on him, he visualizes rather vaguely a conflict between his desire to complete the semester and his probable failure of the final examinations, and the alternative of withdrawing and facing his loss of self-esteem and his parents. Since both alternatives are unacceptable, anxiety builds up while frequently he is not doing anything particularly constructive to solve his problem. A common outcome is that the student succumbs to a form of nervous exhaustion leading the campus doctor to resolve the conflict by sending him home.

NEED FOR ANXIETY

At normal levels, tension resulting from difficulty in meeting the demands of a situation is highly beneficial from the standpoint of the individual's maximum self-realization, because, without this powerful force impelling him to regain equilibrium through the satisfaction of his needs, he would remain forever childish, ignorant, and incompetent. He learns to achieve only when his boasts of alleged accomplishments no longer satisfy him, just as he learns to read when he finds reading essential to status and self-respect. Lynn and Gordon (1961) refer to a golden mean of anxiety for maximal efficiency in performance.

The crucial role of tension in promoting self-realization is evident in any form of learning, whether in the area of social, emotional, academic, or personality development. It is fully recognized in the classroom where a certain level of tension, i.e., of motivation, is accepted as essential to effective learning. Tension also plays a critical role in socialization, because the individual learns acceptable behavior only as a result of the frustration that occurs when his behavior fails to earn the approval of the social group. Social sensitivity results from learned anxiety, and, unless the individual's experiences lead to the development of anxiety over the possible frustration of his needs for social acceptance and recognition, he will not learn self-discipline but will, on the contrary, remain essentially unsocialized, a spoiled brat with no concern for the feelings and rights of anyone but himself. Likewise, a moral conscience and character develop out of the anxiety and guilt feelings resulting from failure to live up to the standards and values he has internalized in the process of socialization.

Although mild tension exerts a facilitating influence upon the discovery of more adequate solutions to one's problems, it must not be assumed that all people who are selfish or shortsighted are lacking in anxiety. On the contrary, it is neurotic anxiety, by forcing the individual to close off the avenues necessary for him to perceive the significant aspects of his environment in their interrelationships, which keeps most people from learning the tasks that are essential to their growth toward maturity and self-actualization.

Research suggests that tension is conducive to increased effort, and it is likely that in familiar and routine tasks, especially those involving gross physical exertion, strong tension may result in increased output, although, since anxiety is energy-consuming and disruptive, excessive tension may just as easily result in perpetual nervous exhaustion, in stupid, erratic, and circular behavior, and in decreased output. It may increase speed of performance, but it is also likely to increase the rate of error (Palermo et al., 1956). When the task involves sheer persistence, the high-anxiety student tends to work harder and to do better (Spence, 1954; Castaneda et al., 1956). However, since excessive tension leads to stereotypy, perceptual rigidity, and closure tendencies, it almost invariably exerts a detrimental effect on the quality of performance in tasks involving complex discrimination in novel material, creativity, innovation, flexibility, originality, and the more subtle aspects of learning as represented by high-level skills and abilities in which there is greater possibility of interference. Sarason et al. (1960), for example, note that on tasks requiring flexible and creative orientation, the less anxious students are more spontaneous, more productive, and show better judgment. The high-anxiety subjects are superior on tasks requiring caution and alertness to error, but they tend to have difficulty when they have to reorganize their thoughts creatively or to improvise. Korchin and Levine (1957) also found that anxiety interferes more with the learning of novel responses to be substituted for old responses and of new contradictory material then it does with the learning of standard material. Highly anxious subjects tend to adhere to a stereotyped approach and have particular difficulty when they have to leave the psychological safety of the memorized solution, the traditional answer, and the routine performance. They are highly vulnerable to situational stress, especially stress based on failure (Sarason, 1957; Krugman, 1958).

A well-known study of the effects of anxiety on problem-solving behavior is that of Maier et al. (1940, 1949). A rat was placed on a jumping stand, facing two doors, one locked and the other unlocked; if it jumped against the locked door, it bumped its nose and fell into the net below. If it jumped against the unlocked door, the door opened and it got a food reward. The rat first learned to identify which door led to the food, but then the problem was made insoluble by making the assignment of which door was locked and which unlocked a matter of chance. Under these circumstances, most animals, when forced to jump, developed a fixed habit of jumping either to the door at the right or at the left, which, even though a stereotyped reaction, was as good as any other inasmuch as the assignment of the correct door was such as to provide inevitably 50 percent reward and 50 percent punishment. Some animals, however, jumped at the post between the two doors—a rather silly compromise. Furthermore, even when the investigators made the problem soluble again by attaching the punishment to the side on which it was fixated, the rat persisted in jumping to the same side even though it was now being punished every time. This behavior lasted through hundreds of trials, even after the door on the other side was entirely removed so that the rat could plainly see on which side the food was to be found.

Anxiety leads to narrowing of the perceptual field so that the anxious individual loses sight of the broader circumstances to which the problem is attached and cannot see effective approaches to its solution. As a result, his behavior is characterized by stereotypy and rigidity (and corresponding ineffectiveness) in performance. It is particularly lacking in abstract qualities and flexibility in higher intellectual functions. A compulsive repetition of errors is characteristic of the anxious child, for example. The more desperately he is in need of love, the more incapable he becomes of refraining from obnoxious behavior; he cannot free himself from tension sufficiently to be able to use his energies constructively. Thus, whereas the secure child is curious and adaptable, the anxious child is rigid; he stays with his ineffectual adjustments simply because his anxiety does not permit him to perceive and to experiment with more effective ways. His anxiety forces him to settle for immediate, although slight and temporary, relief from his tension instead of waiting for more adequate long-range solutions. The worried child may be working at full steam as far as energy output is concerned, but he is likely to expend this energy at cross-directions to his goal so that his net horsepower is often negligible. Not too different is the case of the student who is so worried that he cannot concentrate, who skips classes or forgets assignments (an unconscious withdrawal from an anxiety-producing situation), who becomes aggressive, hypercritical, clinging, or otherwise obnoxious to his instructors and fellow-students, or who resorts to such crash grade-earning techniques as memorizing, cramming, or cheating, all of which reduce rather than enhance his chance of academic success.

In summary, most studies show an overall impairment of performance as a result of stress (Lazarus et al., 1952). It would seem that attention to self-defense mechanisms is distracting to adequate performance. It is also possible that the individual may cease to try as a means of providing himself with a face-saving alibi in case of failure. Although it is true that some people work best under stress, generally, the individual will prosper when he is challenged, but his performance will deteriorate when he is overwhelmed.

IMPLICATIONS FOR EDUCATIONAL PRACTICE

The implications of the concept of anxiety for educational practice are so far-reaching as to warrant careful consideration. This is not to suggest that teachers assume the responsibility for the therapeutic aspects of advanced cases of anxiety. But they have definite responsibility for forestalling the development of anxiety that will interfere with growth.

To the extent that anxiety implies helplessness in meeting situational demands, the importance of building up the child's emotional security cannot be overemphasized. This can be accomplished through providing him with an atmosphere of permissiveness and acceptance in which he can experience tension at a level which is educative rather than disruptive and through ensuring him reasonable success by making sure that what is expected of him is consistent with his level of readiness. The situation must provide the security of clearly defined demands and restrictions. The goal of education is self-direction on the part of the child, but, until such time as he is able to provide his own direction in matters of behavior planning, adult guidance must be supplied if anxiety is to be avoided and learning to take place.

Although considerable individual differences exist in the ability to operate under tension, and although Reed's review of the literature (1960) relates inadequate learning to low as well as to severe levels of anxiety, it is likely that the danger of excess anxiety surpasses that of inadequate tension, and that overemphasis on anxiety will be self-defeating, particularly in the case of the young child. Only when he is relatively free from undue concern over the defense of the self can he gain the perspective necessary to see both himself and his world constructively and to have time and energy to devote to self-improvement. Even though some students may suffer from insufficient anxiety regarding schoolwork, it seems likely that, for the tasks which are of significance in education, anxiety is a most dangerous weapon to use. Most teaching problems appear to arouse a superabundance of anxiety, much of which is teacher-created (through competition, grading, threat, etc.);

when teachers go beyond the lower levels of anxiety, they are probably making difficulties for themselves and risking harm to the child. As Lindgren (1962) suggests, the effective teacher is one who is sensitive to the level of anxiety of students and can manage to keep it at a level where it can be channeled into constructive behavior.

THE PHENOMENAL FIELD

An extension of the self-concept that has direct bearing upon the work of the classroom is that of the phenomenal field, a position which has been getting increasing attention in recent years as a result of the writings of Combs and Snygg, Maslow and Rogers, among others. It is closely related to the life-space postulated by Lewin to describe the effectual environment to which the individual responds, i.e., the individual's total conception of the psychological world in which he lives. The phenomenal field is the universe of time and space in which the person has psychological locomotion as distinguished from the physical environment as it actually exists.

The phenomenal field is based on the concepts of field psychology. It postulates, for example, that greater adequacy in behavior goes hand in hand with greater differentiation of psychological space. It agrees that the characteristics of the parts are determined by the properties of the field and recognizes the *figure-and-ground* character of perception and the importance of the *ground* in determining behavior. Experience has meaning only from the standpoint of the individual's psychological field and relates to the reorganization of that field.

The phenomenal field that governs behavior is the more personal part of the total physical environment in which the individual finds himself. Somewhat more precise and restricted is the phenomenal self, which includes those aspects of the phenomenal field that the individual experiences as part or characteristic of himself. This incorporates the self-concept which refers to the most intimate and personal components of the total situation as contrasted to the still personal but somewhat more distant aspects of the phenomenal field—as might be represented by friends and possessions to which reference is made in terms of *my* and *our*—which generally command a lesser degree of personal involvement. The self is the most highly differentiated element of the total life-space, with the latter so structured that, in the self-centered person, it pivots within narrow and rigid limits around the self-concept. In other less self-centered individuals, the boundaries of the self are less sharp and more permeable so that the self is in greater contact with the rest of the life-space. In all cases, the self does not exist in a vacuum but, rather, has significance only within the total psychological environment which the person experiences. These relationships are shown schematically in two-dimensional space in Figure 4-1. A more complete view is presented by Krech and Crutchfield (1958), who visualize the various levels of the self as layers of an onion ranging from the peripheral to those which constitute the innermost core.

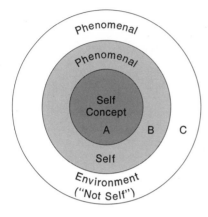

FIGURE 4-1   The phenomenal field. (After Snygg and Combs, 1959.)

These concepts are of major educational significance. To be effective, education must result in a change in the phenomenal field; conversely, education that limits itself to the manipulation of the external environment is doomed to failure. Much of the trouble in our schools stems from our attempts to schedule activities that do not provide enhancement of the personal self or that provide enhancement through indirect means, such as grades and external rewards, to the point where the learner is ego-involved in the rewards but not in the learning. As long as the curriculum—whether divided into separate subjects or integrated into a unified body of knowledge as shown in A and B of Figure 4-2—

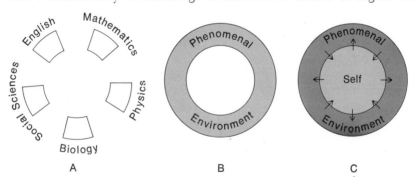

FIGURE 4-2   A. The curriculum (subject matter of traditional education).
B. The phenomenal environment.
C. The phenomenal field (basis of behavior).
(Adaptation of Figure 24, "The phenomenal field and the curriculum," from *Individual Behavior* by Arthur W. Combs and Donald Snygg, Harper & Row, Publishers, 1959.)

remains in the external fringes of the phenomenal field, it will be relatively ineffective in promoting any change in the phenomenal self. Only when classroom experiences become directly involved with the self, as shown in diagram C of Figure 4-2, i.e., only when the individual becomes ego-involved in his studies, can we expect the curriculum to be truly educative. It also follows that, because the phenomenal field is organized as a unit, any learning that takes place affects the whole field. A person cannot learn algebra without its having an effect upon his attitude toward the subject, toward the other aspects of his environment, and especially toward himself. Consequently, the individual can be expected to behave as a whole, i.e., to maintain functional consistency.

Basic Premises

The basic premises of the phenomenological approach have already been presented; we might review the following:

[a] Behavior is the product of one's perceptions; these are phenomenological rather than physical.
[b] Perceptions have to be related to the present structure, the pivotal point of which is the self.
[c] Behavior exists in the present and can be dealt with in the present.

A basic implication of the foregoing is that the child behaves as he does because he sees the situation as he does; as he structures the situation differently, his behavior will change in keeping with his new perceptions and any attempt to change his behavior must proceed indirectly through a restructuring of his perception of the situation.

It is the common properties of the phenomenal field of two individuals that makes communications between them possible. It is always depressing for the farm boy who has moved to the city to realize when he revisits the homeland after a period of years how little he can communicate with the folks back home. Communication between Malayans and Eskimos may likewise be restricted by a lack of commonness in perceptual field. This may in part account for our relative lack of success in converting to our way of life children from the lower classes, inhabitants of other nations, and others whose experiences have led to the development of a different phenomenal organization. Teachers tend to be more effective in promoting a reorganization of the self-concept of children from the middle classes where there is a common meeting ground in perceptual outlook. They are also more attuned to the phenomenal organization that girls are likely to have developed.

Teachers frequently complain that the child is not motivated; actually, they are annoyed that the child does not perceive from the same perspective the goals which the teacher happens to see as important. The child who misbehaves, for example, is trying to accomplish what he considers best, no matter how misguided he may be from the standpoint of the teacher's perceptual outlook. The teacher who laments the child's lack of motivation might profit from perceiving in a new light the effects of his procedures, and while he is at it, getting a new perspective on what constitutes a good education from the standpoint of the child whose education it is.

We sometimes find it difficult to understand the child because we are looking at him from *our* perceptual framework. There is much needless conflict between adults and teen-agers resulting from their differences in perspective. We might profit from the story of the village moron who, having found a lost donkey which his more "intelligent" fellow townsmen had been unable to locate, explained his success by saying that he had tried to think where he would go if *he* were a donkey. Clinicians have rarely seen a parent who deliberately sets out to destroy his child, but frequently they see parents who accomplish just that—parents who do vicious things in the firm conviction that they want the best for their child. People do their best to be adequate according to their perceptions, no matter how futile and misguided their behavior may be to a person whose phenomenal field is more enlightened. They simply need to develop a more adequate perspective. For the same reason, we cannot superimpose our American perceptual outlook and assume that people in totalitarian countries are so unhappy that, given a little encouragement, they would immediately rebel, down to the last man, in casting off their oppressors. Neither can we assume that the neurotic person "obviously" will want to shed his symptoms; he will not. He will remain neurotic as long as his perceptual field is that of a neurotic.

THE CONCEPT OF BECOMING

SELF-ACTUALIZATION

As we have noted, we need to shift our emphasis from the pessimistic and limited view of motivation based on the avoidance or relief of tension to the more positive concept of self-actualization and self-fulfillment. Such a view is most adequately presented by Combs, Kelly, Maslow and Rogers in the 1962 yearbook of the ASCD, *Perceiving, Behaving, Becoming.* Although these authors speak variously of the *adequate person,* the *fully functioning person,* and the *self-actualizing person,* and although some points are more pertinent to one or the other of their separate presentations, there is general agreement on the major points of emphasis and on the underlying view of behavior as the direct outgrowth of perception at the time of behavior. More specifically, they see behavior as ". . . a goal-directed attempt of the individual to satisfy his needs as experienced in the field as experienced." (Combs and Snygg, 1959). For the sake of simplicity in discussion, these positions will be synthesized as basically one; the reader is referred to the yearbook for a more complete statement.

The child is not an inert mass of protoplasm to be molded into something or to be prodded into action by an external force. On the contrary, there is in the child an inner force, an urge, a pressure toward growth and development, an inner drive toward self-actualization. According to Combs and Snygg, the individual is sparked by one basic drive, namely, to actualize, maintain, and enhance the self; all his strivings can be conceptualized as partial aspects of this fundamental need. This basic human drive to push one's self-realization to the limits is discussed in the yearbook under the concept of *becoming*. The basic premise is that there is an all-pervasive force impelling people to grow, that people will actualize themselves in the direction of growth in spite of hardship and the loss of certain advantages. The child will move forward toward greater independence and greater responsibility despite the pain of so doing simply because it is more satisfying to grow than it is to remain a child. It is only when traumatic experiences occur too systematically that this on-going process is stopped and the direction of movement is reversed. Unless they are severely wounded, children will endure the necessary annoyance for the joys of working through challenges toward greater competence and greater maturity.

The four authors identify the following traits as characteristic of the person in the process of becoming:

[a] In contrast to the defensive person, who, in order to protect his existing perceptual organization, sets up a dense selective screen which prevents threatening experiences from coming into awareness except in a distorted form, the self-actualizing person has a more adequate perception of and a more comfortable relationship with reality.

Because he is secure, he is maximally open to experience; he is able to accept into awareness any and all aspects of reality. This openness to experience—with its consequent richness and availability of the perceptual field—is the key to the success of the person in the process of becoming. Because he has free access to available data he is likely to behave more intelligently.

[b] The self-actualizing person is willing to be part of the process of change. Because he is free from having to defend the status quo, each moment is new. What he will do next or the direction in which he will grow cannot be predicted much in advance. The job of reorganizing himself is never complete, but the necessary cues will be provided as he goes along.

Because his failures are not going to overwhelm him and he can rely on an effective system of feedback to get him back on the beam in case of error, he can take a chance on acting impulsively at times. His freedom from rigidity permits him to play spontaneously with ideas and to experiment with the novel. He is capable of what Maslow calls *peak experiences*.

[c] The person in the process of becoming has a positive view of himself and an increasing trust in his ability to arrive at adequate behavior. To the extent that he habitually takes into account all the experiences available to him, his feelings of what is right generally turns out to be an adequate guide to effective behavior. He has a highly differentiated set of values and he has the courage of his convictions; he knows of no way of living other than within his values.

He has a realistic level of aspiration and devotes his talents and his energies to attaining what he sees as attainable. Because his goals are more realistic, his behavior becomes a more precise gauge of what he can and what he cannot do. He then develops confidence in his ability to succeed and also in his judgment of this ability.

[d] His complete openness to experience guarantees a high level of personal integration. Because the shell is permeable he can subject each new experience to an objective evaluation of its validity. He will not necessarily accept each new experience, but he will weigh each for its true worth and, if necessary, remodel a whole new segment of his present structure to incorporate a better arrangement.

[e] He has a strong sense of identification with his fellowmen. He is able to go outside himself and to extend his expanding self to include his family, his friends, and his community. This does not imply slavish conformity; the adequate person has little fear of being unique and no compulsion to sacrifice himself in order to meet the expectations of others. Rather, he has a strong desire to contribute, to accept responsibility, and to serve his fellowmen.

Such a person makes an excellent leader. His openness to experience makes him sensitive to feedback from those whom he serves. He respects the dignity and integrity of others; his trust in himself inspires trust in others. He has no need to usurp authority for self-aggrandizement; being basically fulfilled, he can afford to behave unselfishly for, as Combs points out, the diminished self is the product of deprivation.

The foregoing is, obviously, an ideal picture. It is not achieved in any human being. No one has *become*; rather, we need to think of the person in this process of *becoming*. The self-actualizing person is characterized by psychological freedom to move toward ever-greater adequacy; he makes effective use of his potentialities; he is self-actualizing in the sense that he provides his own power to grow and is moving forward in the direction of a self-actualizing spiral of ever-widening scope.

THE INADEQUATE PERSON

In contrast, the inadequate person is characterized not so much by inability to meet environmental demands—everyone is inadequate in at least a number of dimensions—but, rather, by the fact that his pattern of life is oriented toward his becoming progressively less adequate. When a person is faced with persistent and overwhelming odds against which he has to prove his adequacy, he resorts to such mechanisms as boasting, rationalizing, and other inadequate ways of meeting life's demands. He soon finds himself in a vicious circle of having to resort to the same inadequate mechanisms with progressively greater vigor and frequency. In time, ever-greater threat is met with ever-greater attempt at self-defense and increasing inability to accept reality and develop the necessary competence.

The constructive way of dealing with threatening perceptions is to incorporate them into a more adequate self-structure, but this the neurotic person cannot do. Instead, he defends himself by distorting the threatening experience to fit his present system or by preventing it from coming into his focus of awareness. To the extent that defensiveness leads him to convert his self-concept into an impregnable fortress, access to which is guarded by an impermeable shell, the inadequate person cuts himself off from communication and soon finds, as did the dinosaurs of old, that it becomes progressively more difficult to fit into a changing world. He is operating from false premises. He may, for example, continually complain about mistreatment without giving a cold hard look at the possibility that he himself is to blame. However, even when suppressed, the threatening perceptions hardly remain inactive; on the contrary, they keep him in a continuous state of anxiety. Furthermore, since no action can be taken against them as long as they are kept vague and diffuse, their destructive influence continues to undermine his ability to take positive steps (Jourard, 1963). The person who continually meets threatening situations with rationalization, projection, and other inadequate defense mechanisms consumes his energies in protecting the self-structure and has little energy left for constructive remedial and developmental action. The result is inefficient, if not desperate and stupid, behavior.

EDUCATIONAL IMPLICATIONS

The implications of the concept of *becoming* are all-pervasive; this concept has direct bearing on the adjustment of the individual, it automatically precludes personal inadequacy, and it ensures maximum personal and social success and happiness. It has direct bearing on learning in and out of the classroom. With its implementation, teachers would no longer have to fight recalcitrant students and learning would have personal meaning to the learner. Certainly, teachers can have no greater responsibility than to set each and every child on a spiral of self-fulfillment. The means of doing so are obviously multiple rather than single and certainly no recipe can be given. On the other hand, the implications of the foregoing discussion appear consistent with the best pedagogical practice psychologists have advocated for years.

The following points are worthy of brief mention:

[a] Openness to experience is so crucial to self-fulfillment that its cultivation should be of prime concern to the school. No matter what else we do, it is of no avail if the child simply closes himself off in a shell. We need to pay particular attention to educational practices such as grading, retention, competition, impossible standards, unsuitable curricula, threat, rejection, nagging, and punitive and repressive discipline geared to adult standards, which cause the child to devaluate his self-concept, to become defensive, and to close off the supply lines necessary for continued growth.

[b] We need to evaluate our basic philosophies concerning children. Peak experiences require periods of meditation, of feeling, of thinking, and of enjoyment, all of which, although necessary for the development of self-knowledge, may look like laziness to many adults. Even if we agree that every person must produce, are we sure that the product most likely to result from this emphasis on hurry is what we want? We seem to be suggesting that there is something immoral about being nine years old, that a nine-year-old must know more than a nine-year-old normally would know, that he should be more like a ten-year-old. We give the child the idea (in our misguided way of stretching him to greater heights) that he is never acceptable as he is. We want to get more and more from him, and we want to set up the specifications for his growth. In time he loses his sense of self-direction and begins to look to others for direction; he loses his ability to make decisions as to what is right and what is wrong apart from the standards set by others.

Another factor that hinders self-actualization is our strong preoccupation with the right answer. Schools operate on the premise that the right answers come only from authority figures. The child gets the idea that he has no business trying to think, that he is not entitled to an opinion. Our schools seem to be organized to make standardized individuals, apparently as a way of mechanizing the process of teaching. We must give the child the feeling of belonging and acceptance and lead him to believe that individuality is an asset, not a liability. We need to provide him with opportunities to explore the self as a means of promoting self-discovery, self-understanding, and self-acceptance. This is best done through realistic and meaningful interaction with the environment, and through introducing the self into the classroom as a legitimate subject of study.[2]

[c] Just as we can think of an adequate person, so we can think of an adequate classroom characterized by warmth, acceptance, trust, and openness to experience, as well as stimulation and encouragement. We need to convince the child that we trust him; we need to allow him to participate in decision-making. Frequently we make a sham of it; he soon sees through it and not only feels that we do not trust him but begins to question whether he has any business trusting himself. The child must also have the opportunity to meet with success as the basis for developing trust in his own competence. The adequate classroom permits the child to pursue his curiosity while, at the same time, maintaining acceptance; it thereby promotes self-discovery.

[d] We need to provide the child with meaningful interaction with his environment under conditions that are accepting and stimulating, so that he gets maximum opportunity to discover things about himself in relation to the world. The only way he can develop self-knowledge and self-acceptance is through realistic experiences in which he can make choices and gauge the adequacy of these choices. Incidentally, incorporating into the school the concept of self as a means of encouraging the child to discover himself will not add to the teacher's burdens; on the contrary, it will make his job more meaningful, more significant, and more rewarding. Teaching will no longer be a matter of presenting second-hand whatever comes next in the curriculum guide, but rather it will be a matter of promoting behavioral changes in the pupil through promoting changes in his perceptual field. It is also important that the child be provided with a reasonably stable environment in which he can get his bearings.

A prime determinant of whether children grow toward adequacy as a consequence of classroom experiences is the teacher's handling of the situation, and teachers, just as pupils, need to develop greater adequacy. This is not easy for teachers who—like everyone else—tend to cling to their perceptions as to "correct" classroom procedures. Many see the child as an enemy to be kept in check or to be coerced; they are

[2] Jersild (1951) recommends the study of child psychology oriented toward the understanding and acceptance of self and others as a planned feature of the education which children should receive from nursery school onward. He feels that children from an early age have the capacity to understand the realities of life and that it is rather curious that the subject of self-understanding has been so neglected, when we consider how eager we are to teach almost anything else.

convinced that decisions as to what is good for the child must come from the teacher, who knows best. They conceive of the child's task in the classroom as one of listening and learning; there is no time to explore feelings and attitudes.

If teachers are to assume prime responsibility for developing self-actualizing children, they themselves must be self-actualizing persons, characterized by openness to their experiences rather than by concern for the letter of the law. They must, for example, have an optimistic outlook on life and on children. Teachers, like children, can learn about themselves in a permissive atmosphere, and the administration must make it possible for them to find themselves liked, accepted, and trusted so that they can develop a sense of security and dignity. In view of the compound interest which it bears in the lives of children and their children, self-fulfillment on the part of teachers should be of major concern to the administration and to the community.

HIGHLIGHTS OF THE CHAPTER

A basic premise of field psychology and a point of special emphasis in the writings of Combs, Maslow, Rogers, and other phenomenologists is that the adequacy of one's behavior is a direct function of the adequacy of his perceptions.

[a]

The individual's perception of himself is centered in his self-concept, a system of attitudes, ideals and values developed as he emerges into clearer focus and defines progressively more clearly just who and what he is.

[b]

The well-adjusted person attempts to maintain a small positive gap between his self-ideal and his self-image. Continued frustration tends to promote an unrealistic or erratic level of aspiration.

[c]

Perceptions are phenomenological rather than physical; this is particularly evident in the case of accentuation.

[d]

The self acts as a selective screen, filtering and distorting experiences so as to have them fit in with the existing self, even to the point of closing off from awareness any threatening experience. Under conditions of anxiety, perceptual and behavioral rigidity develop with the inevitable consequence that the individual is no longer capable of taking constructive action to deal with his world.

[e]

The phenomenal field as an extension of the self-concept comprises the various aspects of the individual's life-space from the outermost components of the environment of which the individual is barely aware to the self as the innermost core.

[f]

The concept of self-realization, as incorporated in such terms as the self-actualizing or the fully-functioning person, has more recently been presented under the concept of *becoming*. The person in the process of becoming is maximally open to experience and, therefore, capable of maximal utilization of his potentialities and of environmental opportunities for self-improvement.

[g]

The fact that the individual's behavior will at all times be consistent with his system of attitudes, values, and personal standards has far-reaching implications for every aspect of the educative process. Conversely, any attempt to affect behavior must first work through the self-concept. Teachers could render the cause of education, democracy, and humankind no greater service than to orient each and every child toward a spiral of self-fulfillment.

SOURCES OF RELATED MATERIAL

Combs, Arthur W. (chairman), *Perceiving, Behaving, Becoming*. 1962 Yearbook. Washington, D.C.: Association for Supervision and Curriculum Development, 1962.

———, and Donald Snygg, *Individual Behavior: A Perceptual Approach to Behavior*. New York: Harper & Row, Publishers, 1959.

Gordon, Ira J., "Observing from a perceptual viewpoint," *J. teach. Educ.*, 10: 280–284, 1959.

Hamachek, D. E. (ed.), *The Self in Growth, Teaching, and Learning: Selected Readings*. Englewood Cliffs, N.J.: Prentice-Hall, Inc., 1965.

Hilgard, Ernest R., "Human motives and the concept of the self," *Amer. Psychol.*, 4: 374–382, 1949.

Jersild, Arthur T., *In Search of Self*. New York: Teachers College, Columbia University, 1952.

Lawson, R., *Frustration*. New York: Crowell-Collier and Macmillan, Inc., 1965.

Maslow, Abraham H., "Cognition of being in the peak experience," *J. genet. Psychol.*, 94: 43–66, 1959.

———, *Toward a Psychology of Being*. Princeton, N.J.: D. Van Nostrand Company, Inc., 1962.

Packard, Vance, *The Hidden Persuaders*. New York: David McKay Company, Inc., 1957.

Rogers, Carl R., *On Becoming a Person*. Boston: Houghton Mifflin Company, 1961.

Shlein, John M., "The self-concept in relation to behavior: Theoretical and empirical research," *Relig. Educ.*, 57: S-111—S-127, 1962.

Waterhouse, I. K., and I. L. Child, "Frustration and the quality of performance," *J. Pers.*, 21: 298–311, 1952–1953.
Wylie, Ruth C., *The Self-Concept: A Review of the Literature*. Lincoln, Neb.: University of Nebraska Press, 1961.

QUESTIONS AND PROJECTS

1

Identify from among your acquaintances two individuals who most closely approximate the picture of the fully functioning and the inadequate person respectively. Contrast specific aspects of their behavior. What might be some of the antecedents of their present status?

2

Discuss group pressures as an aspect of the determinants of human behavior. Note the complexity of the situation: Not only must the individual maintain (at times precarious) balance among his various needs each of a given vector strength, but he must also interact in various degrees with the social situation consisting of individuals also directed with certain vector forces along given dimensions. Each must, of course, maintain his individuality in line with the self-concept he has formed. How can one make sense out of a situation of such complexity?

PART II

The Child as a Developing Organism

Surveys the various aspects of growth and development, with special orientation toward the role of environmental influences in the development of inherited potential.

CHAPTER 5

Presents the basic principles of growth; emphasizes capacity as something one develops through interaction with the environment and, therefore, is largely a function of the adequacy of one's experiential background.

CHAPTER 6

Emphasizes the psychological implications of physical and motor development; notes the special difficulties attending early and late puberty.

CHAPTER 7

Discusses the nature of emotions, with major reference to anger, fear, and affection; emphasizes their all-pervasive nature and the school's responsibility in promoting emotional maturity.

CHAPTER 8

Discusses the process of socialization, with special reference to child-rearing practices and the role of the school; considers classroom discipline, group dynamics, and leadership in the light of the school's responsibility for promoting effective functioning in a democratic society.

CHAPTER 9

Presents the basic concepts of the nature and development of "intelligence," with special reference to Guilford's structure of the intellect, Piaget's imaginative analysis of the child's evolving mental processes, and the role of experience in the development of intellectual capacity; focuses on the need for a broader concept of "intelligence."

CHAPTER 10

Considers acceleration, enrichment, and ability grouping as means for dealing with the wide differences in academic adequacy among school children; focuses on the special problems of the gifted and the retarded child, with emphasis on the need for greater flexibility in adapting curriculum and teaching methods to individual needs.

CHAPTER 5

Growth
and Development

We begin with the hypothesis that any subject can be taught effectively in some intellectually honest form to any child at any stage of development. It is a bold hypothesis and an essential one in thinking about the nature of the curriculum. No evidence exists to contradict it; considerable evidence is being amassed that supports it.

Bruner, 1960, p. 33

From a tiny speck at the time of conception, the individual multiplies a millionfold until at birth he exhibits considerable physical development. Shortly thereafter, he begins to display definite signs of motor, emotional, intellectual, and social behavior. Those aspects of growth and development resulting from the interaction of environmental influences upon inherited potential are of special interest to teachers. If these environmental influences are to be effective in bringing out the potential of the child, it is necessary that they synchronize with his maturational processes.

GENERAL PRINCIPLES

MATURATION AND LEARNING

The development displayed by an individual at any given time is the result of both the maturation of his innate potentialities and whatever modification of these potentialities occurs as a result of environmental influences. Whether a person is tall or short, has a pleasing personality, or achieves a high scholastic standing depends upon the interaction of the various hereditary and environmental forces operating in his particular case.

Basic to our discussion is the term *heredity* (or *nature*), which is used to refer to the potentialities with which the individual is conceived. Closely related is the term *maturation*, which may be defined as that phase of development which relates to the unfolding of the characteristics incorporated in the genes transmitted to the individual from his ancestors. In contrast *nurture* and *learning* refer to those changes in behavior resulting from the modification of developmental trends through environmental influences. These terms are somewhat more restrictive than *environment*; the loss of a limb can be attributed to environmental causes but would not qualify as either learning or nurture. *Growth* and *development*, on the other hand, are more inclusive terms referring to the result of the interaction of maturation and learning in making the individual what he is at a given time.

Maturation and learning are so closely interrelated that their influence cannot be isolated. Thus, a person may be short because of an inherited tendency toward shortness or because of inadequate diet. Inherited capacity cannot develop in a vacuum nor can it be measured except through present development which is partially the result of learning. If a person behaves in an unintelligent fashion, there is no way of knowing whether his unintelligent behavior is the result of intellectual limitations which he inherited, or the limitations of his environment in stimulating the growth of which he was capable. Only when we can rule out the possibilities of insufficient opportunity to learn can we consider inadequate behavior to be suggestive of inherited deficiencies.

The relative contribution of heredity and environment to the individual's present level of development has been the subject of considerable speculation and disagreement. Unfortunately, the evidence is, and must remain, circumstantial and open to a variety of interpretations; because of the interaction, interdependence, and functional overlapping of the two sets of factors, any attempt at separating the influence of the one from that of the other is essentially an exercise in futility.

Years ago, McDougal (1908) attempted to explain all behavior in terms of instincts, which he defined as complex behavioral patterns that made their appearance as the result of the maturation of inborn potentialities. Thus, maternal behavior, being characteristic of women in general, was explained on the basis of a maternal instinct; the behavior of the bully was explained in terms of a pugnacious instinct. These behavioral patterns were considered innate; they emerged somewhat as a beard appears on a boy's face when the appropriate maturational stage is reached. Psychologists have rejected the concept of instincts in the sense of complex integrated behavioral patterns which emerge naturally and fully as a result of the maturation of innate capacities, i.e., goal-directed behavior patterns which appear in all members of a given species in the complete absence of learning; certainly, maternal behavior includes many components in which learning plays a significant role.

Instincts probably exist in animals. Warblers migrate by night and maintain road orientation provided they have a clear view of the sky, even if reared in a cage and not previously exposed to the sky. Apparently they have an innate mechanism which is geared to certain features of the star patterns of that particular season. Some of these "instinctive" behavior patterns seem to have a relatively natural explanation. The evidence suggests that salmon swim upstream because they cannot stand the rays of the sun through the shallow waters after their skin pigmentation has decreased. It is also possible that inherited glandular structure is largely responsible for certain behavioral tendencies. Clark and Birch (1945) found that the administration of male and female sex hormones to a male chimpanzee led to social dominance and subordination respectively. Similar results have been found with preadolescent boys (Bize and Moricard, 1937), and it is likely that differences in behavior of men and women are as much a function of differences in glandular balance as of cultural pressures.

The major objection to "instincts" is that they describe rather than explain behavior. As the list of instincts grew ever-longer, psychologists realized that all they were doing was giving names to certain behavioral syndromes and really were not explaining anything. More recently, an essentially similar concept has been introduced by Lorenz (1935), Tinbergen (1951), and other ethologists under the name of imprinting, which they define as a process distinct from associative learning or conditioning, occurring during a relatively brief period early in the life of certain birds and having a lasting effect on selected aspects of their behavior. The main point is that in certain species, a newly hatched bird will follow the first moving object to which it is exposed—be it another bird, a wooden bird, a box, or even the experimenter. Goslings hatched in an incubator and restricted to the company of human beings will follow the experimenter just as a gosling would normally "imprint" upon its mother.

Diametrically opposed to the instinctive point of view is that of Watson (1929), who postulated that all babies were alike at birth, having a certain body structure, certain reflexes, three emotions (love, fear, and anger), and certain manipulative tendencies. The fact that they became different suggested to Watson the influence of differential environmental forces affecting the direction of development from this common starting point. Watson represents an extreme environmentalist position which is difficult to accept in full; certainly, infants do differ in such obvious things as height and weight, and probably also in potentialities in various areas of growth. No one denies the importance of environment in promoting the development of the individual's potentialities, but Watson's position appears to minimize unduly the corresponding role of inherited differences.

Both McDougal's and Watson's views are extreme positions which are difficult to defend. Current opinion would support a more middle-of-the-road position, and it is best to look upon heredity and environment not as rivals but as co-contributors to development, with the relative contribution of each varying on a continuum with the different aspects of development. Thus, it might be logical to postulate that heredity is a more potent factor in physical growth than in social development. Research on the subject yields nothing conclusive. Evidence suggests that the earliest prenatal behavior consists of diffuse and generalized mass activity from which more specific responses are differentiated (Coghill, 1929). These are later integrated into complex unified behavior patterns. But, research does not—and cannot—resolve the issue of the relative contribution of inherited and environmental influences in promoting this differentiation and integration.

PRINCIPLES OF HEREDITY

MENDELIAN PRINCIPLES

The exact mechanism through which heredity exerts itself, particularly as it relates to the significant discoveries which have characterized the field in recent years, is far too complex to permit more than a brief overview in the present text.[1] Heredity is determined at the time of fertilization of one of the egg cells of the female by one of the sperm cells of the male, both of which are unique in that they contain only half the number of chromosomes normally found in other body cells.

The chromosomes contain the genes, the real bearers of heredity. A significant breakthrough has occurred in recent years in explaining the exact mechanism through which the genes exert their influence. The modern view is that the "genes" are giant complex deoxyribonucleic acid (DNA) molecules, the atoms of which are arranged in two long strands twisted into a complex double spiral, with the order of the atoms on the spiral serving as a blueprint or master-code governing the formation of the protein molecules for which that particular gene (or DNA molecule) is responsible. In other words, chromosomes consist mainly of molecules of the chemical DNA which has the capacity of reproducing itself

[1] See such excellent sources as Fuller and Thompson, *Behavior Genetics* (1960); Eichorn (1963); and *Life Magazine*, 55, October 4, 1963.

whenever its environment contains the necessary chemical raw materials; it gathers from its chemical environment the same kind of atoms which are contained in the DNA and arranges them in a perfect replica which then repeats the process. Genes are believed to operate by influencing the chemical processes in much the same way as enzymes do in the digestive tract; apparently each gene has an effect on a particular enzyme which it is in some way responsible for manufacturing. Within this complex organization, the operation of a single gene may so disturb the reaction within the cell that the whole course of development of that particular trait may be changed. Thus, the concept of genes is still useful, but it now seems best to think of a gene as a special function of a region rather than a specific particle.

The determinant of the individual's characteristics is the particular combination of genes involved in the fertilization of one of the many egg cells of the female by one of the many sperm cells of the male. Since each has 23 pairs of chromosomes, and each chromosome contains thousands of genes, billions of combinations are possible, thus providing for unlimited differences among the siblings of a given family. That one sibling is taller, or brighter, than the other does not necessarily call for an explanation in terms of differences in environment, any more than does the fact that one is blond and the other dark, or, for that matter, that one is a boy and the other a girl.

Genes are not manufactured by the parents but are simply transmitted by them to their offspring. As a result, because some of the genes might not be involved in any number of conceptions, a certain characteristic may remain dormant for generations only to reappear unexpectedly in a given individual. Thus, the principles of heredity possess within themselves the means of explaining a relatively unlimited range of variations which can occur in the offspring of a given couple. The only exception is the case of identical twins who are the result of the splitting of a fertilized ovum and thus have identical heredity; whatever differences appear later have to be attributed to differences in environmental influences.

Psychologists agree that heredity sets certain developmental limits and that these limits vary from person to person, depending on the particular combinations of genes involved in conception. What these limits are is a matter of speculation; it seems unlikely, considering the construction of the human hand, that anyone will attain a speed of 200 words per minute on the present-day typewriter. But who can tell? The four-minute mile, thought for years to be out of reach, has been broken many times, and, as time goes on, new records will continue to be established in the various areas of human performance. Recent developments in the learning of both people and animals challenge, if they do not shatter, our conventional views. Skinner (1958b) has had pigeons master performances of a complexity that had long been considered well beyond their capabilities. Moore (1963) has had three- and four-year-olds learn to read.

As teachers, our views on this point are important. If we believe that the usual conditions of everyday living are adequate for the child to achieve a large part of his potentialities, there does not seem to be much adults need to do beyond having him acquire certain specific skills. If, on the other hand, the individual attains only a small fraction of his potentialities unless special efforts are made to provide him with concentrated stimulation—and there is considerable evidence to suggest that this is true—the role of education in promoting effective behavior becomes correspondingly more crucial. Teachers need to be sold on the important role of the environment in the development of inherited potential; it is obvious, for example, that a child is not born a genius but only with the potentialities for becoming one provided certain environmental conditions are met. Furthermore, and this is important from a pedagogical point of view, education plays a crucial part in determining the direction in which inherited potential develops and the use to which it is put. At the same time, teachers must also be fully convinced that the heredity does set limits, and that these limits probably vary from child to child, for a great deal of harm can be done by setting expectations beyond the child's capacities. A realistic view as to what environment can and cannot do in overcoming inherited limitations will serve to save the child from neglect on the grounds that "he'll never make it anyway," and from undue pressure in the belief that "you can do whatever you want to do."

Changes in the Basic Pattern of Development

From the moment of conception, environmental forces influence the basic developmental pattern set by the particular combinations of genes involved in conception. Drastic changes in this basic and presumably inherited developmental pattern can be brought about by the manipulation of environmental conditions. Siamese twins can be developed in fish through cold, insufficient oxygen, or ultraviolet rays, for example (Anastasi, 1958). Likewise, the development of an egg into a queen bee or a worker depends on the food it receives. It would appear that, whereas heredity sets certain developmental patterns, these remain true to form only as long as environmental conditions under which maturation is to take place also remain true to form.

It must be remembered that what is inherited are not actual characteristics but rather a set of genes with accompanying cytoplasm and certain substances which, in certain combinations and under certain conditions, can give rise to the organism having, at a later date, certain characteristics. A germ cell simply contains chemical substances. A certain primrose, for example, produces a red flower if grown at a low temperature and a white flower if grown at a higher temperature; the flower color is certainly an inherited trait, but what is inherited is not the specific color but a norm of reactivity in pigmentation to temperature changes.

Contrary to previous opinion, the fetus in the womb is far from immune from environmental influences. The effects of the Rh factor in some pregnancies, of X-ray in the pelvic region of a pregnant woman, and of German measles in early pregnancy in producing physical and mental abnormalities in the offspring have been known for years. It is now realized that certain drugs, infections, and other forms of maternal dysfunction also affect the development of the unborn child. It is also known that conditions associated with late or difficult delivery may produce permanent degenerative changes in the brain, ranging from relatively complete brain damage to more subtle brain impairment; anoxia may be involved in some cases of epilepsy.

Maternal malnutrition can have drastic detrimental effects upon the offspring. Dietary deficiencies in the mother are presumably connected with a high incidence of malformed fetuses; Ebbs et al. (1942) found drastic differences in such things as frequency of illness between the offspring of women on poor diets while pregnant and those of women of the same socioeconomic status on improved diets. Lack of prenatal care seems to be a major factor in the high infant mortality rate among the lower classes, as well as in the infants' smaller size and various other deformities. Deficiency of certain nutrients at certain critical developmental stages (Cohlan, 1954; Asdell, 1953) can have detrimental effects upon fetal development, the specific effect apparently depending upon which organ is developing at the time of the deficiency; if development is interfered with while the inner ear or the brain is being formed, the result is deafness or mental deficiency. Ingalls (1950), for example, by cutting down the oxygen supply of pregnant mice at specific times during pregnancy, noted that hairlip was produced by anoxia on the twelfth day of pregnancy while incompletely formed skulls resulted from anoxia on the eighth day.

Severe emotional stress on the part of the mother, especially during the last stages of pregnancy, has been associated with hyperactivity, irritability, crying, and digestive troubles in the newborn. In fact, Sontag (1941, 1957), found babies born to highly neurotic mothers to be, to all intents and purposes, neurotic as the result of their unsatisfactory fetal environment. They did not have to wait until childhood for a bad home environment to make them neurotic; it had been done for them before they even saw the light of day.

Because the living organism is capable of learning, relatively drastic changes in behavior can be effected through the manipulation of environmental influences. Sparrows raised with canaries in soundproof cages soon abandon their own chirps and learn the canary call (Conradi, 1905), just as the wolf-girls of India learned to live like wild beasts and were later partially domesticated (Squires, 1927). More commonplace, but no less important, are the behavioral changes that result from everyday contacts with the environment such as might be incorporated under the term *education*. Of course, it must be remembered that all of these changes are restricted by inherited structure; whereas the wolf-girls learned to walk on all fours like the monkeys in the jungle, they did not learn to fly like the birds.

The importance of heredity in determining development must not be minimized. Everyday observation provides ample evidence that tall parents tend to have tall offspring, that bright parents tend to have bright offspring. In a study by Tryon (1940) selective mating of the brightest rats as one group and of the dullest rats as a second group, through eight successive generations, produced two separate distributions of "intelligence" with almost no overlap. These findings were corroborated by Thompson (1954) in a more rigorous study using brother-and-sister matings and more adequate criteria of learning ability.

Similar studies, also with rats, have produced comparable results in the area of emotionality (Hall, 1938) and of activity (Rundquist, 1933). In the latter study, for example, the spontaneous activity displayed by the active group developed by selective mating was, on the average, 20 times that displayed by the inactive group. Selective mating in horses has likewise produced Clydesdales and Thoroughbreds where the fastest Clydesdale is probably not as fast as the slowest of the Thoroughbreds. Similar phenomena have been produced in certain varieties of plants, not to mention similar possibilities with respect to height and intelligence among human beings. It would seem that inherited glandular structure is largely responsible for certain behavioral tendencies; emotional rats have larger adrenal, thyroid, and pituitary glands than nonemotional rats, for example (Yeakel and Rhoades, 1941).

The problem of heredity is, of course, complex. It relates to the concept of survival of the fittest in bringing about an improvement in the species, for example. It is complicated by the fact that inherited characteristics reappear unexpectedly after having remained dormant for generations. It is further complicated by regression toward the mean, i.e., by the tendency for the offspring of parents superior in a given characteristic also to be above average in that characteristic but less so than their parents. In fact, some of the offspring would be definitely below average. Conversely, the offspring of parents below average on a given trait would be less inferior than their parents and some would be superior. In the Carnegie study (Learned and Wood, 1938), for example, it was found that more bright children were produced by average and dull parents than by bright parents (simply because there were more of the former). On the other hand, the fact that each generation tends to be taller than the preceding one probably reflects a tendency for succeeding generations to be progressively less stunted, an explanation that is supported by the findings that physical growth appears to be related to economic depressions and war. The drastic increase in height of the current generation of Korean and Japanese youth is apparently the result of dietary improvements connected with the introduction of high-protein American foods.

Of even greater interest is the effect of superimposing environmental influences on inherited patterns. Uyeno (1960) mated dominant male rats with dominant females, and submissive males with submissive females, then had half the offspring of each group reared by dominant and half by submissive mothers. Hereditary effects were apparent, but environmental effects were even more intriguing. The offspring of dominant parents reared by dominant mothers were less aggressive than those from dominant parents reared by submissive mothers. Thus, the relative role of heredity and environment on development is extremely complicated and no clear-cut conclusion can be reached. The problem is of particular interest in connection with intellectual development, a topic to be discussed in Chapter 9.

PRINCIPLES OF DEVELOPMENT

The amount of research done in the area of development is so extensive as to preclude adequate treatment of its various aspects. The interested reader is referred to Carmichael (1954), Mussen (1960), and other comprehensive sources.

The present discussion is limited to an overview of three major principles of interest to teachers:

[a] The rate of development varies from child to child. Thus, in physical growth where the pattern is more obvious, some children grow at a much slower rate than others. However, the picture is complicated by the fact that, whereas the short child tends to remain short throughout his development, this is not always so, nor is it necessarily so in other aspects of growth. The Harvard Growth Studies (Dearborn and Rothney, 1941), for instance, found some children with a fairly consistent rate of development but also others who were highly variable. The authors concluded that physical and mental growth are essentially individual affairs. On the other hand, the sequence of development is relatively uniform, a fact that bears directly on the question of continuous growth which underlies the concept of developmental tasks to be discussed later in the chapter.

[b] The various aspects of development are highly interrelated and

interdependent, and it is only when considered in relation to other aspects that any phase of development becomes meaningful. In fact, growth in an area can go only so far without parallel development in other areas. Thus, growth consists of a virtuous spiral by means of which the individual can climb higher and higher, the gains in one phase of growth depending on gains in other aspects. For instance, physical growth is necessary for optimal social growth; the crippled child is likely to be limited in opportunity to learn social skills. Physical growth is also important in promoting mental growth; the child whose sensory organs have not matured sufficiently is deprived of the stimulation necessary for mental growth. In the same way, emotional growth is directly dependent on social growth and indirectly dependent on physical growth because of the effect physical size, physical deformities, strength, and coordination have in determining whether a given situation will produce an emotion and what kind. Other relationships could be pointed out; suffice it to suggest that the teacher has to be concerned with the whole child and resist the temptation to think of any single phase of development as more fundamental or important than the others. The various aspects are so closely interrelated that the child can be approached only as a functioning unit. It should be fully understood, therefore, that the breakdown of growth and development into its physical, motor, emotional, social, and intellectual aspects, as will be done in the next few chapters, is for the purpose of discussion only.

The interrelationship and interdependence among the various aspects of growth and development are generally greater for young children than for adults, where the correlation between some of these aspects, although positive, is quite low. Nevertheless, research evidence supports the theory of correlation, and not that of compensation; the evidence shows that a person above average in one trait has a better than 50-50 chance of also being above average in a second trait and vice versa. Terman (1925) found his 1000 gifted children to be superior to their age-mates not only in intelligence, but also in physical size and strength, social and emotional maturity, and other desirable traits. This might be expected from the fact that the various aspects of development operate on a spiral, each contributing to the others.

This correlation is not high and many gifted children are puny and sickly, just as many fine physical specimens are dull or socially or emotionally immature. Nevertheless, the trend is for desirable traits to go together although, to be sure, a person is not likely to be good at everything; if a person is superior in one respect, he is likely to fall below average in at least one area. In the same way, a person who is inferior with regard to, say, intelligence, will, in all likelihood, be above average in at least one characteristic. Furthermore, he may devote special effort in one area as a way of compensating for his weaknesses in others. This does not mean, however, that a student who is failing the academic curriculum is automatically a good prospect for success in the shop program; nor does it mean that failure in the College of Engineering is adequate proof of a student's suitability for the teaching profession.

[c] The younger the child the more he does everything of which he is capable. As we have already noted, one of the basic characteristics of children is their desire to grow, to do those things which maturation permits. Thus, the baby resents being fed and dressed; he wants to exercise his capabilities, to explore, and adults should be particularly careful not to destroy this initiative by penalizing him for mistakes to the point where he finds it pays to play it safe. As he becomes older, his range of possible activities becomes so great that he has to be selective, so that what he does becomes progressively more a matter of choice, with custom, social pressures, opportunity, and likelihood of reward as major consideration in such choices.

Despite this need to grow, there tend to be frequent reversions to earlier modes of behavior. In times of stress, even adults occasionally resort to childish behavior. Also, despite his need to grow, the individual will at times hang on to obsolete forms of behavior. This is particularly true in the area of adjustment in which emotional involvement often prevents him from finding more adequate solutions to his problems. Thus, a person may continue to fear a given situation of which he was understandably afraid when he was young and defenseless, but which he need no longer fear at his present level of competence. Children also tend to overdo a given response. Parents and teachers sometimes become concerned when the child goes out of his way to use a new-found response, and, consequently, they will spend time and energy trying to get him to eliminate a habit which he will drop of his own accord as he matures. Undue pressure tends to increase the child's insecurity and create resistance to new learnings that he would achieve readily if he were left alone.

ATTEMPTS AT EARLY TRAINING

A certain degree of maturation is necessary before learning can take place. Walking, for instance, cannot be undertaken until the necessary bone and muscular structure has developed. However, at any given age, the child is capable of learning more advanced behavior than he would normally attain if he relied solely on maturation and the usual incidental stimulation. He can learn to walk perhaps as much as six months before he normally would. These learnings come naturally when sufficient maturation has been achieved. He will walk when he is ready, and all the parent's coaching may seem a relative waste of time. A question of considerable relevance is the advisability of accelerating the child's development.

That special training can speed up a child's learning beyond what would come naturally through maturation under conditions of incidental stimulation has been shown by such studies as those of Gesell and Thompson (1929) and McGraw (1935), in which special training enabled one member of a pair of identical twins to outdistance in certain skills his twin who was simply allowed to grow at his own rate. After a period of a few weeks, the training of the first twin was discontinued and, in a short time, the untrained twin had caught up with him and they continued to grow at the same rate. It was noted that when he came to them with a greater degree of maturation some weeks later, the second twin could learn quickly and easily tasks which had proven difficult for the first. It is also interesting that, although the untrained twin would not even try complicated skills, such as swimming, which the other twin had mastered under special guidance, the twins learned about equally well the more basic skills of crawling, sitting, standing, and walking.

Maturation that occurs normally does not take place within a vacuum. The untrained twin was still subjected to incidental stimulation; the only difference was that the trained twin received more formal and concentrated practice. Yet, there is evidence to suggest that maturation would prove sufficient for certain tasks. Carmichael (1926), for instance, anesthetized tadpoles with chlorotone which immobilized them but did not interfere with their growth. When a control group of tadpoles in plain water reached the stage where they began to swim, he removed the anesthetic, and the tadpoles that had had no practice in swimming swam as well as those that had. That the ill effects of short periods of deprivation are quickly overcome has also been shown in a number of related studies. Chicks that were prevented from pecking by being kept in darkness from birth, almost immediately become as proficient at pecking in daylight as those that had had continuous practice (Shepard and Breed, 1913). Likewise, Hopi papooses who have been cradled so they cannot move their legs walk as early as those not cradled (Dennis and Dennis, 1940).

Special training can lead the child to master certain skills that normally would not be learned until later in the developmental sequence. The question is whether or not such early training is practical and advisable. Although each case has to be evaluated on its own merits, the following generalizations seem to have theoretical as well as empirical support:

[a] Early training tends to be uneconomical and wasteful because it requires special instruction and many repetitions to learn what later would come readily. In the school situation, where time is limited, there is need to gear the educational program to the maturational level of the child, for teachers cannot afford to spend weeks teaching what could be learned next year in a matter of days. The extent to which special train-

ing leads to performance beyond what would occur naturally varies with the nature of the task. In skills where muscular strength, speed, and precision of movement are crucial factors, maturation is essentially a sufficient determinant of proficiency and special practice is correspondingly futile. In tasks of greater complexity such as those of the classroom, on the other hand, opportunity and training play a more crucial role in determining proficiency; maturation and incidental stimulation would hardly lead to proficiency in advanced mathematics. Nevertheless, even in ideational learnings, early training has its limitations. Pistor (1940), for example, found that training in chronology did not lead to a significant improvement in the understanding of time sequence among sixth-grade children.

[b] Such training may be definitely harmful. Forcing the child to the limit of his ability may well result in frustration and discouragement and, eventually, negative attitudes and personal maladjustment, all of which will interfere with subsequent learning. Even the best teaching may be harmful if introduced too soon or too fast. Stroud (1956), for example, suggests that reading clinics and remedial reading programs stand in "testimony to the unwisdom of our haste."

[c] Early training may also be of great benefit. It may result in outstanding performances which would never be equalled by a person denied this early training. It can also result in positive attitudes, e.g., confidence, which can carry over into all aspects of life. It may forestall the development of the bad habits that can arise when a person learns something by himself, and it may provide the child with a start in learning certain skills which would then be the basis for the early learning of other skills further along the sequence.

There is a limit to the amount of material that may be postponed until "next year," and there is often need to introduce material somewhat in advance of the period of maximum economy of effort and time required to master it. Even more significant, however, are the many indications that early stimulation is essential to later learning. Not only must certain learnings take place by a certain time, if they are not to act as roadblocks to the learning of other material higher on the spiral, but also certain learnings are best mastered at an early age; in addition, early learnings exert a beneficial effect on future learning capacity, including the promotion of the necessary physiological maturation. It also seems clear that we have grossly underestimated the ability of both human and animal subjects to learn under proper learning conditions.

[d] The crucial point seems to be the manner in which training is given. Too often teachers get anxious and try to push simply because the teacher of the next grade expects the child to have covered so much material. Unfortunately, far from building up the background he needs

for the next grade, such efforts are more likely to make him unready by building emotional blocks and a negative self-concept. It is much better for the child to discover that he can read, no matter how inadequately by adult standards, than it is for him to cover the first reader under duress, only to develop attitudes of defeat and frustration. It seems safe to say that the parents' attempt to promote bladder and bowel control, for example, is often misguided in that training is frequently undertaken before the necessary neuromuscular development is present. The child in the meantime may become convinced that he can never please his parents, that his parents are fussy and demanding, or, on the other hand, that his parents are very much interested in his welfare. Recent evidence suggests the importance of early training in the development of the child, but one must not overlook the possibility of harm. In all cases, the approach must be one of positive encouragement; patience and understanding are of the essence.

READINESS

Closely related to early training is the concept of readiness. Involved in both cases is the extent to which the learner has the capability to profit from the experiences to which he is subjected. There is, however, a major difference. The discussion so far has centered on the question of adequate maturation (of inherited potential), whereas readiness does not depend on maturation alone but incorporates such factors as motivation and experience, in which environment plays a far more important role. Readiness is a broad concept covering a wide variety of factors which, for the sake of discussion, may be grouped as follows:

[a] Physiological factors: Behavior cannot take place unless there is sufficient maturation of the sense organs, the central nervous system, the muscles, the glands, and other physiological equipment.

[b] Psychological factors: The individual, to be effective, must have the proper motivation, a positive self-concept, and relative freedom from devastating emotional conflicts and other psychological impediments.

[c] Experiential factors: With the exception of the learning that stems from inborn response tendencies, learning can take place only on the basis of previously learned skills and concepts.

It is important to realize that two of the three components of readiness are clearly amenable to training, and that it is, therefore, possible to make the child ready for a given learning experience much earlier than he would be if left to his own devices. Furthermore, the teacher can make him ready for a given learning experience by adapting his methods to the level of readiness the child has already achieved. As pointed out by Gates (1937):

> . . . statements concerning the necessary mental age at which a pupil can be entrusted to learn to read are essentially meaningless. The age of learning to read under one program or with one method employed by one teacher is entirely different from that required under other circumstances. In the first of the groups compared in which modern and effective instruction, well-adapted to individual differences was provided, a mental age of 5.0 appears to be sufficient. [p. 506]

The fact that children with a mental age of five could be taught to read at essentially the same proficiency as normally found in the first grade led him to conclude that, within limits, there is no mental age that can be set as minimum or even optimum for beginning reading. It would seem that success in reading depends more on the development of skills in visual and auditory discrimination and the method used than on intellectual maturation.

Readiness for a complex task generally entails a number of somewhat independent aspects. It is therefore possible for a child to be unready despite more than sufficient readiness in some aspects of the task and vice versa; because the individual reacts as a whole, strengths and limitations in any one of the many factors involved affect the whole process of learning. Strong motivation can compensate to some extent for limited capacity, just as negative attitudes can prevent learning from taking place despite adequacy in other factors. To the extent that the individual lacks readiness with respect to one or more aspects of the situation, he may not be ready for the task at all. Thus, reading readiness involves a certain level of mental development; sufficient eye coordination to permit clear perception; ability to attend to symbols; a fairly large background of experience which allows the child to relate what he reads to things he has experienced; interest in stories and ability to anticipate what is coming next; favorable attitudes, including a desire to learn to read; social and emotional maturity that permits him to devote his capacities to reading rather than dissipating them in overcoming emotional blocks; and many other developmental aspects, the lack of any one of which can lead to reading difficulty. A great deal of time is spent in kindergarten and in first grade in developing the required readiness through creating interest in stories, expanding experiences, and building gross discriminations, but really, the reading-readiness program begins in the home when the child sees his parents and siblings read, when they read to him, when they relate to him some of their experiences—in short, when they help him develop a desire to read and the experiential background necessary to interpret what he reads. It may even go back to the development of perceptual skills in the crib and the playpen.

Readiness is simply a matter of the child being able to bring to bear on a given task capabilities equal to the demands of the situation; as such, it is basic to coordinating the grade-placement of subject-matter topics and pedagogical procedures through which these materials are taught. Successful educational planning requires that we know what pupils are generally ready for at different ages, what elements enter into readiness, how to judge readiness, what can be done to increase it, and how we can adapt present methods to capitalize on the child's present level of readiness. Two errors can result from failure to understand the concept of readiness: [a] overlooking its importance in the attainment of the competencies in question or taking its presence for granted; and [b] waiting for the various conditions of readiness to appear by themselves. The opposite error is to delay the introduction of materials for which the child is ready.

Unfortunately, in practice there is no simple and sure way of appraising readiness so that, in the final analysis, there has to be a certain amount of trial and error during which an alert and experienced teacher senses the extent to which the material is consistent with the child's present development. Tests are available commercially with which to appraise readiness in a number of areas; a reading-readiness-test, for example, measures certain aspects of intellectual development but it places special emphasis on those abilities of more specific relevance to learning to read. Prognostic (or readiness) tests are also available in such subjects as foreign languages and algebra, but none is foolproof. All we can expect from them is an additional bit of objective evidence to add to the many other evaluations of readiness which must be considered if the best decision is to be reached. However, the number one technique—and frequently the most adequate—is teacher-observation. Readiness for any activity is probably best played by ear from day to day rather than determined for the year on the basis of a test administered in September. It must also be realized that certain children may never attain the readiness required to succeed, say, in mathematics as taught in the traditional classroom; for such children, attempts to introduce the subject are doomed to failure, and harm to a number of them is a definite possibility.

DEVELOPMENTAL TASKS

It is not generally advisable to introduce training too soon in the maturational sequence. There is, however, the complementary problem, namely, that of not introducing it soon enough: "What if a child is ready for a given task but is denied the opportunity to learn it?" The general thinking is that there is an optimal age level for effective learning. Presented at the right time, a task can be a challenge and a source of enjoyment; presented too soon or too late, it becomes a source of frustration or boredom. Havighurst (1952), in his treatment of the problems with which individuals must cope at each developmental level if adjustment is to be maintained, has popularized the term *developmental task* which he defines as one that

> . . . arises at or about a certain period in the life of the individual, successful achievement of which leads to his happiness and to success with later tasks, while failure leads to unhappiness in the individual, disapproval by society, and difficulty with later tasks. [p. 2]

As the individual grows, he finds himself possessed of new physical and psychological resources. His legs grow stronger and enable him to walk; his nervous system becomes more complex and enables him to reason more adequately. But he also finds himself facing new demands. He is expected to talk, to read, to spell and to subtract. A complex of inner and outer forces contrives to set for him a series of developmental tasks which he must master if he is to be successful as a human being. Thus, in the course of development, the child reaches certain stages which not only make it possible for him to master certain tasks, but also make it imperative that he do so in order to be ready to master the other tasks higher in the developmental sequence.

Any number of examples could be given of the difficulties which arise out of failure to master a given task at its most teachable moment. We have seen that maturation is generally sufficient to enable chicks to learn to peck even when they are delayed in pecking for short periods; however, chicks delayed in pecking by being fed in the dark for several days after hatching, experience difficulty in learning to peck, and the more they are delayed, the more practice pecks they require to reach a given level of proficiency (Padilla, 1935). In fact, a delay of 14 days results in such disintegration of the pecking response that most chicks never peck and starve to death "in the midst of plenty." A child entering school for the first time at, say, the age of twelve, is likely to encounter untold problems ranging from self-consciousness to inability to find materials combining the proper level of difficulty and interest. The teacher's responsibility in this connection, then, is to see that the child masters each task reasonably on schedule and to provide whatever assistance is necessary to keep the process on the move. He also needs to synchronize the curriculum with the developmental status of each age group. When the body is right and society requires it and the self is ready to achieve it, then the most teachable moment has arrived.

As we have noted, *the* developmental task of infancy is the establishment of dependency and security. Childhood is also the ideal time for basic explorations of the world, and failure in this task seriously handicaps the future accomplishment of tasks in related series. The adolescent, on the other hand, needs to develop personal identity. One of the most complete formulations of the specific developmental tasks is that of Havighurst (1952), who gives a comprehensive treatment of the tasks to be mastered in each period from infancy to late maturity and discusses each from the standpoint of its biological, psychological, and cultural bases, as well as from its educational implications. Thus, he recognizes that the home, not the school, has primary responsibility for helping boys and girls achieve emotional independence from adults, but he points out that colleges, for example, have the opportunity to help young people who are away from home for the first time, and he suggests that teachers learn to play a useful role in the process of psychological weaning.

It is quite a problem to provide the right experiences at the right time for some 30 youngsters who invariably do not find it convenient to be ready for the same experience at the same time. However, the task is not impossible. First, the child's fundamental drive toward growth is such that he does not have to be pushed over every hurdle. Furthermore, the most appropriate time for mastering a given task is not a matter of minutes or days and children have remarkable ability to catch up when they have fallen temporarily behind; generally all that is necessary is a bit of guidance and moral support.

RECENT DEVELOPMENTS

Although considerable attention has been paid to the problem of ensuring that the tasks with which the child is presented are *down* to his level of readiness, the complementary problem of seeing that the tasks are *up* to his level of readiness has been largely overlooked. Educators have been overly impressed with the immutability of maturation as a prerequisite for learning and have assumed that nothing could be done except to pace the learner as a means of avoiding waste in teaching. A fundamental problem recent research has put into focus, and whose significance for future education may be revolutionary, is that of accomplishing certain learnings much earlier than has been thought feasible in the past. We are shifting from the view of readiness as an aspect of maturation to a more positive and optimistic awareness that many aspects of readiness are amenable to environmental stimulation, and, further, that the child frequently has sufficient maturation for a given task if we modify our methods to fit the degree of readiness he has. Whereas these new developments, sponsored by the work of Hebb, Skinner, Moore, and others, are in need of further validation, they suggest exciting possibilities.

Some educators have asked, "Why so much hurry? Why shorten childhood?" It often seems that parents and teachers are intent about the grim business of having children outgrow their childhood as quickly as possible; apparently nobody wants children to be children. With our middle-class orientation toward achievement and our fever toward precocity, we seem anxious to drive children over the course of learning whether they are ready or not. Education viewed as a matter of a platoon of teachers preparing children to meet the requirements of the next grade can lead to difficulty; it may be better to have a child learn at a comfortable level than to force him into a frustration situation—with resulting emotional blockings and a downgrading of the self-concept.

A number of experiments—most of them outdated—have been conducted on the effects on subsequent competence of postponing formal instruction. In the Winnetka study (Morphett and Washburne, 1940), the formal teaching of reading, writing, and arithmetic was delayed during the first year and a half of school. There were, of course, numerous informal exposures to reading and number experiences. By the middle of second grade, the experimental group was behind; at the end of the third grade they had caught up; then they forged ahead by somewhat more than half a grade, a superiority which they maintained. The experimental group was also rated superior in spontaneity, eagerness to learn, and cooperative, self-directed activities. Supportive data are found in a more recent study by Sax and Ottina (1958). Postponement of formal instruction, however, is hardly the answer, as many critics have noted (e.g., Tyler, 1964). In a sense, such a postponement simply increases the cruciality of informal instruction and the burden on the shoulders of the teacher for the planning of informal learning experiences. This kind of situation could lead to a highly haphazard approach to teaching. Why not rely on the promotion of readiness and the adaptation of pedagogical practices? Certainly reading readiness programs have been shown to promote better reading in the first grade (Edmiston and Peyton, 1950; Bradley, 1956). Kindergarten experiences likewise tend to promote readiness (Fast, 1957; Koenke, 1948). Readiness can be accelerated through experience; the learning of a given skill facilitates the learning of other skills, and, despite the criticism of overemphasis on hurry, there is reason to believe that something is to be gained from the systematic intellectual stimulation of young children as a means of equipping them for effective living in a complex and changing world, and, further, there is reason to believe that this can be done without harm.

Hebb's theory of learning, with its neurophysiological orientation, makes a distinction between primary and later learnings. Early learnings are gained only through a slow and elaborate process (presumably reflecting the slow and tedious process involved in developing cell assemblies); once these basic learnings have been attained, later learnings come more rapidly and easily. At first, the infant is virtually lacking in any knowledge and must spend an apprenticeship acquiring even the most elementary foundation, discriminations, and generalizations from his physical and social world. These primary concepts are more difficult to come by because he possesses no frame of reference to provide conceptual leverage for learning. Even though he hears and sees, he has no experience to which to relate his perceptions, so that his learning is inefficient. What to the adult are tiny insignificant steps represent giant strides for the young child.

Von Senden, in his review of the literature (1932), notes that it takes a great deal of learning for congenitally blind persons who have suddenly gained their sight, as a result of corneal transplants or the removal of cataracts, to perceive even simple forms. These people remain *functionally* blind for some time after their sight has been restored, for they cannot interpret what they see; one girl, a college graduate at the time she regained her sight, required months of practice before she could visually distinguish three of her best friends from one another. Supporting evidence comes from the devastating effects rearing in darkness has upon animals, a handicap which seems to have long-lasting effects upon their visual functioning (Riesen, 1949). In Hebb's experiment (1937), rats raised in darkness took six times as many trials to learn visual discriminations as rats reared in light. Forgus (1956) likewise found that baby rats that had been exposed to cut-out forms of circles, crosses, triangles, and squares from the time their eyes opened until they were 41 days of age were superior in making discriminations to a control group which had been first exposed to the forms at the age of 41 days. Apparently early stimulation is essential for later effective (intelligent) operation.

Of major significance here is Harlow's concept of *learning sets*, i.e., learning how to learn (Harlow, 1949, 1959). In his experiment, chimpanzees first learned basic discriminations pertaining to objects, e.g., a sphere, a cube, a circle, and a rectangle, a black and a white object, etc., through reinforcement with, say, a raisin located under one or the other of the objects. Learning at first was largely a matter of trial and error, but in time the chimps "caught on"; once they had mastered the basic concept of discrimination, they were able to solve new discrimination problems with nearly 100 percent accuracy. They had learned not only the solution to specific problems but, more significantly, had developed *a generalized ability to discriminate*. They had simply become educated monkeys, i.e., adjustable creatures with increased capacity to react effectively to changing environmental demands. Harlow's concept of learning how to learn has fundamental implications with respect to "capacity" and "readiness." Apparently much of the "intelligence" which the organism is able to display is primarily the result of previous background. Gagné and Paradise (1961), for example, theorize that:

> . . . differences in rate of completion of a learning program are primarily dependent upon the number and kind of learning sets (i.e., the "knowledge") the learner brings to the situation, secondarily upon his standing in respect to certain relevant basic abilities, and not in any direct sense upon a general 'learning rate ability.' [p. 3]

A similar point is made by Tyler (1964) who notes that "mental age does not seem to be a particularly useful index of readiness for whatever activity, practice, or skill we are planning to teach." We have now come to recognize that readiness incorporates a host of other factors relatively amenable to training. Kirk (1958), for example, found that systematic day-school experiences in drawing, telling stories, etc., enabled a group of institutionalized preschool children of IQs between 45 and 80 to be relatively successful in Grade 1. The systematic reading of stories to two- and three-year-olds has likewise been shown to result in significant improvement in their language development (Irwin, 1960).

DEPRIVATION OF EARLY TRAINING

Of interest in this connection are the McGill studies in the deprivation of early experiences mentioned in Chapter 1. In one study (Melzack and Scott, 1957), puppies reared in isolation from puppyhood to maturity in specially constructed cages which drastically restricted their sensory experiences showed obvious inability to make appropriate avoidance responses when tested later as adults. They struck their heads over and over again against a water-pipe that ran along the wall just above the floor in the testing room; they walked into a lighted match, poked their noses into the flame, withdrew a few inches apparently reflexively, and walked into the match all over again. The outstanding feature of their behavior was a complete inability to respond adaptively and intelligently to noxious stimuli; they just did not learn to make appropriate avoidance responses that would have prevented further pain. Apparently, contrary to what one might expect, responding to pain, which is so fundamental to normal adult behavior and presumably so important to survival, requires a background of early perceptual experience.

In a similar study, (Thompson and Heron, 1954), Scottish terriers raised under conditions of relative isolation displayed significant sensori-motor disturbances; they bumped into things, they had trouble with stairs, etc. Even after a year of "normal" living, the restricted dogs were still quite stupid by comparison with their litter-mates reared under normal conditions. If food was placed in Corner A of the room and then moved to Corner B in plain sight, they would first go to Corner A. If a screen was placed in front of the food, they invariably went to the screen and tried to go through it. They were short on attention span and generally did poorly on a series of tasks involving what might be called intelligence. When faced with strange phenomena, such as a human skull, a slowly swelling balloon, or an opening umbrella, the restricted puppies became agitated and displayed behavior that was diffuse, undifferentiated, and lacking in purposiveness (Thompson and Melzack, 1956). They did not do any better in social behavior. They were dominated by much younger puppies; apparently their restricted upbringing had even overcome the powerful factor of seniority. According to the authors, the experiments clearly indicate the importance of a rich and stimulating environment in early life as a condition for normal development; restriction of experience during this critical period results in irretrievable retardation in various psychological dimensions.

IMPLICATIONS

These and other studies have raised issues that warrant consideration in any discussion of readiness and developmental tasks in relation to the education of the child. Although the nature of the evidence certainly dictates caution, previous "impossibilities" are now attaining new probabilities. McCullers and Plant (1964, p. 604), for example, referring to Watson's claim (Watson, 1930) that, given a dozen healthy infants and a special environment in which to raise them, he could take any one and produce any type of person desired, boldly assert that:

> . . . the preponderance of current evidence suggests that his claim might have been fulfilled. At any rate, it appears that he would have been hampered more by methodological problems than by the nature of his basic assumptions. Watson's appeal was made nearly half a century ago; it is indeed lamentable that so much time has been wasted. [p. 604]

The concept of the most teachable moment tends to recur in the experimental literature. A number of illustrations have already been noted; many others could be listed: [a] light deprivation for more than a few days results in a breakdown in the pecking response of chicks; [b] early sensory deprivation of dogs leads to irretrievable stupidity; [c] if puppies are not provided with the required experiences in adjusting to new aspects of the physical environment during the critical period (around the twelfth week), they become unable to assume responsibility and cannot complete guide-dog training successfully (Pfaffenberger and Scott, 1959); [d] blind persons gaining their sight have difficulty learning to discriminate (Von Senden, 1932; Hebb, 1937); and [e] extended light deprivation in chimps and kittens results in irreversible chemical changes in the retina, an effect even more marked in higher mammals (Riesen, 1960).

A parallel situation may prevail with regard to academic learning. There are indications that, from the standpoint of accent at least, early childhood is the ideal time to learn a language. The mathematical concept of *sets*, which frequently appears so complex to college students, is being learned apparently without difficulty by first-graders; indeed, there is a considerable downgrading into the elementary school of many concepts once thought to be high school, college, or even graduate material. When these concepts are introduced in an intelligent and matter-of-fact manner, the children respond with interest and understanding. We are learning that it is often not difficulty of subject matter which overtaxes the child but rather the rigidity of the adult thought-mold in which it is presented.

ADAPTATION OF METHODS

Modification of our methods has resulted in learning earlier than hitherto imagined possible. Skinner has had eminent success in teaching complex behavioral repertoires to varied subjects from pigeons to children and psychotic adults. Particularly interesting is the success of Moore at Yale in teaching three-year-olds to read, write, tell a story to a tape recorder, and to type it out as it is being played back (See Chapter 1). We cannot expect to find readiness in precisely the right amount at the moment it is called for in the curriculum, but this need not deter us from attempting to communicate with each and every child; we simply need to incorporate into our curriculum and our procedures sufficient variety and flexibility to permit making the necessary contact. Apparently in 1931, the mental age required for beginning reading was set at 6-6 (six years and six months) (Morphett and Washburne); Gates (1937) suggested that with modification of teaching methods, a mental age of 5-0 is sufficient for learning to read. We might want to know why, over 30 years later, in an era of improved techniques and equipment, it still takes a mental age of 6-6 for children of vastly greater experiential background to learn to read.

PROMOTING READINESS

Readiness is not as immutable as our past emphasis on maturation had led us to assume. Ausubel (1959) takes a particularly strong stand against the unwarranted, fallacious, and overgeneralized application of the concept of readiness to educational practice. Not only are the psychological and experiential factors amenable to development, but they can compensate to some degree for lack of physiological readiness. Furthermore, research suggests that the use of physiological equipment actually promotes its development. Held (1929) found that opening one eye of a baby kitten promotes myelination of that eye. We also know that premature babies have greater myelination than babies of the same age as measured from conception. There are still limits imposed by heredity, but too often we have attributed to inherited limitations what in reality is the product of inadequate previous learning. The stumbling block may be simply a previous step in the spiral which must be taken to release the stoppage.

These and other research findings suggest the need for us to reconsider our position. Could it be, for example, that the intellectual inadequacies that have characterized children from the lower classes are simply the outcome of cultural deprivation, especially in early childhood, and that any attempt at a crash program in the first grade just does not give them time to develop the cell assemblies of which Hebb speaks? By the time they come to school, these children may be so lacking in basic learnings that they cannot be expected to take the longer strides when they have yet to take the smaller, more difficult steps connected with primary learnings. They constitute part of what Chauncey (1963) refers to as a completely untapped potential of intellectual capacity waiting to be developed through the improvement of instruction, on the one hand, and the enrichment of experience, on the other hand. The magnitude of this untapped potential has been shown by such studies as Project Higher Horizons in New York City (See Chapter 1) whose results have been encouraging; a comparable program going back to the preschool years, e.g., Operation Headstart, should be even more productive. Moore, for example, feels that it is a mistake not to capitalize on the preschool years. Hunt (1961) also deplores the neglect of the preschool child, a practice he attributes to the fixed maturation fallacy. Chauncey points to the feasibility of discovering ways that govern the encounters children have with their environment, especially during the early years, in order to achieve a substantially faster rate of intellectual development and a substantially higher adult level of intellectual capacity. He points out that mental processes established very early in life become a permanent part of the individual and exert lifelong effects upon mental and educational development.

It is not the role of a textbook in educational psychology to adjudicate issues that are essentially sociological and philosophical. Nevertheless, the issues are here for us to consider, perhaps in the light of Travers' statement (1963) that in years to come children will learn twice as much with half the effort. A partial answer may be a more vigorous emphasis on kindergarten and nursery school education, perhaps even educational games or teaching machines in the home. We may need to mobilize the home in the education of its children. There would be dangers, but perhaps we stand to gain more than we stand to lose. We need to expand the child's experiential background and increase his understanding through a developmental program from infancy; training in discrimination, including attention to symbols and to sounds, should be stressed as background for reading. Equally important, we need to adapt teaching procedures to the specific nature and level of the child's readiness.

HIGHLIGHTS OF THE CHAPTER

An understanding of the general principles of growth and development is of major importance to the teacher whose task it is to coordinate environmental influences with maturational processes. He needs to be familiar with the following concepts:

[a]

Whatever development an individual displays at a given time is the result of the interaction of environmental influences upon the potentialities with which he was conceived. These two sets of factors are so thoroughly interrelated that it is impossible to isolate their specific influence.

[b]

Recent research has suggested that genes are best conceived as a function of the molecule of the chemical DNA which has the capacity to generate exact replicas of itself when the environment contains the necessary raw materials. Genes presumably influence the chemical processes in question.

[c]

The limits of the individual's capabilities are set in considerable measure by his inherited potentialities. Recent research in early stimulation, however, has caused a major reconsideration of our former emphasis on the immutability of maturational processes and of the scope of human and animal capacity. The possibilities of releasing, through early stimulation and a modification of methods, potential heretofore untapped have found both empirical and theoretical support. Research also suggests a need for a major shift in the meaning of *capacity* from something one *has* to something one *develops*.

[d]

The fact that the rate of development varies from child to child suggests the futility of mass education aimed at the nonexistent average child.

[e]

The interrelatedness of the various aspects of development points to the need for dealing with the whole child. This interrelatedness, along with the fact that the development follows a definite sequential pattern implies that failure to master a certain developmental task at the appropriate time is likely to impede further progress.

[f]

The child has an inbuilt success mechanism in his desire to grow. It is unfortunate that so often adults go out of their way to stifle this enthusiasm by subjecting him to frequent and costly failures. A little more care in establishing readiness before introducing new activities would save teachers a great deal of difficulty in *motivating* reluctant students.

SOURCES OF RELATED MATERIAL

Anastasi, Anne, "Heredity, environment, and the question 'how?' " *Psychol. Rev.*, 65: 197–208, 1958.

Ausubel, David P., "Viewpoints from related disciplines: Human growth and development," *Teach. Coll. Rec.*, 60: 245–254, 1959.

Chauncey, Henry, *Annual Report, 1962–1963*. Princeton, N.J.: Educational Testing Service, 1963.

Flavell, John R., *The Developmental Psychology of Jean Piaget*. Princeton, N.J.: D. Van Nostrand Company, Inc., 1963.

Fowler, William L., "Cognitive learning in infancy and early childhood," *Psychol. Bull.*, 59: 116–152, 1962.

Harris, Dale B. (ed.), *The Concept of Development*. Minneapolis, Minn.: University of Minnesota Press, 1957.

Hunt, J. McV., *Intelligence and Experience*. New York: The Ronald Press Company, 1961.

———, "The psychological basis for using preschool enrichment as an antidote for cultural deprivation," *Merrill-Palmer Quart.*, 10: 209–243, 1964.

Kagan, Jerome, and H. A. Moss, *Birth to Maturity*. New York: John Wiley & Sons, Inc., 1962.

Life magazine, "DNA's code: Key to all life," *Life*, 55 (14): 70–90, Oct. 4, 1963.

Mussen, Paul H. (ed.), *Handbook of Research Methods in Child Development*. New York: John Wiley & Sons, Inc., 1960.

Nixon, R. E., *The Art of Growing: A Guide to Psychological Maturity*. New York: Random House, Inc., 1962.

Passow, A. H. (ed.), *Education in Depressed Areas*. New York: Teachers College, Columbia University, 1963.

Pines, M., "How three-year-olds teach themselves to read—and love it," *Harper's magazine*, 226: 58–64, May 1963.

QUESTIONS AND PROJECTS

1

To what extent is the problem of heredity and environment one of academic interest rather than one of practical significance? one of sociological interest rather than of educational importance?

2

Evaluate the statement: "All that the individual inherits is a certain body structure which is receptive to stimulation; that is both necessary and sufficient."

3

What are some of the further implications for the education of the culturally disadvantaged of the recent view that readiness is not as immutable as previous evidence had led us to believe?

4

Report on a research project designed to promote intellectual and academic readiness on the part of culturally deprived children. How conclusive is the evidence?

5

[a] Specifically, how would you go about enriching the experience of city children about to undertake a unit on "The Farm?"

[b] Discuss the role of television as a medium for promoting readiness.

CHAPTER 6

Physical and Motor Development

Although we can hardly fail to notice the dramatic physical changes which take place in school children, we can all too readily overlook their significance.

Stephens, 1956, p. 71

The question of physical adequacy is of primary concern to students of educational psychology, for it has a significant bearing on every aspect of child development. Not only is physical development of great importance in itself, but it is of even greater significance from the standpoint of its psychological implications.

GROWTH IN HEIGHT AND WEIGHT

NATURE OF PHYSICAL GROWTH

Certainly the most obvious aspect of the child's total development are the changes that take place in the physical realm. His growth in height and weight is particularly rapid during early life as he multiplies a millionfold during the nine-month period following conception and doubles, by six months, his weight at birth. Growth continues at a rapid rate during infancy, moves through alternate periods of rapid and slow gain, and gradually tapers off during the middle teens in the case of girls and a couple of years later in the case of boys.

The growth pattern, as measured in increases in height or weight, can be shown through a curve such as that in Figure 6-1. These curves, it must be understood, represent average status for the various age levels and give the misleading impression that growth is smooth and continuous, although, in reality, the smoothness results from the fact that, at any given age, the rapid growth of one child is offset by the slow

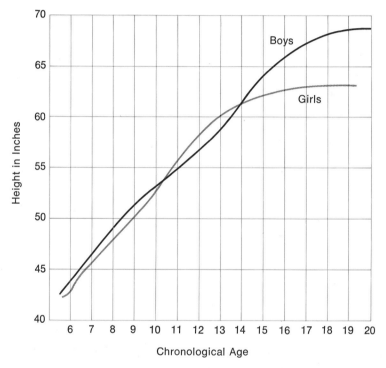

FIGURE 6-1   Height of boys and girls. (After Shuttleworth, 1939.)

growth of another. Consequently, even though such curves are interesting and valuable for general information, the teacher must not forget that each child has a unique growth pattern which may differ by quite a margin from the average pattern characteristic of the group. This does not imply that all is haphazard and chaotic. With few exceptions, the tall infant tends to remain tall and becomes the tall adult while the short infant tends to remain short. In fact, Bayley (1936) has actually devised a scale to predict adult stature from the child's height at various ages. There is, however, considerable evidence to show that growth takes place in spurts, suggesting that predicting future stature from present height is subject to considerable error, especially during adolescence.

As shown in Figure 6-1, the growth patterns for boys and girls differ in several important respects. Boys are taller and heavier at birth and attain a higher final status in both height and weight. Girls, on the other hand, reach physical and physiological maturity some 18 months earlier than boys, and, it is important to note, are on the average both taller and heavier than boys during the period from eleven to fourteen. They are generally taller and heavier than boys throughout the period of growth when growth is measured as a fraction of ultimate status; in fact, they are simply more "mature" than boys of their chronological age.

Growth rates are affected by a number of environmental conditions. Americans are growing taller, heavier, and maturing earlier every generation, apparently as a result of dietary improvement (Tanner, 1955). Japanese and Chinese children in America are taller and heavier than their counterparts on the Asiatic continent (Karpinos, 1961). Physical growth is also related to socioeconomic and cultural status; upper-class children tend to be taller than children of the middle or lower classes (Gray and Ayres, 1931), perhaps because of heredity, if we assume that physical size is an asset in attaining success, or perhaps because of certain nutritional or other advantages. Growth is also influenced by such things as depressions, wars, milk programs, (Laporte, 1946; Palmer, 1935) and, of course, prenatal care (Ebbs, Chapter 5). This may account for the fact that children from homes of limited financial means tend to be smaller than the average (Meredith, 1951). On the other hand, inherited differences may also be postulated, and the general consensus is that physical growth is more dependent on heredity than most other aspects of growth. It is generally agreed, for example, that the usual illnesses that befall growing children have only a temporary effect on their growth and do not affect their final status appreciably, if at all. Endocrine imbalance, on the other hand, whether related to heredity or environmental causes, can effect a considerable departure from normality both in the individual's rate of maturing and his final status.

The one outstanding feature of growth is the vast range of individual differences in the physical size of children at any given age. Thus, from Simmons' data (1944) shown in Figure 6-2, it can be seen that the tallest seven-year-old boy, for example, is about as tall as the shortest thirteen-year-old, while the tallest eight-year-old girl is considerably taller than the shortest fourteen-year-old. Similarly, the tallest 2 percent of seven-year-old boys in Baldwin's sample (1921) were actually taller than the shortest 2 percent of the thirteen-year-olds, while the tallest 2 percent of ten-year-old girls were taller than the shortest 2 percent of the sixteen-year-olds.

Generally, when we plot the height of members of any age group,

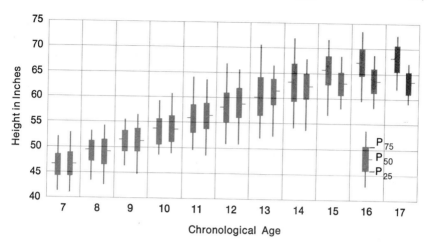

FIGURE 6-2   Range of heights of boys (first symbol at each age) and girls of various ages. (After Simmons, 1944.)

we find they distribute themselves in what is known as the normal curve. Such a distribution is shown in Figure 6-3. Thus, we find a few very short and a few very tall individuals, with increasing frequencies as we approach the average. This is typical of the distribution of most physical and psychological traits, e.g., running speed, strength of grip, intelligence, performance on a test. We do not have separate categories—tall, medium, and short; bright, average, and dull—but rather a continuum ranging from very tall to very short, from very bright to very dull, with

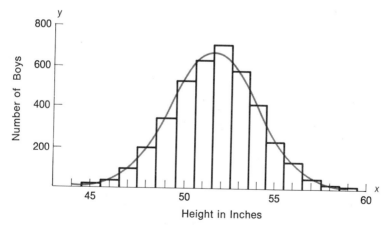

FIGURE 6-3   Distribution of heights of 4451 Canadian boys age nine. (After Blommers and Lindquist, 1960, by permission of Houghton Mifflin Company. Based on data from Dominion Bureau of Statistics, Canada, 1942.)

a definite concentration of individuals of average height, or of average intelligence. In most human traits, individuals differ in degree rather than in kind, and the percentage of cases of a given distribution decreases progressively as deviation (in either direction) from the average increases.

PSYCHOLOGICAL IMPLICATIONS

The psychological implications of physical development can readily be understood in terms of its effect on the self-image and on the difficulty or ease with which the individual can satisfy his needs. What we think of ourselves and what others think of us, and the demands they make of us as well as those we make of ourselves, depend to a large extent upon our physique and the reactions it evokes. Thus, strength and physical size are among the important attributes of the ten-year-old boy just as an attractive figure and a pretty face are valued attributes of the teen-age girl. The individual's whole adjustment revolves in large measure around such ideas as "beautiful," "tall and handsome," "buckteeth," "fatso," "beanpole," or "skinny." In fact, much of one's life might well depend on whether one's image is that of Marilyn Monroe, Jimmy Durante, or Tarzan. The self-concept may also be directly tied to the color of one's skin or even to color of hair, e.g., "carrot-top."

Physical inadequacies can have serious psychological effects. In a study of Stolz and Stolz (1944), for instance, over a third of the 176 boys and girls examined at six-month intervals over an eight-year period expressed concern over some physical characteristic. Similar results are reported by Elias (1949). Being a "runt," a "tub" or "ugly" may easily represent handicaps to adjustment and to success comparable to deformities and other deviations from normality. An extended illness may likewise leave scars on the child's psychological makeup, and the teacher, if he is to be effective in dealing with children, had better become acquainted with the child's past as well as present status.

What is even more important is the child's reaction to his physical characteristics. The statuesque teen-age girl who feels that she is "too tall," the adolescent with a severe case of acne, the smaller boy, all must be led toward increased self-acceptance. Acceptance is circular: if the individual does not accept himself, he cannot expect others to do so. Unfortunately, the way others see us often reinforces the attitudes we would like to overcome. The small boy may be babied longer and denied the opportunity of assuming responsibility. On the other hand, the boy who is tall for his age may be faced with demands and expectations beyond his overall maturity. Youngsters are frequently faced with inconsistent expectations, being told simultaneously that they are too big for certain childhood privileges and too small for adult privileges. The average parent is prone to raise his expectations for more mature behavior and yet reluctant to let go on such matters as allowing the teen-ager to use the car. The adolescent is frequently denied opportunities to explore adult roles.

Physical development is directly and vitally related to other aspects of development. Social and emotional development, for example, are greatly facilitated by such physical assets as attractiveness, size, and strength. The physically adequate boy has more opportunities to lead in games and to learn vitally important techniques of leadership and cooperation so that his total personality development is enhanced by his physical development. It is also possible, of course, for a person endowed with abundant physical assets to feel so complacent that he neglects the development of his potentialities.

THE PREADOLESCENT GROWTH SPURT

The preadolescent growth spurt is of particular interest to prospective teachers because of the complications attending the rapid growth that occurs during this period. A boy, for instance, may add five inches to his height and 25 pounds to his weight in a year. This spurt is very closely timed to taper off with the advent of puberty, although it may occur up to three years before and, in some 10 percent of the cases, up to three years after the attainment of sexual maturity (Dearborn and Rothney, 1941).

Many physical and physiological changes are connected with this growth spurt besides the rapid increase in overall height and weight. Different parts of the body begin rapid growth at different times so that the adolescent boy's feet (or perhaps his arms or even his nose) may temporarily grow out of all proportion. This may result in awkwardness at a time when the adolescent is becoming very self-conscious, and he may trip, or knock over a glass as he reaches for it, simply because he is not used to the new length of his limbs. Even some of the skills he had mastered have to be relearned because his new body proportions make them essentially new skills. To make matters worse, the glandular changes accompanying this growth spurt are likely to result in adolescent acne at the very time when both boys and, perhaps especially, girls becomes conscious of the importance of good looks in attracting members of the opposite sex.

None of the physiological changes accompanying the prepubescent growth spurt is any more important than the attainment of sexual maturity and the resulting need for a major reorganization of the self-concept;[1] especially in the area of social relations. Members of the opposite sex suddenly assume an attractiveness not previously apparent, and

[1] Probably no better illustration can be found of a major change in the individual's phenomenal field.

a new interest in dancing and social sports displaces previous interest in the gang and preadolescent activities. Of major import is the sex drive itself and the conflicts it is likely to introduce because of the sex taboos that are part of the culture.

The drastic changes taking place during the prepubescent growth spurt are bound to have psychological repercussions. This is particularly true where, in addition to the problem attending bodily changes, the youth, trying to think of himself as an adult willing to assume adult responsibilities, is prevented from doing so. In contrast to adolescence in primitive societies or even in pioneer days in America where the adolescent simply took his place as a full-fledged member of society rather early, adolescence for the modern American youth has become a period of considerabe strain and stress. As a result, confusion, insecurity, rebelliousness, and defiance are often as much a part of the adolescent pattern as awkwardness and persistent crazes over teen "idols."

The problems connected with the preadolescent growth spurt and the advent of puberty are complicated when these changes take place early or late. Research has shown that puberty takes place any time from age ten to seventeen for girls and from age eleven to eighteen for boys (Keliher, 1941). The early maturer, who suddenly becomes interested in members of the opposite sex while his age-mates still "can't see it," is likely to find himself out of joint with the gang. This is somewhat more of a problem for the early-maturing girl who, because girls mature some 18 to 24 months ahead of boys, may find herself a year or two out of step with the girls and three or four years out of step with the boys. The early-maturing boy enters adolescence at a time when girls in his age group are appreciative of his interest, and he is simply ready to take advantage of the opportunities presented by his social environment.

The late maturer, on the other hand, is likely to feel left out, to be unable not only to get a date but even to generate any enthusiasm in that direction. This is complicated even further by the fact that when he finally "arrives," he has to compete for dates with the early maturers who have by now polished their social skills relative to members of the opposite sex to the point of making any "Johnny-come-lately" look rather "green" and uninteresting by comparison. The problem is particularly severe for the late-maturing boy who, in our culture, is likely to be exposed to a sociopsychological environment that tends to generate a vicious circle of adverse effects on his personality development. Being less physically impressive, and at a disadvantage in athletic activities, he is regarded and treated as immature by others; he tends to be rejected and dominated, with resulting prolonged dependency, a negative self-concept, and a rebellious outlook. This often interferes with identification with his parents which may, in turn, inhibit the development of mature attitudes ordinarily established through identification with adults. There are exceptions, of course, and the adolescent boy who is fundamentally secure and has warm, accepting parents and generally rewarding social relationships may suffer no ill effects from late maturation. Certainly the early-maturing boy will not develop self-confidence simply because he matures early. Nevertheless, the teacher needs to be careful lest the effects of delayed maturity, by becoming relatively permanent through promoting a vicious circle of immature behavior, be as harmful to the child as an actual defect or abnormality; follow-up studies (Jones, 1957; Jones and Mussen, 1958) have shown late maturers to display a significantly less adequate self-concept and somewhat stronger dependency needs at age thirty three than did the early maturers, for example.

BODY TYPES

The question of body build, a topic of consideration since the time of the Greek philosophers, was the subject of renewed interest in the past couple of decades as the result of investigations conducted by Sheldon (Sheldon and Stevens, 1940), who reported a substantial relationship between temperament and body build. More specifically, he associated [a] the endomorph (rolypoly) with a relaxed social nature dominated by a love of comfort and a greed for approval and affection; [b] the mesomorph (superman), with a personality characterized by activity, energy, and aggressiveness; and [c] the ectomorph (beanpole) with restraint in posture, inhibition, and tenseness. These postulated relationships, in addition to being in line with common stereotypes, also made theoretical sense. The relationships between body build and temperament could have a basis in the individual's biochemical or glandular structure (Harsh and Shrickel, 1959) and/or learning theory, including social expectations.

The possibilities of these relationships are, of course, intriguing. The mesomorph, for example, with his assertiveness and love of power, might be expected to be full of energy and daring, a dynamic leader whether as a business tycoon, labor organizer, or leader in classroom mischief. Twice as many delinquents as nondelinquents in the Glueck and Glueck study (1959) were mesomorphs and less than half as many were ectomorphs. To be a mesomorph is not necessarily to be a delinquent but, if one is to be a delinquent, there is apparently an advantage to being a mesomorph who can be more assertive, impulsive, and daring, perhaps because he can be and perhaps because he is expected to be.

Unfortunately, when subjected to rigorous investigation, Sheldon's postulation of a relationship between morphological and temperamental factors suffered essentially the same fate as other "type" theories of personality (See Chapter 18). Research designed to test Sheldon's hypothesis failed to find an appreciable relationship between constitutional type and temperament, and it now seems that the greatest contribution of Sheldon's somatotypes lies in providing the basis for exact physical descriptions such as might be used in identifying criminals or missing persons.

MOTOR DEVELOPMENT

Also related to physical growth is the development of motor proficiency. Of major importance in itself, it is of even greater significance from the standpoint of its effects upon the satisfaction of needs and the development of the self-concept. Physical and motor adequacy are important determinants of status among preadolescents, for example; the youth who scores a touchdown or bats in the winning run finds himself a hero in the eyes of all, including himself. Fortunately, although motor proficiency is positively correlated with the other aspects of development, it is still sufficiently independent of these aspects to provide the means for satisfying the needs of many children who find very little satisfaction in other areas. Many boys of low socioeconomic status have used boxing, football, and other sports as avenues to success and prestige.

The negative effect of the lack of motor proficiency should also be noted. Just as physical deformity can be a serious liability in the development of a positive self-concept as well as in social and emotional adequacy, so can awkwardness and lack of speed, strength, or coordination. It therefore becomes the responsibility of the school, if it is to be of maximum service to its students, to help them develop the strength, speed, and coordination of which they are capable and to teach them such motor skills as they need to attain maximum self-realization. There is no excuse, for instance, for failing to teach junior high school boys how to dance when such a skill is a *must* if they are to go on with the developmental task of heterosexual adjustment. There is no excuse for the lack of motor skill and ability sometimes encountered among our young people. In America where we *live* such national sports as baseball and football, there are countless children who have never participated in either sport, who in fact have not participated in any organized team sport. Schools spend considerable money on an athletic program which apparently bypasses the very children who need it most. Our military induction centers in World War II reported a rather sorry picture of the fitness of American youth. Similar evidence of a general lack of physical and motor development comes from the study by Cureton (1943) who found some 14 percent of college freshmen to be soft and flabby. Such studies as that of Kirschner and Glines (1957) found American elementary school children considerably inferior to Canadian and European children in minimal muscular fitness.[2] Although this may be the price a well-developed nation must pay for its affluence, perhaps a courageous superintendent might benefit both the children's health and the taxpayer's purse by insisting that children rediscover that walking to school constitutes a very adequate and healthy means of transportation.

A most significant—although still relatively incomplete—step in the area of psychomotor abilities is the formulation by Guilford (1958) of a framework for psychomotor abilities along the lines of strength, impulsion, speed, static precision, dynamic precision, coordination, and flexibility. Also important is the fact that research has shown a difference in the relative importance of the abilities involved in the earlier, as opposed to the later, stages of proficiency in a complex skill (Fleishman, 1957).

Motor development proceeds through two interrelated and complementary processes, differentiation and integration, occurring in simultaneous and reciprocal fashion. The outcome is a gain in strength and an increase in speed, precision, and smoothness of movement. The process is slow and parents and teachers are often impatient over the child's clumsiness and the crudeness of the projects he turns out. But he wants to grow and, if adults don't make a moral crisis out of spilled milk or spilled ink or insist on a degree of perfection which he cannot produce, the child will learn, even if, at times, adults have their doubts! The important thing is that grownups let the child find his own speed, his own level, and that they fight the temptation to take over and do it for him. He learns by doing.

Gesell's extensive studies of various phases in the development of children from birth are of interest to parents and teachers from nursery school through junior high school. In his report of growth in the first five years of life (1940), for instance, he lists developmental sequences in motor development, adaptive behavior, language development, and personal-social behavior. Probably of greater interest to teachers are the sequel studies (Gesell and Ilg, 1946; Gesell et al., 1956) of children from five to ten and from ten to sixteen, in which he discusses significant aspects of the school child's development in self-care, emotional expression, the growing self, interpersonal relations, school life, ethical sense, and philosophical outlook.

---

[2] A major study of physical fitness is that conducted under the auspices of the Association for Health, Physical Education and Recreation of National Education Association (Hunsicker, 1958). Its findings, based on some 8500 boys and girls in grades five through twelve, show, for example, that at almost all levels (and for both boys and girls), the performance of the top student is twice as adequate as that of the poorest performer.

Important sex differences exist in motor development. Although comparisons are difficult to make because boys and girls are generally not involved in the same activities to the same degree, evidence suggests that, from about age eleven to fourteen, girls are physiologically ahead of boys and, in many activities involving motor skills, could probably outplay them. Fortunately for the latter's self-concept, this situation does not last long; after junior high school, boys become so superior to girls in most motor skills that coeducational participation is restricted to a social basis, especially in sports where strength and stamina are important. Of course, part of girls' relative incompetence in sports stems from lack of interest, perhaps resulting from a self-concept that incorporates the notion of helplessness as an attribute of femininity. Girls, on the other hand, are generally superior in skills requiring accuracy and coordination of the finer muscles. These differences may have a partial basis in such inherited characteristics as the slender fingers of girls; it is obvious, however, that inherited sex differences are strongly accentuated by the embodiment into the self-concept of boys and girls of the adult version of what constitutes a man's and a woman's work.

The various motor abilities and skills tend to be interrelated and the phrase "born athlete" is sometimes used to refer to a person who is highly proficient in several sports. Actually, a more correct explanation would have to consider inherited potential, environmental opportunities, motivation, amount of practice, and other factors, each contributing in various amounts. Proficiency in a number of sports might reflect, in part, a high degree of strength and muscular coordination which serves as a common core for success in all activities where this is important. It is also likely that certain skills, once learned in connection with one activity, can be transferred to similar activities. Motivation and opportunity for practice may be important and, of course, some individuals concentrate on athletics as a compensation for relative incompetence in other areas.

Still, the all-round athlete is the exception rather than the rule, and the more diversified the school's program, the greater the opportunity for any given child to excel in at least one area. Unfortunately, although ideally suited to provide additional avenues for children to satisfy their needs, probably no aspect of the school's program is as inconsiderate of pupil needs as is the sports program. With the present emphasis on winning (when it should be on allowing all the children the opportunity for maximum self-realization), participation is more or less restricted to the best players. As a result, the very child who needs the benefits of participation in team sports simply does not go out for them or, if he does, he warms the bench while his more capable colleagues improve their proficiency and outclass him all the more. The situation is even worse for girls, who have essentially no opportunity for any form of organized exercise; even the dance floor is reserved for those who dance well.

The child's play interests are contingent upon his motor development. A boy does not generate much interest in baseball before the age of nine. As his capacity for a greater variety of activities develops, his play interests increase in number (in keeping with his natural desire to grow and do the things of which he is capable) until by the age of eight he is capable of so many activities that he has to be selective and he, therefore, concentrates on a few. As time goes on, there is a further change as the adult, in keeping with his decreased stamina—and his changing self-concept—seeks less strenuous activities or joins the ranks of spectators while younger people become the participants. In view of the very definite decline in participation in rugged sports during late adolescence and early adulthood, children should be encouraged to develop interest in hobbies and less strenuous sports, such as golf, in which they may continue to participate throughout their lifetime. This is particularly important in view of the fact that adults seldom take up hobbies they have not known in childhood.

HIGHLIGHTS OF THE CHAPTER

Physical and motor development has such direct implications from the standpoint of the formation of the self-image and the satisfaction of needs that teachers need to be familiar with the major concepts in this area. The following are among the more important:

[a]

Physical growth curves are based on averages and apply only in a general way to any one child. Each child has a unique pattern of growth and considerable departure from group averages can be expected. In fact, the most outstanding feature of growth is probably the wide variation that exists among children of any given age group.

[b]

Growth is characterized by alternate periods of rapid and slow growth so that the child's current status is of limited value as an indicator of his final status. Nevertheless, the tall child tends to become the tall adult; the short child, the short adult.

[c]

Girls as a group mature earlier than boys and for the period from eleven through fourteen are superior to boys in height, weight, and motor coordination.

[d]

One's self-concept as well as ease or difficulty in satisfying needs revolve in a major way around one's sense of physical adequacy. By influencing the reactions of others, physical and motor development tends to promote a virtuous or vicious circle and, therefore, to be an important factor in determining behavior.

[e]

In view of the importance of motor proficiency in the satisfaction of needs, the formation of his self-concept, and the promotion of various aspects of development, the school needs to encourage the child to develop such skills as might make for greater self-realization. Unfortunately, much of the school's effort in this connection is expended on the few who are already proficient while those who most need to participate in athletic activities are ignored. Evidence from diverse sources points to a considerable lack of physical fitness among American youth.

[f]

Of particular significance are the preadolescent growth spurt and the reorganization of the adolescent's outlook and behavior resulting from the advent of sexual maturity and increased social pressures for more mature behavior. The problems connected therewith may be relatively serious for both the early- and the late-maturer, especially the late maturing boy.

[g]

Although a positive relationship exists between proficiency among the various motor skills, this correlation is sufficiently low that incompetence in one activity may easily be accompanied by considerable ability in another. The school should provide a variety of activities so that each child can find an area in which he can participate with satisfaction.

SOURCES OF RELATED MATERIAL

Bayley, Nancy, "Individual patterns of development," *Child Develpm.*, 27: 45–74, 1956.

Hunsicker, Paul E., "A.A.H.P.E.R. Physical Fitness Test Battery," *J. hlth. phys. educ. Res.*, 29: 24–25, 1958.

———, *Physical Fitness*; National Education Association series, *What Research Says to the Teacher*. Washington, D.C.: National Education Association, 1963.

Kirschner, G., and D. Glines, "Comparative analysis of Eugene, Oregon, elementary school children on the Kraus-Weber Test of Minimal Muscular Fitness," *Res. Quart.*, 28: 16–25, 1957.

Shaffer, Thomas E., et al., "What contributes to physical fitness?" *Childh. Educ.*, 41: 62–81, 1964.

Shirley, Mary M., *The First Two Years: A Study of Twenty-Five Babies*. Child Welfare Monograph, 7, Vol. 2. Minneapolis, Minn.: University of Minnesota Press, 1933.

Tanner, J. M., "The regulation of human growth," *Child Develpm.*, 94: 817–846, 1963.

QUESTIONS AND PROJECTS

1

[a] Analyze your physical assets and liabilities. Do you feel your assets are adequate for the job of teaching?

[b] What hobbies and other recreational interests have you cultivated? Are they of the type that will continue to provide you with relaxation and enjoyment? Will they involve contact with people other than teachers and thereby provide you with an occasional change in viewpoint?

2

What might be done to promote greater participation in sports on the part of high school girls? What benefit might they derive therefrom? Should physical education be required at the college level?

3

What do you consider to be realistic steps that might be taken to minimize varsity-type athletics and, thus, provide more children with the benefits of participation in sports? What are the pros and cons of deemphasizing football?

4

[a] Academically gifted students sometimes contend that their physical education grade should not be included in the calculation of honor roll standing or rank in graduating class. What value-judgment is implied here?

[b] What weight might physical fitness, general health habits, etc. be given (in addition to motor proficiency) in determining physical education grades?

[c] John stays in school simply because of the sports program; he has no interest whatever in the school's academic program. What action might be taken?

CHAPTER 7

Emotional Development

This concept, that self-interest is the dynamic core of affective life, gives the key to effective methods and materials to be used in education. It supplies the cue for the interpretation of the cross-currents of social life. It points the way to national unity and warns of national disintegration. It can render the same service to humanity.

Prescott, 1938, p. 61

Emotions are such dynamic aspects of human behavior that without the usual episodes of affection, love, fear and anger, life would be drab indeed. They add zest to living, and, of course, at times sorrow and grief. The variety of emotional behavior of which man is capable is almost unlimited; there is, however, considerable variation from person to person in the conditions that arouse an emotion and in the nature, intensity, and manifestations of the emotion that results. Emotions are of special importance because of their motivational nature; the energizing function of emotion is quite obvious, for example, in emergencies involving fear or anger. Emotions are involved in the self-actualization of the individual through the anxiety he experiences when, as a child, for example, he fails to meet the demands of those upon whom he depends. Later, as he internalizes external controls, he feels uncomfortable when he behaves in ways contrary to the social code. Emotions are an integral part of the total personality and are therefore of vital concern to teachers.

THE NATURE OF EMOTIONS

ASPECTS OF AN EMOTION

Emotions are generally defined as a stirred-up state of the organism, a definition which, even though not entirely clear, is at least correct in emphasizing the fact that emotions involve the organism acting as a whole. The degree to which the organism is "stirred up" varies from a condition of mild pleasure, as in the case of a child listening to an interesting story, to that of such intense emotional states as blind rage and panic in which considerable disorganization of behavior occurs. However, we must not look upon emotions as aspects of disorganized behavior; on the contrary, emotions, such as love, hate, resentment, tend to be dynamic integrative forces permeating the entire life-space and making for coordination of the various aspects of behavior.

Emotions are composite affairs involving three interrelated components: [a] varying degrees of feeling covering the whole range of such continua as annoyance-satisfaction and pleasure-displeasure; [b] rather extensive visceral changes, e.g., increased heartbeat and circulation; and [c] certain impulses involving the skeletal muscles, e.g., an urge to fight when angry or flee when afraid. The feeling aspect of emotions is, in a sense, the most important phase of the emotion; it may even be considered *the* emotion. Moods are emotional states that are milder than emotions and that last longer. They predispose the individual toward a certain type of emotional behavior; an irritable mood makes one susceptible to stimuli leading to anger. Moods may have a partial basis in inner states of the organism. Ill health and fatigue may lead to irritability, for instance. Moods are also subject to habit, however, and, as a result, are important aspects of personality, for example, the person who is perpetually irritated.

PHYSIOLOGICAL BASES OF EMOTION

Neurophysiologically, emotions are under the control of the autonomic nervous system which—as opposed to the central nervous system that governs voluntary actions—is relatively independent of voluntary control. This system consists of three parts: [a] the cranial, or upper; [b] the thoracic-lumbar, or sympathetic; and [c] the sacral, or lower. As shown in Figure 7-1, all the visceral organs and most glands have dual nerve connections operating antagonistically as a built-in control mecha-

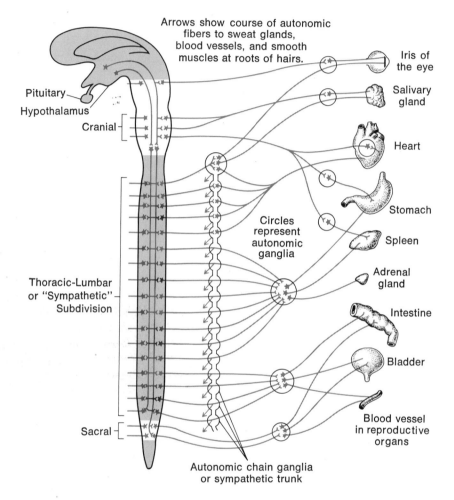

Arrows show course of autonomic
fibers to sweat glands,
blood vessels, and smooth
muscles at roots of hairs.

Iris of
the eye

Pituitary

Hypothalamus

Cranial

Salivary
gland

Heart

Circles
represent
autonomic
ganglia

Stomach

Spleen

Thoracic-Lumbar
or "Sympathetic"
Subdivision

Adrenal
gland

Intestine

Bladder

Blood vessel
in reproductive
organs

Sacral

Autonomic chain ganglia
or sympathetic trunk

FIGURE 7-1   The autonomic nervous system. The brain and spinal cord are
indicated at the left. Nerves from the *cranial* division of the
autonomic system go to organs in the upper part of the body,
from the *sacral* to the lower part. These usually act together and
comprise the cranio-sacral or *parasympathetic* division. The
thoracic-lumbar or sympathetic division originates from the middle part of the cord, and sends fibers to all organs through the
chains of ganglia shown. The action of the sympathetic division
is ordinarily antagonistic to that of the parasympathetic. (Adapted
from N. L. Munn, *Psychology*, third ed. Boston: Houghton Mifflin Company, 1956.)

nism; in fear, the thoracic-lumbar region accelerates the heart, for example, while the other two divisions (known as the parasympathetic nervous system) act to slow it down. A notable exception is the adrenal gland which is connected to the sympathetic division only. In excited emotions, it generally pours adrenalin into the blood, which accelerates the heartbeat and increases the energy immediately available by stimulating the release of blood sugar from the liver. In general, the sympathetic division is active in excited emotional states while the parasympathetic is active in quiescent emotional states. The central nervous system is also active in emotions, being responsible, for example, for muscular tensions. The profound body-wide changes which occur during intense emotions, therefore, are regulated in a complex way by the central nervous system, both divisions of the autonomic nervous system, and, of course, the endocrine glands. The hypothalamus also plays a central role in the activation as well as in the coordination of many types of emotional behavior.

Cannon's emergency theory of emotions (Cannon, 1939), now considered too simple to explain adequately the complexity of emotional behavior, attempted to account for physiological changes in terms of the organism's mobilization of its resources for a fierce physical battle for survival. Thus, in anger, the heartbeat is quickened, adrenalin and noradrenalin are poured into the bloodstream (giving the individual more energy, retarding fatigue, and favoring the quick coagulation of the blood in case of an open wound), the pupils of the eyes are dilated, etc. At the same time, digestion is slowed down to conserve energy. These and the other physiological accompaniments of emotion seem particularly suited to situations involving physical strength and stamina, and stories are told of great physical feats done by persons under emotional tension. John Colter, for instance, is said to have run for miles at full speed while escaping from the Indians.

In the average situation confronting modern man, where solutions are more apt to be found at the conference table than on the battlefield, the changes accompanying violent emotions are likely to be a detriment rather than a help to survival. Mild emotions can be facilitating since they are motivating, but severe emotions often lead to disorganization of behavior, and it may be necessary to help the child ease emotional tensions to the point where he can once again profit from their motivating effects. Strong emotions tend to interfere with clear thinking, and it is common practice to have people prepare for possible emergencies so that, in such events, they can act reflexively to avoid disaster. Fire drills and certain phases of military training are designed for such a purpose. Furthermore, whereas in primitive man, the blood sugar was used up through combat or flight, it tends to remain in the blood of his modern counterpart and to keep him under tension. If persistent, as in anxiety, such tension, besides leading to explosive behavior, could be damaging to physical and mental health.

DEVELOPMENT OF EMOTIONAL BEHAVIOR

EARLY EMOTIONAL REACTIONS

Speculation as to the child's early emotional status dates back to the early days of psychology. Watson (1929), for example, postulated three, presumably inherent, emotions in the newborn, love, fear, and anger. This view is no longer accepted, but research as to the exact nature of the infant's emotional endowment at birth has been inconclusive. Actually, it is impossible to deal with the problem directly since the only behavior of which the infant is capable at that stage of development is essentially in the category of nonadaptive generalized mass activity.

The newborn cannot express his emotions in such a way that people who are unaware of the nature of the stimulus can distinguish between his expression of fear and anger (Sherman, 1928). Goodenough (1932), on the other hand, found that adults did identify with better-than-chance success, the emotions of the ten-month-old baby as registered on photographs. What this means is debatable. It may indicate that the infant at birth has no emotions to express, or it may show that he does not have the necessary physical development to express the emotions which he has. The problem is complicated further by the fact that emotional expression is largely a matter of stereotyping.

It is probably logical to suspect that the infant does not have clearly differentiated emotions. The fact that research in other areas more amenable to investigation has shown that differentiation comes with maturation would suggest that emotional development at birth is not sufficiently complete to permit a full complement of well-differentiated emotions. It is generally agreed, for instance, that the equipment involved in an emotion, such as the hypothalamus and the cerebral cortex, are relatively undeveloped and inadequate for effective functioning at birth. Furthermore, it is unlikely that the neonate would have sufficiently clear perceptions and understandings to permit well-defined emotions; the baby is probably unaware of his complete helplessness, for example.

DIFFERENTIATION OF EMOTIONS

Probably the most thorough investigation of the evolution of the emotions from a condition of general agitation to an almost unlimited variety of specific emotional patterns is that of Bridges (1932), the results of whose study are shown in Figure 7-2. The first stage is that of general excitement from which more specific emotions are gradually differentiated. Thus, excitement becomes differentiated into distress and delight which, in turn, give way to fear, disgust, and anger in the case of distress, and to elation, affection, and later joy in the case of delight. Other emotions such as jealousy appear later. The age at which the differentiation of the various emotions takes place varies somewhat from child to child and, of course, intense emotional situations may cause a regression to more primitive emotions.

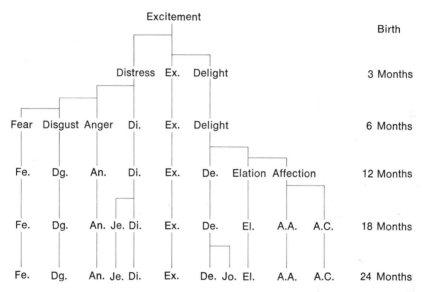

FIGURE 7-2   The approximate ages of differentiation of the various emotions during the first two years of life. A.A. = affection for adults; A.C. = affection for children; An. = anger; De. = delight; Dg. = disgust; Di. = distress; El. = elation; Ex. = excitement; Fe. = fear; Je. = jealousy; Jo. = joy. (After Bridges, 1932.)

The role of maturation in this connection seems relatively clear. Goodenough (1932) found a blind and deaf girl to display the same emotions as normal children despite the restrictions on her ability to learn. The role of maturation is also obvious in the love episodes of adolescence. It is also likely that temperamental differences found among breeds of dogs or horses predispose them toward different emotional reactions. Inherited differences in glandular structure might likewise predispose one individual toward anger and impatience and another toward calmness and self-possession. Inherited differences in physical size and strength might also determine whether a given situation results in fear or in anger.

DECREASE IN OVERT EXPRESSION

An important aspect of the development of emotional behavior is the decrease which takes place with age in its overt expression, a decrease which may or may not be accompanied by a corresponding decrease in the intensity of its feeling tone. Moderation in the overt expression of emotion appears to be essentially a matter of learning to make progressively more socially appropriate responses. Fortunately the child learns that crying at the top of his voice, for example, is frowned upon. Instead of reacting indiscriminately on an all-or-none basis with exaggerated excitement of uniform intensity to all situations, he learns to be selective and to grade his response to the situation at hand. Moderation in expression also reflects the acquisition of other means of expressing his feelings provided through maturation, as well as changes in emotional susceptibility resulting from new needs, new goals, and new readiness. In short, moderation in emotional expression is the result of the same multiplicity of forces which promote the formation of a new self-concept, e.g., "I am a big boy now!"

The influence of social demands on the self-concept is evident in sex differences in the overt expression of emotions. For girls, a display of fear is almost glamorized as an aspect of femininity, but boys must avoid showing fear at all cost. The fact that crying is more prevalent among women probably reflects nothing more than a greater willingness on their part to admit they are sometimes afraid, they sometimes have the blues. Considerable differences in emotional expression also exist from one cultural group, socioeconomic stratum, and even one section of the nation to another.

The decline in the overt expression of emotion, although in general highly desirable, is not without drawbacks. The person who puts on a brave front despite intense fear or who hides his anger behind a smile, the employee who laughs loudly at the boss's jokes, and the hostess who smiles with joy as she welcomes unwanted guests, all are robbing emotional expression of its diagnostic and correctional value. This hypocrisy can be harmful. Besides giving a person the feeling that he is selling his soul, it can result in accumulated tension; as long as the person suffers in silence, there is no way of getting at the cause. There are reasons to believe that a good cry does a lot for women in draining off tension as well as in improving the conditions which brought it about; perhaps punching an offender on the nose, although not recommended as a standard prescription, would do the same for men.

CHANGES IN EMOTIONAL SUSCEPTIBILITY

There is also considerable change with age in the stimuli which lead to emotions. The stimuli affecting the child emotionally are those of his immediate environment and those related to such inner states as fatigue, hunger, and illness. The adult, on the other hand, is susceptible to stimuli relatively remote in time and space; he can become angry at atrocities occurring at the other end of the world. It should also be noted that through his ability to foresee and avoid difficult situations and to set realistic goals, the adult controls, to some extent, the stimuli he encounters and, thus, the emotions he is likely to have.

What constitutes an emotion-producing situation is a function of one's phenomenological interpretation of the nature of the stimulus. Any situation which poses a threat is likely to promote emotional behavior. Fear and/or anger are produced when the individual has some misgivings as to his adequacy relative to the demand of the situation. An object encountered in the dark poses a threat to one's safety; an examination for which one is unprepared or an insult in public poses a threat to one's need for social recognition and self-esteem. All of these situations constitute potential stimuli for the arousal of an emotion. Emotions are, therefore, directly related to the concept of security. The child who is insecure about his status is likely to react with jealousy to any favor done others and to resent even the best-intentioned criticism. Also crucially involved are such predisposing factors as fatigue, illness, hunger, as well as past habits and previously accumulated tensions.

Emotions are also directly related to the self-concept. The child who considers himself both honest and academically competent will probably get quite upset at the prospect of having either to cheat or to fail, while another child with a different self-image could do either or both without a second thought. The individual will also react emotionally to the violation of his dominant values. The person who idealizes fair play may get quite provoked at injustices against helpless people, for example.

COMMON MANIFESTATIONS
OF EMOTIONAL BEHAVIOR

Life is full of episodes in which individuals, singly or collectively, display emotional behavior of varying degrees of intensity and appropriateness. At one extreme, we might consider the violent emotions expressed in the ceremonial dances of primitive tribes or the actions of participants in mob demonstrations. At a more acceptable level in our society, we have the pep rally—whether organized by campus leaders to promote college spirit, or by politicians to generate enthusiasm for a given cause— which also relies on the contagiousness of emotions. Gradually the leader's enthusiasm transfers to the more susceptible listeners, eventually sweeping through the crowd as emotional reactions reinforce one another. This was quite evident in the mass rallies held by Hitler, for example. The exuberance exhibited at football and baseball games reflects some of the same features. Religious revivals generate a similar emotionalized atmosphere in which people faint, fall into a trance, or leave behind crutches upon which they had relied for years.

Of special interest is the concept of patriotism, which also entails an emotionalized reaction toward a group or cause to which one owes allegiance. Interpreted broadly, patriotism might cover group pride in one's country, state, or even a select segment of the community. That patriotism is desirable goes without saying; it is this author's opinion that Americans do too little to instill in youth pride in what America stands for. Pride in one's state, in one's community, and in one's immediate family is undoubtedly desirable; not only does group loyalty provide support to members who need this support while developing enough security to go out on their own, but, if the group goals are sound, it also provides a tremendous incentive toward personal and group achievement and development. The armed forces, for example, encourage the development of *esprit de corps* at the unit level as a means of welding the men into a fighting machine, and even issue special insignia to facilitate group identification. In the same way, some teachers encourage the development of class spirit, all of which is probably sound, for the group with which one is to identify must be sufficiently small to permit a close bond with its individual members.

Nevertheless one cannot overlook the danger that loyalty—whether to country, nationality, sorority, or clique—will degenerate into provincialism, clannishness, and snobbishness. Group loyalty is detrimental when loyalty to the in-group leads to feelings of superiority, rivalry, hatred, bitterness, and rejection of the out-group. When loyalty to a given group makes it difficult to deal with nonmembers on an equal basis, both sides have been hurt, for when our self-concept becomes so narrow and restrictive that consideration of others is based on group designation rather than on individual merit, we deny both ourselves and others the full opportunity for growth and happiness. This does not mean that we must welcome everyone with open arms, but we have to be sure that our basis for rejection is sound. Thus, we might well live by a set of values which involves rejection on the basis of dishonesty, immorality, and cruelty, but not on the basis of nationality, race, or religion.

SOME COMMON EMOTIONS

Space limitations preclude a complete discussion of the many emotions of which man is capable. The present treatment is therefore restricted to a consideration of some of the major aspects of emotional behavior pertinent to an understanding of the child.

ANGER

Watson's claim that anger is one of the three presumably inherited emotions has been more or less discredited by such studies as that of Pratt et al. (1930), who found that anger patterns incorporate a substantial element of learned behavior. Anger appears to be a composite emotion ranging from blind rage to annoyance and general irritation and touching closely upon such emotions as hatred, resentment, and jealousy. Anger generally results from a blow to one's self-esteem or interference with one's purposes. The likelihood of its occurrence is increased by such internal conditions as fatigue, hunger, illness, and tension resulting from previous annoyances. Anger also results from a threat to one's sense of values, and it may generalize from the object responsible for its occurrence to objects relatively remote or even abstract. Anger has the same background as fear, namely, the individual has no ready response to threatening situations; in anger, however, he is not completely overwhelmed by the threat so that he sees a possibility of fighting back, whereas in fear his only salvation appears to be in withdrawal from the situation.

The immediate stimuli which cause anger are numerous and varied depending on the nature of the person, his capabilities, his sense of security, his past experiences, and, of course, the nature of the situation. The greater the discrepancy between his competence and the demands that are made upon him by others and by himself, the more there is occasion for anger. The young child gets angry at restrictions imposed by adults or by his own incompetence, e.g., his inability to get possession of a toy. He finds that as his abilities increase, so does the complexity of the situations with which he must cope: anger among adolescents, for instance, often concerns social situations such as embarrassment before their peers. By that time, the pattern learned as a result of meeting previous situations is an important determinant of the frequency and intensity of their anger reactions.

An important aspect of the stimuli to anger is their cumulative nature. A person gets a bit tense at certain annoyances but he keeps his irritations under control. As more and more frustrations occur, tension mounts until a minor incident triggers action and the individual explodes, much to the amazement of all but those who are willing to think in terms of behavior and its causes. A quarrel on the way to school or a run-in with the first-period teacher may well influence a child's reactions for the entire day in a way even he cannot understand. Early frustrations have left certain persons with a deep-seated sense of hostility and resentment; people who are anger-prone or who display unusually hostile or even competitive behavior might well be suspected of various degrees of unresolved anger. In the same way, whenever a teacher feels especially annoyed at the behavior of a particular child, he might well look for unresolved hostility in his own makeup. It may be a case of projection in which he is annoyed because he sees in others something he resents in himself. Dealing with unresolved hostility is generally a difficult proposition although, in an atmosphere of security, hostile people may gradually lose their defensiveness when they find no need for it.

Not only is there a change with age in the stimuli which lead to anger, but there is a corresponding tendency for the child to express anger more subtly. In fact, he is no sooner able to put on a good temper tantrum—kicking, biting, upsetting furniture—than adults demand that he restrain himself. By the time the child reaches his second year, he begins to learn that it does not pay to express anger too directly and too violently. Thus, Goodenough (1931) found that temper tantrums reached a peak around the third year, after which they declined in frequency and intensity, but she also found an increase in sulking and indirect retaliation. The use of language provides the child with a new tool with which to express his anger more subtly. All in all, unless his temper tantrums are rewarded, he learns less direct and less violent ways of retaliation. The middle and upper-class adult rarely uses his fists; instead he makes a sly remark behind the offender's back, or relies on ridicule or barbed witticisms and other indirect ways of getting even. In school, the child expresses his anger by being noisy, introducing semi-accidental disruptions, engaging in passive sabotage, asking questions just to embarrass the teacher, and generally being annoying. Actually, he must tread a narrow path as he attempts to get sufficient revenge to restore his status and his self-esteem without at the same time incurring the wrath of the teacher to the point where the latter takes further retaliatory steps. In a sense, the child learns a certain hypocrisy in concealing his anger from others, and, to some extent, even from himself. A crucial factor here, as we have noted, is the extent to which the child's anger is controlled through tolerance, consistency, and serenity rather than through counteraggression. As the Sears study has shown, the suppression of the display of anger through punitive and counteraggressive measures results in an increase in the child's aggression and in resentment which influences his behavior in ways that are devious and hard to understand, e.g., cruelty to animals, unprovoked meanness, and prejudice.

The evaluation of anger as an aspect of behavior is a matter of analyzing each individual incident rather than of making a blanket endorsement or condemnation. Quite often anger, especially if violent and if directed at others, only serves to aggravate the situation it is meant to cure. The employee who gets angry at his boss over criticism of his work may lose his job, which will introduce untold new difficulties without resolving the original problem of his incompetence. Actually one needs to learn a certain degree of self-control, especially since the person who displays anger threatens others whose reactions only aggravate his problem; teachers, for example, do not take kindly to the child who displays anger in the classroom.

There are cases where anger may be desirable and conducive to self-actualization. For the milksop, who has always allowed others to walk all over him, to get angry enough to tell somebody off might represent an improvement in adjustment and result in benefit to all concerned. There are times when anger should be expressed in unmistakable terms, when to submerge anger is a sign of weakness and immaturity. Knowing what the situation calls for is a significant part of emotional development. A person may also improve his performance as a result of his own annoyance at his incompetence. No doubt if it were no more annoying to fail than it is to succeed, there would be many more failures than there are.

Anger is not bad *per se*; its worth depends on its orientation. Society's approach has generally been one of suppression rather than of guidance. The child needs to learn to channel his anger into constructive purposes, so that instead of being something he represses, it is something he uses to advantage in self-fulfillment. Actually, inability to blow off steam through the expression of anger is itself frustrating, since it prevents the achievement of the basic purpose of anger, namely, to destroy the frustrating agent. Besides, punishment is itself anger-producing, so that society, in its efforts to suppress anger is actually promoting it by causing it to smoulder inside. When efforts to suppress anger in the child are coupled with rejection and abuse, considerable personality damage can occur, as evidenced by the compulsive desire for vengeance and the complete lack of inner control of certain hostile and resentful children.

The most sensible way of dealing with anger is through the twofold program of building up the child's sense of security and developing in him certain competencies so that there will be less discrepancy between his ability and his aspirations or the demands made upon him. These two aspects are closely related in that the secure child is more capable of devoting his energies constructively to building up skills and competence which, in turn, lead to further success and further feelings of security.

Anger is often aroused by the lack of consideration on the part of others, especially those in authority. Some people have the tact of a bulldozer; they cannot even say "good-morning" without antagonizing someone. In the classroom as elsewhere, occasions arise where criticisms must be given. This is inevitable, but it is possible to criticize without hurting feelings. The first consideration is that the child be capable of accepting the criticism; if he is insecure, his self-concept will only force him to close his mind to the criticism. Under such circumstances, the teacher has only succeeded in making an enemy and in proving to him that teachers use their authority to lord it over defenseless children. It is generally an effective technique to sandwich whatever criticism one has to give between praise, i.e., to get the child in a receptive mood by first raising his ego, presenting the criticism, and then finishing with some positive expression of confidence in his ability to do well. He must be made to feel both more capable of doing better and more eager to do so as a result of this criticism or the teacher has accomplished nothing. Criticism should be constructive and should be directed at unsatisfactory behavior and not at the child, for there is no point in destroying his security. Harping on shortcomings only causes him to become anxious to the point where he cannot devote his energy to the solution of his problems, which, in turn, gives the teacher more cause for criticism.

When the child gets angry too frequently, adults need to review and possibly to revise the demands they make upon him. Anger is merely a symptom of a more fundamental difficulty that needs to be identified. For this reason, a diagnostic approach is better than one of retaliation. It might be noted, for example, that frequently a child does poorly in school just to express his hostility toward his parents. It is good policy to avoid unnecessary restraints particularly when they run counter to basic needs. It is a good idea to limit rules and regulations to those which matter and which can be readily enforced. On the other hand, when a policy has been established (assuming it is basically sound), it should be enforced. Many children rely on anger simply because parents unknowingly train them to use temper tantrums to get what they want. Actually, anger can be too successful in enabling the child to get his way; he should be made to understand that there are more constructive ways of obtaining what he wants and a display of temper should not be rewarded into becoming a habit. Yet, as shown by Sears et al., the parent must not himself resort to anger and counteraggression. In the same way, a teacher gains relatively little in terms of status, respect, and cooperation when he uses his authority to squelch the expression of annoyance stemming from needless restraint, inconsistent or impossible demands, or a poor classroom atmosphere. As Crow and Crow (1956) have stated, the teacher who meets temper with temper, besides giving public proof of his lack of self-confidence and self-control, is not going to be effective in dealing with either offense or offender.

Fear

Since fear arises from situations in which the individual is relatively overwhelmed, the very idea of fear implies incompetence, and the greater the incompetence, the greater the likelihood and severity of the fear. In fact, overprotected children are likely to fear just about everything, including growing up which will involve them in more complicated situations and deny them the protection of friendly adults. Such a situation can only result in self-defeat, for the more insecure the child is, the more desperately he fears failure and the less constructively he can work toward developing his assets to ensure success.

As with anger, the overt expression of fear becomes more subdued with age. This is particularly true among boys, who are led to see themselves as heroes rescuing damsels in distress and who therefore cannot afford to let anybody see they are afraid. In a way, this is desirable, but it has the objectionable feature of forcing the individual to avoid fear-producing situations, thus depriving him of the opportunity to learn.

The stimuli leading to the arousal of fear also change with age. The infant is apparently afraid of any intense and unexpected stimuli. As he becomes older, certain stimuli lose their power over him and are replaced by others. In later childhood, for instance, fear of the imaginary is both common and hard to deal with. Frequently, the child who is afraid of robbers is really expressing a fear of himself, i.e., reflecting a guilty conscience. Because of the guilt he feels over having committed some offense, he associates himself with bad guys like robbers. Fear of examinations may also be a generalized guilt reaction against failure to have undertaken necessary preparation, perhaps going back to earlier occasions when the child was made to feel guilty for having failed. As in the case of anger, the effectiveness of a given stimulus in causing fear reactions depends upon a number of factors, such as the situation in which the individual finds himself, his emotional security, his previous experiences, his health, his current mood, and, of course, the nature of the stimulus.

The child's fears are many and varied: animals, ghosts, robbers, the dark, examinations, failure, the teacher, strange people, men from Mars, rejection, ridicule, social incompetence, noises, fear of falling, bodily injury, sickness, to name but a few. Most of these the child has learned, probably incidentally, as suggested by Hagman (1932), who found a correlation of .67 between the number of fears in children and their mothers. Many fears simply grow through stimulus generalization. A child frightened in a given situation tends to fear similar situations and, for that matter, any situation in which he recognizes some of the elements of the original situation. Fear of animals often includes many animals that are quite harmless and sometimes even all furry things. Fears can be good or bad. Mild fears provide the thrills of roller coaster rides or games of chance and may even be involved in the child's throwing a spitball at the blackboard—a cat-and-mouse situation which may be challenging to students. Vicarious fears make possible the enjoyment of a mystery story. At the opposite end of the continuum, the disruptive fears that cause people to faint or to stand frozen in horror are rarely,

if ever, useful to anyone, except possibly as a drastic deterrent to misbehavior.

In the more normal range, fear makes for a certain degree of pru-
dence, which not only deters people from inadequate behavior but also
may have positive effects, e.g., promote a certain degree of prepared-
ness. It is, of course, questionable whether this could not be done
more effectively through positive motivation; yet, fear of the law and of
hell keep many on the straight and narrow path, and certainly a good
scare has led some people to mend their ways when other means had
failed. On the other hand, many fears are completely out of proportion to
the dangers involved, if any. The child does not always know what to
fear; his reactions range from dread of harmless things to complete un-
concern for things that are definitely dangerous. The harm done by fear,
from a mental hygiene as well as from a success point of view, is often
far greater than any harm that could possibly result from the situation
itself. In the meantime, by causing the individual to avoid the feared
situation, fear promotes later failure. The child who is afraid of showing
his ignorance refrains from reciting; as a result, he becomes progressively more inadequate. Teachers need to be alert to such disguises and
deter the child from continuing on a path that is progressively more
self-destructive. The case against fear is well stated by Kingsley and
Garry (1957):

> The great bulk of the fears that torment children and adults
> are needless and detrimental. Fear is the enemy of mental and
> bodily health. It destroys courage and self-confidence, and under-
> mines morale. It weakens and suppresses purposive action, dis-
> torts perspective, and inhibits clear thinking. It lessens the
> chances for success, and is often the cause of mediocrity and
> failure. [p. 453]

It does not follow that we should—if we could—eliminate all fear-
producing situations, for too few fears might lead to complacency, preclude progress, and invite disaster. However, excessive fear that causes
distress and prevents, rather than promotes, constructive action can only
be detrimental. It is particularly important that fears not be so intense
and persistent as to lead to feelings of inadequacy and foreboding concerning the future, or to anxiety states, phobias, and other abnormalities resulting from inner conflict.

Adults often play on the child's fears as a means of securing his good
behavior, even to the point of threatening him with the bogeyman if he
misbehaves. Such threats are doubly devastating. First, they involve a
mysterious agent which, as far as the child knows, might be tremendously
frightening and against which he cannot prepare a defense; secondly, he
realizes that if he misbehaves he cannot count on the protection of adults

since they were instrumental in getting the bogeyman after him. Besides, since the threat never materializes, it tends to be a rather stupid way to control children. Some parents of preschool children convert the teacher into the bogeyman, thus complicating their children's adjustment to school. Children are far too often disciplined through fear; the more positive approach of inculcating respect for parents, policemen, teachers, and adults in general would benefit all concerned.

Also of primary concern to the teacher is the fact that, for many children, school itself is a fear-producing situation from which they have no escape. For some, the day is one continuous procession of fears—fear of criticism, fear of rejection by the teacher and/or the group, fear of punishment, fear of embarrassment, fear of examinations, fear of ridicule. Our emphasis on academic learning has led us to forget the price some children have to pay in emotional distress. In the meantime, children by the dozen have built their defense against such a situation; they have simply ceased to care about schoolwork. This is a situation with which many teachers struggle—and it is of their own making; or at least, the making of previous teachers who have failed to realize the ineffectiveness of a program based on fear.

The best way of protecting the child against damaging fear consists of the dual approach of helping him build up both his security and his competence. The child who has been able to cope with previous situations approaches life with confidence and uses his energies constructively in surmounting difficulties rather than dissipating his resources in fighting fears. The classroom should be a place in which the child feels secure so that he can devote his energies to learning without fear of jeopardizing his status. It also helps to present threatening situations under conditions where the child is secure—perhaps in his home, when he is with friends, or at least in familiar settings—and at all times he should be able to withdraw if he should want to.

Removing fears, once developed, is generally slow and difficult. To be sure, many fears are simply lost in the process of growth; this is most likely to occur when adults accept the child's fears as normal and limit themselves to providing moral support. It is least likely to occur when they make such a fuss about his fears that he becomes defensive. Precept and ridicule are rarely effective and may be harmful; they also make it all the more difficult to reach him in other matters. Verbal reassurance and explanation may be helpful but emotions are hardly matters of logic. Imitation is somewhat more effective, particularly if the person serving as the model is one the child respects. Parents and teachers should themselves be calm and confident. Social facilitation, i.e., imitation in a social group, is generally more effective than any of the techniques mentioned so far.

The most efficient way of removing fears is through the process of conditioning, which, incidentally is as effective in developing fears as in removing them. As shown schematically in Figure 7-3, the repeated simultaneous presentation of two S-R bonds is likely to result in an association of the stimulus of the weaker bond with the response of the stronger bond so that this stimulus alone is sufficient to elicit the latter.

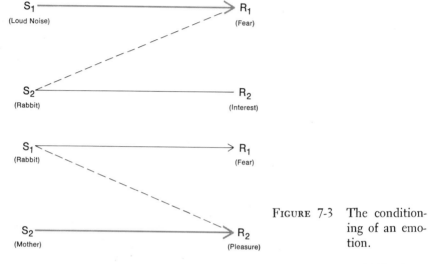

FIGURE 7-3   The conditioning of an emotion.

Thus, in Watson's well-known study (Watson and Rayner, 1920), Peter was conditioned to fear a rabbit by striking cymbals behind his back just as he was reaching for the rabbit. Watson also conditioned the opposite response; he removed the fear by gradually presenting the rabbit while the baby was secure in his mother's arms. The same procedure can be used to eliminate fear of the dark. Parents can, for example, play ball with the child, gradually allowing the ball to roll farther and farther into the next room which is less well lighted. Care must be taken that the desired response is attached to the stronger of the two bonds; otherwise, the process may backfire with the child associating his parents with the idea of fear rather than the dark with the response of pleasure. It is important that the object or situation to be conditioned be introduced gradually so that at no time does it threaten the desired response.

PLEASURE

Pleasure, whether in the form of the quiet satisfactions of daily life or the more violent joys, is essentially a matter of the satisfaction of one's motives. The attainment of food, affection, or social recognition is pleasant only when it gratifies the individual's needs the way he has learned to gratify them. Consequently, if the classroom is to be conducive to maximum development, the teacher must be familiar with the motives and purposes of his students and the means whereby they can be helped to achieve their goals. An important source of pleasure, for example, is activity. The young child enjoys sheer exercise and he will romp and run for the fun of it; the somewhat older child derives pleasure out of exploring and experimenting. The school is missing a good bet when it fails to capitalize on the pleasure involved in accomplishing the things one sets out to do. The child has a zest for doing things that are new, things that are challenging, and certainly the curriculum is not devoid of interesting experiences that can be integrated with his goals and purposes. The school presents unlimited opportunity for the satisfaction of motives; it is up to the teacher to take advantage of opportunities in order to make school experiences more productive by making them more pleasant.

The word *challenging* in the above discussion is, in a sense, the key to successful classroom operation, implying as it does, the need for the child to set for himself goals that are meaningful and realistic, for once he is ego-involved there can be no slipshod work, no halfhearted effort. What is challenging varies, of course, from person to person and from time to time in the same person as abilities and interests change. For the dull child, schoolwork is often a source of frustration rather than challenge. The gifted child, on the other hand, is often consistently denied the pleasure of any real challenge, sometimes with disastrous consequences, because his natural zest for excitement will lead him to seek it elsewhere if schoolwork offers nothing but boredom.

Some teachers are inexcusably incompetent in organizing the work of the school so as to provide experiences that are educationally satisfying. On the other hand, life cannot be a continuous round of pleasure. The true satisfaction of success could hardly be appreciated if one had never experienced failure. However, teachers need not go out of their way to provide children with failure; plenty of failure situations will arise without special effort made to provide them. The successful child is a secure child and a secure child will want to tackle things that are big enough to make the occasional failure inevitable.

AFFECTION

Affection is generally accepted as one of the psychological needs; it is also one of the three emotions postulated by Watson as innate, a claim which psychologists rejected as they recognized conditioning to feeding and other aspects of child care as the possible basis for the child's affection. This latter position has now been shaken by Harlow's experiments pointing to the role of contact comfort in the development of affection (See Chapter 1). What is significant is that the child is born with the capacity for love. Regardless of its origin, affection is crucial to the child's overall welfare. Furthermore, the process is reciprocal and parents and teachers also depend on the affection of their children. This mutual affection helps to satisfy the needs of both children and adults and provides the basis for a happy and adjusted home, school, and community life.

The development of affection is characterized by four somewhat distinct and yet overlapping stages:

[a] Self-love. The infant loves himself. Gradually he learns to associate his mother and other adults with pleasure as they feed, change, and generally minister to him.[1] Whether a person ever outgrows this self-love stage and progresses to what might be called altruistic love is open to question. The "altruistic" love of the person who can never do enough for others is probably motivated, at least in part, by self-interest. Northway (1940), for instance, found that super-helpfulness and present-giving were characteristic of insecure girls. Even Sidney Carton's supreme sacrifice (Dickens' A Tale of Two Cities) apparently had a deep inner reward. Indications are that all love is more or less self-centered, that in romantic love, each is in love with himself or herself rather than with the partner, who in essence serves the primary purpose of helping each satisfy his or her own needs. Certainly for a younger man to have the exclusive affection of a girl particularly if she is in demand, contains many possibilities for satisfying needs of social recognition, self-esteem, achievement, and security as well as affection. Such a view of the situation makes it easier to understand the bitterness that often attends the breakup of the couple.

This idea is of major import from a psychological point of view. We do the child no service by insisting that he love his neighbor if that is not possible. Rather than deny the self-centered nature of love, we may render a greater service by helping him expand his self-concept to include an ever-enlarging circle of people and things. Self-centered love is not a repulsive concept. Friendships are based on the mutual satisfaction of needs, and choosing a mate has to be on that basis if the marriage is to last. In fact, as Jersild (1960) points out, unless the child loves himself he cannot love others. Woodruff (1948, p. 106) makes an important distinction between self-centered and selfish behavior: "Whereas all behavior is self-centered, only that behavior is selfish which consists of obtaining personal satisfactions at the expense of others."

What we need is enlightened self-interest, i.e., we must come to recognize that the individual obtains maximum self-realization only by including others in his phenomenal self. We must realize that the welfare of others is essential to our own welfare and that selfishness is a short-

---

[1] An interesting instance of the development of affection is that cited by Mead (1937), who reports that certain tribes in New Guinea have attained a high level of tribal unity through the verbal conditioning of children. As the young child is happily feeding, the mother is constantly saying: "See that woman over there? She is good; she gives you food, she is good." Eventually, everybody is made good.

sighted policy. There is nothing wrong with self-centered behavior. To quote Woodruff again: "Self-centered behavior seeks the well-being of those who are brought into the personal realm, just as if they were the person himself."

> He drew a circle that shut me out—
> Heretic, rebel, a thing to flout.
> But love and I had the wit to win:
> We drew a circle that took him in!
> *Edwin Markham: "Outwitted"*

The teacher's task, then, is one of helping the child perceive his personal realm broadly enough so as to include all those upon whom he truly depends for maximum self-realization. Such an expansion of the phenomenal self would preclude selfishness, graft, prejudice, and corruption; it would involve full cooperation among people for the good of all, and it would make for good leaders and good followers. If we can implant this idea and help the child to put it into operation through meaningful participation in group goals, human welfare will be assured.

[b] The preschool stage. This is the child's first contact outside his immediate family and constitutes an important learning experience from the standpoint of later school adjustment. During this period the child loves other children of his own age regardless of sex.

[c] The gang stage. In the preadolescent period, the individual's affection is directed toward members of his own age and sex. There is at this time a rather distinct social cleavage between boys and girls.

[d] The heterosexual stage. With the advent of puberty, the adolescent's affection undergoes a drastic redirection toward members of the opposite sex.

Occasionally problems arise in connection with affection; the teacher must understand these problems if he is to be of maximum help in promoting student adjustment in this important area. The discussion will be restricted to a few of the more common problems.

HOMOSEXUALITY Homosexuality is probably best defined as the orientation of one's affection toward members of one's own sex at an age when heterosexual adjustment should have been attained. This definition tends to be preferable to that in which the criterion is the commission (or noncommission) of homosexual acts. Many homosexuals do not commit homosexual acts while, on the other hand, homosexual acts are sometimes committed by persons who are definitely not homosexual.

The cause of homosexuality is not clear. Some authorities lean toward a physiological or medical explanation based on the premise that the orientation of affection is governed by hormone secretions and that homosexuals suffer from oversecretion of hormones of the opposite sex.

Others see homosexuality as a case of arrested development: the individual simply did not advance to the heterosexual stage. This view assumes that, perhaps because of psychological blocking, the individual did not make the transition to loving members of the opposite sex, and, because of the strength of the sex drive, was forced to make a homosexual adjustment. It is conceivable, for example, that a mother who builds in her daughter a strong prejudice against men may make the transition to the heterosexual stage next to impossible for her, since the girl would have to destroy her self-image as well as violate her loyalty to her mother to fall in love with a man. It may also be that, because the adolescent's first contacts with members of the opposite sex were unpleasant, heterosexual adjustment was postponed past the period of optimal ease, thereby preventing the transition from taking place.

Research on the subject is inconclusive, but, in general, it tends to refute the physiological explanation. The administration of male hormones to male homosexuals simply intensifies the sex drive but does not change its direction. There are indications that homosexuality stems from the individual's failure to identify with the like-sex parent. Bender and Paster (1941), for example, found no basic physical femininity in homosexual boys nor basic physical masculinity in homosexual girls, but they did find an absent, abusive, or ineffectual like-sex parent together with a more dominating or considerate opposite-sex parent so that identification took place with the latter. The problem needs further investigation, particularly in view of the lack of acceptance of homosexuality in our present culture.

ADOLESCENT CRUSHES Crushes vary from the violent love of two adolescents of opposite sex to similar situations between two adolescents of the same sex or love of an adolescent for a much older person. Also included are the often near-hysterical reactions of teen-age girls toward a teen idol. It is not uncommon for a young male teacher in high school to be the object of considerable affection on the part of some girls in his classes. This is understandable from a psychological point of view, but it does call for diplomatic handling. Crushes generally reflect, on the one hand, the strength of the sex drive spurring adolescents to seek love and affection and, on the other, the strength of rejection attitudes toward their age-mates of the opposite sex which they incorporated into their self-concept during the gang stage.

MOTHER FIXATION (MOMISM) During the last war, many young men called up for military service were rejected because of emotional immaturity—they were too closely tied to mamma's apron strings. It is not uncommon to find, for example, middle-aged men who are so closely attached to their mothers that they consult her on every decision and generally display toward her behavior that would be appropriate for preadolescents. Often they do not marry—"It wouldn't be fair to Mother!"—or if they do, they seek a maternal woman whom they can cast in the role of mother rather than wife.

The cause of Momism is not clear, but a rather convincing case can be built up in support of the view that it may result from smothering by an emotionally insecure mother. (See Wylie, A Generation of Vipers.) Teachers sometimes have a boy whose mother accompanies him to and from school, who dresses him in such a way that he cannot take part in active play, who is always afraid her "little darling" will get hurt. By depriving him of the usual opportunities to establish his independence, she causes him to depend more and more on her for the satisfaction of his needs. Sometimes the boy will rebel and break away—with much unhappiness to both mother and son—but many of these boys, not having learned to stand on their own two feet, find themselves unable to shed their emotional shackles.

RESTRAINT OF EMOTIONAL INVOLVEMENT At the opposite end of the continuum is the child who, as a result of rejection and abuse, learns that to love is to make oneself vulnerable to deep hurt. Orphanage children who have been shunted from one foster home to another with systematic unhappy consequences, soon learn to protect themselves by avoiding emotional involvement. In time, they become incapable of genuine love—with obvious detrimental effects on their over-all development, especially in the areas of socialization and conscience development, personal happiness, and interpersonal relationships; they tend to be poor marriage risks and poor parents, for example.

EMOTIONAL MATURITY

We constantly encounter instances of infantile emotional behavior—temper tantrums, jealousy, resentment, despondency, overdependence—not only among children but also among alleged grownups. Indeed, such behavior is so commonplace that one is sometimes led to consider it the thing to expect. Perhaps the fault lies in part with the school's emphasis on academic growth and corresponding neglect of the other phases of development. If teachers are to be successful in guiding the child in the area of emotional development, they need to be familiar with the proper goals. Actually, emotionally mature behavior is so complex, and so interrelated with other phases of total growth, that any discussion of its various aspects must inevitably do violence to its true nature. The following signs of emotional maturity are simply illustrative, no attempt having been made to list all its components.

The emotionally mature person is essentially the self-actualizing person discussed in Chapter 4. He is secure and open to experience which, in turn, increases his effectiveness and sense of security. He has a realistic appreciation of his net worth; he accepts himself for what he is so he does not have to resort to prejudice or to keeping up with the Joneses in order to maintain self-esteem. He is relatively free from slavish conformity to group standards and dependence upon others. He is relatively free from anxiety and can devote his energies constructively to solving his problems. He has adjusted his level of aspiration to fit his abilities and has developed competence in areas where it matters so that he has confidence in himself. He has also developed a mature sense of humor and a positive outlook on life and thereby saves himself from devastating emotions such as worry and jealousy.

Because he is secure and has constructive channels through which to drain off emotional strain, he is relatively free from unnecessary tension and, as a result, is capable of exercising control in the face of emotional stress. Furthermore, his sense of security frees him from overconcern about himself. He has achieved a relatively high degree of enlightened self-interest so that he derives pleasure and satisfaction through contributing to the welfare of others.

The emotionally mature person leads a rich emotional life and has a variety of emotional patterns well integrated with his welfare and that of others. Far from being emotionless, he knows what situations call for and, rather than repress his emotions, he channels into constructive behavior the energy which they generate. He maintains a fair balance between work and play; he has found employment which provides both challenge and security; he takes part in creative and recreational activities. He has attained personal stability through a satisfactory marital adjustment, and saves himself from conflict and guilt feelings by acting in accord with a sound moral and social code. Above all, he has a purpose in life and maintains a zest for living.

IMPLICATIONS FOR THE SCHOOL

Competent behavior is as dependent upon the proper education of the emotions as it is upon the cultivation of the intellect and the school must assume responsibility for such education. Not only are emotions of sufficient importance in themselves to warrant our attention, but they cannot be neglected because the effectiveness of the child's learning is directly related to his emotional state. Furthermore, continued emotional tension leads to a disorganization of behavior to the point where the child can no longer deal effectively with life's problems.

Responsibility for the child's emotional development lies primarily with the home. The child who has experienced emotional security in his early years and whose needs are essentially met at home can face the world with confidence and can tolerate the frustrations it presents. This does not imply that there is nothing the school can do for the child by the time he enters the first grade, and that it is, therefore, relieved of responsibility in the matter. Many children are not provided with security at home and have to rely on the school to supply them with a home base and with constructive outlets for the release of the tensions accumulated in other situations. Teachers have to be careful that the school situation does not itself generate harmful emotional tensions. Although the school cannot—and should not—attempt to safeguard the child from all forms of emotional stress, it can and should see that no one is faced with a steady diet of fear, failure, and frustration as a result of school-sponsored activities.

In addition, the school, in its role as an educative agency, will have to concentrate on a positive program for the promotion of emotional maturity. This is best done through a dual approach of giving the child security and competence and of helping him locate constructive outlets through which to channel emotional tension. A democratic classroom atmosphere under a teacher with a sense of humor and a sympathetic understanding of children can go a long way in making the child feel he belongs and that he can experiment in emotional expression without danger of rejection or retaliation. Given this kind of security and a degree of satisfaction for his needs, the child can withstand occasional frustration and profit from the experience.

The school should encourage emotional expression rather than repression. Whereas it would be disastrous if everyone expressed his emotions without any attempt at control, adults are too concerned with having children repress emotional outbursts rather than with showing them how to express their emotions constructively. Restraint is desirable but it can be dangerous and the school would do well to plan for the expression of frustration and resentment as a means of draining away accumulated tension before it reaches the danger point. Sports, for example, are far more effective in releasing pent-up tension, both for players and spectators, than constant bickering and behind-the-back grumblings. School spirit is another effective way to channel emotional energy.

The child can attain emotional maturity only when the adults around him are themselves mature. Unfortunately, many parents and teachers are lacking in this respect. It is not uncommon to see teachers who are so insecure that they forever lose their tempers, who criticize students but cannot accept the least hint of a challenge, who take their frustrations out on children. Obviously, no one is expected to display all the characteristics of the emotionally mature person. Yet, since teachers cannot guide children in areas in which they are themselves lacking, they need to strive for a certain degree of maturity. They can at least be expected to have a positive outlook on life and a sense of humor that will enable them to appreciate the value of a good laugh in clearing away petty grievances and annoyances that interfere with student growth.

HIGHLIGHTS OF THE CHAPTER

Emotions are such an integral part of the total personality that it is difficult to treat the subject as a separate topic without giving a false picture. Consequently, the following points, important as they are, derive their full meaning only when interpreted within the framework of the other aspects of the child's total growth and development.

[a]

Emotions are complex affairs—consisting of various degrees of feeling, certain visceral and skeletal changes, and impulses toward certain reactions—which take place when the individual encounters a situation for which he has no ready pattern of response.

[b]

The intensity of such emotions as fear and anger is roughly proportional to the degree of threat to the self which one perceives in the situation.

[c]

There is a gradual decrease with age in the overt expression of emotions. This is probably the result of cultural pressure as well as the increase in the individual's ability to deal with emotion-producing situations.

[d]

Mild emotional tension, such as might be involved in the usual levels of motivation, is conducive to operational efficiency. Except in situations calling for physical strength and stamina, violent emotional tensions, besides being harmful to physical and emotional health, impede rather than facilitate learning, especially when they cause the individual to avoid the threatening situation. Severe emotional tension is particularly detrimental to clear thinking and flexibility.

[e]

Emotional maturity can be promoted through a dual program of providing the child with security and with outlets through which emotional tension can be channeled into constructive behavior.

SOURCES OF RELATED MATERIAL

Funkelstein, Daniel H., "The physiology of fear and anger," Sci. Amer., 192: 74–80, May 1955.
Overstreet, H. A., The Mature Mind. New York: W. W. Norton & Company, Inc., 1949.

Prescott, D. A., *Emotions and the Educative Process.* Washington, D.C.: American Council on Education, 1938.

Rasey, Marie I., *Toward Maturity.* New York: Barnes & Noble, Inc., 1947.

Weston, G. L., *Emotional Adjustment: A Key to Good Citizenship.* Detroit: Wayne University Press, 1953.

QUESTIONS AND PROJECTS

1

Why is it preferable to speak of emotional balance rather than emotional control? Why is emotional expression preferable to emotional repression? What is to prevent emotional expression from getting out of hand?

2

Discuss specific practices of the school which appear to be clearly detrimental to the child's emotional development. What causes these practices to persist?

3

From the standpoint of present as well as later personal and heterosexual adjustment, what are the pros and cons of coeducational classes at the elementary school level? At the junior high school level? At the senior high school level? At the college level? What might motivate a student and his parents to choose an all-girls or all-boys school? How would such a school face the the problem of the heterosexual adjustment of its students?

CHAPTER 8

Social

Development

The more we broaden our vision and see our responsibilities to the community, to democracy and to the world, the more we see the need to concentrate on learnings that are really important to the children and the young people with whom we live; the more we realize our tremendous responsibilities to them; the more we need to understand the power of group dynamics.

Cunningham, et al., 1951, p. 8

The fact that the child must live in a social setting makes his social development a matter of prime interest to teachers. Social development involves the ability to get along with others and implies ability to get along with oneself. Specifically, it is a matter of integrating one's needs and purposes with those of the social order. In this sense, it bears directly on personal and social adjustment, the concept of enlightened self-interest, the self-image and self-actualization, and other aspects of personal development.

DEVELOPMENT OF SOCIAL BEHAVIOR

THE PROCESS OF SOCIALIZATION

Social development is a continuous process by means of which the individual achieves social adequacy. Involved are two complementary phases:

[a] socialization, which reflects society's attempt to have the child internalize its regulations, values and mores; and [b] individualization, which refers to the child's attempt to retain his individuality while at the same time making certain concessions to the group to obtain group acceptance. In order to maintain itself, society must insist on conformity to its values; however, although the child conforms in certain areas, he does so reluctantly and only so far as he finds it to his advantage in satisfying his needs. It is strictly a business deal involving both cooperative and resistant behavior whereby the individual buys group acceptance at the price of some of his freedom. The ideal stage is reached when the individual can attain maximum satisfaction for his needs within the framework of the values of society to the benefit of both.

Socialization is oriented toward the achievement of social acceptance and social sensitivity. It involves the gradual internalization of social demands as part of the child's reactions to the approval or disapproval of his behavior by significant persons in his environment. For this to occur, as we have seen, the young child must first develop dependency as a result of his experiencing not only many warm, loving relationships with adults, but also their temporary loss when he fails to meet expectations. A necessary condition for the development of social control is learning that other people are necessary and that one must take their wishes into consideration, as well as his own, in guiding his behavior.

From a very early age, the child encounters expectations concerning his behavior. These become increasingly complex and he must develop the ability to adapt his behavior to a complicated set of demands. As a child, he learns that he must do what adults want him to do if he is to get their acceptance. Later, he must do what his peers want him to do if he is to be accepted by them. As a result, his behavior is gradually shaped in the direction of social conformity. He does not have to comply, of course, but then, he must pay a price in terms of social rejection. Unfortunately, he is often put in the position of having to comply with conflicting and contradictory demands imposed upon him by the various groups to which he belongs. Furthermore, many of the outcomes of social learning are intangible and, therefore, provide inadequate reinforcement. The child may find certain tangible rewards such as self-gratification to be more satisfying—as well as more dependably accessible—and he may give up attempting to meet the expectations of others. Some of the demands and expectations to which the child is subjected are unnecessarily rigid and arbitrary; the school often dictates everything from how he is to behave to how he is to solve problems in arithmetic and what answers he is to accept if he is to do well in social studies. Arbitrary controls of this kind tend to have detrimental effects upon his overall growth in that they deprive him of the opportunity for spontaneity, autonomy, and experimentation in manipulating his environment. Anderson (1959), for example, suggests that the brainwashing of children under the guise of child training often produces uncreative, unimaginative, self-conscious, and self-protecting conformists.

Parents play the crucial role in the child's socialization; they not only provide models which, as a result of identification, can exert strong influence on his overall development as an emerging organism, but they also provide both positive and negative sanctions when they approve of certain kinds of behavior and disapprove of others. As we have noted, love-oriented techniques of child-rearing—including the withdrawal of love in the event of noncompliance—tend to be more effective in promoting desirable behavior and the internalization of society's values and constraints in the form of a conscience than object-oriented techniques such as physical rewards. Punitive methods tend to be notably unsuccessful. We have also noted that the middle-class parent is more likely than his lower-class counterpart to use psychological discipline which, by making the child feel guilty when he is disapproved of, tends to be more effective in promoting self-control; instead of being more lenient, the middle-class parent is using methods which are actually more compelling in evoking proper behavior.

The question of socialization is best considered from the standpoint of character development from amoral to rational-conscientious as discussed later in Chapter 17. We might think of four levels of social development:

[a] The child learns to avoid undue trouble, to respect the rights of others, and to refrain from interfering with them. This is essentially a negative phase.

[b] The child is obedient, docile, and conforming. This is a passive type of adjustment which is very convenient for adults.

[c] The child reaches a stage of social interaction and cooperative give-and-take.

[d] The child appreciates the needs of others and cooperates with them for the welfare of all. This stage involves a sense of social consciousness and of personal responsibility for the effective operation of the social group.

Social development goes through a series of "stages" which, although not rigidly demarcated, represent steps in the growth toward social maturity. Parten (1932), for instance, classifies social participation on the part of preschool children into six levels: unoccupied behavior, solitary independent play, onlooker behavior, parallel activity, associative play, and cooperative play. The young child is essentially individualistic; his first attempts at social behavior involve many social contacts in which his desires and needs are in conflict with those of others. It is not before the end of the third year that cooperative play (as opposed to parallel play) becomes relatively fixed, and it is not before the age of ten that effective teamwork can be expected with any degree of regularity. Baker (1942), for example, found that 87 percent of the contributions to classroom discussion in second grade were in the nature of new topics.

Wide differences in social development exist even among children of the same family. These differences may have a partial basis in individual differences in glandular structure (See Chapter 5). This is particularly obvious in the drastic change in social behavior occurring with the advent of puberty, although to be sure, environmental influences are also involved, particularly in determining whether he drags her into his cave or carries her across the threshold of their newly rented apartment. Also suggestive of the role of heredity in determining social behavior is the fact that twins have been found to smile at the same age regardless of previous stimulation (Dennis, 1938). Shyness and self-consciousness likewise develop during the second year with such regularity as to suggest an underlying maturational process (Shirley, 1933). Heredity may also be involved indirectly; the equipment which makes social behavior possible, e.g., physical structure, is largely inherited and a person with such physical assets as beauty and brains is obviously going to achieve social adjustment more easily than one who is ugly or dull. There is also evidence that certain animals are much more socially oriented than others. The rat has few social needs and can be kept in isolation; the monkey, on the other hand, becomes neurotic when denied social contact. It may also be that certain people have fewer social needs than others.

The role of learning, on the other hand must not be minimized, especially since the school has accepted the promotion of socially adequate behavior as one of its primary objectives. This is not contradictory to the position taken in the preceding paragraphs. The problem is one of channeling into socially acceptable behavior whatever predispositions one may have inherited. Behavior is governed not by needs, but by motives, and these are learned, so that assuming an inherited predisposition toward aggressiveness does not deny the role of education in the channeling of this aggression toward constructive behavior any more than accepting the glandular basis of heterosexual attraction implies that there is nothing we can do to help adolescents develop sound boy-girl relationships. It is also true that much of what constitutes socially acceptable behavior is largely a matter of complying with the customs and traditions of one's culture, and this sort of social competence cannot possibly be acquired through heredity, although the capacity to adapt might be.

An interesting aspect of social behavior is that it is cumulative. The person who is socially adept finds himself in demand and has therefore many opportunities to improve his social skills, whereas one lacking in social competence is often denied the opportunity to learn. Social behavior is also reciprocal; aggression leads to counteraggression and to further aggression while, on the contrary, a smile encourages another also to smile, which in turn gives the first person more cause to smile. Thus, through such vicious or virtuous circles which social behavior is likely to generate, not only does environment affect behavior but also one's behavior influences the environment to which he reacts.

Social Development and the School

The child's social development has already progressed a considerable distance by the time he comes to school. Of major importance in this development is the role of identification, particularly with the like-sex parent,[1] in that it provides the child with the security he needs in order to explore his world. Later he identifies with older siblings, his teachers, and other acquaintances. Gradually he incorporates into his self-concept the values of the persons he accepts as heroes. It is, therefore, of major importance that children be supplied with proper models with whom they can identify; the debunking of our national heroes is harmful as it leads to cynicism and to the search for other heroes, frequently less desirable, and the consequent glorification of unsound values.

It follows that people who put themselves in a position where they can be accepted as models by children must exemplify sound values and ideals of conduct. The teacher's life after school, for instance, is not his to live as he pleases, for objectionable behavior on his part may result in conflict or in lowering of the moral standards of the children who have identified with him. There is also need for a variety of personality patterns among the teachers with whom the child comes in contact. There is need on the faculty of a given school for the quiet and reserved scholar and the more rough-and-ready he-man, for the feminine and attractive woman teacher and the more aggressive career girl, so that each child can find among his teachers one or more whose personality and value system fits sufficiently well with the self-image he has already formed that identification can take place. The child also needs to identify with social groups of sound social and moral values, such as the Boy Scouts or Little League baseball.

A number of agencies share in the socialization of the child. The function of the home in this respect has already been discussed. The school also bears major responsibility here. It emphasizes social competence by promoting intellectual and academic proficiency and the

---

[1] Identification with the like-sex parent is easier for girls than for boys; not only is there greater contact between a girl and her mother, but there is also greater similarity in their roles and even in their voices. Besides, even though he is supposed to identify with the father, the boy remains in the care of women at home and frequently at school. The problem is accentuated in many homes where the father no longer lives with the family. This is an area in which male teachers can perform a valuable function in teaching such children the male role in society.

orientation of this proficiency toward the attainment of socially desirable goals. The school also supplements the work of other socializing agencies. It determines to a large extent the intellectual and informational level at which society will operate; it may even determine whether we survive as a democratic nation. It has a special responsibility as a remedial agency for children whose socialization is hampered by adverse conditions.

The school makes a particular contribution as a laboratory for social living and self-discovery, for it is here that the child gains experience in operating within the limits set by the social order. In some cases, this is the first time he has met any form of limits. The school constitutes a miniature social order in which the child can learn social responsiveness. It provides many opportunities for satisfying social needs and guidance in learning techniques of effective group living. In school he learns differentiated social roles and gradually develops a self-concept in relation to the broader social framework, especially since the school provides a diversity of activities and demands as well as opportunities. The school is frequently the first place in which he has had a chance to learn the satisfaction of contributing to group goals. It is particularly important in developing attitudes toward a variety of situations with which the child has not had previous contact.

The nursery school and kindergarten make a special contribution to the child's social development; they provide not only numerous opportunities for children to work harmoniously together, but also a wide variety of creative experiences from which children learn to express themselves in the social context. The kindergarten has two major functions: [a] It promotes social adjustment, especially on the part of children who have been overprotected or whose home background has been unfortunate; [b] It promotes readiness for schoolwork by creating favorable attitudes and by providing opportunities for improvement in the tools of communication. The benefits of kindergarten with respect to intellectual and linguistic development might be expected to be particularly significant for children from the lower classes whose homes tend to be relatively lacking in stimulating qualities. A third and entirely legitimate benefit of the preschool is to free the mother from having the child under foot all day so that, refreshed, she can be more effective in dealing with him when he comes home. The nursery school, however, is best conceived of as a supplement rather than a substitute for the home. Whether a given child should attend nursery school depends on whether he would gain more from the socialization provided by the school and the other children than he would gain from the security and the experiences associated with the home; it may not be wise, for example, to send the insecure two-year-old to nursery school so as to give the mother more time with the new baby.

The selection of preschool teachers is of particular importance, for unless they are especially understanding and adept at seeing that the rewards of attending school outweigh the losses the child has to suffer from leaving his home, more harm than good can result. This is especially important in the case of the insecure child, and particularly so during the first few days when the pattern of maladjustment to the school can easily be set. Bonney and Nicholson (1958) suggest that if the early socialization experiences of the nursery school are to possess significant carry-over in subsequent years, they need to be of particularly high quality from the standpoint of interpersonal rapport between the child and the teacher. They suggest further that educators have been too naïve in their faith in the adjustive and curative value of group socialization in meeting the varying needs of pupils.

Mussen et al. (1963), in their review of the literature, find the outstanding consequences of nursery school to be improved sociability, self-expression, independence, initiative, social adaptability and, interest in the environment. Children who have attended nursery school and kindergarten have been shown to adjust more readily to first grade than those who have not; Fast (1957) found that children with kindergarten experience attained significantly higher scores in reading than children without such experience. In fact, kindergarten children tend to be superior at all grade levels in general scholarship, personality traits, and social development (McLaughlin, 1950); fewer repeat a grade, for example. It must be recognized, however, that, since attendance is often voluntary, nursery school children are frequently from the better homes whose children would be superior whether they attended nursery school or not. Furthermore, the schools in which such studies are conducted tend to be superior schools; the results can certainly not be generalized to all nursery schools, many of which provide little besides custodial care. Logically, it might be assumed that, even if the benefits were to be temporary, preschool attendance would be helpful in getting the child started on the right foot and this in itself might be of major importance.

The issue has attained an entirely new dimension as a result of the modern consensus concerning the importance of the formative years in the child's intellectual development. Research evidence, reviewed in Chapter 5, raises challenging questions as to the role of systematic preschool education, both formal and incidental. More specifically, it places increased emphasis on the need for spanning the early years with a smoothly integrated educational program designed to develop readiness for school. In fact, it stresses the need for incorporating at this level a considerable amount of actual schooling. This would be particularly important for children of the lower classes whose cultural disadvantages are frequently such that they are unready for school. This is, of course, the rationale underlying Project Headstart (See Chapter 1) and the

National Education Association's recommendation for schooling to start at the age of four.

Another powerful socializing agency is the peer group whose influence, as a testing ground for the acceptability of the child's behavior, is of special importance as he shifts from a passive infantile dependence upon his parents and other adults to a more active and assertive dependence upon his peers. The child soon learns that conformity to group standards is the price he must pay for acceptability, and he learns to read the cues, i.e., he acquires social sensitivity. The influence the peer group exerts upon the child can be good or bad. It offers him an opportunity for warm, supportive, and friendly companionship and gives him a sense of security and belonging. It also promotes the development of social skills and provides a strong incentive to behave in ways endorsed by the group. On the other hand, it can encourage snobbishness and engender ill feelings relative to nonmembers, with resulting lowered group morale. It may promote silly rivalries ending in life-long hatreds and prejudices, and even gang warfare. It sometimes ties the adolescent struggling for emancipation from adult control to an even more slavish dependence and conformity to peer group standards. It frequently stifles originality; it may even prompt, as Emerson puts it, a descent to the lowest common denominator.

The child has to sacrifice some of his individuality in order to be accepted. This can be especially disastrous in the case of children whose acceptance by the group is marginal, as for example children from minority groups, for although the individual can generally break away whenever the group gets too possessive and stifling of his freedom, the insecure person is often unable to strike out on his own and is more likely to redouble his efforts to gain group acceptance by sacrificing his freedom further. In the Dittes and Kelley study (1956), for example, the students who were told that they were only minimally accepted by their colleagues conformed more than those who were told that they were highly accepted. However, insecurity and resentment are not conducive to true conformity and their conformity was only superficial, for privately they conformed less than those who felt accepted. On the other hand, individual differences exist; the task-oriented person, for example, being more concerned with accomplishing something than with group approval, is more likely to resist group pressures for undue conformity (Thibaut and Strickland, 1955).

STABILITY OF SOCIAL ORIENTATION

Research evidence suggests that, although there may be changes in the outward manifestations of one's social orientation, the underlying tendencies and predispositions tend to display relative consistency over the years. McKinnon (1942), for instance, found that children classified according to the following social behavior patterns: [a] withdrawing, [b] conforming, [c] invasive (i.e., displaying aggressive tendencies), and [d] cautious (i.e., interested but reluctant to enter into social contacts) tended to remain in the same classification despite the experimenter's attempts to produce shifts. Similar stability in the fundamental personality characteristics of children from nursery school on was also noted by Pinneau and Jones (1959). Neilon (1948) likewise found considerable similarity in the personality of children observed as infants and rated as adolescents 15 years later; although expressed in a different manner, the personality characteristics which had caused excessive crying in infancy, for example, were still evident in adolescence.

The child not only reacts to his environment but he also has a hand in choosing and in shaping the environment to which he reacts, so that the constancy of social orientation is a function of both his inherited potential and the partially self-made constancy of his environment. This does not mean that shifts cannot take place; a child may display relatively different behavior as he takes on different roles in different groups. A gifted child, for instance, may be an outcast in grade school only to blossom out as a leader in high school. The changes involved are probably in outward behavior, however, with the individual maintaining relative consistency in his basic predispositions. On the other hand, there seems to be somewhat less consistency during adolescence (Beilin, 1959; Tyler, 1957), perhaps because of the greater reorganization of social demands characteristic of adolescence in our culture.

Advent of Puberty

Of prime importance in social development is the sex drive and its effect upon both boy-girl relationships and the adolescent's overall self-image. Indeed, heterosexual adjustment is one of the major developmental tasks of adolescence and the promotion of such adjustment warrants high priority among the objectives of the high school. The fact that boys and girls mature at different times complicates the work of the junior high school in providing activities designed to promote boy-girl adjustment. Furthermore, the fact that there may be a span of some seven years in the age at which boys and girls reach puberty, (Keliher, 1941) makes for rather severe problems of adjustment, particularly in the case of the late-maturing boy.

Also of major importance to social development is the effect of socioeconomic and cultural influences. The teacher must realize that not only is different social behavior expected in different socioeconomic and cultural groups, but also that many of the values the school holds dear actually conflict with those of the home and community environment of some children. Thus, lower-class children are likely to have different values from middle-class children with regard to the need for hard work and getting ahead, a fact the teacher cannot afford to overlook if he is to be effective in guiding their growth. In the same way, girls are more likely than boys to value conformity, social graces, and getting along with others. Furthermore, the teacher must not forget that wide variations exist within any one socioeconomic or cultural group and that each child must be understood on his own basis.

FRIENDSHIP

The average child obtains at least minimum satisfaction for his needs of affection and belonging from his immediate family and friends. On the other hand, a number of children have serious problems in this connection; in fact, we need to realize that the child in greatest need of friends is generally the least capable of establishing any kind of friendship, for the more insecure and desperate he is, the less capable he becomes of devoting himself constructively to the task. Furthermore, the picture gets worse as he is consistently denied practice in the art of social give-and-take. An equally undesirable situation prevails where the individual has only one or two close friends (or even a small clique) who monopolize his friendship to the extent that he excludes all others and denies himself the opportunity of extending his social circle and his social skills.

The choice of friends often rests upon rather obscure bases. Research has shown considerable resemblance to exist among friends in such characteristics as age, height, intelligence, interests, and socioeconomic, cultural, and religious background. Geographic proximity (propinquity) is generally more important in determining friendship among young children than is social class, with the latter becoming progressively more important in adolescence and adulthood. But whereas it is sometimes difficult for outsiders to understand what a certain person sees in another —as many parents of teen-age girls can testify—one can be sure that each satisfies some basic need of the other or the friendship would not last.

The choice of friends changes as interests, needs, and goals change. Thus, the preadolescent boy chooses his friends on their ability to play ball or whatever sport is being played at the moment; the adolescent girl may be interested in the playboy who has money and a car. Friendships tend to become increasingly stable with age, but some childhood friendships are tremendously enduring. Attempts to break up friendships must be carried out with tact, for strenuous objections force the individual to defend his choice against the seeming threat to security and independence. A subtle approach such as having a girl bring her unwanted boyfriend into her home, where he is projected against the background of the values the home has always treasured, is more likely to cause her to see his inadequacies than a more open attack.

Popularity is generally based on a number of considerations which vary from age to age and from group to group. Among preadolescent boys, physical size and strength are often the major attributes of popular children, particularly in groups where fighting or sports are important; in high school wealth and social status assume greater importance. To be popular, a person usually has to have a somewhat greater degree of the characteristics the group treasures, such as a pretty face or social prestige; and again, it would appear that these stars help others satisfy certain needs or they would lose their drawing power. Also to be noted is that popularity tends to be cumulative: a person already in demand learns how to deal with people, thus ensuring his continued popularity.

SYMPATHY

An important aspect of social development is the ability to sympathize with others, to show sensitivity to their needs, their joys and sorrows, their fears, and their sufferings. Sympathy is a sign of social maturity: children as a rule are so ego-centered that they have sympathy for no one but themselves. In fact, although love of man has shown itself in countless ways in times of disaster, there are many adults who are incapable of feeling genuine sympathy over the misfortunes of others. Some people have such deep-seated needs of their own that they cannot afford to consider the needs of others; they visit a friend in the hospital not to express sympathy over his illness but to tell him of similar or worse experiences of their own, apparently expecting him to sympathize with them. Some are incapable of appreciating the feelings of others because of conflicting impulses; the person who needs to protect himself against feelings of guilt arising out of partial responsibility for another's predicament may be unable to sympathize with the sufferer. It may also be impossible for certain people to feel real sympathy when misfortune befalls an enemy; the conflict arising from the teacher's need for revenge, for example, may make it difficult to sympathize with the child whose unfortunate home leads him to be defiant. Some individuals seem to enjoy the prestige of their misfortunes and may actually resent the competition of similar misfortunes occurring to others.

Probably the best way to promote sympathy is indirectly through providing the child with a sense of security, for only the secure person can forget about himself long enough to think of others. Beyond that, adult example, together with incidental discussions of the effect of one's behavior upon the feelings of others, is probably all that can be done. It must also be recognized that, to be truly sympathetic, a person must also have experienced misfortunes sufficiently like those of the victim that he can identify with him.

RESISTANT AND AGGRESSIVE BEHAVIOR

The child's desire to maintain his individuality leads him to give in only reluctantly to pressures designed to socialize him. Hence, from early in life, he shows signs of negativism. This resistance generally represents nothing more than an attempt to assert his independence and to test his social powers, or perhaps to avoid being pushed into situations he cannot handle and thereby to save himself from the possible indignities of failure. The child's negativism is often the result of social ineptness: whereas the adult can give a graceful excuse to a difficult request, the child can give only a blunt refusal, whereupon adults are likely to insist on immediate compliance, which only makes him that much more resistant. In time, he may feel that he has to defend himself against everything and he may come to perceive authority as simply hostile. It must also be remembered that, from the child's standpoint, much of his oppositional behavior is really counteropposition since it is the adult who first opposes him. The severity of a given child's negativism depends in large measure on the way adults handle him. If adults do not push him beyond his depth, his natural desire to grow will tend to keep negativism at a minimum.

Negativism reaches a peak around age three or four, after which it tends to decline as the child not only finds it pays to comply, but also develops a greater capacity for complying, for understanding what is expected of him, and for asserting himself in more positive ways. It may also be that adults are more considerate of him as he grows older. Nevertheless, negativism continues throughout life. The adult simply has more subtle ways of expressing his independence. Aggression is a more extreme kind of resistance in that it incorporates an element of attack stemming from the child's desire to assert himself, to appraise his ability to handle others, and especially from a desire for revenge.

The greater the number of contacts between two people, the greater the likelihood of aggressive and/or resistant behavior. Most sibling quarrels, even when continued after the child has learned more subtle ways of dealing with strangers, are not a sign of incompatibility. In a study of preschool children, Jersild and Markey (1935) recorded an average per-child rate of one conflict every five minutes. These are generally brief, self-terminating, and resolved without resentment. Furthermore, despite their frequency, they are generally outnumbered by compatible contacts, and, even at the peak of negativism, resistant and negative contacts constitute only a small fraction of the total contacts made (Mengert, 1931). The child who makes the greatest number of resistant or belligerent contacts also makes the greatest number of friendly, cooperative, or neutral contacts; he is simply more active socially. Thus, resistant and aggressive behavior may be considered a relatively normal phenomenon, or, as Green (1933) puts it, quarreling is part of friendly social intercourse at all ages. Although it may not be desirable except perhaps where the child for the first time begins to stand up for his rights, even aggression represents a developmental stage through which the child must pass on his way to more mature means of asserting himself. Jersild and Markey found that children whose kindergarten teachers had prevented them from fighting fought more the following year than those whose teachers had interfered less frequently. They suggest that fighting is an integral part of learning to deal with others. Even among adults, it may be that the individual's need to attain his purposes and to look after his interests is bound to involve him in an occasional conflict with others who are trying to do the same. Since direct aggression is rarely, if ever, desirable, a definite attempt should be made to channel aggressive feelings into such constructive activities as classwork and sports. Competition as in football, for example, is more effective in removing group tension than petty bickering and scapegoating. On the other hand, if overdone, competition can create resentment and bitterness between the contestants to the point where it serves to generate rather than to dissipate aggressive feelings.

LEADERSHIP

The importance of leadership to the welfare of a democratic society makes its nurture and development a matter of primary concern to the school. Leadership was once considered a quality residing within the leader; certain people were capable of leadership while others were not. This view parallels the "great man" theory of history, which postulates that history is made by significant people whose leadership defines the destiny of mankind. It has an element of truth; there are people whose overall ability, judgment, and sagacity make them potential leaders in a variety of situations. On the other hand, leadership involves followership and, as a result, is far more situational than had originally been believed. We now think of *leadership behavior* rather than leadership as a trait, with the understanding that leadership behavior is a function of many circumstances, and especially of the nature of the group in which it occurs. Since different groups have different objectives and different procedures for attaining these objectives, they are likely to look for different things in, and make different demands upon, their leader. The modern thinking is that everyone has potentialities for leadership behavior and, further, that a leader may be eminently successful in one circumstance and fail in another. This opinion is summarized by Guilford (1959) as follows:

> In the light of considerable investigation and current thinking, the popular concept of leadership cannot be considered a

unitary trait nor is it a very stable composite of traits, since leadership behavior depends upon interactions of leaders, group functions, followers, and situations. [p. 473]

In other words, psychology has shifted from the "great man" view that leaders are molders of human destiny to the sociological view that leaders are merely the expression of the popular need; in this context leaders are seen as riding the tide of history rather than originating it. According to this view, society is a dynamic organism which finds itself a leader as it moves along; in times of war it finds a warrior, in times of peace it finds a peace leader.

Leadership cannot be defined apart from the situation in which it occurs; more specifically, we need to consider the needs and characteristics of the followers as an aspect of the dynamics of group functioning, for in all cases the followers must decide whether they will accept the leadership offered to them, and this decision revolves around their needs in the particular situation and what they feel the leader has to contribute from that standpoint. If the followers need warm, paternal approval, they will accept the person who can supply this kind of support and will reject the task-oriented leader, no matter how competent he might be. In an emergency situation, on the other hand, the competent, task-oriented person might find his leadership accepted despite his inability to relate to individual members.

A number of studies have investigated the characteristics of the successful leader. Leaders are generally somewhat superior in such traits as intelligence, scholarship, verbal facility, social participation, sociability, initiative, originality, enthusiasm, self-confidence, popularity, adaptability, and even in physique and appearance—and yet they must not be so superior as to be different and consequently unable to relate to the group. However, there is no single ability or even pattern of abilities which characterizes successful leaders. Most studies of any one trait have been inconclusive, apparently because of the different goals which are likely to be involved. No one trait alone is found in all situations, and it is reasonable to conclude that, although certain minimal qualities are required of all leaders, those abilities are widely distributed even among nonleaders. As a general statement, leaders possess certain traits and characteristics which, in some way or other, make them superior from the standpoint of the purposes of the group. Physical prowess would be important in a leader of a gang of boys, for example.

Leaders tend to be high in social perception and sensitivity, i.e., empathy. Chowdhry and Newcomb (1952) found leaders more adept at judging and interpreting group feelings on issues relevant to the group's purposes. This is consistent with the view that leaders reflect group opinion rather than mold it to their own specifications or otherwise display initiative that would alienate them from the group. Successful leaders are both sensitive to the pulse of the group and fluent in putting its feelings into words, perhaps as a slogan or formula. A good leader often does nothing more than spread enthusiasm and put into a neat package the feelings and aspirations which the group already has. To quote Guthrie and Powers (1950, p. 467): "He maintains his position by watching which way the group is about to go and putting himself in front just before it starts moving." It follows from the premise that any group that needs a leader will develop one and will keep him as long as he serves the group's major needs, that the permanence of a leader depends on the nature of the group and its purposes in relation to his qualifications and especially his ability to sense, and to adapt to, its changing goals.

The Role of the Leader

The leader plays a number of roles. His primary function is generally to interpret the situation, emphasizing its crucial aspects, clarifying ambiguity, and maintaining focus on major goals. He needs to be particularly skillful at synthesizing group opinions, drawing together the relevant ideas, bringing out the alternatives and issues, and keeping the group on the track. He must be capable of translating the group's feelings into words to permit the members to act as a cohesive and cooperative unit in the pursuit of clearly defined common goals. He may have to coordinate the energies of various members and resolve personal conflicts, thus helping individuals integrate their personal goals into the broader group goals.

Inasmuch as individual differences among the members are the group's most valuable asset, the leader has a particular responsibility in coordinating the resources of the members. His task is primarily that of facilitating the process through which the members can make their maximum contribution to group goals. He must be particularly careful to prevent the exploitation of the group by individual members. It is also important that he prevent the group from depending upon him unduly; he needs to encourage members to share with him the leadership function in order to lighten the load placed upon his shoulders. This is also essential for the group's long-range welfare. It is no less important for him to insist on continuous improvement of his own leadership qualities and skills.

The teacher, as a classroom leader, needs to encourage and inspire students to share the leadership of the group. This may be difficult with young children, although undoubtedly teachers have underestimated the leadership potential of children. As studies like that of Cassell and Shafer (1961) have shown, much can be done when the task is approached systematically and the issues are within the children's frame of reference. Teacher leadership in the traditional classroom has often been unduly directive, if not repressive; in many classrooms, student participation in setting goals and planning work is kept to a minimum, communication is often one-way, and generally students work *for* the teacher. Students, in turn, have responded with apathy to this denial of opportunity to exercise initiative and self-direction. Such an approach fails to provide training in leadership on the part of those who will eventually be responsible for the operation of democratic society.

It is particularly important that children recognize their responsibility to develop and to exercise the leadership potential of which they are capable. Generally the more flexible and the more varied the school program, the easier it is for members to assume leadership with regard to some phase of the group's purposes. It is also important to note that, unless there is considerable turnover in membership, it is relatively difficult for a person to climb within a well-established group, for his fellow members are likely to continue to perceive him in his old role of follower. The organization of new clubs and the movement of leaders as they graduate from grade school to junior high, to senior high, or college, and to an occupation gives newer members a chance to assume leadership, although even then it is generally wise to limit the number of leadership positions which a given student can hold.

In addition to good leaders, a democracy needs intelligent and informed citizens, i.e., followers who have the ability to evaluate leaders, the willingness to insist on knowing what, whom, and why, and the integrity to refuse to go along with the pack unless convinced that it is for the general good. Our new view of leadership makes intelligent followership almost as necessary for survival of the democratic way of life as enlightened leadership. As Bayles (1960) points out, democratic structure places responsibility for the wisdom or nonwisdom of government enactments squarely on the shoulders of the governed. Education for participation in a democracy must continually strive to sensitize the child to the fact that decisions will be wise or foolish as *we* make them, for, as George Bernard Shaw suggested, democracy is a device for ensuring that no one gets better government than he deserves.

How we define our function as educators will in no small way determine whether democratic group processes will be effective or ineffective, for, as we broaden our perspective to see more clearly our responsibilities to democratic society, it becomes apparent that behavior, not knowledge of academic content, is the true substance of education. The development of group and individual standards is a long and slow process of social growth; its final outcome must be understanding and responsibility that will result in improved behavior, not mere outward conformity to rules. Actually, our competitive society has led children to perceive social relations as a matter of surpassing someone; it is very possible that the school's emphasis on excelling, on doing one's best, superimposed upon a rigid grading system complete with honor roll, has stressed that someone must be ahead of someone else to the point of making cooperation difficult. Children must be encouraged to use their competitive tendencies in working for group goals rather than in working to surpass others. What is important is not that people lead or follow, but rather that each make the maximum contribution of which he is capable.

GROUP DYNAMICS

Importance of the Group

The modern emphasis on the classroom as a functioning and interacting unit has focused attention on the concept of group interaction—or, as it is commonly known, group dynamics. The group is a major force—for good or for evil—in determining the behavior of its members, and the greater the group's cohesiveness, the greater its influence. No child exists or behaves in a vacuum, and the teacher can no more understand a group of children by studying each separately than a physicist can understand the action of molecules by studying atoms in isolation. Each group, with its ground rules, standards, and code of conduct makes strong demands on its members to conform, and just as a person has a self-concept, so does the group, when closely knit, have ideals and values it seeks to maintain and perpetuate by rewarding those who further its purposes and invoking sanctions against those who undermine its existence.

Teachers, it seems, fear that the group might become too cohesive and possibly threaten their authority. In an apparent attempt to avoid having to fight a well-organized enemy, they have employed divide-and-conquer techniques such as discouraging group discussion of mutual problems and keeping group interaction to a minimum. In addition, by stressing competition, by playing one child against another, they have fostered group rivalry and prevented the development of group spirit. Perhaps too many teachers are still thinking of the classroom as a teacher-versus-pupils situation.

Having the group work toward common goals makes for more effective motivation and provides a supportive environment within which members are accepted as individuals and co-contributors to group goals, thereby allowing each to use his capacity to best advantage in mutual sharing, and thus promoting maximum individual and group development. The group-centered approach tends to promote learnings in significant directions other than the strictly factual. Under proper guidance, group work might logically be expected to promote the child's ability to get along in a social climate. That is, it should promote effectiveness in leadership, independence of thinking, ability to resolve problems democratically, ability to formulate clearly defined goals, willingness to assume responsibility and initiative, and consideration of and sensitivity to the views of others without sacrifice of one's own ideals—all of which must inevitably be major objectives of education in a democratic society. Group processes are particularly effective in promoting both attitude and behavior changes. Furthermore, the fact that the group expects its members to contribute—or be squeezed out—is a powerful incentive toward pupil growth. Group influences can also be an impediment to wholesome personal and social growth, of course, but in either case—whether an ally or an enemy in the educative process—they cannot be ignored.[2]

For the group to be of maximum benefit to its members, it must be cohesive. Only when each member is reasonably secure within the group can he use his energies for self- and group-fulfillment; otherwise he will dissipate them worrying over his status or he will sacrifice to excess his individuality in order to gain acceptance. This is important inasmuch as the group's most valuable asset is its diversity of talent. Group cohesiveness and loyalty are best promoted through the operation of such factors as commonness of purpose, adequacy of the channels of communication, mutual responsibility and cooperation, and accepted norms of conduct. A group cannot exist without a sense of purpose, for then it has no reason for existing. It is essential that the group formulate meaningful objectives, operationally defined and significant to the individual members as well as to the group. Each subactivity must also have a definite purpose so members can see how their individual contribution fits into the overall plan. Group decisions must not be imposed upon the minority by majority rule, because, unless each member is sold on the goals, the quality of his contribution will suffer, group spirit will deteriorate, and the group will eventually disintegrate. There is also a need for continuous evaluation of the group's attainment of its goals and purposes; not only does this give the group a sense of contribution and achievement, but it also enables it to appraise its mode of operation, to reorient its efforts, and to realign itself for greater effectiveness.

In any group, the members play various roles, depending upon their talents, their status, and even their preferences in relation to the needs of the group as a whole. This is again the case of the group providing itself not only with the necessary leadership to direct its operations but also casting its members in complementary roles to promote its overall success. A person also plays different roles in different situations; he may be the life of the party in one setting and a senior member and consultant in another. These roles must be compatible within the broad frame-

[2] Every school tends to have its own traditions and its own group spirit. This is particularly evident in the "traditioned" private colleges. Certain high schools value athletics as their major consideration to the point where concern for athletic excellence sometimes interferes with academic excellence. The faculty has a responsibility for seeing that academic standards become a major aspect of the "image" each school forms of itself.

work of the individual's self-concept if he is to avoid internal conflict; they can vary in terms of outward behavior but not in terms of fundamental values.

GROUP CLIMATE

Group climate is of prime importance in the achievement of both personal and group growth. This, in turn, is largely a function of group leadership. Translated to the classroom situation, this means that the teacher is largely responsible, by action or by default, for the climate in which pupil growth is to take place. Under proper leadership, effective learning can be fostered; under different conditions of leadership, the group may deteriorate to the point of fostering negative attitudes which impede growth. Probably the most common symptom of faulty group relations is apathy, which tends to occur under autocratic control, especially when the leader is unpopular or the goals unsuitable. In such cases, there is a need for a redefinition of group goals in terms of individual and group purposes as a means of building up the group and encouraging greater ego-involvement.

The best known study of social climate and group leadership is that of Lewin, Lippitt, and White (1939) in which groups of boys were placed, in successive periods of seven weeks' duration, under three types of leadership: autocratic, democratic, and laissez-faire. The autocratic leader decided everything—what was to be done, when, and how. He praised and criticized but remained impersonal and aloof. The democratic leader allowed maximum freedom in the determination of policy; he participated as a senior member, giving help and encouragement as well as objective praise and criticism. The leader under laissez-faire conditions did nothing beyond answering questions when asked; he allowed the boys complete freedom in decision-making, did not participate in the group's activities, and did not praise, criticize, or attempt to guide the work.

The results favored democratic control. The autocratic group displayed signs of apathy, listlessness, and general distaste for the work. As might be expected from the fact that autocratic control relies on authority, work in the autocratically controlled group declined as soon as the instructor left the room, whereas under democratic control work continued as before. The laissez-faire group had difficulty in arriving at group goals and what began as cooperative work often degenerated into horseplay. Frustration mounted as a result of lack of leadership to the point where mutual interference prevented even those who wanted to work from doing so. From the standpoint of emotional climate, least tension was found in the democratic group, which suggests that a democratic organization is more conducive to the satisfaction of individual and group needs. Hostility was 30 times as prevalent in the autocratic group; this group also showed less cohesiveness in the sense that contacts between members were largely of the one-to-one variety. The laissez-faire group was characterized by a vicious self-perpetuating circle of frustration-aggression-frustration.

A democratic social climate seems best. It is difficult, of course, to set up an experiment of this kind without prejudicing the results; it is possible, for example, that a more understanding autocrat might have had more success. Anderson (1959), who summarized the literature on autocratic-democratic leadership, suggests that available evidence fails to demonstrate that either autocratic or democratic leadership is consistently associated with higher productivity, for example. In most situations, democratic leadership promotes higher morale, but this too must be interpreted cautiously because the authoritarian leader has often been conceptualized as unreasonably harsh and rejecting. Not to be overlooked is the personality of the student; it is very possible that a task-oriented student, or even the insecure student, would do reasonably well in the highly structured authoritarian situation.[3]

The Lewin et al. study was not conducted in an educational setting and, inasmuch as the authoritarian leader was most atypical of teacher leadership, the results are probably not valid for the classroom. Nevertheless, there are reasons to believe that autocratic control is conducive to frustration. Autocratic control is also conducive to the attitude that someone has to dominate, an idea foreign to our democratic ideals and detrimental to effective classroom functioning. It is generally difficult to prevent the impersonal attitude of autocratic leadership from degenerating into a dictatorial atmosphere. Denied the assurance of group acceptance and the satisfaction of a warm personal relationship with the group leader, children often resort to antisocial behavior which, in turn, causes the leader to become more dictatorial and critical. The relationship soon deteriorates from neutrality to animosity and, as the children disassociate themselves from the leader, they simply work to avoid censure rather than to attain meaningful goals. Laissez-faire, on the other hand, suffers from lack of leadership and, although occasionally a leader will arise from the ranks, he is not likely to be as well trained as he might be and may have all the deficiencies of the autocratic leader.

Supporting the Lewin et al. findings are the educationally more pertinent conclusions presented by Anderson and Anderson (1954):

> The children with the more dominating teachers showed significantly higher frequencies of behavior defined as non-conforming to teacher domination, which supported directly the hypothesis that *domination incites resistance*. In addition . . .

[3] See Stern, George G., "Measuring noncognitive variables in research on teaching," in N. L. Gage (ed.), *Handbook of Research on Teaching*, 1963, p. 427.

the children with the more dominating teachers had significantly higher frequencies recorded as conforming, looking up at seat work, "undetermined" child-child contacts (including whispering), and playing with "foreign objects," most of which represents the degradation of energy in the classroom. [p. 1193]

Our schools are relatively autocratic in orientation. This is perhaps understandable: it may seem illogical that the teacher should share his leadership with immature children. It is also true that most of the research findings are based on studies comparing extremes in autocratic, democratic, and laissez-faire climates, and it is conceivable that a more middle-of-the-road position may be as good as, if not better than, any of these extremes. There is always the temptation to feel that democratic processes are slow and occasionally lead to confusion and, by adult standards, to unsatisfactory results. At such times, the teacher is likely to want to take charge and expedite matters, forgetting that the important thing is the learning children do and not how well the job is done. Unfortunately, it is easy to be democratic with a cooperative, well-bred group, but the more children need understanding and democratic handling, the more likely they are to make it difficult by their unruly behavior for the teacher to be democratic with them. In such cases, progress tends to be so slow that many teachers give up in the face of the need for orderliness in the immediate situation. When this is achieved at the expense of spontaneity, enthusiasm, and responsibility, the teacher has made a bad bargain.

Teachers must draw the line between too much leadership (which results in undue docility and apathy) and too much freedom (which, because of lack of coordination and achievement, generally leads to frustration). This does not mean that the democratic approach never leads to confusion; but confusion is probably preferable to a procedure that avoids all confusion by having the teacher dictate at every moment what is right, what is wrong, and what constitutes a satisfactory performance. On the other hand, damage can also result from indiscriminate use of an ultrademocratic approach. Democratic procedures need to be scaled down to size; there are many decisions related to their present and future welfare that we cannot possibly expect young children to make for themselves. We must refrain from putting on their shoulders a heavier burden of responsibility than they can constructively bear. It is also true that when the teacher becomes overly democratic a small group within the class often takes over much of the control relinquished by the teacher.

The belief that a happy, cohesive situation is conducive to productivity cannot be considered apart from the circumstances involved. Some children display social facilitation; they work more efficiently in a group situation than alone. The group may provide competitive striving as well as interstimulation and imitation among the members. A great deal depends on the leadership, the nature of the group, the adequacy of available talents, the training of the members in working together, the meaningfulness of the goals to the members collectively and individually, and, of course, the ground rules by which the group operates. Overemphasis on consensus, for example, can act as a barrier to the expression of bold and imaginative ideas; to the extent that members are sensitive to the criticisms of others, they may refrain from voicing and defending unusual ideas. As a result, creative democracy often gives way to conformity at any price, with mediocrity as the inescapable consequence.

Of particular significance in the success of a given group is the extent of communication, for, to be successful, the group must tap the resources of each of its members. Unfortunately, certain people tend to monopolize and dominate the situation for selfish ends. As Jersild et al. (1941) suggest, the extent of a child's loquacity and his ability to get a hearing are determined primarily by factors other than knowledge. This is complicated further when not all members are of equal status, when the opinions of prestiged individuals go unchallenged while lesser members who have contributions to make feel reluctant to do so. Even cohesiveness may at times interfere with the attainment of group goals in that members may hesitate to contradict their friends.

What constitutes optimal group size depends on the situation. Ideally, the group should be large enough to provide the variety of competencies necessary for the success of the overall venture. On the other hand, the usual class of 30 is probably too large to function effectively as a discussion group. On a logical basis, it would seem that breaking the class down into subgroups would ensure greater unity of purpose and greater ego-involvement and acceptance of responsibility for the attainment of group goals as well as provide greater opportunity for each participant to make his contribution, to develop communication and leadership skills, and to experience first hand the operation of democratic processes. A small group may actually be more productive inasmuch as it is less likely to deter the more timid members from making their contribution; this would at least contribute to their personal development.

The group has an important influence upon personality development. One group may consist of docile, unimaginative conformists; another of confused, purposeless drifters or perhaps competitive overstrivers; while a third may consist of cooperative, flexible, purposeful, and group-spirited individuals. The difference is largely a matter of the group climate which the leader is able to generate. To be beneficial, the situation must be sufficiently free from personal threat that the individual can afford to try things without fear of jeopardizing his status. Group climate also determines group morale. A wholesome group spirit is generally reflected in pupil satisfaction, feelings of security and acceptance, and a minimum of conflict. It is conducive to openness to experience and to the promotion of creativity, ingenuity, imagination, originality, spontaneity, and cooperation. On the other hand, we must recognize that a given group climate is not necessarily or equally good for all children, and that it takes time as well as guidance for children to learn to operate as a group. There is need for a continuous appraisal not only of the effectiveness of group processes in the classroom but also of the progress being made in improving this effectiveness. What is significant is the extent to which students are assuming greater personal responsibility, are becoming progressively more capable of working together in the solution of group problems, are able to agree on group goals without domination by a few, and are developing the security necessary for them to use their full potential in the attainment of individual and group goals.

SOCIOMETRIC TECHNIQUES

In view of the importance of social climate in promoting the all-round development of their pupils, teachers should make periodic appraisal of group structure within the class. Sociometric techniques, which have been devised for that purpose, consist of asking each child to list his first, second, and third choice of a companion in various settings: "Whom would you like to sit next to in class?" "Whom would you like to have as your discussion group leader?" etc. The tabulation of these choices provides an index of the acceptance of each member and the cohesiveness of the group. The results can then be shown in a sociogram, a particular version of which is the "target" sociogram (Gronlund, 1959) in which the degree of acceptance of the different students is shown by their position on a series of concentric circles marked off from the center of maximum attraction. (See Figure 8-1.)

Research has shown that teachers are often unaware of the social structure of their classes; they tend to overrate children who are prominent in class activities, those who are amenable to teacher direction but are socially inhibited, and those who are courteous and responsive to adults but unskilled in interpersonal relationships with their peers. Conversely, they tend to underrate children who are academically inept, those who antagonize the teacher by disregarding regulations but who are nevertheless well liked by their peers, and those who create a poor impression but who manage to establish intimate relations with a small circle of friends (Bonney, 1947). On the other hand, substantial differences in the ability of teachers to appraise the sociometric status of their children have been noted, with these differences apparently unrelated to the child's sex or the teacher's sex, age, experience, and college training.

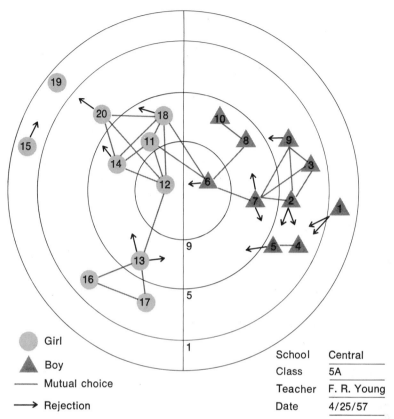

Girl

Boy

—— Mutual choice

——→ Rejection

School	Central
Class	5A
Teacher	F. R. Young
Date	4/25/57

FIGURE 8-1 Sociogram of choices and rejections of work companions. (Adapted from Norman E. Gronlund, *Sociometry in the Classroom.* Copyright © 1959 by Norman E. Gronlund.)

A number of studies have been made on the characteristics of accepted and non-accepted group members. Gronlund and Anderson (1957) identified three major categories of pupil acceptance among seventh and eighth graders:

[a] The socially accepted, who were characterized as attractive, friendly, likable, neat, and outgoing.

[b] The socially neglected, who received neither positive nor negative mention; theirs were simply neutral personalities lacking in stimulus value; they were overlooked rather than disliked.

[c] The socially rejected, who were rated as unlikable, restless, and talkative, untidy, and not good-looking. They attempted to make social contacts but lacked the necessary social skills.

Essentially similar findings concerning the criteria of prestige and acceptance among early adolescents are reported by Bonney (1947). At age twelve, socially successful boys tend to be good-looking, enthusiastic, friendly, aggressive, boisterous, fearless, and skilled in games and sports, while popular girls are neat, attractive, friendly, docile, good-humored, and conforming to adult standards. At fifteen, the social requirements for boys have changed; boisterousness and hyperactive behavior are regarded as childish, and higher value is placed on social poise in heterosexual situations. Athletic ability and leadership qualities are still important. For girls at fifteen, acceptance and popularity are achieved through attractiveness to boys and cheerful good fellowship in mixed groups.

Sociometric techniques have their limitations and should generally be used only in connection with supportive data from other sources (Cunningham, 1951; Ausubel, 1958). Yet, they can be of definite help to the teacher. Their primary purpose is to focus attention on the group structure within the class as a preliminary step in improving intragroup relations. They orient the teacher to the child whose annoying characteristics lead to his rejection, for example. Regrouping and reseating sometimes help break up cliques and bring in the isolate; it might help the isolate become accepted if he were allowed at least one of his choices in connection with the activities listed. It must be remembered, however, that he will become accepted only insofar as he makes a contribution, so it is generally necessary to find a group in which his abilities can be useful, even if it means providing him with guidance in developing skills which are in demand or increasing his overall acceptability. In the meantime, the teacher should accept the child; not only will this serve as an example to the other children, but it will also help him relax enough to do something constructive toward his acceptance by the group. There are times, on the other hand, when it would be advisable to have him transferred to a more compatible group in which he can make a new start.

DISCIPLINE AS AN ASPECT
OF SOCIAL GROWTH

Of the many problems facing teachers—especially beginning teachers—none is more immediate than those concerning the maintenance of classroom discipline. Studies generally rate discipline as one of the major problems faced by new teachers, for even though a beginning teacher can make a stab at teaching a lesson, it is sometimes quite a problem to settle down 30 youngsters who are all at once bent on talking, moving around, and generally doing everything but what they are asked to do. In such a situation, the young teacher tries to recall some specific set of rules or magic formula. Finding none that takes care of the situation, he turns in desperation to punishment and other forms of autocratic control. Then he rationalizes that students are rowdies, that a teacher must be realistic. At times, he will recall his psychology and alternate between democratic and autocratic classroom techniques, much to the confusion of all.

Discipline must be seen in the context of socialization and character development; it falls into the broader category of motivation and needs to be understood from that standpoint. At the lowest level, the child learns to balance what he would like to do against what others expect him to do; more significantly, he learns to synchronize his goals and purposes with those of the social order in the manner of enlightened self-interest. The crucial element is the internalization of society's values and standards to the point where the penalty for misbehavior is no longer external punishment but rather guilt feelings; the ultimate goal is for the child to develop a positive valuing of social standards as a dynamic force toward constructive personal and social behavior.

Discipline is a matter of progressive development in which the child needs considerable guidance and support as he works out the details of self-direction. Much of his misbehavior is simply the manifestation of normal growth; no matter how annoying his behavior, he needs the opportunity to experiment with immaturity. The teacher must realize how normal it is for children to get into trouble as they experiment with better ways of conduct. In a sense, then, misbehavior is desirable from the standpoint of the child's overall growth. He needs to be encouraged to assert his initiative with the understanding that things do not always work out right; he can improve only by trying and by accepting the consequence of his behavior. If he is to take his place in a democratic society, the child must have practice in democratic living as he undergoes his internship training preparatory to his becoming an adult member of that society. If personal and social responsibility rather than conformity and obedience are to be the true criteria of discipline, he must be given the freedom to make decisions—and occasionally mistakes. Only thus can he become increasingly capable of self-direction.

The child must be allowed freedom to test the reality of the limits imposed upon his behavior by the social order; this is necessary for him to arrive at an adequate grasp of the situation within which his behavior is acceptable or unacceptable, adequate or inadequate. Learning to deal with these limits is a major task of childhood. Too much guidance is bad in that it deprives the child of the opportunity to learn; a laissez-faire approach is equally bad, because, although self-direction is the goal, the development of control and the integration of the ideals and habits upon which it is based require the guidance and, at times, the firm hand of the adult. The child needs to know the specific limits to which he can go, for, although he will continually struggle against them, he needs these limits to provide security. When the limits are nonexistent or movable, he is not only prevented from learning self-discipline but he is left anxious and bewildered as to where he stands.

A crucial aspect of discipline is a sensitivity to the social consequences of one's actions and a deliberate orientation of one's behavior
toward the promotion of the social good. Unfortunately, classroom discipline is frequently pitched at the level of irrational conformity, in which
the child respects certain standards not because of consideration for the
welfare of others but simply because of mechanical adherence to a rule.
True discipline is based on an understanding of what constitutes appropriate behavior and why and a positive valuing of such behavior as
an integral part of the self, rather than on mere conformity to external
or even internal standards. These concepts, to be discussed in Chapter 17,
constitute the foundation on which any attempt at discipline must rest.
In this sense true discipline and character are essentially synonymous.

Sheviakov and Redl (1956) emphasize that constructive discipline is
a much more exacting task than reliance on simple punitive tricks. First
of all, discipline in a democracy must recognize the inherent dignity of
each and every child, and while there is a need for external control in
the classroom, for example, the sooner teachers shift from external to
internal control the sooner they can expect children to display adequate
behavior. Unfortunately, many teachers, overburdened with large classes,
only have time to grasp at autocratic measures as expedients "for the
time being"; the problem is that they never get around to using more
constructive measures. Children, however, become apathetic under repressive classroom discipline; they comply, but they do only what is necessary
to avoid punishment. Eventually, some can stand it no longer and drop
out of school. The remainder behave, but all that the teacher has
accomplished is a change in surface behavior and not in basic attitudes
as is necessary if good behavior is to be made self-sustaining. Some changes
have actually taken place in basic attitudes, but these changes have been
essentially for the worse: dislike for school, dislike for teachers, a belief
that might makes right, to name a few.

Need for Discipline

Discipline in the sense of self-direction is necessary everywhere—on the
street, in the home, in the classroom, and on the playground. Rules and
their enforcement are a necessary part of efficient living, as would be
obvious to anyone stopping to consider the confusion that would result
if everyone had to make individual decisions on every occasion which
presented itself. Such discipline is constructive; it spells the difference between an army and a mob. The child must perceive rules and regulations
not as limitations or taboos but rather as facilitators of social interaction
enabling people to realize their individual and collective goals with
maximum efficiency; it is only by restricting the in-flow of traffic to limited accesses that the freeway is able to handle the volume of traffic it does.
On the other hand, much of the discipline found in schools simply

deters the child from misbehavior; too often it is just plain vindictive or retributive.

A major difficulty involved in the child's development of favorable attitudes toward rules and regulations is that so many of the rules he is to obey do not make sense to him in terms of the concept of orderliness expressed above. It is difficult to set down regulations that apply in all cases. The rule of quiet in the classroom, for example, although sound, may actually interfere with efficient operations when the class is working on certain class projects. Rules are not good or bad except in terms of the purpose to be achieved at a particular time and the stage of development of those involved. This only points to the need for a democratic viewpoint of discipline as individual self-control based on an understanding of the purposes of rules and regulations, for in the final analysis good behavior must be a matter of good sense and goodwill. When this is coordinated with practice in self-direction under the guidance of an understanding teacher, effective behavior patterns are likely to result.

Origin of Misbehavior

All behavior—including misbehavior—is an attempt at satisfying needs; the child who misbehaves has apparently learned from experience to gratify his needs through misbehavior and needs help in finding more suitable ways to satisfy these needs. He may have found that he can gain status among his peers by annoying the teacher or that continuing in misbehavior and taking the expected punishment is less anxiety-producing than trying something new. Misbehavior can be explained on the basis of the same psychological principles as acceptable behavior and only when teachers approach it from this point of view can they be successful in dealing with it.

Under productive circumstances, the child is likely to find socially acceptable outlets for satisfying his needs. On the other hand, an unsuitable curriculum or a tense emotional atmosphere arising from pupil-teacher or pupil-pupil dissension tends to promote unrest and misbehavior. It is probably true, for instance, that many of the discipline problems encountered in school stem from a curriculum that is too easy or too hard, or that is unrelated to the child's goals and purposes, so that, instead of being a source of satisfaction and self-fulfillment, it makes for frustration, tension—and misbehavior.

Years ago the primary purpose of discipline was to suppress misbehavior—which it did. But it also increased the tension that caused misbehavior in the first place. Modern discipline, on the other hand, is based on the philosophy of helping the child learn to satisfy his basic needs in socially acceptable ways by providing guidance in finding suitable outlets and practice in acceptable behavior. Providing such guidance and practice is as much the school's responsibility as providing guidance and practice in the academic aspects of the curriculum; both are oriented toward the attainment of the purposes for which the school exists.

Dealing with Misbehavior

The school's task is not so much curbing misbehavior as promoting constructive and positive behavior. Yet, as every teacher can testify, instances of misbehavior inevitably occur and he must be prepared for such situations. What is important is for him to realize that misbehavior is an indication that the child is having difficulty satisfying his needs through acceptable channels. Unfortunately, many teachers are so busy dealing with the symptoms that they never get around to the underlying causes; the sooner they come to view misbehavior from the standpoint of individual development rather than as a violation of classroom decorum, the more successful they are going to be.

The misbehaving child is one who has not yet found socially acceptable solutions to some of his major problems. Like all other children, he is trying to satisfy his needs but he is not going about it in the right way. Before we blame him, we need to remember that he may not be one of those hypothetical "average" students for whom the curriculum is supposedly devised or that he may have to contend with particularly difficult conditions at home. Faced with unrealistic demands and unable to run away from the situation—often not understanding what it is all about—he may be desperately trying to tell us that something is wrong. "Getting after" such a student, as Woodruff (1948) points out, merely adds to the unpleasantness of the situation without removing any of its frustrating features. Thus, it seems illogical to punish the child who cheats when cheating constitutes his only way of meeting requirements and maintaining status among his peers. Teachers must realize that children behave the only way they know how or in which it is possible for them to behave considering their potentialities, their experiential background, and the forces operating on them.

In dealing with misbehavior, the teacher must first be clear as to what "discipline" is supposed to accomplish. He needs to develop criteria for determining which incidents may be ignored, which may be corrected informally, and which should be of greater concern. It is easy to lose perspective in the heat of battle to the point where immediate goals become all-important while the real goals are overlooked. Too frequently, prohibitions are simply denials of the expression of healthy constructive motives. The teacher needs to be particularly clear as to just how disciplinary measures are to operate in helping the child develop new patterns of conduct. Specifically, how is severe punishment more effective than mild punishment, for example? The teacher's approach must be positive; berating, scolding, and expounding on pupil shortcomings in a moralizing tone only serve to foster the development of a negative self-image, with resulting damage to future growth potentialities.

A diagnostic approach generally accomplishes more than repressive and punitive measures. The wise teacher realizes that inattention is more likely to occur when children are tired or preoccupied with some pressing need, that they have so much energy that being noisy and mischievous is almost natural, that some would like to cooperate but can't because cooperation with the teacher would involve rejection by the group, and that some find the gamble involved in misbehaving interesting—in fact, it may be the only relief from the monotony of an unsuitable curriculum. An understanding of these principles is fundamental for dealing constructively with misbehavior; each case is different and the treatment will sometimes be difficult and complicated, but at least the approach is constructive and is more likely to be effective in the long run. Certain groups of children suffer more from the school's disciplinary procedures than others. Boys, for example, tend to receive more punishments than girls (Meyer and Thompson, 1956). We must remember that aggressive, outgoing behavior is as normal for boys as docile and nonassertive behavior is for girls; perhaps special steps should be taken to drain off the excess energy of boys in constructive activities. The lower-class child also has difficulty with the discipline of the classroom where the standards are often in conflict with those of his culture.

Although even a good teacher has occasional disciplinary problems, it is certainly a fact that problems are multiplied by an unsuitable curriculum, poor teaching methods, and a disliked teacher. Experience has shown that one of the better ways of promoting effective discipline is by keeping children occupied with meaningful activities; a well-motivated child who sees a definite purpose in what he is doing does not have to look elsewhere to satisfy his needs. The child who finds school interesting is not likely to be a truant just as the boy who enjoys baseball is not likely to violate the rules of the game even though both must give up a part of their freedom. Failure in discipline represents a failure in the direction of the child's motivation. It is also desirable to adopt a businesslike approach to classroom management. Starting promptly, making clear what is to be done, expecting only mature behavior, and not letting the class bog down are important; certainly we cannot expect children to be quiet and attentive when nothing is happening.

Teachers sometimes expect too much too soon in the line of improved behavior. After all, progress toward self-control is a gradual process and it is necessary to start where the child is, giving him only the freedom he can handle. The child must proceed from adult control to group control and to self-control and not all children have reached the maturity necessary to take one or the other of these steps. Consequently, the teacher must accept the fact that he is not going to be completely successful with all children; the important thing is that they progress toward the ultimate goal, self-direction.

If discipline is to be cumulative in the sense that the child can profit from his previous attempts at self-direction, it is necessary that disciplinary measures be consistent, but it is equally important that this consistency be in terms of the spirit rather than the letter of the law. The child needs to realize that regulations have no point apart from their purpose. It has long been an established tenet of democracy that people should have a voice in the policies that affect them directly; children should have practice in planning and enforcing the rules concerning school behavior. This removes discipline from a pupil-versus-teacher basis; when the class is responsible for its own behavior, misbehavior becomes a violation of the rights of one's fellow-students and would-be offenders are deprived of the opportunity of gaining peer status by disobeying the teacher. When discipline is a matter of self-imposed restrictions based on an understanding of both group and individual needs, misbehavior is relatively rare. Under such conditions, the teacher will generally have to attend only to major infractions while leaving the group to pull individual children in line on minor violations. Student courts are useful in enforcing conformity while, at the same time, providing an important lesson in self-direction on a group basis. They do require faculty supervision, however, not only to provide the maximum learning experience but also to prevent unfair or unduly harsh punishment.

Discipline cannot be reduced to a set of rules. Suggestions for maintaining classroom discipline must, therefore, be evaluated from the standpoint of their agreement with the psychological principles underlying behavior rather than simply accepted as rules of thumb of obscure validity. For instance, in view of the importance of the self-concept as a determinant of behavior, it is essential that the teacher convince students that he has confidence in their capacity for mature behavior. Many teachers treat children as immature and undependable and then wonder why they get immature behavior. It is also true that many children perceive the classroom as a place where pupils and teachers wage a perpetual battle or where students waste time between more pleasant activities such as sports. Until such time as they change their phenomenal field to construe the classroom as a place where one works toward worthwhile goals under the direction of an understanding teacher, little can be expected from superficial attempts at discipline.

Probably the most helpful suggestion for maintaining effective classroom discipline is to provide students with a program of challenging educational experiences geared to their motives and purposes. When children become mischievous, explosive, rebellious, or apathetic, the teacher had better check into the appropriateness of the work assigned or the demands made on them. It follows that teachers would save themselves a good deal of the time and energy which they spend coping with mis-behavior if they oriented themselves with a little ingenuity in the direc-tion of good teaching.

Disciplinary Measures

The question of punishment must invariably come up in any discussion of discipline for, although the emphasis should be on the positive, teachers occasionally have to punish children as a means of helping them toward self-discipline. This is particularly true inasmuch as there is a limit to the extent to which the teacher can allow the misbehavior of one child to disrupt the class. Punishment, however, is essentially negative in that it is directed primarily toward suppressing misbehavior; it should generally be accompanied by constructive guidance in what to do if it is to contribute to adequate behavior. Punishment has a history of ineffective-ness in situations ranging from schools to penitentiaries. In disciplining children, for example, teachers and parents usually administer punish-ment some time after the deviation has occurred and fail to make the removal of the punishment contingent upon the child's expression of self-punitive responses, so that the disciplinary techniques are generally more conducive to avoidance of the disciplinary agent than to the de-velopment of adequate inhibitions through the acquisition of guilt. With-holding positive reinforcement is more likely to be effective, especially when used in an atmosphere of warmth and mutual understanding, since the reinstatement of the reward is usually made contingent upon com-pliance with adult demands. Punishment tends to be detrimental to the development of the democratic principles of self-direction and respect for human dignity, especially since methods of discipline based on au-thority, domination, hostility, and violence are soon learned by the chil-dren on whom they are exercised. There is a tendency to build up a long list of annoyances and then crack down as patience wears thin, so that punishment is frequently triggered by some rather minor misdeed—which places punishment out of proportion to the offense. It would be desira-ble not to punish children who are already psychologically damaged as a result of previous abuse; unfortunately, such children often have a way of exasperating the teacher until he can contain himself no longer, so that he ends up by adding further damage.

The negative attitudes which punishment tends to generate toward the punisher are most detrimental when the latter is the parent, inas-much as the outcome may be feelings of ambivalence and failure to de-velop the identification and dependency necessary for later socialization and character formation. Damaged children tend to be children who were punished too early and too frequently and who were thus prevented from achieving proper identification with the social values of the culture. Punishment in the classroom is likely to result in resentment and antagonism which destroy morale and the teacher-pupil relationship to the point where the teacher no longer has the child's confidence, which he needs in order to promote his growth.

Punishment can be of many kinds, none of which is necessarily any better than any other except insofar as it is more appropriate to the individual case and can be integrated more readily with constructive measures. For example, punishment through natural consequences is often considered best in that it is impersonal and thus less likely to create resentment against the dispenser. Unfortunately, natural punishment is rarely sure and immediate enough to be effective. Often it is too drastic; obviously, the adult cannot let the child be struck down by a car so that he can suffer the consequences of his disobedience. In the final analysis, discipline is an individual matter and the disciplinary measure must fit the child rather than the offense. Each case must be analyzed on its own merits in the light of whether or not it promotes growth in self-discipline.

FAILURE IN DISCIPLINE

A certain degree of misbehavior in the classroom can be expected; there is a limit to the extent to which the school in a short school day can promote mature behavior on the part of all its students. Nevertheless, when we find perpetual misbehavior by a sizable number of students, something must be wrong, and part of the blame must fall on the teacher. That certain teachers fail in discipline and encounter undue student misbehavior is well known. Not so obvious is the fact that a much larger number of teachers fail in discipline in that, by using autocratic meaures to forestall misbehavior, they deny their students the opportunity to learn effective self-discipline. And, of course, if we emphasize the positive aspects of discipline—for it should be as much a part of discipline to inspire children to do their best as it is to discourage misbehavior—then probably every teacher is somewhat of a failure.

The reasons why teachers fail in discipline are as varied as there are combinations of pupils and teachers. For the sake of discussion, they are grouped here as follows:

[a] Lack of understanding of children and the dynamics underlying their behavior. Teachers are often unaware of the characteristics of children, of their needs, and of the means whereby these needs can be satisfied. This often leads to an unsuitable curriculum, unrealistic goals, and impossible demands, all in the setting of autocratic classroom management.

[b] Lack of a constructive program. A common failing among teachers lies in their failure to have a program which is challenging to

students. Two errors can be made in this connection: [1] Some teachers have no program at all so that the first and the last ten minutes of each period are wasted and even those who want to work cannot do so because of interference from others; [2] Others have a program often very meticulously planned but not related to student purposes. In either case, the students get nothing but frustration from classwork and consequently resort to misbehavior.

[c] Lack of understanding of the purpose of discipline. Many teachers judge discipline in terms of classroom orderliness rather than pupil growth; they glorify the docile child who may actually be far from well-disciplined. Some conceive discipline as a matter of suppressing anything they, for whatever reason, do not like, rather than of providing children with the opportunity to grow in self-direction. They insist on conformity to rigid rules of absolute quiet—presumably for their own benefit and comfort, since it has never been shown that pupil growth is promoted by such orderliness. They thereby destroy individuality and spontaneity and encourage apathy and discouragement.

[d] Poor personality or incompetence on the part of the teacher. In the final analysis, discipline revolves around the teacher; disciplinary problems reflect failure in leadership. Constructive discipline is based on a meaningful pupil-teacher relationship; it reflects the teacher's inner strength and security, his personal integrity, his kindness and understanding, as well as firmness; it implies a sense of mutual trust and respect and especially the teacher's ability to inspire children. On the contrary, teacher incompetence or personality quirks are likely to have repercussions in student misbehavior. Many teachers are insecure, perfectionistic, lacking in a sense of humor, and afraid to let go. They insist on unrealistic standards and take as a personal affront the child's failure to meet their demands. They meet aggression with superaggression and leave him, not with a greater appreciation of the teacher's sense of fairness, kindness, and understanding, but with increased resentment and hostility. Others have learned, instead of effective self-discipline, a neurotic rigidity and conformity to rules for rules' sake and cannot tolerate even intelligent deviations from the rule of the book. Schools need teachers with integrity who can promote feelings of mutual respect, trust, and understanding without which children will find it difficult to profit from classroom discipline.

An equally important aspect of the situation is the teacher's own growth. Not only must the teacher become increasingly proficient in helping children become more self-directive, but he too must gain in self-direction. As he grows in competence and security, he can afford to lose his defensiveness so that he no longer feels it necessary to repay rudeness with rudeness and resistance with resistance, and discipline is no longer a contest of wills or a show of strength. As a result, not only does a higher quality of pupil-teacher relationship evolve, but, as he develops a greater sensitivity to the problems of children, the teacher can forestall misbehavior by adapting his procedures to their needs.

SOCIAL MATURITY

Social maturity is relative in the sense that it is not restricted to a single behavioral pattern and that, even within the framework of a given cultural setting, there is room for considerable variation in the behavior which can be considered healthy social adjustment. Since we are dealing with children, we can expect some degree of immaturity as part of the normal pattern of social development; all that can be expected is progress toward social adequacy. Any attempt at relating the various aspects of social maturity to a given individual must make allowance for his assets and his goals as well as for the situation.

Social maturity is essentially a matter of effective relations between the individual and the group; it involves the twofold problem of integrating one's goals and purposes with those of society and of making the maximum contribution to social welfare. The socially mature person is characterized by the following attributes: [a] He has attained relative freedom from domination by his parents and his peers and no longer seeks security in childish dependence upon others, nor does he display adolescent rebellion and explosiveness; [b] He assumes responsibility for himself and his actions; [c] He has achieved social sensitivity to the point where he can integrate his needs and actions with the needs and rights of others, and he can communicate effectively in promoting effective action in social situations; [d] He is able to meet various situations without sacrificing his basic values and standards of conduct "just to be accepted"; [e] He has attained sexual adjustment in the sense of being motivated by the moral, spiritual, and personal aspects of sex rather than the biological and he has many close friends of both sexes; [f] He evaluates issues critically on the basis of their long-term effect on the group and on himself rather than from a selfish point of view; [g] He participates effectively in social relations but keeps his participation to a level consistent with his personality, his resources, and his own needs as well as those of the social group. The socially mature person is again the self-actualizing person described in Chapter 4.

IMPLICATIONS FOR EDUCATIONAL
PRACTICE

The school has accepted responsibility for the child's development of socially adequate behavior; more and more it provides opportunities for building social competence through contacts with other children in both its curricular and cocurricular programs. This is particularly necessary for the child who is late in maturing, isolated, or overprotected through either indulgence or domination by his parents and who, as a result, has not mastered the developmental tasks for his age.

The school has responsibility for providing the encouragement, the opportunities, and the guidance whereby the child can attain greater social maturity. This calls, first of all, for building up his sense of security; only when he feels secure can he be free from overdependence on others and from slavish conformity to group demands. Classes organized on a student-centered basis present excellent opportunities for social growth; there the child comes to recognize the interdependence of the individual and the group in the attainment of their mutual goals. Student government is another example of the type of activity through which the school can promote social competence. Sports and free play also exercise a vital role in teaching the child fairness, loyalty, cooperation, friendliness, and other social skills which are needed in the development of socially adequate behavior.

The school should be as concerned with teaching social skills as it is with the more academic phases of its program. Rather than simply providing the opportunity for children to learn social competence, it must also provide definite guidance whereby these social experiences can be effective and practice so that such behavior will become self-sustaining. Democratic attitudes are not inherent in children, and allowing them to make their own plans and decisions will not necessarily result in a democratic outlook. Student government can result in training a few "political bosses" and in convincing children that the way to obtain favors is to get along with those who are "in." The school's cocurricular program often falls short of its potentialities for helping children attain social skills because those who are already socially competent hog all the offices while those who need the training most are denied the opportunity to learn. On the other hand, the school must not supervise such programs so closely that children are denied the opportunity to learn through actual doing. On the playground, for example, it is generally best to let children settle their own quarrels if they can reach an equitable solution without adult interference. In the same way, the teacher should give children as much opportunity to do their own planning as their maturity will allow, although, to be sure, there is little point in having the teacher abdicate in favor of a demagogue who springs up from within the group.

HIGHLIGHTS OF THE CHAPTER

The fact that the individual does not live in a social vacuum makes the development of socially adequate behavior of immediate interest to the school. The following are among the major concepts relative to social development:

[a]

Socially adequate behavior is essentially a matter of enlightened self-interest, i.e., of developing a self-concept in which one's needs and purposes are integrated with those of the social group for the mutual benefit of both.

[b]

The child is an individualist; he becomes socialized only as he finds it to his advantage to internalize the values of society and to comply with its demands. Love-oriented child-rearing practices have proven more effective in promoting adequate socialization than object-oriented or punitive techniques.

[c]

Social behavior is influenced by predisposing factors of an inherited nature. Its specific orientation, on the other hand, is determined largely by social and cultural forces.

[d]

Identification is important in orienting early social development; there is need for worthy heroes with whom the child can identify.

[e]

Resistant and aggressive behavior can be expected as part of the process of attaining social competence.

[f]

Recent evidence has cast new light on the role of preschool education. The importance of the formative years in the development of the intellect may point to the need for an integrated educational program from early preschool years oriented to the promotion of intellectual as well as social growth.

[g]

The new view of leadership as a function of the group rather than of the leader emphasizes the importance of developing both the leadership and the followership potential of every member of democratic society.

[h]

Discipline is an aspect of social growth which can be understood only in terms of the basic determinants of behavior; the emphasis should be on discipline as a factor promoting group and individual welfare rather than restricting individual freedom.

[i]

Social maturity is best promoted by providing the child with security and the opportunity for practice in socially effective behavior.

[j]

A democratic social climate tends to be more conducive to effective learning and group relations than either an autocratic or a laissez-faire atmosphere. Although group work does not necessarily lead to greater productivity, democratic group work should be encouraged for the training it provides in effective democratic living.

[k]

Sociometric techniques enable the teacher to appraise the social structure of his class as a preliminary step in improving intragroup relations.

SOURCES OF RELATED MATERIAL

Anderson, Richard C., "Learning in discussions: A resume of the authoritarian-democratic studies," *Harv. educ. Rev.*, 29: 201–215, 1959.

Barry, H., et al., "A cross-cultural survey of some sex differences in socialization," *J. abnorm. soc. Psychol.*, 55: 327–32, 1957.

Cassel, R. N., and A. E. Shafer, "An experiment in leadership training," *J. Psychol.*, 51: 299–305, 1961.

Elam, Stanley M., et al., "Discipline and delinquency," *Phi Delta Kappan*, 41: 89–117, 1959.

Getzels, J. W., and H. A. Thelen, "The classroom group as a unique social system," in N. B. Henry (ed.), *The Dynamics of Instructional Groups*, 59th Yearbook, National Society for the Study of Education, Pt. II. Chicago: University of Chicago Press, 1960. Pp. 53–82.

Jennings, Helen H., *Sociometry in Group Relations: A Work Guide for Teachers*. Washington, D.C.: American Council on Education, 1948.

Jensen, G. T., "The social structure of the classroom group: An observational framework," *J. educ. Psychol.*, 46: 361–374, 1955.

Pressey, S. L., and D. C. Hanna, "The class as a psycho-sociological unit," in A. P. Coladarci (ed.), *Educational Psychology*. New York: Holt, Rinehart and Winston, Inc., 1955. Pp. 246–253.

Sheviakov, G. V., and F. Redl, *Discipline for Today's Children and Youth*. Washington, D.C.: National Education Association, 1956.

Thelen, Herbert A., "Group dynamics in instruction: Principle of least group size," *Sch. Rev.*, 57: 138–148, 1949.

Trow, W. C. et al., "Psychology of group behavior: The class as a group," *J. educ. Psychol.*, 41: 322–337, 1950.

Withall, J., "The development of a technique for the measurement of social-emotional climate in classroom," *Educ. psychol. Measmt*, 12: 440–451, 1952.

QUESTIONS AND PROJECTS

1

In what specific ways can teachers and parents make maximum use of the childhood gang for educational purposes?

2

In the discussion of leadership, it is implied that a leader must be somewhat of an opportunist ready to lead in the direction in which the group wants to move but reluctant to exert real leadership lest he be left without followers. Discuss the validity of this position and the implications for the school and for democratic society.

3

[a] To what extent is "socialization" of the child a matter of indoctrination to our American middle-class way of life? How would socialization in a totalitarian country differ from that in a democratic country?

[b] Can a person overdo the development of social sensitivity?

4

[a] To what extent is the teacher, in the final analysis, responsible for the misbehavior that occurs in his class?

[b] Evaluate: Autocratic discipline is a shortsighted expedient which is neither easy nor effective.

CHAPTER 9

Intellectual Development

It is no longer unreasonable to consider that it might be feasible to discover ways to govern the encounters children have with their environment especially during the early years of their development, to achieve a substantially faster rate of intellectual development and a substantially higher adult level of intellectual capacity.

Hunt, 1961, p. 363

Although educators are concerned with all aspects of the child's growth and development, none has a more direct bearing on the work of the school than the intellectual. This is particularly emphasized in the thinking of those who consider the learning of academic materials to be the primary, if not the sole, justification for having schools at all. The recurring emphasis on academic excellence does not let the teacher forget that Johnny must learn to read, to add, to subtract, and to spell—and up to a certain standard, too, if unpleasantness is to be avoided. On the other hand, the fact that Johnny does not mix with his peers, that he is moody, that he pouts, is, to the general public, less associated with failure on the part of the school. It is only when juvenile delinquency (or some other problem) gets out of hand that someone remembers that the school should have done something about it; just what, how, and when is not clear.

ASPECTS OF MENTAL GROWTH

Although the layman has a fairly clear idea of the meaning of intelligence, no such unanimity of viewpoint exists among experts in the field. There is, however, general consensus as to the following aspects of intellectual development:

[a] Mental development involves a widening of intellectual and temporal horizons from those stimuli immediately impinging upon the child to those more remote in time and space. As he grows older, the child is progressively more capable of thinking in terms of yesterday and tomorrow, in terms of what is there rather than merely what is here, and of displaying foresight and memory.

[b] Mental development involves an increase in the ability to deal with symbols, particularly abstract symbols, in manipulating the environment. Probably no other aspect reveals more clearly the child's mental development than his ability to use language. This development, as other forms of development, is most rapid in the early years, with his spoken vocabulary growing from 100 words at age two to some 2500 words when he enters school (Smith, 1926). In addition, there is a corresponding increase in the clarity of his concepts and in the length and complexity of the sentences with which he expresses his ideas.

Of special interest are the vast differences in the size of vocabulary among individuals, among socioeconomic and cultural groups, and between the sexes. There is, for example, a very definite sex difference favoring girls in all aspects of language development (McCarthy, 1954). Perhaps showing an environmental slant are McCarthy's findings that the average sentence length of five-year-old twins is slightly below that of three-year-old singletons. It is also worth noting that the feeble-minded child is always late in talking whereas the child who talks early is almost always of above-average intelligence. The reverse statement cannot be made, however. The gifted children studied by Terman (1925) talked some four months earlier than average, although some of them did not talk until they were two or even three years of age.

[c] Mental development involves an increase in memory. Contrary to popular claims that childhood is the golden age for memorization (often used as an argument to have children memorize things which they do not understand), the child's memory, like his other functions, is far from having reached its peak. This can be expected for a number of reasons: [1] his use of language as the tool by means of which things can be remembered is far from fully developed; [2] his background within which to integrate experiences is as yet limited; and [3] the clarity of his perceptions and his understandings, which are essential to memory, do not reach a peak until early adulthood. On the other hand, even the very young child can remember.

[d] Mental development involves a gradual increase in reasoning ability. Even the baby can reason, as can be inferred from the way he manipulates his environment in order to get what he wants. Ling (1941) found that infants as early as six months of age were able to choose between a circle, a cross, or a triangle, one of which had been sweetened with saccharine. On the other hand, childhood reasoning is often naïve and faulty—as might be expected inasmuch as [1] the child has not reached the peak of his mental development; [2] he is lacking in experience, and particularly, in the generalizations and principles which are necessary for the discovery and evaluation of hypotheses; [3] he is lacking in vocabulary and other tools with which to manipulate ideas; [4] he is generally lacking in persistence and attention; and [5] he tends to be swayed by emotional factors which color reason. However, it must be noted that adult reasoning is also often naïve and faulty and that there is no fundamental difference—except in degree—between the thought processes of adults and children.

THE NATURE OF INTELLIGENCE

Probably no area of psychology has been the subject of so much controversy as that of intelligence. Not only have psychologists been unable to agree on a definition but also they have been unable to agree on its nature or even its basic components. Many authors dealing with the topic simply accept the layman's use of the term and make no attempt to define or analyze it. Those who do give a definition display considerable difference in viewpoint, although such phrases as composite of abilities to grasp relationships, abstract reasoning, ability to learn, ability to solve problems, effectiveness in dealing with one's environment, ability to manipulate symbols, ability to act purposefully, etc., tend to be used with a certain frequency by authorities in the field. The definition is, of course, related to one's preferences with respect to the various "schools" of psychology. Perceptual psychologists, for example, use intelligence to refer to the effectiveness with which the individual interacts with his psychological environment. They suggest that vagueness or ambiguity in the perceptual field is likely to result in ineffectual, i.e., unintelligent, behavior.

The first successful attempt to measure intelligence was that of Alfred Binet, who at the turn of the century was asked by the French government to investigate the causes of retardation in the schools of Paris. Conceiving of intelligence not as a unitary trait but rather as a composite of many abilities, he set up a number of questions dealing with areas with which every child, while lacking in knowledge of the specific questions, would nonetheless be somewhat acquainted. His sampling of many different types of performance in which intelligent behavior might be displayed proved sufficiently successful that in 1905 he devised the first intelligence test.

The relatively wide difference in viewpoint as to what constitutes intelligence can be noted from a study of the content of the intelligence tests on the market. Probably the most basic intellectual function involves the ability to perceive relationships such as might be involved in: "A bird flies; a fish—" and "In what way are an orange and a baseball alike, and how are they different?" (Terman and Merrill, 1960), and most tests include at least some items of this nature. Some of the better tests incorporate a variety of items designed to measure different aspects of intellectual ability, e.g., vocabulary, verbal comprehension, abstract reasoning, memory for words and digits, ingenuity, and spatial relations; others rely on a simple combination of verbal and numerical items with emphasis on the former. In fact, some tests measure the verbal factor almost exclusively, much to the chagrin of some psychologists who feel that intelligence tests, supposedly designed to measure intelligence, do nothing more than deal with the material encountered in the classroom and, as a result, penalize students who do not do well in schoolwork. More recently, considerable concern has been expressed at the failure of current tests of intelligence to incorporate an appraisal of abilities in the area of creativity.

THEORIES OF INTELLIGENCE

The theoretical picture of the nature of intelligence is no clearer than the practical problem of measuring it. Even though the problem has received considerable attention, relatively little agreement has been reached with respect to such issues as whether intelligence is a unitary trait as proposed by Spearman (1904) or whether it is a composite of many factors as proposed by Thorndike (1927), Thurstone (1935), and more recently, Guilford (1956, 1959c, 1967).[1]

The two-factor theory proposed by Spearman postulated that intelligence is composed of a general factor g underlying all mental functions and a multitude of s factors, each specific to a given task. It is also possible to combine the s factors dealing with tasks of the same general nature into a group factor. According to this theory, a child's ability to do a problem in arithmetic depends on the quality of his g factor and of his s factors dealing with that particular problem. People differ in the amount of g as well as in the quality of the specific or the group factors involved in a given task, so that it is possible for a person who is relatively more intelligent than another by reason of a superior g to be less capable in a given area, e.g., mathematics, because of relatively inferior s factors in that area. On the other hand, since Spearman postulated g

[1] See Bischoff (1954) for a discussion of Thurstone's Primary Mental Abilities, and Burt (1955) for an exposition of the Spearman position.

as a form of mental energy permeating all mental operations, it would be unlikely for a person who is grossly lacking in general intelligence to be particularly capable in a specific field.

The theory of specific intelligence proposed by Thorndike conceived of intelligence as made of a multitude of specific and independent neural connections; intelligence was simply the summation of all the abilities involved in mental acts, each separate and independent of the others. According to Thorndike, a bright person simply has more neural connections of an adequate nature than a dull person, a view consistent with his S-R Bond theory of learning.

Somewhat better known in America is Thurstone's theory of primary mental abilities, which conceives of intelligence as made up of a number of mental abilities in the relative amount of any one of which people differ not only from one to another but also within themselves. A person may, for example, have relatively less of most of these abilities than another person and so be generally less "bright," but he may have considerably more of one ability which makes it possible for him to excel in the tasks where this ability is important. Of course, to the extent that many tasks involve a combination of these abilities, a person would be restricted in intelligence by a particular weakness in any one area.

The most comprehensive conceptualization of the complex structure of the human intellect is that recently presented by Guilford in which he classifies the intellect according to three dimensions:

[a] the process or operation performed: cognition, memory, convergent thinking, divergent thinking, and evaluation
[b] the kind of material or content: figural (i.e., concrete intelligence), symbolic or semantic (abstract intelligence), and behavioral (social intelligence)
[c] the kind of product resulting from the application of certain operations on certain kinds of content.

These three components of the intellect can be represented by a $5 \times 4 \times 6$ three-dimensional solid model, each of the 120 cells of which can be construed as a factor, as in Figure 9-1. For example, among the cognitive abilities at the figural level, there is the recognition of familiar picture objects and silhouettes which can be made as difficult as necessary by blotting out some of the parts. They can also be auditory figures, e.g., melodies and rhymes. At the cognitive-semantic level, there would be verbal comprehension as represented by the use of vocabulary tests.

Of particular interest is the distinction between convergent and divergent thinking. The former is oriented toward solving a problem to which there is a known (or, at least, an expected) answer; this is generally known as logical (critical) thinking, or simply reasoning. Convergent production dealing with relationships, for example, is generally

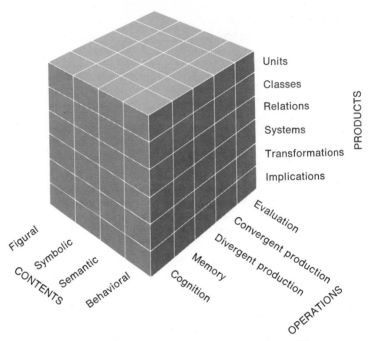

Units
Classes
Relations
Systems
Transformations
Implications
PRODUCTS

Figural
Symbolic
Semantic
Behavioral
CONTENTS

Evaluation
Convergent production
Divergent production
Memory
Cognition
OPERATIONS

FIGURE 9-1   Theoretical model for the complete "Structure of Intellect." (After Guilford, 1959.)

measured as an aspect of the eduction of correlates through the usual analogies test. Divergent thinking, on the contrary, seeks a new and different solution and might be considered imaginative thinking, or perhaps, simply creativity. Among the divergent thinking abilities, we have word fluency or ideational fluency at the semantic level. The divergent production of class ideas may be considered a factor of spontaneous flexibility; a typical test might have the examinee list varied uses for a common brick. If he suggests building a house, a barn, or a church, he has remained in the same class; if, on the other hand, he uses the brick to make a doorstop, throw at a dog, drown a cat, or drive a nail, then he reflects a higher degree of class flexibility since he has gone from one class to another.

These theories of intelligence are not conflicting; they merely represent different emphases and different levels of comprehensiveness. The Guilford model is presumably an extension of the Thurstone approach to the identification of mental components. Spearman's group factors might well be the counterpart of Thurstone's primary mental abilities. Contrariwise, since Thurstone's abilities do not account for the total variance in the mental performance of different individuals, there is room for a general factor. The differences reflect differences in purpose. Spearman's emphasis on a general factor leads to the calculation of a single measure of general intelligence which may satisfy the needs of the elementary school; the multifactor approach, on the other hand, provides a measure on each of a number of relatively independent abilities and therefore permits drawing a profile of abilities in specific areas which may be used as the basis for vocational guidance.

Guilford's model is, of course, complex and, even though it structures the various aspects of the intellect into a logical system, it does complicate the task of measuring "intelligence." As Guilford suggests, some people long for the good old days of simplicity when we got along with a single unanalyzed measure of intelligence. Simplicity has its appeal but human nature is extremely complex and we might as well realize that, for most purposes, only multiple scoring, with each score representing a different aspect of intelligence, will provide a meaningful picture of the individual's status. The implication of the Guilford model from the standpoint of classroom practice is not clear but it does suggest that, inasmuch as intelligence is not a single composite factor, a given student would not be uniformly capable of doing all things. Guilford's system should also deter educators from thinking of only one kind of intelligence to the neglect of other talents they have ignored in the past, particularly in the area of divergent thinking. We need to adopt a broader basis of intellectual quality and to adapt our teaching methods to the various kinds of intellectual potential.

Of special significance is the recent shift from intelligence as something one has—or perhaps is born with—to intelligence as something one develops. Substantial scientific evidence has converged from varied sources to focus on the need for educators to abandon their previous emphasis on the immutability of development as essentially a maturational process in favor of a more positive view of development as amenable to systematic environmental influences. As has been noted, stimulation appears necessary to intellectual development. Without it, puppies become irretrievably stupid; mice raised in complex environments are more "intelligent" than their litter-mates raised in simple environments. Although he does not deny the genetic basis of intelligence, Hunt (1961) feels that, in practice, the limits set by the genes in no way act as a ceiling to intellectual development. All indications are that the fixed maturation outlook led educators to grossly underestimate animal and human potential. Such concepts as the development of cell assemblies and the most teachable moment point to the cruciality of early environmental stimulation, and both Hunt and Moore, among others, emphasize the need for systematic preschool experiences in the development of untapped potential which then becomes a permanent part of the individual's intellectual assets.

More and more, psychologists are seeing intelligence as *intelligent behavior*, a major determinant of which is readiness, which, in turn, is recognized more and more as a function of the number and quality of previous learning sets that the learner brings to the situation rather than any general intellectual ability. Intelligence, as might be reflected in various forms of effective behavior, e.g., learning ability, is best conceived as an ability that develops through the process of interaction with the environment. In this setting, the concepts of motivation, N Ach., and especially openness to experience, take on special significance. Hayes (1962) suggests that what distinguishes the bright from the dull person may be not so much differences in learning capacity as the amount of information and problem-solving skills each has acquired. The latter are a function of the degree to which people expose themselves to experience which is, in turn, according to Hayes, a function of genetically controlled differences in experience-producing drives.

THE WORK OF PIAGET

A major contribution to the field of intellectual development is that of Piaget (1948, 1950, 1952, 1954),[2] a Swiss psychologist whose investigations dating back to the 1920s have centered on the growth of logical concepts, especially in the areas of numbers, time and space, and causation, as well as various aspects of moral development. His methods have been essentially clinical in the sense of a combination of observation and interview from which he has classified the spontaneous conversation of children from the standpoint of logical sophistication. Unfortunately, his earlier approach was very loose; his failure to control significant variables, for example, made it extremely difficult to evaluate the inferences he has drawn from his data. He has been criticized for his failure to standardize his methods, which apparently have varied at times from subject to subject even in the same study, and for his failure to specify the criteria on the basis of which responses were assigned to one category or another, so that we are expected to accept on faith his interpretation of the data. Besides, by burying their findings in lengthy and ponderous discourse, Piaget and his co-workers have left themselves vulnerable to misinterpretations.[3]

Piaget views intellectual growth as a matter of sequential stages in the maturation of the child's capacity to utilize increasingly difficult logical operations. He describes the intuitive thinking of the young child, for instance, as egocentric and syncretic—egocentric in the sense that his thoughts are self-centered, and syncretic in that his ideas of objects and

[2] See also Berlyne, 1957; Braine, 1959, 1962; Carroll, 1960; Flavell, 1963; Hunt, 1961; Inhelder and Piaget, 1958; Oakes, 1947.
[3] As implied, these criticisms pertain more clearly to his earlier studies and his earlier writings.

events are not based on an analysis of their qualities. The young child thinks of individual objects rather than of classes of objects having common characteristics. At seven, the child does not realize the need to satisfy others as to the validity of his solutions; he simply reaches decisions to suit his fancy and accepts them uncritically. He is so egocentric that he cannot step outside himself to view things objectively; it is only as social pressures develop that he begins a more objective appraisal.

Piaget categorizes the child's thought process into three main stages of development, each of which he divides further into substages:

[a] Sensori-motor control (birth to age two). Here the infant reacts to each object on the basis of its physical characteristics; symbolic activity is at a minimum.

[b] Concrete operations (age two to twelve). This stage involves a gradual increase in the child's ability to extract concepts from experience and to gain control through anticipation of consequences. It includes three subphases:

[1] a preconceptual phase (age two to six), during which objects gradually take on symbolic meaning (e.g., a bottle as a source of milk).

[2] an intuitive stage (age six to eight), during which the child's concepts become more elaborate and complex. He gradually shifts from seeing a tall and narrow jar as containing more candy than a shorter but wider jar, i.e., from equating tallness with bigness to a greater appreciation of the concept of the conservation of quantity.

[3] a stage of concrete operations (age nine to eleven), during which the child is still handicapped in dealing with abstract concepts and prefers concrete objects.

[c] Formal operations (age twelve through adulthood) during which there is a gradual increase in the youth's ability to master formal operations through logical deductions of possibilities and consequences.

An important aspect of Piaget's study of the development of the child's intellectual processes concerns the analysis of language from the standpoint of their function in his mental life. The language of the child of three or four is largely egocentric; in contrast to the sociocentric speech of the older child, the preschooler either talks to himself or talks for the pleasure of associating others in whatever he happens to be doing. Piaget notes a transition from: [a] a syncretic stage in which superficial associations are made among experiences to an intermediate stage in which the child is able to reason in the presence of the objects of thought to a final stage in which he is able to engage in abstract thought;

and [b] an animistic and magical mode of thought characteristic of children and primitive people to the logical mode of thinking characteristic of adults.

Piaget has devoted considerable attention to the development of the concept of causality which he views as a matter of relatively universal stages in the progression of the child's ability to see physical relationships as a matter of physical law. His approach consists of classifying the responses of children of various ages to such questions as "What makes the clouds move?" and "Why does a stone thrown into a pool of water sink to the bottom?" into three major stages. Each stage is subdivided so as to give a total of 17 levels of physical causality ranging from the least to the most mature, e.g., from "the stone falls to the bottom because it is white" (phenomenistic), to "the clouds move because they are alive" (animistic), to "the wind pushes the clouds" (mechanistic), and to a final stage of explanation by logical deduction.

Piaget has been criticized for his postulation of relatively distinct stages through which the child presumably proceeds. Although it is entirely possible that Piaget uses the term *stages* in the sense of qualitatively identifiable sequential phases in the orderly progression of development rather than of a rigid age-scale of cognitive development (Ausubel, 1962), the latter view is apparently a misinterpretation to which Piaget has left himself open as a result of his failure to present his material systematically. At any rate, to the extent that psychologists have accepted the concept of continuity in human development, Piaget's "stages" (regardless of his intent) are best conceived of simply as a matter of designation of developmental levels for the purposes of convenience.

Piaget's views have been both confirmed and refuted:[4] Berlyne (1957) gives Piaget's findings favorable treatment; Klingberg (1957), on the other hand, rejects Piaget's claim of animistic reasoning in children. In an early study Deutsche (1943) pointed to a number of inadequacies in Piaget's 17-point system of the development of causality; not only did she find it unusable as an instrument for classifying children's thinking but there was considerable evidence of overlapping among "stages." Her findings also challenge Piaget's concept of thinking as a general ability; she found that a given child's reasoning was not restricted to a single level of logical sophistication but rather the level of his causal explanations appeared to be specific to the problem.

The consensus of psychologists who have reviewed Piaget's work seems to be that: [a] the child can handle problems in which he is informed at a fairly high level in Piaget's classification while giving much more naïve answers to problems in which he is not as well versed; the adult also often reverts to egocentric, syncretic, and other primitive

[4] See Wallach (1963) for reference concerning Piaget's work in the area of children's thinking.

modes of thought; [b] children can give logical answers much sooner than the age postulated by Piaget; and [c] the age sequence is not as rigid as Piaget has suggested, nor is it as exclusively a matter of maturation. As Stacey and DeMartino (1958) suggest, Piaget asks many of the right questions but his conjectures need to be refined and put to the test in a manner more convincing to American psychologists. Nevertheless, his investigations constitute a most significant contribution to the psychology of child development. His conception of growth in operational thought as a matter of building one level on another, for example, bears significantly upon the concept of the spiral curriculum in which the child is given repeated opportunities to comprehend a given concept at progressively higher levels of logical sophistication and insight.

MEASUREMENT OF INTELLIGENCE

BASIC CONCEPTS

Mental development is measured in terms of mental age (MA). A large representative group of children who are, say, exactly ten years of age would automatically have a mental age of 10, i.e., the mental development that is average for ten-year-olds. In the same way, an MA of 6 represents the mental development that is average for children who are six years old, and so on, for an MA of 1 through at least 13.[5]

The child's mental age is obtained from his performance on an intelligence test; his successes on the various items of the test are added and the total converted into a mental age through a table derived from the standardization data. Thus a raw score of 115 might represent a mental age of 9 simply because the nine-year-old segment of the standardization population averaged a raw score of 115. Intelligence, however, is a relative term: a person is not bright or dull but rather is brighter or duller than other children of his own chronological age. To state that a child has a mental age of 9 is relatively meaningless since it would be important to know if he is chronologically six, nine, or twelve. Thus, the child's mental age has to be considered in terms of his chronological age (CA), or more correctly, in terms of the mental age of children of his own chronological age. This relationship or ratio between one's mental age and chronological age is known as the Intelligence Quotient or IQ.[6]

[5] This working definition of MA breaks down after the age of approximately thirteen, but it is still useful to understand its basic meaning as it applies to children.

[6] This method of calculating the IQ as a ratio of the mental age to the chronological age has been relatively abandoned by modern test constructors in favor of the deviation method in which IQs are simply read off a table. A child's IQ is a matter of the deviation, plus or minus, of his performance from the average of the group. There is also a trend toward abandoning the IQ altogether in favor of *standard scores*, as more clearly indicative of relative status.

The computation of the IQ involves only simple arithmetic, even when either or both the MA or the CA are fractional. Thus if a child has an MA of 11 years, 5 months (written 11-5) when tested at a CA of 9 years, 6 months (written 9-6), his IQ would be computed as follows:

$$IQ = \frac{\text{Child's MA}}{\text{Child's CA}} \times 100 = \frac{11\text{-}5}{9\text{-}5} \times 100 = \frac{137 \text{ months}}{114 \text{ months}} \times 100 = 120$$

In this case, the child's mental development is somewhat accelerated by comparison with that of children of his own chronological age; actually his mental development is proceeding at the rate of 120 percent of that of the average child. The IQ is an index of relative brightness and is the basis for estimating the mental level the child will reach at a given age. For example, we might expect this child to have an MA of (approximately) 12 when he reaches a CA of 10. This, of course, assumes that the child's IQ remains constant, an assumption that is only relatively true, as we shall see.

THE MENTAL GROWTH CURVE

Mental growth does not continue throughout the entire period of one's life; in fact, it begins to slow down in rate during the early teens and reaches its peak somewhere in the middle twenties.[7] The general shape of the mental growth curve of three different IQ levels is shown in Figure 9-2, but it must be remembered that these curves represent an hypothetical average and that sizable departures from average can be expected in the individual case.

Because of the gradual tapering off of mental growth in adolescence and early adulthood, an adjustment in the divisor must be made when the ratio method of calculating the IQ is used. The usual compensation made to take care of this problem in computing the ratio IQ is to use a chronological age of fifteen (or possibly sixteen) as the maximum divisor so that the person with an MA of 15 when tested at age twenty will have an IQ of 100, not 75. The problem is handled directly through the norms when the deviation IQ is used.

The age at which mental growth ceases is open to debate. Wechsler (1958) postulates that most mental functions reach their peak in the mid-twenties.[8] Corroborating evidence comes from the well-known fact

[7] Probably the best representative of the mental growth curve up to age twenty-one is that of the Berkeley growth data presented by Bayley (1955).

[8] To the extent that intelligence is a composite of many abilities, each maturing at its own rate, the age at which the peak is reached is a function of the particular composition of the "intelligence" test used. Bloom (1964), for example, points out that, whereas 80 percent of adult proficiency in perceptual speed is attained by age twelve, this relative level of ability is reached only at fourteen in the case of reasoning and spatial perception, at sixteen in numerical ability and memory, and after twenty for word fluency.

that college seniors do better on intelligence tests than they did as fresh-man, and from the results of the Harvard Growth Studies which show intellectual gains up to approximately age thirty, with some 2 percent taking place after twenty-one or twenty-two.

To the extent that intelligence tests are essentially tests of achieve-ment, performance cannot cease to improve at sixteen, but whether to accept or reject these increments in test performance as evidence of in-creased intelligence revolves around what we mean by intelligence. Cer-tainly, as a person grows older, he gains experience which contributes to his ability to solve problems of the kind included in intelligence tests. But the interpretation of this increased ability is a matter of controversy between: [a] those who hold that the concept of intelligence should eliminate at least in a large part the improvement in performance that is the direct outcome of experience—who, for example, feel that the increase in test performance between the freshman and the senior year in effect reflects a type of coaching not entirely unlike giving the student the answers to the questions before beginning the test; and [b] those who hold that intelligence can only be defined in terms of intelligent be-havior, that intelligent behavior is intelligent behavior regardless of its origin as long as it has relatively wide applicability. For example, the data provided by Tuddenham (1948) show the test performance of the draftees of World War II to be superior to that of their World War I counterparts beyond what might be accounted for by the better sampling, higher motivation, and greater familiarity with test material on the part of the more recent draftees. But some might contend that this superiority is really a spurious effect of better schooling and a more intellectually adequate environment rather than a result of biological improvement of the American intellect over the period of a generation—which is proba-bly true. On the other hand, if these environmental advantages enable the present generation to deal more adequately with complex problems in a wide variety of situations, is this not what is meant by being more in-telligent?

The converse problem exists at the upper levels of the chronological age scale. Since the mental growth curve shows a decline with advancing age, the IQ of older people is bound to show a continuous drop especially after age forty when a gradually accelerating decline sets in. It should be noted from Figure 9-2 that the mental level of gifted people probably never drops below the maximum level of people with average intelli-gence; in fact, there are many examples among the older educators and statesmen of people exhibiting great mental alertness despite advanced age. Others, especially the uneducated, suffer early and sharp losses, al-though it is doubtful whether a test could be devised that would give a true picture of the intelligence of such persons.

The amount of decline in IQ registered with age depends in a fun-

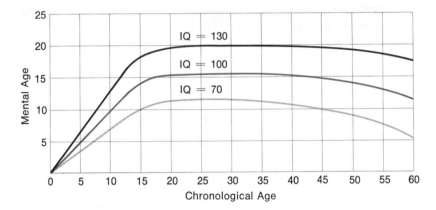

FIGURE 9-2   Hypothetical mental growth curves for three IQ levels. The shape of the curves is only approximate. The extent of the decline with age, for example, depends greatly upon the nature of the test material used.

damental way upon the material included in the test. Results of the Wechsler scale of intelligence show that performance on the subtests on information, comprehension, vocabulary, object assembly, and picture completion holds up well with age whereas performance on the subtests on digit span, similarities, block design, arithmetic, and digit symbols undergoes considerable decline. It would appear that, in general, the more complex intellectual abilities have a slower rate of growth, reach maturity at a later date, and undergo earlier decline. The greatest loss on test performance seems to occur in tests emphasizing speed and the identification of relationships.

The extent of mental deterioration with age is difficult to appraise. The cross-sectional approach generally used in the study of this problem suffers from obvious limitations in sampling, not only because of mortality (which could be selective), but also because of the difficulty of enlisting the cooperation of older subjects to engage in the test with enthusiasm. The educational factor also should be considered in measuring the extent of mental deterioration; many of the things the aged do not know may simply be things they never learned in their limited schooling.

Friend and Zubek (1958) suggest that the marked difference between older and younger subjects in their ability to think critically can be largely explained on the basis of the former's subjectivity and inflexibility. There was a tendency for the aged to evade the evaluation of arguments on the basis of their logical merit and to prefer to base their conclusions on what they *believed* to be the truth involved. The general consensus, based on such studies as those of Miles and Miles (1932), Wechsler (1944), and Jones and Conrad (1933), is that the losses in actual intellectual capacity occurring up to the middle fifties are relatively minor. Furthermore, from the practical point of view of learning ability and effectiveness of behavior, the added store of experience of an older person may well compensate in good part for whatever decline in "intelligence" may have occurred.

INTELLIGENCE TESTS

A relatively large number of intelligence tests designed for subjects from preschool to the adult level are available on the market today. Most of these are of acceptable quality from the standpoint of the purpose to be served by the conventional IQ, and it is up to the teacher and school officials to select the particular instruments which will serve their special needs. Evaluating intelligence tests calls for a considerably greater understanding of the principles of tests and measurements than this text can provide in the limited space available. The following paragraphs are simply for purposes of orientation, and the reader is referred to the many excellent texts on educational and psychological measurements for a more complete discussion.

In order to provide meaningful results, tests of intelligence, just as any other instrument of measurement, must possess certain characteristics, primary among which are validity and reliability. These terms will be discussed in Chapter 16 and it may be well for the student who is not familiar with these concepts to turn to the appropriate section of that chapter now.

The present discussion is limited to the following points:

[a] To be valid, a test of intelligence must measure intelligence and not some other aspect of the personality. This poses quite a problem inasmuch as there is no agreement as to what intelligence is or even as to what factors are to be included or excluded. Test makers generally rely on agreement of the scores provided by their tests with such criteria as teachers' judgment of pupil ability, success in school, and results of other tests purporting to measure intelligence. It is, of course, obvious that these are relatively inadequate criteria of intelligence and the lack of more substantial agreement of intelligence test scores with these criteria can be blamed on the test, on the criteria, or on both. The failure of present-day tests to incorporate more of the factors of the Guilford model, especially in the area of divergent thinking, can be construed as lack of validity.

[b] There are certain groups of people for whom the average intelligence test cannot give a valid measure of intelligence. To the extent that the average test was designed to measure the intelligence of children without a language handicap, the bilingual or the foreign-born child is going to do poorly, not necessarily because of a lack of mental ability but simply because of a lack of opportunity to learn the language

in which the test is given. In the same way, a child with a reading problem will tend to be underestimated as to IQ if he is given a test involving a considerable amount of reading. Other groups for whom the average intelligence test does not give "valid" scores include children who are emotionally upset, who are uncooperative, who are timid, or whose home background has been relatively limited in intellectual stimulation. All that can be said in such a case is that the obtained IQ is, in all likelihood, a relative underestimate of the examinee's "true" intelligence— although again it could be argued that the obtained IQ, no matter how depressed, may actually give a "valid" estimate of his educational potential since his handicap is likely to operate to depress both his test and his classroom performance. In other words, the validity of a test of intelligence cannot be considered apart from the purpose it is to serve.

[c] A test of intelligence should also be reliable, i.e., consistent. The average intelligence test is fairly reliable, although fluctuations of up to five IQ points can be expected upon retest in two thirds of the cases and even greater fluctuation in the remainder.

RANGE OF INDIVIDUAL DIFFERENCES
IN INTELLIGENCE

Results of intelligence tests indicate that the distribution of intelligence scores, like the distribution of many human characteristics, tends to approximate the normal curve. The distribution of IQs obtained from such tests as the Revised Stanford-Binet has been calibrated at 100 as the average of the general population, with approximately one third of the IQs ranging from 84 to 100 and another third from 100 to 116. Percentages for other IQ intervals can be estimated from Figure 9-3. It is impossible to say how far the curve extends toward either extremity but it is probably true that some idiots have IQs relatively close to zero, while at the opposite extreme some of the famous people of history had

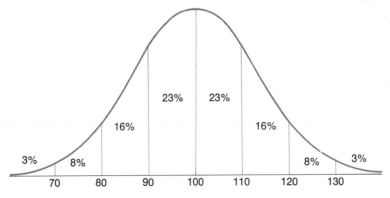

FIGURE 9-3   Distribution of IQs in the general population.

IQs approaching 200 as a minimum estimate. In a typical unselected class of 30 pupils, there are likely to be one or two relatively gifted and one or two relatively dull, so that from the standpoint of classroom performance, there is likely to be perhaps one child who has the mental development necessary to do work two to three grades in advance of his present grade placement, while there is also likely to be another child whose mental age would be average for children two or three grades below the grade in which he is currently enrolled.

USES OF INTELLIGENCE TESTS

RELATION TO ACADEMIC SUCCESS

Despite their limitations, intelligence tests have been shown to be of definite value in promoting a greater understanding of the individual with a view to predicting some aspect of his future behavior. Consequently, they are indispensable tools in such fields as psychology, sociology, industry, and especially education; intelligence tests were devised in connection with school problems and well over 75 percent of the intelligence tests given are administered in school-connected situations.

Intelligence tests serve their primary function in helping the teacher determine the ability of the individual child as a prerequisite to gearing the instructional program to his ability level and to determining the quality of work to be expected from him. Intelligence tests also serve as a partial basis for the classification and assignment of students to special classes.

That imbeciles and idiots cannot succeed in the standard academic program is so generally accepted that they are usually denied admission to regular classes. At the opposite end of the intelligence scale are the gifted, whose brilliant academic records sometimes border on the fantastic: John Stuart Mill studied Greek at the age of three; Ruskin was writing poetry at six; some 2 percent of Terman's gifted children learned to read at three. Even in the more normal range, there is a definite tendency for academic achievement to go hand in hand with IQ. In Bradley's study (1943), high school students with IQs above 140 obtained 16 times their proportional share of A's; no one with an IQ of 110 or above got a D. In a similar study by McGehee (1938), 63 percent of the students in the top three decile intervals in intelligence got A's while only 10 percent of those below the fourth decile obtained A's. Research has repeatedly shown correlation in the .50s to exist between IQ and success in the more academic subjects.

It generally takes an IQ of 120 to do acceptable work in a first-rate college with an average expenditure of energy and time; an IQ of 130 is about average for graduates of good colleges (Traxler, 1940). Cronbach

(1960), in a relatively comprehensive table of expectancies associated with various IQ levels, lists an IQ of 115 as average for freshmen in a typical four-year college, for example. Keys (1940) has estimated that for IQs from 70 to 84, chances are two out of three that a person will not go beyond high school and chances of graduating from college are nil, as opposed to only one chance in five of stopping after high school for those of IQ from 120 to 129. These data do not mean that academic success is denied the person with a low IQ; they only mean that his chances of success are somewhat less and that he will have to have special assets or will have to work harder in order to compensate for his intellectual limitations.

It must be realized that intelligence is not the only factor that has a bearing on school success and that there is a wide range of achievement levels among pupils of the same IQ. In fact, all that can be expected from an intelligence test is for it to indicate what the child could do, not what he will do, since motivation, emotional blocking, work habits, other responsibilities, ability to get along with the teacher, and many other factors have an effect on his success in the classroom. Bright children, for example, often avoid working to capacity for fear that achievement beyond the level of their classmates will cause them to be isolated from their peers. It must also be recognized that present-day intelligence tests leave unmeasured many of the components of the human intellect postulated by Guilford's recent work, many of which are undoubtedly involved to various degrees in academic success.

Nevertheless, to the extent that learning ability is accepted as an important aspect of intelligence, however defined, there must of necessity be a relationship between IQ and success in school, especially since test makers deliberately incorporate into their tests situations that are closely akin to those common in the classroom; years ago, Kelley (1927) wrote of a 90 percent overlap between the material included in tests of intelligence and that incorporated in tests of academic achievement. More recently, Coleman and Cureton (1954) have estimated the overlap at 95 percent. Actually the principal point of difference between a test of intelligence and a test of academic achievement is one of orientation. The items of any test—whether of achievement or intelligence—are necessarily samples of what a person can do here and now, i.e., of achievement. From these samples an inference is made as to the person's ability to deal with similar situations at a later date. An achievement test is concerned with the student's ability to use in a meaningful situation the material covered in a given course; it is unquestionably prognostic of later success in this and related activities. Intelligence tests, on the other hand, presumably assay present abilities having applicability in a wider range of activities than those specifically related to a given course, but certainly the courses a student has taken can be expected to contribute to this performance. What would a curriculum be for if it did not contribute to intelligent behavior?

Among the severest critics of the orientation of present-day intelligence tests are Davis (1948) and Eells (1953) who argue that test designers have accentuated the socioeconomic differential in IQ by choosing items that are unfair to children of low socioeconomic status. They point out that, while test makers deliberately choose items that do not discriminate between boys and girls on the supposition that the two sexes are of equal ability, they, on the contrary, deliberately choose items that discriminate on the basis of scholastic success which, because of the unsuitability of school material to children of the lower class, is the equivalent of deliberately seeking items that discriminate against them. In other words, they feel that the IQ differential among the social classes reflects primarily a cultural bias in the test material rather than a real difference in ability.

Davis and Eells argue further that this unfairness of the tests for children of lower socioeconomic status has resulted in considerable harm to them. Because the tests are loaded with material that is relatively meaningless in terms of their interests and background, these children are first mislabeled as dull which leads the teacher to expect relatively little from them and to deny them the benefit of more meaningful learning experiences. Soon everyone, including the children themselves, is convinced of their dullness and, as a result, they are deprived of the opportunity of achieving the success that could be theirs were new objectives and new approaches to be stressed.[9] Davis and Eells present as a solution the Davis-Eells Games (1952), in the construction of which they attempted to abandon the conventional middle-class-oriented emphasis on academic and verbal material and to emphasize instead practical problems presumably fair to all cultural and socioeconomic groups.

The answer to the Davis-Eells arguments involves many considerations. There is, in a sense, some validity to the charge that children from the lower socioeconomic classes are undermeasured as to intellectual potential by current tests and, conversely, that children of higher socioeconomic backgrounds are overmeasured. The whole problem stems from the fact that we cannot measure intelligence directly but must estimate it indirectly through performance on tasks calling for intelligent behavior. As a result, we measure ability rather than capacity, what has been learned rather than what can be learned: this is undeniable—and unavoidable.

[9] The same argument can be used for the child who has an educational problem. A child with a reading difficulty, for instance, would tend to have a low IQ score, and as a result the teacher is not likely to see his need for remedial work which would permit him to improve his academic performance and his intelligence-test score. The same can be said for the creative child.

That IQ differences exist among the various socioeconomic groups has been shown repeatedly. In the Harvard Growth Studies, for example, the children of white-collar parents had an average IQ of 108, while children of unskilled parents had an average IQ of 96. In the study by McGehee and Lewis (1942) professional parents were found to produce two-and-one-half times their proportionate share of superior children while unskilled day-laborers produced only one third of their quota.

The interpretation of this IQ differential, however, is another matter. The basic question to be answered is what purpose do we expect intelligence tests to serve? If we are interested in the testee's true intelligence (whatever that means), it seems obvious that our present tests are not fair to children of the lower socioeconomic strata; but if we are interested in IQs for what they lead us to expect by way of academic and occupational performance, our present tests reflect a relatively appropriate differential. No doubt we could select items on which children from the various socioeconomic levels would perform equally well, but surely many arguments could be advanced to the effect that this would not give a correct picture of the relative intelligence of the various groups. Whereas current tests may not give a valid measure of the intelligence of children with extremely poor or extremely good background, the extent of the adjustment that could be made to narrow down this difference before discrimination in the opposite direction sets in is difficult to establish. Kingsley and Garry (1957), for instance, point out that this discrimination resulting from the nature of the content of the tests is probably not as important a factor of bias against children of lower socioeconomic status as differences in motivation and personality. Should we, while we are at it, make adjustments in these areas also? Others have questioned the validity of making such adjustments; Stroud (1956) argues that "It makes no sense to say he is intelligent despite our inabilities to detect it, no more than to say a child who is stunted in growth is of normal size only he doesn't show it." He also suggests that the limitations of these children do not end with poor performance on intelligence tests. The point is well stated by Anastasi (1953):

> Cultural differences in information, motivation, and work habits manifested in test performance also influence the individual's overall development. Removing the culturally biased items from a test does not eliminate cultural differences in behavior. The criteria against which the tests are validated are themselves culturally loaded and "intelligence tests," are operationally meaningless unless defined in terms of such criteria. [p. 152]

The solution proposed by Davis and Eells has also been questioned; not only have Tyler (1953) and Darley (1952) criticized the methodology of the study upon which the Davis-Eells Games were based, but Russell (1956) found that they did not give as good a prediction of reading progress in first grade as the Stanford-Binet. Rosenblaum et al. (1955) likewise concluded that the Davis-Eells Games did not "tap a hidden intellectual potential missed by other tests"; the children from the lower socioeconomic levels were lacking not in familiarity with the material but rather in ability to make correct associations and discriminations. It would seem that the Davis-Eells Games have sacrificed predictability without any clear-cut gain in the elimination of cultural bias.

In view of the modern emphasis on the whole child, the school should abandon a concept of intelligence so narrow that it relates almost exclusively to the ability to do schoolwork as presently structured in American classrooms. Teachers need a broader basis that will allow them to make use of a variety of teaching techniques for the self-fulfillment of each and every child. Certainly, educators must divest them of any notion of intelligence as innate ability. In the meantime, caution in the interpretation of the results of testing the intelligence of children of different backgrounds seems in order.

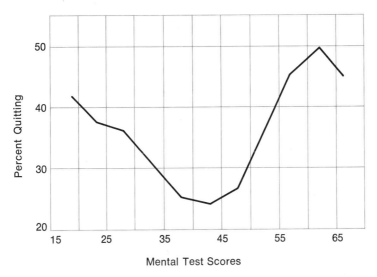

FIGURE 9-4   Relation between intelligence and job turnover. (After Scott, 1931.)

RELATION TO VOCATIONAL ADJUSTMENT

Intelligence tests are also of considerable value in predicting vocational success, especially from the standpoint of predicting what the examinee is not likely to be successful in doing because of too little or too much intelligence. A person with limited intelligence is not likely to achieve success as an engineer, nor is the genius likely to achieve success as a file clerk. This is illustrated in Figure 9-4 (Scott, 1931), showing how labor turnover increases with deviations, both positive and negative, from what might be considered an optimal ability level for maximum satisfaction in a given job. The role of intellectual limitations in vocational success is obvious in the case of the feebleminded. As anyone connected with the training of the mentally retarded can testify, not only is their learning very slow but there is also a very real limit in the level of complexity of the tasks they can master. Vanuxem's well-known study (1925) of the difficulty of training feebleminded women to do ordinary chores is reproduced in part in Table 9-1 to illustrate the point.

TABLE 9-1

RELATION BETWEEN MENTAL AGE AND LEARNING
IN FEEBLEMINDED WOMEN*

Mental Age	Task	Time or Trials to Learn
Below 2	Fetching and carrying a single object	15 trials
2—2–11	Weeding one kind of weed	3 days
3—3–11	Gathering one kind of fruit or vegetable	3 days
	Gathering several kinds of fruit or vegetable	5 days
	Sorting and hanging clothes	5 days
	Drying and putting away dishes	17 trials
4—4–11	Simple handwashing of clothes	7 days
	Dishwashing	18 trials
5—5–11	General handwashing of clothes	8 days
	Preparing vegetables for table use	8 days
	Bedmaking	52 trials

* From Vanuxem (1925), by permission of the Bureau of Publications, Teachers College, Columbia University.

Further evidence of the relationship between vocational and intellectual status comes from the study of the Army General Classification Test scores of World War II draftees classified according to preinduction occupation (Stewart, 1947). The data in the accompanying chart (See Figure 9-5), and similar findings by Simon and Levitt (1950), point to a steady progression in intellectual caliber with increases in occupational status from unskilled labor to the professions. Furthermore, even within a given occupation, progress is associated with increases in intelligence, and top-level accountants, for instance, score higher than those whose chores consist largely of bookkeeping. On the other hand, there is a wide range of IQ's within any one occupational group, and the overlap from one occupational group to another is such that the most intelligent la-

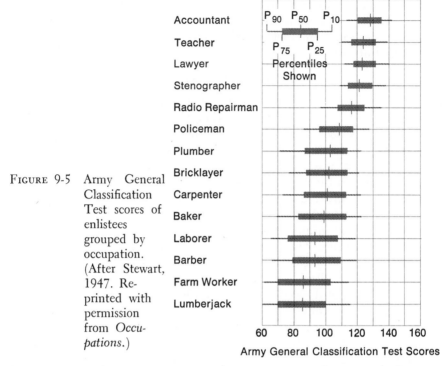

FIGURE 9-5 Army General Classification Test scores of enlistees grouped by occupation. (After Stewart, 1947. Reprinted with permission from *Occupations*.)

borer may well be more intellectually adequate than the least intelligent member of any profession.

RELATION TO MORAL ADJUSTMENT

Intelligence is also related to moral adjustment, although since adjustment is more a matter of the satisfaction of one's needs than of mental alertness, the relationship is far from perfect. Nevertheless, Terman, for instance, found 85 percent of his gifted subjects to score above the average of an unselected group in tests of moral knowledge and conduct. Hartshorne and May (1928) found a correlation of .50 between scores of intelligence and honesty, and numerous investigations, including those of Glueck (1959), have found delinquency to be more prevalent among children of below-average IQ.

The antecedents of this relationship are probably multiple rather than single. The higher incidence of delinquency among children of low intellectual status may reflect in part the greater ability of bright children to avoid detection and/or the greater likelihood of their having influential parents who can get them out of the hands of the law when they get caught. It is also true that not only can they foresee consequences more clearly but they generally find it easier than the dull to satisfy their needs through the usual channels of socially acceptable behavior. Furthermore, whereas bright children tend to come from homes whose values are generally in harmony with those of society in general, dull children often come from homes whose moral and social code is in direct conflict with that of society.

EVALUATION OF INTELLIGENCE TESTS

The previous discussion suggests that, despite their weaknesses, intelligence tests serve a definite function, particularly with respect to the work of the school. Certainly, they are not magic nor do they give foolproof answers to all the questions relating to ability but there is considerable empirical as well as theoretical evidence of their overall effectiveness.

They are, on the other hand, subject to a number of limitations which need to be clearly understood if we are to avoid their misuse. What they measure, for example, is a controversial matter and when we say that a person is lacking in intelligence, we are not clear as to the specific nature of his deficiencies. There are indications that they are essentially oriented toward the prediction of scholastic success and, in a sense, they undermeasure children, who, because of cultural differences or academic difficulties do not do well in school or whose talents lie outside the traditional mold of convergent thinking. This may lead to incorrect expectations from such children and result in harm to them. Furthermore, that fact that the IQ is only relatively constant complicates the problem of using it effectively. It tells us only what the child is likely to be able to do, provided conditions remain the same, but our prediction could be in considerable error under a different set of conditions. Intelligence tests measure only a relatively narrow segment of the many factors typically involved in school performance. There is an urgent need to incorporate into our measure of academic and vocational potential more of the factors postulated by Guilford, and especially the aptitudes and talents associated with different cultural backgrounds.

Nevertheless, intelligence tests are indispensable as scientific tools in the hands of the teacher or administrator who uses them for the purpose for which they were designed and interprets the results with caution and in relation to other aspects of the whole child. When used in this way, they form the basis for dealing with the child at his own level. The school's primary concern is to help the child make the most of his capabilities; intelligence tests, although in need of improvement, are the best indicator of these capabilities currently available.

CONSTANCY OF THE IQ

The question of the constancy of the IQ has received a great deal of attention, for the very usefulness of the IQ rests upon the assumption that it will remain relatively constant over the years, an assumption which is generally sustained for the majority of individuals. Whereas there is considerable empirical as well as theoretical evidence to indicate that such consistency is far from absolute, the dull child generally becomes the dull adult, the gifted child, the gifted adult. This does not imply that, if a determined effort were made, considerable change in IQ could not be effected.

There is considerable empirical evidence pointing to sizable IQ changes occurring over a period of years. Honzik et al. (1948) found that between the ages of six and eighteen, 60 percent of the group changed 15 or more IQ points and 9 percent actually changed 30 or more IQ points. Bayley (1949, 1955) reports similar IQ changes. Lack of constancy of the IQ over the years is also evident in the correlations obtained in the Harvard Growth Study (Dearborn et al., 1938). (See Table 9-2.)

TABLE 9-2

CORRELATION OF IQs AT DIFFERENT AGES
WITH THOSE OBTAINED AT AGE 16*

Age	Boys	Girls
7	.58	.54
8	.64	.58
9	.58	.53
10	.74	.70
11	.75	.73
12	.79	.78
13	.78	.81
14	.83	.82
15	.90	.91

* From Dearborn et al. (1938).

That the IQ does not remain exactly constant over the years should come as no surprise; fluctuations can be expected to occur for a number of reasons ranging from the unreliability of the test, the effects of practice or other factors operating from one test to another, to differences in the content of the tests in relation to the various abilities of the testee. The latter is of particular importance when the results of childhood tests with their emphasis on sensori-motor tasks are compared with those of later tests where the emphasis is on abstract reasoning. Actually, the correlation between the IQ of infants and their IQ a few years later is typically negative. As pointed out by Jones (1954), it is not until the age of twelve months that this correlation reaches zero and then begins to become positive. It is not until the fourth year that any degree of stability in the IQ is attained and certainly, for the first year at least, a better indication of the infant's subsequent IQ can be obtained by testing the mother. Various attempts have been made to supplement or to correct infant test scores to make them more predictive of later IQ, but, as Bayley (1955) points out, eventually investigators ran across the hard reality that infants exhibit a very limited range of behaviors beyond sensori-motor functioning upon which to base an estimate of intellectual ability.[10] She suggests that instead of continuing to think of intelligence as an integrated or simple entity or capacity which grows through childhood by steady accumulation, intelligence is better seen as a dynamic succession of developing functions with the more advanced and complex functions in the hierarchy depending on the prior maturing of the earlier and simpler ones.

A good part of the fluctuation occurring in the IQ stems from the fact that no test is completely reliable. Thus (assuming no practice effects) we would expect one third of the testees on the average test to gain upon retest up to five IQ points and another third to lose up to five points. Another 14 percent would lose from five to ten points while 14 percent would gain from five to ten points, and the other 2 percent at each end would gain or lose more than ten IQ points. (See Figure 9-6.) These fluctuations can be expected on the basis of chance alone and have nothing whatsoever to do with any change occurring as a result of an increased or decreased rate of intellectual growth. They simply reflect fluctuations to be expected as a result of the limitations of the measuring instruments, the carelessness of the psychometrist, and fluctuations within the testee arising from fatigue, loss of motivation, distractibility, and other personal factors. It is also possible that mental growth, like physical growth, goes by spurts and stops.

In addition, directional shifts in IQ may result from exposure to special environmental influences. Thus, since most IQ tests include vocabulary questions, one might raise his IQ if he were to be subjected to intensive vocabulary drill. Whether such directional shifts in IQ actually represent a shift in intelligence or just an invalidation of the norms of the test is the crucial question around which the whole controversy of the constancy of the IQ revolves. Thus, to use an extreme example, coaching on the items of the test would certainly result in increased IQ but would not imply a corresponding increase in intelligence, since we could

[10] On the other hand, physicians have been reporting correlations of around .5 between IQ at six months and at five years. Apparently, knowledge of neurology and physiology is providing them with valuable cues not available to psychologists. (Knobloch, H., and B. Pasamanick, "Predicting intellectual potential in infancy," *American Journal of Diseases of Children*, 106: 43–51, 1963.)

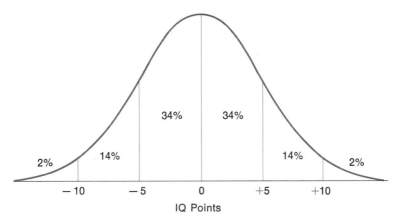

FIGURE 9-6 Theoretical distribution of changes in IQ upon retest due to test unreliability.

hardly assume its applicability to a wide variety of situations calling for intelligent behavior.

A significant study is that of Sontag (1958) who investigated the factors concomitant to directional shifts in IQ from infancy to ten years of age. He found that twice as many boys as girls were among the top gainers in IQ while twice as many girls were in the group of greatest decline in mental growth rate. Emotional dependence upon the parents during the age from three to six was found to be detrimental to intellectual growth; many of the girls revealed what Sontag called a "slide into femininity," i.e., an adoption of the adult female role in which achievement is important only in the area of being more feminine and charming. In contrast, the child who learns to meet some of his needs through aggressive, competitive problem solving is apparently laying the groundwork for a high need for achievement which, in turn, relates to an accelerated mental growth rate. The traits associated with gains in IQ included aggressiveness, self-initiation, competitiveness, and interest in problem solving—all of which are masculine traits. Of special significance in this connection is the growing belief that intellectual development can be promoted through early stimulation.

THE ROLE OF HEREDITY AND ENVIRONMENT

The problem of the constancy of the IQ is directly related to the relative influence of heredity and environment upon intelligence. If heredity were the sole determinant of intelligence, the limits of intelligence would be set at conception and IQ fluctuations would be restricted to those arising from the unreliability of the tests and the irregularities connected with the spurts and stops of the mental growth curve. If, on the other hand, intelligence is readily susceptible to environmental influences, additional fluctuations can be expected from test to test as a result of the actual changes in intelligence coinciding with changes in the adequacy of the environment.

The relative influence of heredity and environment upon intelligence has been the topic of considerable investigation since the turn of the century. Actually the problem is incapable of solution because studies do not touch upon the problem of heredity and environment but simply upon the susceptibility of the content of a particular test to environmental forces. The difficulty stems from our inability to measure intelligence except indirectly through performance, which incorporates both an inherited and a learned component so closely entwined that their relative influence in making this performance possible cannot be separated.

Considerable research evidence is available to show that intelligence runs in certain families more so than in others. In the Kallikak study (Goddard, 1912), for example, only 46 out of the 480 descendants of the son Kallikak fathered through a feebleminded girl were judged to be normal, whereas the descendants of his regular family were all essentially normal. At the other end of the continuum, for every 15 of Terman's gifted, there was at least one relative in the Hall of Fame. Nearly one third of them came from homes of professional parents, even though the professional group constituted less than 3 percent of the population studied. On the other hand, these children had definite environmental advantages; one quarter of them had at least one parent with a college degree, and the homes from which they came were rated especially high in parental supervision. Another factor here is the definite tie-in between socioeconomic status and complications of pregnancy and childbirth (with resulting psychological malfunction in the offspring). Pasamanick et al. (1956), for example, found a significant relationship between inadequate prenatal care and the occurrence of mental defects and psychiatric disorders in the child. Also of definite pertinence are the patterns of child-rearing and family atmosphere associated with socioeconomic status. Lower-class parents tend to discourage mealtime conversation, for instance, a practice likely to have detrimental effects upon intellectual development (Milner, 1951). Lower-class mothers also tend to interact less with their children than middle-class mothers (Zunich, 1963).

Pointing to the effect of environment on intelligence are the many studies showing IQ gains connected with the placement of foster children into good homes (Freeman et al., 1928; Burks, 1928). The Iowa studies (Skeels, 1940; Wellman, 1945; Skodak and Skeels, 1949), reported substantial gains in IQ resulting from nursery and other preschool experiences. These studies have been severely criticized on a number of counts centering on the validity of the testing (McNemar, 1940; Woodworth, 1941; Kirk, 1948). It is well known, for example, that young children are very negative, particularly when treated in an impersonal manner as might occur in an orphanage, and very often refuse to answer questions even when they can. In Mayer's study (1935), for example, 75 percent of his sample of two-, three-, and four-year-olds showed negativism during testing. Rust (1931) found that lessened resistance enabled some children to pass on later presentation up to 58 percent of the items they had refused to answer, with a resulting gain of as much as 35 IQ points. McHugh (1945) found essentially similar results. It should also be noted that orphanage children tend to be markedly retarded in language, perhaps because of lack of association with adults (Moore, 1947), and that Dawe (1943) was able to raise by some 15 points the IQ of orphanage children by giving them some 50 hours of training in the use of language.

The most pertinent evidence on the relative role of heredity and environment on intelligence comes from the study of the similarity in IQ of twins. Identical twins, even when separated at birth, show remarkable similarity in IQ (Newman et al., 1937). On the other hand, adoption tends to be into homes of relatively equal stimulation value; when the separation involves sizable environmental differences, the similarity in IQ decreases correspondingly. Because tests of "intelligence" are heavily loaded with academic content, differences in schooling, for example, are bound to produce differences in IQ; whether this implies corresponding differences in intelligence is a matter of debate. A child's IQ is supposed to reflect his intellectual status and it does this rather well for the majority of children, but it must be remembered that the IQ, like any other score, is valid only to the extent that the background of the examinee is comparable to the background of the group upon which the test was standardized. Consequently, care must be taken in interpreting the IQs of children whose backgrounds are grossly different from the average.

The research evidence on the subject lends itself to conflicting interpretation. It certainly does not permit us to specify the relative contribution of heredity and environment to mental status or to approximate the extent of the constancy of the IQ to be expected under various conditions of environmental differences. We must recognize that constancy in IQ is frequently the direct reflection of the constancy of the environment impinging upon the average individual. It does not speak to the changes that could take place were the environment to be made drastically different. It does not preclude, for example, the possibility that a systematic attempt at early stimulation might provide an entirely different set of results. Perhaps the failure of many studies to promote greater IQ gains simply reflects the ineffectiveness of our current approach. It is also very possible that our efforts have not been exerted at "the most teachable moment." As we have seen in Chapter 5, there are definite indications that the preschool years are the most academically and intellectually profitable years in the individual's life and that, consequently, making the child's early environment more intellectually stimulating would result in a faster rate of intellectual development and a higher final level of intellectual capacity (Moore, 1963; Hunt, 1961; Chauncey, 1963; Fowler, 1962). This would be of particular significance for the culturally disadvantaged.

Teachers and especially parents need to concentrate on providing each child with a psychologically productive environment within the framework of which he can realize his maximum potentialities in the pursuit of self-actualization. On the other hand, they need to be cautioned against applying pressures to make the child perform like a genius which he was never intended to be; the sooner they accept the fact that there are limitations in intelligence as there are in all areas, the more effective they will be in helping children attain their maximum growth. In the meantime, the amenability of intellectual development to systematic early stimulation is an exciting possibility deserving of our best research and pedagogical efforts.

HIGHLIGHTS OF THE CHAPTER

The emphasis on the learning of academic material in the classroom makes intelligence a topic of primary importance to the teacher. This chapter considered some of the major aspects of intellectual growth as it relates to the work of the classroom.

[a]

Mental development is characterized by an increase in the use of language and in the ability to remember and to reason. A major contribution in the area of intellectual growth is Piaget's imaginative exploration of the development of logical concepts in children, particularly as they relate to causality.

[b]

Mental growth tends to be relatively constant until the early teens; then it tapers off, eventually reaching a peak in the middle twenties, and finally undergoing a gradually accelerating decline. The age at which intellectual growth reaches its peak revolves around the question of what we mean by intelligence.

[c]

There is considerable disagreement among psychologists as to the definition of intelligence as well as to its nature and its components. The concept of intellectual capacity as something one develops has placed emphasis on the operational definition of intelligence as intelligent behavior. It has also placed emphasis on the amenability of intelligence to improvement through intellectual stimulation in the early years of life.

[d]

A particularly significant contribution to the modern conception of human intelligence is Guilford's structuring of the intellect in terms of processes, contents, and products in a three-way solid model comprising 120 factors. His approach highlights the inadequacy of the traditional IQ, especially from the standpoint of its disregard of the dimensions of divergent thinking and of the nonintellective factors. It points to a definite need for an expansion of the concept of intellectual potential beyond that measured by current tests of "intelligence."

[e]

The mental age refers to the level and the IQ to the rate of one's mental development. The IQ follows a normal distribution with 100 accepted as the average, and some two thirds of American-born whites having IQs within the range from 84 to 116.

[f]

Intelligence tests are particularly useful in connection with the work of the school, e.g., in enabling the teacher to set classroom experiences at the level of the child's insights, to determine what can be expected of him, and to predict his future academic success. The teacher's concept of both intellectual and academic excellence must be broadened.

[g]

The IQ is relatively constant under the usual environmental conditions confronting the average child. Recent developments present exciting possibilities for promoting the child's intellectual development through systematic early stimulation.

SOURCES OF RELATED MATERIAL

Bayley, Nancy, "On the growth of intelligence," Amer. Psychol., 10: 805–818, 1955.

Bruner, Jerome, "The course of cognitive growth," Amer. Psychol., 19: 1–15, 1964.

Burt, Cyril, "The inheritance of mental ability," Amer. Psychol., 13: 1–15, 1958.

——, "Is intelligence distributed normally?" Brit. J. statist. Psychol., 16: 175–190, 1963.

Cattell, Raymond B., "Theory of fluid and crystallized intelligence; A critical experiment," J. educ. Psychol., 54: 1–22, 1963.

Clarke, P. R. F., "Complexities in the concept of intelligence," Psychol. Rep., 11: 411–417, 1962.

Combs, Arthur W., "Intelligence from a perceptual point of view," *J. abnorm. soc. Psychol.*, 47: 662–673, 1952.

Eells, Kenneth, "Some implications for school practice of the Chicago studies of cultural bias in intelligence tests," *Harv. educ. Rev.*, 23: 284–297, 1953.

Fromm, Erika, and L. D. Hartman, *Intelligence: A Dynamic Approach*. New York: Doubleday & Company, Inc., 1955.

Fuller, J. L., *Nature and Nurture: A Modern Synthesis*. New York: Doubleday & Company, Inc., 1954.

Guilford, J. P., "The structure of the intellect," *Psychol. Bull.*, 53: 267–293, 1956.

————, *The Nature of Human Intelligence*. New York: McGraw-Hill Publishing Company, Inc., 1967.

Hunt, J. McV., "How children develop intellectually," *Children*, 11: 83–91, May-June, 1964.

Jenkins, J. J., and D. G. Paterson (eds.), *Studies in Individual Differences: The Search for Intelligence*. New York: Appleton-Century-Crofts, 1961.

Jones, H. E., "The environment and mental development," in L. Carmichael (ed.), *Manual of Child Psychology*. New York: John Wiley & Sons, Inc., 1954. Pp. 631–696.

Michael, W. B., et al., "J. P. Guilford: Psychologist and teacher," *Psychol. Bull.*, 60: 1–34, 1963.

Meyers, C. E., and H. F. Dingman, "The structure of abilities at the preschool ages: Hypothesized domain," *Psychol. Bull.*, 57: 514–532, 1960.

Olin, E. G., "Maternal language styles and their implications for children's cognitive development," *Amer. Psychol.*, 20: 540, 1965.

Stroud, James B., "The intelligence test in school use: Some pertinent issues," *J. educ. Psychol.*, 48: 77–86, 1957.

Wann, Kenneth, et al., *Fostering Intellectual growth in Young Children*. New York: Teachers College, Columbia University, 1962.

QUESTIONS AND PROJECTS

1

[a] Evaluate: The evidence of the constancy of the IQ bears a direct relationship to the constancy of the environment and to the susceptibility of test items to environmental influences and only an indirect relationship to the constancy of the individual's intelligence.

[b] What are some of the educational and sociological implications of the recent views on the role of environmental influences on the development of the intellect?

[c] What evidence do we have of the effectiveness of the various programs designed to promote intellectual and academic adequacy among the culturally disadvantaged? On what premise do they base their general approach?

[d] To what extent should nonintellective factors (for example, motivation) be considered part of "intelligence"? How might the school promote and capitalize on the nonintellective talents of children?

2

Insofar as it is known, what is the neurophysiological basis of intelligence? What research has been done in this area?

3

Make a list of some of the better known tests of intelligence. Check in Buros' *Mental Measurement Yearbooks* and other sources for an evaluation of these instruments. Check in the manuals for evidence of validity.

CHAPTER 10

Individual
Differences

Fortunately, the demands to educate everyone
up to the level of his ability and the demand
for excellence in education are not incompatible. We must honor both goals. We must
seek excellence in a context of concern for all.
*The Rockefeller Report
on Education, 1958, p. 22*

Dedication to the philosophy of equal educational opportunity does not
mean the *same* education for all. On the other hand, trying to be all
things to all children in the face of the marked differences that exist
among them has complicated the task of the school to the point where
it has not been particularly effective with a sizable portion of them.
Some administrators have become reconciled to the view that only so
much can be done and that inevitably someone will suffer; others,
spurred by pressures and criticisms, have tried various innovations with
varying degrees of success. Common among the latter are the special
programs for exceptional children. What needs to be recognized is that
everyone is, in a sense, exceptional and in need of a special program,
for, as any classroom teacher will testify, there is no typical child for
whom a standard program would be suitable without alteration.

RANGE OF INDIVIDUAL DIFFERENCES

Everyone recognizes that individuals differ from one another; seldom appreciated, however, is the extent to which people differ, especially with respect to psychological traits where differences are not as obvious as in the physical domain. Although this discussion will be oriented primarily toward differences relating to the learning of academic material, we might review briefly some of the highlights of differences in other areas.

PHYSICAL DIFFERENCES

Individual differences in physical size are particularly evident at the approximate age of puberty when some youngsters are nearly twice as tall and twice as heavy as others of the same age and sex. Vast differences also exist in physical fitness, motor coordination, and motor proficiency.

SEX DIFFERENCES

Males are generally taller, heavier, and stronger than their female counterparts; females, on the other hand, mature earlier. Boys tend to surpass girls in spatial and mechanical aptitude while girls show a definite language superiority from infancy. Girls get better grades but they generally do not do as well on standardized measures, especially in high school. They tend to be more motivated and cooperative, perhaps because school materials and procedures are more compatible with the feminine personality.

The interpretation of certain sex differences is complicated by the nature of the measurement through which they are determined. As we have noted, intelligence test makers deliberately mask sex differences in intelligence. Differences are also due, at least in part, to social expectations and cultural pressures incorporated in the self-concept. Girls are generally not subjected to the same pressures to achieve; they tend to lead more sheltered lives, and to have more restricted experiences. Up to recently, at least, girls were not supposed to be good in science and mathematics; they were not supposed to surpass boys, whether in sports, achievement, or brain power. In the Sontag (1958) study, girls were found to display a declining IQ pattern; Terman's sample of 1000 gifted children consisted of 120 boys for every 100 girls.

Girls are more emotionally and socially mature than boys of the same age; they display greater social sensitivity and greater skill in interpersonal relations. They tend to be more quiet, docile, friendly, and responsive to social demands—perhaps because of inherited predispositions (see Chapter 5), perhaps because of social expectations, or even because civilized culture is more compatible with certain aspects of the feminine social pattern. On the other hand, the aggressiveness and rebelliousness characteristic of the masculine role in our culture are undoubtedly nurtured by social expectations.

AGE DIFFERENCES

Physical height curves extending from birth to maturity follow the expected pattern of progressive, although not smooth, growth with gradual tapering off in the late teens. Weight curves reach their peak later. The decline with age in physical competence varies from function to function; agility and fine muscular precision tend to decline sooner than gross muscular strength, for example. There is, of course, a decline in sensory acuity. Research suggests that only a minor decline in mental functioning occurs till middle age, that a good part of the later decline stems from an increase with age in personal rigidity and a decrease in motivation. Research has also shown that intellectual ability declines differentially with the various mental functions; in areas where knowledge and judgment play an important role, the greater experiential background of older subjects more than compensates for the loss, if any, in mental ability. Learning ability in certain areas remains good till late in life, but it falls off rather sharply when the material to be learned conflicts with old habits or evokes motivational resistance.

SOCIOECONOMIC DIFFERENCES

Socioeconomic differences have been noted in physical size, in physical and mental health, and especially in values, attitudes, and intellectual and academic status. Of particular importance from the standpoint of later development are the socioeconomic differences in prenatal care and child-rearing practices.

INTELLECTUAL AND ACADEMIC DIFFERENCES

Student differences in intellectual and academic potential are well known to teachers; indeed, each child is unique in the totality of his personality, and no two children, even with the same IQ, are intellectual equals, for the whole child is more than the summation of his characteristics. Thus, when, for the sake of discussion, reference is made to gifted children, no implication is made beyond their relative similarity with respect to intellectual ability, for even among the gifted tremendous differences exist.

To appreciate the range of individual differences among children in the classroom, we might consider the implications of the range of IQ noted in Chapter 9. If, for instance, we consider sixth grade children of CA = 12 and, for the sake of simplicity, ignore the top 2 percent and the bottom 2 percent of the distribution, we find the mental age of the remainder to range from 8 to 16 (see Figure 10-1). Thus, there are children in the average sixth grade class who are capable of working at the tenth grade level while others are fully challenged by second grade work. This range of ability exists in any subject area.

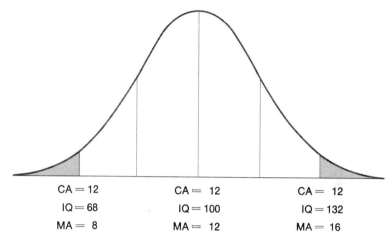

CA = 12	CA = 12	CA = 12
IQ = 68	IQ = 100	IQ = 132
MA = 8	MA = 12	MA = 16

FIGURE 10-1   Range of individual differences.

There is considerable overlapping from grade to grade. As shown in Figure 10-2, IQ data suggest that one sixth of the sixth graders are above the median for Grade 8 in ability and, conversely, one sixth of the eighth graders are below the median for Grade 6. There is a one third overlapping between consecutive grades. The upper 10 percent of high school seniors in any one area are more competent than the median college senior and, conversely, the lower 10 percent of college seniors fall below the median of high school seniors. In Project Talent, 20 percent of the ninth graders surpassed the twelfth grade average (Flanagan, 1964).

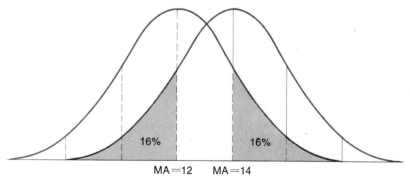

MA=12   MA=14

FIGURE 10-2   Degree of overlapping in ability between Grades 6 and 8.

Learned and Wood (1938) found that, if graduation from college had been based on accumulated knowledge rather than accumulated credits, the graduating class would have consisted of 28 percent of the seniors, 21 percent of the juniors, 19 percent of the sophomores, and 15 percent of the freshmen. The average score of the class that would have graduated had graduation been based on test performance would have fallen at the 84th percentile of the class that did graduate. Many other examples could be given, including the fact that there are high schools and colleges in America where the dullest pupil is a mental giant by comparison with the brightest student in some other high school or college. Suffice it to say that individual differences are real and that they are large. The more important question is what to do about them.

Our schools are not well organized to deal with such differences; children start the first grade at the same age, move one grade per year, use the same textbooks, follow the same curriculum, do the same assignments, and face the same standards—all much after the pattern of an industrial assembly line. Teachers, forgetting the importance of individual differences to the welfare of society, are frequently intolerant of children who drag or who race ahead of the others. It is difficult to adjust to the pace of each and every child, and it might be nice (perhaps) if everyone were exactly alike and equally capable of profiting from a standard program, just as it would be nice if everyone wore the same size shoes. But things being what they are, procrustean education is no more comfortable than procrustean shoes would be.

Yet despite all that is known about individual differences, many teachers still operate on the assumption that grade levels mean definite stages of educational achievement and that all children can do the work "if they will only apply themselves," or that, with large classes, there is nothing teachers can do about children who "can't" or "won't" learn. Both views are bad; the more or less inevitable outcome is that students become frustrated and apathetic, misbehave in the classroom, and even drop out of school. Gardner (1961), for example, sees the apathetic student who has to be trapped into learning as the obvious result of failure to individualize the school's program. Wolfle (1960) suggests that our sabre-tooth curriculum approach "where all the animals have to take all the subjects" may result in homogeneous mediocrity. Certainly, the same education for all is very likely to be an education for no one. Recent research suggests that inadequacy on the part of a minority of our students, far from being inevitable, may well be the natural outcome of inadequate background. A more suitable approach might well duplicate in human learning the success obtained by Skinner and others in animal learning. Such an approach would, perhaps, increase rather than decrease the range of individual differences but it would, at least, raise the bottom of the distribution.

DEALING WITH INDIVIDUAL DIFFERENCES

Although none of the many schemes advanced to deal with individual differences has been a complete solution to the problem of the classroom teacher faced with 30 or more children representing all possible combinations of differences, it is profitable to consider at least the major plans. Generally, these proposals fall in the category of promotion, instruction, and grouping.

PROMOTIONAL POLICIES

The oldest attempt at dealing with individual differences in the classroom revolved around what might be called rigid standards of grade placement. A child was retained in a given grade until he had mastered its content and, conversely, he could get a double promotion if he had already mastered enough of the content of the grade following that which he had just completed.

Acceleration was particularly common in the old one-room school where a gifted child could go through the first eight grades in perhaps four or five years. In fact, repeated double promotions could result in college graduation perhaps as early as age fifteen. It has been frowned upon in recent years on the argument that it overemphasizes the intellectual and the academic at the expense of the other phases of the child's all-round development and that the accelerated child may become a misfit from the standpoint of physical, social, and emotional adjustment.

At the other end of the continuum are those whose work is below par and who, according to the older view on the subject, needed to be retained lest they got hopelessly bogged down and interfered with the progress of students in the next grade. Before we proceed to a discussion of the validity of this position, let us consider the question: "Why fail students?" Whereas the specific answer to that question varies, the policy of failure "where warranted" is said by its advocates to serve three important functions:

[a] To motivate students who apparently will work only when the threat of failure is kept constantly before them. This is not true. Otto and Melby (1935), for example, found no difference in the achievement of children threatened with failure and those assured of promotion—and fortunately so, for it would be a sad commentary on the appropriateness of our curriculum and our methods if it were. Failure is a last-ditch attempt at motivation and it ought to be possible for the few teachers who still rely heavily on fear of failure as a motivational device to locate more positive measures.

[b] To maintain standards. Some people feel that the high school is losing its academic reputation by graduating students who have been

carried along for years, and community groups have on occasions demanded a return to the "good old standards" where one did not graduate without a certain amount of knowledge. They overlook the fact that the solution in those days consisted of forcing the student to drop out, sometimes long before he got to high school.

[c] To reduce the variability within the classroom. It is argued that his increased mental development and the general overview of the work will enable the child who is retained to do much better as he repeats the grade. This has not been realized in practice. As early as 1911, Keyes showed that repeaters do worse, rather than better, than they did the first time. Cook (1941) and Klene and Branson (1929) likewise showed that potential repeaters profited more from being promoted to the next grade than from being retained. Thus, Cook, in his comparison of schools with rigid standards as represented by an average retardation of nearly two years in Grade 7 with a matched sample of schools having liberal promotional policies with a corresponding average retardation of only .17 of a year, found a significant difference in achievement favoring the schools with lenient promotions; but he found no difference in the range of individual differences in the two sets of schools. Coffield and Blommers (1956) found that children who reached Grade 7 in eight years (because of failure) knew less than comparable children who had been promoted. Evidently, the standards of the school cannot be raised by accumulating the dullards any more than the standards of a ball team can be raised by keeping the unfit for an extra year or two. Of course, emphasis in school must be on the individual child but, if our concern *has* to be for the standards of the school, let us at least be logical and eliminate, not retard.

Also to be considered, in view of the modern emphasis on the total child, are the effects of retention on his personality. Although the evidence is not entirely conclusive, the consensus supports the statement by Goodlad (1952, p. 449) that "throughout the body of evidence runs a consistent pattern: undesirable growth characteristics and unsatisfactory school progress are more closely associated with nonpromoted children than with promoted slow-learning children." In view of his need to maintain a consistent self-image, the child who is retained is likely to see himself as dumb, tough, or unconcerned, as many teachers who have repeaters in their class can readily attest. Having been separated from the group to which they belong and being out of step physically, socially, and emotionally with the new group, these children find it difficult to get accepted and often react to the whole situation with discouragement, hostility, and misbehavior.

Evidence points to the fact that retention is not effective in reducing the range of individual differences and that it tends to have negative effects on academic achievement and personality development. It does not follow, however, that children should never be retained; no doubt a child who is retarded physically, socially, and emotionally as well as mentally and academically, may profit from being put into a somewhat younger age group; each case must be evaluated on its own merits. The decision to promote or to retain should be made only after consideration of all the factors—not just the academic—and generally the teacher should have to show cause why the child should be retained in terms of how he can be helped more by retention than by promotion. The important thing is not to promote or to retain but rather what the teacher does after having made this decision, for the element of failure is not eliminated by universal promotion. Unless the teacher is prepared to take the child at his level—as he must do with all the other children in the class—and make the necessary adjustment and adaptations of instructional methods and materials to bring the curriculum down to his level, the child had better be retained, for otherwise classwork will become progressively more baffling to him. If he has to be frustrated, it is debatable whether it is more devastating to be frustrated once a year or continually throughout each day of the year.

Retention should not be thought of as a form of punishment but rather as a matter of optimal grade placement for maximum growth. At all times, the child's instructional needs should take precedence over the teacher's convenience and, if by special help and remedial procedures, he can be kept with his group without taking too much of the teacher's time and energy away from the other children, he should be promoted. Furthermore, if he is to be retained, he should be prepared for the decision; it is especially important that the parents be in on the decision for their opposition might well render unwise an otherwise wise decision to retain.

To avoid the objections to complete failure, various compromises have been suggested, e.g., partial failure or even conditional failure where the child is given the option of attending summer school. A proposal that seems to have merit is that of having fewer promotion periods. A number of schools operating on a nongraded basis have a primary block consisting of six semesters which can be shortened or extended by two semesters before the child moves into Grade 4. There is no passing or failing: the child simply covers the material of the first three grades at his own speed. The effectiveness of these solutions varies from case to case but none can be considered a cure-all.

INSTRUCTIONAL PROCEDURES

Teachers are in a difficult position in that they have to get children of widely different ability and background up to grade standards by the end of the year. In other words, they have to extract similar performances out of children who are far from being similar. And they manage to do just that through the simple expedient of limiting their objectives. Thus, in spelling, the teacher announces that all the words children need to know for the examination are those in certain lists; in history, the material to be mastered to pass the course is found in the certain chapters of the prescribed text, and so on. Thus, whether it is the 100 addition facts or the work of Grade 9 algebra, it makes no difference if the bright child knows it all before he enrolls: he can sit and be bored while the teacher prods and pushes the dull past the finish line by the end of the year. For the same reason, teachers emphasize facts and other aspects of the course that can be memorized, since this is an

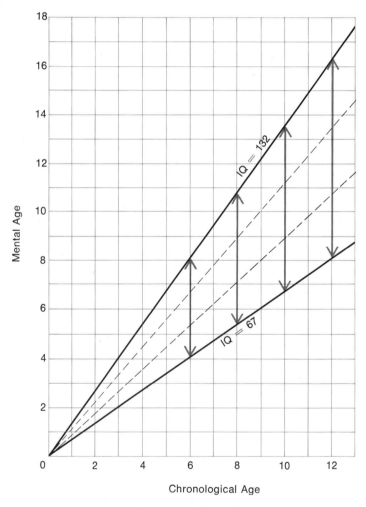

FIGURE 10-3   Increase in intellectual differences with age.

in which the gifted are grouped homogeneously for half a day and returned to their regular classroom for the other half.

[b] Grouping on the basis of mental ability gives some students a feeling of superiority and others a feeling of inferiority. This argument tends to overlook the fact that the gifted child can also feel superior as a result of his being cock-of-the-roost in an ungrouped class and that we have already accepted ability grouping for the retarded child.

[c] Grouping does not result in sufficient homogeneity to warrant the trouble, especially in a small school where there may not be enough students from whom to choose so as to effect any degree of homogeneity in the subgroups. Even when children are grouped according to ability, teachers still have to take care of individual differences in the various subject areas. This point is well taken. The ideal is to place each child in the educational setting that will give him the best opportunity to achieve optimal well-rounded growth, but one must not assume that ability grouping is the only way of dealing with children at their level. A competent teacher can make provision for differences among individual pupils whether his class is grouped according to ability or not; it is not uncommon to have students in the primary grades, for instance, sectioned into three ability levels for a particular activity and reshuffled among the groups for a different activity. Such subgrouping can be partially effective in that it takes maximum advantage of the benefits of homogeneity in grouping while maintaining the whole-group feeling. Of course, subgrouping entails certain difficulties but none is insurmountable. Teachers who have had experience with eight grades in an ungraded rural school feel little sympathy for the teacher of a single grade who finds the fact that his students do not happen to be of a single ability level in all subjects an insurmountable obstacle. The teacher who complains that he does not have time to individualize the work of the classroom needs to realize that he had better find time before minor troubles become real difficulties; after all, the number of children requiring extended special attention is generally relatively small.

Ability grouping is not an end in itself; it is a means which, some schools find, facilitates the teacher's task of dealing with children of widely different ability. When ability grouping is used, the term *ability* should be interpreted in the broad sense and made to include such factors as IQ, special aptitude, and special talents, past scholarship, motivation, perseverance, social competence, and general maturity.[1] Let us no longer ignore the creative child, for example. Admission to the various classes should involve an evaluation of each individual case on its own

[1] Perhaps the term *readiness* as defined in Chapter 5 would be more suitable than *ability*.

merits. What is even more important, however, is that all such alloca-tions be considered tentative and reversible. It should also be empha-sized that ability grouping implies a differentiated curriculum fitted to the abilities and needs of the group and of the individual students in the group; presenting the same material at a slower or faster pace just will not work.

THE GIFTED CHILD

The advent of the space race has once again focused attention on the gifted child who becomes alternately our most valuable natural re-source and the forgotten student. Because he is able to take care of him-self academically, he gets less attention from the teacher, and because he can get by without effort, he is not encouraged to develop his talents. Hollingworth (1926) estimated that children with IQs of 140 or better waste half their time in the usual classroom and those with IQs of 170 or better waste practically all their time. Terman and Oden (1947) noted that more than half of the children with IQs of 135 or above had already mastered the school's curriculum to a point two full grades— and some, three or four grades—beyond the ones in which they were enrolled. Some educators are convinced that, whereas we have accepted the idea of special provisions for the dull, we still discriminate against the bright, boring them, and causing them to seek outside of school the feeling of achievement and self-esteem we deny them in school. Many display signs of apathy, boredom, unhappiness, and even maladjust-ment. Nearly 15 percent of Terman's gifted did not go to college, for example, despite the fact that they averaged exactly the same on a con-cept mastery test as a group of Ph.D. candidates at a leading university; another 30 percent did not graduate. The result is a tremendous loss of the type of potential we can least afford to lose.

Generally speaking, the teacher in the regular classroom cannot take care of the gifted along with the average and the dull. As a result, the gifted are simply neglected. Often their intelligence is not even recog-nized, partly because many conceal their true ability so as not to appear different. Instead of being encouraged to make a contribution in keep-ing with their superior ability, they are often forced into habits of in-difference, carelessness, and indolence by being made to adjust their pace to that of the class.

Suggestions for doing something for the gifted child generally fall along one of three lines: acceleration, adaptation (or enrichment), and grouping. All three have merits and limitations and the most desirable procedure to follow depends on the particular situation. It must be em-phasized that intellectual superiority is a matter of degree and that it is impossible to devise a standard program that will take care of the needs of the gifted for, just like their more average counterparts, gifted children display individual differences in all areas, including the intellectual. The only saving feature is that they tend to possess ingenuity and initiative (when it has not been beaten out of them) so that, in contrast to duller children who often hang on to the teacher's neck like millstones, the bright can make their own adaptations of the curriculum when given the freedom and encouragement to do so. They tend to do well on independent research projects, for example.

Acceleration has definite possibilities. Allowing the gifted to go through the second and third grades in a single year, or to enter the first grade a little earlier, is often desirable, especially since many of them are superior in other aspects of growth as well as the intellectual and, therefore, fit in well with an older group. Not to be overlooked is the very real possibility that emotional and social development can be promoted through association with older children. Acceleration of the gifted is recommended by no less an authority than Terman (1954). Its advantages are relatively well documented in Pressey's comprehensive review of the literature on the subject (Pressey, 1949). Not all accelerates have turned out well but Pressey emphasizes the following: [a] Many of the failures were victims of exploitation by overambitious parents and/or unwise or excessive acceleration, or they were maladjusted children who would have been failures whether accelerated or not; [b] Maladjustment resulting from acceleration is far from inevitable, especially when adequate care in selection is exercised; [c] Maladjustment and waste can also result from holding back a child ready to be accelerated; and [d] The problem of the accelerate would be decreased further if acceleration were to become somewhat more prevalent as in the case where a whole class is accelerated together. According to McCandless (1957), research evidence indicates that the very superior child tends to benefit on all counts from a discreet application of special techniques such as acceleration (if done in a psychologically sophisticated way), segregation (with the same qualifier), and enrichment. Experience with war veterans and other college students has suggested that acceleration through college is also possible and, in many cases, desirable.

It seems that a much more flexible view of acceleration all across the board is indicated; not only can such acceleration save educational costs but, where warranted and wisely handled, it can do so without harm and with considerable benefit. It can, for example, add two or more years to the period of professional productivity.

Early admission of the gifted child to first grade on a selective basis is in order. The concept of the most teachable moment demands that the child who is ready to read at four or five not be delayed until he is six;

barring him from school on the basis of administrative expediency is simply psychological nonsense. Worcester (1956) found that children admitted earlier than normally did as well as their older classmates and suffered no ill effect from early admission. They were rated by their teachers as socially and emotionally adjusted; they displayed good motor coordination, were well accepted, and they liked school. In view of the unreliability of our present formal instruments for determining readiness, however, entrance into first grade might be based on long-term observation in kindergarten and nursery school; such an approach provides maximum flexibility in admission together with maximum accuracy in the appraisal of readiness. In keeping with the research evidence on the benefits of early stimulation as presented in Chapter 5, this approach should probably be extended into the early preschool period.

Progress through the elementary and the high school can also be accelerated. Early maturing gifted youngsters could easily complete junior high school in two years instead of three. The nongraded school has greater flexibility in this connection since acceleration is preferable to grade skipping—although children who have skipped a grade seem no worse for it. Early admission to college and the granting of college credit for special work done in high school are also definite possibilities. The program of the early admission of gifted high school students to college sponsored by the Fund for the Advancement of Education has shown that carefully selected high school students allowed to skip their senior year are at least as successful academically in their freshman year as their equally gifted age-mates granted regular admission one year later. The early entrants also show adequate social and emotional adjustment. The general consensus (e.g., The Fund, 1957; Shannon, 1957) is that the acceleration of gifted students carefully selected from the standpoint of intellectual and academic adequacy, emotional maturity, and freedom from excessive parental pressure does not harm them personally, socially, or academically.

Earning a college degree in three calendar years through heavier class loads, summer sessions, advanced credits, and credit by examination generally results in benefit rather than harm. Greater flexibility with prerequisites (especially prerequisites based on class standing alone) may be to the benefit of all; the Learned and Wood study (1938) has shown that the number of college credits accumulated are hardly indicative of student knowledge. Furthermore, if we believe in the benefits of outside employment in rounding out the student's education, we might also allow a greater flexibility in his outside work load. We might also rid ourselves of the belief that day-to-day attendance in formal course work is the only source of educational benefit. Flesher and Pressey (1955) found that outside employment had not affected adversely the health, schooling, or social life of wartime accelerates. They had participated somewhat less in undergraduate activities, but about twice as many as regular graduates had obtained further degrees, perhaps partly because of the greater challenge of their accelerated program.

Ability grouping has already been discussed; it has definite possibilities for dealing with the gifted and many school systems have successfully implemented a program of this sort. Not only does experimental evidence (Miles, 1954) tend to favor ability grouping from the standpoint of academic progress, but grouping is also endorsed by the gifted themselves (Goodenough, 1941). The general consensus is that, while not conclusive, the evidence concerning special classes "indicates certain advantages and minimizes the claimed disadvantages." (Norris and Noonan, 1941.) Of course, grouping is not sufficient in itself; its effectiveness depends on what adaptations of standards, materials, and methods are made to provide the gifted child with experiences at his level, and the extent to which this is done may account for the conflicting evidence as to the superiority of grouping over nongrouping. Partial grouping may be a satisfactory compromise in view of the arguments against complete segregation of the gifted.

Enrichment or adaptation of the material to the child's level of ability is a *must* whether or not he is accelerated, for the highly gifted child could not be accelerated enough without danger of social and emotional harm. Enrichment can take place in special classes or in the regular classroom where the child is encouraged to pursue the subject beyond the regular requirements. Unfortunately, although ideal in principle, enrichment as the sole means of dealing with the gifted is seldom adequate in practice. Too much effort is wasted by having the gifted child do the same work as the other children—in fact, often more of the same when he should be doing less—and the teacher is often too busy with the rest of the class to give the needed encouragement. Some schools allow gifted children to use the study period to work on projects of their own, but they are entitled to more positive direction from the teacher if they are to make the most of their abilities. Excusing them from routine work and allowing them to take an extra subject during the study hall is generally to be recommended wherever feasible, but probably the best approach involves a combination of acceleration, enrichment, and segregation. Most school systems of any size ought to be able to work out some arrangement along these lines.

THE RETARDED CHILD

The slow learner also has special needs but these are generally much more obvious to the teacher than those of the gifted child so that, whereas the gifted child is often neglected, the dull is constantly being prodded. Although this may lead him to greater use of his limited talents, it can also lead to frustration and maladjustment. The special provisions that need to be made for the dull child depend on the situation. It is generally agreed that for children whose IQs are below 70, special classes are preferable to attempts to deal with them in the regular classroom. What these children need is special help and understanding and especially freedom from the emotional distress that results from unrealistic demands. Teaching these children is not a matter of covering the same material at a slower rate. The curriculum must be oriented toward the specific and the concrete—with a strong vocational bent. It is also necessary that they be given practice in effective living under conditions of contentment. For children somewhat less retarded, ability grouping into special areas where their lack of intelligence will be less of a handicap is advisable, but it must not be assumed that the child will be good in shop or that he will have a lot of drive in motor mechanics simply because he lacks academic ability.

As pointed out in Chapter 9, Davis and Eells make a strong case for the slow learner from the lower socioeconomic strata. They point out that these children make slow progress in school, not so much because of lack of mental ability as because of the unsuitability of the middle-class oriented curricular diet served in our schools. Regardless of the validity of their contention, the fact that taking care of individual differences also implies orienting the curriculum toward the child's needs and purposes must not be overlooked. Special education may not accelerate the mental growth of the retarded child but it can facilitate achievement as well as personal and social adjustment. Such studies as that of Charles (1953), for example, have shown the overall adult record of a group of former students of special classes for the mentally deficient to be surprisingly good in view of the early prognosis.

THE ROLE OF THE TEACHER

None of the proposals we have discussed can by itself take care of the wide range of individual differences found in the classroom. Any administrative plan can perhaps facilitate the work of the classroom teacher but it cannot solve the problem for, in any grade—whether with liberal or strict promotion, whether with or without ability grouping—there will always be differences and, even if pupils were to be equated today, by tomorrow some would already have separated themselves from the rest. Perhaps the most significant factor in the adaptation of educational forces to individual differences is security on the part of the child; if he is open to experience and free to explore his environment, he will generally be able to make his own adaptations. The child in the process of *becoming* can be expected to make the most of environmental opportunities in developing his potentialities. He will still need sympathetic guidance in making his explorations more effective; he will need practice in library and study skills; he will need moral support as he develops the ability to take hold and to rely progressively more upon himself. But his own sense of self-propulsion will keep the need for outside help to a minimum and his ability to profit from such help to a maximum.

In the final analysis, it is the teacher who is the key to any plan for dealing with individual differences in the classroom, for it is he who has contact with the "customer." We need teachers who are not only familiar with the principles of individual differences and their implications for educational practice, but who are also sensitive to individual needs and are sufficiently dedicated to want to adjust requirements and standards to the level of the child. They also have to be ingenious in vitalizing the curriculum and competent in the use of pupil-centered techniques which can be more easily adapted to the differences in ability and background than the more regimented chapter-at-a-time approach. A project in transportation or sanitation, for instance, contains aspects that would challenge both the first grader and the college senior. Given a part in the selection of the goals for which they are to strive and provided with a classroom atmosphere of understanding, encouragement, and psychological safety, children can be depended upon to find their own level.

Teachers need to accept individual differences as both a challenge to their professional competence and a blessing. What if everyone were equally adept at mathematics and no one had any ability in motor mechanics? They need to know and to capitalize upon the resources of the class in connection with group projects as a means of building group spirit and of giving individual members a sense of worth and belonging through contributing to the attainment of group goals. There is also need for a much greater emphasis on independent work in which the student can not only take care of his special interests at his level of competence but can also develop initiative, self-direction, and self-dependence. Special hobby clubs, discussion groups, and various cocurricular activities, besides providing education geared to the level of interest and ability of individual children, also constitute a most worthwhile preparation for effective democratic living.

Unfortunately, a number of forces tend to operate to regiment education to the mass production philosophy of the industrial assembly line where the goal is to have the product emerge capable of meeting the specifications of quality control. These forces range from lock-step grade placement and school-wide standardized testing beginning in the primary division to standardized curricula punctuated by periodic examinations on prescribed content and complete with prescribed Carnegie-unit patterns and College Boards. Our schools overemphasize conformity: too frequently the marks of the good student are not resourcefulness, spontaneity, and intellectual curiosity but rather promptness, obedience, dependability, social sensitivity, and orientation toward *the* correct answer.

Getting acquainted with each and every child is obviously a prerequisite for dealing effectively with the problems of individual differences. This calls for the teacher to have at his disposal various test scores, family data, developmental history data, and any other information that will help him understand the child as a unique individual. Implied is the need for a thorough testing program and for mutual sharing of information with the home for the welfare of the child. An up-to-date, concise, and convenient cumulative folder where this information is readily available is essential and a lightened teacher-load would certainly help. The core program in which a high school teacher has the same students for two periods a day would help him become familiar with his students. There is also need for a wide variety of course offerings and cocurricular activities together with an effective guidance program that will orient students into areas of greatest suitability.

HIGHLIGHTS OF THE CHAPTER

An understanding and appreciation of the differences among and within individuals is fundamental to implementing the American ideal of providing each and every child with educative experiences geared to his potentialities, his interests, and his experiential background. The following are among the major points to be grasped:

[a]

People seldom appreciate the wide range of differences among individuals in all aspects of physical and psychological status. As an example of the many differences which exist in the classroom, the top third of the students in the typical Grade 6 class have the ability that would permit them to do above-average work in Grade 7 while the lowest third would probably do below-average work in Grade 5.

[b]

Our schools are not too adept at dealing with individual differences. Procrustean practices ranging from uniformity in age at entrance to standardization of curriculum and of textbooks, to single standards of evaluation, etc. are unfortunately too much part of the present pattern of classroom operation.

[c]

A number of schemes have been advocated for dealing with individual differences. Of these, ability grouping appears to be among the more effective. When used in high school and college, ability grouping should be based on special aptitude as well as past scholarship, general maturity, motivation, social competence, and other aspects of readiness peculiar to the individual case.

[d]

It is difficult to deal effectively with the gifted child within the framework of the regular classroom and special provisions in terms of acceleration and special grouping are generally necessary. Enrichment is essential regardless of what else is done.

[e]

The needs of the duller child in terms of special classes, special curricula, and special methods are generally more obvious.

[f]

None of the schemes discussed is, in itself, an adequate solution to the problem. At best, these plans can only facilitate the work of the teacher in dealing with the wide range of individual differences in the classroom, but it is the teacher who, in the final analysis, must adapt classroom experiences to fit the individual child.

SOURCES OF RELATED MATERIAL

Broudy, Harry S., et al., *Democracy and Excellence in American Secondary Education*. Skokie, Ill.: Rand McNally & Company, 1964.

Coffield, W. H., and P. Blommers, "Effects of non-promotion on educational achievement in the elementary school," *J. educ. Psychol.*, 47: 235–250, 1956.

Cook, Walter W., "Classroom methods: 1. The gifted and the retarded in historical perspective," *Phi Delta Kappan*, 39: 249–257, 1958.

——— and T. Clymer, "Acceleration and retardation," in N. B. Henry (ed.), *Individualizing Instruction*. 61st Yearbook, National Society for the Study of Education, Pt. I. Chicago: University of Chicago Press, 1962. Pp. 179–208.

Drews, Elizabeth M. (ed.), *Guidance for the Academically Talented Student*. Washington, D.C.: National Education Association and American Personnel and Guidance Association, 1961.

Flanagan, John C., et al., *The Talents of American Youth*. Boston: Houghton Mifflin Company, 1962.

Gardner, John W., *Excellence*. New York: Harper & Row, Publishers, 1961.

Henry, N. B. (ed.), *Individualizing Instruction*. 61st Yearbook, National Society for the Study of Education, Pt. I. Chicago: University of Chicago Press, 1962.

Lawson, D. E., "An analysis of historic and philosophic considerations for homogeneous grouping," *Educ. Adminis. Supervis.*, 43: 257–270, 1957.

Murphy, Gardner, *Human Potentialities*. New York: Basic Books, Inc., 1958.

Otto, Henry J., and D. M. Estes, "Accelerated and retarded progress," in C. W. Harris (ed.), *Encyclopedia of Educational Research*. New York: Crowell-Collier and Macmillan, Inc., 1960. Pp. 4–11.

Pressey, Sidney L., *Educational Acceleration: Appraisal and Basic Problems.* *Res. Monogr.*, No. 31. Columbus, Ohio: Bureau of Educational Research, Ohio State University, 1949.

Reynolds, M. C. (ed.), *Early School Admission for Mentally Advanced Children.* Washington, D.C.: Council for Exceptional Children, National Education Association, 1962.

Rockefeller Brothers Fund, *The Pursuit of Excellence: Education and the Future of America.* New York: The Fund, 1958.

Torrance, E. Paul, *Gifted Children in the Classroom.* New York: Crowell-Collier and Macmillan, Inc., 1965.

Tyler, Leona E., *The Psychology of Individual Differences.* New York: Appleton-Century-Crofts, 1965.

Vernon, P. E., "Education and the psychology of individual differences," *Educ. Rev.*, 20: 91–104, 1958.

QUESTIONS AND PROJECTS

1

[a] Comment on the "incompatibility" of providing for individual differences and maintaining academic standards.

[b] What might be the role of standardized tests of academic competence in the enforcement of standards at the local level?

[c] What are the assumptions as to the nature and purpose of American education underlying the current emphasis on academic excellence—complete with College Boards, National Merits, etc., as the basis for college admission?

2

Evaluate: Dull children should be allowed to leave school whenever the school feels they are accomplishing nothing for themselves and are interfering with the education of more capable students.

3

What specific adaptation of the curriculum and of teaching procedures can be made for children of the lower classes while keeping within the framework of the curriculum prescribed by school authorities?

4

To what extent is it legitimate for the teacher to set aside the curriculum of the school in order to attain individual objectives in other aspects of pupil growth?

PART III

The Process
of Learning

Covers the basic principles underlying the
promotion and measurement of academic
progress; considers both the traditional
aspects of classroom learning and the newer
emphasis on creativity, learning how to
learn, proactive inhibition, etc., and stresses
the role of measurement and evaluation as
integral components of the teaching-learning process.

CHAPTER 11

Considers points of both agreement and disagreement with respect to such aspects of learning as its definition and theoretical perspective, the "steps" of the learning process, the various "laws" of learning, and insight.

CHAPTER 12

Attempts to clarify a number of issues around which efficiency of learning revolves, e.g., the role of the teacher in the guidance of pupil learning, the relative effectiveness of the lecture and discussion and of massed and distributed practice, the nature of perception, and the use of audiovisual aids.

CHAPTER 13

Relates the problem of motivation to the promotion of academic learning, emphasizing the need for meaningful goals and the role of the teacher as the key to effective classroom motivation; discusses the various incentives available to the teacher within the framework of the satisfaction or nonsatisfaction of dominant motives.

CHAPTER 14

Introduces forgetting and transfer as interrelated (if not identical) phenomena, subject to the operation of essentially the same set of factors, and points out their educational implications.

CHAPTER 15

Clarifies the nature of problem solving by relating it to Dewey's steps of critical thinking and Piaget's analysis of the development of logical thought, and presents critical and creative thinking within the framework of Guilford's structure of the intellect; stresses the need to broaden the concept of "ability" beyond the confines of the traditional IQ, noting the special responsibility of the school in identifying and developing the creative potential of each and every child.

CHAPTER 16

Presents the basic concepts of measurement and evaluation of academic performance within the setting of the overall teaching-learning process, with special emphasis on the psychological implications of current grading and reporting practices.

CHAPTER 11

General Nature
of Learning

Learning is the heart of the educational enterprise.

Haggard, 1955, p. 156

Learning has always been of primary interest to teachers responsible
for having children master the academic curriculum of the school. It is
of even greater concern to the modern teacher interested in the child's
all-round growth, for the principles of learning apply just as surely to
emotions or personal adjustment as to the multiplication tables. Learning
is part of the larger and much more significant process of adjustment to
environmental demands. The orientation of the present chapter toward
the learning of academic material constitutes, therefore, an artificial
segmentation of behavior justifiable only for purposes of discussion. If
they are to fulfill their obligation of guiding pupil growth toward desirable goals, teachers must be familiar with the principles on the basis of
which desirable behavioral changes can be brought about.

THE NATURE OF LEARNING

To the layman, the nature of learning is clear: learning refers to the acquisition of knowledge and skills. The psychologist is far less sure. He can immediately reject the layman's definition as naïve and generally reflecting the viewpoint of philosophers at the turn of the century when it was the educator's task to fill the originally blank mind of the child with "knowledge" to be reproduced parrotlike on demand. The modern psychologist, whose concern is with behavior rather than the accumulation of useless information, can see little value in "filling the bowl" with learnings; neither is he impressed with the efficiency with which most of this "filling" operation proceeds.

One of the earlier attempts to explain learning from a physiological point of view postulated the lowering with exercise of the resistance to the passage of a neural impulse. This view was abandoned when research (Franz and Lashley, 1951) showed that learning is more than simply a telephonic-type connection between a given receptor and a given effector. To the psychologist, whose interest in neurophysiology is only secondary, a behavioral definition is more functionally profitable, and modern definitions simply equate learning with behavioral changes resulting from experience.

The word *change* here warrants elaboration. Throughout life the one thing that is inevitable is change. Change results from both maturation and learning, with the two so highly interacting that their influence cannot be separated. Learning refers to those changes taking place as a result of special stimulation; it deliberately excludes the changes directly associated with maturation of inherited structure and predispositions, or such changes in effectiveness of reaction to stimulation as might be associated with fatigue or drugs. Learning can also be defined as *improvement* in behavior in the sense that the person becomes more proficient at whatever he is learning. One can *learn* to become a pickpocket or *learn* a bad habit; as he learns, his behavior becomes more efficient, more smooth, more precise, more probable, and more direct with respect to the goal, although not necessarily *better* from the standpoint of desirability.

There is basic agreement among psychologists that learning refers to change in performance arising from experience. Beyond this, the question is one of considerable controversy and, as noted in Chapter 2, certainly any attempt at definition would make some psychologists happier than others. The controversy is directly related to the basic difference in point of view between the association and the cognitive theorists. The former emphasize the association between stimulus and response under conditions of reinforcement; the latter see learning as the reorganization of cognitive structure functioning as a guide to more adequate and more satisfying adjustment. The problem stems in part from the fact that certain explanations fit certain learning situations better than others. Operant conditioning appears to fit particularly well the development of specific response patterns of animals and people along Skinnerian lines. It would seem less appropriate for the clarification of relationships, discriminations, and problem solving where the cognitive interpretation would seem more convincing. On the other hand, each theoretical position is supposedly self-contained and Skinner argues that problem solving, creativity, etc., being logical processes, can be programed like all others forms of learning. (See Skinner, 1966, for an operant analysis of problem solving.) Frequently, psychologists adopt an eclectic point of view. The development of skills involves certain components that are adequately explained through connectionism and reinforcement and others requiring understandings better explained through field explanations. Explaining the development of attitudes likewise is perhaps best done on a multiple basis—conditioning, reinforcement, perceptual reorganization, etc. Mowrer (1947), for example, identifies conditioning and problem solving as dual aspects of learning. Sanford (1961) also divides learning into simple learning (e.g., conditioning) and serial learning (e.g., concept formation and problem solving). Staats (1966), on the other hand, presents an integrated-functional approach to complex human behavior.

Learning involves two complementary processes: differentiation and integration, i.e., a breakdown of the whole into its component parts and a combining of the parts into a new whole. In a Gestalt sense, differentiation may be considered as the process in which regions of the perceptual field are divided into smaller and more highly defined subareas. Integration, on the other hand, is a matter of the reorganization of the individual parts into a new meaningful structure in which the components fall into place in their proper interrelationships. A back-and-forth movement between differentiation and integration is involved in all aspects of learning. Hence, the changes taking place during learning are rarely sudden, immediate, and complete but rather are developmental processes which may extend over a considerable period of time. It is also to be noted that the learner must do his own differentiating and integrating; even though the teacher may point out various components and their relationships to each other and to the learner's previous experiences, it is the learner who, in the final analysis, must discover the parts and the relationships and fit the individual responses of a complex behavioral pattern into the system in which they belong.

STEPS IN THE LEARNING PROCESS

Despite the relatively large amount of theoretical and empirical data available on the subject, there is, as we have seen, considerable disagreement as to the specific aspects of the learning process and considerable variation in the technical terms used by the different psychologists to label and describe them. Fortunately, there is general agreement on the concepts with which an introductory course in educational psychology needs to be concerned. Most psychologists agree that learning takes place as a result of experience generally connected with the individual's attempts to satisfy his multiple motives and purposes.

A well-known formulation of the steps of the learning process, considered from a reinforcement point of view, is that of Dashiell (1949) shown diagramatically in Figure 11-1: the motivated organism (1) encounters an obstacle (2) which prevents the attainment of its goal and the satisfaction of its motives. It makes exploratory responses (3) until some response (4) gets around the obstacle to the goal. A simpler

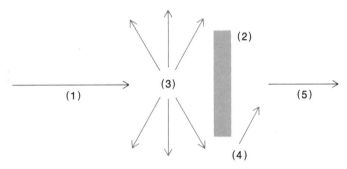

FIGURE 11-1 Diagram of cardinal features in readjustment behavior. (After Dashiell, 1949. By permission of Houghton Mifflin Company.)

statement of the essential aspects of the learning process, also approached from reinforcement premises,[1] is given by Miller and Dollard (1941, p. 2) as follows: "This may be expressed in a homely way by saying that, in order to learn, one must want something, notice something, do something, and get something." A more detailed analysis of the reinforcement view of learning might include the following steps:

MOTIVATION Learning takes place as a result of response to internal or external stimulation. Psychologists agree that motives play a part of various degrees of directness and cruciality in the organism's learning.

GOAL The motivated individual orients himself toward a goal which past experience leads him to believe, unconsciously perhaps, will be effective from the standpoint of his motives. Behavior does not just hap-

[1] Most lists of specific steps in the learning process have been devised from associationistic specifications; the more global cognitive viewpoint is not so easily identified by subcomponents. (See Chapter 2 for a presentation of the cognitive position.)

pen: it is caused by some need and is oriented toward some goal, i.e., it is purposive. The teacher spends much time and energy in setting up goals of various kinds toward which the child is to strive, but these will be effective only insofar as they become the child's goals, for if they do not, his behavior will be directed toward goals of his own and toward circumventing those of the teacher.

READINESS We must assume the individual is basically capable of satisfying his needs; the premature infant whose physiological growth has not progressed to the point of his being able to take in food cannot learn to do so. The question of readiness is of major concern to the curriculum maker; unless the curriculum is adjusted to the learner's developmental level, the likelihood of his learning its contents is relatively small and that of his developing attitudes of disinterest or defeatism is correspondingly great.

OBSTACLE An obstacle arises between a motivated individual and his goal. If no barrier existed, the goal would be reached according to some previously learned behavior pattern and the situation would involve no learning. Inability to reach his goal results in tension which propels the individual toward its attainment. Such tension is beneficial in that it forces him to find a solution, i.e., *it forces him to learn.* The teacher's task is to put realistic obstacles in the path of the child's goals and encourage him, with guidance when necessary, to deal effectively with the situation. Changing the requirements of a geometry problem so that it can no longer be handled by the solution given in the text will provide the occasion for learning. Obstacles may take any number—or even any combination—of forms. They are frequently social or societal, e.g., rules and regulations dictating what constitutes adequate social behavior; they can also be physical, personal, (e.g., incompetence) or psychological.

RESPONSE The individual is led to action, the nature of which depends on his interpretation of the situation. He may feel that direct attack will overcome the barrier, or he may decide to go around, or to seek a different goal. His behavior, though varied, is nevertheless still governed by the need he is trying to satisfy.

REINFORCEMENT A response that is successful in attaining the goal is reinforced and will tend to be repeated on subsequent occasions of a similar nature. An unsuccessful response, on the contrary, leads to continued trying until one response provides reinforcement.

GENERALIZATION The last, and certainly a vital, step in the learning process is the integration of the successful response with previous learnings so that it becomes part of a new functional whole.

SOME ASPECTS OF THE LEARNING PROCESS

LAWS OF LEARNING

Psychologists have derived a number of laws and principles to express empirical relationships between certain conditions and the effectiveness of the learning that results. Thus, Thorndike (1913), as a result of his experiments in animal learning, postulated such laws as the laws of effect, exercise and others. These laws no longer carry the prestige they held earlier in the century; in fact, Hilgard (1956) suggests:

> There are no laws of learning which can be taught with confidence. Even the most obvious fact of improvement with practice and the regulation of learning under reward and punishment are matters of theoretical dispute. [pp. 457–458]

Yet inasmuch as they still bear upon classroom learning, we shall devote a few paragraphs to a brief consideration of their nature in relation to the basic concepts presented in Chapter 2.

The Law of Effect which states that, other things being equal, those responses followed by satisfying aftereffects tend to be learned, besides being the most important of Thorndike's laws is also the most widely accepted. In fact, as pointed out by Melton (1950), whether the idea is in terms of effect, reinforcement, need-reduction, or purposive behavior, the concept of relating the learning or nonlearning of a response to its consequence is accepted almost universally. To appreciate the full significance of the Law of Effect, one must realize that *satisfying* is to be interpreted from the standpoint of whether or not the response is successful in attaining the learner's goal. If the learner sets a grade of A as his goal, those responses which lead to the attainment of the A will be satisfying even though they involve considerable self-sacrifice. Thus, the Law of Effect relates learning to the concept of motivation and is best understood when considered in this light.

The Law of Effect is usually considered as an aspect of the broader principle of reinforcement, a concept first postulated by Pavlov in connection with his experiments in classical conditioning. As we have noted in Chapter 2, reinforcement is fundamental to association theories, e.g., Hull's drive-reduction theory and Skinner's operant behavior theory, and, although somewhat less emphasized, reinforcement is also fundamental, to cognitive theories under the concept of the purposiveness of behavior. Unless there is some awareness of the consequence of one's behavior— whether called reinforcement, confirmation, or feedback—it seems unlikely that any significant degree of purposeful learning would occur. It seems further that to be effective, reinforcement must follow immediately upon the response, and, although it is dangerous to relate the results of animal studies to the learning of human beings who have a greater power of association, Skinner argues that ineffectiveness in school is related in no small way to its failure to provide immediate reward. This is less of a problem in meaningful material where the learner does not have to rely so exclusively on the teacher to tell him whether his performance is adequate or inadequate, especially when he has formulated clear-cut goals against which to gauge his performance.

The Law of Effect has been the subject of considerable controversy. At the empirical level, there can be little disagreement that the organism tends to repeat the responses which, on previous occasions, it has found effective in attaining its goals. The theoretical picture, on the other hand, is less clear; as we have noted in Chapter 3, nonreinforcement theorists reject both the notion of reward as necessary for learning and drive-reduction as the mechanism through which reinforcement (or the Law of Effect) operates. Regardless of its theoretical status, however, the Law of Effect and its underlying concept of motivation is of definite pedagogical value: learning effectiveness is in relative proportion to the extent to which [a] children have accepted as theirs meaningful goals and [b] their responses are rewarded through the attainment of these goals. Teachers often assume, for example, that the child is committed to certain goals related to schoolwork when, in reality, the goals as seen in the perspective of his overall motivational structure are such that their attainment (or unattainment) is of little moment to him.

Thorndike's Law of Exercise, used years ago to justify drill in the classroom,[2] has been more or less discredited. The present consensus is that although practice is necessary, it is not a sufficient condition for learning and that the Law of Exercise operates only indirectly through the fact that practice permits reinforcement of correct responses—or, in cognitive language, practice provides an opportunity for cognitive reorganization and the development of structural insight. A realization of this point has helped revolutionize school practice from emphasis on drill to emphasis on motivation and meaningfulness. "Practice makes perfect" only under proper conditions of motivation and effective practice; unless the child cares about the outcome, practice until doomsday will not improve his performance. The futility of unmotivated drill is well illustrated by the old story of the boy made to write "I have gone" one hundred times in order to break him of the habit of saying "I have went." The teacher was out of the room when he finished so he left the following note: "You were out, so I have went home."

Thorndike's other laws are also of doubtful validity. His Law of Recency, for instance, probably pertained to retention rather than learning. On the other hand, other concepts, e.g., readiness, even though no

---

[2] Actually, drill was advocated by Herbart years before Thorndike's Law of Exercise.

longer considered as *laws*, have direct educational implications; the concept of belonging, for example, emphasizes the importance of meaningfulness, relatedness, and integration of learning into a unified frame of reference.

TRIAL AND ERROR VERSUS INSIGHT

When the learner finds himself in a situation where his previous solutions are not adequate, he has to devise some new means of dealing with it. Whether the solution comes suddenly or only after a gradual and laborious process of trying this idea and that until the solution finally evolves has been the subject of considerable discussion between the followers of the connectionist and the Gestalt schools of learning.

Thorndike's experiments in animal learning led him to see learning as the result of trial-and-error behavior. In a typical experiment, a hungry cat was placed in a cage outside of which was a bowl of fish; the experiment might be set so that the key to the cat's getting out of the cage lay in its learning to push against a post somewhere in the cage and thus trip the lever on the door. After having tried to squeeze through the bars and claw the door down, the cat would move about, meow, etc. in semi-random fashion. Eventually, perhaps by accident, it would hit the post and be released. When it was made to repeat the experiment, the cat would tend to repeat that part of the performance which led to its release, even to the point of backing into the post if that is how it got out the first time. In time, it became more adept at repeating that part of the total performance that had been effective in releasing it; in other words, it learned to short-circuit the random aspects of the process, to limit the useless movements, and to get to the post more directly, even though it frequently did not know what it was all about. Thorndike concluded that learning was essentially a trial-and-error proposition (or more correctly, trial-and-success) with reward, rather than understanding, the key to learning.

Present emphasis on insight has resulted largely from the influence of Gestalt psychologists. In Köhler's study (1929), an ape, after having tried unsuccessfully to pull in a banana lying outside the cage just beyond his reach, suddenly saw the possibility of a stick lying in the cage and proceeded to use it to pull in the banana. In another study, the ape suddenly saw how he could fit two sticks together to make a longer pole to pull in the banana. In other words, the ape was able to see the means-end relationships involved in the situation, i.e., to structure his perceptual field to include the stick, the cage, and the banana into a meaningful whole. Implied is a sudden mental reorganization and integration of the various aspects of one's previous experiences into a new pattern so that a new, although not entirely different, situation is seen in its basic relationships.

The word *sudden* in the above statement is troublesome and some psychologists question the existence of insight on the basis that, unless the situation is identical with a previous situation in the learner's experience (in which case there is no learning), there is bound to be some trial and error, although it may be mental rather than physical. They feel that insight does not differ, except in degree, from other aspects of learning and therefore requires no special treatment. They point out that trial and error is not blind, haphazard, and purposeless groping in all directions until, quite by accident, one response is learned in accordance with the principle of reinforcement. On the contrary, unless the means-end relationships are completely obscure and illogical, the trials are very definitely oriented toward what the learner feels will lead him to his goal: it is *trial and error* only insofar as the means-end relationships of the situation are not clear. Furthermore, insight is rarely complete; it is more likely to be a matter of ever-greater clarification of a given point through the clarification of related ideas.

The most damaging evidence against the concept of insight as a unique phenomenon is that presented by Harlow (1949, 1959) in connection with the concept of learning sets (See Chapter 5). After a period of trial and error, the chimps "caught on;" experience in solving discrimination problems of a given class resulted in the formation of learning sets which permitted them to solve not only subsequent problems of the same class but also related problems with almost complete accuracy. Presumably, insight is essentially a case of generalized experience. As Harlow has said, "No animals can solve problems insightfully with maximal efficiency without a history of earlier solutions of similar problems." According to Harlow, thinking does not develop spontaneously as the expression of innate ability but rather as the end result of a long learning process. Köhler did not know the history of his apes; they apparently had had previous related experiences in their natural setting and were simply adapting abilities they had previously acquired.

Learning involves various degrees of both trial and error and insight. As Brownell (1942) points out, a given situation may [a] be so familiar to one person as to involve no learning; [b] for a second person constitute a problem calling for considerable enlightened trial and error before insight is achieved; while [c] for a third, be a puzzle to which he can bring only haphazard trial-and-error behavior. Probably learning is on a continuum with the extent of trial and error and insight involved in a given situation determined by the difficulty of the task in relation to the capacity, motivation, mind-set, and especially the experiential background of the learner. Learning would also depend on whether the solution is predicated on logical means-end relationships; in Thorndike's experiment, for example, the relationship of the center post to the opening of the cage was not, to the cat, a logical relationship so that, having exhausted in vain such "insightful" approaches as trying to push down the gate or to slip through the bars, it has no alternative but to resort to trial-and-error behavior. Whether classroom activities involve trial and error or insight depends largely upon the way they are conducted. When the child is expected to cope with material he does not understand, he has to resort to trial and error. Number combinations, for example, can be learned by rote in which case there is little, if any, insight, or they can be presented in such a way as to involve considerable discovery on the part of the student.

Inasmuch as insightful learning makes for progressive growth in understanding, the school must emphasize insight and encourage the child to discover relationships, to go beyond the memorization of isolated facts, and to strive for generalizations. This is not to say that there is no room for trial and error in the classroom; on the contrary, because insight generally comes only after considerable persistence with the material, students might well be encouraged to stay with a task until the relationships become clear, whether the insight involved is foresight or hindsight.

PROCESS VERSUS PRODUCT

A distinction must be made between the products of learning and the process through which they are attained. To some extent, this distinction bears upon the relative role of educational philosophy in setting the goals (the products) to be attained and of educational psychology in pointing to the process through which these goals can be achieved most effectively. Teachers are primarily involved in the process of learning so as to govern not only the specific products of learning but also the efficiency with which they are to be attained. It is also true that, if the process is right, the product tends to be right, whereas the fact that the product is right does not guarantee that the process was also right: a person can type a perfect copy by the hunt-and-peck method or arrive at the correct answer in addition by counting—or copying! Teachers should be more concerned with helping the child develop skills by means of which he can find his own answers than giving him ready-made answers to memorize.

This does not imply that the school can ignore the products of learning, particularly those in the area of motivation, attitude and character development, as well as reasoning and problem solving—all of which are often neglected in our overemphasis on facts and skills. Nor is it implied that process and product are separate and independent. The school must be concerned with both, but its primary concern should be with the *how* rather than the *what*. At least, it must not let overconcern with passing examinations (i.e., with limited products) divert its attention from the process through which a true education is achieved.

FORMAL VERSUS INCIDENTAL LEARNING

A distinction can be made among: [a] formal learning in which the teacher deliberately plans to have the child achieve certain specific learning through the operation of a formal program of instruction; [b] informal learning in which instruction is organized on an informal basis; [c] incidental learning in which learning takes place without definite intent, perhaps as a by-product of other learnings; and [d] instrumental learning in which the learning of certain outcomes occurs as an intermediate step in the pursuit of some other learning activity, e.g., learning the Pythagorean theorem in order to lay out a baseball diamond.

The vast amount of material the preschool child learns without apparent intent is often given as evidence of the effectiveness of informal learning. Although it is true that a great deal of learning takes place through the informal experiences of the kindergarten, for example, the very existence of schools is a monument to the ineffectiveness of learning on a catch-as-catch-can basis. Instrumental learning is also efficient largely because it is meaningfully related to the child's goals and purposes. It is often difficult, however, to prevent gaps from developing in areas that do not lend themselves to integration within projects in which the child is particularly interested. If something is worth learning, it should generally be made part of a carefully defined sequence of experiences so that its occurrence is a matter of design rather than accident. One cannot rely on the child's knowing how to spell words simply because he has come across them in his reading. This does not mean there should be a formal period of instruction devoted to the learning of everything the school considers important, but it does mean that at no time should *informal* become synonymous with *haphazard*. On the other hand, formal learning need not be drill based on a compulsion to have the child learn or else. There is nothing in the concept of formal education that says it *has* to be dull, meaningless, or unrelated to the child's purposes.

Of special interest in the promotion of all-round growth are what Dewey (1938) calls *collateral*, i.e., incidental, learnings, which invariably accompany—and often overshadow in importance—the primary learnings the teacher deliberately sets out to implant. Thus, to quote Dewey:

> Perhaps the greatest of all pedagogical fallacies is the notion that a person learns only the particular things he is studying at the time. Collateral learning in the way of the formation of enduring attitudes, or likes and dislikes, may be and often is much more important than the spelling lesson or lesson in geography or history that is learned. For these attitudes are fundamentally what counts in the future. [p. 49]

Whereas the purpose of education is to enable the student to deal more effectively with related situations in the future, this would not be true if, while learning mathematics, for example, he gets to dislike the subject, to doubt his competence, and generally to become less rather than more capable of further growth as a result of his experience. The teacher's methods, his personality, and the classroom atmosphere affect not only the effectiveness with which academic learnings take place, but also determine whether the experience will be helpful or harmful from the standpoint of continued growth. He must therefore take care that, in his concern over primary learnings, he does not lose sight of the by-products. Indeed, in view of the importance of the latter and the fact that they inevitably occur, the teacher must plan for the occurrence of positive learnings in these areas just as deliberately as he does for primary learnings.

HIGHLIGHTS OF THE CHAPTER

The school exists for the purpose of promoting and guiding the child's growth. There is perhaps little the teacher can do concerning the maturational components of this growth, beyond coordinating its efforts with the various aspects of maturation; the learning component, on the other hand, is not only susceptible to manipulation but its formal aspects are the primary responsibility of the school.

[a]

Learning refers to changes in behavior resulting from experience. Beyond this, the explanation of the learning process or even a precise definition is a matter of theoretical dispute. Its neurophysiological basis is also unknown.

[b]

Learning ranges from simple conditioning to the more complex processes of problem solving, creative thinking, concept formation, etc. Complex learning, according to reinforcement theory, generally proceeds through such steps as: [1] motivation, [2] goal, [3] readiness, [4] obstacle, [5] response, [6] reinforcement, and [7] generalization. There is not complete agreement on the cruciality or even the relevance of these steps; field theorists, for example, emphasize perceptual reorganization rather than reinforcement.

[c]

Thorndike formulated a number of laws relating certain conditions with effectiveness of learning. The most important of these, the Law of Effect, can be considered a special case of the principle of reinforcement; as such, it bears directly on the concept of motivation.

[d]

Learning involves various degrees of trial and error and insight depending on such factors as the difficulty of the material relative to what the learner brings to the situation and the extent to which the problem involves logical means-end relationships. Harlow has raised serious questions concerning the nature of insight.

[e]

Teachers should be more concerned with the process whereby learning takes place than with its products. This is not to minimize the importance of the latter.

[f]

Although incidental learning is often efficient, whatever is worth teaching should be deliberately planned for rather than left to chance. This is particularly true of collateral learning such as attitudes which arise as byproducts of what the teacher sets out to have the child learn and which are often of vastly greater importance.

SOURCES OF RELATED MATERIAL

Estes, William K., "Learning," in C. W. Harris (ed.), *Encyclopedia of Educational Research*, New York: Crowell-Collier and Macmillan, Inc., 1960. Pp. 752–770.

Hilgard, E. R. (ed.), *Theories of Learning and Instruction*. 63rd Yearbook, National Society for the Study of Education, Pt. I. Chicago: University of Chicago Press, 1964.

Mednick, S. A., *Learning*. Englewood Cliffs, N.J.: Prentice-Hall, Inc., 1964.

Mowrer, O. H., "On the dual nature of learning—A reinterpretation of conditioning and problem solving," *Harv. educ. Rev.*, 17: 102–148, 1947.

Postman, Leo, "The history and present status of the law of effect," *Psychol. Bull.*, 44: 489–563, 1947.

QUESTIONS AND PROJECTS

1

Why must each law of learning be predicated by the phrase "other things being equal?" Are laws of science ever universal in application?

2

How might teaching based on the theory of learning as an active process of reconstruction differ from teaching based on the theory of learning as a passive process of absorption?

3

Single out what you consider the three most desirable features of the teaching of your current college courses and the three most frustrating. What might account for the differences?

CHAPTER 12

Guiding
the Learning
Process

Basically, the aim of educational psychology is
to understand how learning processes may be
more effectively guided.

Bernard, 1965, p. 6

That the child is born with capacity and the need to grow does not imply
that he will on his own make the most of his potentialities. That schools
exist at all testifies to his inability to assume responsibility for his growth.
Growth results from the individual's responses to environmental demands and, although the learner must learn for himself, it remains a
fact that the process can be made more certain and more effective by
competent guidance. Teaching has been defined as the facilitation of
learning: this chapter will consider some aspects of the process by
means of which this can be done.[1]

---

[1] As we noted in Chapter 2, Gage (1964) makes a strong case for the theories of
teaching, apart from the theories of *learning* which he considers relatively incapable
of meeting the practical demands of education.

ROLE OF INSTRUCTION IN LEARNING

NEED FOR GUIDANCE

Providing children with a carefully selected sequence of experiences constitutes but part of the school's task; it must further provide the guidance necessary to make these experiences effective in promoting growth. Everyday experience provides ample evidence that, without guidance, the learner will usually stumble upon a method which is somewhat short of the best. In fact, it is illogical to expect the learner to strike upon the best of the many possible methods of doing a given thing; because he is lacking in background, he would hardly be able to conceive of all the methods, let alone appraise their relative merits and proceed to master the most efficient. A person learning to type without instruction is likely to use the two-finger hunt-and-peck method, for example. More effective methods are generally more difficult in the early stages. Thus, in golf, it would seem so much more natural just to go out and club the ball without all the fuss about stance, grip, position of the elbow, of the shoulder—but it would lead to disappointing results. In a study by Davies (1945), for example, the group instructed in the use of the bow made greater gains in archery than an uninstructed group of equivalent ability. This is perhaps more obvious in the learning of skills but it is equally true in the learning of meanings, concepts, or problem-solving techniques, Furthermore, the more complicated the task, the more important instruction becomes in terms of final gains.

ROLE OF THE TEACHER

Whereas the learner must do the learning, instruction can undoubtedly save time and effort and, more important, can prevent the development of ineffective techniques which will preclude any degree of proficiency. Thus, instruction is a determining factor with respect to both the learner's progress and the final status he will attain. If the teacher is to provide the child with effective guidance in learning, it is imperative that he know specifically what role he is to play and the techniques by which effective learning can be promoted.

His task can be divided into three broad categories.

[a] Help the learner develop insight into the nature of the product to be attained and the process through which this is to be accomplished. Thus, in teaching motor skills, he needs to direct the learner's attention to adequate techniques and the reasons underlying their use, e.g., the purpose of the follow-through in golf.

[b] Anticipate the use of faulty techniques and provide continuous diagnostic and remedial help to prevent the consolidation of bad habits.

Thus, the instructor must be able to recognize good and poor form, i.e., he must be able to provide a critical evaluation of the learner's performance. Yet, he must allow flexibility, for, although certain methods tend to be more conducive to success than others, even these must be modified in keeping with individual differences among learners. In fact, within limits, the learner should be allowed to develop a style of his own.

[c] Give the learner moral support. The teacher should concentrate on what to do rather than on what to avoid and should refrain from adverse criticism, especially in the early stages. A study by Holodnak (1943), for example, showed that emphasizing correct responses led to greater improvement in learning a skill than emphasizing errors. The relative emphasis to be placed on these aspects of the teacher's role varies; giving moral support would be somewhat less important for a person who is relatively secure and beyond the novice stage of learning.

FORMS OF GUIDANCE

The teacher, in his attempt to help the learner, can proceed in a number of ways. He can rely primarily on verbal or perhaps manual guidance; he might rely on a visual approach via diagrams, mechanical devices, or other aids, or he might use a combination of these by having a demonstration. The form most effective in a specific case depends on the particular situation; manual guidance is obviously more appropriate for teaching a skill than for teaching a verbal concept.

Verbal guidance can be very helpful in the development of meanings and concepts, but it tends to be particularly ineffective for teaching skills to beginners. It is next to impossible to give an adequate description of a skill without being either inaccurate or tedious and labored, as can be demonstrated readily by having a boy scout explain verbally how to tie various rope knots without benefit of demonstration. Verbal guidance is more effective in improving the skills of a person already familar with their basic aspects. Films have certain advantages in that they can combine the visual and the verbal approach and, in the case of a skill, can provide a slow motion demonstration without distorting the performance, but they too have definite limitations. Often the film presents too much material for the beginner to grasp at one time, and as a result, as any other medium improperly used, it causes confusion. Films, charts, and graphs are of definite value in conveying such ideas as the structure of molecules or chemical reactions that are difficult to describe by words alone.

Regardless of the form in which it is given, guidance is generally most effective in the early stages of learning. It facilitates learning to the extent that it helps the learner understand what the task involves. But, in the final analysis, one learns by doing so that if he is ever to learn, the learner must actually go through the process of learning on his own. The exact amount of guidance required for maximum efficiency of learning varies from case to case but the teacher must recognize that guidance can be overdone.

Excess guidance tends to be detrimental inasmuch as it destroys the learner's initiative and causes a shift in the sense of personal responsibility for the learning from the shoulders of the learner where it belongs to those of the teacher. Once the learner has grasped the general nature of what he is to do, he must go ahead on his own. Teachers often talk too much: they direct the solution of a problem step by step; they tell the child when to multiply, divide, add, or subtract to the point where he is learning, not arithmetic, but simply how to follow directions. Some teachers feel they are shirking their responsibility if they do not cover every minute detail, when actually their responsibility should be limited to providing the general framework and encouraging students to tie the pieces together for themselves. In the same way, science manuals often do nothing more than teach students to follow directions step by step. Guidance is necessary for effective learning, but as a rule it should be kept to a reasonable minimum. Generally an overview of what is to be learned, perhaps, a demonstration or two where appropriate, should suffice. Where tools are involved, their use should be made clear, of course, but once again the important thing is to let the learner do the learning.

LEARNING CURVES

As learning proceeds, it is sometimes possible to plot behavioral changes as they take place. Thus, in typing, one might plot the number of words typed per minute on the vertical axis against the number of practice periods on the horizontal axis. The resulting curve[2] provides a graphic representation of progress per unit of practice time. It should be noted that although reference is often made to *the* learning curve, there is no single or typical curve that characterizes learning. Logically, the basic curve (see Figure 12-1) would display a slow initial rise followed by a more rapid rise and a gradual leveling off. However, the shape of the curve varies with such factors as the stage of learning, the nature of the material, the capacity of the learner, his motivation, etc. In practice, the learning curve is usually abbreviated at both ends because the plotting of the learner's progress in an actual case rarely covers the period from zero to the attainment of the limits of improvement.

[2] Learning curves are more correctly *performance* curves from which learning is inferred.

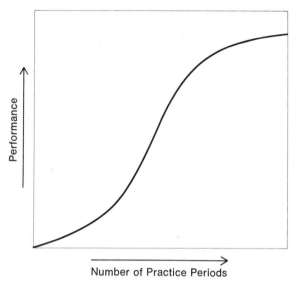

Number of Practice Periods

FIGURE 12-1   Theoretical learning curve.

When a person has to start learning a given activity from scratch, his early progress tends to be slow. He may have to unlearn conflicting skills or habits, he may begin by using an ineffective approach, or he may have to develop the necessary background. In learning to type, for example, the student generally shows slow initial progress largely because he has to learn the keyboard and develop eye-finger coordination. Feelings of uncertainty will also slow the learner's progress by preventing him from devoting his whole energy to the task. On the other hand, when initial progress is rapid, it is generally caused by positive carry-over from related learning; a person's batting average in softball might show rapid progress in the early stages simply because of previous experience with baseball. Rapid initial progress also occurs when the earlier phases of the total activity are the easiest.

PLATEAUS

Learning curves frequently display what is known as a plateau, a period of no apparent progress which is then followed by further gains. In typing, for example, a person may reach a point where, perhaps for weeks, he shows no improvement—only to have progress eventually resume. Whereas plateaus are not an essential aspect of the learning curve and can perhaps be avoided, their occurrence can be explained in any number of ways:

[a] It may be necessary to reorganize previous learnings into a new pattern before further progress can evolve. In typing, for example, one has to move from typing one letter at a time to typing a word

at a time and to typing a phrase at a time. Thus, a plateau may represent a period of actual progress even though performance does not show it.

[b] The learner may have to replace bad habits before he can advance to a higher level of achievement.

[c] His lack of progress may be caused by decreased motivation or emotional tenseness which prevents him from using his abilities effectively.

[d] The task may not be of uniform difficulty throughout.

[e] Undue attention to one of the subaspects of the total performance may be throwing the performance out of kilter. This is particularly true when the subaspects are learned separately and have to be put together into an integrated performance.

[f] Plateaus may also reflect the transition from one performance limit to another.

Whereas short-lived plateaus are not particularly harmful, the teacher should detect their presence early and take steps to forestall bad habits, tenseness, and discouragement. His effort should be directed toward analyzing the student's performance to discover if perhaps some aspect needs correction and toward maintaining adequate motivation. The learner must be kept from worrying about his lack of progress and from losing confidence in his ability. It is probably best to minimize the occurrence of plateaus by pacing the learner (Kao, 1937); in first-grade reading, for example, only so many new words are introduced in each lesson so as to permit the child to consolidate his gains as he goes along.

PHYSIOLOGICAL LIMITS

Improvement cannot continue forever and, regardless of the activity, the learning curve will eventually have to reach a limit beyond which further improvement is not possible. These limits are generally known as *physiological limits*, i.e., limits beyond which further gains are precluded by the limitations of one's physiological equipment. Actually, physiological limits are often more properly *methodological, mechanical,* or *materials* limits since the limits are set not so much by limitations in physiological structure as by limitations in the method (e.g., the hunt-and-peck method in typing), the equipment, or the material used; and it is quite possible that, with a better method or with better equipment or material, new gains could be made. It might be pointed out that these limits are hypothetical, since probably no one has ever reached these maxima—or at least no one can be sure he has reached them. Recent research on early stimulation suggests that we have no more approached the limits of human potentialities than pre-Skinnerian psychologists had exhausted the potentialities of pigeons. A planned program in early years along the lines suggested by Harlow, Hebb, Hunt, and Moore may well add new dimensions to what people can really do.

In practice, the limit of performance that is reached is not set by the limits mentioned above but rather by the individual's judgment as to what is adequate in the light of situational demands. Thus, a typist goes on for years typing 60 words per minute, not because that is as fast as her fingers can go but simply because she does not have to type any faster to hold down a job. If promotion were to be made conditional on her typing faster, she could probably increase her speed to a new motivational limit. Of course, just as physiological limits vary from person to person, so do motivational limits; in fact, successful people in this world are frequently people who set their motivational limits very close to their physiological limits, people who are not content to operate at 50 percent efficiency. It is not unusual, for instance, for professional musicians and athletes to practice by the hour to get one small skill down to perfection.

Short-time Fluctuations

Whereas the learning curve tends to show a gradual improvement in performance, the advances are, in actual practice, anything but smooth. In fact, short-time fluctuations are to be found in all learning curves whenever day-to-day performance is plotted without averaging. This is fully understandable in view of the innumerable factors that affect performance: difference in motivation, health, and other conditions of the learner; distractions; errors of measurement; etc.

Use of Learning Curves

Learning curves are of considerable value, particularly from a motivational point of view, in that they give the learner graphic evidence of his progress. On the other hand, they can bring discouragement to those making only minor gains, and a certain degree of caution in their use seems in order lest the child, seeing his lack of improvement, become discouraged or so tense that progress becomes well-nigh impossible.

A real limitation in the use of learning curves is that the number system on the basis of which performance in certain areas is measured does not lend itself to graphic representation. A learning curve can be drawn for "words typed per minute" or "seconds to run a hundred yards," but the fact that most educational measurements are based on a displaced cardinal series presents serious problems when plotting, say, progress in a history course. If John stands at the 50th percentile of his group on the first test, at what percentile should he stand on the second test to show improvement? This question will be considered in Chapter 16.

ROLE OF PRACTICE IN LEARNING

Current interpretation of the Law of Exercise is that practice is a necessary, but not a sufficient, condition for learning since as a result of practice performance may improve, remain at a standstill,[3] or even worsen. Practice gives the learner an opportunity to restructure the situation, to discard errors, and to telescope, refine, and integrate its various aspects into a rapid, smooth, accurate, and effective sequence so that he can operate on an automatic and comfortable basis without any need to analyze and reanalyze each step. Practice also permits the generalization of responses to multiple cues. Whether the learner takes advantage of this opportunity, however, depends on whether he wants to improve and whether he is given adequate guidance. Dunlap's success (1932) in ridding himself of typing *hte* instead of *the* by deliberately practicing the wrong response, and his success in removing facial tics by forcing the client to repeat the tic until he became very reluctant to do so, is evidence that the individual does not always learn what he practices. Nevertheless, even though practice does not ensure improvement, improvement cannot take place without practice, and the school needs to encourage practice in order to promote greater understanding, retention, and transfer.

To be effective, practice must take place in a meaningful setting. It is important, for instance, to have the learner develop insight into the nature of the required performance. A basic postulate of the Gestalt position is that practice should come after understanding; drill in advance of insight is likely to lead to a consolidation of bad habits. Good form must first be established, then consolidated through practice. In typing, for example, practice must integrate accuracy and speed from the beginning; the student cannot build up accuracy once and for all and then concentrate on speed, since introducing the element of speed changes the performance into an essentially different skill.

The most effective type of practice is generally that in which the learner uses his previous learnings in dealing with more advanced work. This can be done readily in sequential subjects such as mathematics where it is probably better to have the child practice division in connection with a problem than to subject him to artificial drill. Teachers need to devise meaningful experiences which permit the child to use his knowledge in his climb to new heights. He can, for instance, practice correct grammar in writing reports in his other subjects. Classroom discussion can be particularly effective in forcing the child to consolidate previous learning. There is still room in the modern curriculum for drill

---

[3] A distinction can be made between *learning* a skill or a fact and *using* it once it has been learned.

but it must not be of the monotonous variety which so often leads only to negative attitudes toward the subject and toward the school, especially when it is prescribed for a whole class even though needed only by a few.

The fact that we learn by doing has been misinterpreted to imply that the child must be doing something physical or overt. Actually mental practice can be equally, if not more, profitable inasmuch as it often promotes the structural organization of materials as the basis for their effective use in actual practice. Even in physical skills, imagining better modes of attack can produce improvements particularly in complex skills calling for development of strategy where, as in football, thinking of what might occur generally leads to more effective performance as well as greater insights for the future than simply going ahead and doing something.

A number of suggestions can be given for efficient practice. On the other hand, none can be considered conclusive; no one approach is superior, except in the light of what is to be learned, by whom, under what circumstances, and for what purpose. Thus, such studies as that of Knapp and Dixon (1950), showing as much improvement to result from 70 minutes of distributed practice as from 126 minutes of massed practice, led psychologists to conclude that practice distributed in a series of relatively short periods promotes more efficient learning than the same amount of practice massed into periods of longer duration. Intensive study of the problem by Underwood (1961, 1951-date) now shows this generalization to be of limited applicability. Spaced practice seems to facilitate learning only under relatively specialized conditions, and, for immediate memory at least, cramming may well result in acceptable performance—as students have always hoped it would. It was also believed that spaced practice facilitated retention, but it now appears that spacing facilitates retention through eliminating interfering associations; therefore spacing would be clearly recommended only when forgetting is caused by the interference of unwanted associations and not by other school tasks, the retention of which is also at stake.

It is still believed that, under certain circumstances at least, short sessions extended over a period of time tend to produce greater efficiency in learning, e.g., from the standpoint of the long-term retention of material when spaced learning promotes a deeper grasp of its content. Just how short is short, however, depends on many factors in the task, the learner, and the learning situation. Short periods have certain advantages over longer practice sessions; the latter lead to fatigue and tension which may destroy the rhythm and flexibility necessary to achieve a good performance. Periodic rest allows interfering factors to dissipate. Duncan (1951), for example, found that introducing rest periods equivalent to two thirds of the total practice time did not have detrimental effects on final performance, even though the rest group had only one third as much actual overt practice as the control group. Intermittent practice allows errors—which tend to be less thoroughly learned—to fade during the rest period so that it prevents the consolidation of bad habits; it also permits a certain amount of surreptitious practice in the form of rehearsals between sessions. Perseveration of neural circuits continuing after the practice sessions may also be involved in the consolidation of learning. Distributed practice tends to promote more efficient learning when there is a lot of material, when the material is long and not particularly meaningful, when the probability of erroneous response in the early stages is high, or when motivation is likely to be low. On the other hand, changing from one activity to another involves waste, particularly when it calls for getting out equipment or for a warm-up period, and this waste has to be balanced against the disadvantages of extending the learning period. The time between practice periods should be neither so long that excessive forgetting takes place between sessions nor so short that wrong responses do not have time to drop out. The teacher has to work out his schedule according to what he considers the optimal distribution of lessons for the children in his care. Actually, the length of practice periods as they pertain to academic material is perhaps not crucial. In the modern curriculum with its emphasis on planning, doing, and evaluating, the child engages in such a variety of activities that negative effects from long periods are relatively minimal. Many schools are finding the two-hour block in core subjects, for example, less troublesome from the standpoint of pupil efficiency than the more formal 50-minute period.

PARTS VERSUS WHOLE

Research evidence concerning the relative superiority of learning a given unit by parts or learning it as a whole is also somewhat conflicting. Whereas early studies had given indications of the superiority of the whole method, later studies (e.g., Jensen and Lemaire, 1937), although still favoring the whole method especially when combined with distributed practice, have not been so conclusive. Actually, the issue is difficult to resolve; perhaps the answer varies from task to task and from learner to learner. The whole method may be inadvisable, for instance, with material of uneven difficulty or with an insecure learner who needs constant reassurance that he is making progress. Furthermore, in an experiment of this kind, it is difficult to prevent the group learning by parts from vitiating the experiment by getting an overview of the material.

The problem itself is ambiguous in that it revolves around the question: "What is a whole and what is a part?" Any whole is part of a bigger whole and, in the final analysis, all learning has to deal with a part of some larger whole. The question then becomes, "What constitutes the optimal unit of study for a given person under given conditions?" It seems the answer to the question must be sought in the concept of meaningfulness. Learning a passage one word at a time would obviously be inefficient from the standpoint of both learning and retention since it would rob the passage of its meaning and would, therefore, be the equivalent of learning nonsense material. On the other hand, taking too broad a unit would make it difficult to grasp its meaning and would lead to ineffective learning. Thus, the learner should probably choose as his unit of study whatever he can grasp clearly and meaningfully, whether this be a chapter, a section, or a paragraph. It follows that, because of differences in intelligence, experience, organizational ability, attitudes, and motivation, the optimal unit for one person is not necessarily the optimal unit for another.

The parts method tends to be ineffective because it does not provide the structure which would enable the learner to make use of the relationships and the continuity of the material to relate one part to the other and to previous learnings. In addition, putting the parts together after each has been learned may prove troublesome, particularly in a complex skill where fitting the parts into perspective is the crucial part of the learning, and where, no matter how effective one part may be, unless it is coordinated with the other components of the skill, the whole performance will be relatively poor. In general, a bright person learning meaningful material would find the whole method advantageous, particularly as he got accustomed to its use. In fact, whenever one can impose a structure on a unit to the point of perceiving its relationships, he should probably study it as a whole, regardless of its size (within limits, of course). Even in the case of nonsense material, it is usually possible to impose some kind of structure upon it to facilitate its acquisition. Furthermore, even when the parts method is used, for whatever reason, the learner should first get an overview of the material and structure the field so that the parts fall into place.

RECITATION VERSUS REREADING

Another problem of interest to teachers is the relative emphasis to be placed on the reading and rereading of material as opposed to devoting a certain amount of the time and effort to recitation. Experimental evidence has shown rather conclusively that recitation is generally more effective than rereading, particularly from the standpoint of delayed recall. Forlano (1936), for example, found that one can profitably spend up to 80 percent of the total learning time in recitation. This percentage would vary with the nature of the material, of course; it is probably high for meaningful material where rereading would be more efficient. Recitation must not be guesswork; one has to get a good grasp of the contents before concentrating on recitation. The superiority of recitation over rereading can be attributed at least in part to the fact that, by providing immediate goals, recitation makes for a greater degree of ego-involvement and effort on the part of the learner. It also provides immediate feedback and enables the learner to devote his attention to those aspects of the total learning that he does not know. Furthermore, recitation gives him an advantage by familiarizing him with a situation similar to that on the basis of which gains are to be measured.

It must also be noted that rereading is a relatively passive process, whereas to be effective learning must be active. In fact, unless one reads with a purpose, he may find himself just reading words without comprehension. As a rule, having a child read a single source over and over as a means of increasing his understanding of its contents is relatively futile. If the meaning of the passage is not clear, he will probably get nothing for his pains but verbalisms. An extensive coverage of related sources would be more profitable. Children should be trained to skim so that they can cover a number of references quickly looking for what is new or expressed in such a way as to clarify their understanding of the first source.

METHODS OF PRESENTATION

Our current conviction that the important thing going on in the classroom is *learning* on the part of the children does not minimize in the least the importance of good teaching. The student must do his own learning but the teacher is hired to facilitate his learning and effective presentation is an essential aspect of this facilitation. As presently organized, the average classroom relies almost exclusively on visual and auditory presentation of content; the child gets most of his information from listening to his teacher and from looking at the printed page, chart, graph, or film. Research evidence suggests that the difference in the relative effectiveness of these two principal sensory avenues of instruction is generally slight. Goldstein (1940), for example, found a correlation of .78 between learning through reading and through listening. The difference, of course, may be relatively great in the case of a given individual. Differences in ability to profit from a given presentation would also exist with differences in intelligence and experience. Thus, the gifted may get more out of reading a great deal of material silently whereas the dull may profit more from discussion or explanation by the teacher. Generally, the more sense organs stimulated, the more effective the learning; the use of a picture to complement a verbal explanation, for example, is likely to result in more adequate learning of what is presented than if either is used alone.

An issue of long standing concerns the relative merits of the discussion and the lecture as teaching methods. The extensive literature on the subject suggests that the relative superiority of the two approaches centers primarily around the choice of the criterion, i.e., what is to be accomplished. As pointed out by Stovall (1958):

> In summary, research indicates that the lecture is equal or superior to the group discussion method if the criterion is acquisition of information but that discussion produces better results in terms of retention of this type of learning. Discussion has been found to be more effective than lecture as a means of stimulating critical thinking and in aiding students to attain a deeper understanding of subject matter which is reflected in the ability to make application of knowledge newly acquired to interpret and to draw inferences. Likewise, the discussion has a greater effect on attitudes and is more conducive to the development of desirable inter-personal relationships in the classroom. [p. 256]

Discussion is not effective simply because it is discussion. Certainly it often degenerates into a bull session characterized by a pooling of ignorance, endless arguments over inconsequentials, or worse, the loud expression of unverified opinions and endless verbiage by a few empty heads and domination by a few demagogues. Discussion can result in a vocal minority imposing its views upon the group and monopolizing class time to the point that no one learns very much. When conducted in an atmosphere of argument, it simply leads everyone to reaffirm his point of view or to align himself with his friends and close himself off from any learning in the matter. The teacher must be particularly skillful in moving the discussion along, keeping it on the right track, and preventing a few individuals from monopolizing the conversation and making a mockery of democratic processes. It would seem logical to assume that, if someone has to dominate the group, it might as well be the teacher who is at least better informed and better trained. It must also be recognized that ability on the part of the brighter members of the group to verbalize the main points of the discussion cannot be taken as evidence that the whole class has grasped the principles involved; if that is all there is to it, the teacher might as well present the lesson himself as a lecture.

The choice between lecture and discussion hinges in large part on what we want to promote, i.e., on how concerned we are with the more intangible but generally more significant objectives of education—ability to reason, ability to draw inferences, attitudes, democratic social orientation, etc. Critics of modern education argue that these objectives can be achieved only at the sacrifice of "academic competence," narrowly conceived as knowledge of the fundamentals to be revealed through test performance. Actually, the question is not which is better, lecture or discussion, but rather under what conditions one is better than the other. The research evidence as to their relative superiority is far from conclusive; it seems reasonable to believe that neither is better for the attainment of all educational objectives. As Spence suggested in 1928:

> The decrying of the wholesale use of lectures in college teaching is probably justified; the wholesale decrying of the use of the lecture in college is just as certainly not justified. [p. 462]

A similar pattern exists with respect to the student-centered versus the teacher-centered classroom. The Eight-Year Study (Aiken, 1942) showed the former equal or superior to the traditional approach on nearly all counts, especially in the area of critical thinking. Apparently it is possible to attain the significant objectives of a good education without sacrificing the fundamentals. The superiority of the student-centered classroom is not universal, however, as will be noted in Chapter 20.

The problem is related to the controversy regarding class size. Contrary to popular opinion, there is no convincing evidence that students necessarily or even generally, suffer from attendance in large classes (e.g., Siegel et al., 1959). It would seem that, if the general purpose is to transmit course content, the large lecture class tends to be more effective; on the other hand, if the objective is to develop problem-solving abilities, attitudes of inquiry, group spirit, communication skills, etc., the small discussion group should, logically, prove more adequate. Although the evidence supports this point of view, it is inconclusive. In the study by Beach (1960), for example, the less sociable students achieved more in the large lecture section, while the more sociable achieved more in the smaller groups.

PERCEPTION

Psychology has devoted considerable research to perception; it is known, for instance, that a person's attention shifts back and forth to a given object or phenomenon very much like a series of shots taken by a movie camera. Young children particularly cannot keep their attention on a given thing for an extended period of time. The teacher should attempt to keep rather short the periods in which they have to pay close attention, to vary procedures, and, most important, to get them interested, for even though their attention span is short, they can stay for surprisingly long periods with a task that genuinely interests them. Teachers must concern themselves not only with keeping the child's attention on his work but especially with directing his attention to the important things which need to be noticed. Children and even adults in unfamiliar settings notice relatively little. This is illustrated dramatically when witnesses of an accident are questioned, for instance. It is probably just as true that many children who misspell or misread words consistently are troubled by faulty perception of either or both the written or spoken form of the word, e.g., "goverment" instead of "government."

Fortunately, perception can be improved, not only by increasing sensory acuity (as with glasses or hearing aids, when needed), but also by cultivating effective perceptual habits and developing experiential background. Clear perception is often a matter of understanding the field, of having a framework into which details must fit in order to complete the picture. Without this framework, the learner does not realize the details are missing, does not look for them, and does not realize their significance when he perceives them. Thus, the teacher should be more concerned with presenting the outline of a lesson than with presenting its details; in fact, overemphasis on details only serves to obscure the structure of the material and often leaves particularly the dull child with a great number of unorganized details. Clear perception also implies negative adaptation; i.e., ability to withstand stimuli that are extraneous to the task at hand. The child who does not understand clearly the nature of a given problem is likely to be attracted by irrelevant details in attempting to solve it, and the teacher should provide him with well-directed questions to orient his attention toward significant aspects of the situation.

Perception involves a great deal of patterning or filling in from one's personal makeup. Not only does the individual display a tendency toward closure as evidenced by his ability to see a familiar word from a vague outline, but his unsatisfied needs also sensitize him selectively toward certain stimuli. As we have noted in connection with accentuation, this often causes perceptual distortion in the direction of his phenomenological orientation; in order to maintain a consistent self-concept, he approaches his environment with certain expectations as to what he is likely to perceive and he interprets various stimuli in terms of these expectations. This is particularly true of children, whose interpretations are inadequately geared to critical evaluation.

AUDIOVISUAL AIDS

Audiovisual aids are particularly necessary for the presentation of certain materials where actual experience is difficult to acquire; the geographic relation of one continent to the other, e.g., Australia and South America, are best conveyed through the use of a globe, for example.

The same is true of current events presented on television programs such as *You Are There*, which, in a very real sense, provides each child with a front-row seat at a variety of worldwide events.

One of the more common technological media used for instruction is closed-circuit television, a comprehensive example of which is the Midwest Program on Airborne Television Instruction in which educational telecasts are transmitted from Purdue University to an aircraft flying over northcentral Indiana in a seven-state broadcast region covering five million students in 1300 schools and colleges. The program is designed to provide better education than is economically feasible for any one school, e.g., permitting the broadening of the curriculum of the small school, making outstanding instructors accessible, and, in general, stretching the school dollar, while at the same time raising the quality of instruction.

Extensive use is made of modern technological instructional equipment in the teaching of modern foreign languages. In the more elaborate electronic language laboratories, the student works in a semiprivate booth with headphones, microphone, and tape recorder; he listens to prerecorded materials spoken at normal speed by a native voice, repeats what he hears into a tape recorder during the pauses provided for that purpose, and plays back alternately his own recording and that of the native model. Not only is it possible for him to compare his rendition with the original, but it is also possible for the teacher to listen in to his speech as it is being recorded. Some systems provide two-way communication: the teacher located in an instructional control booth can tune in to any student's station to ask questions or to provide remedial help and the student can, likewise, contact the teacher for any help he may need.

Even more elaborate are the various simulators (e.g., those used in driver education),[4] most of which are modeled on the Link trainer used by the Air Force. Basically, the Link trainer is an aircraft cockpit, complete with controls, designed to provide the student pilot with a concentration of experiences in handling a plane in a variety of situations without having to be in regular flight. Its advantages, in addition to factors of safety and cost, include a considerable saving in training time and a greater control of the learning situation. More recently, teaching machines of various degrees of complexity and the more elaborate automated equipment used by Moore in teaching three-year-olds to read has added a new dimension to the use of instructional equipment in aiding the teacher to accomplish more—more effectively.

On the basis of extensive use in teaching all kinds of people from elementary, high school, and college students to military personnel as well as housewives and IBM salesmen, it can be concluded that televi-

[4] See Fox (1960) for an orientation to the research on simulators in driver education. See also Gagné (1962).

sion has proven relatively successful as an instructional medium; the results of its use in schools (e.g., Siegel et al., 1959, at the college level) have shown that achievement in subject matter as measured by course examinations is as high in the television situation as in the small self-contained classroom. Television instruction can be misused, of course, and certainly the prescription of a given television program is no better than the prescription of a given number of pages from the adopted text.[5] The simple fact that students have viewed something that could have been instructive does not guarantee that the experience has been educationally profitable. Programs must be adapted to the needs of the class; frequently commercial films, for example, are oriented toward visual effectiveness rather than academic clarity. Broadcast television is often unsatisfactory and, except where live television gives the child a feeling of belonging in events as they take place, it is generally better to recast the film and schedule it at a time when it can be integrated into the regular activities of the classroom.

It seems that, as in all aspects of classroom operation, the success of television depends largely on the competence of the personnel operating the program; we need to investigate the traits and competencies which characterize good television teachers and also the type of student who can profit from television instruction. In the meantime, teachers need to be clear as to specifically what these modern media are to accomplish. In summary, television has undoubtedly made an important contribution to educational practice, not the least of which is to highlight the need to redefine the role of the various components of the classroom, and especially the function of the teacher. It has opened the way to a consideration of the broad question of the extent to which materials and equipment made possible by technological advances can contribute to classroom effectiveness. This question is receiving increasing attention as a result of the current emphasis on "teaching machines," a brief orientation to which is presented in the appendix.

PSYCHOMOTOR SKILLS

Although primarily motor, psychomotor skills are governed by the same psychological principles as underlie the more intellectual, verbal, and perhaps academic aspects of behavior. In fact, because of their essentially overt nature, psychomotor learning provides especially good examples of some of the psychological principles of learning. Psycho-

---

[5] Instructional aids, at times, become the robots who use the teacher; certain teachers, it seems, give films top priority to the point where other instructional activities are fitted around the showing of the film. To let the availability of instructional aids dictate curricular and pedagogical practices reflects professional incompetence, whether the aids be textbooks, television programs, or other technological hardware and electronic gadgetry.

motor performance, particularly in complex skills, involves a considerable element of mental activity; Twining (1949), for example, found that even in such simple activities as ring-tossing, mental practice results in considerable improvement in performance. Not only is there a considerable shift in the patterning of abilities required for success in the early and later stages of proficiency but also competence becomes more and more a function of specific habits acquired in early training (Fleishman and Fruchter, 1960). Also involved is the ability to resist stress and to eliminate awkward and useless components. An essential aspect of the learning of skills is the organization of subskills into successively higher levels of integration and of "automation" in performance. A parallel aspect is the elimination of intervening symbolic interpretations and the reduction of the number of cues necessary to identify the situation as the basis for orienting one's behavior; the batter, for example, must be able to cue his performance on very subtle differences in the pitcher's delivery.

An important factor particularly noticeable in the learning of a skill is the concept of feedback, i.e., the interpretation and reinterpretation of the situation in the light of the consequences of one's behavior: a person driving a car does not drive in a straight line but rather continually readjusts his driving to allow for shifts from one side of the road to the other. This readjustment is especially evident in mirror drawing where feedback, being reversed, is particularly difficult to interpret. Both experienced and inexperienced performers rely on the continuous correction of error; the skillful performer, however, is more sensitive to cues and adjusts more quickly to the results of feedback. There is also a difference in the nature of the feedbacks by which they operate; the beginning typist may have to see the wrong letter she has typed before she realizes her mistake whereas the more experienced typist feels the error as she hits the key. Later still, kinesthetic feedback through the stretch of the finger tells her when she has gone far enough and actually prevents errors from occurring. The importance of feedback is shown in a study by Fairbanks and Guttman (1958) in which delayed feedback of speech (through earphones) resulted in a stumbling disorganized speech pattern very similar to stuttering. Placing a shield between the subject and his writing caused a similar deterioration in handwriting; the deterioration is particularly drastic when the subject watches his handwriting through television which has been delayed one second (Smith and Smith, 1966).

Adequacy of performance is generally more immediately and objectively obvious in psychomotor skills than in ideational learnings; one knows when he has hit a home run or struck out. Because he is less able to protect his ego in the event of inadequate performance, the learner is always tempted to emphasize quality of performance at the

expense of the adequacy of the process. The beginning typist often orients herself toward the avoidance of error by adopting an accurate but
inadequate style of typing. Such overconcern with errors interferes with
effective learning and one of the teacher's primary tasks is keeping the
learner's sights on the long-range rather than the immediate but shortsighted goals.

EFFECTIVENESS IN LEARNING

Effectiveness of learning depends upon a multitude of specific factors,
most of which can be synthesized under the concept of readiness broadly
interpreted as the relative adequacy of what the learner brings to the
situation in relation to its requirements. A most important aspect of this
readiness consists of the learner's self-concept, his motivation, his self-
confidence, his relative freedom from competing motives such as might
be involved in distraction and fatigue, and especially his relative freedom from anxiety and emotional blocks. Also involved in a direct and
most crucial way is the relative adequacy of the teaching and learning
methods used in promoting said learning.

EFFECTIVE STUDY HABITS

This section will be brief, not because of its unimportance to prospective
teachers, but because it tends to overlap what has already been covered
in the text and because most college students have had considerable
acquaintance with study methods in their freshman orientation classes.

Learning is a complex task; no one learning method is best for all
combinations of learners and materials. There are, however, certain
general rules which tend to make for effective learning. Periodic review
has been shown to be an effective procedure, while cramming generally
should be discouraged because of its apparent ineffectiveness with respect
to the long-term retention required when advanced material is based on
prerequisite courses. These rules are based on the principles of educational psychology, which in turn, have been derived from research.
Determining the best method of learning, however, is made difficult
by our relative inability to control the multiplicity of factors involved,
and any conclusion must consequently be interpreted in the light of
the specific factors operating in the situation from which they are
derived. Research in the psychology of learning has produced conflicting
results at both empirical and theoretical levels. Furthermore, the conclusions stem from the superiority of one method over another in terms
of group averages and do not imply an exception-free situation.

Because of their self-sustaining nature, study habits are of major
importance in determining the effectiveness of the learner's efforts.
Even the most effective method does not necessarily yield outstanding

results immediately and the learner should be cautioned against continuing to use ineffective methods simply because they are more comfortable or because previous attempts to use better methods did not automatically lead to an immediate improvement in learning efficiency.

The following are among the rules of study which have been found effective for the majority of students:

[a] Make efficient use of study time. Time, like money, must be budgeted or it will be wasted. The student must make a habit of scheduling his study periods and getting to work promptly. The habit of "studying later" or putting off assignments until "tomorrow" can be academically fatal. Studying when "in the mood" has obvious advantages from a motivational point of view but it is undependable. Once the habit of studying is established it will stimulate the proper mood; furthermore, the proper mood can be induced by going through the motions of studying.

[b] Emphasize understanding. Getting an overview of the material before studying in detail is psychologically as well as empirically sound because it structures the field and makes for greater meaningfulness. The practice of organizing, outlining, and synthesizing generally pays off in increased understanding, greater retention, and greater transfer. Effective learning calls for a critical attitude and the ability to digest rather than merely to accumulate. The student should also strive to increase his vocabulary, his comprehension, and his reading speed.

[c] Get acquainted with the library. Rarely can the student rely on a single source; ability to skim several sources for additional information is an important contributor to scholarship.

[d] Make periodic reviews of the material. Students should learn to take functional notes in connection with class and library work as well as their basic texts; identifying the main ideas is important for quick and effective review. Review periods should be spaced at gradually increasing intervals, the first, second, and third review occurring perhaps a day, a week, and a month after the original learning. It is also wise to overlearn the material somewhat.

[e] Become ego-involved in the learning. Commitment to meaningful goals is an essential aspect of a functional education.

Many other rules could be given, but space does not permit further discussion of a topic on which so much is readily available. The student is urged to refer to the many sources to be found under *Study, Methods of,* in the card catalog of the library. In reading these references the prospective teacher, whose task it will be to help children develop effective study habits, should relate the suggestions given to basic psychological principles rather than merely accept them as arbitrary rules; he should attempt to learn not only what works but also why.

HIGHLIGHTS OF THE CHAPTER

Even though the child must learn for himself, his learning can be made more certain and more effective by competent instruction. Schools exist for that very purpose. This chapter deals with some of the considerations involved in the facilitation of learning.

[a]

The teacher's main contribution to the child's learning consists of: [1] helping develop insight into the nature of the product and the process by which it is to be attained; [2] preventing the development of faulty techniques; and [3] giving the learner moral support.

[b]

Whether the guidance given by the teacher is verbal, visual, manual, or a combination of these, it is generally more effective in the early stages of learning. Furthermore, it can be overdone.

[c]

Learning curves show graphically the learner's progress. Plateaus which are common characteristics of such curves can probably be avoided by pacing the learning.

[d]

Practice is a necessary, but not a sufficient, condition for learning. Short distributed practice periods tend to produce more efficient learning. Recitation also tends to promote more efficient learning than rereading.

[e]

Learning by wholes tends to promote more efficient learning than does learning by parts—when *wholes* are defined as the largest meaningful unit (within limits) the learner can grasp.

[f]

The lecture (and large classes) tend to be as effective as the discussion (and small class) for the transmission of information. Discussion seems more effective from the standpoint of some of the more intangible—and also more significant—aspects of education (e.g., the promotion of citizenship, problem-solving ability, and communication skills).

[g]

Modern technological instructional media are becoming progressively more an integral part of the modern classroom. Whereas they have been shown to be of direct instructional value, perhaps their most significant contribution to the cause of education has been to force a redefinition of the role and function of the various components of the instructional machinery, including the teacher.

[h]

Prospective teachers should be familiar with sound study techniques not only to improve their own learning efficiency but also to provide competent guidance for their students in the cultivation of effective study habits.

SOURCES OF RELATED MATERIAL

Association for Supervision and Curriculum Development, *Learning and the Teacher*. Washington, D.C.: The Association, 1959.

Calvin, A. D., et al., "Studies in adult learning since 1930," *J. educ. Res.*, 50: 273–85, 1956.

Gagné, R. M., and R. C. Bolles, "A review of factors in learning efficiency," in E. H. Galanter (ed.), *Automatic Teaching: The State of the Art*. New York: John Wiley & Sons, Inc., 1959. Pp. 13–53.

Mathieu, G., "Automated language instruction: A new deal for student and teacher," *Autom. teach. Bull.*, 1: 5–9, 1959.

Rivlin, H. N., *Improving Children's Learning Ability*. Chicago: Science Research Associates, Inc., 1953.

Robinson, F. P., *Effective Study*. New York: Harper & Row, Publishers, 1961.

Trace, A. S., "New look in foreign language instruction: Threat or promise?" *Mod. lang. J.*, 43: 382–386, 1959.

Underwood, Benton J., "Ten years of massed practice on distributed practice," *Psychol. Rev.*, 68: 229–247, 1961.

QUESTIONS AND PROJECTS

1

Evaluate: Educational practice has in many cases deteriorated into soft pedagogy and false humanitarianism. Actually, it doesn't make too much difference how children are made to learn worthwhile material, as long as they know it. In this day of scientific advances and world uncertainty, it is time we brought the importance of knowledge back into proper perspective.

2

College professors often display more interest in increasing their mastery over subject matter than in increasing their pedagogical skills. What does this imply about the way they perceive their role?

3

Teachers-in-training often complain that college professors of education operate on the "Do-as-I-say, not-as-I-do" basis. Is this a valid criticism?

4

Outline the next couple of chapters in the text and be prepared to hand them in to your instructor. Do not forget to incorporate your outside readings.

CHAPTER 13

Motivation
in the Classroom

> Striving for self-enhancement is not a whim
> of the individual which can be suspended at
> the teacher's command while the business of
> education goes on. It is the basic, constant, all-
> pervading life purpose of every individual, the
> sole motive of his every act.
> *Snygg and Combs, 1949, p. 237*

Motivation is of particular significance to the classroom teacher whose task it is to direct the growth of his pupils toward worthwhile goals. The present text recognizes this fact in its orientation toward the psycho-dynamics of human behavior. The purpose of this chapter is to make explicit with reference to the classroom some of the principles discussed in the previous chapters; it is not intended to provide a bag of tricks for use as a cure-all for the indifference toward schoolwork often encountered among children placed in unsuitable school environments, nor is it meant as an antidote for ill-fitting curricula, pedagogical malpractice, or other inadequacies in our schools. Motivation is certainly more than a rabbit that can be pulled out of the hat at the beginning of a lesson to make the students, individually and collectively, eager to participate in whatever the school has to offer, regardless of suitability. It must be especially noted that there is nothing in the concept of motivation that infers soft education. On the contrary, a sound motivational program implies greater academic competence for, to the extent that properly motivated students can profit from their learning experiences to a greater extent than indifferent or overanxious pupils, motivation should make for greater educational adequacy. True motivation implies a real challenge, from which meaningful education can proceed.

NATURE OF MOTIVATION

MOTIVATION: A PERSISTENT PROBLEM

In probably no area of pedagogical endeavor is the teacher so inadequate as in the area of motivation. Not only have such studies as that of Davis (1940) found motivation to be the number one problem of teachers at all levels of public school, but even a casual visit to the average classroom is likely to reveal anywhere from one to several children apathetically going through the motions of participating in class activities but really accomplishing very little, if anything. After contending with the repeated "I can't understand that," "That's sissy stuff," "I'll never use that," and the even more common instances of passive resistance, some teachers give up and rationalize their ineffectiveness by pointing out that one child is absent a lot, another is lacking in background, a third is not interested, parents do not cooperate, etc. Other teachers do not give up easily and, by alternating threats, appeals, punishment, and reward, try to evoke some semblance of activity from the student, but very often their frantic attempts to *motivate* him only serve to aggravate the problem. When activity does take place, the operation seems to be powered by a low octane mixture, complicated further by an unreleased emergency brake in the form of academic deficiencies, emotional blockings, lack of maturation, or lack of experience. Yet, contrary to what the teacher would prefer to believe in order to excuse his inability to reach him, the student is not lazy; on the playground, he is as active as the genius of the class, and after school he may delight his employer at the service station with his pep and willingness to oblige. It is just schoolwork that leaves him cold!

What the problem amounts to is that the teacher does not understand what makes children tick. He does not understand that perhaps the student has been led to form a self-image that causes him to reject everything connected with school, or that schoolwork is not related to his needs and purposes. Nor does the teacher know how to effect a change in the situation. There is need for him to become more conversant with the psychodynamics of human behavior as they pertain to behavior in general and to classroom learning in particular; only thus can he be effective as a teacher, for, as stated by McConnell (Gates et al., 1948): "There can be no more important problem in teaching . . . than that of motivation."

MEANING OF MOTIVATION

The background for the present discussion, as outlined in Chapters 3 and 4, includes the following considerations:

[a] The question of motivation concerns two distinct questions: "Why is the organism acting at all?" (the energizing aspect); "Why does the activity take the particular form it does?" (the directional aspect). Teachers are concerned with a third question: "How does one 'motivate' children?"

[b] Since motives persist until the motivating condition is satisfied, they force the organism to keep trying until he makes a response leading to the goal. Thus, motives, besides energizing the organism and directing its behavior toward a goal, also determine what behavior will be learned.

[c] Despite lack of complete agreement among motivational theorists, the fact that learning results from the goal-seeking behavior of the organism is, in a sense, the central theme of modern psychology. The view that behavior is purposive rather than accidental, even though only a theory, has proven productive in the study of human as well as animal behavior.

Motives can be conceived as predispositions toward certain kinds of behavior which have developed within the individual as a result of the relative success of his previous attempts at satisfying his needs. Peer approval, for example, becomes a motive to the adolescent to the extent that it is effective in satisfying his needs of belonging and social recognition. Thus, motivation can be understood only within the framework of the concepts of needs, goals, values, the self-image, and the phenomenal self, a good grasp of which is essential to the understanding of the present discussion. In a sense, this chapter does nothing more than spell out how the learner can be encouraged to satisfy his needs through participation in activities that lead to the attainment of desirable educational goals. The child does not learn because he has an innate interest in the intricacies of algebra; he learns because by so doing he can satisfy his needs for social recognition, self-esteem, and belonging—because it contributes to self-enhancement. Conversely, a child may not be motivated toward schoolwork simply because past experience has shown him that it does not help him to attain his purposes. Much time and effort devoted to improving the child's use of the English language is wasted, for instance, because such improvement has no meaning in his phenomenal field. The child has needs which he has to satisfy; it is up to the teacher to see that he derives satisfaction for these needs through participation in activities the school considers worthwhile.

Motivation implies a state of tension directing behavior toward the attainment of certain goals with a force roughly proportional to the net vector strength of the motives operating in the situation.[1] The child's motivation may be such as to generate too little or too much tension; it varies along a continuum ranging in intensity and effect upon behavior from: [a] inadequate motivation in which the individual is relatively apathetic and easily diverted from his goal by extraneous factors; to [b] a level that is facilitating to learning, in which the individual's behavior is characterized by direction and flexibility in the pursuit of the goal; and to [c] a higher level of intensity that interferes with effective functioning. Excessive motivation promotes rigidity in behavior which interferes especially with the more significant aspects of learning.

The school's responsibility is to keep motivation at a level that promotes maximum learning efficiency; it needs to avoid the complete lack of tension which is reflected in indifference to schoolwork and in irresponsible behavior, and at the same time to avoid excessive levels of anxiety which have such detrimental outcomes as compulsive overachievement, neurotic self-protection, and the downgrading or alteration of the self-concept to exclude anxiety-producing areas. Maintaining such an optimal balance is among the teacher's most delicate and important tasks.

MOTIVATION IN THE CLASSROOM

The motivation of children with regard to schoolwork calls for a thorough understanding of both psychology and education so that the material of the classroom can be related to the child's goals and purposes. Because of the complexity of the child, the experiences he has encountered, the self-image he has formed, and the ways he has found effective in satisfying his needs, any generalization reached on the subject is likely to be an oversimplification. Motivation has to be an individualized affair involving a consideration of the effect of any given motivational device in terms of the individual's need structure in relation to the situation in which he finds himself. In fact, nowhere does the concept of the whole child apply with so much force as in the area of motivation. Whereas a good report card may be an effective motivational device for most children, for instance, it is often perceived as something to be avoided by a child from the lower class since it not only conflicts with his sense of values but may also cause his rejection by his peers.

NEED FOR MOTIVATION

Whereas the question of whether all behavior is motivated is a matter of controversy, it is generally agreed that some degree of motivation is

[1] Ineffective behavior can result from strong but incompatible needs essentially neutralizing each other into a weak net behavior-directing force.

necessary for the effective learning of the complex material of the classroom. It also seems logical to assume that, whenever significant learning takes place, there must be some motivation, conscious or unconscious. Many children can recognize cars by make and by year, a feat most adults cannot duplicate. By the same token, it is no more unusual that a child should not know the spelling of a word he has just read than it is that the adult should not know which president is pictured on a ten-dollar bill. It is all a matter of one's motivation.

The teacher need not worry about creating motives in children. His task is to capitalize on the many motives already present in sufficient abundance in any child and to harness them toward the attainment of desirable objectives. Not only has the child many needs to satisfy but the most basic human quality is an inborn drive toward self-realization: he wants to do something for himself, to be somebody! He enjoys working through challenges toward greater competence and, unless he has been too severely hurt by past failure, he can be depended upon to propel himself forward with a minimum amount of encouragement. All that teachers need to do is provide guidance for his efforts at self-enhancement. Their task is to help the child identify suitable goals through the attainment of which he can satisfy his needs, i.e., to encourage him to develop more and more adequate motives, for not only do motives serve the purposes of learning but they are themselves subject to learning. Teachers needs to capitalize on the child's present motives, but, more important, to direct current motives into evermore appropriate channels.

When the child sees a real purpose in schoolwork, there will be no problem in motivating him, for he will work with enthusiasm, initiative, and perseverance—and coercion and artificial incentives, as well as endless repetitions, will no longer be necessary. As pointed out by Neugarten and Wright (1950), much of the problem of motivating the child will disappear if we learn to bridge the gap between those things which he should learn and those things he wants to learn. The child can be said to be motivated when the task becomes part of his psychological structure. To the extent that he is ego-involved, he can be depended upon to make adequate effort to identify with the material and to react to it wholly and creatively. Self-involvement will result in greater effort, greater understanding, and greater enjoyment; under these circumstances, education becomes *education for what is real.*

Unfortunately, much of the school curriculum, it seems, is not related fundamentally and critically to the child's needs, goals, and purposes. In fact, much of what he is made to do in the classroom does not, in his estimation, have much bearing on anything anywhere but in the classroom. Much of the training in English, for instance, does not seem to relate to out-of-school communication. The youngster who would be interested in local politics or in student government must instead study the civilization of Phoenicia. As Karpf (1961) points out, too many social studies teachers label such topics as the population explosion and medicare as peripheral—peripheral because they are not in the textbook, because they are too current to be discussed, perhaps because they contribute nothing to the teacher whose only concern is preparing students for passing standardized examinations. It may not be just coincidental that, as the child moves up the grades, there is frequently a decline in both his interest in school and in his achievement. As Jersild (1960) suggests, the curriculum becomes progressively more abstract, more coldly academic and arbitrary, and less and less of vital concern for the child's immediate purposes. Even the textbook is tailored progressively more along rigid lines of adult organization.

To make matters worse, the high school student is likely to have so many more competing interests and so much greater ability to satisfy his needs in ways that are more fundamental to him that schoolwork often becomes a very secondary matter. Under the circumstances, the teacher often has no alternative but to resort to various extraneous means of coercion in order to promote any learning, with a resulting adverse effect on the child's attitudes, not only toward the subject but also toward all that the school stands for.

To be effective, the curriculum not only must relate to the child's needs but also must be made sufficiently dynamic to meet the competition of the other activities bidding for his attention. One might even go so far as to say that generally, although not always, he should not be expected to learn anything which he has not been shown to be meaningful in terms of his goals and purposes. When exceptions to this rule occur, it should be easy enough for the teacher to capitalize on such crutches as the average student's desire to please his teacher—and even on firmness—to carry him over such humps, but, when used as a steady prop to push over meaningless material, these devices soon lose their effectiveness.

Need for Effective Goals

Teachers are not always effective in selling to children what, from an adult point of view, they see as desirable. Burton (1962) points out that teachers frequently have on their hands groups of pupils who have undergone years of conditioning under archaic curricula and incompetent teaching procedures, pupils who have to be policed and bullied into learning. We have in our schools a number of damaged children who have just given up in the face of the meaninglessness of it all. They compromise by working for a grade or the avoidance of punishment while waiting for the day they can drop out.

The problem of making schoolwork meaningful to the student is particularly acute when dealing with lower-class children whose values are often completely different from those incorporated in the curriculum. Teachers subscribe to the typical middle-class view of education as the royal vehicle for improving one's status. They forget that their value system is not universally accepted and assume that the child will want to learn to read, to get good grades, and to please the teacher, when actually for many children these middle-class values are in direct conflict with their present self-structure and that of their social group. Whereas needs do not differ appreciably from person to person, the specific goals one sets and the behavior he displays vary directly with differences in experiential background. If they are to be successful in relating the curriculum to his needs, teachers must know more about each individual child—his background, his values, and his purposes. It may even be necessary that special curricula be provided for certain children or that they be guided into certain courses.

Because behavior is directed toward a goal, the child must develop a meaningful grasp of the situation in relation to his needs so that he is aware of what the goals are, how they fit in with his purposes, how they can be attained, and how progress toward them can be evaluated, for only then is he in a position to proceed with efficiency to his destination. Often a child does not improve in composition, for instance, because he sees no real purpose in improving nor does he see how his attempts can be improved. The teacher is more often concerned with pointing out errors than in showing him how he could have turned out a better product and, when models are used, they are often too far removed from his present level for him to profit from them. In the same way, the child going through the book page by page is not likely to be aware of the goals toward which he is proceeding.

For goals to be effective, particularly for young children, they must be broken down into smaller, more immediately attainable subgoals. Although some reinforcement may derive from long-term goals and these may at times be sufficient to carry some people through a considerable amount of work, the average child needs periodic reinforcement. In fact, each phase of the work must provide its own satisfaction if effective learning is to take place. It is unrealistic to expect, "You will need it when you get to college," to be a convincing or motivationally effective answer to the twelve-year-old's question, "What are we doing all this for?" Teachers often approach the task of providing for the child's education from the standpoint of normative needs. It is frequently said that children *need* to know this, they *need* to do that, in order to be educated. Unfortunately, these normative needs do not always coincide with psychological needs and, as Wright (1948) has suggested, teachers have tutored, have implored with an awful sense of obligation, but all to no avail. It is only when children see a purpose in what they are doing that we can expect their wholehearted participation.

INTERESTS

Interests are closely related to habit motives in that they are acquired as a result of satisfying experiences and, once established, tend to perpetute themselves as long as they are effective from the standpoint of the individual's goals and purposes. They are, therefore, related to such factors as age, sex, and background. Thus, interest in love stories blossoms in adolescence and tends to die off as the individual finds more adequate ways of satisfying his need for love. Similarly, the child's interest in "cops" may reflect a need for mastery and self-assertion at a time when he is most dependent upon others, just as participation in sports provides for those needs as he becomes older, only to decline as the adult finds other interests more compatible with increasing age.

The fact that the school must relate school experiences to the child's motives and purposes does not mean that it must orient its curriculum toward his present interests. On the contrary, one of the school's primary responsibilities is to foster new purposes, new motives, and new interests. The teacher who criticizes students for not being interested might well remember that there are no primary motives that lead a child to study history; the only innate aspect of the situation is his capacity for growth. His present interests and purposes, being based on limited experience, tend to be narrow and oriented toward the trivial, but, even though temporary and perhaps silly, they are very real to him and can be used as a wedge to pry him toward more mature purposes. Thus, an interest in model airplanes can be used as a take off for developing interest in airplanes, mechanics, or science in general. In the meantime, it can serve to promote learning at his present level.

The teacher must remember that satisfaction is necessary for the development of interest. It is essential that the child be spared premature failure either to master reading techniques (perhaps because of excessive difficulty) or to get satisfaction out of reading (perhaps because of uninteresting or unduly simple content). It should also be noted in passing that meaning is an important aspect of motivation. Without the challenge involved in discovering the relationship between the old and the new, ego-involvement is not likely to develop. It is rather too much to expect a person to generate any great interest in nonsense material. This may explain the disinterest in schoolwork often found among dull children.

The teacher is often faced with the task of teaching material which does not have a great deal of appeal for children. There are things obviously worth teaching that do not carry immediate interest to students, or at least to all students. The fact that there are wide variations among children in intellectual background makes it difficult for the teacher to find material of interest to all. To make matters worse, some students take the view that they must be entertained, that responsibility for their education lies with the teacher, and that they should be free to reject anything which is not "interesting" to them. Even college students sometimes complain that they are not learning a thing from a course because the instructor is "so dull." It might occur to them that a serious attempt to learn something on their own would not only give them a good grasp of content but also might induce interest in the field. To be sure, the fault is not always with students. In too many cases, the distaste for a given subject stems from the dry and uninteresting way it is presented as well as from its inappropriateness from the standpoint of the pupils' goals and purposes. An ingenious teacher should be able to extend the child's current interests to cover most topics in the curriculum. The teacher's own enthusiasm is an important factor here. Unfortunately, teachers often become discouraged by their inability to promote pupil progress commensurate with their standards and resort to pressures which, according to Dreikurs (1957), tend to destroy the true desire to learn. Coercion is too successful in forcing children to surface compliance. Unfortunately, it generally brings only limited returns at a tremendous cost; Dreikurs believes the prevalent pressures on children are responsible for many of their bad working habits, for example.

THE ROLE OF THE TEACHER IN MOTIVATION

Inspiring children to use their potentialities for maximum self-realization is obviously the most important task facing the teacher for, in the final analysis, it is he who is the key to motivation in the classroom. It is particularly important, therefore, not only that he understand children and the ways in which they can be "motivated," but also that he be the type of person by whom they can be inspired. What this involves cannot be listed in terms of specific rules, procedures, and characteristics, for it implies all that the teacher is and all that he does as it affects the children in his care, but if special mention had to be made of relevant qualifications, sensitivity to children's needs and ingenuity in harnessing their motives in the direction of desirable goals would be among the most important. It means the teacher will have to provide moral support to the child who is frustrated by the demands of the school, a change of work for the child who is bored, special projects for the child whose interests have not yet been tapped by the school's routine. He will have to keep a nice balance between difficulty and ease of material so that the child is neither frustrated nor bored, and this he will have to do not only for one child but for some 30 children, each of different ability, interests, and background. He will have to get children to learn material in which they have no great interest and to develop those interests, relying in the meantime on his personality and his prestige as a person concerned only with their welfare. This will not always be easy. Some children have developed a negative outlook on anything academic; many have been damaged by long-continued frustration, both in and out of school. In addition, television, travel, and other modern educational opportunities have made many of them relatively blasé with respect to a number of the things that would have been exciting to the previous generation.

Professional competence is essential. In addition to being the kind of person with whom children can identify to the point of being sensitive to his approval and disapproval, the teacher needs to be ingenious in the use of his personality and his professional skills as a force in tipping the scales of their multivector motivational structure in the direction of desirable behavior. It is especially important that he provide children with sufficient success in significant situations so that they can develop a positive self-concept and thereby place themselves on a self-actualizing schedule. He needs to safeguard them from the disruptive and damaging effects of premature and continued failure by making sure that they are ready for whatever task is assigned. He also needs to give them moral support while they experiment in tackling difficulties and in setting realistic goals. In summary, the teacher needs to help children develop personal adequacy as well as academic competence and enthusiasm for schoolwork through a planned sequence of relative successes in an atmosphere of psychological safety.

This implies that the teacher must know the ability level, the interests, and the experiential background of each child as that child gradually evolves; he must develop a sensitivity to pupil needs which permits him to keep tension at a level from which children can profit and avoid the severe tensions which can only result in disorganization and damage. It also implies a judicious degree of differentiation of the curriculum where indicated. It does not imply a soft education but rather curricular experiences which allow the child's natural capacity for growth an opportunity to operate for the welfare of all. Perhaps more fundamentally, the teacher needs to decide whether the school's prime responsibility is that of inculcating certain skills and facts or whether its primary purpose is to develop self-actualizing persons in the process of *becoming*. It makes a difference: whereas emphasis on the fully-functioning person will result in greater academic competence, overemphasis on academic competence *per se* can easily operate to the detriment of self-actualization.

That the classroom is a social group is of fundamental importance from the standpoint of motivation, for the group exerts a powerful influence upon its members to conform to group values. If, therefore, the class and the teacher can agree on mutually acceptable goals, the pressure of the group upon the individual to contribute toward the attainment of these goals will ensure the motivation of the individual members. The teacher's task will then be one of selling the group on certain goals and of maintaining group cohesiveness so that the members remain subject to group influence. Since social reinforcement is probably the teacher's greatest ally in motivating children, he needs to pay particular attention to promoting a high classroom morale and to working through the group in orienting students toward worthwhile objectives from which the members can obtain individual and collective satisfaction.

INCENTIVES

Incentives are objects or conditions that have possibilities for satisfying needs and that therefore can become goals toward which behavior is directed. Their effectiveness in orienting behavior is a function of the expectations they hold for the individual from the standpoint of his needs. Thus, whereas food may be a powerful incentive to a hungry person, it has no incentive value to a person whose hunger is completely satisfied. Furthermore, partly as a result of the specific experiences on the basis of which their motives have evolved, certain foods would probably never be an incentive to certain persons, no matter how hungry. An incentive may also derive its effectiveness from being something the learner wants to avoid (e.g., punishment). The picture is complicated by the fact that the organism is always besieged by a multiplicity of unsatisfied needs and that a given incentive may have positive valence with regard to one motive and negative valence with regard to another. Incentives also act in combination: the child may not only be attracted by a good grade but also be pushed in that direction by fear of punishment if his grades are low. What behavior will result in a given situation is determined by the net force of the various need-goal sequences in the individual's overall motivational structure in relation to situational realities.

Incentives may be: [a] intrinsic, i.e., inherent in the activity itself, as in the case of the person learning to play the violin for the aesthetic pleasure he derives from playing; or [b] extrinsic, i.e., external to the activity, e.g., the child studying algebra to get a monetary reward or a good grade. It should be noted, that the terms *extrinsic* and *intrinsic* apply, not to the motivation since motivation is always within the learner, but rather to the relationship between the task and the goal. Some incentives, e.g., food, derive their appeal from their ability to satisfy a need directly; others, such as money, have appeal of various degrees of indirectness from the standpoint of prestige, self-esteem, etc. Actually, the distinction between intrinsic and extrinsic incentives, as they operate in a given situation, is not always clear. Running and playing for the pleasure of muscular release involves an intrinsic incentive but the minute a person tries to outrun others—and thereby satisfy his need for social approval—the incentive is extrinsic. An activity often involves both extrinsic and intrinsic incentives; a teacher may enjoy working with children but still appreciate being paid. It might be noted in passing that extrinsic incentives are not artificial; even though extraneous to the activity, they cannot be extraneous to the motives of the learner. If they were, they would not be incentives.

INCENTIVES IN THE CLASSROOM

The teacher uses many incentives to stimulate the learner to action. Incentives derive their effectiveness through their potentiality in tapping the motives the learner already possesses, and the teacher must think, not in terms of incentives, but rather in terms of needs and the way they can be satisfied in the course of the child's doing what the school considers worthwhile for him to do. If the child can be led to find satisfaction for his needs in doing the classwork expected of him, the desperate jiggling of artificial incentives will be unnecessary, and misbehavior and indifference to schoolwork will cease to be problems.

A certain amount of the trouble teachers experience in motivating children stems from too exclusive a reliance on extrinsic incentives. Rather than concentrate on making their subject interesting, challenging, and satisfying from the standpoint of pupil needs and purposes, too many teachers attempt to force learning through punishment and rewards which are related only artificially to the activities of the school. This does not imply that extrinsic incentives have no place in the classroom but they have definite limitations that must be recognized. They can be ineffective, and even harmful, under the following conditions:

[a] When they stem from the authority of the teacher rather than from the relationship between the task and the goals of the learner. This tends to be part of the authority-centered approach to teaching in which the learner works for the rewards provided by the teacher; it is more conducive to docility and deference to authority than to self-initiated, self-regulated, and self-rewarding learning.

[b] When they lead to emotional disturbances. When there is but one prize or reward, it automatically means that all but a few—namely, the winner and those who, convinced that they are not in the running, have ceased to care—are bound to be disappointed. Under such conditions, incentives are not only ineffective; they are definitely harmful.

[c] When they are emphasized to the point of superseding the real goals of education. When rewards, no matter how good, are emphasized,

the significance of a given activity tends to be measured in units of the rewards it brings. Grades are so important to some students that accumulating a good scholastic record or surpassing others becomes the measure of academic and personal worth. Others restrict their learning to the minimum necessary to obtain a passing grade. The precaution teachers take to protect the security of examinations, for example, is a reflection of the objectionably extrinsic nature of grades in the overall learning process. Under these conditions, grades actually impede learning by forcing the student to study not what is important but what is likely to be covered in the test. Under these circumstances, grades simply serve to teach the child shortcuts such as cramming, cheating, apple-polishing, and other means of circumventing true learning. Furthermore, although overemphasis on incentives can promote some learning, this learning tends to cease the minute the incentive is removed. The emphasis must remain on the real goal, for that is what will continue to be significant after the reward is removed. This is the true test of the adequacy of motivation.

Overemphasis on incentives tends to be self-defeating, especially in that rewards are generally offered on a rationed basis. The honor roll must be restricted to the few if it is to maintain its incentive value. Furthermore, the rewards are not always fairly apportioned. The gifted child can attain success, praise, etc., without much exertion whereas the dull child cannot even come close no matter how hard he tries. As a result, the latter would often prefer not to try for the reward, except that the threat of punishment is often added to reinforce the goal which was not basically attractive in the first place. The threat of punishment, however, is conducive only to minimal effort, so that rewards actually discourage the dull child from his best efforts. Eventually he decides he must look elsewhere for the satisfaction of his needs. But in order to do this and still maintain a consistent self-image, he may find it necessary to reject many of the values for which the school stands. The end result is that he is no longer subject to the beneficial pressures which the school as a social agency should exert upon him for the good of all.

Sanford (1961) presents a convincing argument that, with our emphasis on extrinsic motivation, we may actually be deemphasizing the inherent importance of education and the simple enjoyment of learning. We seem to suggest that an activity that has to be controlled by reward is not worth doing in its own right. We seem to imply that the only thing that counts is the grade, and we may be issuing a subtle invitation for students to get grades by any and all available means. Even such benevolent incentives as praise tend to be objectionable in that they imply that there must be an external paymaster sitting in judgment over his workers. Bruner (1961) argues against heavy reliance on external rewards on the grounds that they tend to orient the child toward teacher-prescribed goals rather than toward self-discovery which thrives best under a self-rewarding schedule.

Nevertheless, there are times when one has no alternative but to rely on extrinsic incentives. They are acceptable, for example, when they are used to start an activity on a self-sustaining basis, or perhaps to reinforce the rewards inherent in the activity. Any new activity can be motivated through intrinsic incentives only after the child has actually tried it at least once under rewarding conditions. External motivation may be necessary in the early stages of learning. However, the teacher must see that extrinsic rewards are gradually deemphasized and that the intrinsic quality of the relationship is promoted as soon as possible.

This may be difficult in a large class of heterogeneous ability but it is fundamental and within the capabilities of a skillful teacher. One thing is sure: presenting a large assignment without provision for adequate reward is likely to result in discouragement. We need to present material in units small enough to permit the satisfaction of success to propel the child along, while at the same time providing whatever extrinsic rewards are necessary in the early stages to tip the scale toward the positive side. There is nothing wrong with praise added to the natural satisfaction which the child gets out of work well done. But, what is important is for teachers to realize that, if they could lead children to set realistic goals and deal with meaningful materials, the need for artificial rewards would be correspondingly reduced; it might behoove educators to improve their curriculum and pedagogical skills rather than to continue to rely on crutches.

Intrinsic incentives are probably best in that they are more fundamental and, in many cases, more dependable. The boy for whom planning the family's summer trip really means something can be depended upon to participate with enthusiasm and effectiveness. Yet extreme opposition to extrinsic incentives is not warranted and as early as 1935 Thorndike pointed out that the advantages of intrinsic over extrinsic motivation had been exaggerated. This opinion finds support in such studies as that of Symonds and Chase (1929), for example, in which the group extrinsically motivated through tests was found to have made nearly five times the gains of an intrinsically motivated group and six times the gains of a third group stimulated by no particular incentive. Perhaps, rather than making a sharp distinction between the two, the teacher might concern himself with cultivating in children interest in school activities and in having them develop a self-concept oriented toward schoolwork as an important avenue to self-realization. But he might also make judicious use of extrinsic incentives to reinforce intrinsic rewards and thus ensure the harnessing of their motives in the direction of activities which will promote such self-realization.

A number of studies have been conducted on the relative valence strength of various incentives. To the extent that incentive appeal varies with the individual situation, however, these studies are of relatively limited generalization value. Whether a given incentive has positive or negative valence depends on the individual's motive structure at a given time, although certain incentives are perhaps essentially negative or essentially positive to most people most of the time. It might also be surmised that such incentives as ridicule and sarcasm, besides being relatively ineffective, tend to be debasing and objectionable regardless of their empirical effect. It must also be recognized that incentives do not work singly but rather are involved in complex interaction.

REWARD AND PUNISHMENT

Since every response of the motivated organism is either "rewarded" or "punished" depending on whether or not it serves to attain its goals, all incentives can be grouped into broad categories of reward and punishment. In general, the former is more effective in promoting learning than the latter, but that the evidence should be far from clear is not surprising in view of the many complicating factors involved. What constitutes reward and punishment for a given person depends on his phenomenological appraisal of the situation. We would have to consider, for example, the penalties one must pay in peer status for the praise which the teacher provides. Actually, reward and punishment refer to relatively superficial aspects of the situation; the more fundamental aspects of motivation concern motive satisfaction and these can be considered only from the individual's personal point of view.

Probably no other motivational factor has attracted as much attention as punishment. This is more in keeping with the prevalence of its use by parents, teachers, and society in general than with its effectiveness, for all evidence points to both its relative futility as a motivational device and its potentially damaging effects. Whereas arguments can be advanced in favor of its use in special cases, the continued emphasis on punishment is more a reflection of social approval based on ignorance than a matter of psychological endorsement. On the other hand, the evaluation of its effects must take into consideration such factors as its intensity, its fairness, the setting in which it is administered, and the relationship between the punished and the punisher. As a result, any conclusion as to its effectiveness as an incentive in both an academic and disciplinary setting cannot be generalized to all situations. The general consensus is that a punitive approach, especially if it entails severe punishment, is particularly detrimental in the case of the young child, who is relatively incapable of making adequate discriminations as to the pertinence of the punishment and who generalizes too easily to areas where it does not pertain. This is especially true when the punishers are his parents on whom he is totally dependent for security. If introduced too soon, punishment by the parents tends to interfere with normal identification and promotes the development of blind inhibitions reflected in rigid, stereotyped behavior with no integrative basis for learning to deal with the future.

Sears et al. (1957) in their classic study noted that "The unhappy effects of punishment have run like a dismal thread throughout our findings." The mothers who punished toilet accidents severely ended up with bed-wetting children; the mothers who punished dependency had more dependent children; the mothers who punished aggressive behavior severely had more aggressive children. This does not mean that punishment is to be avoided at all costs; on the contrary, Sears found that a completely permissive atmosphere is also bad. Punishment in the sense of disapproval or nonreinforcement is effective and essential; physical aggression, on the other hand, is self-defeating and damaging.

The effects of punishment must be considered from the standpoint of the anxiety it produces and again we must distinguish between various degrees of punishment and the corresponding levels of anxiety which they generate. Mild punishment in the sense of nonreward or even disapproval may serve an informational function; certainly the child needs to be made aware of the fact that his response was not adequate. What active punishment would contribute beyond this point is, of course, a complicated proposition. Moderate punishment tends to suppress the undesirable outward behavior but may not affect the underlying motivation. Severe punishment, on the other hand, tends to have more drastic side effects ranging from personality distortion to compulsive stereotyped continuance of the undesirable behavior. It often results in a closing off of experience, with personal inadequacy as the inevitable eventual outcome.

The effects of punishment are not all negative; certainly some punishment is essential, if the alternative is a continuous series of success experiences. This does not mean that punishment needs to be introduced deliberately. The child in the process of *becoming* seeks challenges and generates his own failures and punishments. As a disciplinary measure, punishment may be effective in stamping out undesirable behavior, e.g., as a deterrent to the child's touching the stove; it fails as a motivational device in that it emphasizes what not to do but does not tell what needs to be done instead. Punishment may be of value in setting definite limits beyond which the child cannot go, e.g., not crossing the street. That this is not particularly effective seems rather clear from the fact that delinquents know what the limits are; they are simply not motivated to abide by what they know. It may be better to explain what is expected in an accepting manner and to show disapproval of violations without resorting to severe punishment. Punishment may make the child more careful; the loss of a grade may draw his attention to careless errors that would otherwise be sloughed off, for example. As anxiety sets in, however, there is a greater focus on routine aspects with correspondingly less openness to subtle cues and less insight into the important things to the point where the child simply becomes more "stupid." Punishment can sometimes be effective in jarring the child out of his complacency and leading him to put in the effort required to attain a desirable goal. On the other hand, it needs to be used judiciously with full awareness of its dangers and its limitations.

That punishment of incorrect responses is less effective than the rewarding of correct responses has been known since the days of Thorndike (1931), and psychologists are agreed that the emphasis, particularly as it applies to classroom learning, must be on reward rather than punishment. Besides being relatively ineffective, punishment has definitely harmful side effects: it frequently results in antagonism, counter-aggression, and a desire for revenge. It creates emotional tensions which become a distracting element in an already difficult situation. It may cause emotional disturbances to the point of a disorganization of behavior. The severe punishment of a given response tends to promote its fixation; by generating anxiety, it leads to restriction of the perceptual field in which the individual, rather than face the uncertainty of a novel approach, simply repeats the incorrect response and takes the expected punishment. Applied too frequently, it tends to make the child progressively less capable of self-direction. It often promotes psychological withdrawal and a closing off of the avenues of improvement; it tends to generate a negative self-concept in which the child ceases to care whether he improves or not. He simply strives to avoid the punishment and if there are other ways out of the situation, he will take them, so that the teacher needs to be ready with adequate secondary defenses. It sometimes has unusual outcomes: for example, parents often follow the punishment of their child with lavish guilt-produced affection so that they end up by rewarding the undesirable behavior they are attempting to eliminate. This does not deny that punishment may have a place in the socialization of the child and in the motivation of his learning, but those who use it need to be clear as to the purpose they want it to serve. For example, it is sometimes claimed that punishment is necessary to teach children respect for authority and to act as a deterrent for potential offenders. But is it? Does it? And is punishment the best way to promote these objectives? It must also be recognized that punishment will not work when the activity is self-reinforcing, e.g., misbehavior in the classroom which may get periodic reinforcement through approval by the child's fellow mischief-makers.

The situation is not completely hopeless, however. The fact that punishment temporarily suppresses the objectionable response provides the basis for learning, for, to the extent that suppressed behavior leads to increased tension, it increases the likelihood of the occurrence of a desirable response which can be rewarded and therefore learned. It is the general consensus that punishment is most effective when used in conjunction with the rewarding of a more appropriate response. In the study by Penny and Lupton (1961), a combination of reward and punishment was found to be more effective than either reward or punishment alone. In other words, punishment appropriately combined with reward of correct responses may be used to redirect behavior; the net result of punishment depends on what it leads the child to do that can be rewarded into improved behavior.

SUCCESS AND FAILURE

Although the effects of failure vary considerably with such factors as the security of the individual, research suggests that people reach new heights as a result of their success in meeting challenges and that they reach new lows as a result of their continued failure. In a study by Postman and Bruner (1948), the group that had been frustrated by inability to keep up with the speed at which pictures were flashed on a screen did more poorly than a control group when confronted with the simple task of perceiving three-word sentences presented at a reasonable speed. Similarly, scholastically successful students have been found to improve on tests of intelligence while scholastically unsuccessful students do more poorly.

The effects of failure are best considered from the standpoint of the self-concept. Most people like to think of themselves as capable. When first faced with failure, the individual is likely to redouble his efforts in order to maintain a consistent self-image. When faced with continued failure, however, he cannot help but lose in self-esteem as a result of the unfavorable comparisons he makes or which are made for him. He is thus forced to alter his self-image, and having conceived of himself as inadequate in a given area—or as a complete failure, if his failures cover a number of areas—he proceeds to live up (or rather down) to this self-image, thereby confirming his image of incompetence.

The teacher should be particularly careful that the child's early contacts with a given activity be successful. Most activities have some degree of inherent motivational appeal once the activity gets under way; failure before the student has had a chance to capitalize on this inherent appeal should be kept to a minimum. The teacher can set the stage for success through providing readiness exercises, setting clear-cut goals, giving him evidence of his progress, and not expecting too much too soon. It may even be necessary for the teacher to find areas which matter to the child and in which he can be successful in order for him to build a positive self-concept. Furthermore, inasmuch as what is success and what is failure is a function of one's level of aspiration, it is important that the child be helped to set realistic goals as means of ensuring some measure of success and thereby promoting self-actualization.

Success and failure have far-reaching consequences. The child whose self-image is one of confidence will do better than one who views each new situation as the occasion which will once again prove him a failure. And, to allay the fears of those who might argue that the absence of failure will develop a spoiled, spineless individual unable to meet any form of crisis, it can be said without fear of contradiction that success is a better preparation for both success and failure than is failure. Furthermore there will always be enough failures to strengthen moral fiber, especially as success tends to develop secure individuals unafraid of tackling difficult and challenging tasks. There is nothing wrong with the occasional failure, but it can do definite harm when it causes the child to feel unworthy or to become less capable of dealing with the future.

Unfortunately, some teachers emphasize failure as their basic motivational device. Many teachers in their first grading period, apparently with the idea of putting students on notice that standards will be maintained, give low grades to the whole class, regardless of performance. Some pride themselves on being tough; they operate on the premise that this is the way to make men out of boys. Grades are an important aspect of success and failure in school; they *should* represent an index of the caliber of the pupil's performance, but they frequently turn out to be weapons teachers hold over the heads of children. Furthermore, grades violate the fundamental criterion of adequate incentives in that, besides being relatively meaningless as symbols of achievement, they are not available to all on an equitable basis.

Other incentives such as praise and reproof, reward and punishment, have direct bearing on the present discussion inasmuch as they serve to emphasize the success and failure component of performance; their value and limitations must therefore be considered in the light of the principles above. This applies also to knowledge of results which has motivational value in that it provides reinforcement and may be important in schoolwork where the success and failure of one's efforts is not always clear. In addition, knowledge of results has feedback (informational) value which is essential in redirecting the learner's performance; not only does it identify areas in need of further practice, but it also spells out how much of a correction he needs to make in his next attempt.

PRAISE AND REPROOF

The praise and reproof continuum is another aspect of reinforcement and needs to be considered from that standpoint. Furthermore, it must be interpreted phenomenologically. One has to know who is being praised, for what, and by whom, the price being paid in terms of peer status, whether it is given in a spirit of helpfulness, and many other aspects of the psychological situation. Considerable research has been conducted on this subject, much of it contaminated by the inherent reinforcement of the activity itself. As a child gets interested in an activity for its own sake or for the status it gives him among his peers, praise or reproof by the teacher becomes a progressively more inconsequential aspect of the overall situation. In the Silberman study (1957), the teacher's commendation or reproof had little effect on learning, presumably because the teacher is a relatively unimportant source of reinforcement in the case of meaningful material where the learner can be his own judge of his success.

Research has shown praise as a motivational device to be superior to reproof which, in turn, tends to be more effective than no comment. Hurlock (1925), for example, compared the arithmetic performance of fourth- and fifth-grade children subjected to different levels of praise and reproof. At the end of each day, the reproved group, regardless of the quality of its performance, was called to the front of the room where it was admonished for its mistakes, its careless work, and its failure to improve. The praised group, on the other hand, regardless of how well or how poorly it had performed, faced the class each day and was complimented on its fine work. The ignored group heard the praise or reproof administered to the other groups but was neither praised nor berated. A control group in a separate room was not subjected to any of the three experimental factors. The data showed considerable superiority of the praised group; as shown in Figure 13-1, the performance of the reproved subjects deteriorated badly after the second day.

Research (Thompson and Hunnicutt, 1944) has also shown reproof to be relatively more effective with boys than with girls, with the bright than with the dull, and with the extrovert than with the introvert. But these findings are far from conclusive. Schmidt (1941), for example, reviewing the evidence on the subject, found no basis for the claim that praise is more effective than reproof, a conclusion which is understandable considering the complexity of the situation; a student may, for example, see reproof from a much disliked teacher as rewarding from the standpoint of the resulting gain in peer status. A distinction must also be made between constructive criticism given by a friendly teacher in a spirit of helpfulness and the vicious abuse sometimes showered upon students by frustrated teachers. Constructive criticism is essential for effective pupil growth, but little good is likely to result from a situation in which the child, because of insecurity, the way the criticism is given, or the person giving the criticism, feels compelled to shut himself off from attack to protect his self-image.

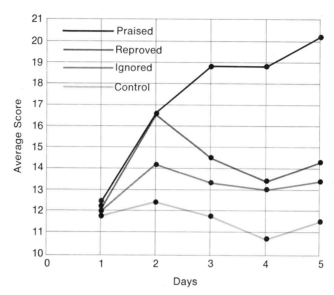

FIGURE 13-1   The effect of different motivating conditions on solution of arithmetic problems.
Note that the scores of all four groups were
initially equivalent. (After Hurlock, 1925.)

Unfortunately, despite its relative ineffectiveness, many of our deal-
ings in the home, the school, and elsewhere emphasize reproof rather
than praise. Teachers, in common with people in general, believe in
praise, but in practice tend to use reproof more often. Dreikurs (1957)
charges that we know how to discourage; we find it easy to criticize
but, when faced with the need to encourage, we are clumsy and end up
doing the opposite. When we want to help somebody, we resort to correction, pointing out his mistakes; we rationalize that we are doing it for
his own good, unaware that more benefit accrues to our own ego than
to his. Even when we encourage the child, we often do so in a discouraging way, telling him that he could do so much better if only he . . . ,
thereby implying that he has not done well up to now. Gordon (1963)
makes the same point concerning the nagging teacher who, every time
he attempts to reward behavior by praising it, inadvertently also punishes it by accusing the child of not having made the correct response in
the past. Of course, there is much unspoken praise, but teachers would
do well to remember that achievement without recognition is relatively
unsatisfying. Praise should be given judiciously, of course, and without
flattery, but it should be possible to find, in the course of the school day,
numerous occasions deserving of honest praise. It is also important to
note that, whereas praise tends to be cumulative in its effects, reproof

soon loses its effectiveness and probably nothing could be more senseless from a motivational point of view—and as harmful to mental health—than the constant berating of students.

COMPETITION AND COOPERATION

The potential benefits and evils of competition have been debated on many occasions; a more profitable undertaking might be to consider the circumstances and conditions under which it can be harmful and those under which it can be beneficial. Competition can have harmful effects under the following circumstances:

[a] When success is over-restricted, when there are few winners and many losers to the point where the losers, in self-defense, must decline further participation. Generally the weak ones are eliminated or withdraw for fear of coming up short so that competition denies participation to the very ones who need it most.

[b] When it is so intense that losing means loss of status, even in the case of individuals who did not wish to participate in the first place and whose fear of losing was a major factor in their defeat. Competition is harmful when everyone is so busy protecting himself from the threat of the achievements of others that no one can do his best.

[c] When winning at all costs overshadows all other considerations; when children become obsessed with the need to surpass others; when values get lost in the pursuit of self-aggrandizement; when the success of others is a source of threat rather than happiness and good fellowship; when the need to win at all costs leads to dishonesty, rivalry, bitterness, and reprisals in the case of defeat. As Jersild (1960) points out, competion becomes rather sick when the child becomes vindictive, gloating over his rivals and enjoying their defeat. There is also a sick quality when the child who loses feels bitter toward himself and has revenge as his goal, or feels that he must prove that he can beat others, even when the contest has little or no value for him.

[d] When it interferes with creative social participation. Some people just cannot participate even in social situations unless there is some way of excelling.

[e] When attention has not been given to a gradual moving toward more intrinsic incentives so that learning ceases the moment the competition is removed.

Competition is not necessarily bad: research suggests that it can promote superior performance. In fact, individual competition tends to be more effective in promoting learning than group rivalry which, in turn, is more effective than group cooperation. Thus Sims (1928) found the individually motivated group to make a 35 percent gain as opposed to a 15 percent gain for the team-motivated group and a 9 percent gain for the group with no special motivation. Similar results were obtained by Leuba (1933) and Maller (1929). On the other hand, its relative effectiveness would undoubtedly vary with such factors as the nature of the task, the personality and experience of the participants, and the cohesiveness of the group.

Competition is necessary to provide the child with a basis for appraising his capabilities as background for realistic goal setting. It can lead him to overcome personal limitations and thereby promote greater adequacy. Ordinary competition in making friends, for example, leads to socialization and sensitivity to the rights and feelings of others. It can provide the challenge that stimulates greater individual productivity and thereby raises standards, and it can do this without the emotional upset and the compulsive striving which we have mentioned.

It is often said that competition is so basic to our way of life that the school has a responsibility to teach children how to compete, that business thrives and that nations prosper under the impetus of competition. In rebuttal, Combs (1957) points out that ours is not a competitive society but rather the most interdependent society the world has ever known; that competition is not a powerful motive but rather that it discourages scores of people from trying; and that competition is not a strong incentive for improving quality but rather that it produces people more willing to cheat than to produce. Moreover, as he points out, the fact that competition exists in our society is no reason why we ought to have more competition in our schools, especially since certain teachers make their classrooms much more competitive—with the degree of success relative to that of others much more obvious and the freedom to withdraw much less—than is generally encountered out of school. Although the judicious use of competition can increase interest in schoolwork, it is essential that this competition not be of the dog-eat-dog variety and that everyone have a chance of winning. Certainly, there is no justification for forcing the child into competition in which he must inevitably lose.

It is also argued that competition is relatively innate, presumably on the premise that we ought to go along with what is "natural." Actually it is relatively difficult to deal with the question: it seems likely that competition has both native and learned components. There is evidence that aggressiveness is tied to glandular secretion, for example (see Chapter 5). On the other hand, competitive tendencies are susceptible to environmental modification, especially from the standpoint of the social acceptability of the behavior through which they are expressed. Kittens and rats have not only been trained to live together but also to cooperate in getting food for one another (Ruch, 1963). On the other hand, in Fredericson's study (1951), mice trained to compete for food in early

infancy and then allowed to grow into adulthood without further competition were found to be highly competitive with regard to fighting over
food many weeks later.

But none of this evidence answers the question as to whether competition or cooperation is the more fundamental. Actually the issue is
ambiguous. Cooperation can be visualized as organized group competition and, of course, many activities involve a good measure of each both
alternately and simultaneously. Team sports, for example, involve competition between two cooperative groups and, even within each team,
there is much competition (as well as cooperation) as to who plays a
given position.

Competition in the classroom may stimulate greater output, for it
subjects the child to the full force of the dynamics of a closed peer group
culture, one of the most fundamental and powerful motivational influences available. It suffers, however, from a number of severe limitations
as we have already noted. Unless it is reinforced by coercion, overemphasis on competition almost invariably leads to indifferent performance
on the part of the weaker students who cannot afford to try. When
the child encounters continuous failure, the line of least resistance, and
the most intelligent, is to stop trying. Generally speaking, competition
is a part of the autocratic pattern of classroom management and often
leads to a need for further autocratic measures. Even more important
is the effect which it has upon the participants. Competition can lead to
a downgrading of the self-concept and to an attitude of indifference toward schoolwork as a means of maintaining an image of personal
adequacy in the face of poor scholastic performance. It can also result
in the destruction of group loyalties and of the child's capacity to cooperate; it tends to cause resentment, jealousy, and poor intragroup relations.
In fact, it can negate the very values for which the school and democratic
society stand.

Competition, as do all incentives, has its dangers and its limitations.
However, much of the criticism of competition has been directed at its
abuse rather than its use, and the position taken by Jersild (Gates et al.,
1948) appears both educationally and psychologically sound:

> From an educational point of view, the proper attitude
> toward competition is not to deplore it on general principles,
> not to try to stamp it out by grudging rewards to those who are
> deserving nor by placing a handicap on those best able to
> achieve. The practical attitude rather should be to turn com-
> petitive impulses into the most constructive channels; to avoid
> emphasis on ulterior or artificial rewards; to provide each indi-
> vidual as far as possible with opportunities that are com-

mensurate with his abilities; to provide opportunities for children with different types and degrees of ability to have a taste of achievement; to prevent inequalities in the rewards for useful service; and to avoid a policy of continually placing children in competitive situations in which they are bound to fail. [p. 150]

Competition is neither good nor bad in itself. Undoubtedly, there is need for greater emphasis on cooperation in the classroom to offset the competitive training the child is going to get. On the surface, it would seem that cooperation requires a greater personal maturity and a more self-fulfilling approach to life, but certainly one cannot generalize to all cases. Competition need not have the adverse effects we have noted. When groups are well-matched, when the emphasis is on good sportmanship and character development, when the goals are realistically attainable so that the individual does not have to compete compulsively and recklessly, little harm need result. Phillips and D'Amico (1956) have shown that competition does not necessarily have adverse effects on group cohesiveness, for example.

There are many achievements that can result from healthy competition and whereas we condemn aggression, we know that competitive feelings can be channeled into a high degree of leadership. It is a matter of the way the competition is exerted, and certainly such traits as courage, initiative, persistence, and self-dependence which are promoted through healthy competition are good old American virtues. Whereas we note the abuses and view with alarm the athletic scandals, we must not overlook the dozens of "real nice guys" who have come out of our sports program; we must not overlook the many leaders in industry, business, and government who have come up through our competitive ranks. Unfortunately, as indicated by Blair et al. (1962), American schools have fostered competition without teaching children how to compete. We need not condemn competition, but we need to emphasize that what is important is not besting the next person but rather dealing with problems with progressively greater effectiveness. The emphasis should be on personal growth rather than superiority to others.

Competition needs to be used cautiously and, in general, the less personal the rivalry, the less potentially dangerous it is. Thus, group rivalry tends to be less intense and less harmful than individual rivalry, although here too teachers need to be careful lest group rivalry assume the proportions of gang warfare. Nor should group rivalry pit boys against girls, for this could interfere with the necessary heterosexual adjustment that must take place in adolescence. The often repeated suggestion that children should compete against their own record rather than against those of others is probably psychologically sound, but it does pose a problem in terms of the mechanics of execution when dealing with learning in the classroom. In order to compete successfully against himself, must the child convert all his C's into B's and all his B's into A's? This problem will be discussed further in Chapter 16.

HIGHLIGHTS OF THE CHAPTER

Motivation is one of the more troublesome aspects of teaching. Part of the difficulty apparently stems from the teacher's failure to understand the *why* of the child's behavior and the experiences through which his growth is promoted. The following are among the major points with which the teacher should be familiar if he is to be successful in classroom motivation.

[a]

Motivation stems directly from the concepts of needs, the self, and the phenomenal field as discussed in Chapters 3 and 4 and incorporates both the energizing of the individual and the orientation of his behavior toward the attainment of certain goals as potential satisfiers of his needs.

[b]

A reasonable level of motivation is generally considered essential to effective classroom learning. Both inadequate and excessive motivation are to be avoided.

[c]

The child is always motivated. The teacher's task is to harness his motives in the service of education through the promotion of worthwhile goals meaningfully related to his needs and purposes.

[d]

Numerous incentives are available to the teacher to tap the motives existing in the child. Extrinsic incentives are often emphasized to the point where they supersede the real goals and provide rather convincing evidence that the activity is not worthwhile apart from the incentive.

[e]

All incentives are best understood in terms of reward and punishment, i.e., in terms of whether or not they satisfy the purposes of the motivated organism. The positive incentives (reward, success, praise, etc.) are generally more effective than their negative counterparts. Punishment is particularly ineffective, except as part of a punishment-reward sequence.

[f]

Knowledge of results not only has motivational value, but it also provides direct feedback as to the areas to which the learner needs to devote his efforts and the extent of the correction needed.

[g]

Success is important from the standpoint of motivation, particularly as it leads to the development of a positive self-concept and, hence, to further success and further motivation. Teachers too often emphasize failure in a misguided attempt to have the learner improve. Success is a relative term and the child should be encouraged to develop a realistic level of aspiration.

[h]

Competition is a powerful incentive since it brings the full force of group pressure to bear upon the learner. On the other hand, it can be dangerous and should be used judiciously.

[i]

The fact that the classroom is a social group is of fundamental importance since social reinforcement is the teacher's greatest ally in "motivating" children.

[j]

The teacher is, in the final analysis, the key to motivation in the classroom.

SOURCES OF RELATED MATERIAL

Combs, Arthur W., "The myth of competition," *Childh. Educ.*, 33: 264–269, 1957.

Dinkmeyer, D., and R. Dreikurs, *Encouraging Children to Learn: The Encouragement Process.* Englewood Cliffs, N.J.: Prentice-Hall, Inc., 1963.

Dinsmoor, J. A., "Punishment: 2. An interpretation of empirical findings," *Psychol. Rev.*, 62: 96–105, 1955.

Marx, Melvin H., "Motivation," in C. W. Harris (ed.), *Encyclopedia of Educational Research.* New York: Crowell-Collier and Macmillan, Inc., 1960. Pp. 888–901.

Sears, Pauline S., and E. R. Hilgard, "The teacher's role in the motivation of the learner," in E. R. Hilgard (ed.), *Theories of Learning and Instruction.* 63rd Yearbook, National Society for the Study of Education, Pt. I. Chicago: University of Chicago Press, 1964. Pp. 182–209.

Young, Paul T., *Motivation and Emotions: A Survey of the Determinants of Human and Animal Activity.* New York: John Wiley & Sons, Inc., 1961.

QUESTIONS AND PROJECTS

1

[a] Evaluate: Whereas most of the learning primitive man does has direct need-reduction, if not survival, value, much of the learning expected in our schools is related only indirectly and, often remotely, to the needs of students.

[b] Evaluate: The less the teacher has to depend on external incentives, the better a teacher he is.

2

Teachers are often accused of being stingy with rewards. How can they deal with the fact that when rewards become plentiful inflation destroys their valence value?

3

How realistic is it to tell students they should not be working for grades? Can a subject ever be made interesting *for its own sake*?

4

[a] Some teachers rationalize: "Why should I break my neck to teach children who 'just do not want to learn'?" How might the impasse be resolved? Do certain teachers operate under misconceptions of their role and function? Is it possible that some teachers "just do not want to teach"?

[b] Just what can be done for the child who has given up in the face of his inability to meet school and home pressures?

5

Evaluate: Teachers throughout the elementary and high school have so played up to the interests of their pupils in the choice of academic content and teaching procedures that colleges are filled with students who have not learned to discipline themselves into mastering what is important if it should happen to be the least bit hard and not immediately interesting.

6

Specifically, what would you do with the boy who admits in all candor that he will not study Shakespeare because he sees no point in it?

CHAPTER 14

Retention
and Transfer
of Training

> . . . the central educational task is not the
> passing on of accumulated knowledge, but
> rather it is to master the process of learning—
> to learn how to learn.
> *Bowman, 1963, p. 38*

Probably no other aspect of the classroom situation is more frustrating to teachers and pupils than the extent to which the latter not only forget by tomorrow what they learn today but also seem unable to make effective use of the knowledge they have in dealing with new situations. Because they are closely interrelated, these two aspects of the learning process will be considered together in the present chapter.

RETENTION AND FORGETTING

Retention and forgetting are complementary processes, retention referring to the preservation of what is known, forgetting to its loss. That a great deal of what is learned is soon forgotten is obvious, particularly to teachers; it would be even more obvious to them if they were to check how soon after the final examination students forget what they knew at the end of the course. Pressey et al. (1959) suggest that approximately two thirds of the concepts learned in high school and college courses are forgotten within two years. During the summer vacation, children may forget from 10 to 50 percent of the content of a given course, depending on such factors as the functionality and appeal of the content, the method used in teaching and learning, and the nature of the learner.

The situation is probably not as bad as it appears on the surface. Forgetting is selective and although in some areas there is an almost complete loss, in others gains may actually occur during a period of disuse. Thus, Schrepel and Laslett (1936) found a loss in arithmetic computation over the summer vacations but a gain in word meaning, literature, and social sciences. Tyler (1933) found the ability to apply principles and interpret new experiments in zoology to be equal or better than at the completion of the course 15 months before, even though no other course had been taken in the interim. Furthermore, not only can forgetting be minimized, but a good deal of what is forgotten is really not overly important in and of itself. The learner needs details to gain a good grasp of the principles involved, but, once they have enabled him to go beyond to generalizations, their loss is of no great moment. A person's memory of the Hitler regime may be vague, but he will still have attitudes, generalizations, and viewpoints based on the facts of his career even though the facts themselves are almost forgotten. On the other hand, the importance of facts must not be minimized. One needs facts to use as stepping stones to higher levels of understanding and, although they are often forgotten and although the mere possession of facts does not ensure insights, generalizations, and principles, the latter would not be possible without facts. Yet it is these higher levels of understanding, and not the facts upon which they are based, which are the important outcomes of education—and these, fortunately, are relatively resistant to forgetting.

RELATION TO LEARNING

Ability to learn and ability to retain are positively related; this should cause no surprise since these two abilities are really phases of the same process. One would be unable to learn unless he could retain things as he goes along, so the relationship in question is really that between immediate and delayed retention. It is true that occasionally a student learns something quickly—more correctly, superficially—only to have it fade away almost completely in a matter of days, while another student who takes time to grasp the interrelationships of the ideas to each other and to previous learnings will take longer but will also retain it longer. The statement "It takes him a long while to learn something but when he's got it, it really sticks," has some basis in truth, but what is being compared is not differences in retention but differences in adequacy of learning. When practice time is held constant, as in the classroom situation, rapid learning is associated with greater retention. This might be expected since speed in learning tends to imply greater intellectual and/or experiential background, leading to greater meaningfulness; effective study habits and efficient procedures for organizing the material; or strong motivation—all of which tend to promote retention.

MEASUREMENT OF RETENTION

The rate and extent of forgetting was first investigated by Ebbinghaus (1885) whose well-known forgetting curve deals with the retention of nonsense material learned by memorization. The retention curve for meaningful material would display a considerably less rapid and less complete loss[1] but it would have the same general shape; all retention curves show the greatest drop immediately after the learning period, followed by more gradual losses, for example.

The steepness of the decline and the final level of retention are determined in large part by the method used in their measurement; greater retention can be expected, for example, when retention is measured through recognition than through recall. The steepness of the decline and the final level of retention also depend on such factors as meaningfulness of the material and interrelatedness of its components which, in turn, are a function of the nature of the material; the intelligence, experience and motivation of the learner; the degree of overlearning; the amount of review; and other factors to be discussed presently.

EXPLANATION OF FORGETTING

The older view among psychologists—and still that of the layman—was that forgetting resulted from disuse or decay with the passage of time. In a sense, it is true that, with the passage of time, omissions, additions, or condensations take place, particularly in points not too clearly understood or interconnected with the main aspects of the material. But mere passage of time does not explain why forgetting is selective, why we forget some things and not others, and why we forget more in certain instances than in others. The modern view is that forgetting is the result of active interference of what is learned by previous or subsequent learnings. Thus, the child having learned that $7 + 6 = 13$ and later that $8 + 4 = 12$ confuses the two to the point where he is no longer sure whether the sum of $7 + 6$ is 13, 12, or what-have-you. In the same way, the teacher has no trouble remembering the names of one or two new students but, faced with another 28 besides, he confuses one name with another to the point that he can not remember a single one. This

---

[1] Ebbinghaus estimated some 75 percent loss over a 24-hour period. Underwood (1957) suggests that this is a gross exaggeration: he feels that 25 percent might be a more correct estimate.

interference of previous learnings by *subsequent* learnings, first investigated by Müller and Pilzecker (1900), is generally known as retroactive inhibition.

Although details tend to drop out, forgetting is more than a mere loss; rather it is a reorganization in which the individual fills in from his own experience for some of the aspects of the situation he has lost or perhaps displaced. In this reorganization, there is a tendency to give a more simple, economical, and personally logical version of the event. For example, the witness having come to a conclusion as to the guilty party in the accident fills in from his general understanding and "remembers" that "he came this way," when he really means: "It seems to me he would have had to come this way for me to have reached the conclusion I did as to his guilt." This does not mean lying any more than in the case of the student who identifies CaCl as table salt. The extent to which our memories are colored by our interpretations is well brought out in the study by Carmichael et al. (1932) in which two groups of subjects were shown ambiguous figure stimuli with different word stimuli. As shown in Figure 14-1, the group led to associate the first figure with the phrase "curtain in a window" tended to draw it as curtains, whereas the group to which the figure was presented with "diamond in a rectangle" drew it more like a diamond in a rectangle.

After a half-century of relatively complete acceptance as the primary basis of forgetting, the concept of retroactive inhibition was challenged in 1957 by Underwood, who suggested that interference to retention came from tasks learned previously rather than those learned subsequently to the material in question. In his classic study, subjects learned a list of ten paired adjectives to a criterion of eight out of ten correct answers. Forty-eight hours later, they recalled the list. The following day, they learned a new list which they again recalled 48 hours later and likewise for a third and fourth list. The results showed a sharp decrement from 69 percent recall for the first list to 25 percent for the fourth, suggesting that decrement in performance is a function of *proactive* interference, i.e., interference from previous lists. Underwood argues that what a student has learned in the 20 years before coming to college is likely to interfere with his retention of college material to a greater extent than the few experiences intervening between learning a list one day and recalling it the next. Ausubel et al. (1957), whose experiment with meaningful materials supports Underwood's contention that it is proactive rather than retroactive interference that accounts for the bulk of the loss, suggest that retroactive inhibition is important in forgetting only in the artificial laboratory setting and that it would normally be a minor factor in the retention of meaningful materials.

Evidence also suggests that some forgetting results from repression. First emphasized by Freud, repression is rather clearly shown in am-

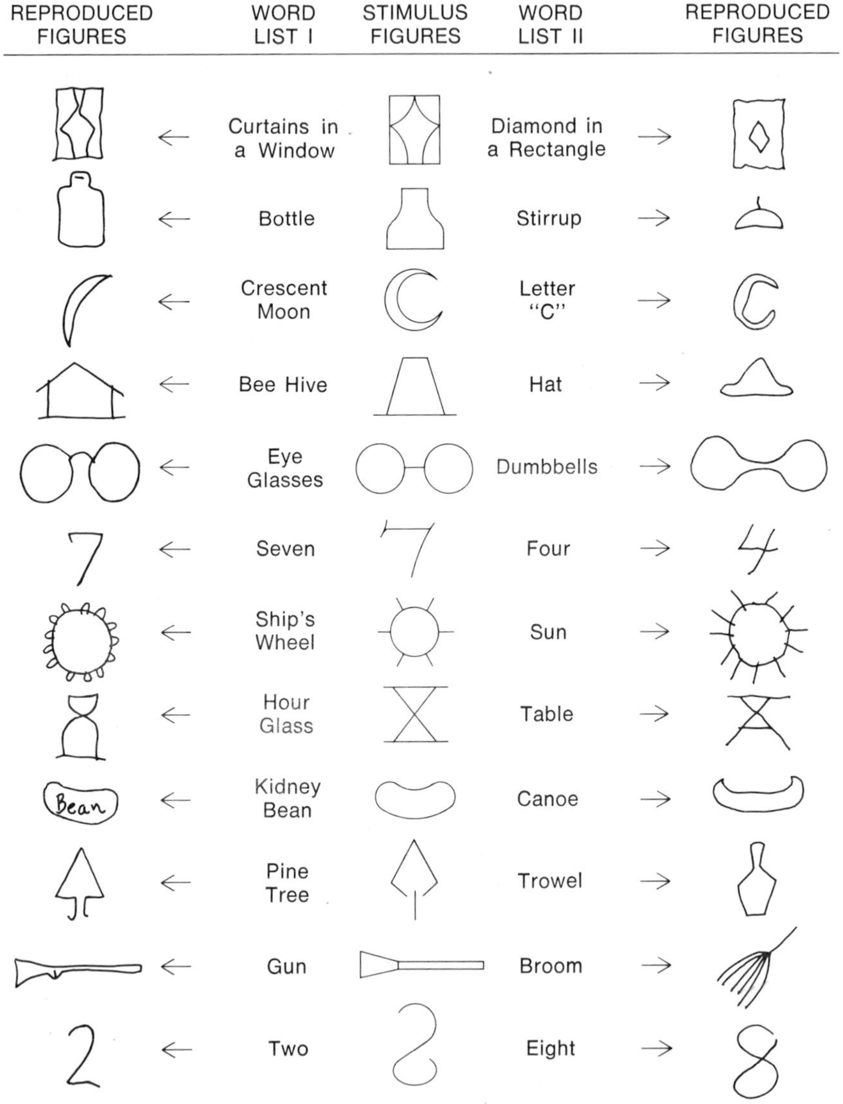

REPRODUCED FIGURES		WORD LIST I	STIMULUS FIGURES	WORD LIST II		REPRODUCED FIGURES
	←	Curtains in a Window		Diamond in a Rectangle	→	
	←	Bottle		Stirrup	→	
	←	Crescent Moon		Letter "C"	→	
	←	Bee Hive		Hat	→	
	←	Eye Glasses		Dumbbells	→	
	←	Seven		Four	→	
	←	Ship's Wheel		Sun	→	
	←	Hour Glass		Table	→	
	←	Kidney Bean		Canoe	→	
	←	Pine Tree		Trowel	→	
	←	Gun		Broom	→	
	←	Two		Eight	→	

FIGURE 14-1 The stimulus figures in the middle column were presented to two groups of subjects with a different word list. Later when the two groups were asked to reproduce the stimulus figures, they tended to make them conform to the stimulus word with which they had been presented. (Adapted from Carmichael et al., 1932.)

nesia where the victim forgets selectively items of personal reference he *wants* to forget. In a cognitive sense, forgetting is not so much a matter of the fading out of what was learned as it is one of relegating certain perceptions, perhaps relatively undifferentiated in the first place, into the *ground* (in a *figure-and-ground* sense); this takes place as a result of the reorganization of the perceptual field in the course of subsequent learning or as a result of the recovery of previous learning so that it becomes less available for recall into clear focus upon demand.[2] Many things are not so much lost as simply not immediately available, but they can be recovered through the removal of inhibitory forces through hypnosis, for example. A person in delirium may speak a language he had not used since childhood.

Factors Affecting Retention

Considerable research has been conducted on the various factors that make for a greater or lesser degree of interference. Before we review this evidence, however, we need to consider the design of such experiments and here we must first distinguish between retroactive and proactive inhibition as the major cause of forgetting.

Since in the retroactive design, what is learned is interfered with by subsequent learning, i.e., by the activity interpolated between the learning of the material and its testing, it is a matter of comparing the relative extent to which performance is impaired by the introduction of different activities subsequent to the learning of a given set of materials. Thus, if we wanted to determine whether memorizing a list of the largest city in each state interferes with the recall of its capital more than does the memorizing of the list of the respective governors, for example, we would have to start with two groups of subjects, one the *experimental*, the other the *control* group. These groups would have to be equated in all respects relevant to retention, i.e., they would have to be equally familiar with the state capitals; they would have to have the same level of intelligence and motivation, and equal skill in memorizing. Both groups would learn the state capitals to the same degree of mastery, e.g., to the point of one correct repetition. Then, for a given period of time, one group would study the list of the largest city in each state while the second studies the list of state governors. Finally, both groups would be tested for their retention of the state capitals and, if the group that had studied the list of largest cities, say, were to display less retention than the other, we would conclude that, to the extent that other things were

[2] Travers (1963) suggests that the brain, just like a computer, has limited storage capacity and that forgetting is a matter of shedding certain information to clear storage space for other material. A person remembers what he considers important. Perhaps the student at the end of the semester simply sheds the material he no longer needs along with the semester's notes.

equal, the study of the list of largest cities causes a greater interference with the retention of state capitals than does the study of the governors. In schematic form, the experimental design would look like this:[3]

	Original Learning	Interpolated Learning	Test of Original Learning
Group I (Experimental)	Learn: State capitals	Learn: States' largest cities	Test: State capitals
Group II (Control)	Learn: State capitals	Learn: States' governors	Test: State capitals

Among the factors that have direct bearing on retention the following can be mentioned:[4]

SIMILARITY OF ORIGINAL AND INTERPOLATED LEARNINGS   Research supports the Skaggs-Robinson Hypothesis (Skaggs, 1925; Robinson, 1927), which postulates that the more similar the interpolated and original learnings, the greater the interference up to a point. As the two become more similar beyond this point, interference decreases and eventually as the materials become essentially identical, the interpolated learning naturally reinforces the original learning. (See Figure 14-2.) Where interference reaches a peak and begins to give way to reinforcement depends on such factors as the intelligence and background of the learner and the meaningfulness of the material. Thus, the bright child might find that learning $(a - b)^2$ after he has just learned $(a + b)^2$ reinforces his understanding of $(a + b)^2$ whereas, for the duller child, the second example may only serve to confuse his meager understanding of the first. Interference would probably be greatest when the same (or similar) stimulus calls for different responses on different occasions, e.g., studying two lists of response words to the same list of stimulus words. Watson (1938) suggests that incompatibility, rather than similarity, is the significant factor in interference. It is probably better, for example, to master one foreign language at a time rather than to undertake two at once.

A more elaborate representation of the relationships between similarity and forgetting is Osgood's three-dimensional model summarizing the relationships to be expected with various combinations of stimulus

[3] The development of the proactive experimental design is left as an exercise for the student.
[4] The role of these factors is discussed from retroactive premises. The arguments can be extended to the proactive design.

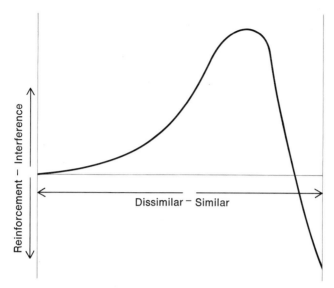

FIGURE 14-2   Theoretical curve of interference with increasing similarity of interpolated and
original learning.

and response similarity (Osgood, 1949). It incorporates at once retroactive interference and transfer results, with the Skaggs-Robinson hypothesis apparently a special case of the more complex relationships
covered by the Osgood model. On the other hand, it has not escaped
criticism; some of the findings of the Bugelski and Cadwallader study
(1956), for example, actually agree more closely with the Skaggs-Robinson viewpoint.

TEMPORAL POSITION OF INTERPOLATED LEARNING   Although the relationship is not entirely clear, there is some evidence to suggest that
retroactive inhibition is at its maximum when the interpolated learning
takes place either immediately following the learning or immediately
preceding the testing of the original material (Sisson, 1939; Swenson,
1941). Thus, one should avoid cramming for a couple of examinations
the night before the tests, or even arranging his schedule so that classes
follow without a break.

SIMILARITY OF LEARNING AND TESTING SITUATIONS   The more associative
cues the learner can form, the more likely he is to retain what he has
learned. Contrariwise, the lack of certain features of the learning situation
tends to present distracting elements which prevent the recall of the
learned response. We are more likely to recognize Mr. Jones if we see him
in the office where we first met him than if we meet him on the street.

DEGREE OF MASTERY   All indications are that the crucial variable in retention is the degree of original learning (Underwood, 1964). In fact, it seems that, although such factors as intra-list similarity, meaningfulness, or student ability can generate enormous differences in the learning of the material, they do not seem to be reflected in appreciable differences in the rate of forgetting when equivalent levels of learning are involved. If slow and fast learners achieve the same degree of learning before the retention interval is introduced, there is no evidence that the rate of forgetting will differ appreciably; what determines the rate and level of forgetting is primarily the degree of learning, regardless of the time and effort required to get the material up to a given level of acquisition. If it is learned only to the point of one correct reproduction, retention will tend to drop sharply almost to zero, as shown in Figure 14-3,

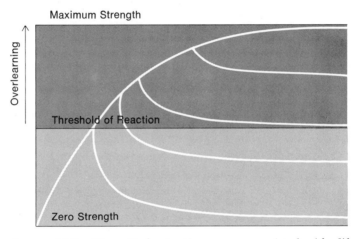

FIGURE 14-3   Theoretical retention curves associated with different degrees of overlearning.

whereas if it is learned considerably beyond the point of bare mastery, it may never drop below the level necessary to permit its reproduction. Americans would never forget the pledge of allegiance, for example. The factor of overlearning is also involved in the retention of many skills such as riding a bicycle for, contrary to popular opinion, there is no reason to expect skills to be retained any more than verbal material when the two are learned to the same degree and are relatively equivalent with respect to various factors relating to retention.

Excessive overlearning tends to be uneconomical. As can be noted from the shape of the learning curve, the law of diminishing returns in the form of a ceiling and a decline in motivation sets in so that, after a certain mastery has been attained, relatively little improvement in performance accompanies further efforts to learn. Nevertheless since good retention revolves around good learning, some overlearning, say 50 percent, is probably a good investment of time and effort from the standpoint of immediate and long-range retention (Krueger, 1929, 1930).

To the extent that meaningful material is likely to be more adequately grasped than meaningless material, the more structured, compact, self-contained, and interrelated are the various components of a given lesson, the less affected it tends to be by interference from subsequent learnings and the less it will interfere with other learnings, either previous or subsequent.[5] Obviously involved in the degree of meaningfulness of material are such factors as its clarity and continuity, the intelligence and experience of the learner, his motivation and persistence as well as the time he has to devote to getting a clear picture of its content. Thus, difficult material tends to be forgotten quickly simply because it has not been adequately grasped. As long as facts remain isolated bits of information, they not only tend to impede rather than facilitate further learning but they are also quickly forgotten. On the contrary, when they attain functionality in terms of interrelationships, applications, generalizations, interpretations, and implications, they resist forgetting. The fact that so much of the learning in school fades away so quickly and so completely almost suggests that it borders on nonsense for many children.

REVIEW   Review is probably one of the best means of maintaining retention above a given level. Spitzer (1939), for example, found that more forgetting occurred in one day when retention was not aided by review than in 63 days when two review periods were introduced. As shown in Figure 14-4, review overcomes the forgetting that has occurred and brings the material back above the threshold of reaction. As the learner reviews periodically, the loss becomes progressively less to the point where the material may remain above the memory level almost forever. Depending on the thoroughness of the original learning, the first review should probably come within 24 hours after the initial learning, the second perhaps within a week, and the next within a month.

Periodic reviews are generally more effective than overlearning from the standpoint of economy of time and effort. This is especially true inasmuch as effective review is more than just bringing the material up to the original level. In meaningful material, review involves a systematization

[5] Deese (1958) suggests that one can remember a constant number of items (chunks or bits) of information regardless of the amount of information in each. A person might have a memory span for a group of five words or five ideas. People do not code by letters; they code by words, ideas, sentences, i.e., they recode what they hear into so many chunks with relatively more pieces of information per chunk. In remembering numbers, we group them into so many thousands, etc.; even nonsense material is generally given some structure as a means of promoting its grasp and retention.

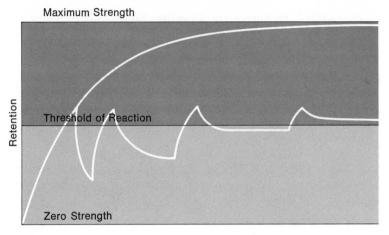

Maximum Strength

Retention

Threshold of Reaction

Zero Strength

FIGURE 14-4   Theoretical retention curve with periodic review.

and reorganization of the learning to bring about deeper understandings and new insights into relationships that are more functional as well as more permanent than the original.

Except when the material has faded to the point where recitation would be essentially guesswork, review should not be a matter of re-reading. Skimming related sources for new ideas, working through a quiz, thinking through the implications of the material, or using the knowledge as a stepping-stone to more advanced work are generally more profitable. Unfortunately, instead of being encouraged to gain insight through seeing the material from a broad and diverse point of view, the student is often required to become letter-perfect in a limited area, e.g., one chapter of the basic text. Also of direct bearing in this connection is the question of how much repetition and overlapping of material there should be from course to course in order to promote a sufficient review of the material needed as foundation. Review is essential but it should be organized as a stepping-stone to more advanced work; mere duplication should generally be avoided.

SET OR INTENT TO REMEMBER   Retention is facilitated by having the student learn with full expectation of being tested on the material. Intent to remember is related to motivation, which makes for maximum retention by leading the student to make periodic reviews and, above all, by making for a more intense impression at the time of learning. Parents often get reminded with the common "But you said ...." of a promise given casually; children do not forget when they have been promised something they want but they conveniently forget having been told to do certain chores. The more ego-involved the child is, the less likely he is to forget. Getting him interested in a problem but giving him only half the answer and leading him through thought-provoking questions to go the rest of the way by himself—or at least to keep the material clearly in mind until the discussion is resumed next day— is a procedure that can be used effectively in promoting retention.

EDUCATIONAL IMPLICATIONS

Research has identified some of the factors that make for greater retention. As might be expected, these relationships do not apply equally to all learning situations but, to the extent that they do, it is the teacher's task to work—and have the students work—in harmony with these principles in order to minimize the forgetting that would otherwise occur.

Research supports the following suggestions:

[a] Promote effective learning as a means of promoting retention. Stress should be on meaningfulness, organization, distributed practice, intent to remember, and other psychologically and pedagogically sound practices. The material should be presented, not as isolated fragments, but rather structured into relatively large units which are meaningful in terms of the student's ability and background, with emphasis on generalizations and applications. Avoid introducing more material in any given period than can be covered adequately in the time allowed. Material introduced in a hurry is not only forgotten in a hurry but it also tends to interfere with other learnings.

[b] Encourage a certain degree of overlearning. The extra effort is a wise investment in terms of retention, especially because, in the case of meaningful material, it generally makes for greater meaningfulness.

[c] Encourage periodic review. This is done most effectively through scheduling frequent quizzes and insisting that students make use of the material in climbing to higher levels. This is more obvious in sequential subjects like mathematics. Distributed practice makes for economy as well as permanence of learning; it is also more likely to promote the shedding of errors through differential forgetting.

[d] Encourage intent to remember. The student who anticipates being tested on the material or who is self-involved is not likely merely to go through the motions of studying, nor is he likely to dismiss the material from his mind the minute class is over.

TRANSFER OF TRAINING

The purpose of educational experiences both in and out of school is to enable the individual to meet new situations more effectively. Throughout life, the intelligent person "profits from experience" in the sense that, as a result of experience, he is better prepared to meet situations of various degrees of relatedness and similarity. This is of special significance in the classroom where experiences are deliberately planned in sequence so that one serves as a stepping-stone to the next.

Life—and especially the school—is predicated on the assumption that what we learn in one occasion will facilitate our dealing with related situations. Since it is impossible to teach the child all the things he will need as an adult, even if we could foresee what he would need,[6] it is necessary to assume that, by virtue of what we have led him to learn, he will be able to adapt to new situations. Thus, such important decisions as to what and how to teach revolve around our views on transfer, for any curricular offering is justified only to the extent that it serves as the basis for more effective behavior in a later situation. It would follow that the more pessimistic a person is as to the amount of transfer that can be expected from a given educational experience, the more he would insist on a practical "social utilities" curriculum.

Measurement of Transfer

As in the case of retention, the amount of transfer to be expected from a given situation can be determined through experimentation. If, for example, one is interested in whether experience in playing the piano facilitates the subsequent learning of typing, he might start with two groups—one with experience on the piano, the other without—making sure they are equated with respect to such relevant characteristics as chronological age, coordination, motivation, and relative unfamiliarity with the typewriter. The two groups might be subjected to equivalent instruction in typing for a period of, say, three months. If the group having had experience on the piano were to make greater typing progress than the other, he could conclude that transfer from the piano to typing has taken place. The schematic form of this experiment is shown below:

	Previous Learning (Learn A)	Present Learning (Learn B)	Gain (Test B)
Group I (Experimental)	Play piano	Learn typing	Test typing
Group II (Control)	Nothing related	Learn typing	Test typing

In this case, we are likely to have *positive* transfer, i.e., the previous learning experience is likely to facilitate the subsequent learning. Transfer can also be negative, in which case previous learning interferes

---

[6] It is estimated that half of what a top-level engineer will need to know ten years from now is not known to anyone today.

with the subsequent learning of another activity. Thus, having learned to judge the flight of a softball might at first cause a fielder to misjudge the flight of a baseball. Generally, transfer from one activity to another involves both negative and positive aspects and the transfer involved is then the net sum of the facilitation and interference of the second learning by the first. For instance, many skills in softball are sufficiently similar to those in baseball that a person would be helped by previous knowledge of softball, but there are also skills sufficiently incompatible that he would have to readjust the old skills before he could get on with the new ones. The extent to which he would be ahead or behind as a result of his previous knowledge of softball would depend on the relative balance of the positive and the negative phases of the transfer between the two sports. In the same way, experience in driving a car in the United States involves both positive and negative transfer to driving in a country where cars move on the left side of the road.

RELATION TO FORGETTING

We need to distinguish—to the extent that such a distinction is possible—between transfer of training and forgetting. In retroactive inhibition, we are concerned with the interference (or reinforcement) which subsequent learnings may have on the retention of previous learnings; in transfer, we are interested in the extent to which previously learning facilitates (or hinders) subsequent learnings. The distinction can be represented as follows:

Retention (Retroactive design)	Learn fractions	Learn decimals	Test fractions
Transfer	Learn piano	Learn typing	Test typing

On closer inspection, the distinction becomes rather artificial. As pointed out by Melton (1950), Morgan (1961), and others, forgetting is simply a special case of negative transfer. The study of the permanence of learning in a situation essentially duplicating that of the original generally is considered a question of retention, while the study of the effects of old learning in mastering new situations generally is considered transfer of training. Since no two situations are ever identical—and certainly the testing situation is not identical with the original learning situation—what is measured in a retroactive inhibition problem is really transfer, i.e., the interference or facilitation of interpolated learnings with the recall of the original learning. What has been learned in class on fractions transfers to the examination situation where the student's knowledge of fractions is to be appraised; the learning of decimals might interfere with (or facilitate) the performance on the test on fractions just as learning piano might interfere with (or facilitate) typing performance. The case of proactive inhibition as an explanation of forgetting is even more clearly a case of transfer of training. It should also be noted that, in educational practice, the distinction is relatively trivial since both the original and the antecedent or interpolated learnings must be learned and remembered—for the examination, if nothing else—so that the particular pattern of interference or facilitation between Learning A and Learning B is of concern only from the standpoint of experimental design.

EXPLANATION OF TRANSFER OF TRAINING

Early psychologists explained transfer of training on the basis of the theory of formal discipline. They postulated that the mind was made up of a number of faculties or powers which, like a muscle, could be developed through training and which would then be capable of effective performance in all relevant areas. Thus, the training of memory through practice with, say, nonsense syllables was supposed to improve one's memory for names, for meaningful material, in fact, for anything involving memory. Accordingly, education was largely a matter of training (or disciplining) the mind by means of rigorous mental exercises in the classics, logic, and mathematics on the assumption that such training would make the person effective in all areas where a given faculty was involved.

This view was challenged by James (1890) who found that a month's practice in memorizing Victor Hugo's *Satyr* did not result in improvement in his ability to memorize. Following the question raised by James' simple experiment, the theory of mental discipline was challenged by such studies as that of Sleight (1911) in the area of memory; of Thorndike and Woodworth (1901) in perception; and of Briggs (1913) in reasoning. In these studies, the expected improvement in performance in related tasks did not materialize; in some cases, previous practice actually led to an impairment in performance, i.e., to negative transfer. In a study by Kline (1914), for example, practice in canceling letters interfered with performance in canceling words.

Transfer is probably best explained on the basis of the theory of identical components (Thorndike, 1916) which postulates that transfer from one situation to another occurs to the extent that the two situations have certain elements in common, e.g., eye-finger coordination in transfer from piano to typing. In other words, transfer occurs to the extent that the learner can carry certain aspects of his previous learnings to a situation which is then only partially novel. The Gestalt concept of transposability, Judd's theory of generalization (Judd, 1908), and Bagley's transfer through the formation of ideals or generalized attitudes (Bagley, 1922) are essentially equivalent positions. Harlow's "learning sets" (See

Chapter 5) are a more recent version of the same view. As the monkeys figured out the "common elements" they were able to deal with related discrimination and even reverse discrimination problems with almost 100 percent accuracy. Ausubel (1963, 1966) presents a parallel view in his "advanced organizers"; on the assumption that cognitive structure is organized in terms of concepts arranged in a hierarchy of inclusiveness, he postulates that the learning and retention of meaningful material is facilitated by introducing in advance broad overriding concepts under which the less inclusive concepts and information can be fitted.

All these explanations can be subsumed under the concept of identical components, where the "components" can be specific facts or skills, principles or relationships, or generalizations (whether cognitive or attitudinal). We might, for example, distinguish between [a] specific factors involving some identifiable similarity between two situations such as might occur in the transfer of computational skills to the solution of more advanced mathematical problems, and [b] nonspecific factors such as might be represented by a positive self-concept or even warm-ups in physical education, both of which permeate a relatively large spectrum of learning situations.

Factors Affecting Transfer of Training

That transfer of training usually materializes is a matter of common as well as experimental evidence. Webb's review (1936) of 167 investigations dealing with transfer showed 28 percent with considerable transfer and 48 percent with appreciable transfer. Certainly all education is predicated on the assumption that learning experiences will transfer to further learning and to effective living.

Transfer may range from the simple case of stimulus generalization, in which a response evoked by one stimulus is attached to similar stimuli, to the more pervasive effects of anxiety and openness to experience, and to the new possibilities of developing human potential introduced by Hebb, Harlow, Moore, Skinner, and others. Of particular importance to transfer in the classroom is the promotion of positive attitudes on the part of the learner, a conviction that his previous learnings are probably adequate for solving the problems he currently faces. The mere presence of identical components in two situations will not result in effective transfer; many children apparently do not see the grammar they learn in their English classes as having any bearing on everyday communications. Transfer can be expected only to the extent that the learner is encouraged to become transfer-conscious, to form attitudes of self-confidence, to apply what he knows, and to the extent that he is helped to develop effective procedures for dealing with novel situations.

Transfer relies heavily on meaningfulness, generalizations, and principles in contrast to facts whose applicability to other situations is much more restricted. The degree of transfer occurring in a classroom situation is essentially proportional to the degree to which one teaches for transfer, i.e., the extent to which the learning is brought to a generalization, to which relationships, implications, and applications to various situations are pointed out, or better still, the extent to which the child is encouraged and helped to discover these for himself. Overman (1930), for instance, found that the group for which arithmetic solutions were generalized outscored by a significant margin one group in which the procedures were simply shown and a second group in which the reasons for the procedures used were discussed. The child should be made to see the usefulness of the materials he is asked to learn, and the school's evaluation program should emphasize applications to novel situations as a measure of real understanding. Teachers are often too eager to tell everything, thereby depriving children of the opportunity to seek applications and relationships for themselves. Departmentalized teaching is often a drawback to transfer in that it is conducive to fragmentation of learning experiences and corresponding underemphasis on relationships and other aspects of learning that promote transfer.

The curriculum should be such as to have transfer value in terms of the learner's goals and purposes. Thus, a course in homemaking tends to have greater transfer possibilities for a girl who plans to marry and raise a family than does a course in Latin or Greek. This does not imply an outright rejection of all classical studies or unconditional endorsement of the social utilities approach to curriculum selection. Neither extreme is warranted: we can no more justify a social utilities curriculum solely on the basis of its transfer to the attainment of immediate (practical) goals than we can justify the inclusion of classical subjects strictly on the basis of their alleged disciplinary value.

Three important studies have shown that the superiority of the classical subjects in improving reasoning ability has been grossly exaggerated. In the first study, Thorndike (1924) measured the growth in general reasoning ability of over 8500 senior high school students over the period of a year's enrollment in various curricula. The same study was repeated by Broyler et al. (1927) and by Wesman (1945). Although the results did not show a high degree of consistency from study to study, they did indicate that the relative contribution of various academic curricula to the improvement of reasoning ability is not appreciably different, and they certainly refuted the alleged monopoly of the classical subjects on the development of intellectual competence. Or, as stated by Andrews et al. (1950): "There is no superior subject matter for transfer, there are only superior learning experiences."

It is interesting to note that, despite the fact that empirical as well as theoretical evidence has led psychologists to discard the theory of formal discipline years ago, there are still people who advocate hard courses to "toughen the mind," who feel that the curriculum has become "soft" and that what we need is a return to Latin, the classics, logic, the great books, and other courses of yesteryear. They point to the capable people among those who have followed such a curriculum as evidence of the benefits to be derived therefrom. Apparently their tough curriculum did not improve their own reasoning ability enough for them to see that it did not make these people capable but simply eliminated those of lesser ability.

The study of Latin is often advocated on the basis that it helps in learning English grammar and vocabulary. As was shown over four decades ago (Hamblen, 1925), it helps when—and almost only when—English derivatives are stressed. Furthermore, it stands as a fact that it is not an economical way of learning English: many English words have a Latin derivation, but a study of Latin roots as they apply to English vocabulary is a more economical and more effective way of learning English vocabulary than the study of Latin as a language. In other words, one should teach directly what he wants children to learn rather than expect indirect benefits through transfer. The question is not whether Latin and the classics are useful; undoubtedly they are useful, but are they more useful than other subjects which also have transfer value in addition to a much larger degree of direct value? A course in mathematics likewise has to be evaluated primarily on the basis of what it can contribute to the solution of mathematical and related problems rather than the improvement of reasoning ability, for no subject has a monopoly on that.

The degree of transfer is closely related to the learner's intelligence. In Thorndike's study, for example, the bright gained 20.5 points in reasoning ability while the slower students gained only 1.5 points. This is consistent with the view that greater transfer results from the higher level of learning, meaningfulness, and generalization made possible by greater intellectual and experiential adequacy. Thus, it might be noted that the dull child is triply penalized; he learns slowly because the material is not meaningful to him (partially because he is lacking in transfer from his previous experiences), he forgets more quickly because it is less adequately grasped, and he has more difficulty in having it transfer and form the basis for subsequent learning. The teacher dealing with dull children must be particularly conscientious in pointing out the transfer possibilities of the material.

Educational Implications

The implications of transfer of training for educational practice have been indicated throughout the discussion. It may be well to reemphasize that transfer is not automatic but rather that it occurs in proportion to the extent that one teaches and learns with transfer in mind, and to reiterate some of the effective techniques through which transfer can be promoted. Whatever the school does necessarily affects (i.e., transfers to) the child's later life. It is, therefore, a matter of major responsibility to discover how best we can perform for the benefit of the child and the adult he is to become the task which has been delegated to us.

First, an appropriate curriculum is essential. Since without transfer, education is a relative, if not a complete, waste of time, the transfer potentialities of the various academic experiences should be a primary consideration in curriculum planning. However, since the transfer value of a given experience depends more upon the way it is handled than on its inherent nature, transfer finally becomes the responsibility of the teacher who, in setting the objectives of a given course, unit, or lesson, must spell out the specific ways in which transfer is to be promoted. It is nevertheless true that the curriculum must be closely related to the child's experiences and purposes so that he can bring something to the curriculum material and, in turn, see enough benefit to be derived from it for him to generate interest in using it in connection with some other aspects of his purposes. We must avoid both overemphasis on an education geared to the development of the intellect based on discredited mental discipline premises and overorientation toward fads and frills disguised under the cloak of "practical" education. Neither is acceptable. Nor is there any ground for worry that attempts to promote transferable general skills through life adjustment approaches automatically implies sacrifice of intellectual and academic competence.

Probably all subject matter has transfer value, but certain aspects of education have wider application than others and every child should be familiar with such things as common roots of words, suffixes, prefixes, basic numerical concepts, certain rules of grammar, certain principles of science, basic rules of study, and effective modes of problem solving. A course in geometry, for instance, might better stress the nature of proof, which has wide transfer potential rather than the proof of individual theorems. Ulmer (1942) found that an experimental course in which geometric reasoning was tied in with reflective thinking about nongeometric problems resulted in much greater ability to draw sound conclusions from given facts than a conventional course in geometry. Fawcett (1938) reports similar results. It is the teacher's responsibility to emphasize those outcomes which have the greatest transfer possibilities; verbalizing the principle underlying a given point, for example, tends to promote transfer to related instances. The teacher must capitalize on a variety of procedures promoting insight, meaningfulness, the organization of experience, and the discovery of interrelatedness among ideas and techniques and emphasizing the applicability of knowledge to a variety of situations.

Other suggestions could be given: [a] Relate learning experiences to the situations to which transfer is expected; [b] Provide practice in transfer; [c] Force children to become transfer-conscious by emphasizing as a major aspect of evaluation the transferability of knowledge to novel situations; [d] Encourage mastery of content; [e] Promote the development of efficient learning habits and tools (e.g., self-discovery tends to promote greater transfer than does memorization). Undoubtedly, however, the most crucial single aspect of transfer lies in the kind of person we develop. If we can only develop a person characterized by positive attitudes toward the experiences he encounters, by a constructive self-concept, by relative freedom from anxiety, and by openness to experience along the lines presented in Chapter 4, we will have developed a person who can approach new situations with eagerness and confidence in his ability to meet life's demands—and our efforts at education will not have been in vain.

HIGHLIGHTS OF THE CHAPTER

The school's effectiveness depends in a fundamental way upon the retention and transfer of the material the child has learned. The teacher must, therefore, be familiar with the psychological principles underlying these two functions.

[a]

Some forgetting is not only inevitable but actually desirable. The problem is to maximize the retention of those learnings which are important from the standpoint of the individual's further growth.

[b]

The explanation of forgetting most commonly cited by modern psychologists centers around the interference by subsequent learnings with the recall of material previously learned. More recently, the role of proactive inhibition as a major factor in forgetting has also been noted. The extent of this interference depends primarily upon the degree of learning, important aspects of which include meaningfulness, overlearning, and review. Some forgetting may result from repression.

[c]

Transfer of training is the cornerstone upon which education must ultimately rest; unless the child's learnings help him to meet more effectively situations further along the academic sequence or in later life, he is essentially wasting his time.

[d]

Transfer from previous to subsequent situations occurs to the extent that the learner is aware and encouraged to take advantage of the similarities of the two situations. The degree of transfer occurring in the classroom is a function of the way one teaches for transfer; no subject matter has a monopoly on transfer.

[e]

Harlow's concept of "learning how to learn" is of special importance in view of the knowledge explosion and the obvious consequent impossibility of covering all the material the child will need in later life.

[f]

To the extent that forgetting is best conceived as an aspect of transfer, the factors operative in the one are also relevant to the other. Thus, meaningfulness, emphasis on generalizations, the cultivation of positive attitudes, overlearning and periodic review, all tend to reduce memory losses and to promote transfer.

SOURCES OF RELATED MATERIALS

Broadbent, D. E., "The well-ordered mind," *Amer. educ. res. J.*, 3: 281–295, 1966.

Ellis, Henry, *The Transfer of Learning*. New York: Crowell-Collier and Macmillan, Inc., 1965.

Grose, R. F., and R. C. Birney (eds.), *Transfer of Learning*. Princeton, N.J.: D. Van Nostrand, Inc., 1963.

Harlow, Harry F., "The formation of learning sets," *Psychol. Rev.* 56: 51–65, 1949.

Orata, P. T., "Recent research studies on transfer of training with implications for curriculum, guidance, and personnel work," *Harv. educ. Rev.*, 11: 359–378, 1941.

Sassenrath, J. M., "Learning without awareness and transfer of learning sets," *J. educ. Psychol.*, 50: 205–212, 1959.

QUESTIONS AND PROJECTS

1

Why is meaningful material retained longer than nonsense material? Is anything ever completely forgotten?

2

Devise an experiment to determine the transfer effects of a course in general science upon critical thinking. Locate the report of such a study in the professional literature.

3

Specifically, how much transfer might the average student expect from the content of this course? What might the instructor do to ensure that transfer does take place?

CHAPTER 15

The Higher Mental
Processes

> . . . I have dared to believe that providing a
> basis for the understanding of children's think-
> ing may eventually help many to think more
> clearly.
>
> *Russell, 1956, p. vii*

The school has major responsibility for promoting effective problem solving that will enable future citizens to think critically concerning the
problems of democratic living as well as those of scientific and material
progress. This is particularly crucial in these times of social upheaval
and evermore rapid technological advances. Although there has been
greater recognition of the fact that reflective thinking is the cornerstone of
education, there is still far too much emphasis in the average classroom on
covering a curriculum of half-digested facts. Horn's criticism that the
average adult does not have the information he needs to think effectively
about modern problems and that he cannot locate adequate sources nor
read them intelligently even if he found them is perhaps only slightly less
valid today than it was when made in 1937.

REASONING AND PROBLEM SOLVING

The Nature of Problem Solving

Problem solving, reasoning, and thinking are terms used more or less synonymously to refer to a broad variety of complex mediating processes such as the eduction of relationships and correlates, the synthesis of isolated experiences, the reorganization of cognitive structure, etc. In contrast to learning, which entails the grasping of a fully structured situation, problem solving is a matter of reorganizing experience with respect to a problem whose solution is not readily available. It involves a somewhat greater emphasis on flexibility of approach and on insight (or hindsight) in discovering means-end relationships. Yet, problem solving is an aspect of learning essentially similar in nature and subject to the same laws as other complex forms of learning; the difference is one of degree and emphasis rather than of kind. One can, for example, distinguish between inductive reasoning in which the thinker derives generalizations from the investigation of a number of elements and deductive reasoning in which he extends known relationships to new situations. One can also isolate critical (evaluative) reasoning, which is concerned with the appraisal of the soundness or appropriateness of an idea or solution, from creative (divergent) thinking, which deals with the evolvement of a novel idea. Each of these is probably a composite of abilities rather than a single unitary trait. One might also consider various (overlapping) levels of thinking ranging from common sense, which generally involves a rather ill-defined problem and vague premises, to the systematic derivation of a solution along the lines of the formal steps of logic.[1]

Steps of Critical Thinking

The nature of problem solving is probably best understood by considering the steps of critical thinking (sometimes referred to as the steps of the

[1] An interesting development in the area of problem solving is that of computer simulation of human reasoning (Hovland, 1960; Newell et al., 1958, 1962). Once it is provided with the basic data in the form of premises, axioms, rules of operation, and other pertinent information—whether in playing a game of checkers or in deriving the theorems of Euclidean geometry—the computer can be programmed to test (at fantastic speeds) every single possibility among the data. It can locate conflicts in the various projected solutions and eventually isolate solutions that are not in conflict. The computer performs essentially the same operations as the human brain and can, therefore, provide an understanding of the process of human reasoning. The computer, however, is restricted to the strategy for which it has been programmed; the human operator, on the other hand, is not as thorough in checking through his solutions, but he has much greater flexibility in shifting from one strategy to another. (See also Glaser, 1962.) In other words, even though the computer can simulate human problem solving, one must not assume that the computer goes about it in the same way as its human counterpart.

scientific method) as formulated by Dewey (1933). These will be discussed in order of their theoretical sequential arrangement even though they rarely occur in a 1-2-3 order in an everyday problem.

AWARENESS OF THE PROBLEM   Problem solving cannot take place without a problem, but problem-solving behavior is initiated not by the existence of a problem in an objective sense but rather by its recognition as a problem situation by the individual. Dewey defines a problem as a "felt need," implying thereby that what constitutes a problem for one person may not be a problem for another. Problem solving in school occurs when the child is faced with a problem that is genuine to him in terms of his needs and experiences; i.e., it is the encountering of an obstacle to the attainment of his purposes that leads the learner to think in order to remove the obstacle and reach his goal. A real problem is more than an idea to be manipulated. It represents a threat to the individual's equilibrium and, unless he gets sufficiently ego-involved to feel discomfort over the fact that a given problem is not solved, he does not have a *problem*. Under these circumstances, the problem simply remains the teacher's problem; to the student it is just a task and his real problem may be how to avoid having to do the assignment.

The investigator's first step is to clarify the exact nature of his problem for, unless he has identified the issues involved, he is not likely to find a solution. This generally calls for a relatively adequate background enabling him to structure the problem so that it can be examined with effectiveness. Actually, having a problem implies having information on the subject; it is only the intrinsic relationships that are not clear to the individual involved. Nevertheless, it is generally necessary to supplement one's present knowledge by further clarification of the problem area.

A major component of effective problem solving is the review of the literature as the basis for deriving more intelligent and productive hypotheses as to potential solutions, for evaluating these hypotheses, and for planning more effective modes of attack. This step—which may range from a quick survey of the data at one's fingertips to a systematic review as required in a thesis or dissertation—is important. Too often classroom discussion, even at the college level, consists of superficial, if not erroneous, remarks by students who have not taken the trouble to look up the facts. Furthermore, these data must be assimilated and organized to the point where they can be seen in the perspective of the problem. The teacher must help students learn effective ways of locating data; of organizing those data through outlining, summarizing, and synthesizing; of checking them for accuracy; and of reconciling seeming contradictions. Above all, the teacher must instill in them a respect for accuracy. Failure to encourage the development of these important skills and attitudes is to promote superficial reasoning, if not error.

EMERGENCE OF THE HYPOTHESIS   The definition of the problem in the light of what is already known about its relevant aspects generally leads the investigator to the formulation of a hypothesis as to its likely solution. Hypotheses may come as sudden insights, occurring perhaps after a period of inactivity has broken the mental set blocking the solution, but more commonly they occur to the individual only after he has systematically and laboriously considered the evidence in relation to the problem. Good hypotheses unquestionably require a good grounding in the subject without which crucial relationships are likely to go unnoticed.

TESTING OF THE HYPOTHESIS   Coincident with the review of the literature is the continuous evaluation of emerging hypotheses from the standpoint of their implications relative to what is accepted as true: Is it consistent with this principle? with this fact? Failure of a given hypothesis to meet this deductive test of agreement with present knowledge should lead to its rejection or modification and a similar check of substitute hypotheses. In the meantime, more information might come to light and the learner may find it necessary to clarify his problem further.

The good thinker can not only devise a large number of hypotheses, but he can readily separate the good ones from the poor ones and avoid chasing down blind alleys. Some of the factors which make for effectiveness in this area include intellectual and experiential background, flexibility, originality, and not least, a critical attitude that prevents the learner from accepting half-baked ideas. All of these are *necessary* conditions for success in deriving fruitful hypotheses but none is *sufficient*; thus, the child who has never seen a blizzard cannot reason about its dangers, but if other factors are absent, he may have seen a dozen blizzards and still not be able to reason about them effectively.

A hypothesis which has stood the deductive test of the validity of its logical implications must still be subjected to empirical validation. If the evidence points to a dead battery as the reason the car will not start, this hypothesis can be tested empirically by exchanging the battery for one known to be functional. Again failure of a hypothesis to be sustained in such a test leads to its rejection, and the investigator has to start anew with another hypothesis. This may involve going back to redefining the problem and reconsidering the literature as the basis for finally formulating a hypothesis that is both logically and empirically valid. Problem solving entails various degrees of trial and error; it is not uncommon for the learner to hit upon the solution by accident and then to develop hindsight as to why this particular solution worked while previous attempts failed.

GENERALIZATION   Problem solving is not complete until the investigator has generalized his results and has identified the areas and conditions in which his solution holds and the areas and conditions in which it does not. The ability to extend the applicability of a solution from one situation to another is the real test of understanding; it is also the basis for scientific progress.

FOSTERING PROBLEM SOLVING

Reasoning in the Classroom

To the extent that critical thinking is probably the major component of the traditional IQ, the development of reasoning in children very closely parallels that of intelligence as traditionally defined. The recent emphasis on creative thinking as an aspect of intelligence simply presents a broader concept of both thinking and intelligence. Of particular interest in this connection is the work of Piaget whose investigation of the intellectual development of children, especially as it relates to critical thinking, has already been presented. His formulations represent one of the most comprehensive and, in a sense, most imaginative approaches to the study of the development of reasoning in the child.

Both common observation and research have pointed to inadequacies in the reasoning of children. This is sometimes interpreted as evidence that reasoning is a capacity that appears relatively late in the maturational process, an argument used by the school of yesteryear as a justification for drill and memory work. It has been suggested that the elementary school is a period for the accumulation of data, a period of preparation for thinking later on. These views have been discredited; true, the reasoning of children is relatively ineffective and often faulty, primarily because of their lack of experience and their failure to impose upon the problem the necessary structure. Often they do not have a well-defined problem and, as a result, proceed in all directions at once. Furthermore, because of limited experience, they are relatively blind to the existence of problems. However, there is no magical point of transition from inability to ability to think and adults, even experts outside their field of specialty, commit many of the same errors in reasoning as children. Furthermore, there are wide differences in reasoning ability among children as well as among adults, and many children reason more effectively than many adults; it is all a matter of whether the problem and the relationships among the parts, which they must understand to reach a solution, are within their understanding and experience. In other words, the reasoning of children is subject to the same conditions and limitations as that of adults.

The discussion on transfer of training led to the inevitable conclusion that the reasoning process can be improved; this can be done through the introduction of both general factors such as interest, persistence, and self-confidence, and specific factors such as skill in locating information, in formulating precise hypotheses, in defining terms, etc. Certainly, providing the child with a good background of information, particularly of principles and generalizations, can lead to improved problem solving. That critical thinking can be taught has been demonstrated in any number of areas from historical fiction, to reading newspapers, geometric proof, mathematics, social studies, and propaganda analysis (Russell, 1960). Such studies as those of Fawcett (1938) and Ulmer (1942) have shown that a generalized approach to reasoning as a process results in improved reasoning ability of wide applicability. Torrance (1953) found that conducting critiques of good problem-solving performances led to a significant improvement in problem-solving behavior. Research has also shown that critical thinking can be promoted at the elementary school level (Grener and Raths, 1945; Harris, 1948). Harlow's more recent study in learning how to learn provides further evidence that problem-solving abilities can be developed.

Actually, the school has been relatively misguided in its efforts to promote problem solving. Although mathematics is ideally suited to such training, geometry, for example, is often taught through memorization, despite evidence suggesting that it leads to an improvement in reasoning ability only when it is meaningful. Arithmetic problems are often exercises in imitating what the teacher has demonstrated so that the child becomes progressively less capable of reasoning at a more advanced level. Frequently mathematics is presented as a mechanical process of applying formulas. As a result, the student gets the erroneous image that mathematical relationships are the expression of mathematical realities rather than simply deductions evolving from a set of assumptions—assumptions which may be changed. Likewise, science courses often involve nothing more scientific than memorizing predetermined answers. Too frequently, the orientation is toward outcomes and conclusions rather than toward the image of science as a process of discovery; too often, teachers present conclusions as ultimate truth instead of simply as tentative beliefs.

Obviously, the teacher in charge of 30 children of various degrees of intellectual and experiential adequacy is faced with a difficult situation. A problem suitable for one child is a hopeless puzzle for another, and "child's play" for a third. Yet, our modern civilization in all its complexity should be able to provide the ingenious teacher with a variety of problems capable of accommodating differences among children. To be functional for classroom study, problems should deal with situations difficult enough to be challenging and yet simple and familiar enough for children to grasp. There are many social problems that could be of tremendous educational value but for which the students' background is so sketchy and disorganized that, until greater clarity is attained, any attempt to deal with them is not going to be very productive. Nevertheless, knowledge must begin somewhere. Educators can always promote adequacy in reasoning by developing the experiential background of their students. It is also possible that many national and international problems have their counterparts at the local level, or even within the framework of the school. The teacher can often convert a technical problem into one stated in everyday language. On the other hand, the teacher must realize that classroom discussion does not necessarily and inevitably lead to effective thinking.

Teachers in their eagerness to help children over every bump often deprive them of the opportunity to do any real problem solving. Many lessons are so thoroughly premasticated or presented in such mechanical fashion that the child is left with nothing to do but implement on a prescription basis the teacher's solutions. When they do not supply the answers themselves, teachers often refer students to the textbook as another source of wisdom and unconditional truth. And so the three proofs that the earth is round become: [a] Teacher said so; [b] My father said so; and [c] The book says so. If teachers are to be successful in fostering reasoning in the classroom, they must come to realize that more education from the standpoint of both the present and the future is likely to emerge from the solution of real problems than from the wholesale application of ready-made solutions. Teachers have a responsibility for fostering independence by helping the child only after he has made a fair attempt to find the solution on his own; they have a responsibility for breaking his blind allegiance to the *right* answer, to the *right* way of doing things.

Some teachers actually discourage problem solving. To be sure it takes more ingenuity, originality, and competence to use the problem-solving approach effectively than to rely on a page-at-a-time routine. But, whereas the latter restricts the student's progress more and more, the former places him on a self-perpetuating spiral, for once accustomed to solving his own problems, he is no longer satisfied with ready-made answers and he resents being denied the opportunity to solve things for himself. Teachers can encourage problem solving by asking leading questions rather than by supplying answers, by refusing to accept either in class or on examinations pat answers given verbatim from the book or from class notes, by having students validate their findings in terms of their implications, and by insisting on the clarification of terms and concepts used in reasoning. They should at all times emphasize the "if . . . then," approach as means of discouraging both superficial thinking and glib memorization of material as a substitute for understanding.

Prerequisites to Problem Solving

A number of suggestions can be made for promoting effectiveness in problem solving among school children. The teacher must first ensure that children are working on a problem of psychological as well as academic significance to them. Then, by asking well-directed questions, he can help them clarify the problem and devise an effective approach to its solution. He must act as a resource person while the students look up the necessary information and carry out the investigation but he should not provide answers before they have even noticed that answers are needed. In other words, as pointed out by Thorndike (1950), teachers should be more interested in creating problems for students to solve and in providing them with methods whereby they can get their own answers than in providing them with ready-made solutions. The problems assigned should not, of course, be puzzles from which little learning can be derived.

A good background of experience is essential to both the identification and the solution of problems. The school has a primary responsibility for providing children with systematic experiences, in the perspective of which problem situations stand out as gaps or conflicts and on the basis of which they can formulate imaginative hypotheses. If reasoning is to involve reorganization of experience in relation to a goal, children have to have experiences to reorganize. They learn through reasoning; they also improve their reasoning ability as a result of their learning, and the teacher must see that they gain adequate grasp of the field in which they are to work. They simply must "have their facts straight," for instance. The contribution of experiences to problem-solving ability, however, is a function of the nature of these experiences; education is not to be equated with filling the bowl with facts that answer questions children do not have.

One should not minimize the importance of facts and of the skills through which facts can be obtained, but facts alone are relatively sterile; they are means, not ends, and the teacher must emphasize the use of facts in connection with new problems rather than their mere accumulation. As Hullfish and Smith (1961) point out, little is to be gained from fact-grinding classroom procedures which reduce knowledge to the level of meaningless items to be placed in unmarked storage bins. Bruner (1961) insists that what is crucial is not memory or storage but rather retrieval, i.e., availability for transfer to other situations. To be useful in other situations calling for productive thinking, knowledge must be so integrated, structured, and familiar that it can be seen in perspective and the components relevant to a particular problem located surely and efficiently.

Research has shown a low correlation between knowledge and the ability to apply this knowledge in a reasoning situation, and even though one cannot reason without knowledge, its mere possession is no guarantee that he will be able to reason with it, especially if the material is merely memorized to pass the examination. The student must be encouraged to generalize his experiences as a means of clarifying and classifying them according to a meaningful storage system. Only then can knowledge contribute significantly to problem solving.

The child's growth in problem solving must be made the object of definite and systematic concern. The school must help him develop the necessary skills; it must also provide experience in the application of these skills in solving novel problems. A number of specific skills conducive to effective problem solving could be listed, e.g., efficiency in defining and clarifying the problem and locating and evaluating information, skill in analyzing data and synthesizing experience, etc. We can also identify approaches generally considered inappropriate; the formal steps of reasoning would rarely be used, for example, except perhaps when thinking reaches the proportions of the investigation of a complicated scientific problem. Such a formal approach may actually stifle successful problem solving as it puts emphasis on the method rather than on the problem. Likewise, mechanical formulas of the what-am-I-to-find, what-am-I-given variety are generally indicative of rigidity of approach which is inimical to successful reasoning. The student should also be discouraged from using cues such as "difference means to subtract" since they put problem solving on a mechanical basis. This is not to say that students should be left to reason in a haphazard fashion; on the contrary, they should be encouraged to develop a reasonably systematic approach to problems but not to the point of rigidity.

Of prime significance is the student's motivation. Glaser (1941) found the aspect of critical thinking most susceptible to general improvement to be the willingness to consider in a thoughtful way problems within the scope of one's experience and an attitude of wanting evidence for one's opinions and beliefs. The school needs to foster in its students a critical attitude, a willingness to ask *why* rather than simply *what*. It is more productive for the child to reason out why Chicago was bound to become an important industrial and trade center than to memorize the reasons given in the book. Such an aproach gives knowledge which is more penetrating and more personally satisfying and operational than the study of the text, even though it may not be as well formulated or organized from an adult point of view. Students often want to be provided with pat answers; they are likely to be annoyed when their questions are thrown back at them with a "What do you think?" Actually, pat answers are much more reassuring to the student who has been kept dependent on the teacher or the text for his answers. When his curiosity and initiative have been blunted, he prefers being told to having to dig up all the complications, exceptions, and provisos—especially when very often all he wants is to pass the examination, in which case the expedient thing to do is to find out what answer the teacher will accept.

Motivation makes for greater persistence and for the development of a more adequate background, both of which facilitate problem solving. Excessive motivation—or more correctly anxiety—interferes with effective problem solving as we noted in connection with Maier's experiment showing frustration-induced fixity on the part of rats (See Chapter 4). Closely related is the concept of *functional fixity*, a form of rigidity or blocking off of possible solutions as a result of mental set resulting from previous experience. The classic study here is Maier's two-string experiment (1931) in which the subject is to tie together two strings suspended from the ceiling far enough apart so that he cannot reach both at once. The trick is to tie any object to one of the strings to serve as a pendulum and to set it swinging so that it can be caught in the upswing while the subject has the other string in hand. It has been found, for example, that engineers accustomed to using a switch or a relay as a piece of equipment are blinded to its possibilities as a pendulum (Birch and Rabinowitz, 1951); in other words, the preexperiment utilization of the switch or relay blocks out its general characteristics of mass which is basic to the problem. In line with this, some people have argued against too thorough an orientation to the present status of a given problem on the ground that, by chaining the investigator to the past, such a background may be a hindrance to productive thinking. It is felt that familiarization with a problem forces the prospective investigator into the mold of previous approaches to the point where he loses any fresh perspective he might otherwise bring to the situation. This argument is not completely devoid of validity; such a loss can—but need not—occur. Certainly, some familiarity with the situation is essential to effective problem solving. The moral is that experience must be kept sufficiently general and flexible that it does not restrict its availability for a dissimilar purpose in subsequent problem situations.

Incorrect information and incorrect mental set can preclude productive thinking. Scholars of the Middle Ages were stymied by erroneous beliefs that the world was flat and that the sun revolved around the earth. Galileo succeeded only when he broke away from the prevailing set. Incorrect set, deliberately planted, is often the basis for riddles and jokes. On the other hand, the educated person has many sets readily available which enable him to move directly to a solution. Certainly, a good quarterback has a large number of preplanned options—against which the opposition also has a number of preplanned defenses.

A common form of fixity stems from routine: the subject simply approaches all problems of a category from a given set without considering whether a different approach might be more productive in certain individual problems in the category. This frequently reflects a sort of mental laziness, where routine is used as an excuse for avoiding problem solving or for not examining the effectiveness of current approaches. Overlearned habits frequently constitute a set which interferes with effective problem solving. Biases, prejudices, and other forms of stereotypes operating as mental sets are also generally a hindrance to effective problem solving. In fact, any form of strong emotional involvement tends to interfere with rational processes; a person may not be able to think straight about problems concerning his immediate family, for example.

A number of instances of erroneous thinking can be cited; in rationalization, the person focuses on one acceptable feature of the situation, while blocking a whole segment of unacceptable aspects of greater relevance. A common cause of poor reasoning is ambiguity, e.g., failing to define the problem, or not getting a clear understanding of the exact meaning of the crucial terms on which it pivots. Faulty reasoning can also stem from failing to consider all the evidence or from stating the problem in an either-or dichotomy with the blocking out of alternative solutions. One can also mistake the cause for the effect, or assume a direct cause-and-effect relationship between what are really two consequences of a third factor.

The Problem-solving Approach

Proponents of the view that the schools of a democratic society should place maximum emphasis on reasoning have advocated what might be called the problem-solving, problem-centered, or reflective approach to teaching (Hullfish and Smith, 1961; Bruner, 1961; Bayles, 1960), an approach which, as the various names imply, refers to a variety of classroom procedures centering on problem situations. Problem-centered teaching— or more correctly, learning—is a group activity; a problem of interest to the group, collectively and individually, is selected and clarified through discussion. Inherent in the method is the emphasis on discovery: rather than being told the solution, the students discover it. The teacher's task is to act as general consultant and coordinator, keeping the group on the track and on the move.

This approach is also known as the pupil-centered or even the progressive method and will be discussed further in Chapter 20. Where appropriate, it tends to result in increased insight into individual problems as well as increased ability to engage in problem-solving behavior. Ideally, it results in greater interest and motivation; in more penetrating, although perhaps less extensive, education; in more meaningful learning; and in greater understanding. Furthermore, it is relatively effective in changing attitudes and behavior (Lewin, 1958). It also promotes a feeling of group belonging and provides training in democratic resolution of problem situations. On the other hand, it is a rather slow-moving procedure which is sometimes difficult to adapt to a systematic coverage of the curriculum, and it may have to be supplemented by other more systematic approaches, if gaps are to be avoided (Hermanovicz, 1961). It is also difficult to handle well. Its effectiveness revolves in a crucial way on the effectiveness of the discussion as a teaching-learning device, an approach which has both strengths and limitations.

Research, although generally favoring the problem-centered approach over the cut-and-dried version of the "traditional" method, has not been consistent. Kersh (1958) found the discovery group superior, but Craig

(1956) found that the teacher-directed method promoted greater learning and retention. Kittell (1957), on the other hand, found the group that received an intermediate amount of guidance superior in learning, retention, and transfer to the groups which had received either more or less direction. Ausubel (1963), in a strong critique of the discovery method, recommends the organized presentation of subject matter. It seems that discovery is conducive to greater learning, retention, and transfer only insofar as it raises the level of motivation and encourages continued study of the problem. It seems, further, that a good education entails more than one teaching method, whether teacher-centered or student-centered.

The views expressed in a discussion, when judged by adult standards, are often relatively inadequate. Yet the teacher must suppress, at least in part, the desire to take over and present a more elegant, or even a more correct, version. Children reason and speak as children because they *are* children; they cannot absorb answers appropriate to adult insight simply because they are not adults. Complete answers come in degrees; what can be absorbed meaningfully at a given time is restricted by maturational and experiential limitations. To be concerned that children do not possess the complete truth regarding a given point is to fail to understand children and their development. Children often do not care to have a complete answer in all its scientific aspects; they simply want to know what they can use for the time being. This is a significant fact in what constitutes a meaningful education, i.e., an education oriented toward student needs rather than toward an adult version of what children ought to have in order to be adequately educated.

The group situation is generally conducive to the encouragement of problem solving; a group working at the solution of a common problem is likely to come up with more hypotheses and to have more experience to bring to bear in evaluating such hypotheses and devising effective plans of attack. The group is more likely to pick out errors in logic, e.g., false assumptions, false analogies, and unwarranted generalizations. But its greatest potential contribution to problem solving is probably social reinforcement which permits the interstimulation of members, and forces each to make his best contribution toward the attainment of group goals. This is especially true in a group characterized by cohesiveness and group morale where the atmosphere is sufficiently permissive that each is free to make his contribution without fear of losing status. Only then can the members mobilize their energies toward solving problems rather than dissipate them in self-protection.

A group approach is not superior simply because it involves a group; we need to clarify just what we can expect to be achieved through group methods and what is unlikely. Research, most of it done in a nonschool setting and involving relatively small groups working on an *ad hoc* basis, suggests that group work is most effective in dealing with complex tasks requiring a background more extensive than any one individual is likely to possess. Its effectiveness in problem solving depends on a number of factors including the nature of the problem, the resources, background and involvement of the members, the quality of the leadership, and various other considerations peculiar to the situation.

MEANING

The realization that, without meaning, all that goes on under the guise of education is to no avail has led to a major shift in educational practice from emphasis on drill and memory work to the current emphasis on understanding and meaningfulness. More specifically, the shift toward meaningfulness represents an awareness that meaningful material is: [a] learned more readily; [b] retained longer; and [c] more readily available for transfer to novel situations. Also implied in meaningfulness is the factor of patterning or structural organization; it is easier to learn and to remember the prime numbers as a sequence than to deal with each individually, for example. This can be related to Deese's postulation (1958) that the mind can grasp only so many "bits" of information, whether the bits be symbols, words, or ideas; meaningful material, because it has continuity, simply condenses into fewer interconnected units.

NATURE OF MEANING

Civilized man has come to place heavy reliance upon symbols—especially verbal and written symbols—for conveying meaning. This is particularly true in the classroom where language is almost exclusively the medium of instruction. Thus, words, i.e., a specific sequence of letters and sounds, by common agreement, have come to mean a particular object, event, or relationship, to symbolize certain experiences, or to express relationships among experiences. Because they are so easily manipulated, symbols are effective means of classifying as well as communicating experiences and they are indispensable tools in the process of reasoning, particularly at the higher levels. Symbols facilitate the manipulation of ideas and experiences; they not only permit one to deal more effectively with tangible objects but also to go beyond to abstract and hypothetical entities, relationships, and concepts. Modern scientific advances could hardly have been possible without the use of mathematical and verbal symbolism; in fact, unless concrete experiences are synthesized and generalized through symbolism, they tend to be relatively nonproductive.

PROBLEMS IN DEVELOPING MEANING

Symbols can only mean what they represent in one's experience; hence, meaning lies in the individual, not in the symbol. We cannot convey meaning to the child; it is the learner's personal organization of experiences that counts. The teacher's logical presentation of the materials of the curriculum is important only insofar as it facilitates the organization which the learner must do for himself. Furthermore, since learning is dependent on experience, the more the learner carries into the situation the more he is likely to gain; conversely, when his experiences are meager, his understandings will be correspondingly vague. Thus, a person born and raised in Florida may have difficulty in getting accurate meaning out of the word *blizzard*. Many a farm boy has a very inadequate idea of a skyscraper; most people are not particularly clear as to the size of an acre. We can sometimes extend the learner's experiences so that he gets at least a vague notion of experiences he has not had. Indeed, he must, if he is to learn anything. Thus, an octopus might be described to a person who has never seen one by relating it to a squid, a jellyfish, or any other animal with which he is acquainted. Of course, this process of relating one experience to another always carries the danger of inaccuracy and general vagueness; the use of pictures, for example, would not give too clear an idea of the size of an octopus.

Fuzziness in meaning is not the monopoly of children. In adults, as well as children, there are various degrees of clarity of meaning depending on such factors as: [a] the learner's intellectual and experiential background; [b] his motivation; [c] the difficulty of the concept and, [d] the terminology in which the concept is presented. Rarely are meanings complete, even in a restricted area; we generally see only one side of an issue; we fail to relate our experiences to all the other experiences to which they could be related. Few adults really understand the concept of democracy in all its implications. On the other hand, children are even more likely to possess inadequate or incorrect concepts, for, in the course of an average day, they are expected to make a large number of constructs, many of which are of considerable difficulty in relation to their intellectual and experiential background. Thus, we have come to expect the occasional boner or expression of half-baked ideas as normal and unavoidable, when in reality they reflect the teacher's failure to communicate with the children whose growth he is paid to guide. As stated by Horn (1942):

> . . . the inadequate and erroneous conceptions formed by pupils in various curricular fields, far from being something to wonder at, are precisely what one should expect. For while, of course, instruction is not deliberately planned to foster the development of inadequate and erroneous ideas, it is, nevertheless, organized in such a way that those results are sure to follow. [p. 406]

The same viewpoint is expressed by Morse and Wingo (1962), who state that, while occasional boners may be funny, there is nothing funny about an educational system which systematically produces them.

Since we interpret symbols in terms of our experiences, the use of symbols is predicated upon the presupposition that the listener has an experiential background sufficiently similar to that of the speaker so that the symbols evoke the proper meaning in the listener.[2] Horn, for example, suggests that the average college instructor is a man of many words, both literally and figuratively. He may be saying very different things to the many students in front of him, each with his own background; to some he is not saying much of anything; to others he is probably saying approximately what he means to say. For others still, the meaning is distorted by various "noises" on the line. Failure in communication is probably greater in elementary school, especially with children from different cultural or socioeconomic strata. Language is so easy to use that it is dangerous in that it can be used to replace meaning. The use of symbols degenerates into verbalism when the learner has a word or a symbol but does not have the corresponding experience or referent. The class, for example, may be able to verbalize a given concept or use a certain term without necessarily comprehending its meaning; the manipulation of a symbol (unlike the manipulation of an object) does not lead to its clarification. James' well-known story is appropriate here (James, 1899):

> A friend of mine, visiting a school, was asked to examine a young class in geography. Glancing at the book, she said: 'Suppose you should dig a hole in the ground, hundreds of feet deep, how should you find it at the bottom—warmer or colder than on top?' None of the class replying, the teacher said: 'I am sure they know, but I think you don't ask the question rightly. Let me try.' So, taking the book, she asked: 'In what condition is the interior of the globe?' and received the immediate answer from half the class at once: 'The interior of the globe is in a condition of igneous fusion.' [p. 150]

Our schools are so highly verbal and bookish that the child is often virtually swamped by a flood of words and other symbols concerning which he has no experience. Occasionally, the confusion reaches such Babelic proportions that he has no choice but to rely on parrot memory if he is to meet examination requirements. Frequently, he does not realize the

---

[2] The role of language in meaningfulness is best seen from the standpoint of communications or information theory. A communication system consists of five basic components: a source, a transmitter, a channel, a receiver, and a destination. The operation of converting information into transmittable energy is known as *encoding*, and the messages that pass along the channel are coded signals. The receiver must decode the message if he is to get the intended message. In any communication system, there are "noises," or unwanted events which tend to interfere with the communication, e.g., static on the radio. Two kinds of transmittal distortion can occur: one in decoding where the individual does not receive the message that has been sent, the other in encoding where the individual does not send the message he intends to send. If he is to be effective, the sender must have some form of feedback to tell him whether he is getting through to his audience.

inadequacy of his understandings or he may not be sufficiently interested to clarify meaning through a dictionary or related sources. Teachers need to realize that much of the difficulty the child encounters in learning classroom materials stems from a lack of experience that would give meaning to many of the symbols with which the classroom is concerned. It may be necessary to undertake a systematic program of field experiences along the lines of Project Higher Horizons as a way of building the background necessary for effective communication.

Getting meaning from a textbook is not easy; the child must first perceive and recognize each word; any error here is likely to garble the message. Then he must determine the meaning of the words he has read, select from his experiences the meaning to be associated with each, and organize these experiences into their proper relationships to give meaning to the paragraph. Where individual words have multiple meanings—and some words have a dozen or more different meanings—he must withhold judgment as to which meaning is relevant by relating each possible meaning to the context of the passage. Add to this the fact that vocabulary loads are often excessive, that the vocabulary used is not always the most understandable and one can get an idea of the difficulty confronting the learner when he attempts to develop precise meanings. To complicate the situation further, the average text or course contains too many ideas to be assimilated. Often it contains so many new words that it is almost impossible for beginners, especially those below average, to acquire the new vocabulary of, say, a science course, let alone understand the meaning of the content and its relation to actual problems. Numerous readability studies have shown that many textbooks are too difficult for their intended level. A vocabulary development program emphasizing student reports of the constructs they have formed may be beneficial, provided it is kept meaningful rather than a matter of drill. The discussion approach may provide greater opportunity for detecting misconceptions and various forms of verbalism.

IMPROVEMENT OF UNDERSTANDING

Many of the understandings of the average person are vague and even self-contradictory: people who "believe in democracy" harbor strong prejudices against minority groups; others who "believe in honesty" see "nothing wrong" with loafing on the job. Children often misbehave because they fail to see a certain act as a violation of a given rule. Complete understanding is, of course, difficult to achieve if we define it in terms of the grasp of facts and concepts and their complete integration and organization into the larger wholes of which they are a part. Woodruff (1948), for instance, mentions three stages in the development of understanding: [a] the assimilation of the facts and ideas which constitute the subject matter; [b] their organization and integration into larger meaningful wholes;

and [c] the development of the ability to use these facts and ideas in new situations. Unfortunately, the child—particularly the dull child, who is less capable of interrelating his experiences—at times does not master even the first stage.

Bearing directly on this problem is the common criticism that teachers teach facts rather than understandings, apparently unaware that the mere accumulation of unassimilated facts serves to confuse the child rather than to facilitate his reasoning or clarify his future experiences. Teachers often stress facts in isolation of the things that make them meaningful and the child, frequently concerned only with passing the examination, relies on memory rather than understanding. In fact, teachers sometimes discourage understanding by giving a higher grade to the student who parrots the words of the book than to the one whose answer, being in his own words, is not as polished as that of the text.

Actually there can be no objection to teaching facts; reasoning, understandings, and applications would be impossible without facts. What is objectionable is that children are taught not *facts* but mere words which they do not understand and which they can use only on the examination.[3] Mursell (1952), for instance, insists that there can be no quarrel between facts and understanding since to *know* a fact is to understand it. The solution, then, lies in teaching facts in such a way that they are understood and available for subsequent understandings. The teacher must ensure that the child has the experiential background to understand facts in their interrelationships. It is easy for the teacher, eager to cover the curriculum, to forget the slow tedious process through which genuine understandings develop, or even to forget that children are not always helped by glib explanations: "Rainbows are formed as a result of the refraction of the sun's rays by moisture particles."

Although concrete experiences are essential, excessive reliance on concrete experiences can be as fatal to understanding as excessive reliance on symbols; the child must have the concrete experiences backing up the symbols he uses but it is also imperative that he organize these experiences in terms of symbols, for unless they are tied together according to some principle or concept, they will remain isolated, unassimilated and again of no value in understanding later experiences. Nor are all concrete experiences vitally meaningful; laboratory experiences, for example, often provide nothing more than practice in following the manual; they may actually introduce an artificiality which stifles effective dealing with an actual science environment.

Learning experiences should be synthesized into cognitive structure and integrated with other learnings through some form of generalization which, as much as possible, should be in the child's own words since this is what

[3] There are different levels of understanding a fact: what is involved in water boiling at 212° F?

is meaningful at his level of understanding. One can generally encourage him through questioning to extend his level of comprehension but he especially needs guidance and practice in synthesizing his experiences; synthesizing them for him is hardly the answer. Nor is the answer to have him copy the generalization in the text, for then it simply becomes another fact with all the limitations thereof. What we want to encourage is a generalization in the child's own words, no matter how inadequate, for generalizations, like all forms of complex learning, are not mastered on first contact; rather, generalizations at one level structure related experiences at a higher level from which he formulates new and more adequate generalizations on a spiral of ever-greater meaningfulness.

Difficulty in promoting understanding stems from the complexity of the concepts to be learned in relation to the adequacy of the language in which they are expressed and the learner's readiness, e.g., his ability, his experiential background, his motivation, his work habits, his mind-set, etc. Efforts to improve the clarity of the child's understanding must, therefore, be oriented toward improvement in one or more of these problem areas.

[a] Curriculum-makers have attempted to minimize the difficulty of concepts by delaying their introduction. Thus, numerical concepts are introduced only informally in the primary grades, and decimals and fractions have been pushed into the upper elementary grades. As we have noted in Chapter 5 postponement is, at best, only a partial solution; if we accept the view presented by Hebb, Moore, and others that development feeds on itself and the early years are among the most intellectually profitable, it may even be misguided. Children in the primary grades are forming—with reasonable ease and accuracy—concepts in newer mathematics that had heretofore been considered advanced college work.

[b] A number of issues are involved in improving clarity of understanding through improved adequacy of presentation. It is true that concepts are sometimes presented in vocabulary that is unnecessarily complicated; we can no more expect the child to understand unfamiliar content presented in unfamiliar language than we can expect him to lift himself up by his own bootstraps. The problem has received considerable attention in recent years as more stress has been placed on readability. On the other hand, simplification of vocabulary is not an entirely adequate solution: different shades of meaning call for the use of different words and to use *wait* synonymously with *delay, linger, tarry,* or *loiter* will only cause confusion.

Understanding is facilitated by clarity and effectiveness in the use of language. People sometimes speak all around the topic without ever getting to the point or they get there by way of the most confusing details. Teachers and textbook writers are not exempt from this failing. Clarity of expression is related to clarity of thinking and generally the more familiar a person is with his topic the more lucid he can make his explanations.

It also follows that, if they are to be effective in the classroom, teachers must develop a certain facility in conveying ideas clearly and concisely. On the other hand, it remains unavoidably true that complex ideas tend to call for complex explanations.

Understanding is also promoted by using varied approaches in presenting the material. Using many examples in different settings so that, through the process of contrast, the learner can isolate the relevant from the irrelevant and the essential from the incidental is likely to promote clearer understanding than emphasizing a single illustration. For the same reason, the student should generally read different sources rather than dwell exclusively on a single text.

[c] Probably the most effective means of improving understanding is through raising the learner's motivational and experiential background. Any attempt to lower the vocabulary level of instructional material must be accompanied by a corresponding attempt to promote vocabulary development through systematic instruction based on meaningful experiences. The school must make a deliberate effort to enrich the experiential background of the students directly through firsthand contact with the environment, or vicariously through various aids where personal experience is not possible. Increasing the learner's motivation is also likely to result in greater understanding through the extra effort he is likely to devote to synthesizing details into structural unity. The child who is interested is likely to use the dictionary in clarifying meaning rather than rely on the context to give him the general idea, for example.

The self-concept is an important factor in this connection. The boy who feels that his status as a boy calls for his knowing about motorcycles will learn the operation of the carburetor, for it has meaning to him; it is no longer just a word in his spelling lesson. Not only will he read about internal combustion engines, but he will also understand material which, by all standards, is rather difficult. This, despite the fact that in most school subjects he cannot understand even simple material. On the other hand, a student may have difficulty understanding certain concepts because they have an emotional overtone which prevents him from devoting his whole attention to clarifying their meaning, or because they do not fit in with his system of values. The adolescent boy may be handicapped in understanding poetry by his views of poetry as sissified.

Whereas teachers cannot do much to raise the child's intelligence (in the traditional sense), they can do a great deal in promoting intelligent behavior through promoting greater experiential and motivational adequacy. They must also realize that extra help will be needed for the duller child if comprehension is to be achieved. Research has shown that good students get as much from one reading as poor students from two readings and that the lowest 10 percent in hearing comprehension gain little more from three hearings than the top 10 percent do in a single hearing (Good,

1926). Research has also shown that those children who have difficulty in understanding what they read also have difficulty in understanding what they hear (Young, 1936). What it amounts to is that the poor student is often unable to get much from either his text or the lectures and, unless special help is provided, he soon becomes thoroughly confused as he piles unassimilated material on unassimilated material. On the other hand, the situation is not hopeless; research has shown that not only can listening comprehension be improved, but, even more important, such improvement tends to be accompanied by parallel increases in other comprehension skills (Trivette, 1961, Pratt, 1956).

DEVELOPMENT OF CONCEPTS

The mere accumulation of experience is of little value in itself, for experience becomes meaningful only when it is organized. Thus, the young child, seeing various animals for the first time cannot determine what to expect from each until he manages to categorize them as cats and dogs. He now has formed a couple of concepts, i.e., he has assigned a general label, not to a particular cat or dog but to a generalized category of animals having common cat or dog characteristics in terms of which other cats, dogs, and noncats, and nondogs can be identified. In order to develop adequate concepts, the child must first be exposed to a wide variety of situations from which he can identify the crucial aspects that cause dogs to belong to the dog category and cats to belong to the cat category, i.e., he must resort to the complementary processes of abstraction (the observation of similarities in otherwise different things) and generalization (the combining of these common properties). That this is an extremely slow process has been noted in connection with Hebb's concept of primary learnings. It follows that children cannot logically be expected to gain complete conceptual clarity at first contact;[4] the clarity of their concepts depends directly on the clarity of previous concepts and it is only as deeper understandings develop that more adequate concepts can be formed.

The fact that the child must form his own concepts does not imply that he must do so without help. A primary purpose of education is to facilitate the formation of functionally effective concepts and to sharpen into cognitive clarity the child's present fuzzy concepts. The teacher, by drawing out of the *ground* the significant features, for example, can focus the child's attention on certain aspects of a given phenomenon and thus help him identify its crucial properties. In order to help the child clarify his concepts, it is necessary to present the essential elements of the situation in a reasonable variety of nonessentials, but it is best not to

[4] This also points to the ill-advisedness of setting grading standards of 90 percent, etc. Reliance on such illogical standards may explain in part why the typical test measures facts which can be memorized rather than concepts in which such approximations to perfection are impossible.

clutter the presentation with so many details that the essential aspects are obscured. On the other hand, sufficient details should be presented so that the picture is not left incomplete. Both too many details and too few are to be avoided; however, it is rather difficult in view of the differences in ability and background among students to decide the point at which the optimal degree of explanation has been reached. It is generally wise to present an overview, a framework into which the details must fit if they are not to become the trees that prevent the learner from seeing the forest. Thus, the concept *democracy* may be unnecessarily obscured by introducing in the first lesson all the complications involved in electing a president or a prime minister. Or, if reference is made only to such democracies as the United States, England, Canada, Australia, and New Zealand, the student may mistakenly conclude that the English language is an aspect of democracy.

The teacher must make the essential elements conspicuous in different interrelationships and give the student practice in seeing the various aspects of a situation in relation to each other and to previous learnings, since it is an understanding of these relationships, rather than of the separate elements, which enable him to grasp a given concept. Studying by wholes is generally conducive to the formation of clear concepts since it makes for greater continuity and emphasis on interrelationships among component ideas. Finally, if the child is to develop clear concepts, it is necessary for the teacher to insist that he use these concepts accurately in connection with their applications and implications in related situations. The teacher must guard against children viewing concepts as new words to be committed to memory. Many word lists in spelling, for example, simply involve arbitrary associations totally unrelated to anything in the child's experience. Meaningful vocabulary drill can increase one's vocabulary, but studying wholesale new words that have no basis in experience is rather futile; not only will they soon be forgotten but they are of little value because only functional information can be used in solving day-to-day problems.

CREATIVITY

The Nature of Creativity

An aspect of personality which, up to recent years, has been grossly neglected is creativity. In fact, except for the talented musician and artist, the creative individual in our society is still largely unappreciated. The outcome has been to the considerable detriment of our democratic society in which progress is as crucially dependent on imagination as on the more conventional "intelligence." To date, our schools have given the recognition—grades, honors, scholarships, college education, and as a result, later executive positions—to the youngster who is gifted along narrow traditional IQ lines. There has been a growing annoyance on the part of educators and business leaders with the conformist, the stereotyped individual the educational system has been turning out, and the relative lack of people who are freely creative and original thinkers. We have plenty of technicians, but the people who can originate and innovate are relatively scarce. The problem is not necessarily peculiar to our times; it simply reflects the greater inventiveness necessary for survival in a well-developed society. Culture cannot remain static; it must be dynamic and growing. We have been too concerned with preserving the culture; our aim has been to inculcate rather than to promote its advancement. We have concentrated on people able to accumulate a great deal of what is known but who are not necessarily those who can create new knowledge. We need to differentiate between talented conformists who can be trained to become manipulators of the ideas of others and original and inventive nonconformists who may make imaginative breakthroughs to new knowledge. Especially we need to conceive of students as thinkers, producers, and creators rather than solely as learners—or, as Taylor (1963) puts it, as "spongeheads" and "regurgitators."

We are becoming progressively more aware that we do our society a disservice when (by virtue of the approval we provide) we are a party to placing in leadership positions persons who are incapable of imaginative leadership. The future businessman, the industrial tycoon, the inventor, the poet, the artist, the essayist—to whose talents their later success clearly attests—are far too frequently mediocre students whose potentialities go unrecognized while the school caters to the conventionally bright. We are beginning to question why we do not produce more creative geniuses; among Terman's gifted children, we have seen as yet little promise of a Darwin, an Edison, or a Eugene O'Neill. Despite the best educational system in the world, our space program, for example, has had to rely heavily on imported scientists. Our traditional academic value system is oriented toward the conventionally gifted; we provide scholarships to the academically gifted while we deny the potential creator or inventor a chance to develop his talents. We may be squeezing out of our executive ranks the analytical, the intuitive, the creative person while we emphasize conformity patterned to "organization-man" specifications. This, in a sense, constitutes a bias in our present cultural orientation as devastating to our national welfare as that connected with the inappropriateness of our present middle-class oriented curriculum for lower-class children.

Creativity bears directly upon problem solving. It can be conceived as a combination of realistic thinking and imagination, a sort of problem-solving activity without a predetermined answer, frequently with self-expression as the dominant feature. The person who creates, whether the product is in the area of the literary, the artistic, the scientific, or the practical, goes through essentially the same process as in reasoning, the difference being that a greater emphasis is placed on the novelty of the solution.

We must avoid conceiving of creativity along the more spectacular lines of the paintings of da Vinci, the plays of Shakespeare, or the inventions of Edison, Morse, or Bell. We must include, for example, social innovations as represented by the Magna Carta, the Bill of Rights, and by constructive interaction with one's neighbors, even though this kind of creativity may not qualify one for a Nobel prize. In that sense and contrary to previous views on the subject, everyone is capable of creativity; not everyone can create a masterpiece certainly, but to the extent that creativity is a matter of self-expression, the difference is one of continuity rather than dichotomy. The school needs to encourage the child to express himself in a way that is novel to him—and anyone can draw, paint, design a dress or a house, write a theme or a letter, even though for most people none of these productions will ever gain public acclaim.

The present emphasis on creativity stems largely from the work of Guilford (1950, 1956, 1967) and is best conceptualized in the context of divergent thinking as postulated in his structure of the intellect. A major aspect of creativity is originality as revealed through uncommon and clever responses (e.g., suggesting apt titles for stories). Also basic to creativity are various forms of novelty, flexibility, and fluency. Another important aspect is the capacity to grasp a vast, complex, or intricate conceptual structure, to organize ideas in novel juxtaposition, and to synthesize the familiar into novel and more inclusive structural patterns. An evaluative component is also involved, permitting the examination of the product for fitness and thus preventing aimless wandering, but this component must not be so dominant as to impede flexibility.

THE RELATION OF CREATIVITY TO INTELLIGENCE

That "intelligence" and creativity are not synonymous has been shown by Getzels and Jackson (1962a, 1962b) and by Torrance (1952, 1962, 1963), who found that roughly two thirds of the top 20 percent in creativity in various student populations did not qualify in the top 20 percent on the intelligence scale, while, conversely, roughly two thirds of the highly intelligent did not qualify as highly creative. Relative independence between creativity and intelligence was also noted by MacKinnon (1962, p. 493) who concluded that ". . . if a person has the minimum of intelligence required for mastery of the field of knowledge, whether he performs creatively or banally in that field will be crucially determined by non-intellective factors."

Up to now, psychology has been oriented toward intelligence in the sense of the traditional IQ which, according to Guilford, would probably encompass no more than six or eight of the 61 intellectual factors postulated in his structure of the intellect and presumably few, if any, of the nonintellectual factors such as sensing a problem, originality, and various other traits which may be fundamental to creativity. In other words, our present tests focus on convergent thinking as synonymous with intelligence to the neglect of other forms of academic excellence, particularly as it relates to creativity. Actually, there are probably many different talents including giftedness in the area of planning, decision-making, and communication.[5] Certainly, the human intellect is not adequately represented by the single dimension of critical thinking.

Contributing to our present narrow and erroneous conception of intelligence is our equally narrow orientation in academic matters. As long as we structure schoolwork along the same lines of convergent thinking oriented to grasping predetermined answers, present IQ tests will continue to provide a reasonably adequate appraisal of this kind of ability. The system is self-consistent and self-perpetuating but also narrow and, in some cases, vicious in that it causes us to overlook other talented children. Taylor (1959) criticizes traditional measures of intelligence on the grounds that they were designed to predict academic performance of the kind that was valued most highly at the time of their derivation and that this has tended to freeze both the nature of the tests and of academic values. Much of the older mathematics, for example, seems better suited to training systematic bookkeepers than intuitive mathematicians. Education has been oriented toward a traditional system of academic values not too closely related to life outside the system; only recently have we begun to recognize that many things can be learned more economically by exploring, manipulating, questioning, and experimenting.

The situation is compounded by the fact that the creative child is not appreciated by his teacher. In both the Getzels and Jackson and the Torrance studies, teachers exhibited a preference for the high IQ group even though the "creative'" equalled the "intelligent" in academic performance despite a substantial IQ handicap. The "creative" were rated by their teachers as lower in ambition and studiousness, so that apparently the highly creative learn as much as the highly intelligent ". . . at least in some schools, without appearing to work as hard." (Torrance, 1962). They are relatively indifferent to grades. Drews (1961), for example, found that, while the other children were preparing for an examination, the "creative" might be reading science fiction or philosophy, or otherwise engaging in activities which have no bearing on their grades. As a result,

---

[5] Thorndike (1963) makes the important point that, as presently used, creativity is a global term covering a considerable conglomeration of abilities. Just as creativity has been found relatively independent of the traditional IQ, so have the various abilities measured by tests of "creativity" been found relatively independent of each other so that the concept of the "creative child" (just as that of the "gifted child") may be so encompassing as to warrant considerable caution in its use. Wallach and Kogan (1965) emphasize the same point.

they obtained the lowest grades, but by virtue of their wide, self-initiated readings, they out-performed both the social-leader and the studious-conformist groups on standardized (achievement) tests.

The IQ has been useful. As suggested by Miles (1960) we have yet to devise an index as effective as the IQ in identifying the talented and potentially successful in school and various areas of human endeavor. Perhaps this is so, however, because of the way we teach, i.e., because of the way the creative child is handicapped academically by the authoritarianism typical of the average classroom. The creative child rebels at the rigid approach in which he is told what he should learn and what he should accept as true. Ornstein (1961) found that when science is taught so as to encourage creative learning, the traditional predictors lose their validity. Some of the gifted children did not do well; presumably they were better at memorizing facts and formulas, i.e., learning by authority, than at analytical intuitive thinking as required in creative learning.

CHARACTERISTICS OF THE CREATIVE PERSON

The creative person is characterized by spontaneity, flexibility, adaptibility, and especially originality; he is particularly open to experience. He tends to get involved and often displays a high level of persistence, but he relies on a flexible approach rather than a stereotyped mode of attack. In a very real sense, the creative person represents the person capable of *becoming* as presented in Chapter 4.

The creative person tends to be an individualist, inclined to follow his own system. He seeks adventure and tolerates disorganization and ambiguity; he enjoys the risk and the uncertainty of the unknown. He abandons old ways of thinking and strikes out in new directions; he rarely preplans activities. His adventuresomeness and willingness to take a chance is often reflected in the way he is likely to change plans on the spur of the moment and in his willingness to test the limits of his capacities as well as the limits of conventionality. On the other hand, Guilford (1959) found no indication that the original person is necessarily less inclined toward cultural conformity in moral values; certainly his unconventionality is not a matter of bohemian or beatnik reactions. Of interest in this connection is Hilgard's observation (1959) that having to take responsibility for earning a living may actually interfere with creativity. Few college professors of English, for example, are first-class creative writers. Apparently, anyone who can meet classes regularly, take committee responsibilities seriously, grade papers conscientiously is not likely to have the freewheeling drive generally associated with creativity.

An interesting aspect of creativity is that of its two basic traits, sensitivity is a feminine characteristic while independence is a masculine virtue. Thus, creative boys tend to be somewhat effeminate and creative girls to be somewhat masculine, all of which does not help them fit in with their peers. Torrance points to a number of creative children who have sacrificed their creativity to maintain their masculinity or femininity.

PROMOTING CREATIVITY

To the extent that creativity is essential to social progress as well as personal self-realization, the school should consider its promotion a matter of primary responsibility. This implies, first, recognizing its importance and making it one of the definite and enumerated goals of American education. This, in turn, calls for major modifications in the traditional conception of educational objectives; it calls, for example, for the elimination of the overemphasis on uniformity, conformity, and routine which currently characterizes our schools. To the extent that we have responsibility to make everyone creative within the framework of his potentialities, we need to expand the objectives of our various courses to include the development of the skills of creative thinking and further we need to develop teaching methods that will enable everyone to capitalize on his creative talents. We especially need to get away from one standard educational program which every child must fit. This is not an impossible task: teachers can promote creativity if they will simply devote the same energy and imagination to its promotion as they have to the teaching of facts which frequently stifles rather than promotes education along significant dimensions.

An obvious necessity is that we expand the present IQ beyond the narrow confines of the academically and convergently capable. Already a start has been made: Guilford and Torrance have constructed tests to measure uncommonness of response, ability to make remote associations, cleverness, etc. This will necessitate a major revision in current tests of intelligence; Guilford suggests that certain creative abilities can be measured only by a completion test since multiple-choice items simply force the child to choose from conventional alternatives. We must also incorporate some of the nonintellectual factors postulated in Guilford's structure of the intellect.

Rogers (1954) identifies two factors basic to constructive creativity:

[a] Psychological safety—which implies accepting the individual as of unconditional worth, understanding him empathically, and providing him with an environment from which external evaluation is relatively absent. Only as he is provided with this sense of safety can he afford to act spontaneously.

[b] Psychological freedom—which implies giving the individual complete freedom of symbolic expression, freedom to think, to feel, and to be whatever he is and, thereby, encouraging the spontaneous juggling of ideas, concepts, and meanings.

The creative person needs both psychological safety and psychological freedom in order to be free to juggle impossible juxtapositions, to shape wild hypotheses, and to express the ridiculous. It is this spontaneous exploration of ideas that eventually leads to a hunch, a creative seeing through of new and significant possibilities. Maslow (1959), for example, sees absence of fear as characteristic of the great people he has known; they were less inculturated, i.e., less afraid of what people would say or laugh at; they were free to express their impulses, their emotions, their thoughts, and their insights. The insecure individual is rarely creative, regardless of his brilliance; he is characterized by rigidity in approach, overconcern over his adequacy, and a negative self-concept. He walls himself off in order to protect his deeper self; he dissipates his talents and energies in protecting himself against himself.

Of fundamental importance here is the definite relationship between creativity and personality. Intelligence and a thorough grounding in one's field are important, but perhaps even more crucial are the nonintellectual factors of motivation, versatility, and unwillingness to fit a mold. That men are apparently more creative than women, for example, may be due to their greater nonconformity, daring, adventuresomeness. A fundamental psychological condition for constructive creativity is openness to experience, for creativity is essentially a by-product of self-realization rather than something one strives for directly. Rogers' fully-functioning person, for example, is by definition a creative person; his sensitive openness to his world and his trust in his ability to form new relationships with the environment make him the kind of person for whom creative products and creative living are likely to emerge (Rogers, 1962). If we accept the fact that every person has the capacity for creativity, the problem of education is not the production of creativity but rather the release and encouragement of the creativity which is already present.[6]

Undoubtedly, the greatest single factor in promoting creativity is a permissive atmosphere predicated upon concern for human dignity, freedom from pressure, and opportunity for and encouragement of self-initiated activities. Not only must the teacher foster an atmosphere of permissiveness and acceptance so that the child can afford to try novel ideas even if they fall flat, but he must also tolerate (perhaps encourage) a certain departure from tradition. He also needs to provide for leisure, meditation, and even daydreaming as a means of fostering creative ideas; rushing students from one 50-minute period to another is not particularly conducive to creativity. Nor do creative ideas emerge overnight; the short homework assignment structured around predetermined answers, complete with

[6] This is again the idea that educators do not have to vitalize an inert mass but rather simply channel and direct existing potentialities. Not the least of the teacher's tasks is to refrain from damaging and stifling these potentialities.

grading, to be handed in the next morning does not promote the whole-hearted involvement that characterizes creative productivity.

The creative child is not a particularly easy person to have around. Teachers tend to become irritated at his endless curiosity; his persistent questioning and experimenting can be most disrupting to a teacher with 29 other children to tend to and a curriculum to cover, especially since, in addition, he often has difficulty in conforming. He refuses to fit the established pattern; this is the very essence of his creativity. Many of the traits that characterize the highly creative child—nonconformity, adventuresomeness, nonsociability, impulsiveness—tend to be traits teachers identify with pupils they do not like. On general principles, he might be expected to have trouble in fitting the traditional mold designed by teachers who, by their very position, tend to be culture-bound conformists. The very fact that creative thinking is fundamentally unconventional thinking creates problems in the classroom.

The traditional classroom atmosphere, although very reassuring to the highly structured child, is relatively incompatible to the self-directing, self-initiating, and spontaneous child, whose screwy ideas often antagonize others. His very display of creativity, i.e., his deviations from the norm, tend to make him obnoxious. It must be recognized that any novel idea automatically makes its originator a minority of one. Rarely is the creative child understood; he tends to be unpopular and to have few friends, for example. Because of the psychological estrangement, if not rejection, and the inevitable consequent difficulties in identifying with adults, he is frequently eccentric, immature, narrow, and in some cases, maladjusted. The counselor and the teacher have a special responsibility—as they have to each and every child—to provide opportunities for him to satisfy his needs within the framework of the school situation and to provide him with guidance in channeling his personality traits into effective social patterns without, at the same time, sacrificing his creativity.

It is often difficult to adapt a program to students who deviate from the established classroom pattern; as a result, the creative child is often presented with a program in which he can only be judged educationally inadequate. Even when his creativity is recognized, it is not always easy to make the necessary modifications, so that he is often sacrificed in the interest of administrative expediency. The classroom atmosphere tends to inhibit creativity by typically forcing the student into the role of learner rather than seeker of new and better ways of doing things. For too long our schools have emphasized that the only way of doing things is that prescribed by authority; even in sports, there is only one way of swimming, one way of playing basketball—all of which presents difficulties for the creative child whose approach is typically unorthodox.

The specific ways in which creativity can be promoted are not clear;

we can much more easily suggest a number of ways in which creativity can be stifled. A number of social forces, including the present level of affluence and the drift toward the easy life which characterizes modern American culture may restrict opportunities for creative problem solving. Much of our life is routinized; we have drifted toward the organization-man concept. Social pressures toward conformity are particularly detrimental to creativity. Furthermore, our society does not give creative artists, composers, and inventors the recognition that was given Michelangelo, Mozart, or da Vinci; Nobel and Pulitzer prize winners rate nothing more than a bare mention while the wild acclaim goes to the football hero, the movie star, or the television idol.

On the other hand, the emphasis on hard reality which also characterizes our present culture may likewise be detrimental to the development of creativity. Torrance points out that many parents eliminate fantasy from the child's thinking too soon. Eventually, creativity must come in contact with reality, but fantasy must be kept alive until the child's intellectual development reaches a level where he can engage in sound creative thinking. Indications are that many children with impoverished imaginations are those who have been subjected to premature rigorous efforts to eliminate fantasy; they have simply become afraid to think creatively. Our schools' expectation of a firm answer to all questions likewise tends to create an atmosphere in which ambiguity and probabilistic thinking are not tolerated.

Probably the greatest deterrent to creativity on the part of the child is adult insistence on perfection and conformity to adult standards. Whereas the emphasis should be on self-expression, adults are usually concerned with the product, and often simply with pointing out inconsistencies and errors rather than with praising the child for the ideas behind his productions. With our concern for perfection in the product, we rob the child of the opportunity for creativity; we dictate not only what he is to do but how it is to be done and what the finished product is to look like. We discourage him by our criticisms when the product does not come up to our standards—which often he is not ready to meet—with the result that, while there is no limit to the ideas the young child wants to express through drawing, the ten-year-old refuses to draw anything at all.

This does not deny the importance of basic rules, whether in mixing colors or in organizing a theme, but originality of content is often stifled by emphasis on form and technique so that, as a result of the education they receive, children become correct from a technical point of view but dead from the standpoint of creativity. Kettering (1944) defines an inventor as a person who doesn't take his education too seriously; he points out that the probability of an engineer making an invention is half that of a nonengineer. It well may be that employers selecting potential executives from the ranks of the college graduates have been fishing from the wrong pond; to the extent that many creative students do not get to college, present practices probably assign a number of creative persons to production line work where they have no opportunity for creativity and assign many who are not particularly creative to positions calling for creative leadership.

Our standards of achievement are often in terms of trivial points of mechanics, e.g., copying neatly or listing every single step in the solution of an algebra problem. The student is not expected to write particularly imaginative themes, but should he use double negatives, that is a serious offense! Many of our assignments and methods of operation show marked inflexibility, not only must problems be solved the prescribed way but adults often become impatient and attempt to take over. As long as we insist that children draw horses that look like horses, we may be taking a direct route to the destruction of any creative ability they possess. As they grow older, the need for evaluation will emerge naturally and they will want to meet standards, but overemphasis on evaluative restraint is fatal to the birth of new ideas, especially in the early stages and with the young child. Furthermore, this evaluative restraint must have an internal locus; external evaluation, e.g., grades, tends to introduce an element of threat which is detrimental to the development of creativity. It is also possible that, to the extent that those two abilities are relatively incompatible, the person who is most capable of creativity may not be adequate in evaluation.

As Nelson (1963) points out, the more effectively we organize to educate the intellectual conformist, the more effectively we organize to eliminate his opposite. We need to concern ourselves with overorganization and overvaluing of authority. We must avoid the danger of a stereotyped education geared to a lockstep, textbook-centered curriculum; we must also avoid such mechanical approaches as filling in the blanks or operating according to formula, all of which tend to breed conformity rather than functionality. Perhaps as Rogers (1962) puts it, we need to choose between institutional order and dogmatism, on the one hand, and flexibility and freedom, on the other.

CREATIVITY IN TEACHERS

If we are to foster creativity in our future citizens, we must begin with those who will teach them. Although it is probably not true that only creative teachers can teach the creative child, the teaching profession could profit from greater creativity and we need to give greater consideration to selecting prospective teachers who can understand the creative child and with whom he can identify. The selection process in teacher education is perhaps overly oriented toward the conventional student who prefers security to creativity. Even though we cannot expect every teacher to be a creative genius, all teachers should at least understand the nature and the special needs of the creative child. They especially need to learn to teach creatively many of the things they now teach by authority.''

Teachers themselves need freedom to be creative, to teach differently, to experiment with new approaches even at the risk of the inevitable occasional failure. It must also be recognized that, just as creative children are not easy to work with, neither are creative teachers. Many characteristics common to creative teachers may be highly upsetting to their colleagues and to the administration. They are likely to tackle tasks which are too difficult—with resulting overwork, irritation, and at times, failure. Many display the immaturity and nonconformity characteristic of the creative child; they can be a pain in the neck to their staffmates and a nuisance to the principal who does not know quite what crisis they are likely to generate next. To be creative is to be unpredictable and this always makes those in charge uneasy to the point that, for the sake of stability and consistency of operation, many principals prefer more conventional teachers. On the other hand, under imaginative administration, creative teachers can display the same effectiveness which characterizes the creative child. If the administrator's personal security allows him to tolerate a few mistakes, most creative teachers are worth the trouble, especially to the administrator who values innovations and experimentation over routine.

HIGHLIGHTS OF THE CHAPTER

Although educators have recognized the importance of problem solving, meaningfulness, concept formation and creativity in promoting the objectives of democratic society, the emphasis in the classroom is still too often on the memorization of half-digested facts. Teachers must be conversant with these higher mental processes if they are to provide youngsters with a meaningful education.

[a]

Problem solving is best understood in terms of Dewey's steps of scientific thinking. Actually, except for a greater emphasis on insight (or hindsight) and understanding, problem solving is a form of learning subject to the same laws as other types of learning.

[b]

Problem solving in the classroom is best fostered by orienting classroom experiences toward the development of: [1] an adequate background of experience, [2] effective problem-solving skills, and [3] interest in the pursuit of truth.

[c]

Of particular importance is the recent shift in pedagogical practice from drill to a greater emphasis on meaningfulness in promoting effective learning as well as greater retention and transfer.

[d]

Civilized man relies heavily upon symbols to help him manipulate and convey ideas. Unfortunately, symbols can mean only what they represent in one's experience; when the child is lacking in the required experience, boners, verbalism, and misunderstandings inevitably occur. There is need for both concrete experiences and generalizations to integrate isolated experiences into cognitive structure.

[e]

Much of the child's difficulty in getting clear meaning stems from the relative complexity of the concepts he must develop; the inadequacies in the way they are presented, and the large number of such concepts he must form. Clear-cut concepts are not made on first contact but rather evolve on a spiral of ever-greater meaningfulness.

[f]

Creativity is at last receiving some degree of recognition. Yet largely because of our orientation toward the conventionally bright as the epitome of academic excellence, the creative child in the classroom is still neglected and unappreciated. It is time we broadened our concept of "intelligence" beyond the confines of the traditional (convergent) IQ.

[g]

Everyone is capable of creativity. It is not a special gift restricted to the few, nor is it the property of the bright; creativity has been found to be relatively independent of the traditional IQ.

[h]

Among the characteristics of the creative person are flexibility, adaptability, spontaneity, originality, and tolerance of ambiguity. Many of these traits make him a difficult person to get along with.

[i]

Psychological safety and psychological freedom are essential to the encouragement of creativity. Probably the greatest deterrents to creativity are conformity to adult standards and insistence on perfection geared to the traditional "right" answer.

[j]

The encouragement of creativity among teachers is as crucial to our welfare as its promotion among children.

SOURCES OF RELATED MATERIAL

Barron, Frank, *Creativity and Psychological Health*. Princeton, N.J.: D. Van Nostrand Company, Inc., 1963.
Bennett, G. K., et al., "What is creativity?" *Trans. N.Y. Acad. Sci.*, 26: 779–797, 1964.

Berlyne, D. E., *Structure and Direction in Thinking*. New York: John Wiley & Sons, Inc., 1965.

Bingham, A. I., *Improving Children's Facility in Problem Solving*. New York: Teachers College, Columbia University, 1958.

Bruner, J., "Learning and thinking," *Harv. educ. Rev.*, 29: 185–192, 1959.

Burton, William H., et al., *Education for Effective Thinking*. New York: Appleton-Century-Crofts, 1960.

Dressel, P. L., "Critical thinking—The goal of education," *NEA J.*, 44: 418–426, 1955.

Duncker, Karl P., "Recent research on human problem solving," *Psychol. Bull.*, 56: 397–429, 1959.

Flesch, R., *The Art of Plain Talk*. New York: Harper & Row, Publishers, 1946.

Getzels, J. W., and P. W. Jackson, "The meaning of 'giftedness,' " *Educ.*, 82: 460–467, 1962.

Golan, S. E., "Psychological study of creativity," *Psychol. Bull.*, 60: 548–565, 1963.

Rogers, Carl R., "Toward a theory of creativity," *ETC: Rev. gen. Sem.*, 11: 249–260, 1954.

Russell, David H., *Children's Thinking*. Boston: Ginn & Company, 1956.

Smith, B. O., "Critical thinking," in American Association of Colleges for Teacher Education, *Recent Research and Development and Their Implications for Teacher Education*. 13th Yearbook. Washington, D.C.: The Association, 1960. Pp. 84–96.

Stein, M. I., and S. J. Heinze, *Creativity and the Individual*. New York: The Free Press of Glencoe, 1960.

Taylor, Calvin W., and F. Barron, *Scientific Creativity: Its Recognition and Development*. New York: John Wiley & Sons, Inc., 1963.

Torrance, E. Paul, *Education and the Creative Potential*. Minneapolis, Minn.: University of Minnesota Press, 1963.

———, *Rewarding Creative Behavior*. Englewood Cliffs, N.J.: Prentice-Hall, Inc., 1965.

Tyler, Ralph W., "The knowledge explosion: Implications for secondary education," *Educ. Forum*, 29: 45–53, 1965.

Vernon, P. E., "Creativity and intelligence," *Educ. Res.*, 6: 163–196, 1964.

Wallach, M. A., "Research on children's thinking," in H. W. Stevenson (ed.), *Child Psychology*. 62nd Yearbook, National Society for the Study of Education, Pt. I. Chicago: University of Chicago Press, 1963. Pp. 236–276.

Witty, Paul A., "Recent publications concerning the gifted and the creative student," *Phi Delta Kappan*, 46: 221–224, 1965.

———, and R. A. Sizemore, "Studies in listening," *Elem. Engl.*, 35: 538–552, 1958; 36: 59–70, 130–140, 297–301, 1959.

QUESTIONS AND PROJECTS

1

Evaluate: The best, if not the only way, to promote fruitful thinking in children is to promote knowledge and a deep respect for truth. If this doesn't do it, nothing will.

2

Clear thinking calls for the clarification of terms; should we first clarify the meaning of the term *thinking*? Relate *thinking* to [a] problem solving; [b] convergent and divergent thinking; [c] logic; [d] reasoning; and [e] imagination.

3

Devise three multiple-choice questions designed to measure reasoning in connection with some topic in educational psychology.

4

Appraise the scientific sophistication of your fellow-students relative to a sociological issue. Should a course in logic be required for a college degree? (Note: Evaluate the clarity of your own thinking in answering these questions.)

5

What constitutes having "proven" something? Distinguish between logical (e.g., mathematical), legal, and empirical proof.

CHAPTER 16

Measuring Academic Achievement

Any activity which takes the time of students
and teachers can be justified only if it contributes to the attainment of educational goals.
Ebel, 1963, p. 28

The measurement of academic achievement and the assignment of marks
on the basis of performance are viewed by many teachers with mixed feelings ranging from an apologetic, "I don't believe in tests," to a cocksure
conviction that tests are practically infallible. Since measuring academic
achievement is an integral part of the overall teaching-learning process, it
is necessary for teachers to develop in this area the same degree of competence they display in other aspects of teaching. Specifically, this implies
greater competence in defining the goals of education and of particular
courses in terms of student needs and in appraising student progress toward
these goals. Thus, an academic testing program should involve both the
measurement of academic progress and its evaluation in relation to educational goals.

ASPECTS OF A PUPIL-APPRAISAL PROGRAM

Since the school is responsible for the child's all-round growth, its pupil-appraisal program cannot be restricted to the mere testing of academic skills. To be of maximum benefit, the program must concern itself with the appraisal of:

[a] Intelligence: The measurement of intelligence has been discussed in Chapter 9; it might be added that the child's IQ cannot be interpreted apart from the other aspects of his total personality.

[b] Special aptitude: Aptitudes are of particular importance in vocational guidance; they also have a direct bearing on the particular strengths and weaknesses the student displays in the various subjects, particularly at the high school and college level.[1]

[c] Interest: Vocational interests are also of fundamental importance in vocational guidance. Nonvocational interests (e.g., hobbies, cultural and recreational interests) are also important inasmuch as they provide a point of contact through which the teacher can tap the student's motivation.

[d] Personal and social adjustment: The promotion of pupil adjustment is one of the school's major objectives. Adjustment also has a direct bearing on classroom achievement and classroom behavior.

[e] Attitudes, appreciations, values, and ideals: The very essence of pupil development, whether considered from an academic, a character-development, or an adjustment point of view is to be found in the system of appreciations, attitudes, and values which he has developed. Inadequacy here may well mean that all other aspects of the child's education will be to his detriment and that of society. Unfortunately, this is an area that is extremely difficult to appraise.

[f] Academic achievement: Even though the school has accepted responsibility for the child's total growth, when it comes to measurement of this growth, the teacher inevitably finds himself more directly involved in the measurement of the academic than of any other aspect of this development.

Although all aspects of growth are of fundamental concern to teachers, the appraisal of their various components need not necessarily entail a formal program of testing and evaluation. The elementary school teacher who has the same children for some six hours a day for a whole year can learn quite a lot about their particular strengths, weaknesses, and other characteristics through simple observation, perhaps together with such informal techniques as interviews and offhand conversations. In the same way, he should be able to learn something about their personal and

[1] See Wesman (1956) for the distinction between aptitude, intelligence, and achievement.

social adjustment without having to resort to formal instruments of measurement. In the departmentalized high school, on the other hand, where perhaps no teacher really gets to know a given student, there is a correspondingly greater need to rely on tests, inventories, sociometric techniques, and other formal and semiformal instruments. These aspects of pupil growth are too involved to be covered adequately in a course in educational psychology; the student should refer to any one of the many excellent texts in pupil appraisal available in any college library. It should also be realized that a pupil-appraisal program is a time-consuming proposition; it is generally worth the effort, but a half-job rarely pays off and can do a great deal of harm.

MEASUREMENT IN THE CLASSROOM

Teachers have always measured the extent to which pupils have mastered the content of their teaching. It was not until the turn of the century, however, that testing the effectiveness of the classroom in promoting learning came to resemble the science it really is. Yet, despite the rapid progress of the past half-century, much remains to be done particularly in the interpretation of test results and their utilization in promoting the child's all-round growth. The following are among the recent trends in this area: [a] a greater tendency to relate academic achievement to other phases of development; [b] a greater emphasis on growth and continuity rather than simply status with reference to a norm group; [c] a greater orientation toward the more complex types of learning and of the higher mental processes; and [d] a greater appreciation of testing as an aspect of the problem of promoting and guiding child growth. Implied in these developments is a need for a multiple approach to pupil appraisal, for greater validity and greater year-to-year comparability in the instruments, and for a recording system which synthesizes this information so that it can be seen in perspective by teachers and counselors.

Functions of an Academic-Testing Program

Every enterprise, whether in business, industry, or education must make a periodic appraisal of the success of its efforts and the adequacy of its present status in relation to its future goals. It is perhaps because schools have not had to demonstrate success or account for failure that their efforts at evaluation have until recently been so ineffective. We need to become more aware of the function of the school's testing program in providing basic information as to the extent to which educational goals are being realized.

Benefits to the Student   The primary function of academic tests from the standpoint of the student is to appraise his mastery of the various aspects of the curriculum as an indication of his progress in attaining current goals and as the basis for reorienting his efforts toward the attainment of progressively more advanced goals. It serves a vital informational purpose in keeping the student on the beam, enabling him to set realistic immediate and long-range objectives. Viewed in this light, tests are essential to the work of the classroom, for, only insofar as the child is given the basis for evaluating his performance in relation to his objectives, can he assume responsibility for his own learning, and only then can the teacher provide effective guidance.

Tests promote learning; not only do they serve as motivational devices by providing short-term goals, but they are in themselves effective learning experiences. The child learns while preparing for the test, he learns while taking the test, and he learns while reviewing after the test has been taken. Tests also constitute a highly motivated way of individualizing instruction. They should be given frequently and kept short so that they can be graded and reviewed in the same period to provide immediate reinforcement.

BENEFITS TO THE TEACHER   Academic tests, along with other instruments such as intelligence tests, serve their main function by helping the classroom teacher: [a] determine the child's educational needs; [b] set realistic goals and reorient classroom experiences to the level of his present status so that these experiences will be conducive to his maximum growth; and [c] evaluate his progress toward these goals. They serve as a partial basis for determining optimal grade placement, predicting college and vocational success, and providing guidance and diagnostic and remedial work for children who are experiencing difficulty. Tests also enable the teacher to appraise the effectiveness of his teaching and can be as instrumental in promoting teacher growth as in promoting pupil growth.

BENEFITS TO THE ADMINISTRATOR   For the administrator, tests serve many —perhaps secondary but nonetheless essential—purposes. First, they are useful in orienting the curriculum and in improving instruction by providing a criterion on the basis of which the effectiveness of both curriculum and instruction can be appraised. Tests supply evidence of the status and the progress of pupils, individually and collectively; they help in maintaining standards, and serve as the basis for reports to parents, school officials, and the community.

ROLE OF TESTING IN THE LEARNING PROCESS

Academic testing is not a matter of the occasional day-of-reckoning situation superimposed upon, but relatively apart from, the teaching-learning process. On the contrary, it is a fundamental aspect of this process, and its full value is realized only when it is integrated with the total process of education. Rather than an end in itself or a means leading only to the report card, testing should lead to the setting of more appropriate goals and the planning of more effective attempts to reach these goals. Thus, testing and evaluation are not the last steps of the instructional program, but rather, since planning, doing, and evaluating represent a continuous process, one of the steps of a spiral by means of which the child's growth is furthered. What is needed for effective learning is continuous, rather than periodic, appraisal.

Pupils should be directly involved in planning and evaluating their educational experiences and in setting new goals in the light of that evaluation, perhaps even to the point of collaborating in determining their grades and reporting their own progress. Not only do such procedures involve the student in his own education, but they also lead to self-knowledge and insight in setting realistic and meaningful goals.

The testing program is not without danger of abuse. If improperly stressed by administrators, tests can come to dominate the teaching process to the point where teachers become test monitors and feel compelled to ignore all aspects of pupil growth not specifically covered therein. This is often the situation when the end-of-year standardized testing program is allowed to become the sole criterion of pupil growth.[2] Similarly, if misused by teachers, tests can mean to children, not an opportunity to measure what they have learned, but simply another occasion to fail, and, certainly, little can be said in favor of the battle of the grades waged periodically in some of our schools in which, by means fair and foul, teachers and pupils attempt to outwit each other. Tests are generally harmful to the student when: [a] they become objectives in their own rights causing him to become so engrossed in getting a grade that learning becomes an insignificant aspect of getting an education; [b] they are given for the purpose of separating the sheep from the goats, of labeling children as adequate or inadequate; [c] the results are interpreted as final and infallible indications of all we need to know about the child; [d] when they have harmful effects with respect to other aspects of his growth we are trying to promote; or [e] they become the only means of communications between the school and the home regarding pupil progress. On the other hand, the fact that the testing done in some of our schools can be criticized on any one of these counts does not imply that tests are bad *per se*. Working for a grade is not incompatible with getting an education, and it is just not true that, whenever grades are given, examinations have to be proctored and students seek the easiest instructor. The testing program does not necessarily lead to distortion of the various objectives of the

---

[2] As Brownell (1947) points out, when teachers are rated on the basis of the marks their students make on examinations, the prudent teacher will see that, by hook or by crook, his pupils pass the examinations regardless of how many other considerations have to be neglected.

school, nor does it mean that every student has to be evaluated according to the same standards. When properly used, measurement and evaluation cannot have a detrimental effect upon the child for they become an integral part of the process by which his growth can be promoted most effectively. The teacher needs to understand, however, specifically what role tests are to play in the overall teaching-learning process; he also needs to be fully aware of their strengths, their limitations, their use and their abuse.

CHARACTERISTICS OF A GOOD MEASURING INSTRUMENT

Whenever one undertakes to measure anything—distance, weight, achievement, etc.—he must be sure that the measuring instruments possess such characteristics as will make for dependability in the results. The characteristics, previously mentioned in connection with intelligence tests, apply with equal force to academic achievement tests, whether formal or informal, standardized or teacher-made.

VALIDITY First and foremost, a test must be valid, i.e., it must measure what it claims to measure.[3] Thus, a test in American history designed for a given eighth-grade class must deal with the phase of American history taught in that particular class. It would not necessarily be valid for another class on the same phase of American history where perhaps a different emphasis had been given to the various aspects of the subject. Validity is a specific concept: a test is valid for a specific purpose under specific circumstances.[4] Even within a course in American history, there are many different aspects that can be measured: a teacher may, for instance, emphasize dates and names, or he can emphasize relationships and understanding, or relative amounts of each.

Many questions arise: "Should the teacher make deductions for misspelled words on the test? . . . for bad grammar? . . . for sloppiness and general illegibility?" "Should the grade reflect the student's attitude toward the course and toward school in general?" These questions can be answered only in terms of the course objectives, and determining these objectives is necessarily the first step in constructing a test and in evaluating it from the standpoint of validity. In keeping with the definition of learning, these

[3] What is measured is performance from which learning is inferred.
[4] Psychologists think of four kinds of validity (American Psychological Association, 1966): [a] curricular validity; [b] predictive validity; [c] construct validity; and [d] concurrent validity. Teachers are generally more concerned with the first two. Curricular validity, sometimes known as content or face validity, is a matter of relating the content of the test to the material of the course. Predictive validity refers to the ability of the test to forecast subsequent attainment of a given criterion: the College Boards have predictive validity to the extent that performance on the tests is related to subsequent success in college.

objectives should be stated in terms of specific changes in student behavior which the course is designed to promote: specifically what behavior patterns is the student to display to give evidence of progress toward these objectives? Although we have to think of the whole child, it is not enough to refer to his all-round growth when it comes to measurement; the expected changes must be stated in specific and measurable terms.

These objectives can generally be broken down into three main areas: functional information, skills, and attitudes, and these can in turn be broken down into more basic components. Thus, under functional information may be listed facts, dates, names, technical terms, definitions, principles, and generalizations. Likewise, skills can be broken down into ability to look up a reference and ability to present a report in clear concise English, etc., while attitudes might be subdivided into appreciation of the contribution of political and scientific leaders, pride in one's social heritage, loyalty to certain ideals, etc. A formulation of the objectives of a course in educational psychology was presented in Chapter 1. It will be noted that each objective is stated in terms of certain behavior changes expected to result from the course.

Not all objectives can be measured and the table of objectives is generally reduced to a table of specifications which contains only those objectives to be covered, together with the emphasis to be placed on each in the test. Thus, objectives serve as instructional guides while specifications are guides to evaluation—and certain objectives, even though pertinent to instruction, would not be listed in the table of specifications.[5] Whatever objectives are carried into the table of specifications should be so stated that the teacher can determine whether or not the child has attained the objective: "Does he or does he not know a certain fact?" "Can he or can he not deal with the technical vocabulary of the course?" This must be done very carefully for, in a very real sense, the test determines the amount and the kind of learning the child does, and objectives that are not stressed on the test tend to be overlooked by the student—and by the teacher too. As pointed out by Kirkendall (1939, p. 644): "The avidity with which pupils work for marks is equalled only by the assiduity with which teachers teach for marks." Unless all aspects of pupil growth are stressed, those which are measured will be emphasized at the expense of those which are not and testing will distort educational goals.

If a test is to be valid, it must cover not just one area of the table of specifications but all of them in proportion to the emphasis which has been placed on each area. Thus, a test that measures only facts is not valid unless the course is designed to cover only facts. In the same way, whether or not to deduct for misspelled words depends on whether this is one of the course objectives. One might well expect the objectives of a

---

[5] There is generally no point in listing high-sounding objectives that are never measured and probably never attained.

course in American history to include the ability to spell the names of the people who made American history, and, if they do, the teacher should expect students to demonstrate their ability to spell such names. On the other hand, a history instructor might not deduct for the misspelling of common words if he felt spelling of ordinary words is only vaguely and remotely one of the objectives of his course. The question of what to test is therefore answered in terms of what learnings the course is intended to promote.

Unless all teachers work as a team in emphasizing correct English in every class, students may get the idea that English is something which is used in the English period but which has no relation to any other course, let alone to out-of-school situations.[6] From the standpoint of validity, however, if a student gets an A with regard to the content of American history but that grade is reduced to a C because of inadequacies in English, penmanship, or deportment, the grade he gets is not a valid indication of his knowledge of American history: it does not reflect what it purports to reflect, namely, achievement in American history. Inasmuch as another student may also get a C out of limited knowledge of American history presented in superb English, the two grades do not mean the same thing and the students would have no basis for improving their performance.

Most academic achievement tests overemphasize facts simply because they are easy to measure. Correspondingly, they underemphasize the more complicated, but usually more significant, outcomes of education such as ability to organize and integrate raw material into meaningful structure and to use it in situations calling for problem solving, understanding of relationships, interpretation of data, application of principles, drawing of inferences, testing of hypotheses, and the other higher mental functions. These are measured in various degrees by some of the better commercial tests. Teachers should become acquainted with such tests as the Watson-Glaser Critical Thinking Appraisal (Watson and Glaser, 1964) as an example of what can be done to measure the important goals of education (see Figure 16-1).[7]

In order for a test to provide a valid score, we must assume that reading poses no special problem in tests where reading is not what is being measured, that the child is properly motivated, and that he is relatively free from emotional blocking that might impair his performance. Inadequacies in vocabulary, for example, may be of considerable importance in

<hr>

[6] Teachers must work as a team toward maximum pupil growth, rather than toward the attainment of individual glory. In high school, where responsibility for the student is divided, there is need for coordination (perhaps through the homeroom) of the forces designed to promote his overall growth.

[7] Hurst et al. (1961) report an attempt to measure the significant aspects of educational psychology. The test describes certain school situations and asks the student to make decisions and judgments, with the criterion being the extent of his agreement with the experts. (See Burton et al., 1960, for other examples.)

EXAMPLE	TEST 3	
Some holidays are rainy. All rainy days are boring. Therefore —	Conclusion	

EXAMPLE

Some holidays are rainy. All rainy days are boring. Therefore —

1. No clear days are boring. (The conclusion does not follow. You cannot tell from the statements whether or not clear days are boring. Some may be.)........................

2. Some holidays are boring. (The conclusion necessarily follows from the statements, since, according to them, the rainy holidays must be boring.)..

3. Some holidays are not boring. (The conclusion does not follow even though you may know that some holidays are very pleasant.).........

TEST 3

Conclusion

	Follows	Does not follow
1	|¦	**▮**
2	**▮**	||
3	¦|	**▮**

FIGURE 16-1 An example from the Watson-Glaser Critical Thinking Appraisal.

an essay examination where the misreading of a question or two can cause the student to get a score much lower than he deserves.

The modern emphasis on all-round growth has complicated the task of evaluation by increasing its scope to include phases that are relatively difficult to define in terms of measurable objectives, let alone measure and relate to the child, his capacity, his maturity, and other aspects of his background. In fact, evaluation should also cover his out-of-school behavior for, when education is defined in terms of experiences which are meaningful from the standpoint of the child's purposes, the distinction between in-school and out-of-school becomes essentially irrelevant.

RELIABILITY

An achievement test must also be reliable, i.e., it must measure consistently whatever it measures. This consistency can be determined by comparing the performance of students on successive administrations of the test, for example.[8] Reliability is generally measured in terms of the coefficient of correlation. This correlation can be converted into the *standard error of measurement*, which refers to the magnitude of the fluctuations in the individual's score which might be expected upon retest—the lower the reliability, the greater the fluctuations that are likely to occur. It must be noted that a reliable test is not necessarily a valid test since it may measure consistently something other than what it purports to measure. On the other hand, a test that is totally unreliable cannot be valid, but if a test is to be valid it must be reliable.

[8] Reliability is generally measured in one of the following ways: [a] equivalent forms; [b] test-retest; and [c] chance-halves. The student is referred to the library for appropriate sources on these techniques.

Students occasionally get a score on a test which is not typical of their performance. This is particularly true in high school and college courses where the content is so extensive that, unless a number of tests are given, the final grade will be based on a relatively small sampling of the course, especially with essay examinations. It is also obvious that, as a rule, tests are not sufficiently reliable for a grade to be decided on the basis of a difference of two or three points; student performance should be scattered over a wide range if grades are to be assigned with a certain degree of fairness.

USABILITY

Usability combines such features as costs, ease of administration, ease of scoring, and attractiveness. These are, of course, secondary in importance, but, if two tests are of essentially comparable validity and reliability, factors such as cost and labor should be considered. If only a few students are to be tested, for example, the relative ease of constructing an essay examination might outweigh the labor of scoring, whereas, if large numbers are involved, a teacher might save time and effort by devising an objective test.[9] It might also be noted in passing that unless he goes about it in a systematic way, the teacher will find the construction of a good teacher-made test expensive in teacher time and energy.

KINDS OF TESTS

Academic tests can be classified according to any number of dimensions depending on the purpose they are to serve and the basis of classification. Some of the more common distinctions include:

TEACHER-MADE AND STANDARDIZED TESTS

A teacher-made or informal test is one constructed by the teacher, generally with the particular objectives of his course in mind; logically, therefore, it should be reasonably valid. Its validity is frequently vitiated, however, by violations of the principles of testing ranging from failure to relate the items to clearly defined objectives to simple noncompliance with the basic rules of item construction. Its greatest weakness lies in the lack of a standard of comparison on the basis of which class performance can be evaluated.

Standardized tests, in contrast, are generally constructed by experts, standardized on a representative sample of the population for which the test is intended, and made available commercially. Their greatest advantage over the informal test is that they provide an outside standard or

---

[9] Such features as excessive length, unattractiveness in format, difficulty in administration and scoring are often reflected in lowered validity and reliability.

norm[10] for evaluating pupil performance. Their greatest weakness is that they are often oriented toward a set of objectives different from those emphasized in a given class. They operate on the assumption that there are broad general objectives common to all courses of a given title; that despite variations that may occur from instructor to instructor, there are common objectives that apply to all high school courses in American history, for example.[11] To the extent that this assumption is correct—and it is likely to be reasonably correct in such fields as reading where relative uniformity of objectives can be expected—a standardized test tends to be valid for a number of classroom situations. If local objectives differ from those toward which the test is oriented, however, the class will be at a disadvantage by comparison with the standardization group and the test norms will not be valid for that class. Standardized tests are available for most elementary and high school areas and it is up to the individual teacher to decide whether a given test has sufficient validity for his particular purpose and circumstances to warrant its use.

OBJECTIVE AND SUBJECTIVE TESTS

Tests can be either objective or subjective, depending on the objectivity or subjectivity of the scoring. In objective test items such as multiple-choice, true-false, and matching, the answers are either right or wrong. The completion and simple recall items also call for a relatively high degree of objectivity in scoring. Grading essay examinations, on the other hand, calls for the grader to have a sufficient grasp of the subject to make a subjective appraisal of the adequacy of the answers given.

The relative merits of objective and essay tests have been debated on numerous occasions. Most teachers prefer the objective test, especially once accustomed to it, but this view is not universal. Students also are divided as to preference. Obviously much depends on the course content, the way the questions are asked in relation to the way the course is taught, the instructor and his ability to devise good questions, and the student's experience with the two types of tests. Actually, neither is superior to the other. Each has its relative advantages; the problem is to locate the

---

[10] Norms are neither standards of excellence nor minimal standards; they are simply standards of comparison.

[11] Some educators are concerned that national standardized tests may come to dominate American education to the point of dictating to the local school what is important and what is unimportant, regardless of individual peculiarities in the local situation. They fear that when student performance on a national scale becomes the yardstick of the school's effectiveness, teaching and all other school activities become good or bad depending on whether they promote successful performance on this scale. As long as the tests keep ahead of practice, they may serve a purpose in upgrading American education; they can just as easily discourage experimentation on the part of the more advanced schools who might fear that revising their curriculum will result in lowered student performance on the narrow dimensions set by the national scale.

situations for which each is the more appropriate. Each type of item has its purpose and there are certain aspects of the content of almost any course that lend themselves to the true-false type of test, others to the multiple-choice, and certain contents and certain objectives call for the essay test. It is not a question of which is superior but rather where to use each most advantageously. It follows that measuring devices almost of necessity have to be varied in order to deal adequately with the different objectives, the different subject-matter contents, and the different psychological processes to be measured. It is probably safe to say, for example, that teachers who condemn objective tests as completely inappropriate for their purposes have not explored too closely their possibilities.

The major advantages of the objective test are wide sampling, the correspondingly greater likelihood of covering more of the course objectives, and as a result, a tendency toward greater validity and reliability in most situations. Relatively greater reliability also results from objectivity in scoring. Another advantage, ease of scoring, is of particular importance in large classes where the extra work necessary to construct an objective test is more than compensated for by the saving in scoring time and effort. This is especially so when the computer[12] or an IBM scoring machine is available but even a stencil used over separate answer sheets can save the teacher many tedious hours of scoring. On the other hand, the essay-type test also has its advantages; in fact, it measures certain objectives that are difficult to measure effectively in any other way, e.g., ability to organize and express ideas. Preparing for an essay examination tends to bring into play a higher level of learning, e.g., getting an overview of the material, organizing the data into meaningful structure, clarifying issues, etc., than its objective counterpart (Meyer, 1936); it may even promote more as well as better learning, inasmuch as the objective test, requiring recognition rather than recall, may give the learner a false sense of knowledge. The essay test is also more effective in revealing the process used by the student to arrive at the answer and is, therefore, useful for diagnostic purposes. On the other hand, it must be remembered that none of the various items has a monopoly on the quality and quantity of the mental processes it activates. Contrary to criticisms, for example, objective examinations can be made to measure precise forms of reasoning, interpretation of data, application of principles, etc.; probably the only thing objective examinations cannot do well is to measure the ability to write essays.

As implied in the previous discussion, the weakness of the essay test stems largely from limited sampling and subjectivity and labor in scoring. Because it requires the writing of many words in order to bring out an

---

[12] The computer also permits item analysis and, hence, progressive improvement of the test.

idea, the essay is very wasteful of the testing period (courses calling for ability to organize and express ideas excepted) so that only a small segment of the course content can be covered in a one- or two-hour test. Hence, it has limited reliability and in some cases, limited validity—especially in that penmanship, verbal fluency, ability to make shrewd guesses as to what will be included in the test, ability to bluff, and ability to avoid misinterpreting questions occasionally play an important part in getting a good score. For the last half-century, educators have been concerned over the fact that not only is an instructor unable to agree with other graders on the quality of a given essay, but he is not even likely to agree with himself in rescoring the same paper. In one study (Starch and Elliott, 1913), the grades given a geometry paper by different raters ranged from 28 percent to 92 percent. A similar inconsistency in grading is noted in the results of a study by Arny (1953), shown in Figure 16-2, in which

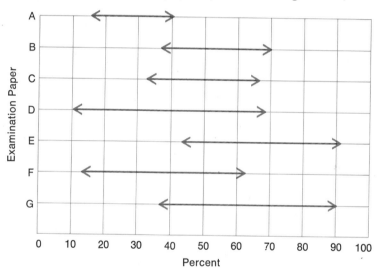

FIGURE 16-2   Range of scores assigned by twelve teachers to seven essay examination papers. (From *Evaluation in Home Economics*, by C. B. Arny. Copyright © 1953, Appleton-Century-Crofts, Inc. By permission of Appleton-Century-Crofts, Inc.)

twelve raters, grading seven papers in home economics, disagreed by a minimum of 18 percentage points on one paper to a maximum of 61 points on another. Similar inconsistency in grading is noted in the results of a more recent study in which 53 judges graded 300 essays in college English on a scale from 1 to 9; one third of the essays received grades ranging the full scale from 1 to 9; 60 percent received seven or eight of the nine possible grades; and no essay received fewer than five different grades (Educational Testing Service, 1961). Crow and Crow (1956, p. 452) report the case in which a group of experts had prepared a model to act as a guide in scoring—only to have a colleague who did not know that the model had been included actually fail the model.

The essay examination can be frustrating to both rater and student. It often takes great concentration on the part of the teacher to decipher meaning out of the student's clumsy expression, and it takes infinite wisdom and patience to decide whether he is just awkward or whether he is trying to cover his lack of knowledge. Students often do not know what the instructor is after and how deeply they are to go into the question. Thus, the essay test has a number of limitations, some of which are inherent in this type of test. It may also be that the strengths of the essay have been overstated; many of the fine examples of reasoning the essay is said to promote represent nothing more than parroting from memory the reasoning which has been covered in class. Other weaknesses stem from misuse; many can be reduced by devising clear-cut questions and by working out a system for scoring papers more objectively.[13] Stalnaker and Stalnaker (1934) report reliabilities in the .80 and .90 when essay examinations are graded by experienced raters operating according to precise scoring rules.

POWER AND SPEED TESTS

A power test consists of items of increasing difficulty which is usually administered with liberal time limits so that a student's score is determined by the difficulty of the items he can answer. The items of a speed test, on the other hand, are of relatively equal difficulty throughout but the time limits are such that the more a student has to ponder over the answers, the fewer he will cover during the time allowed. There is a definite trend away from speed tests and current standardized instruments incorporate some increase in item difficulty along with liberal time limits. Research evidence (Cook, 1932), for example, suggests that maximum validity is obtained when time limits are set so as to allow approximately 80 percent of the class to finish.

SURVEY AND DIAGNOSTIC TESTS

A survey test is one that gives in a single score an all-round measure of achievement in a given area, e.g., the child's grade level in reading. A

---

[13] Teachers sometimes ask questions of the variety of "Discuss the implications of the Treaty of Versailles." (Why not: "Describe the universe and give two examples"?) On the other hand, making questions too narrow and specific defeats the very purpose for which essay questions should be used in preference to objective items. "List three characteristics of a good measuring instrument" is not an effective essay item, so that, in a sense, the essay is weakest in the very area for which it is supposed to exist.

diagnostic test provides subscores and separate norms for each of the various subskills such as speed of reading, vocabulary, and comprehension so that strengths and weaknesses can be determined. It must be remembered, of course, that frequently these subscores are based on relatively short subtests and, as a result, may incorporate a substantial element of error and should, therefore, be interpreted cautiously.

Prognostic Tests

A prognostic test is one designed to predict probable achievement in a given area. Thus, a Latin or an algebra prognostic test indicates likely achievement in those fields. Actually, all tests are in a sense prognostic. An intelligence test, for example, is prognostic of success in those fields in which performance is related to IQ.

CONSTRUCTION OF TESTS

Space limitations do not permit adequate treatment of the techniques of test construction; the discussion is, therefore, simply for purposes of orientation and the student is referred to the many books on educational tests and measurements for a more thorough coverage.[14] The following suggestions might be given as examples:

[a] Use a variety of measuring devices; different objectives call for different testing methods.

[b] Sample widely and use a variety of test items.

[c] Keep the difficulty level of the items such that the average student will obtain a raw score approximately 50 percent of maximum.

[d] Make essay questions sufficiently restricted that the student can organize his ideas on the subject.

[e] Make the questions clear; avoid trick or controversial questions and avoid giving clues to the answers.

[f] Do not give optional questions; it is difficult enough to compare performance on the same task without complicating the problem by giving choices.

Probably the most helpful advice that might be given the young teacher on this subject is for him to organize a file of evaluative material. Keeping such a file of test questions on 3 × 5 or IBM cards will make good testing possible without an undue expenditure of time and effort. This does not mean using the same test over and over any more than accumulating instructional material implies using the same notes year after year. The best way to make out the individual file card is to

---

[14] Stated bluntly, if all the reader knows about testing is what is covered in this chapter, he does not know enough to be effective in this important area of teaching.

place the test question on the front of the card. The following is an example of a multiple choice question:

The factor most clearly involved in the stability of the self-concept is

[a] environmental consistency
[b] functional autonomy (habits)
[c] human aversion to change
[d] innate behavioral predispositions
[e] selectivity of perception

The reverse side of the card should show the correct answer (in this case, [e]), the source of the concept (*Psychology for Effective Teaching*, Chapter 4), the dates on which the question was used, and how many students out of the top and bottom quarters of the class answered it correctly; the last of these items can be used as the basis for an overall difficulty index and discrimination index, which should give the teacher a good idea of the level of difficulty of the question and how well it discriminates between the best and least capable students in the class. The evaluative portion of the reverse side of the card might look like this:

Date	Top	Bottom	Difficulty	Discrimination
1/66	12/15	: 7/15	19/30	12/7
6/66	5/6	: 3/6	8/12	5/3

These data show that, when used in January 1966, the item was answered correctly by 12 students in the top quarter and by 7 students in the bottom quarter of the class (actually two classes combined), for an overall difficulty index of 19 out of 30 students in the top and bottom quarters combined and a discrimination index of 12 to 7. The item was used again in June 1966 with results as shown above. These cards can be coded to allow sorting according to a system decided upon by the teacher, such as by chapter or by objective or thought process involved.

  Good testing calls for a multiple approach. Each type of test has its particular merits and it is up to the teacher to make effective use of the many testing procedures at his disposal. As situations vary, testing procedures should also vary. In general, the most meaningful way of evaluating learning is to ask the student to apply what he has learned to a somewhat different situation, preferably one in real life, but this is not always easy or even possible. Discussion, student reports, and question-and-answer procedures are often effective means of appraising student progress; such techniques incorporate immediate reinforcement, correction of errors, and clarification of issues under conditions of high motivation. However, they are ineffective and impractical in a large class, for example. In other words, the test must be tailor-made to the particular situation for which it is intended.

INTERPRETATION OF THE RESULTS OF TESTING

MEASUREMENT AND EVALUATION

A testing program involves two interrelated processes: measurement and evaluation. So far we have considered the first; namely, the construction of a good test from which to derive a valid and reliable score. The more important and, in many ways, the more difficult question of interpreting this score now lies ahead. A score has no meaning in itself; it takes on meaning only as it is interpreted in the light of such other factors as the goals of education, the objectives of the particular course, the caliber of the student, and the nature of the test upon which it is based. Thus, 60 items right out of 100 may represent adequate or inadequate performance depending on the difficulty of the test and the scoring, for example.

Implied in the distinction between measurement and evaluation is the fact that performance is not to be interpreted in relation to an absolute standard of perfection but rather in terms of a realistic standard of what level of performance it is reasonable to expect. This is, of course, a matter of subjective judgment: as we evaluate a student's performance, we may feel that it leaves much to be desired but that it is satisfactory considering the particular circumstances involved. In a given situation, we may judge as unsatisfactory a performance actually superior by objective measurement to one we judged satisfactory in another instance.

THE NUMBER SYSTEM

To interpret the results of testing, we need to be familiar with the nature of the number system underlying measurement. Numerical series can be either ordinal (e.g., first, second, third), or cardinal (e.g., 1, 2, 3,). Cardinal series, in turn, can be either absolute or displaced depending on the nature of the zero point. An absolute cardinal series is one which starts with a true zero; a displaced cardinal series starts from an arbitrary zero point other than the true zero. Both then proceed in equal units, e.g., feet, minutes, or degrees of temperature.

The distinction is fundamental to an understanding of educational measurements. In displaced cardinal series, e.g., the Fahrenheit temperature scale, all that can be indicated is "more than" or "less than"; we cannot say that a temperature of 20 degrees above zero is "twice as hot" as a temperature of 10 degrees. Except for speed in typing and certain skills in physical education, nearly all the measurements with which teachers come into contact are on displaced cardinal series. Thus, a score of zero on a test does not imply complete lack of knowledge of the subject but simply zero performance on the test material, the difficulty of which may be well above true zero. A child may miss every word on a spelling test and still be able to spell many words not included in the test. Since the teacher has many choices as to which words to include in a test, it is possible for a student with a given spelling ability to get 95 percent of the words on an "easy" test, only 50 percent on an "average" test, and practically zero if the teacher selected only difficult words. This situation, shown graphically in Figure 16-3, demonstrates the fallacy of the common

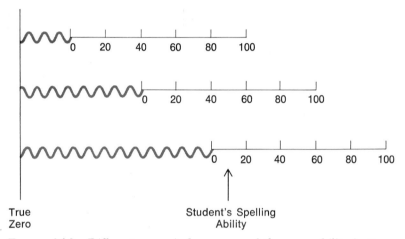

FIGURE 16-3   Different numerical measures of the same ability in three different displaced series.

percentage scale in grading student performance; percentage of maximum is completely meaningless unless we know the level of difficulty of the questions and the severity of the scoring.

RAW VERSUS DERIVED SCORES

For a student to obtain, say, a score of 60 out of a maximum of 100 on a spelling test means nothing more than that he has a spelling ability greater than zero. Since scores in spelling are based on a displaced cardinal series, the only thing that can make them meaningful is to convert them into a *derived* score that relates his performance to that of other students who have taken the test. We will now consider some of these derived scores:

PERCENTILE RANK   If a high school senior's performance puts him at the fifth percentile of high school seniors, i.e., his score is equalled or exceeded by 95 percent of the group of which he is a member, we can picture his performance as relatively poor. This is more meaningful than saying he has a raw score of 60 percent on a test of unknown difficulty—which could represent, for all one knows, the highest or the lowest score on record.

AGE OR GRADE EQUIVALENTS   When the test maker of, say, a reading test has completed his final draft, he administers it to a representative sample of children in the grades for which the test is designed. Then in scoring the papers, he can score separately the papers of children in each specific age or grade (e.g., CA = 11–0; 11–1; . . . . or Grade 5–0; 5–1; . . . .) and publish the average of each group in a table of norms. Thus, if a raw score of 42 turns out to be average for the children in the standardization sample of CA = 11–0 and for children of Grade 5–6, then any child who obtains a raw score of 42 on this test can be said to have a *reading age* of 11–0 and a *reading grade equivalent* of 5–6. Educational age and grade equivalents can be obtained in the same way for standardized tests in arithmetic, spelling, etc.

EDUCATIONAL AND ACHIEVEMENT QUOTIENTS   We can get further meaning from the child's educational age by relating it to his chronological age and his mental age by means of the Educational Quotient (EQ) and the Achievement Quotient (AQ) which are defined as follows:

$$EQ = \frac{EA}{CA} \times 100$$

$$AQ = \frac{EA}{MA} \times 100$$

Thus, a student of CA = 10 and MA = 12 (i.e., IQ = 120) who scored 42 on the reading test above and who would therefore have a reading age of 11–0 would have:

$$EQ = \frac{11}{10} \times 100 = 110$$

$$AQ = \frac{11}{12} \times 100 = 93$$

Since the average child of ten has both a mental age and a reading age of ten (by definition), both his EQ and his AQ would be 100. Therefore, the student above is accelerated by comparison to his age-mates but is retarded by comparison to children of his mental age. Similar comparisons can be made of the EQ and the AQ in other academic areas in which standardized tests provide an educational age.[15] These can be plotted on

[15] Current test manuals generally give only grade equivalents and percentile ranks. It is felt that academic growth is more directly tied to grade placement than to chronological age.

a profile showing his standing in each area in relation to an EQ and an AQ of 100.

In practice, gifted children are generally accelerated from the standpoint of EQ and dull children are retarded. This is understandable since academic progress is certainly related to intelligence. However, the gifted child is generally retarded in AQ while the dull child is accelerated, i.e., the bright child's educational growth does not keep pace with his mental growth, whereas the dull child is more advanced academically than bright younger children of the same mental age. Why this should be is not entirely clear; it is partly a statistical artifact.[16] On the other hand, some educators feel that the lag in the gifted child's educational growth stems in part from the neglect of the gifted in the average classroom where the pace is set by average students and the teacher's energies are often expended on behalf of the dull; some argue that the lag is unnecessarily large, especially in view of the 90 to 95 percent overlap in the contents of academic and intelligence tests (see Chapter 9). They feel that providing the gifted child with an enriched curriculum geared to his potentialities would result in some narrowing of this gap. At any rate, plotting individual profiles for both EQ and AQ (where the required educational ages are available) can help identify children whose performance is apparently out of line with general expectations. It will be found, of course, that most students are more advanced in some areas than others; this may be explained on the basis of relative strengths and weaknesses of their different aptitudes or special motivation, but it might also identify areas where remedial work is needed.

The comparison between educational and mental growth represented by the AQ can also be shown in terms of underachievement and overachievement. If we plot mental age on one axis and educational status on the other and if furthermore, we draw in the averages, we will have four quadrants as shown in Figure 16-4. In a belt comprising Quadrant 1 and 3 and a small corner of the other two quadrants (since tests are always short of complete reliability) are students who are achieving more or less in accordance with their ability. In Quadrant 4 are students whose achievement is lower than their ability should make possible and who are, therefore, called underachievers. In this group are children who need remedial help; many have struggled with unrealistic demands and unsuitable curricula until they finally lost interest. To the extent that they are no longer trying, they save the teacher from guilt feelings: "It's their own fault, they deserve to be failed. Me—I've tried everything!"

In Quadrant 2 are the overachievers who do better than their measured ability would lead us to expect. Some are "overachievers" simply by virtue

[16] The concept of regression toward the mean serves as an inbuilt mechanism to cause underachievement among the gifted and overachievement among the dull. In general, the concept of underachievement should be used cautiously.

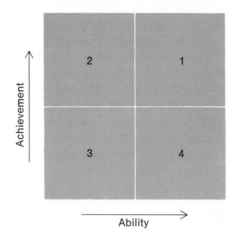

FIGURE 16-4 Comparison between educational and mental growth.

of the undermeasurement of their true ability. But that still leaves a sizable group who perhaps have effective study habits or special talents; the creative group in the Getzels and Jackson and the Torrance studies (see Chapter 15) achieved at the level of the gifted despite a 23 point handicap in IQ. Others are strongly motivated and we might be tempted to pat them on the back and say, "More power to you!" Yet some may be displaying signs of neurotic perfectionism and the question may well be raised: "Are they perhaps paying too high a price for their achievement in terms of neglected social participation and other aspects of personal growth?" Mitchell (1959) found the self-rejectant overachiever to be ambitious, highly motivated, and highly competitive; he makes desperate attempts at setting goals of academic excellence to convince himself and others that he is a worthy person after all. Mitchell also found, however, a self-acceptant overachiever group consisting of well adjusted and good, hardworking students who had been consistently successful. These perhaps were simply efficient people who used their talents and energies constructively rather than dissipating them in self-defense. At any rate, the teacher has responsibilities to both underachiever and overachiever, and, whereas differences exist from person to person, a definite possibility for helping both groups lies in reducing the anxiety level—of the overachiever so he can accept himself at a more comfortable level and of the underachiever so he can afford to try.

GRADING

RATIONALE UNDERLYING GRADING

The grading period is rough on teachers and pupils alike. Many teachers are not too sure of the purpose pinning a grade on the student's achievement is to serve in the school's function of promoting his all-round growth.

To many conscientious teachers, grading has the flavor of a postmortem—in some cases, of retaliation for what is past—whereas evaluation should be directed toward the future. Many feel that grading actually interferes with sound evaluation in that one single mark cannot provide the diagnostic basis for orienting the child's growth during the next grading period. Likewise, except for the gifted and those who have ceased to care, students also eye the grading period with considerable discomfort. All this coming after an exhausting period of preparing for, or grading, examinations leaves everyone rather cold.

The obvious questions is, "Why grade at all?" And, in this connection, it must be made clear that accepting the necessity for evaluation does not mean that evaluation has to eventuate in a grade. All that a grade can do is to provide a synthesis—perhaps a misleading synthesis—of the various aspects of the evaluation. Thus, a good grasp of computational skills, a limited understanding of problem solving, and a relative weakness in the use of formulas might be synthesized into a D. Whether this synthesis is desirable depends on the purpose involved.

Examinations frequently seem designed to satisfy the needs of the teacher rather than those of the student. Whereas examinations should have primarily an educational function, their administrative purposes often take precedence to the point that grading is essentially a judgmental proposition with the outcomes a question of pupil success or failure, promotion or retardation, classification into grade level, recommendation for college, etc., all according to adult specifications often applied on a wholesale basis. Grades are often used to determine eligibility for sports, for example, when depriving the youngster of the one thing in which he is interested simply causes him to drop out of school. Examinations and grades are often teacher-centered and oriented toward the discovery of pupil inadequacy rather than potentiality for growth. Too frequently, teachers see failing on the part of the child as the child's failure, rather than failure of the school to relate education to his needs and of the teacher to present materials in such a way as to make them educationally profitable. The overall testing program is often used as the basis for passing judgment on the child rather than on the school's program and its failure to reach its "customers." As a result, the child learns to fear and to worry about examinations rather than to use them as a means of appraising his adequacy and guiding his further growth.

When grading is considered from the standpoint of purpose, a distinction must be made between what might be called the public school and the professional school philosophy. In a professional school, e.g., the medical school, grades serve to protect society from professional incompetence. In teacher training, the college sets certain standards of attainment, and, for the protection of the children who might be harmed by having an incompetent teacher, fails any prospective teacher unable to meet these standards. Here grades are a screening device and the welfare of society takes precedence over that of the individual aspiring to professional status. In the public school, on the other hand, the primary purpose of measurement and evaluation is to determine the student's status as a prerequisite for planning his further growth. Presumably, then, a student would be failed only when his teacher is convinced that his growth can be promoted more effectively in his present grade than in the next. The teacher who gives a child a low grade on an assignment would likewise have to be reasonably sure that this is the best way of promoting his subsequent growth. To deny this would imply that the school is operating at cross-purposes.

Objections to Grading

Grading is not without danger: when misused, it can easily negate all the school is trying to accomplish through sound teaching and evaluation. Whereas when they are used wisely grades are essential to the effectiveness of the school's operations, some people feel that it is a pity that they are so thoroughly entrenched and taken so seriously.

From a psychological point of view, the following objections can be raised against most of the grading done in our schools:

[a] Grades are inadequate indicators of the child's total development and a single letter grade or even two cannot possibly cover all aspects of child growth the school is trying to promote in any one subject-matter area. Schools with but a single grade must have but a single objective; a single grade cannot reflect multiple goals. When teachers are forced to concentrate their whole evaluation of a child's performance into a single letter grade, this mark becomes such a composite that it is essentially meaningless. Since, like all other symbols, a grade is useful only to the extent that it evokes the same meaning in the child and the parent who receive it as it did in the teacher who sent it, it tends to be wasted motion, except that it can do harm. Some schools give separate grades for the academic and the citizenship aspects of school behavior but probably most teachers, consciously or unconsciously, include as part of the academic grade such things as effort, docility, and attitudes along with a number of academic considerations.

[b] Grades exert a strong influence in raising the child's motivational level. This can be desirable for some students but, for others, grades have detrimental effects ranging from psychosomatic disorders to feelings of resentment, hostility, frustration, and discouragement.[17] Children often interpret grades not as an evaluation of their work but as an evaluation of themselves, with resulting conflict in their self-image. Furthermore,

---

[17] Grades and promotion, along with recitation, homework, examinations, and marks headed the list of serious school handicaps to mental health in the 1938 Commonwealth Fund Report on Mental Health and Education.

grades lead to worry over past and future failures and thus detract from effectiveness in dealing with the present and planning for future improvement. Grades often raise the wrong kind of motivation: they tend to breed competitiveness and various antisocial attitudes and behaviors; overemphasis on grades often causes motivation to degenerate into anxiety which deters from, rather than promotes, productivity. There are more positive and less dangerous means of motivating children. Grades appeal to a few and actually repel the rest who have to build up a front of indifference in order to maintain status and avoid conflict (see Chapter 4). As we noted in Chapter 10, the threat of academic failure does not increase academic output and it would seem fair to suggest that teachers who rely on grades as their principal incentive must be pretty poor teachers indeed.

[c] Grades often become ends in themselves so that learning is cast into a secondary role of vehicle toward a grade. Grades represent a sort of academic currency to be exchanged for a diploma, a symbol of academic respectability valued for its own sake, which often detracts from the real purposes of education. Grades tend to orient education toward whatever is emphasized on the test at the expense of what would have greater functionality in the lives of students; they encourage cramming, cheating, and catering to the personal views of the teacher. Often the result is a mediocre standard on the part of students who are capable of much more, while the slow student is discouraged and antagonized by this continuous exposure to, and recording of, inevitable failure.

Burton (1962) suggests that one might look at the marking system as a necessity stemming from the inadequacy of the present curriculum or teaching methods; apparently, school practices are so inadequate that a grading system had to be invented to make them work at all. On the other hand, the grading system is perhaps largely responsible for making the curriculum unsuitable and our practices inadequate. It seems that as students progress from elementary school to college, they get progressively more grade-conscious and, in a sense, more convinced of the unimportance of education apart from grades. They often cannot afford to pursue items of interest inasmuch as it will detract from the study of what the test will cover. The only conclusion that can be reached under such circumstances is that the students are working *for* the teacher. In the meantime, education becomes a shallow proposition: the school becomes a mill for passing out information which students recite on call but which is not expected to have functionality and vitality at the behavioral level. Whereas grades do not have to have any of these adverse effects, it is essential that we define specifically what grades are to contribute to education's major goals of providing children with a positive self-concept and a sense of worth as well as a functional education.

[d] Teachers often find that giving the child a low grade destroys the pupil-teacher relationship they have been trying to cultivate. Many chil-

dren, rather than blame themselves for a low grade, project the blame onto the teacher—and parenthetically, there is enough invalidity and unreliability in the average test to make this entirely plausible, especially to a child who needs to protect his self-image.

[e] A more common criticism of grades is their undependability from the standpoint of validity and reliability. Students often get lower grades than they deserve because of undue difficulty in the examination or in the grading. Some teachers set standards in terms of what they could have done—or would have liked to have done—when they went to school. Some pride themselves on being tough and proceed to appoint themselves as watchdogs of academic standards. Besides reflecting personality problems of potential interest to a psychiatrist and considerable lack of understanding of the principles of sound evaluation, these teachers are only deceiving themselves, while doing considerable harm to some students. The unfortunate students who are assigned to these teachers are automatically deprived of the recognition for academic performance supposedly available to all and they get to feel, "What's the use?" so that performance goes down, not up. In the meantime, students are being penalized, not for lack of preparation, but simply for the poor choice of an instructor. There ought to be more constructive ways of maintaining standards and the teacher who, year after year, turns in grades lower than those of his colleagues only shows himself a poor teacher or a misguided reformist whose objectives are out of line with reality. Whose failure is it when wholesale grades of F are given? Far from being a matter of virtue or standards, failing a large number of students is undoubtedly a reflection on the suitability of the course content, the appropriateness of the goals, or one's adequacy as a teacher, all of which are at least as much the responsibility of the teacher as they are of the student. Whereas every teacher is bound to have a different point of reference in assigning grades, the school should agree upon a common grading policy consistent with its philosophy, its student body, and its faculty, and there should be a reasonable uniformity in the grading standards of the different teachers.

Grades often incorporate more than just a bit of downright injustice. It has been shown repeatedly that both men and women teachers give higher grades to girls for equal or lesser performance (Burton, 1950); in one of Lobaugh's studies (1942), for instance, girls had a grade-point average of 2.19 in contrast to 1.97 for boys although on standardized tests the median score for boys was 46 and for girls 36. In three consecutive years, eight out of the ten top scorers on the objective tests were boys, but girls were more frequently on the honor roll. In another study, the boy who ranked first in performance on standardized tests actually failed to graduate while the valedictorian ranked 36th and the salutatorian ranked 105th. The evidence applies to groups and does not deal with the student who gets an undeserved grade simply because the teacher consciously or unconsciously likes or dislikes him or her. Goodenough (1940), for example, reported a correlation of .40 between errors in scoring papers and the teacher's rating of the children's personal attractiveness.

SELF-EVALUATION

The psychological implications of these criticisms of grading must be clearly understood by the teacher. Whereas each case has to be evaluated on its own merits, the teacher must remember that giving the child an *F* or writing a comment about his being "lazy" or "undependable" is more likely to have major negative effects than to bring about an improvement in his performance. Some of the problems associated with grading are difficult to handle. What is to be done when the teacher knows the child's parents will beat him unless he brings home a good report? Or when reporting the low grade will make a boy ineligible for sports which is the only thing that keeps him in school? It may be true that he is at least partially responsible for his low grade but is this the best way to help him? And if his grade is adjusted, is it fair to the other children? These problems can be quite a hazard to the mental health of the teacher who may feel he has to choose between being disloyal to the child and killing whatever chance he may have had of helping him—especially when he is convinced the low grade will serve no useful purpose—or betraying his trust as a teacher and sacrificing his integrity. The fact that the teacher has a basic need to be loved and that he is likely to resent the hostility and hurt feelings of students to whom he gives low grades only serves to increase the conflict with which he is faced.

Worthy of consideration as a partial solution is to have the child participate in the evaluation of his performance. This represents nothing more than the logical outgrowth of the modern philosophy of pupil-teacher cooperation. If we accept evaluation as an integral part of an effective learning situation, we have to involve the child in the clarification and continuous appraisal of his goals and the effectiveness of his attempts at attaining these goals. From a psychological point of view, self-evaluation has considerable merit. Not only does it promote effective learning, but it also provides the child with an important lesson in self-understanding. No more desirable educational objective can be imagined!

The validity of these self-evaluations is, of course, an important consideration. Research (Steier, 1948; Sumner, 1932; Tschechtelin, 1945, 1956) has shown that girls tend to overestimate and boys to underestimate their performance, and that the tendency to overestimate one's performance is inversely correlated with scholarship. On the other hand, Clark (1938) found that, with the A, B, C, . . . system, from 50 to 80 percent of the students give themselves the same grade as the instructor—with the majority of the remainder (comprising a heavy concentration of duller students) giving themselves better grades. This is probably to be expected. Ego-involvement which is almost certain to exist is likely to cause some distortion in self-evaluation and each person probably has a systematic tendency to overestimate or underestimate his performance—simply because he is the person he is. Occasionally a child will need help in arriving at self-insight and self-acceptance; this is more likely to occur under conditions of psychological safety and freedom from undue pressure to meet unrealistic external standards.

CONVERTING PERFORMANCE INTO GRADES

The form in which grades are given is perhaps not of major consequence; yet, in view of the strong conviction sometimes encountered relative to the percentage method or grading on the curve, a word of discussion might be in order. We know whether performance is creditable only by comparing it to that of others. This is particularly true in displaced cardinal series which can tell us only that one performance is better or worse than another. Even in absolute cardinal series such as typing speed, we agree that 80 words per minute is "good" only because we know that few typists type at that rate. To illustrate the point: How would you rate the performance of the one-year-old colt that supposedly galloped the mile in two minutes flat?

Converting a student's performance into a grade has to be arbitrary; preconceived limits such as 93–100 = A are essentially meaningless as we have pointed out. The only reason the percentage method works at all is that the teacher can set the severity of the scoring in inverse proportion to the difficulty of the questions so that approximately the "right" number of students get A's, B's, C's. Years ago, it took only 50 percent to pass, then the minimum passing mark was raised to 60 percent, and then to 70 percent, but the same number of A's, B's, C's is given now as before. Teachers simply make whatever adjustment is necessary to have the "proper" percentage of students in each grade interval. On an essay test, the answer to a given question by objective standards might be worth no more than perhaps 13 of the 20 points assigned to the question, but the teacher, realizing that no one is perfect and that this is the best answer he is likely to get, scores it 18 or 19; otherwise, no one would get 93 percent of the maximum required to get an A. In objective tests, the teacher emphasizes facts and limited objectives which have been drilled over and over, e.g., "List three types of sedimentary rocks," "Who was president before Truman?" And so examinations stifle education! Authorities on testing are unanimous in recommending that the average item difficulty be set at approximately 50 percent of maximum so that all students—good, mediocre, or poor—have room in which to demonstrate their knowledge or lack of it without interference from a ceiling or a floor. Under these conditions, the highest grade, if we were to abide rigidly to a percentage scale, might be no more than a C.

Grading on the curve follows directly from the previous discussion. Whenever grading is based on a displaced cardinal series, there can be no grading other than grading on the curve—although not necessarily grading on the normal curve. Grading on the curve is based on the readily acceptable proposition that, if education is to be a matter of helping students make the most of their ability, the distribution of performance on an appropriate evaluative instrument must approximate the distribution of ability among the group members. In an unselected group, the distribution of the factors involved in learning such as intelligence and motivation tend to follow the normal curve, and it seems logical, therefore, to expect the distribution of performance also to be normal.

From this distribution of performance, the teacher has to select cutoff scores so as to derive letter grades. This process is entirely, and unavoidably, arbitrary. Thus, some authorities suggest *as a rough guide* for dealing with unselected groups, the percentages of A's, B's, ... shown in Figure 16-5.

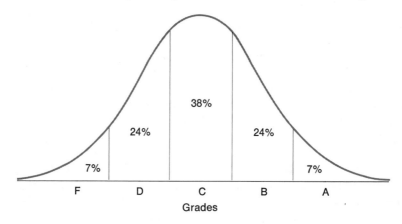

FIGURE 16-5   Theoretical distribution of grades for an unselected group.

It must be emphasized that grading on the curve does not imply that a set percentage of the class must fail or that there must be no more and no less than 7 percent A's. Depending on its philosophy, a school might set other percentages as points of departure for its teachers in their grading, and, certainly a teacher need not give a single F unless he feels that some student's performance is so much below acceptable levels as to warrant being labeled unsatisfactory—whatever the basis used in establishing what is to be considered unsatisfactory. It also follows that with the proportionally greater incidence of academic mortality among the less able in, say, the sophomore and junior year in college, the distribution of ability gets weighted more heavily toward high ability, and the distribution of grades ought to be correspondingly weighted toward a greater concentration of A's and B's. It must also be noted that there is nothing in the concept of grading on the curve that says a teacher cannot adjust the grade of a student whose performance, although below class average, is nevertheless in line with his limited ability.

The point is sometimes made that, in view of the undependability of marks, the only grades we should assign are S for satisfactory and U for unsatisfactory. Actually, such a scheme solves nothing. When accompanied by verbal or written comments, it may be a way of minimizing the emphasis sometimes placed on grades, but, from a tests and measurements point of view, it is a step in the wrong direction. Admittedly, marks are subject to error but lumping all the A's, B's, C's, and D's into a single "Pass" category magnifies the distinction between the D's and the F's, which distinction is still subject to the same error as ever. As a result, teachers using the S-U system generally give everyone an S which is equivalent to grading no one. The present letter-grade system is not a particularly effective means of communicating with students and parents, but the S-U system, by itself, is almost completely devoid of meaning; if teachers want to report to students and parents only in cases of unsatisfactory progress, it would be easier to say it that way.

REPORTING TO PARENTS

The report card exists primarily to keep parents informed of their child's progress, to enlist home-school cooperation, and to improve public relations. The report card in use in many schools is essentially ineffective in all three and Kingsley and Garry (1957) make the categorical statement that, for all practical purposes, grades and report cards could be eliminated without serious loss. Teachers are not always clear as to how these purposes are to be realized; it is one thing to report the "grade" the child receives in each of the academic areas, but is this all the school stands for? Is the amount of material he has mastered the most significant aspect of the responsibility the school has assumed for the welfare of each and every child?

A letter grade in each subject-matter area, and even a comment or two on the child's emotional and social development hardly give an adequate picture of status or growth. Low grades and negative comments are more likely to arouse resistance and resentment than cooperation. Parents do not appreciate being told the shortcomings of their offspring for it reflects on them. The child is likely to resent being tattled on and to view teacher-parent cooperation as nothing more than a conspiracy against defenseless children, especially when, at the very time he needs the understanding of his parents in order to profit from his past errors, he is deprived of their support as a result of the report card. Pupils and parents tend to look upon the report card in an emotional way so that it loses whatever value it might otherwise have; they often see it as a symbol of teacher unfairness and society's rejection of children who do not meet the approval of the reigning dynasty. In a sense, the report card is designed to be too negative for the child who does badly and perhaps too positive for the child who does well.

Crow and Crow (1956) express the opinion that some report cards have done more than anything else to bring about misunderstanding between parents and teachers, parents and children, and teachers and pupils. An equally strong stand against some of the present reporting practices is taken by Redl and Wattenberg (1959):

> To thoughtful adults, the glee of those pupils who 'did well' is more than balanced by scenes in less fortunate homes. Here a 'cooperative' parent administers a beating, cuts an allowance, or indulges in third-degree interrogation. There, to avoid a scene, a parent's signature is forged. Elsewhere ambitions crumble amidst sorrows and vows of vengeance.
>
> That a ritual so fraught with nasty feelings for so many people should endure is a puzzle for sociologists to study. Mental hygienists have dutifully registered their disapproval for decades. [p. 397]

It all adds up to the fact that teachers need to be aware of the potential harm that can result from the misuse of the report card lest they unwittingly allow it to sabotage their efforts on behalf of the child. Most teachers were relatively adequate students when they were in school; perhaps they do not appreciate the crisis a poor report card can generate.

The form letter used in some schools to report to parents has greater flexibility but it too has its drawbacks. Not only is it time consuming, but it frequently deteriorates into a series of meaningless clichés. Teachers find it difficult to convey information without antagonizing parents. The form letter does not, for example, allow the teacher to lay the groundwork for the parents' acceptance of adverse comments by dwelling on strengths before going on to the weaknesses.

The feeling on the part of teachers that a better understanding, better relations, and greater cooperation between parents and teachers can be fostered through personal contact has led many schools to adopt the conference as a partial or complete substitute for the report card. Unfortunately, the conference has some of the same shortcomings as the form letter; it is time consuming and is subject to clichés and stock phrases. In addition, having to come to school for a conference may cause resentment on the part of certain parents, e.g., parents who work, especially because some have been conditioned to expect to talk to the teacher only when their child is in trouble. It has special limitations in the departmentalized high school where the parents would have to see five or six teachers, some of whom can hardly identify their child, let alone discuss his problems. Nevertheless, the conference has much to recommend it if teachers and parents, rather than exchanging hypocritical niceties, will discuss objectively mutual problems concerning the pupil's growth, emphasizing not the symptoms but their probable causation and the steps to be taken to alleviate them. The conference enables the teacher to discuss the more personal and confidential matters concerning the child, e.g., that he is of limited ability, matters which he could not handle via the report card since it does not permit him to build up the background necessary for parents to understand and accept the information, and since potentially damaging information should never be made part of a semipublic document.

Another recent trend in reporting to parents involves self-reports by pupils. This is a logical sequel to self-evaluation. Once the student's evaluation of his work—done under the direction of the teacher—has reached the point of mutual agreement, it is sent home under their joint signature in lieu of, or as a supplement to, the more formal report card. The teacher should provide guidance if the report is to go in meaningful directions and if it is to be objective and sufficiently detailed, but, when well done, such a procedure can embody the best in pupil-teacher-parent cooperation.

HIGHLIGHTS OF THE CHAPTER

A comprehensive pupil-appraisal program is essential to the understanding of children for whose all-round growth the school has accepted responsibility. Some aspects of such a program are of such a technical nature as to belong more appropriately in a text in educational tests and measurements. This chapter is concerned with certain aspects of the appraisal of academic achievement.

[a]

Measurement and evaluation are integral aspects of the total teaching-learning process. They provide information on the basis of which the child's further growth can be planned and guided most effectively.

[b]

Sound evaluation begins with sound measurement derived through valid and reliable instruments, but it goes beyond measurement in that it appraises the results of measurement in the light of the goals of education, the objectives of the course, and the particular circumstances involved.

[c]

An academic test is valid when it is relatively free from factors which are extraneous to the objectives of the course in which achievement is being measured. The specific nature of these objectives is a matter of the school's philosophy and the function the course is to serve in the child's education.

[d]

A test should be reliable and teachers should be cautious when evaluating the results of a short test. The essay examination is notoriously low in reliability.

[e]

Tests can be *standardized* or *informal*, *objective* or *subjective*. Objective test items, in turn, can be of various types. None is "better" than any other; each is most valid under certain circumstances, and it is a matter of choosing the right type of test and of test item for one's specific purpose.

[f]

Most educational measurements are based on a displaced cardinal series. Consequently, the results can be interpreted only on a relative basis.

[g]

Grading is a matter of synthesizing the evaluation of the various aspects of the student's performance into a single symbol. The process is obviously arbitrary and any attempt to derive the grade directly from the test as implied in the system of 93–100 = A is misguided. The primary point of reference available to the teacher in assigning grades is the performance of other members of the class (or of previous classes) and grading must inevitably be "on the curve."

[h]

Many relatively valid criticisms have been aimed at grading and its abuses, and the teacher needs to be cognizant of the fact that grading can negate many of the more important things he is trying to do.

[i]

Improperly done, reporting to parents can be harmful, and, whereas no one method has been found completely satisfactory, parent-teacher conferences and self-reports by students are among the more psychologically sound approaches to the problem.

SOURCES OF RELATED MATERIAL

Berdie, R. F., et al., "Symposium—Tests: Tools of value," *Teach. Coll. Rec.*, 64: 183–203, 1962.

Buros, O. K., *Tests in Print*. Highland Park: Gryphon, 1961.

Carter, L. F., "Psychological tests and public responsibility," *Amer. Psychol.*, 20: 123–146, 1965.

Cook, Walter W., and T. Clymer, "The impact of school organization," in W. G. Findlay (ed.), *The Impact and Improvement of School Testing Programs*. 62d Yearbook, National Society for the Study of Education, Pt. II. Chicago: University of Chicago Press, 1963. Pp. 62–81.

PART IV

The Child
and his
Adjustment

Concerns itself with the development of effective personality patterns which will enable the child to live in wholesome and constructive interaction with his environment.

CHAPTER 17

Attitudes
and Character
Development

Among the various tendencies and predispositions which are acquired and modified by
learning, none is more important to individual
and social welfare than attitudes and ideals.
Kingsley and Garry, 1957, p. 471

Educators are becoming progressively more aware of the importance of
attitudes in the overall educative process. Whereas, up to the turn of the
century, schools existed primarily for the purpose of imparting knowledge
and skills, it now has become evident that the attitudes which are by-
products of whatever is taught are often much more important than the
primary learnings from the standpoint of both the learner's academic
progress and the effect these attitudes will have throughout his life. Too
often in their eagerness to force the child to learn at whatever the cost,
educators have succeeded only in fostering attitudes antagonistic to those
upon which his long-term welfare and that of society depend. The importance of attitude is recognized in the orientation of the present text
toward the self-concept, accentuation, and other emphases on the phenomenal nature of perception.

NATURE OF ATTITUDES

Attitudes may be thought of as learned patterns of behavior which predispose the individual to act in a specific way toward certain persons, objects, or ideas. A more comprehensive definition is that of Allport (1935, p. 45), who defines an attitude as a "state of readiness organized through experience exerting a directive and/or dynamic influence upon the individual's response toward all objects or situations with which it is related." Attitudes are best approached from the standpoint of the motivational structure of the individual as discussed in Chapters 3 and 4; they constitute the nucleus of the self-concept, for example. Attitudes are also closely related to emotions; in fact, they can be defined as emotionally toned ideas, a definition the validity of which is apparent even from a cursory analysis of prejudices, for example.

Attitudes underlie behavior in such a fundamental way that it is necessary to understand attitudes if we are to understand behavior, especially that they tend to become generalized into an overall outlook permeating all aspects of life. Actually, attitudes constitute a highly complex system of variables, and any attempt to analyze their nature or operation is likely to lead to oversimplification. Attitudes can be considered from the standpoint of three basic components:

[a] An affective component, i.e., a certain feeling tone, sometimes quite irrational, which influences the acceptance or rejection of the attitude-object

[b] A cognitive component consisting of the intellectualized aspects of one's views regarding the attitude-object

[c] An action component, predisposing the individual toward specific overt behavior

These components exist at various levels of intensity and in various degrees of independence of one another. A person may have a rather clear cognitive view of a given idea or object but have no great feeling about it and have no inclination to take any action concerning its promotion, while another may die for his country, for example, without knowing quite what is at stake. On the other hand, attitudes with a strong affective content generally lead to some form of overt action—whether they are correct or incorrect, and whether they are clear or unclear from a cognitive point of view; violent action may result from challenge to ignorance and prejudice as easily as from a violation of a well-defined principle of integrity.

Attitudes tend to be definite and specific from the standpoint of the object or the value to which they are attached. They differ, therefore, from ideals, which tend to be more generalized and abstract and to represent a higher level of conceptual organization. Thus, tolerance toward a minority group is an attitude whereas tolerance as an abstraction is an ideal. Both attitudes and ideals imply generalizations, and individuals who are limited in their ability to generalize, e.g., persons of limited mental development, may have to rely on habits that are more restricted and hence influence a smaller segment of their lives. Attitudes can be differentiated from values in that values have reference to social and moral worth; they are also more stable and more general and, of course, of greater significance to society. Whereas values are related to broad goals residing within the individual, attitudes have more specific (external) objects of reference and are more closely related to narrow channels into which activity can be directed.

Attitudes permeate our very existence. The self-concept, for example, is best viewed as the complex system of attitudes and values which the individual has developed concerning himself in relation to the external world with which he has psychological contact. The individual who sees himself as honest simply has favorable attitudes toward the class of experiences involving honest behavior; the adolescent who considers himself a "tough," on the contrary, has negative attitudes toward the social and moral codes, law enforcement, and other social values. Consequently, the cultivation of favorable attitudes toward the values that society treasures is tantamount to promoting behavior in line with the code and the mores of the social order. In the same way, promoting favorable attitudes toward a given school subject is the equivalent of encouraging the student to pursue the subject with eagerness and persistence.

DEVELOPMENT OF ATTITUDES

If it is to fulfill its responsibility to society, the school cannot escape from its responsibility of embarking upon a deliberate campaign to influence for the good the attitudes of children. Children are going to form attitudes anyway—good or bad—and society cannot afford to be indifferent to the outcome. Educators do not tolerate haphazard learning in academic areas and it just would not make sense to let this most important phase of education be a matter of accident. It follows that teachers need to be familiar with the general nature of attitudes and the process by which they develop.

The formation and maintenance of attitudes is subject to the principles and laws which govern any other form of learning. To the extent that attitudes are learned in the process of the attainment of one's purpose, differences in attitudes can be expected with differences in age, sex, socioeconomic status, and cultural and experiential background. The essential difference between the learning of attitudes in contrast to more exclusively cognitive material is the greater affective and evaluative component of the former. Favorable attitudes toward honesty are not only cognitively correct and appropriate, but also good from the standpoint of social well-being.

Attitudes tend to develop incidentally, gradually, and generally unconsciously. They arise as by-products of one's day-to-day experiences and, conversely, everything that goes on in the classroom as it affects the child leads to the formation on his part of certain attitudes. If the teacher is pleasant, enthused about his subject, and sensitive to the needs of his students, the latter may develop favorable attitudes toward the teacher and the subject. Furthermore, these attitudes will tend to spread from the situation to which they are attached to related situations in ever-wider circles. If the teacher is punitive, on the other hand, the child will tend to develop negative attitudes toward the teacher and toward the subject. This will prevent him from doing well and will serve to reinforce his dislike for the subject and may spread to include a dislike for the whole school and all that it stands for—society, social values, etc. As a result, the school experience, rather than serving as the basis for self-realization, may well have highly detrimental repercussions on his whole life; a negative self-concept, rebelliousness, and even delinquency are among the more or less natural adjuncts of an unsuitable curriculum forced upon children through autocratic pressures. Furthermore, these attitudes will remain long after the subject matter has been forgotten—as might be expected when one considers that much of the academic content of the average course is only remotely related to the child's goals and purposes so that he is relatively impervious to it, while, on the other hand, the aspects of the situation which lead to the formation of attitudes affect him in a vital way. Thus, he may not care particularly about the dates of historical events or the theorems of geometry, but he is definitely involved in the fact that the teacher makes him look stupid or brilliant.

Once developed and incorporated into the self-structure, attitudes force the individual to react in a way consistent with his present self-image. The child who has a favorable attitude toward school and the teacher is not likely to misbehave, for to do so would lead to internal conflict. Only those attitudes that are consistent with the present self-concept are assimilated and they, in turn, serve to restrict future behavior.

The development of attitudes is probably best explained on the basis of a combination of psychological principles, and most authors (e.g., Jones 1960) have accepted a multiple rather than a single approach.[1] Attitude formation may be a matter of imitation; many of our attitudes are simply borrowed. The child accepts the views of his parents and other significant

---

[1] The fact that such a multiple approach has to be based on an eclectic theoretical position may be disturbing to those who believe in scientific purity. Eclecticism appears to be justified on the basis of the relative inconclusiveness of the present theoretical positions and the introductory nature of the present discussion.

persons in his environment. Later, as he identifies with his peers, with fictitious characters like the Lone Ranger, with sports and screen stars, with older siblings as well as with teachers, he incorporates their attitudes and general outlook. Reimann (1951), for example, concluded that prejudices are generally transferred unconsciously to children by adults and playmates. The child probably derives some sense of belonging by reacting toward minority groups in the way his parents and siblings do. Attitudes also develop as a result of deliberate cultivation, especially by parents and teachers.

What the teacher is as a person and the way he acts is generally more important in fostering desirable attitudes on the part of children than what he preaches. Positive attitudes cannot be developed as a result of a 15-minute period set aside for attitude formation if the procedures of the rest of the day constitute a negation of the principles involved; the child cannot develop attitudes of fairness when he is continually the victim of unfairness. By the same token, positive attitudes toward democracy are not developed by lecturing about the glories of democracy when the whole tone of the class is autocratic; all the child can get out of such a situation is the ability to verbalize the benefits of democracy and a sense of puzzlement at the hypocrisy and contradiction of it all.

To the extent that teachers are often used as models by children in the formation of their attitudes, it is imperative that they meet definite standards of suitability from this all-important standpoint; it seems essential, for example, that they have a positive outlook on life and that they be stable people whose integrity, sincerity, and loyalty to the things our society holds dear are unquestioned, who can embody such beliefs into living lessons, and who can use their prestige to inspire children in the development of wholesome attitudes which will serve as a foundation of wholesome behavior. It is essential that teachers exemplify the basic values of our culture. On the other hand, teachers cannot *give* the child attitudes; they can only arrange for him to have satisfying experiences that will lead to the formation of positive attitudes on the basis of which desirable behavior can become integrated into a pattern of life.

Some attitudes are learned as a result of conditioning through emotionally toned experiences. As the individual is presented simultaneously with two stimuli, one of which is already associated with a given affective tone and the other neutral, he is likely to associate the feeling tone with what was originally the neutral stimulus. A student may develop a strong dislike for a certain subject as a result of its being taught by a teacher who habitually ridicules him in front of his peers.

Desirable attitudes are probably best developed through meaningful participation in worthwhile activities designed to influence attitudes. Thus, pupils with experience in self-government tend to be more favorably inclined toward the observance of regulations than are pupils without such experience (Peters and Peters, 1936). Attitudes underlying moral behavior are not developed by preaching but by providing the child with systematic practice in integrating moral concepts into his total behavior patterns and, whereas part of this integration must involve a verbalization of the basis for one's behavior, sermons are of limited benefit.

ATTITUDES TOWARD THE SCHOOL

An important set of attitudes from the standpoint of the basic purpose of education concerns those attitudes which the child holds with regard to the school itself and the values for which it stands. Unfortunately, we have not been too successful in this area. Eight to 12 years or more of attendance in our schools has led a sizable number of our students to have anything but favorable attitudes toward literature, teachers, education, schools, desirable behavior. Schools should provide the tools and the desire whereby the individual can promote his self-realization. But, whereas one's education should be just beginning when he leaves school, many youngsters, on the contrary, are finished with education the day they graduate or drop out. They take with them a few facts or skills, but, all too often, the bonus in the form of a dislike for any kind of learning is by far the most significant aspect of the total situation.

The reason underlying such negative attitudes should be of primary concern to the teacher. The excitement of going to school makes most beginning children highly susceptible to the development of favorable attitudes toward school. But, in a few short years—for whatever reason—a good number of children do not like school, do not like teachers, do not like what they are studying. They attend only reluctantly for want of a choice in the matter. The school needs to evaluate its offerings and its procedures to see if perhaps it is not responsible, at least in part, for this state of affairs. Unfavorable attitudes, it seems clear, develop out of unsatisfying experiences; it is likely that, in many cases, these unfavorable attitudes are the direct outcomes of an unsuitable curriculum, of rigid, frustrated, and unenthused teachers, and other aspects of the school situation for which the primary responsibility rests with the teacher and other school officials. Unfortunately, administrators and teachers are very often unaware of unsatisfactory conditions in their schools; children, on the other hand, are reluctant to complain. And so the matter drags on, with the morale of the students dropping lower and lower.

Children from the lower socioeconomic classes are more likely to hold antischool and antieducation attitudes than those from the middle and upper classes (Hieronymus, 1951). Many harbor these negative attitudes even before they come to school. Furthermore, they get continuous reinforcement from their parents and siblings, who hold similar views; in fact, they are likely to feel disloyal if they like school. On the other hand, the school very often deserves full credit for an "assist" in the development and maintenance of these negative attitudes. By providing them with an unsuitable curriculum from the time they enter first grade, by labeling them as dull because they are not oriented toward schoolwork, and by continually punishing them when they fail to internalize the values of the school, even though these attitudes are incompatible with those of their culture and socioeconomic background, the school only intensifies these attitudes and causes them to be transmitted from generation to generation. Children who are pushed to the limit day by day, often under conditions of threat, to learn things that are not only meaningless in terms of their goals and purposes but often incompatible with the orientation of their home and community, are bound to develop negative attitudes. These attitudes not only will preclude success but also will set into motion a vicious cycle, a major component of which is the rejection of the school in all of its values and the development of counterattitudes which are detrimental to all from both an immediate and a long-term view.

Fortunately, the current emphasis on the culturally disadvantaged is, at last, focusing attention on the special characteristics and the special educational needs of lower-class children. The teacher working with these children needs to be particularly understanding as well as adept at relating the curriculum and his procedures to their needs and background. He needs to understand these children so that he can have his influence in the development of attitudes harmonize with their present set of values as the point of departure from which to foster a more acceptable outlook. In the meantime, he must realize that they are no more "troublemakers" because they live out the values of their cultural group than are children from the middle class, the values of whose homes happen to coincide with those of the school.

CHANGING ATTITUDES

RESISTANCE TO CHANGE

That attitudes should be relatively resistant to change follows from the discussion of the self-concept. As we have noted, stimuli do not have an absolute stimulus value but rather each new experience is perceived, appraised, interpreted, and reacted to in relation to the present self, a major component of which is the individual's current attitudes. Perceptual resistance and distortion stemming from the individual's attitudinal structure is particularly noticeable in the case of the prejudiced person who, having a system of beliefs that he cannot afford to have shaken, simply maintains a consistently closed position. To the extent that attitudes are broad predispositions affecting one's perceptions and thus one's learning, they are themselves selectively maintained and, as a result, enable the person to maintain personality and behavioral consistency.

Yet despite their resistance to change, attitudes are constantly being modified. Although this occurs more readily and more smoothly in people open to experience, every individual is constantly being forced to reappraise his attitudes as he interacts with his environment. In this connection, parents play a crucial role particularly in shaping the basic personality and thereby orienting later personality developments. The child who suffers from insecurity as a result of parental rejection, for example, is susceptible to the development of rigid moralistic attitudes, including hostility toward minority groups. In addition, because of their many contacts with the child during his formative years and the consequently greater likelihood that he will identify with and be responsive to them, parents are also more influential than anyone else in the modifications that occur in the basic personality.

The school also plays an important role. The interaction of the attitudes developed by the child as a result of home and peer contacts with those of the school causes him to clarify, reappraise, and readjust his views. Such reappraisal, under proper guidance, can lead to attitudes of openmindedness and willingness to question the validity of his previous views and his interpretations of the facts at his disposal. The school thus provides him with the basis for developing valid, meaningful, and functional attitudes and thereby equipping himself for effective behavior beyond the immediate situation. The school also needs to help the child verbalize and generalize his attitudes in order to extend the scope of their applicability. Its contribution is especially important inasmuch as it relates to areas in which he is, up to then, relatively uninformed and free from personal conviction.

The difficulty in changing attitudes stems from the fact that they are so closely related to the total personality. A person can generally change rather easily his views on a certain make of car, but it is not so easy for him to change his attitudes toward race, religion, or other issues in which he is ego-involved. This would vary from person to person, depending on the extent to which these attitudes are anchor-pins in the individual's value system. Attitude changes cannot be considered apart from the nature of the attitude in question and the person and the circumstances involved. Some people are more open to experience than others. Identical attitudes may have different motivational bases and may have to be approached differently. A possibility in dealing with a person whose attitudes are at the level of personal conviction based on adequate information might be to attack the cognitive object in the frame of reference in which it is perceived through a rational, matter-of-fact approach. Social rewards and punishments might be more effective in the case of the conformer who values social approval. Another possibility is through exploiting the system of dominant values to which the person subscribes; one might point out that racial intolerance is incompatible with the person's concept of fair play.

Certain attitudes may be more effectively influenced through an attempt to give insight into the self rather than insight into the problem itself (Katz et al., 1957). Attitude changes can sometimes be effected by attacking ego-defensive forces through the use of catharsis and direct interpretation; they would be most effective in the case of people who want to change, e.g., persons suffering from guilt. A group interpretation and group discussion approach might help to promote insight into the mechanics underlying the development and maintenance of attitudes, e.g., the role of rationalization and projection in the case of prejudice. Group decision would also provide security for the person who fears that a change in viewpoint might jeopardize social acceptance.

The effectiveness of any approach to changing attitudes depends on the congruity between what is presented and the current self-concept. A factual approach would be most effective in modifying attitudes when it clarifies an unstructured situation which the individual is approaching with an open mind. Naturally, facts form a good starting point for thinking about certain issues. But the mere presentation of facts generally has limited effect on a person with definite feelings on a given subject. Carlson (1956) found that attempts to promote a more tolerant outlook toward racial integration resulted in more favorable attitudes on the part of subjects with moderate initial attitudes but effected little change in the strongly prejudiced. In the study by Wagman (1955), information-giving was also relatively ineffective with the more authoritarian subjects.

Because attitudes are so basic to the individual's total self-structure, a direct attack often only serves to intensify and solidify his attitudes as he sets up his defenses to ward off attack and, thus, to maintain self-consistency. Remmers (1934), for example, found that attitudes can be changed by direct instruction when they are not too well integrated but that direct instruction produces only negative reactions when they are well organized. When the listener feels threatened either by the evidence or by the speaker, he is likley to reject the argument and close himself off as a means of warding off anxiety. In the Janis and Feshbach study (1953), for example, a strong fear appeal listing the dire outcomes of failure to brush one's teeth apparently promoted a state of emotional tension which tended to be resolved through the defense-avoidance reaction of ignoring or minimizing the threat.

A relatively gradual and subtle approach generally brings about greater and more permanent changes in attitudes than does a head-on attack, whether based on a well-documented argument of the superiority of the position advocated, the untenability of the listener's present position, or simply an emotional hardsell approach. A person is less likely to generate resistance if he is led to believe that his position is basically sound and that the new position is simply a minor readjustment of the original attitude. It is also necessary that the change be undertaken in a permissive atmosphere in which he can admit his error without fear of losing status. The more insecure the person, the less flexible his attitudes, and, as we shall see, the more likely he is to have prejudices and other negative attitudes in need of change. It follows that any program designed to reduce prejudices, for example, would do well to consider first how necessary these prejudices are to support the self-structure of the people toward whom the program is directed.

On the other hand, the answer to the question as to whether a person trying to influence someone should begin from a position relatively close to that of the person he is trying to influence, or, on the contrary, take a position which is completely divergent, tends to be situational. Harvey and Rutherford (1958) claim that greater changes occur when a completely divergent position is taken. It is difficult, however, to generalize to all situations. Certainly, if the subject finds the arguments presented completely inconsistent with his present views, he will simply reject the whole proposition. The successful politician is generally a champion of causes which the public has already accepted.

Attitude changes are best effected through a relatively deliberate and systematic approach; an incidental approach, on the other hand, is essentially ineffective because, in an unconscious attempt to safeguard his self-image, the individual simply finds evidence to support his present system of values and ignores or reinterprets conflicting data. A general factual approach would be more effective when a person has no information on the subject and no vested interest to protect. Dictators, for example, have been more successful in cultivating certain attitudes by using a relentless campaign directed at children than they have been in campaigns directed at adults. On the other hand, adults, too, are frequently lacking in the experiences on the basis of which they can form valid attitudes. They may react to atypical incidents and fail to understand the confounding conditions that might explain these incidents, and, often, they have no way of checking the validity of their "data."

Role-playing has been found effective in promoting changes in attitudes. In the study by Janis and King (1954), students who actively played the role of the sincere advocate of a given point of view—i.e., who participated with ego-involvement—tended to shift in the direction of the role they played. Similar results were reported by Festinger and Carlsmith (1959) and by Culbertson (1957). Apparently a person, having said or done something, adjusts his attitudes to bring them into correspondence with what he has said or done. Perhaps he is affected by his own arguments, although rewards may also play a part. In a study by Scott (1957), in which the subjects debated in favor of a position opposite to the one which they personally held, the group which was rewarded by being named the winner made greater changes toward the position they presented in the debate than the group which was declared the loser.

The effect of role-playing can be extended to participation in a given group. Undoubtedly, one's attitudes and values are molded by the constant pressure of the attitudes and values of those about him, and particularly by those with whom he identifies. There is probably no better way of rehabilitating a juvenile delinquent than by having him participate in a wholesome group, although the exact effect of such participation would depend upon the leadership, the cohesiveness and identification of the group, the commonness of purpose, and, of course, his self-concept.

Of particular interest are the experiments conducted by Lewin (1958) pointing to the effectiveness of group decision and personal commitment not only in promoting changes in attitudes but also in ensuring action in line with the new attitudes. In a typical study undertaken with the objective of increasing the consumption of beef hearts, sweetbreads, and kidneys, three groups were given attractive lectures linking the problem of nutrition with the war effort and emphasizing the vitamin and mineral values of these meats; in three other groups the emphasis was on discussion, eventuating in group decision. Only 3 percent of the women in the lecture groups actually served the meats, as against 32 percent of the women in the decision groups. Similar results were obtained in connection with the consumption of fresh and evaporated milk, the use of cod liver oil in the baby's milk, and the use of orange juice. Apparently for the women to perceive the changes in food consumption as a matter relating to housewives like themselves helped to minimize their resistance. Lewin emphasizes that it is not the group discussion but rather personal commitment to a group decision that leads to action; not only is it often easier for a group to reach a decision collectively during the discussion than it is for each to do so individually after the lecture, but reaching such a decision has the effect of freezing the motivational constellation for action.

Presenting both sides of an argument is generally more effective than presenting only one side, especially with the better educated (Hovland et al., 1949; Lumsdaine and Janis, 1953). Presumably it increases the listener's confidence in the integrity and competence of the speaker when he sees that the arguments with which he is already familiar have been taken into account. Furthermore it tends to discount the arguments the listener may hear later which otherwise might tempt him to change his mind, especially if he felt that he had been "sold" a partial picture.

The approach must be congruent with the setting of the reference group. Torrance and Mason (1958) found that making food indoctrination a regular part of military training was the most effective of six approaches to convincing recruits into accepting army rations. In other words, in a military setting where indoctrination is expected, an official role was found more effective than low-pressure techniques such as personal persuasiveness, the setting of example, or the presentation of objective evidence concerning its use.

Generally the speaker should be a person of acceptability to the listeners so that identification can take place. In the study by Scollon (1957), a Korean veteran was more effective in influencing army trainees to use army field rations than was a food specialist. Della-Piana and Gage (1955) found that pupils with strong affective needs preferred teachers who were high in benevolent attitudes toward children, but that the teachers' status in this regard was of lesser significance for children with strong cognitive needs. In other words, the characteristics of the teacher depend for their significance on the value system of the pupils. Obviously, pupils are not likely to be influenced in the modification of their attitudes by a teacher who rejects them; students have been found to cheat more in classes where the atmosphere is coldly formal and where the teacher uses autocratic techniques than where truly friendly democratic procedures prevail (Lodge, 1951).

Of significance in this connection is the question of whether teachers have the prestige or status in the eyes of students necessary for them to be effective in promoting attitude changes in the latter. This may have a bearing on the type of person we should sponsor as future teachers and also the effect which public criticisms may have in undermining the usefulness of teachers in this important area of attitude development. It might also suggest that a course toward which favorable attitudes are to be developed, e.g., the tenets of democracy, might be assigned to the most popular and prestigeful teacher on the staff. Having a popular boy who has gone to college visit as a guest of his former high school may influence many students as to the desirability of a college education. Of prime interest here is the observation by Bauer (1964) that in the past we have placed too much emphasis on the role of the communicator. He suggests that, outside the laboratory, the prospective audience exercises considerable initiative as to what it listens to, even to the point of dictating to the speaker the line he had better expound if he wants to be heard. This is, of course, in keeping with the newer concept of leadership presented in Chapter 8.

It must be remembered that a change of attitude, like any other learning, is predicated upon motivation. To the extent that his current attitudes serve a need, the individual is not likely to want to discard them unless he is assured that the new attitudes provide greater satisfaction. Furthermore, he must be given the opportunity to experience satisfaction in connection with these new attitudes so that they will be reinforced. Many students have developed a liking for a subject taught by a well-liked teacher and vice versa. When adequate motivation is present, attitudes can be changed; just note, for example, the rather drastic change in the adolescent's attitude toward members of the opposite sex resulting from the intensification of the sex drive and the accompanying social pressures to join the crowd.

INDOCTRINATION

In view of the relative ineffectiveness of an incidental approach to attitude formation, one needs to consider what might constitute a more constructive program and the school's function in the matter. The development of desirable attitudes on the part of school children cannot be left to chance; indeed, the school has a definite responsibility to orient their attitudes in the direction of the values of society. In view of the vast bulk of evidence on such topics as selective perception and the maintenance of the self, a teacher has to be rather naïve to think that touching upon a given subject, mentioning a few basic facts, and orienting their readings to certain passages will automatically convert their illogical prejudices or antisocial views into positive attitudes. If we are to be successful in influencing children's attitudes, we need to give the matter the deliberate and systematic attention which we devote to the attainment of other significant educational goals. This implies indoctrination and, of course, raises a question of ethics.

Indoctrination can be particularly effective when used on young children whose minds are pliable and whose background of information on the basis of which to evaluate evidence is relatively limited. In Nazi Germany, for instance, young children learned to read to captions of "Mein Führer," "Mein Führer ist güt." There are people in our country who feel we need to sell democracy with some of the fervor and zeal the Nazis and the communists use in spreading their ideologies; that we should cultivate in youngsters an intelligent understanding of the meaning of democracy and emotional attachment to its principles and practices. It is their contention that we should condition the attitudes of our children toward democracy and toward moral values by subtly introducing passages about George Washington, Thomas Jefferson, etc., after the style of the old McGuffey readers. Others object on the grounds that indoctrination is part of the totalitarian pattern of operation and that it has no place in the schools of a democracy, which should address themselves to teaching children *how* to think and not *what* to think.

The argument that indoctrination is not democratic is untenable. Certainly since the beginning of time parents (and teachers) have indoctrinated their children in such attitudes as honesty, integrity, and morality—and, let us hope, will continue to do so. All education involves teaching values, and when we say that schools should turn out scholars rather than burglars or skillful exploiters of the public, we are subscribing to a point of view that implies the use of indoctrination to achieve the ultimate aim of education. This is unavoidable, but more important, it is desirable and essential: children *have* to be indoctrinated into the dominant values of their society, if that society is to survive. Further, it is the responsibility of the school as a major representative of society to indoctrinate children in those basic values. This is a direct mandate, and negligence in the fulfillment of this responsibility constitutes gross neglect of duty in an area of maximum sensitivity.

Teachers just cannot avoid taking sides on basic issues in order to avoid the possibility of indoctrinating impressionable young children. Society has the right to expect its teachers to espouse and to expound the dominant values upon which this nation stands. To argue that one does not have the right to indoctrinate children in favor of democracy because not all people believe in democracy is akin to saying that teachers should not take a stand on sexual morality inasmuch as some people take a more liberal view of the subject than others. It is hardly a matter of choice; children will form attitudes anyway. The school itself cannot avoid promoting attitudes. In fact, every element of our society—some not particularly wholesome—has an effect on the development of the child's attitudes. Educators cannot subscribe to a policy of making the child's orientation toward the more significant values of the social order a matter of accident. They cannot avoid taking sides—either by willingness to stand and be counted or by default.

In this connection, two questions need to be considered: With respect to what values should the teacher, or need the teacher, indoctrinate? And how is this to be effected? It would be rather difficult to defend a position against the indoctrination of children in such values as honesty, integrity, and morality. It would not make sense to argue that teachers ought not to plug for democracy—that, even though the communists teach their children the virtues of communism, we ought to let our children, with their limited perspective of information and their immaturity of judgment, make their own choices in the matter. This does not mean that the teacher should go out of his way to impose his personal views on children with respect to every controversial subject, but rather that there are dominant values on which teachers must take a stand. A similar opinion is expressed by Bernard (1965), who feels that attitudes are part-and-parcel of the educative process and that they will be formed through evasion, if not through planned education. Horn (1937), in discussing the teaching of social studies, rejects the claim that schools in a democracy should teach children how to think and not what to think; he presents a convincing argument that it is impossible to teach the *how* apart from the *what*.

In other words, there may be questions as to where the line of indoctrination should be drawn, but there can hardly be arguments as to the basic position itself. The alternative—namely, that every child should chart his own course—is clearly unacceptable. This is, of course, an issue in philosophy. A problem which is more within the province of psychology is the means whereby this indoctrination is to be effected. It might be argued, for example, that despite our psychological know-how, our attempts to bring the lower classes around to our middle-class point of view, or to win the backward nations of the world to our side, despite the considerable financial outlay, has so far been somewhat short of a rousing success. Attempts at indoctrination frequently achieve the opposite effect. The English teacher, for example, instead of crusading against cheap literature might be more effective in getting rid of it, if he would actually encourage its study as a means of letting the students on their own discover and agree on its shortcomings—a more subtle and more effective form of indoctrination!

The school needs to embark on a systematic and constructive program designed to promote desirable attitudes on the part of the pupils relegated to its care. However, it must be realized that attitudes cannot be taught like an academic subject. Formal instruction can help crystallize attitudes that are already forming, but attitudes are better absorbed gradually as they permeate the whole atmosphere of the school. The school needs to capitalize on the many opportunities for value development presented by the constant interaction of pupils with teachers and fellow-students and also with significant academic content. Shakespearean plays are typically studied as literature; rarely do students grasp their many life lessons. Attitudes are also established as a result of living. Desirable attitudes are formed and gradually adjusted over the years as the child's interpretations are confirmed or denied as they meet or fail to meet social expectations. The school plays a special role in helping students see where their views are inadequate, for example. Attitude formation and attitude change cannot be rushed. It is not possible to build at the last minute a crash program capable of effecting wholesale changes in the attitudes of delinquents or the salvage of drop-outs.

It is particularly important that the child experiences success, not only as a student but also as a person. The failure of the school to improve the attitudes of children from the lower classes stems in large part, no doubt, from the inability of these children to achieve success within the framework of the school's program—or perhaps more specifically, from the school's failure to provide them with activities that are worthwhile and self-fulfilling and thus promote identification. They need to be allowed some leeway in the choice of goals for which they are to strive, if their education is to be meaningful in terms of their backgrounds and their purposes. It is also essential that they do not find themselves rejected by the school's dominant middle-class peer structure.

PREJUDICE

Prejudices are examples of negative attitudes and, therefore, can be understood only in terms of the concepts previously discussed. They are given special treatment here because of their importance in view of the harm they do to both the persecutor and the persecuted. The latter suffer from feelings of humiliation and inferiority which are reflected in increased hostility and aggression, which, in turn, serve to intensify the prejudices others hold against them. The persecutor, on the other hand, denies himself (and society) the benefits of the contribution of the persecuted. Prejudices are best seen as complex and dynamic attitudinal systems developed during the process of social learning which are generally oriented toward the rejection of a particular class of attitude objects. From a different point of view, prejudice involves putting social labels or group designations on individuals and attributing to every member certain negative characteristics which one has associated with the group.

Prejudices may stem from the normal preference for the familiar and the natural resistance to strangers who tend to accentuate one's insecurity. Foreigners, strangers, and reformers disturb the *status quo* and are generally resented by the average person who likes a certain degree of stability. Prejudice may also stem from the natural feeling of competition for the satisfaction of one's needs. The infant is egocentric, and, although later he expands his self-concept to include his immediate family and a few friends, only reluctantly, and to a limited degree, does he attain a positive attitude of enlightened self-interest that will include out-groups.

Prejudices tend to have a basis in the concept of identification, which automatically implies a certain degree of rejection of nonmembers, i.e., it tends to promote the concept of in-group and out-group, with boundaries of various degrees of permeability and flexibility. The interests of the group often lead the members into conflict with nonmembers and to the extent that such a possibility of conflict and out-group rejection does *not* exist, the benefits of belonging to the in-group are automatically minimized. Prejudices are often the direct outcome of persecution and victimization. The rejected person tends to develop strong in-group bonds with corresponding out-group rejection. It is a well-noted sociological phenomenon that persecuted groups frequently display the very same types of prejudices of which they themselves are the victims (Steckler, 1957; Engel et al., 1958).

Although some prejudices, particularly in young children, probably reflect nothing more than a tendency to imitate others, prejudices are more commonly the outgrowth of insecurity. The intolerant person is the immature, insecure individual who needs so desperately the support of the in-group that he has to reject nonmembers. He *needs* prejudices and the individual who has cause for being prejudiced will tend to be prejudiced against a large number of groups—even nonexistent groups (Hartley, 1946). He is simply an intolerant person who needs to compensate for feelings of insecurity and inferiority. The personality of the prejudiced individual has been rather thoroughly investigated; Frenkel-Brunswik (1946), for example, found him to be characterized by less detachment; by admiration of strength and power and rejection of weakness; by submission to, but strong resentment against, authority; by excessive concern with status, with conventionality, and with external moral values including strong moralistic condemnation of transgressions; by a fearful and catastrophic conception of the outside world; and by more inclusive and diffuse manifestations of aggressiveness. He is intolerant of ambiguity and rigid in his interpretation of events.

Adorno et al. (1950), in their discussion of the authoritarian personality, give the following composite picture of the highly ethnocentric person:

[a] He is an authoritarian: he sees the world and the people living in it as dangerous and unfriendly, so he seeks security by submitting uncritically to a powerful authority in order to gain strength.

[b] He is rigidly moralistic: he seeks security in strict adherence to standards of morality and propriety. He is safe as long as he is conventional.

[c] He strongly represses socially disapproved tendencies within himself and projects them on the others: "I don't have these aggressive desires, the minority group has them."

[d] He places people in oversimplified black-and-white categories.

[e] He typically possesses conservative political and economic attitudes. He makes patriotic speeches, but he acts as an antidemocratic agitator in trying to realize his political ambitions.

The prejudiced person represents the insecure personality who has to shut off his supply of experiences in order to maintain the security of his present position. He tends to operate on a closed-mind basis even when an adequate complement of facts is readily available; he prefers to act on the evidence which he already has and which his need to protect his self-concept does not allow him to disturb. He wants no data concerning minority groups; he certainly wants no contact with them, and if he has contact with them he approaches them with a negative outlook and confirms his original position. He performs poorly under conditions of ambiguity, and the greater the stress, the more he distorts his experiences. Here is the case of the cigarette smoker who was so disturbed over newspaper reports of the possible cancer-producing effects of smoking that he stopped—reading the newspapers! He is a person with a narrow perception of his phenomenal field; a person who feels that loyalty to his country implies the rejection of others, who fails to see that the love of one's family is actually increased by a generous, tolerant, and accepting view of other families.

Tolerance is not an inborn trait; if it is to be developed, parents, teachers, and other adults have to work at it by precept and example. The school needs to be careful that it does not unwittingly foster prejudices. It seems logical to suspect that an overemphasis on competition will tend to create distrust and suspicion of others. Offhand remarks by the teacher of social studies as to the motives of people may likewise form the basis for cynicism and distrust. A fertile source of prejudice is to be found in the concept of group spirit. The teaching of patriotism, although highly desirable, may degenerate into provincialism and clannishness which is nothing more than prejudice on an organized basis. Allport (1954) voices the opinion that the patriotism taught in our schools is often narrowly conceived, that the fact that loyalty to the nation automatically implies loyalty to all the subgroups within the nation is seldom pointed out, and that the teaching of exclusive loyalty—whether to nation, school, fraternity, or family—is the equivalent of instilling prejudice. He refers to the "institutional patriot" and the "superpatriotic nationalist" as "thorough-going bigots."

Sociologists have devoted considerable attention to the elimination of prejudice. Unfortunately, success has been relatively limited: the phenomenon is far too complex to permit the formulation of an easy prescription. The causes of prejudice are many and varied; the cure is correspondingly complex. As with any attitude, prejudice can be eliminated only insofar as the new and more tolerant outlook can be incorporated into the individual's present personality structure; he is not likely to forego his prejudices if they support his whole phenomenal organization on the basis of which he can maintain his feelings of worth and bear his feelings of insecurity. Giving information is generally not effective. The prejudiced person can learn all the facts without its having much effect on his attitudes; education simply makes it possible for him to express his prejudices in a more sophisticated way, or perhaps to verbalize "tolerant arguments," but it does not affect his basic feelings.

Where prejudices stem from basic personality needs, not only is their removal difficult but, even if they were removed, they would simply be replaced by others as long as the needs remain. Removing prejudices is complicated by intermittent reinforcement; parents, for example, often feed prejudices which the school is attempting to eliminate. It is also likely that overemphasis on a point of view contrary to that of the child and his parents will lead to resistance, and the teacher's approach, if it is to be effective, generally should be gradual and subtle. Too vigorous an attempt by the teacher to develop more tolerant attitudes among his students will probably lead to his outright rejection, although, on the other hand, the child may remain well identified with the teacher by simply rationalizing that the teacher "just says that because it's his job."

The best way to eliminate prejudices is undoubtedly to build up secure people maximally open to experience and minimally in need of the support of prejudices. The more secure one is, the more he can focus on the crucial aspect of his fellowman's adequacy and the more irrelevant cues like race or class distinction fade into insignificance. Joint participation in the face of a common enemy is often effective in eliminating prejudice; the soldier who has to depend on the fellow next to him on the firing lines is not likely to notice too carefully whether he is Negro, Jewish, or what-have-you. Nations and peoples have cooperated in times of disaster. Identifying a common enemy which is a greater threat and possesses even greater differences than that which is involved between two groups has been used by dictators and even democracies in times of war as a means of consolidating their nation and overcoming internal dissent, but it is not a tool which can be used too easily in the classroom.

A program of education directed at the removal of prejudice can help children recognize that they are rationalizing, that their evidence is not conclusive. It can, up to a point, lead them to see the irrationality of their prejudices; it can help them see intolerance as a function of ignorance, and to appreciate the contributions of other people and other cultures. Such a program must not be simply verbal; it must provide actual practice in tolerance and acceptance. However, it must be realized that, although pleasant association between parties generally leads to greater understanding and tolerance, unpleasant association, on the other hand, may lead to an intensification of prejudice. Prejudice against a given national group does not necessarily disappear as a result of the study of its language; if taught by an autocratic teacher, such a course is more likely to engender or intensify prejudice than it is to eliminate it. At a more complex level, such techniques as role-playing, particularly where the prejudiced person is given the role of the victim, has been found relatively more effective (Moreno, 1945).

The persecuted must also realize that their own reactions can be an important contributor to the continuance of prejudices against them; many are rejected because of their relative unacceptability with respect to such simple things as boisterous and inconsiderate behavior or lack of personal habits of cleanliness which, because of their upbringing, they do not see as objectionable. It must also be recognized that the victims of prejudice are frequently the results of social, educational, and economic disadvantage which is at once the product of prejudice and the cause of its continuance. Furthermore, as a result of past victimization and discrimination, persecuted people frequently become defensive and aggressive, banding together and continuing in ways which set them apart and intensify the negative reactions of others toward them.

CHARACTER DEVELOPMENT

Much of the child's education is oriented toward the development of sound character dominated by positive moral values as the basis for desirable conduct. No aspect of education can be more crucial from the standpoint of the welfare of both the individual and society. As Fromm points out (1944, p. 381):

> In order that any society may function well, its members must acquire the kind of character that makes them *want* to act in the way they *have* to act as members of society. . . . They have to *desire* what objectively is *necessary* for them to do. *Outer force* is replaced by *inner compusion*, and by the particular kind of human energy which is channeled into character traits.

Character relates directly to attitudes and values as major determinants of behavior. The individual's basic need to maintain self-consistency will not permit him to act in violation of his dominant values, and we can depend on him to keep in check impulses toward behavior inconsistent with these values. By directing his attitudes, therefore, we direct his behavior and, conversely, any attempt to control behavior by other means, unless accompanied by the development of appropriate attitudes, is doomed to failure.

Character refers to behavioral consistency as it relates to moral and ethical behavior. It differs from personality, which is a more inclusive concept relatively devoid of moral evaluation so that, generally speaking, personality is not good or bad but simply adjusted, rigid, or pleasant, for example. Character underlies the integrity and the consideration with which a person deals with others and is reflected in the reputation he holds among his fellowmen; however, it is his reputation rather than his character *per se* which determines the impact he will have upon others.

Character tends to be reflected in conduct which is in conformity with social values and relates, therefore, to the degree of internalization of the control and constraints of the social order. A person whose behavior is in keeping with the values and standards of the social group is said to have character, while the drunkard, the swindler, and the prostitute are said to be lacking in character. On the other hand, conformity to the standards of society is not, in itself, the criterion of character. The person who conforms simply to get social approval, even if it means sacrificing his own values, is a chameleon entirely devoid of character. Character also implies conformity in matters where nonconformity is possible but in which the individual chooses to act in a way consistent with the welfare of others. The drunkard who remains sober simply because he cannot obtain liquor is not displaying character, and the child who does not cheat solely because he is afraid of detection is nothing more than a coward.

Character is not the equivalent of morality, for character implies volition and creativeness whereas morality is more specifically geared to the accepted standards of a given time and place. Character implies a willingness to stand and be counted in the advancement of morality beyond the accepted norms of the present social order. Havighurst and Taba (1949), for example, postulate two levels of character, one controlled by praise and reward from the immediate situation, the other controlled by ideals, so that a person may actually displease his associates in the pursuit or implementation of his moral values. Character incorporates morality as a minimum standard but is not restricted to this minimum. History identifies a number of persons who were willing to fight for an improvement in the moral tone and the standards and practices of the day. Underlying character is an internal compulsion to live by one's system of values rather than by mere rules and sanctions geared to external standards. True character implies a rational choice based on an understanding of the consequences of the behavior at issue and a consideration of the welfare of all concerned in line with the concept of enlightened self-interest. The child who does not know why he should behave in a certain fashion in a given situation can only be amoral. Likewise, the individual who has a blind allegiance to honesty as an abstract concept and who tells his hostess that, frankly, he is bored is displaying more rigidity than character, morality, or integrity.

Character relates to the ways the individual satisfies his needs, which, in turn, relates to both his potentialities and environmental circumstances. Character is the resultant of two sets of forces in dynamic interaction: forces within the individual and forces of the social environment in which he operates. It may be easier for the bright child to refuse to "stoop to cheating" than for the duller child who must choose between cheating and failing, for example. This does not imply the inheritance of character. Inherited assets and liabilities are best seen as predispositions to the development of certain character traits; physical inadequacies, for example, may predispose the adolescent toward insecurity and hence to excessive need to conform. Character is also indirectly related to heredity through the relationship between the individual's glandular balance and his temperament, e.g., hormone secretion and aggressiveness (see Chapter 5). However, character is a matter of the direction in which, say, aggressiveness is oriented rather than of its mere existence, and it should be as readily possible for an aggressive person to display integrity or honesty as it is for a more submissive individual. In this orientation of personal traits, environment plays a major role; Mead (1937), for example, found that treachery and suspiciousness formed the basis of the typical pattern of interpersonal relationships in certain primitive tribes, while in others the emphasis was on cooperation.

The child is constantly finding that his behavior meets or does not meet with the approval of the significant people in his environment. As he grows older, he grasps the common elements in the different situations in which his behavior was approved or disapproved and builds up a generalized concept of what is good and what is bad. Conscience develops (or fails to develop) in large measure as a function of the nature of the various approaches used in the socialization process. As we have noted, love-oriented child-rearing techniques tend to promote dependency and socialization. If the parents are wise in the giving and the withholding of love, the child soon finds that he must gear his behavior to their expectations if he is to retain their approval. He becomes socialized as he adopts the values and the behaviors which bring him social approval and save him from disapproval. Later this need to please his parents is generalized to other persons and eventually he comes to include himself as a socialized member of the social order. From this moment on, he is his own reward-giver or punisher, i.e., he has developed a conscience; any violation of his code results in feelings of anxiety and guilt. This is an important step: the individual becomes his own keeper and is guided not so much by fear of detection or of punishment as by an inner code of right and wrong. This internal code is much more severe than that imposed by external authority since, with an internalized code of values, the watchdog is on the alert, ready every minute of the day to generate anxiety for any transgression or even for thoughts and desires in this direction. The individual's conscience thus leaves him with relatively little choice but to act according to expectations.

It is also significant to note that the child's reactions at first are neither good nor bad in a moral sense; he simply tests various responses to situations and learns from his experiences to identify those which are encouraged and those which are condemned. This requires a good deal of trial and error under conditions of permissiveness and consistency in an atmosphere of love and acceptance in which the child learns to gauge the acceptability of his behavior and gradually shifts from behavior geared to external rewards and punishments to behavior that is based progressively more on internal constraints. This process extends over many years and involves the child's experiences at home, at school, at church, and in the community at large. If the total environment is sound and consistent, the child is likely to develop acceptable character traits.

VALUES

Because values are subjective, they have not until now been granted a high level of scientific respectability among psychologists. Yet values, along with attitudes, ideals, and other motivational concepts are such a significant part of the phenomenal field that we need to determine the conceptual properties to be attributed to them as well as to determine how they become established in the individual's life-space, how they become activated, and in what way values differ from other aspects of his motivational structure. Taylor (1960), for example, feels that the study of human values is of primary importance in the study of human motivation.

Behavior is affected by a hierarchy of values within the individual's self-structure. This hierarchy is phenomenological, and research has shown that children often give priority to trivial values while ignoring major values (Mitchell, 1943); they might, for example, rate sportsmanship higher on the continuum than kindness. In fact, few people organize their behavior in accordance with the true significance of the values involved. A person might be very sanctimonious about petty things while violating basic values, or he might subscribe to a given value in one situation and violate it in another. Society in general and teachers in particular have a responsibility to help children to clarify their values and to incorporate them into a meaningful self-concept capable of generating consistently desirable conduct. If we are to be successful in this area, we need teachers who themselves have fairly well-defined values which they display and express in consistent and significant ways so that children see that values are something one lives rather than something one talks about.

Society undermines the child's development of a clear system of values by presenting a relatively inconsistent pattern of moral practices at almost all levels of family, local, and political life. The same pattern of inconsistency too often prevails in school where teachers preach honesty, for example, and yet continually provide a situation which makes cheating almost necessary and almost always profitable. The Hartshorne and May study (1928) showed honesty to be relatively situational; Sister Gross (1946) found an essentially similar inconsistency. Equal inconsistency can probably be found in the school's way of promoting desirable values: What does it mean to proctor an examination supposedly held on the honor system?

Helping children develop a functional set of values is obviously a complex task; generally we know more about what is not going to work then we know about what will work. Moralizing, or even formal instruction in the values of honesty and integrity, generally remain at the abstract level; unless skillfully woven into the child's value-structure, they have relatively little effect upon his behavior. Sunday school instruction, for example, like much of the teaching in our schools, is too frequently at the verbal level, essentially divorced from the basic concepts of socialization, enlightened self-interest, attitudes, the self, and other aspects of human motivation. As a consequence, it seems it has not been particularly effective in helping children develop an integrated system of values capable of meeting the moral demands of modern life.

Of major interest is Jacob's recent summarization of the literature concerning value changes during college (Jacob, 1957). It would appear that the main effect of four years of higher education on the student's value system is to bring about a general acceptance of a body of standards and attitudes characteristic of college-bred men and women in America. The values of American college students are remarkably homogeneous considering the variety of their backgrounds and the relatively unrestricted opportunity and freedom in matters of personal thought. Whether students pursue a liberal arts program, an integrated general education curriculum, or a professional option is not reflected in their values, nor is there any solid evidence of a delayed reaction; the college alumnus exhibits no special trademark identifying his undergraduate curriculum.

Certain personality characteristics are apparently responsible for the immunity of student values to the rich educational opportunities provided by four years of college. Jacob suggests that some students have their minds set so rigidly, their outlook on human relations so stereotyped, and their reliance on authority so compulsive that they are incapable of understanding, much less accepting, new ideas. These students quail in the presence of conflict and uncertainty; they crave the right answer and recoil from creative discussion. Jacob pictures the current student generation as gloriously content in its present status and in its outlook toward the future. They are self-centered, aspiring above all to material gratification for themselves and their families. The traditional moral values of sincerity, honesty, integrity, and loyalty are apparently esteemed but there is little inclination to censor laxity, which the students consider to be widespread. There is little inclination to contribute voluntarily to the public welfare.[2] In short, Jacob reports few changes in values during the college years, with the most striking of the few changes that can be noted being in the direction of greater conformity to the prevailing profile.

MORAL DEVELOPMENT

The question of moral development can be approached from a number of viewpoints. Jones (1954) refers to the conflicting theory of moral development in children as indicative of the difficulty of arriving at a comprehensive and integrated concept of moral character. He notes that the mainsprings of moral behavior are probably not few and simple but rather many and complex. As Peck and Havighurst (1960, p. 5) point out:

[2] In contradiction to this point of view is the commendable participation of prospective teachers as volunteers in various projects for the education of culturally disadvantaged children and the widespread involvement of college students in civil rights and Peace Corps activities. Also to be mentioned, although more difficult to interpret as to motivation, are the student demonstrations, teach-ins, and riots.

"There is perhaps no study of human behavior more fraught with the risk of subjective bias and culture-bound prejudice than is the study of moral character."

The older view of character was oriented to the development of sound moral habits; it emphasized moral knowledge and rigid conformity to rules of moral conduct. Unfortunately, habits tend to be narrow; habits formed under adult supervision rarely carry over into situations in which the child is on his own. Character must be based on something more substantial, such as well-defined attitudes and values. The child must have contact with a variety of examples of a given standard of moral behavior in different settings so that he can visualize morality in its different manifestations. Because moral behavior tends to revolve around unconscious motivation, it is also necessary that it be generalized through the verbalization of underlying principles acting as a tool, not only for considering the present but also for reconstructing the past and planning for the future.

Knowledge of right and wrong is not enough. Delinquents have been found to have more moral and religious knowledge than nondelinquents (Bartlett and Harris, 1936). However, even though knowledge does not guarantee proper conduct, we must not underestimate its role in character development. Knowledge is not a sufficient condition but it is a necessary condition if we insist that, to be truly moral, behavior must be deliberately selected with the welfare of others in mind. Good character training incorporates a balance between the development of insight into what constitutes moral conduct and practice in implementing these insights into a pattern of enlightened sociomoral behavior.

Moral standards develop according to the same principles as underlie other forms of learning; Havighurst and Taba (1949) suggest that character is learned in three ways: [a] through reward and punishment; [b] through unconscious imitation; and [c] through reflective thinking. To the extent that the child learns desirable behavior in accordance with the principles of reinforcement (Jones, 1954), a significant aspect of successful character formation lies in making ethically and socially acceptable behavior more satisfying than undesirable behavior. The child needs to realize that honesty is the best policy; that greater satisfaction can be obtained by being considerate than by being inconsiderate, by working for the welfare of others than by taking advantage of the situation. Rewards such as approval are useful means of making sure that certain responses are satisfying. They are beneficial to the child's overall character development, however, only to the extent that they become progressively more unnecessary as the child gets inner satisfaction from compliance with the standards he has internalized.

Unfortunately, the various social forces playing upon the child are not only often in conflict with each other but many are self-contradictory. Thus, both desirable and undesirable behavior are at times punished and rewarded as the child is intermittently (if not indiscriminately) ignored and praised for his honesty while the cheater is both punished and allowed to profit from his cheating. The result is confusion and ambivalent attitudes, the net vector strength of which as it leads to moral behavior is generally weak and easily overcome by conflicting motives which are operative in the situation. Jones feels that parents and teachers wait too long and overlook too many opportunities for giving early moral training. They are often so lackadaisical in enforcing basic rules that children see conformity as an optional matter. After a period of such inconsistency, it becomes difficult to reorient the child to the internalization of more adequate standards, especially since our relatively inconsistent and only partially moral society is likely to provide intermittent reinforcement of violations.

Character involves a deliberate choice among moral alternatives. Consequently, even though we expect someone with a highly developed character to be a person of action, he will also be somewhat hesitant and introspective, and he might be less spontaneous and devil-may-care than average. On the other hand, even though moral training implies the development of conditioned anxiety, we must not conceive of morality as a matter of generalized habits of inhibition or of resistance to temptation, but rather as positive forces in the orientation of the individual's behavior.

Parents and teachers affect the character of children through some or all of the principles of learning. They provide models for the stimulation of the growth of the self and the development of feelings of personal worth, which is at the very core of character formation. Teachers often exert their strongest influence on the character development of their students just by being the kind of people they are. Subject matter can also serve as a potential contributor to the value systems of boys and girls; the school offers many opportunities to discuss problems of conduct and to arrive at a better understanding of what constitutes moral behavior. Literature is full of people worthy of emulation and of episodes having definite character-building possibilities. Inspiring thought along these lines without moralizing is likely to be more profitable than simply hammering away at facts. We need to think of a subject less as an end in itself and more as an instrument for developing life lessons, for only as these are achieved does education have any real reason for being. The school is actually in an excellent position from the standpoint of character development: not only is the child still in his formative years when he comes to school but the years of his attendance are characterized by increasing capacity for understanding the reasons underlying desirable behavior. Besides, the school provides a laboratory for learning moral lessons by putting into sharp contrast rewards for appropriate behavior and punishment for improper behavior.

THE ROLE OF THE HOME

The home is undoubtedly the greatest single factor in character formation. Peck and Havighurst (1960) suggest that the peer group appears to be less of an originator than simply a reinforcer of the moral values and behavior patterns developed in the home; the school likewise seems to crystallize character rather than to shape it. As has been noted in Chapter 3, the young child first develops dependency needs as a result of the warmth and acceptance of his parents. In time, parents begin to impose demands and conditions upon their love and he comes to realize the need for acceptable behavior. As we also noted, the internalization of moral standards and the development of guilt and anxiety are best promoted when the young child's feelings of acceptance and personal worth are maintained at a high level.

Conscience grows out of the parent-child relationship in which the child gradually takes over and exercises the same control over the ego that the parents would have exercised over him. If he learns to depend on his parents, he has something to work for in meeting their expectations; he has something to lose if he fails. If, on the other hand, the child-rearing practices to which he is subjected are punitive, then his parents and other people like his parents are simply perceived as the possessors of punitive properties. Under these conditions, why should he add himself to the list of his tormentors? Why should he become socialized if the only reward for so doing is the privilege of punishing himself? He then has no reason to internalize parental standards and, therefore, remains low in anxiety and oriented toward direct self-gratification with his only concern that of avoiding punishment. Children from autocratic homes, for example, tend to be fearful of authority, untrusting, rule-bound, resentful, and lacking in genuine affection and in independent judgment (Frenkel-Brunswik, 1946).

Parents frequently deny the child certain satisfactions for the sake of denying them, presumably on the premise, not so much that denial will promote fortitude and frustration tolerance but rather that giving in on everything will convert the child into a spoiled, demanding brat, interested only in his immediate self-gratification. This does not make psychological sense. It is only when the child learns to balance one satisfaction against another and to organize his motives to the point of providing such a balance that moral growth ensues. Furthermore, it is only when the environment is friendly and free from undue frustration and privation that the child can experiment with foregoing certain satisfactions with the reasonable guarantee that he will get greater satisfactions at a later date. In a hostile environment, one gets what he can—now!

Conscience consists of the moral values the child has internalized. Unless he establishes these standards of right and wrong, his only basis for acting properly will be external control. Difficulty arises when discipline is so inconsistent that the child cannot decipher which behaviors earn him approval and which behaviors earn him disapproval. Difficulty also arises when discipline is so severe that he develops a fear of authority and ambivalent attitudes of hostility and resentment toward adults. As a result, he becomes either unmanageable and capable of being governed only by external punishment, or, on the contrary, he develops rigidity of conduct based on severe guilt feelings which tend to be repressed, thus preventing the behavior from coming out in the open where its acceptability can be appraised. The result is a blind allegiance to rules for rules' sake.

PIAGET'S CONCEPT OF MORAL DEVELOPMENT

A significant series of studies of the development of moral concepts is that of Piaget (1932), whose contributions to the field of child development, especially in the area of logical and moral concepts, are receiving increasing recognition. His research has been oriented toward the identification of the various stages through which the child's development proceeds. According to Piaget, the first stage in his development of moral and ethical behavior is one of blind obedience in which his concept of right and wrong is based on what his parents permit or forbid. His interpretation of a rule is literal; he operates by the letter of the law. A rule is a rule: it is sacred and inviolable. He also expects absolute regularity in his world. He wants to count on things being the way he perceives them. When he is told a story a second time, he insists on hearing it with exactly the same details as he did the first time. Nor does he tolerate deviations in his relationships with others. In the case of damage, it is the absolute extent of damage, rather than the intent, that counts; breaking three cups accidentally is a more serious offense than breaking one cup on purpose. Violations call for punishment by the authority whose rule has been violated, rather than retaliation by, or compensation of, the victim.

By contrast, the older child judges conduct in terms of its intent rather than of its material consequences, and, at the approximate age of twelve, his concept of justice passes from a rigid inflexibile notion of right and wrong to a sense of equity which takes into account the subtleties of situational circumstances. As he develops a better understanding of social roles, and recognizes the reciprocity between himself and others, he gradually sees that rules derive their sacredness from mutual agreement rather than from authority, and he gradually moves from moral behavior based on external authority to a more general and more adequate conception of morality based on an internal code.

A fairly large body of research on Piaget's conception of moral development has been accumulated.[3] His work has been criticized for failure to meet the standards of scientific objectivity set for themselves by American psychologists, and it is felt by some that perhaps his conclusions are too dogmatic. Some of his ideas have received relative confirmation while others have been questioned. Bandura and McDonald (1963), for example, did not find the sharp demarcation between stages postulated by Piaget. There is also evidence to the effect that the child shifts from moral realism to moral relativism at a younger age than Piaget has indicated, that this varies with the individual child, and that it is not as predetermined by heredity or by age as Piaget seems to suggest. Durkin (1959, 1961) concluded that Piaget has minimized environmental effects on the development of the child's ideas of justice. Parochial school children tend to have more mature moral concepts than public school children, for example. More fundamental is the fact that the specific level of conscience development which the child displays varies with the specific situation (Boehm and Nass, 1962). Some children display concepts of justice ranging from very mature in some situations to rather immature in others, with the differences in the same individual from situation to situation at times much greater than class differences. On the other hand, Piaget's work has been highly stimulating and, even though his findings may have to be modified in part to allow for socioeconomic, cultural, and individual differences, it actually represents a major advance in the investigation of moral development.

CHARACTER (PERSONALITY) PATTERNS

A most productive study of character formation is that presented by Peck and Havighurst (1960) who first identify six components contributing to overall maturity of character:

[a] Moral stability: the ability to follow the moral code willingly
[b] Ego strength: accuracy of insight, rational judgment, and appropriate affect
[c] Superego strength: the strength of inner control over behavior (conscience)
[d] Spontaneity: direct expression of wishes and feelings
[e] Friendliness: general warmth of feeling for others
[f] Hostility-guilt complex

On the basis of the relative strength of these six factors, the authors define five basic character patterns which they describe as follows:

[a] The amoral (low in moral stability, ego strength, superego strength, and hostility-guilt): Such a person has not internalized moral values and

---

[3] See also evaluation of Piaget's work concerning logical development (Chapter 9).

disregards the moral connotations of his behavior and its effect on others. He is the center of the universe and others are simply means of self-gratification. If his basic attitudes are hostile, he is apt to commit delinquent acts; on the other hand, if he has a positive view of others, he may be charming but irresponsible. He may form temporary alliances with people but he will abandon them the minute he sees a richer source of gratification. This is the picture of the one-year-old child. Adults who exhibit such a pattern are said to be fixated at the infantile level and, in extreme cases, are known as psychopathic personalities.

[b] The expedient (below average in ego-strength, superego strength, moral stability, and friendliness; high in spontaneity and hostility-guilt): Such a person is primarily self-centered; he considers other people's welfare only in order to gain his personal ends. He behaves in ways society defines as moral only as long as it suits his purposes. He may be honest in order to obtain a position of advantageous reputation, but, if he can gain more by being dishonest, he does so. He is the only person who really counts, but he is more aware of the advantages of conforming to the social requirements in order to achieve long-term advantages.

The key to his low level of morality is his me-first attitude. Such a motivational pattern is characteristic of many young children who have learned to respect the reward-punishment power of adults and to behave correctly whenever adults are present. External sanctions are always necessary to guide and control their behavior and to keep it moral, for in the absence of such control they immediately relax into doing what they please.

[c] The conforming (moderate in ego and superego strength and friendliness; low in moral stability, spontaneity, and hostility-guilt): This individual has one general internalized principle: he conforms to all the rules of the group; he does what others do and his only anxiety centers on possible disapproval. He has no generalized or abstract principle of honesty, integrity, or loyalty. He follows a system of literal rules specific for each occasion, with no overall consistency as to the degree of morality in different situations. If the rules that he lives by call for kindness to some people and cruelty to others, that is all right. He differs from the expedient character pattern in that social conformity is accepted as good for its own sake. A conformist may frequently ignore chances of personal advantage if they require departure from prescribed rules of conduct. He has a crude conscience and may feel very uncomfortable about departing from the rules, but he does not follow the rules for a moral purpose.

[d] The irrational-conscientious (weak to moderate ego strength; low in friendliness; high in hostility-guilt, superego strength, and moral stability): This individual typically judges a given act according to his own standards of what is right and wrong. The issue is not conformity to group rules but rather conformity to a code which he has internalized. If he approves of an act, he is so honest that he carries it out whether or not

people approve. He appeals to an abstract principle of honesty and applies it as he interprets it to any situation whether or not it is relevant. If he fails to live up to his own standards, he suffers anxiety-guilt, i.e., a feeling of having violated his own integrity.

The irrational component is visible in his rigidity in applying a preconceived principle somewhat in the manner of the conformist; an act is good or bad because he defines it as such, not necessarily because it has positive or negative effects upon others. This is a blind, rigid morality best represented by Javet in Victor Hugo's *Les Misérables*. It is characteristic of children who have internalized parental rules but who have not learned that rules are man-made and intended to serve a functional human purpose. This approach is reasonably effective in ensuring outward moral behavior at all times; if the parental code fits in well with the social code which has been produced by long and careful testing of what is good for people, then it probably contains few seriously destructive elements, but the irrational-conscientious pattern can operate just as well in the case of a criminal subgroup.

[e] The rational-altruistic (high in ego and superego strength, moral stability, spontaneity, and friendliness; low in hostility-guilt): This represents the highest level of moral maturity. Such a person not only has a stable set of moral principles by which he guides his actions, but he also assesses the results of his behavior objectively against the criterion of whether or not it serves others as well as himself. In the ideal case, he is dependably honest, responsible, and loyal because he sees such behavior as contributing to human well-being. He does what is morally right because he wants to, not because it is the thing to do. This kind of behavior involves emotional maturity and personal and social adjustment characterized by the use of one's potentialities to the fullest. Here again is the fully functioning person—the person in the process of *becoming*.

Peck and Havighurst point out that there is need for society to agree on the kind of character children should emulate. It must be recognized, for example, that even though the school is vitally concerned with the moral development of the child, its emphasis on the promotion of conformity is too often an orientation toward the irrational-conscientious character pattern. Effective morality demands the understanding of the nature, meaning, and purposes of the rules and principles by which one guides his behavior. The rigid inculcation of cultural standards without explanation of why conformity is expected coupled with inconsistency in discipline lead to behavioral inflexibility by their discouragement of cognitive clarity; they force the child to develop a behavioral pattern which is rigid and unchangeable simply because it is not clear. This lack of clarity concerning the basic rules of society would present no major problem in a stable culture in which the standards and expectations remain constant from generation to generation, but it would be unfortunate should the child ever need to improvise either because society or his role has changed. The school needs to clarify how it can best cultivate rational-altruistic character in children as an aspect of the process of *becoming*.

HIGHLIGHTS OF THE CHAPTER

There is no more important aspect of the work of the school than the development by the child of positive attitudes that will direct his behavior along constructive lines. The organization of this text around the dynamics of human behavior, the self-concept, the phenomenal field, motivation, and self-actualization emphasizes this viewpoint. The prospective teacher needs to be acquainted with the following highlights of the present chapter:

[a]

Attitudes are an important aspect of the self-concept; operationally, they incorporate an affective, a cognitive, and an action component.

[b]

The development of attitudes is best explained through a multiple approach. Attitudes may be the outcome of imitation of significant persons with whom the child has identified. Teachers need to be solid citizens who can inspire children and with whom children can identify in the formation of sound values. Attitudes can also occur as the result of deliberate teaching and as by-products of emotionally toned experiences.

[c]

Once developed, attitudes tend to resist change, especially when they are part of the anchor system of the individual's personality structure. Generally, a relentless and systematic but subtle campaign is more effective than an incidental approach or a head-on attack.

[d]

The school cannot make the development of attitudes on the part of the children delegated to its care a matter of chance. Indeed, it has no greater task than the promotion of sound attitudes and character through a program of attitude and character development which permeates the whole educative process. Arguments to the contrary notwithstanding, the school is charged with the responsibility of molding the child in the dominant values of society, and, within the framework of democratic processes, indoctrination in these major values is not so much a right as it is a duty.

[e]

The school has not been too successful in promoting favorable attitudes toward itself, its teachers, its curriculum, and in some cases, the values for which it stands. Special efforts should be devoted to making the curriculum more suitable, the demands more realistic, and the classroom atmosphere more pleasant.

[f]

Prejudice is an example of negative attitudes. It generally involves an insecure person who needs to maintain strong defenses in order to protect a weak ego.

[g]

Character development is a major component of the socialization of the child. Love-oriented child-rearing practices leading to early dependency together with the withholding of love in cases of unacceptable behavior and a certain freedom to explore are essential to the adequate socialization of the child and the internalization of social constraints into a social-moral conscience. True morality operates at the rational-conscientious level; it implies more than compliance with the demands of the social order.

[h]

The development of a sound pattern of values is frequently undermined by conflicting standards existing among and within the various social agencies and forces with which the child comes into contact. The fact that the influence of a college education on values is relatively nil is a tribute to the ineffectiveness of an incidental program.

[i]

Piaget's investigation of the growth of the child's moral concepts from moral absolutism to moral relativism constitutes a significant contribution to the field.

SOURCES OF RELATED MATERIAL

Adelson, J., "The teacher as a model," in N. Sanford (ed.), *The American College*. New York: John Wiley & Sons, Inc., 1962. Pp. 396–417.

DeBoer, J. J., "What shall we teach in high school English?" *Sch. Rev.*, 67: 305–319, 1959.

Dreikurs, R., *Character Education and Spiritual Values in an Anxious Age*. Boston: The Beacon Press, 1952.

Elam, Stanley M., et al., "The school's responsibility for moral education," *Phi Delta Kappan*, 46: 41–94, 1964.

Francis, E. F., "Fundamentals of character education," *Sch. Rev.*, 70: 345–357, 1962.

Hovland, Carl I., "Yale studies of communication and persuasion," in W. W. Charters and N. L. Gage (eds.), *Readings in the Social Psychology of Education*. Boston: Allyn and Bacon, Inc., 1963. Pp. 239–253.

Jacob, Philip E., *Changing Values in College*. New York: Harper & Row, Publishers, 1957. (See also *NEA J.*, 47: 35–38, 1958).

Jones, V., "Character development in children: An objective approach," in

L. Carmichael, (ed.), *Manual of Child Psychology.* New York: John Wiley & Sons, Inc., 1954. Pp. 781–832.

Katz, B. and E. Stotland, "A preliminary statement to a theory of attitude structure and change," in S. Koch (ed.), *Psychology: A Study of a Science,* Vol. 3. New York: McGraw-Hill, 1959. Pp. 423–475.

Kohlberg, Lawrence, "Moral development and identification," in H. W. Stevenson (ed.), *Child Psychology.* 62d Yearbook, National Society for the Study of Education, Pt. I. Chicago: University of Chicago Press, 1963. Pp. 277–332.

Mitton, B. L. and D. B. Harris, "The development of responsibility in children," *Elem. sch. J.,* 54: 268–277, 1954.

Plant, Walter T., *Personality Changes Associated with a College Education.* C.R.P., No. S-042. San Jose, Calif.: San Jose State College, 1964.

Rogers, Carl R., "Toward a modern approach to values: The valuing process in the mature person," *J. abnorm. soc. Psychol.,* 63: 160–67, 1964.

Sears, Robert R., "The growth of conscience," in I. Iscoe and H. W. Stevenson (eds.), *Personality Development in Children.* Austin, Tex.: University of Texas Press, 1960. Pp. 92–111.

Webster, H., "Changes in attitudes during college," *J. educ. Psychol.,* 49: 109–117, 1958.

QUESTIONS AND PROJECTS

1

[a] How might the school approach the problem of cheating once it has become widespread? of general violation of parking restrictions?

[b] Should teachers appoint "monitors" when they have to leave the classroom? How can such situations be made into effective learning situations?

2

What is the basis of socioeconomic differences in attitudes toward the school? toward education? toward certain moral values?

3

How might teachers of English at the junior high school level overcome the negative attitudes of boys toward the feminine overtones of poetry?

4

Why do mass media like television have such impact on children's attitudes despite a relatively haphazard approach, while parents and schools—operating on a supposedly systematic basis—appear to be so inept?

CHAPTER 18

Personal and Social Adjustment

> No person has an unlimited amount of energy
> available and the anxious child invests so much
> of his energy in his problems that there is little
> left over to conduct the ordinary affairs of life.
> *Peck and Mitchell, 1962, p. 15*

Of special significance among the major educational changes of the past two or three decades is the school's increased concern over the child's personal and social growth. From a rigid emphasis on academic learning, often at considerable cost in terms of his adjustment, schools have come to recognize the importance of the latter, and have not only organized elaborate guidance programs designed to promote the more personal and social aspects of development, but have also made the classroom more guidance- and adjustment-oriented. The primary responsibility for the child's adjustment lies with the parents who set the basic personality pattern through the security they provide, particularly in his early years. The teacher's influence is only slightly less important, for it is he who holds the key to whether the experiences the child undergoes in school will lead to satisfaction and self-fulfillment—or to frustration and self-defeat.

485

THE NATURE OF ADJUSTMENT

THE CONCEPT OF ADJUSTMENT

Throughout life the individual has to adjust to environmental as well as internal demands. Thus, he is continually eating, drinking, seeking approval, trying to gain status. The adjustments he makes in response to these demands are not always wise from the standpoint of his long-term welfare but they are nevertheless adjustments in the sense of attempts to satisfy his needs.

Adjustment may be defined as the process by means of which the individual seeks to maintain physiological and psychological equilibrium and propel himself toward self-enhancement. Implied is a state of harmonious relationship between the individual and his environment. Adjustment is specific to a given individual under specific conditions and "adjustment" is meaningful only in terms of "adjusted to what?" Adjustment is relative and temporary. A person can never be *adjusted*, for no matter how contented he may be over the fine meal he has just had, he will be out of harmony with his environment in a matter of hours if his next meal is not forthcoming. Furthermore, he almost invariably has personal or business problems that disturb his adjustment. When we speak of promoting the child's adjustment, we really mean we are trying to develop his capacity for *adjusting*, on the premise that, if he can learn to deal with the problems confronting him today, he will be adequate in meeting the problems of tomorrow.

A question may be raised as to the desirability of promoting adjustment: is it in society's best interest to have people adjust to conditions of poverty and crime, for example? A different aspect of the same question concerns the extent to which progress on both the social and the personal level is being promoted by maladjusted people. The producer, the achiever, the reformer are maladjusted in the sense that they are not in harmony with the conditions they find. We do not want the child in school to be too content with his present ignorance: we want him to feel a certain degree of tension, to be sufficiently anxious so that he will learn more adequate behavior.

Adjustment refers to the adequacy of the behavior patterns the individual habitually uses to satisfy his needs. Inasmuch as everyone has, at all times, multiple needs to satisfy, everyone is perpetually faced with adjustment problems, and, therefore, is potentially capable of being adjusted or maladjusted, depending on the adequacy of his need-satisfying behavior. A person is considered maladjusted, for instance, if, while he concentrates on satisfying his immediate needs, he actually increases the severity of the problem of satisfying his future or his more basic needs, e.g., the child who habitually daydreams rather than develop the skills that would permit him to convert his fantasies into actualities. Adjustment also implies that the individual must satisfy his needs within the framework of the expectations and constraints of the social order, for unless he satisfies his needs in ways consistent with social standards, he is likely to increase rather than alleviate his problems of adjustment.

The adequacy of the adjustment the individual makes depends in considerable measure on the severity of the problems with which he is faced. If the situations to which he must adjust are in line with his potentialities, he can generally resolve his problems without having to resort to atypical behavior. Severe and continued frustration, on the other hand, tends to lead to maladjustment as the individual in desperation grasps at any straw that promises even a momentary reduction in the tension associated with the frustration of his needs.

Conflict, Frustration, and Anxiety

The question of adjustment revolves around such concepts as conflict, frustration, and anxiety. If all conflicts were to be resolved automatically, the individual would have no adjustment problem and, of course, no cause for learning; the fact that difficulties arise is the basis for both self-realization and self-destruction. Frustration and anxiety are inevitable and generally desirable components of any conflict situation, for they lead the individual to redouble as well as redirect his efforts to resolve his problem. This does not deny the wisdom of avoiding frustrating situations from which nothing but further frustration can be expected.

Lewin (1935) lists four types of conflict situations:

[a] *Approach-approach,* in which there are two or more positive reinforcements in opposite and conflicting directions (This is the case of the donkey caught halfway between two great piles of hay, who, being unable to choose one in preference to the other, starved to death.)

[b] *Avoidance-avoidance,* where two negative reinforcements are present, one or the other of which cannot be avoided (The student may find himself a couple of weeks before the final examination with the choice of withdrawing from school or risking failure in his courses.)

[c] *Approach-avoidance,* in which a given situation has both positive and negative reinforcement (The student may have to choose between a good grade and the approval of his peers.)

[d] *Double approach-avoidance,* in which each of the alternatives in a given situation has both attraction and repulsion value

Frequently, the source of conflict lies in the lack of clear perception of the alternatives. It is also possible for a person to avoid conflict by acting on a problem without considering the alternatives; the headaches may come later, of course.

Anxiety is an unpleasant emotional state involving an ill-defined feeling of apprehension occurring in situations in which the self is threatened. The anxious individual is afraid something terrible is going to happen, but he does not know what or when. As a result he is tense, fearful, disturbed, and driven to do something to reduce the unpleasant state of affairs. Anxiety is normal when there is a reason for the apprehension and the response is constructive and generally proportional to the danger involved. The difficulty arises when anxiety becomes so severe that ineffectiveness or even disintegration of behavior sets in. Mira (1943) points to the complete disintegration of behavior that sometimes occurs in combat. As danger mounts, control becomes increasingly difficult; the individual becomes obsessed with the danger; he can no longer inhibit the restlessness, tremors, and other overt signs of anxiety. Thought and judgment deteriorate and actions become erratic and poorly coordinated; the panic-stricken soldier may rush wildly about, laughing, shouting, crying in rapid succession, scarcely aware of what he is doing. This reaction may last for days in soldiers exposed to prolonged fire. Marshall (1947) estimates that less than one third of the soldiers under orders to fire actually fire their rifles, and then not always in the direction of the enemy.

The classic study of the consequences of experimentally induced frustration is that conducted by Maier et al. (1940), in which rats developed behavioral fixity (see Chapter 4). What is interesting is the amazing strength of the fixation: strong punishment persistently administered did not seem to break the stereotyped reaction. Marquart (1946) found similar nonadaptive behavior in people; when confronted with a difficult but not insoluble problem, many just kept repeating a solution which had been adequate at one time but which they knew was no longer effective. Fixation is probably involved in many forms of inadequate behavior. For the very young child, temper tantrums, thumb-sucking, and aggression are reasonable patterns of adjustment but they become a problem if continued beyond the developmental stage to which they belong. Too vigorous an attempt to have him shed these inadequate behavioral patterns may simply fixate them; the child who puts on a temper tantrum comes out ahead sufficiently often to produce fixation, especially because his anxiety restricts his perceptual field so that he is blinded to more adequate alternatives.

A somewhat similar phenomenon is noted in experimental neurosis. Pavlov found that experimental dogs conditioned to respond differentially to a circle and an ellipse underwent disintegration of behavior as the circle and ellipse were made to look progressively more alike. Not only did their ability to discriminate deteriorate badly, but they began to whine and struggle and finally had to be taken out of the experiment. They had developed experimentally produced neuroses as a result of the conflict caused by inability to make the required discriminations. In similar experiments by Masserman (1943), cats developed a phobic reaction to the experimental apparatus; in fact, some displayed behavior closely paralleling that of disturbed people. There is, however, one significant difference between experimental and ordinary neurosis: the former is likely to be situational, i.e., conditioned to a specific stimulus or situation. Animals tend to be protected from overinvolvement by their inability to engage in symbolic and linguistic behavior. Man, on the other hand, generalizes and extends his fears and conflicts because he can face conflict symbolically, even when the situation does not demand it. In fact, he anticipates and generalizes his anxiety from one situation to another, thereby producing an ever-increasing spiral of neurotic involvement leading to a generalized fear of himself. Included as part of the cycle are perceptual distortions, repressions, progressive neurotic stupidity, increased social and self-disapproval, intensified anxiety and guilt, leading to further distortion and further stupidity—all on a self-sustaining cycle (Shoben, 1953).

The concepts of frustration and anxiety are relatively basic to all theories of psychology. According to field theories, for example, to the extent that tension causes a reduction in the variety of the individual's available life-space patterns, frustration tends to produce regression to a more infantile level of behavior. Horney (1937) makes basic anxiety the central concept of her theory of neurotic behavior; she postulates that basic anxiety is aroused by any situation that makes the child fearful. As a result of his attempts to alleviate the aroused anxieties, the child learns certain modes of adjustment. If he learns to cope with anxiety by turning to his mother for security, for example, he may develop a neurotic need for affection and approval.

Two major theories of frustration have been advanced, neither of which has complete acceptance. The frustration-aggression hypothesis (Dollard et al., 1939) presents aggression as the natural consequence of frustration—or more correctly, frustration as the natural antecedent of aggression. Actually, our culture places a premium on certain forms of aggression. Even our schools promote the image of American society as a vigorous, competitive social order in which initiative, enterprise, leadership, and ambition are both prized and rewarded. The idea of doing things with all one's might, never giving up, trying and trying again, and other maxims implying that the world steps aside for the man who knows where he is going, all emphasize aggressiveness so that aggression is not so much a matter of maladjustment as of social "adjustment." In the middle classes, aggression is channeled into conventional forms of initiative and overcoming of obstacles; in the lower classes, on the other hand, it appears too frequently in the form of outright—and not particularly constructive—physical attack.

The second major theory concerning frustration is that of Barker et al. (1943) which ties frustration to regression. The theory is based on their well-known experiments in which the play activities of preschool children were rated as to constructiveness both before and after a frustration situation. The children were first allowed to play in a room containing standard play materials. Then a partition was removed and the children were allowed to play with much more elaborate and attractive toys; then they were returned to the standard toy situation and a wire screen was lowered to separate the standard and the more elaborate setup. This was the frustration period: they could play only with the less attractive toys while the more desirable toys remained visible but inaccessible. The children's play during the frustration period was far less constructive than it had been during the earlier free-play situation; they displayed significantly more escape reactions and more aggressive behavior. It must be recognized, on the other hand, that not all the children regressed; a few actually improved.

Learning and Adjustment

Adjustment has to be approached from the standpoint of learning, for adjustment reactions—whether constructive or detrimental to the individual's welfare—are learned according to the same principles as govern the learning of any other material. Adjustment patterns may develop through a long and complicated process; they may occur unconsciously and outside of deliberate intent; they may have a partial basis in heredity, but they are nevertheless learned. Thus, according to reinforcement theory, as a consequence of the confirmation or denial of the adjustment he makes in a given situation, the individual learns not only a certain response to a specific situation but also certain response patterns for dealing with situations in general. Some response patterns are adequate and effective from the standpoint of self-fulfillment; others are unhealthy. Yet the individual may persist in their use despite their shortcomings. Perhaps he does not know of other approaches; more frequently he is afraid of the risk involved in leaving the safety of his present (albeit inadequate) position to strike out in a more constructive direction. A person can withdraw, for example; this is sometimes the wisest thing to do, but, more commonly, he had better develop competence if he is not to become progressively more inadequate in relation to the situation. And again we need to remember that unwise approaches are sometimes reinforced often enough to be learned and also to make them particularly resistant to extinction.

We need to consider the development of adjustment patterns from the standpoint of the various theories of learning as presented in Chapter 2. Probably the best way of dealing with nonadjustive reactions, for example, is to ignore them; spanking the screaming child is often rewarding since it brings attention with it. According to reinforcement theory, the individual learns those reactions which provide relief from the tension connected with the frustration of some of his needs. Maladjustment results from the reinforcement of shortsighted approaches; neurotic behavior, for example, provides only partial relief, and yet, because it does provide some relief, it is often learned in lieu of a more constructive approach to the problems of life. From a cognitive point of view, maladjustment reflects lack of perceptual insight. All behavior has a purpose according to the individual's interpretation of the situation; this interpretation may be shortsighted, of course, when his overconcern with the immediate situation causes him to select goals that are not compatible with his long-range welfare.

The development of adjustment patterns must also be considered from the standpoint of anxiety. The fact that learning takes place only when the individual's present behavior patterns are no longer adequate in meeting situational demands implies that inadequacy is characteristic of any learning situation. A situation with which the individual can cope using his present behavior patterns is simply handled routinely. But when the situation is such that he cannot attain his goals through the use of past response patterns, he is faced with an adjustment problem, and the greater his insecurity, the more likely he is to develop atypical and ineffective behavior.

Once learned, behavior patterns tend to maintain themselves through the satisfaction they provide, and they develop into habit motives, thus giving stability to behavior; hence, Shaffer and Shoben's definition of personality (1956) as the individual's persistent tendencies to make certain kinds and qualities of adjustment. As a result, ineffective behavior, for example, may become such an integral part of the total personality that it is highly resistant to change. It is especially resistant to change in the case of the insecure person who cannot afford to experiment with more adequate modes of adjustment. If he keeps trying long enough the motivated individual can generally overcome or circumvent the obstacle to his goal or reach a reasonably satisfactory substitute. If this behavior is completely ineffective, he will be forced to continue trying other reactions until some degree of satisfaction is achieved. There are times, however, when the individual's behavior is only partially ineffective, leading to goals that are only partially satisfying. Unfortunately, since it provides some satisfaction, such behavior will tend to be learned in accordance with the principle of reinforcement even though it is not in the individual's best interest from the standpoint of his long-term adjustment.

It may also be that the individual reaches a goal, which, although satisfying in terms of his motivation, may involve him in difficulty with social standards. If he is not sold on the standards involved, his only concern lies in not getting caught. On the other hand, to the extent that society is successful in having him internalize its rules and regulations, he will not be able to violate social constraints without automatically upsetting some value of importance to his continued adjustment. There may also be times when he cannot attain his goal without outside help. This may entail coaching in a special skill or perhaps psychological counseling, which, when provided, will allow the individual to achieve reasonable adjustment. On the other hand, the obstacle may be of such magnitude and resistance in relation to the individual's potentialities, that he may be completely overwhelmed. He is then likely to become desperate and aggravate rather than solve his problem. His only salvation may lie in being removed from the situation or in being provided with considerable support. If this is not possible, his only escape may be an emotional breakdown, with possible eventual recovery with psychiatric help and improvement in the conditions which caused the difficulty.

PERSONALITY

At a superficial level, personality refers to the unique and distinctive characteristics which set one person apart from another, and as such relates to the reaction one evokes from his fellowmen. Personality is more than this; it represents the whole person, his physical, mental, social, and emotional assets and liabilities and their integration into a behavioral pattern which is characteristic of, and peculiar to, the individual. It has particular reference to the concept of the total organism interacting dynamically with his environment, i.e., affecting as well as being affected by the field forces of his psychological world as he attempts to attain his multiple purposes. What is important, however, is the integration of the personality acting as a totality and, of course, the direction in which the totality is oriented. We must recognize, for example, that a person may have one personality at home and a different personality at the office, so that personality cannot be considered apart from the situation in which the various traits and characteristics are exhibited.

Yet behavioral consistency is fundamental to the concept of personality, for only then can the individual remain the person that he is. Because personality is derived in part through identification with a variety of people, the child may at first display inconsistencies in his personality makeup. He gradually finds himself, however, as he experiments with various roles and finally achieves personal identity, at least in connection with his dominant values. Although adults display inconsistency of behavior, this inconsistency, as we have seen in connection with the self-concept, is probably from the standpoint of the observer rather than from that of the individual's own perception of the situation. Personality orientation also reveals considerable consistency over the years. Kagan and Moss (1960) found that girls who were highly dependent upon their mothers at age six through ten were still highly dependent upon their families as adults. Dependent behavior was not as stable for males, presumably because it conflicts with the male self-concept and is in-hibited by dependent boys as they mature.[1] It should also be noted that once a person gets known, people expect certain kinds of behavior from him and reinforce the role he has selected or they have selected for him. Personality stability then becomes a function of environmental stability.

Psychologists from the days of Freud have placed particular emphasis on the role of early experiences in determining the individual's basic personality. Considerable support for this position comes from animal experimentation; Hunt (1941), for example, found that rats deprived in infancy hoarded more pellets as adults than their nondeprived controls. A certain amount of the immature behavior displayed by children and adults is the result of intermittent reinforcement received in the formative years. Rosenzweig (1954), for example, suggests that the infant is con-ditioned to use crying as a form of communication by the failure of adults to respond to his other modes of expression. The mother, instead of recognizing his precrying cues and promptly satisfying his needs, waits until distress reaches a point where he begins to cry. Then she provides relief which conditions him to substitute crying for the more natural squirming and smacking of the lips.

The child maintains himself in precarious equilibrium between his external world, to whose expectations he must conform at least to a degree in order to be accepted, and his own private idiosyncratic world, which he must protect and maintain, often at considerable psychological cost. He is continually reorienting himself to the present, rehearsing the past, and modifying his perspective. As a result, he is continually discover-ing himself anew, revising his self-image with each revision within his world. When experiences are traumatic, however, this reorganization may be too difficult to manage and, as the emotional concomitants persist, his personality may become progressively more incongruous and jeopardize his capacity for further growth. Frank (1955) suggests that play serves an important function in this connection by translating the child's private world and feelings into a semiobjective situation where he can revise them to the pattern of the external world without danger to himself and others.

PARENTAL INFLUENCE

The child's personality is molded by a vast array of interacting forces. The school, for example, plays an important role in providing a relatively objective basis from which he can get his bearings and assess his potentiali-ties for growth. The foundation for personality, however, is unquestionably set in the home.

The climate of the home is of primary importance. Mussen et al.

[1] See Stone and Onque (1959) for an excellent annotated bibliography of longitudinal studies concerned with behavioral stability. Kagan (1964) also provides an extensive bibliography of major longitudinal studies. See also Bloom (1964).

(1963) found marital maladjustment to be the factor most consistently and highly correlated with problem behavior in children. They noted that, if only one or two aspects of the home are psychologically unfavorable, development usually proceeds without too much disturbance, provided the parents are themselves secure enough to give the child security and affection. A large number of unfavorable aspects, on the other hand, is likely to lead to emotional difficulty. As Kaplan (1959) points out, it is one of the ironies of life that many people who want children cannot have them, while many who have children do not want them. Some reject their children openly and brutally, even to the point of abandoning them in ashcans and beating and starving them; others are more subtle but the results are often the same. These children build up hate and hostility which they vent through retaliation against people and their property. In extreme cases, they become the unsocialized aggressives who fear neither man nor beast and who take on all comers in a compulsive desire for revenge. (See Redl and Wineman, 1951.)

There are also the overprotected, the children whose parents insist on prolonging their infancy by rendering service far beyond what is customary for their age. Then there is the dominating pattern in which parents simply rule their children with an iron grip and drive them toward the achievement of goals often far beyond their capabilities, frequently in the belief that it is in their best interest that high standards be set for them. Some children submit meekly; if they can meet their parents' expectations, they may internalize parental pressures and themselves become drivers. They often achieve considerable academic and professional success—and occasionally, peptic ulcers. Those with less ability may lie, cheat, and otherwise give the impression that they are fulfilling parental expectations, and thus stave off unpleasantness at home. Others simply rebel, especially in adolescence when psychological forces normally reduce parental influence over their children.

The home exerts a major influence on the child's likely success. Besides determining his inherited potential, it is a major factor in accelerating or retarding all aspects of his development. The crucial role of the home in the character and moral development of the child has already been presented (Chapter 17). There is need for freedom from excessive pressure, whether with respect to eating habits, toilet training, or other aspects of socialization; discipline, for example, must provide adequate ethical guidelines but must not unduly restrict natural exploratory behavior. Parents must strike a happy balance between complete permissiveness, which leads to the development of a weak conscience, and excessive prohibition, which produces unrealistically severe moral constraints.

There are a number of patterns of parental behavior, classified on the basis of different emphases and combinations of acceptance-rejection, warmth-cold, democratic-autocratic orientation, indulgence, etc., that have a crucial effect upon the development of the child (See Chapter 2). Children from homes with strict control show less disobedience, less aggression and less nonconformity, but they also show less curiosity, planfulness, and sociability. Apparently control suppresses spontaneity of behavior, both constructive and antisocial. A number of studies have indicated that dominant mothers create submissive children. Symonds (1936) notes, however, that this apparent submissiveness simply represents a fearfulness of assuming a dominant role in a situation governed by authority. As these children become adults their pent-up aggression causes them to create the same family pattern all over again, and they become the dominant parents of another generation of submissive children. The dictatorial German father, for example, does not let fear of losing their love deter him from punishing his children. He expects not love but respect. He may love his children but he never unbends lest he impair his reputation as a wise, powerful, and infallible father. As Kaplan (1959) points out, this type of family life breeds people who have a strong dependency on authority. These are the people who become the followers of a Hitler, who need a father-image in their political as well as their family life.

The consensus concerning the influence of various parental patterns on child development can be noted from a brief summary of Radke's findings (1946):

[a] The rejecting home promotes submissiveness, feelings of insecurity, nervousness, and noncompliance; the overprotecting home promotes infantile and withdrawal reactions, submissiveness, feelings of insecurity, jealousy, and nervousness.

[b] Dominating parents have dependable, shy, submissive, polite, self-conscious children; submissive parents have aggressive, careless, disobedient, independent, self-confident children.

[c] Disharmonious homes promote aggressive, neurotic, jealous, delinquent, uncooperative children; calm, happy, harmonious, and compatible homes promote cooperation, good adjustment, superior achievement, and independence.

[d] Defective home discipline promotes poorly adjusted, aggressive, jealous, delinquent, and neurotic children.

PERSONALITY THEORIES

Personality is the result of the interaction of many factors, the relative contribution and effect of which vary in the individual case in keeping with the uniqueness and yet the basic continuity of the individual's personality makeup. These factors can be grouped under two major classifications:

[a] Inherited predispositions. Kallmann (1953) found that whereas the

incidence of schizophrenia in the general population is less than one in 100, the odds increase to 10 in 100 if one parent is schizophrenic; the odds are increased to 15 in 100 if one child in the family develops it. The odds for fraternal twins are still 15 in 100, but for identical twins the odds jump to 80 in 100. Identical twins reared apart have the same odds as identicals reared together. It is not clear as to how this takes place; explanations range from the linkage of the genes to metabolic processes, to the endocrine glands, and to the influence of the assets and liabilities which the individual brings to his adjustment problems. Inherited potentialities and tendencies also play a major role in personality development; physique, for example, has an important bearing on the demands, expectations, and problems one faces.

[b] Cultural factors. Anthropological evidence shows a strong relationship between certain cultural patterns and certain personality orientations. Important here are the various child-rearing practices as previously discussed. It must also be noted that the person who has not learned the appropriate sex role or who has not developed adequate independence or social skill may be considered to have a poor personality (i.e., to be maladjusted) with respect to any society which makes these demands upon its members.

A number of theories of personality have been presented, none of which is completely acceptable to all psychologists. The field of personality, covering as it does the whole gamut of psychology, is too complex for a single system to place all of its various aspects into meaningful structure. Personality theories must sooner or later be reconciled with the principles of learning, for example. There is need for clinical psychologists to orient their efforts toward the psychology of learning just as learning theorists must come to grips with such concepts as a permissive atmosphere in which the individual can deal with his anxieties symbolically. The different theories of personality vary in their emphasis; in a survey by Hall and Lindzey (1957), for example, heredity was found to have high priority in seven theories, moderate emphasis in six theories, and little emphasis in four theories. The role of experience in personality development was given a major role in five theories, a moderate role in five, and little emphasis in seven. The self-concept was given high emphasis in eight theories, moderate emphasis in six, and little emphasis in three.

The various theories can be considered from the standpoint of a number of relatively overlapping classification schemes, none of which is completely satisfactory. They can be grouped as follows:

[a] Type theories, most recently represented by Sheldon's classification of body build on a seven-point scale in each of three continua—endomorphy, mesomorphy, and ectomorphy—and a relating of this classification to the individual's temperament (Sheldon and Stevens, 1940).

Unfortunately, Sheldon's theory, like the other type theories before his, is now essentially discredited.

[b] Trait theories, represented, for example, by Allport's theory of functionally autonomous traits (1937) and Cattell's theory of surface and source traits (1950), in which personality is described in terms of a minimal number of basic traits generally identified through factor analysis.

[c] Development theories, as for example, the psychoanalytic theories with their emphasis on the origin of personality in early life and the continuity of development. Psychoanalysts, for example, postulate that overrigorous toilet training in early infancy leads to the development of a compulsive personality structure characterized by excessive cleanliness, orderliness, obstinacy, and stinginess.

[d] Learning theories, which, as expected, place first importance for forming habits, including habits of anxiety, on the rewards and punishments administered by the significant people in the child's environment. Fixation, for instance, may be the result of overlearning not corrected by new learning.

[e] Role theories which emphasize the way the individual typically meets the various demands society places upon him in his role as parent, child, worker, citizen. These are essentially learning or development theories, but they stress the restrictions on the individual's freedom imposed by his role in life and the extent to which many of the decisions have already been made for him, perhaps even before he was born.

Other personality theories include the theory of personality dynamics, e.g., Lewin's group dynamics which primarily concern itself with contemporary manifestations of personality in inevitable interaction with the physical and social environment. Hilgard (1962) suggests that the most hopeful way of characterizing individuals according to some common plan seems to be the concept of personality syndromes, i.e., a pattern of traits which arises through common experience, even if, at present, clear-cut syndromes can be specified only for certain individuals, especially for those with abnormal orientations, e.g., the neurotic personality.

Of particular interest in view of the orientation of the present text are the phenomenological theories, a loosely organized system which, in common with the field theories of learning, places maximum emphasis on the present relationship of the individual to his environment as perceived by him at the time of reaction. They view behavior as a function of the vector forces operating in the field and thus bear directly on the theories of personality dynamics. The organismic view (Hall and Lindzey, 1957) places emphasis on the overall unity of personality as achieved through a natural unfolding of potentialities. Barring excessive environmental stress, the individual's basic need for self-actualization is an adequate guarantee of an integrated and functional personality. The self theories, as emphasized in the present text, take a similar position. Rogers' theory of personality which combines organismic and Freudian theory, for example, is predicated on the premise that, given the opportunity to reexamine his conflicts in a permissive atmosphere, the individual's basic drive toward self-actualization is sufficient for him to generate a higher level of personality integration and to actualize himself along the lines of the fully functioning person. Combs and Maslow present essentially equivalent views.

ADJUSTMENT-MALADJUSTMENT: NORMALITY-ABNORMALITY

Although of prime usefulness, adjustment has never been a particularly satisfactory concept from the standpoint of either scientific or operational clarity. Just what should an ideally adjusted person be like? What should he do? Is the well-adjusted person the equivalent of the "normal" person and is maladjustment the equivalent of abnormality? As Shoben (1957) points out, we have an abundant supply of empirical knowledge and an impressive body of theory concerning the deviant, the diseased, the neurotic, the disturbed, the anxious, the maladjusted, but very little information, and even less conceptual clarity, about the nature of the psychologically normal.

The concept of adjustment has been approached from a number of points of view, none particularly acceptable. In fact, a considerable reaction has set in against the use of *adjustment* and *normality*. The statistical view, for example, makes adjustment a matter of conformity to the majority. Shoben objects to thinking of normality in relativistic (statistical or cultural) terms. Delinquency is bad, not because it is infrequent, but because it *is* bad. Even at best, the statistical view of normality implies a descent toward mediocrity; if it is to imply a desirable situation, normality cannot be made a matter of group norms. The pathological view of normality is simply a variation of the statistical position and besides is objectionable in that it is oriented toward the negative end of the continuum. To identify a normal person as one who is relatively free from abnormal symptoms is dealing with the dimension of pathology—the idea that everybody is a little queer except thee and me. A third criterion of normality, the acceptance of social responsibility and conformity to social standards, is also unacceptable since conformity is again a statistical norm and is not always in the best personal and social interest.

Shoben sees normality as a matter of integrative behavior rather than a condition of minimal pathology. He suggests that the acts themselves are what counts and that we must come to grips with the concept of values. Smith (1961), in a similar vein, feels that, although some lament the intrusion of values in psychology, mental health inherently involves an evaluative aspect and psychology as a science cannot divorce itself from values. Shoben also argues that the concept of normality cannot be developed apart from moral considerations, and that conduct must eventually be evaluated in terms of human satisfaction and happiness.

Adjustment can be considered from a number of basic dimensions:

[a] The perceptual and cognitive domain. Ideal adjustment is characterized by efficiency in dealing with situational demands. Involved is the concept of competence which permits the individual to adapt to situations calling for a shift in role, to distinguish between the important and the trivial, the relevant and the irrelevant, etc., but especially it relates to contact with reality based on openness to experience and relative freedom from perceptual distortion.

[b] The personal domain. The well-adjusted individual accepts himself. He has confidence in his adequacy.

[c] The social domain. The adjusted individual displays social sensitivity; he conforms to social expectations not because it is the thing to do, but because it promotes his self-realization and that of others. He neither violates rules for the sake of violating them nor conforms for the sake of conforming. His behavior is dominated by the rational-conscientious character pattern portrayed in Chapter 17.

[d] The affective domain. While happiness is neither a criterion nor a primary goal of adjustment, it is generally a by-product of positive personality orientation characterized by spontaneity, zest, creativity, a sense of humor, and openness to experience. The adjusted person lives in harmony with his world and derives pleasure from life.

[e] The self-actualization domain. Orientation toward self-actualization is an important criterion of personal and social adjustment.

Adjustment is the resultant of two sets of forces in dynamic interaction: forces within the individual and forces from the environment. The individual must maintain his equilibrium while at the same time growing toward greater adequacy and greater complexity. Adjustment is not a simple matter of satisfying one's needs, but rather of integrating one's purposes and needs with those of the social order in which one lives. The integrated person either conforms to social standards because their acceptance eventually leads to greater rewards, or, if he rebels, he does so on considered grounds and is willing to pay the price for behaving according to his own values. It is not a question of his fitting into a preconceived behavior mold which can be considered adjusted or normal, but rather a matter of operational functionality. It follows that we need to emphasize the positive, i.e., the promotion of mental health, with the prevention of pathology as a vital but secondary aspect.

On the other hand, we cannot define the normal person as one possessing all the desirable traits; nor can we assume that the well-adjusted individual is free from conflict, that he is happy, successful, etc. It might be expected that a mentally healthy person would be characterized by spontaneity, productivity, zest, freedom from severe conflicts, with positive orientation toward value ends, freedom to use his ability to the fullest, etc., but we must recognize that these traits exist on a continuum and that no one is completely adjusted; perhaps no one is completely maladjusted. Some degree of "maladjustment" in children is characteristic of development, i.e., "normal"; the preadolescent is typically quarrelsome. Many signs of maladjustment among young children may well represent nothing more than the immaturity of youth. We might heed Olson's suggestion (1959) that the best guarantee of normal maturity is a normal immaturity; forcing children through phases of their immaturity to the standards of adult "normality" cannot be a goal of mental health.

Since it relates to every aspect of the individual, the concept of normality is perhaps best defined in terms of a multidimensional criterion, such as presented by Jahoda (1958) and Smith (1959), to include attitudes toward the self, growth in self-actualization, integration, creativity, autonomy, perception of reality, and environmental mastery. Other dimensions might include efficient perception of reality, acceptance of self and others, spontaneity, detachment, and openness to experience, all of which are related to the actualization of potentialities—which is again a slippery concept, since one can actualize himself in a number of ways, some of which are not particularly acceptable.

Adjustment differs from maladjustment in degree rather than in kind, and, despite objections, normal adjustment simply entails behavior within the range of tolerated differences, where the limits of such a range are uncertain and flexible. More specifically, the adjusted person shows a relatively high degree of personal integration; he displays behavior that is effective in attaining his goals; he faces problems realistically, and devotes his energies to the attainment of his purposes. He has found satisfactory solutions for his major problems and has effective ways of releasing tension so that he is relatively free from conflict and stress. In effect, he displays emotional and social maturity. On the other hand, when the individual is caught between a resistant obstacle and a persistent motivation, frustration mounts to the point of causing excessive interference and even disorganization of behavior. Internal conflict may cause him to be at cross-purposes with himself, with resulting indecision and inability to coordinate his efforts in the attainment of his goals. When this pattern becomes typical of his behavior, he may be said to be maladjusted, although there is no sharp dividing line separating the maladjusted from the adjusted.

Maladjustment is revealed through any number of symptoms, many of which—at least in their milder forms—are also characteristic of normal adjustment. Among the more common, we might mention explosive behavior, general restlessness, preoccupation (daydreaming, absentmindedness, worry), withdrawal (excessive reading for vicarious excitement, shyness, and general avoidance of social situations), and physical dysfunctions. Another set of symptoms such as crying, temper tantrums, fixations or delays in normal growth, dependence upon others, lack of motivation, inability to assume responsibility, attempts to win sympathy, and selfishness are often signs of immaturity rather than maladjustment, i.e., they reflect failure to learn more mature ways of behaving rather than the learning of undesirable behavior patterns. Regardless of differences in antecedents, however, both immaturity and maladjustment are difficult to deal with; to the extent that they are incorporated into the self-image, changing them calls for major reorganization of the total personality. Furthermore, improvement in behavior cannot take place in a vacuum, and immature and maladjusted persons are likely to have difficulty finding people endowed with sufficient patience to put up with them, let alone provide the supportive environment they need in order to improve.

ADJUSTMENT MECHANISMS

The individual learns certain behavior patterns by which he attempts to resolve his conflicts. Thus, the boy who is frustrated by his inability to gain social recognition and self-esteem by getting on the honor roll *compensates* by making the football team, or *rationalizes* that only sissies are interested in grades, or perhaps develops *neurotic symptoms*, e.g., headaches, that make his failure to get on the honor roll understandable. These habits, known as *adjustment mechanisms*, are neither disorders nor symptoms of maladjustment; they are simply the adjustments the individual makes when confronted with certain needs, on the one hand, and certain situational realities, on the other.

Adjustment mechanisms can be classified according to any number of systems, none of which is particularly satisfactory; behavior is the resultant of multiple causation and is invariably so complex that it does not fall into neat categories. A given mechanism may resemble the others in its category from one standpoint but also resembles those in adjacent categories in other respects. Furthermore, a certain situation may give rise to a different adjustment mechanism so that being able to identify the display of a given mechanism is of limited value in dealing with the underlying problem. Yet, despite the obvious necessity of considering any classification of adjustment mechanisms merely suggestive, an attempt in this direction may be justified on the grounds that it brings out their common features and tends to make for greater understanding of their nature. The present discussion follows in an abbreviated form the classification used by Shaffer and Shoben (1956).

DEFENSE MECHANISMS

The mechanisms in this category represent an attempt by the individual to defend himself against feelings of inferiority occasioned by his failure to attain his goal by minimizing his failure or attaining success by other means. Included in this category are a variety of reactions, the more common of which are attention-getting devices, compensation, and rationalization.

In compensation, the individual attempts to overcome feelings of inferiority arising from personal limitations in a given area by striving for success in the same or a different area. Thus, Demosthenes is said to have overcome a speech impediment by practicing speaking with pebbles in his mouth. A boy may compensate in a peculiar area, e.g., collecting snakes, or college banners where, because the competition is less keen, he is more likely to attain relative success. A common form of compensation is compensation through others in which a person identifies himself emotionally with another and gets vicarious satisfaction for his needs through the latter's achievement. Compensation through others is involved in the popularity of sports and movies, for example. Parents who compensate through their children occasionally make it rough on them; the father who harbors a sense of inadequacy over his inability to get past the fourth grade may insist that his son meet unrealistic standards of academic achievement. Compensation is also involved in such attention-getting devices as boasting, lying, and exhibitionism. Sublimation refers to socially desirable compensation, particularly as it applies to the area of sex; teaching and nursing can be considered forms of sublimation of the sex drive.

Rationalization consists of giving plausible but untrue reasons for one's behavior as a defense against having to admit that, by objective standards, it is irresponsible or otherwise unacceptable. Rationalization is a face-saving device dating back to Adam's "The woman whom Thou gavest to be with me, She gave me of the tree and I did eat." It may take any number of forms from "sour grapes" to blaming the incidental cause, e.g., kicking the stool for having been in the way. Rationalization is an unconscious mechanism; when false reasons are given knowingly, they are lies, not rationalizations.

A more serious form of rationalization is projection, in which the individual perceives in others the traits and motives for which he himself feels inferior; he not only represses the feelings which he finds intolerable in himself but unconsciously attributes them to others so that he feels justified in directing his aggressions toward them rather than toward himself. The selfish person sees selfishness in others; he condemns others for being selfish and convinces himself that his self-interest is made necessary by their selfishness. Sears (1936) found that college students who were rated by fraternity brothers as stingy and obstinate showed a marked tendency to rate themselves favorably and to rate their brothers unfavorably on those traits.

WITHDRAWAL MECHANISMS

In withdrawal mechanisms, the individual is no longer seeking satisfaction for his needs through the attainment of his goal, but instead runs away from the frustrating situation. Withdrawal is generally undesirable inasmuch as it does not solve the problem and yet removes the pressure that would force the individual to do something more constructive than simply withdraw. Teachers should be particularly aware of the relationship between simple withdrawal and more serious forms of maladjustment such as schizophrenia. They should realize that the model child who never misbehaves may be in grave danger of later difficulty and is, therefore, a more serious case of maladjustment than the "troublemaker" who is fighting to satisfy his needs.

Probably the most common forms of withdrawal are bashfulness, timidity, negativism, and general seclusiveness in which the individual, perhaps as a result of having been the victim of frustration and failure along with repressive discipline, avoids situations which may mean further failure. Another common form of withdrawal is fantasy (daydreaming) in which the individual becomes the conquering hero for whom success and revenge are unlimited, or the suffering hero whose misfortunes cause even his enemies great sorrow. Fantasy is not harmful in itself. There is a danger, however, of its being used in lieu of more constructive behavior, for as long as the individual finds no satisfaction for his needs, he will be forced to seek a solution, but when he gets partial satisfaction from his fantasies he is more likely to rely on them more and more, and, as a result, becomes progressively less capable of more positive adjustment. Fantasy can become a habit: it is always readily available and satisfying since one can always make the story come out right.

Another common form of withdrawal from frustrating conditions is regression, i.e., a movement back to the lesser maturity of an earlier period. The preschool child who has become quite grown-up may revert to infantile behavior when a new sibling is born. Procrastination is another common variety of running away from difficult situations which is indulged in by very normal people. A more elaborate withdrawal reaction is nomadism, which is characterized by frequent shifts of residence, repeated divorces, excessive job changes, and general shirking of responsibility. Less obvious forms of withdrawal include plunging into a number of activities, becoming drowsy, and turning to alcohol or narcotics or even sweets. A person with a severe problem which he can neither avoid nor resolve may turn to his work with a vengeance or get involved in numerous activities in an attempt to forget. The nervous breakdown that sometimes follows is more directly the result of the personal difficulty than of the hard work.

MECHANISMS INVOLVING FEAR AND REPRESSION

Fear (i.e., insecurity) is a basic component of all adjustment mechanisms; in compensation, fear is dispelled by overassertion of adjustment, while in withdrawal, the individual avoids fear-producing situations. On the other hand, persistent and excessive fears may be indicative of maladjustment. A person might have an intense fear of dogs, but it is something else to have frantic dread of high places, low places, crowded places, open places— none of which is a normal stimulus for fear.

Such abnormal fears—i.e., phobias—are generally the outcome of a traumatic experience in connection with which the individual feels some degree of guilt, the latter causing him to repress the incident to avoid anxiety. But a repressed incident is not a dead incident and it enters the consciousness in disguise. The girl who has been sexually assaulted under circumstances in which she feels partly to blame finds that her fear of the original situation transfers from one object or situation to another, until, for no apparent reason, she fears being in a large room or being alone, stimuli which are symbolic of being without protection. Repression serves the purpose of protecting the self but it is a most dangerous mechanism, for when problems are no longer in the open, they become difficult to deal with. Repression also underlies *reaction formation* in which a person overacts in a given direction in compensation against opposite feelings which he harbors with some guilt. Thus, the mother who strongly resents the fact that the birth of her child ended her career may react by granting his every wish and working well beyond the call of duty in seeing that no harm befalls him.

Repressed guilt often leads to obsessive-compulsive reactions. An obsession is a persistent, irrational anxiety-laden thought—often centering on such morbid themes as death and suicide—which comes into consciousness inappropriately and cannot be banished voluntarily. Compulsions refer to bizarre recurrent impulses which are highly compelling and yet have no observable value. They are usually symbolic, like the handwashing of Lady Macbeth whose compulsive reaction had to be repeated over and over in a desperate effort to relieve the tension which seemed to accumulate faster than it could be dissipated by such relatively indirect and ineffective means. The term *disassociative reaction* is often used to include such forms of withdrawal as amnesia, fugues, multiple personality, and other forms of psychological escape involving repression. Amnesia resulting from organic causes is usually permanent; more frequently, amnesia is psychological in nature, in which case memory losses tend to be selective and subject to recovery through hypnosis, for example.

The term *neurosis* describes a wide variety of ineffective adjustment reactions ranging from those which interfere very little to those which are quite incapacitating. Neurotic disorders are based primarily upon anxiety, i.e., generalized feelings of apprehension growing out of unresolved frustrations. The child who is systematically subjected to severe punishment for expressing socially disapproved impulses comes to regard the impulses themselves as dangerous and to feel anxiety whenever he experiences them. As a result, he represses these impulses to obtain relief but this causes the anxiety to become "free-floating." When it becomes attached to some object in the environment, it results in irrational fear, i.e., a phobia, so that, phobias are abnormal fears with a locus displaced on some object in the environment. In hysteria, on the other hand, the anxiety is displaced to a limb or organ of the body where it produces physical dysfunction.

Because neurotic reactions are only indirectly related to the goal and yield only partial satisfaction; they have to be repeated persistently in order to keep anxiety under control. The individual may be under constant tension as evidenced by digestive upsets, insomnia, and diffuse motor activity. However, to the extent that he fears taking the risk involved in an outright attempt to reach the goal, he is incapable of taking positive action; the worrier, for example, simply continues to worry, often not knowing what he's worried about. By keeping the *field* relatively undifferentiated, he keeps his anxieties at a tolerable level.

It is generally easier to prevent the development of hysterical symptoms than to remove them. A good rule is never to make illness a pleasant experience. The child who has too much of a headache to go to school should be put to bed for the day—minus comics and television. If he is really sick, the rest will do him good; if the headache is of psychogenic origin, putting him to bed will discourage the development of hysterical patterns of adjustment. Of course, it is necessary to deal with causal factors; perhaps some of the pressures at school need to be lightened or the child helped to realize that it is not necessary for him to be sick for people to notice that he exists.

Evaluating Adjustment Mechanisms

All people have needs; therefore all have to rely on adjustment mechanisms. In fact, the adjusted as well as the maladjusted make use of most of these mechanisms. Adjustment and maladjustment are a matter of degree, and even adjusted people daydream, rationalize, and develop migraine headaches. On the other hand, some of these mechanisms are potentially objectionable; they can be considered dangerous when they interfere with rather than contribute to personal adequacy. They tend to develop into rigid behavior patterns to the point that the individual becomes a victim of his own defenses. The insecure child who rationalizes his shortcomings denies himself the opportunity of developing greater adequacy and thereby promotes his own downfall through closing off his avenues of experience. Generally speaking, adjustment mechanisms are undesirable when they displace more constructive modes of behavior, when they are relatively ineffective in satisfying basic needs, or when they introduce greater problems than they solve. Perhaps a more adequate—although less explicit—guide is that only those adjustments that fail to satisfy individual and social needs are maladjustments (Shaffer and Shoben, 1956).

UNDERSTANDING THE CHILD

Teachers must understand the child as an individual if they are to provide educative experiences maximally conducive to his growth. Actually, the teacher can be only partially effective in this regard; not only does he not have the time to make a thorough study of each child, while at the same time attempting to have the class as a whole attain certain academic standards, but he is also relatively untrained in the psychodynamics of behavior. To make matters worse, behavior, being the product of multiple causation over a period of years, is complicated. In medicine, illness can often be identified by the symptoms, and, once this is done, a rather complete understanding of the disease, including its etiology and treatment, is achieved. In the area of maladjustment, on the other hand, symptoms rarely identify the trouble; each case is unique so that labeling a child a "bully" does not tell us what needs to be done about it.

Nevertheless, in the final analysis, it will be the teacher who will do most for the vast majority of children in the development of effective behavior. Qualified or not, he must make understanding children and their behavior one of his primary responsibilities, for understanding children is an integral aspect of teaching, not something one undertakes when things get out of hand. And whereas love is not enough, it is essential, and, when coupled with sensitivity and a reasonable grasp of basic psychological principles, it goes a long way. In fact, it will go the whole way with most children, for children have a wonderful resiliency to stress and strain, and all they want—all they need—is perhaps a little help here and there, but mostly, just a chance to grow.

The lazy way is not to bother—simply to present academic material, make assignments, and ignore the fact that children are people with individual characteristics and problems. To understand children takes time, and the more understanding a teacher is, the more they will come to him rather than to other teachers who will not help them. But it is time and effort well spent, for it pays dividends in pupil adjustment and in teacher satisfaction. A little help at the right time will often put the child back on his feet and it is surprising how many children, who perhaps were drifting in the wrong direction, have found themselves as a result of a little understanding on the part of a sympathetic teacher. In fact, it is debatable whether any saving is effected by ignoring students except in the case where, in final desperation, they drop out of school. When they remain in school, whatever saving is involved, if any, is very shortsighted even from a purely selfish point of view, for neglected students soon fall behind, become disciplinary cases, and multiply the teacher's problems a hundredfold.

JUVENILE DELINQUENCY

CHARACTERISTICS OF DELINQUENTS

If the teacher is to understand the child, he must know something of the experiences and the forces to which he has been subjected. The child who has been mishandled may well have deepseated problems that defy superficial treatment. This is true of the delinquent, who, besides being the product of unhappy child-rearing practices, rarely finds the understanding and help he needs in order to change his pattern of behavior. Jackson (1950), for example, found that while normal children described themselves as good and nice, delinquents and neurotic children saw themselves as naughty and disobedient. The normal children saw their parents as affectionate, accepting, and as sources of love and protection. The neurotics and the delinquents, on the other hand, thought their parents disliked, rejected, and maltreated them; as might be expected, they viewed strangers with fear and distrust. The neurotic children reacted to injustices they had suffered and showed hostile rejection of their parents, intense jealousy of their siblings, and fear of aggression from more powerful brothers and sisters. The delinquents showed less hatred of their parents and siblings and less anxiety and self-pity than the neurotics; they simply felt less emotionally involved with their families. In the Glueck study of delinquent and nondelinquent boys, 66 percent of the mothers of the nondelinquents and 56 percent of the fathers were rated firm but kindly, as against 4 percent and 6 percent of the mothers and fathers of the delinquents (Glueck and Glueck, 1959). The delinquents displayed greater hostility, defiance, resentment, suspicion, and emotional stress arising from inadequate identification and unsatisfactory relations with their parents.

Each child is unique and no general statement can be made as to the cause and treatment of delinquency. Many delinquents simply have not internalized the constraints of the larger society, a situation likely to occur when adults make unreasonable or inconsistent demands, or when they allow the child to grow like Topsy without making any demands on them at all. Children need discipline, but only when it is consistent and based on love and security does discipline lead to character formation. The delinquent is often confused by the conflicting demands made upon him by the different groups to which he belongs. Furthermore, he is not helped to improve his behavior by the harsh treatment he receives when he is caught. Actually delinquency is more than a matter of the commission of an act in violation of the law; it generally involves the whole child, his values, his goals, and his purposes, and delinquents have been found to be more independent, extrovertive, vivacious, impulsive, aggressive, and adventurous than nondelinquents, but also to exhibit less self-control. They tend to be more courageous and many delinquents have become war heroes, for example. Delinquents tend to show emotional shallowness and lack of empathy; they are more likely to act out their conflicts in overt retaliatory aggression and are apparently unable to assess the consequences of their contemplated behavior.

Bandura and Walters (1959) found that delinquents had been less consistently reinforced for dependency and more frequently rejected by their parents. As a result, they are relatively immune to social approval as a guide to, and reinforcement of, adequate behavior and generally have little incentive to help them keep out of trouble. According to Kvaraceus (1960), who summarized the literature on the subject, delinquents tend to come from homes which are atypical and generally socially, ethically, economically, educationally, and culturally inferior. The parents and the neighborhood reflect a high incidence of mental inferiority, broken homes, and criminality. Many delinquents live with foster parents in a relatively confused family situation after having been shunted from home to home in early life. Many parents display indifference to their children, if not downright rejection; discipline tends to be lax, erratic, and punitive. This has left many youngsters without adequate ethical moorings. Delinquents do not seem to be lacking in moral knowledge; it simply has not been internalized. Nor are they usually socially maladjusted. In fact, gang delinquents may be very secure in their subculture. They simply belong to a subgroup whose values are incompatible with those of the larger social setting.

It is easy to jump to conclusions, however; in one of the Glueck studies, 84 percent of the persistent delinquents felt unwanted and unloved, but so did 88 percent of the nondelinquents. Perhaps a more realistic way of looking at the situation is from the standpoint of basic motivation. When the barriers are resistant and yet the motivation is too insistent to be denied, the resulting frustration leads the individual to turn to anything that offers help, even though it may involve him in socially and psychologically undesirable behavior. We might think of the problem child as one who has important problems for which he has not found a socially acceptable solution. He is striving to satisfy the same basic needs as any well-adjusted boy or girl, and it is not realistic to suggest that he does not *have* to misbehave, since this may be the only way he knows of to handle the situation. We can think of the delinquent child as one who has not been adequately socialized, who perfers immediate gratification of his needs to the satisfactions connected with the more adequate long-range goals of the social order.

Although delinquency is certainly not restricted to any one social class, its incidence is greatest among the lower socioeconomic strata where a series of adverse conditions generally interact to induce behavior contrary to the social code. The difficulty stems in part from the fact that lower-class values are in some degree of conflict with those of the overall society. In addition, lower-class children meet a great deal of frustration at school and in the greater community where everything operates according to middle-class standards. While the school is really an extension of the home of the middle-class child, rewarding and punishing the same things, it is a strange place to lower-class children who are not oriented favorably toward the school or anything it has to offer; they have had no encouragement by way of precept or example at home and, as a result, many of them from an early age band together and express their defiance by attacking the middle-class status system.

Teachers, belonging almost exclusively to the middle-class and subscribing to middle-class standards, have difficulty in understanding lower-class values and behavior. Lower-class children tend to express aggression more directly, for example; not to fight when provoked would be to lose self-esteem and peer status. They tend to be somewhat authoritarian and punitive; above all, reflecting the self-concept they have developed as a result of the experiences they have undergone, they subscribe to a set of values, particularly as it relates to education, which is so different from that of the predominating middle and upper social groups that for them to adjust to the demands of the school is often a matter of considerable difficulty.

The school is an important instrument in raising social standards and encouraging upward mobility among the more able. Unfortunately, this opportunity is definitely class-linked. As Kaplan (1959) points out, the school's conveyor belt drops the lower-class child pretty early in the education route. Even the children categorize one another along rather rigid lines of socioeconomic caste, with middle- and upper-class children looking down on their lower-class counterparts for being poorly dressed, aggressive, unpopular, and generally lacking in sundry status symbols ranging from sports cars to social graces. This feeling is frequently shared by teachers who find the middle-class child clean, neat, orderly, discreet, and respectful of authority; in other words, the middle-class child displays attitudes in line with their own. The lower-class child, on the other hand, tends to be rejected for not measuring up to middle-class expectations. His problems are complicated by the fact that curricular offerings and the demands made upon him are frequently, if not generally, unrealistic from the standpoint of his background, his goals, and his purposes. The textbook poses a problem; readers invariably present as their main characters a pair of well-scrubbed, attractive children, who live in a neat house complete with fence and lawn. The father is invariably a professional man carrying a briefcase; grandpa lives on a ranch. Even the vocabulary is different. All this makes the school so foreign to the lower-class child that he has difficulty in identifying with its values.[2] The result is frustration, academic failure, and eventual withdrawal from school. A cynic might add, that our society provides the lower-class child with up to 12 years of academic failure as preparation for his later social and vocational success!

With the current emphasis on education as a dominant American value, scholastic achievement plays a major role in the child's adjustment; conversely, inability to achieve success in school-related activities is undoubtedly a significant factor in some youngsters turning to delinquency. It would seem logical to suspect that many of those who *cause* trouble in school (and in the community) are also those who have *had* trouble at school. When school regulations seem arbitrary and the demands always out of reach, the child comes to regard authority as an enemy. His role is then one of reluctant compliance with regulations and defiance and retaliation whenever it is safe. Educators need to challenge these children through interesting activities from which they can derive sufficient satisfaction to develop positive identification with the school and society.

DEALING WITH DELINQUENCY

Aggression and delinquency, although understandable from a clinical point of view, pose quite a problem to the classroom teacher. Whereas in clinical work, the expression of hostility is often the key to psychotherapy, there are limits to the aggression, hostility, and other forms of antisocial behavior the teacher can permit in the classroom. The social situation demands that they be channeled into constructive ends rather than allowed to interfere with the growth of other children and the operation of the school. In the meantime, when delinquency does occur, the teacher must remember that it is a symptom of something more fundamental than a mere undesirable act. Misbehavior must be considered against the total background of the setting in which it occurs; it may take on a more positive coloring, for example, when we realize that the rejected child strikes out against authority as a means of sustaining

[2] This has to be balanced against what is to be gained, if anything, from displaying drunkenness, fights, slums, etc. with which he may be more familiar. If we accept the view that the school should be an agent for upgrading social standards, perhaps the question is whether the step might not be too high for him to take.

his personal integrity. We must visualize the problem child as a child with a problem who is trying to tell us in his own way that the demands made on him are impossible, that the school's standards are unrealistic. It is particularly important that the school not contribute to delinquency through the persistent frustration of the needs of certain children over the period of their formative years.

Unfortunately, the delinquent's behavior often provokes annoyance and counteraggression rather than understanding; we tend to become emotional and find it difficult to maintain a rational outlook. Our first thought is that the delinquent child should be punished—when, actually, he may already have been punished too often. The average teacher is not attuned to the delinquent's frame of reference and, being unable to understand him, resorts to punishment, presumably on the assumption that the child is a free agent deliberately choosing misbehavior. If we really believe that behavior is the result of multiple forces, many beyond the individual's immediate control, we certainly ought to be more understanding. Whereas it is easy to get annoyed at the tough teenager, we need to use more enlightened methods than to get tough in return. Our past attempts at altering behavior through advice, persuasion, ordering, forbidding, and punishment, whether used by parents, teachers, or probation officers, have been grossly ineffective. It is only as the child identifies positively with those in authority that social constraints provide him with a basis for self-reward and self-control; conformity under duress to values incongruent with his present self-structure cannot lead to positive identification. Nor does severe punishment move the delinquent toward the middle-class pattern of behavioral respectability (see Havighurst, 1958).

Asking the school for due consideration for potential delinquents is asking nothing special. These are children who need and who deserve our help in exactly the same way as any other child. As Larsen and Karpas (1963) point out, these are the gang leaders, the Robin Hoods, whose talents we need to utilize, whose motivation needs to be redirected for their own sake and that of society. We cannot sell them short and keep the doors of our jails open for them to fall into. The least we can do is to give up the pessimistic view that nothing can be done for these unfortunate victims of societal mishandling.

Actually something can be done. Studies like that of Karacki and Toby (1962) have shown that delinquency can be reduced, even in blighted areas, by providing opportunities for youngsters to develop allegiance to the values of our culture. It must be noted that cures are not achieved overnight; this is a matter of the long pull. Teachers must also be careful not to break down the values of the home and thus aggravate home-school conflict; rather they need to help the child integrate the values of the groups which are important to him with those of the school by working with parents in a spirit of cooperation and mutual responsibility.

THE DROP-OUT

Considerable emphasis is being placed on the drop-out, a problem of alarming proportions when gauged in terms of the tremendous loss of talent involved. Research has identified a number of reasons why children leave school, many of which are relatively superficial. It would seem that when the youngster feels he is getting nowhere and that further efforts to succeed are useless, he just drops out. Actually dissatisfaction with school is generally part of the larger picture of psychological discontent, embracing the student's overall view of himself in relation to his world. The lower-class child, for example, often finds himself incompatible with almost all aspects of the school ranging from curriculum to teachers and the dominant middle-class peer group. Except for a few athletes, most lower-class children feel unwanted and generally left out of things. Even when the drop-out is persuaded to return to school, for example, the same old curriculum presented in the same old way is bound to have essentially the same old results and wear down rather quickly his renewed motivation. There is only so much that can be done with one, single-standard curriculum which every child must accept.

Probably the most significant reason for dropping out of school is a relative lack of orientation to the value of education in the first place. Schreiber (1963) reports that 70 percent of the mothers and 80 percent of the fathers of the drop-out had not completed high school; 25 percent of the mothers and 30 percent of the fathers had not gone beyond the sixth grade. Other studies have shown that two thirds of the parents of the drop-outs held negative or indifferent attitudes toward the value of education and did not consider the lack of an adequate education to be a serious obstacle in later adjustment or success. Lack of orientation of the home toward education has also been found to be a major factor in the talent loss among students of high caliber (Thistlethwaite, 1958).

Closely related to the drop-outs are the underachievers, who, in a study by Frankel (1960), were found to evidence more negative attitudes toward the school, to conform less, to be less happy, to have a poorer attendance record, and to participate less in extracurricular activities than a matched group of achievers. The fathers of the underachievers had significantly less formal education and more of them were of lower occupational status. From the standpoint of personality, underachievers generally have been found to be low in need for achievement and lacking in a sense of responsibility, seriousness of purpose, and self-confidence, all of which can be interpreted as much the result of underachievement as its cause. Of similar origin perhaps is their relative hostility (Shaw and Grubb, 1958). Research has also shown some degree of self-rejection on the part of the underachiever, but the picture is complicated by the appearance of self-acceptant underachievers, who, according to Mitchell (1959), apparently satisfy their needs in nonacademic areas or perhaps do not require a high level of achievement in order to attain self-contentment. They appear well-adjusted and, in Mitchell's study, showed less anxiety than the other group studied.

PUPIL APPRAISAL

Logical considerations suggest the value of pupil appraisal to the promotion of effective education. Travers (1963) looks forward to the day when teachers will begin the school year by spending a couple days collecting data on pupils, systematically feeding these data into a computer in order to gain a better understanding of the children they are to teach. This view is not shared by all: Rogers and other phenomenologists argue that emphasis on testing frequently causes teachers to lose sight of the real problems. In line with this objection, it has yet to be shown that the teacher's understanding of his pupils has a significant bearing on his ability to promote their welfare. Both Gage (1958) and Di Vesta (1961), for example, point to the lack of convincing evidence that teacher-pupil relationships affect the pupils' learning efficiency in any manner. Whether this implies that the difference among teachers in understanding their pupils is not great enough to make any discernible difference in their effectiveness, or that the source of the differences in teacher effectiveness lies elsewhere than in their understanding of their pupils, is not clear. It would seem that pupil understanding alone does not guarantee efficiency of operations; on the other hand, this does not deny the value to a conscientious teacher of adequate information concerning his pupils.

To be effective, a pupil appraisal program must be systematic and theoretically sound. The problem is that of accumulating whatever data are pertinent to the uniqueness of each individual child, including his own reactions to these data and to himself as a person. Since behavior involves the child as a functioning unit, we need to see the total child in the totality of his environment. It is also necessary to see him in perspective by considering his present status in terms of his previous experiences, his unresolved difficulties, his present values as well as his present and future goals. This calls for taking a number of appraisals at different times and in different settings so as to arrive at an understanding of his typical behavior patterns rather than be misled by unusual incidents.

Furthermore, educators must tap all relevant sources of information, among the more important of which are the following:

[a] The child. Obviously, no other source can give us as good an under-

standing of the child as he can. The teacher must get acquainted with him—in the formal situation of the classroom and especially in the freer homeroom or playground situation. The child cannot be expected to give a psychiatrist's analysis of his underlying motivational structure, but informal contacts in a permissive and accepting atmosphere can be helpful; allowing the rebellious child to tell his side of the story, for example, can give the teacher valuable insights into what makes him tick.

[b] The home. Since the child cannot be understood apart from the home, the teacher needs to know its general status, and especially the attitudes which his parents, siblings, and even the community hold toward the school, the teacher, and education. He should know the parents' views toward discipline, their system of values, their goals, and their general expectations from the child. But most of all he needs to know something about the home's emotional climate, for the child's problems at school are often those he brings from home. It is also important that the teacher appraise its socioeconomic and cultural status, because, when the home and the school subscribe to different cultural values, the child may be involved in a conflict between accepting the school and remaining loyal to his home. Peer ratings are also important, not only because they put a different perspective on his status, but also because his reputation as such is also important.

[c] The child's former teachers. The child's former teachers can be valuable sources of information. In most schools, for instance, teachers are encouraged to write anecdotal records which can provide valuable insights. Unfortunately, anecdotal records are time-consuming and busy teachers often report only the unusual and the negative rather than the more typical aspects of the child's behavior. Where this is the case, their use should be discouraged, for they can do more harm than good. Even at best, care must be taken that they do not prejudice future teachers and Rogers (1948) questions keeping pupil records for this reason. The same comment can be made concerning gossip often exchanged among teachers.

[d] Tests and other formal instruments. Information concerning the child's intellectual capacity, his special abilities and talents, his academic status, and perhaps his interests and personal adjustment cannot be obtained with sufficient precision by the observational and anecdotal techniques just discussed and recourse must be made to more formal instruments. When used with due awareness of their limitations, these instruments provide objective evidence which, when combined with the informal, and even the incidental, appraisals made by the teacher, give a broader and more adequate basis for pupil evaluation.

Of primary interest to the school are the child's motives, aspirations, attitudes, and values, for these are the prime determinants of just who he is and what he will do. Most of these, unfortunately, are difficult to appraise. Of special significance are his attitudes toward the school itself. These can usually be determined by observation and interview in the case of an individual child, but a more adequate appraisal of the morale of the student body can probably be obtained by means of an unsigned questionnaire covering the various aspects of the school program such as that used by Hand (1948) in his Illinois survey.

The child's personality, his emotional balance, and his habitual traits are of immediate concern to the teacher for the bearing they have on other aspects of his behavior and growth. Much of the information the teacher needs in this area can be obtained by observation, particularly in the elementary school. On the other hand, teachers must be alert to the limitations of observation; Gronlund (1950) and Moreno (1953) have shown the relative inadequacy of teacher observation as a means for appraising the social composition of the classroom, for instance. Whenever possible, observation should be supplemented by other techniques or confirmed by other observers. Yet observation is often the only means available for obtaining certain data, and all that can be done is to strive to make it as valid and reliable as possible.

Additional information can be obtained from student themes on such topics as "My Biggest Problem." A number of standardized "personality" inventories are also available but most are easy to fake and it is essential that students be convinced that the only reason for their filling them out is to enable the teacher or counselor to be of greater help to them, and that, therefore, it is in their best interest to give candid answers. Even then, the results should be interpreted cautiously.

These data should be incorporated in a cumulative folder available to all teachers who have contact with the child. This folder must be complete, accurate, and concise, or it is not worth the teacher's time to consult it. Clerical assistance should be provided for putting these data on a profile which will tell at a glance the things that an interested person needs to know. In addition, special cases will occur in which the teacher will want to consult the principal, the counselor, the doctor, or the social worker to get additional insights into the problems of a given student. It may even be necessary to carry out a case study in which all who have had contact with the child contribute what they know about him. Such detailed studies are, unfortunately, time-consuming and have to be restricted to a few cases, often too far advanced for any major improvement to be effected.

HIGHLIGHTS OF THE CHAPTER

The personal and social adjustment of the child has received considerable attention in the modern school, and the teacher, even though not clinically trained, must be familiar with the major principles of adjustment if he is to be effective in contributing to this important aspect of education. The following are among the more significant concepts covered in this chapter.

[a]

Adjustment refers to a state of harmonious relationship between the individual and his environment; it must, therefore, always be considered in relation to the question "adjusted to what?"

[b]

Adjustment is not a static condition; rather it is a continuous process of adjusting. Adjustment is relative; complete adjustment cannot be achieved, nor would it be desirable for people to be adjusted to some of the conditions in their environment. Motivation, for example, is essentially a matter of jarring the individual out of his complacency and forcing him to make new adjustments.

[c]

Objections have been raised against the normative concept of adjustment. It is difficult to devise a satisfactory criterion.

[d]

Adjustment is learned according to the same principles as govern other forms of learning. Shortsighted behavior may be explained on the basis of the individual's lack of cognitive clarity into the means for attaining his purposes, for example. A basic tenet of nondirective counseling is that, as the individual perceives himself and the situation differently, his behavior will change accordingly.

[e]

Child-rearing practices play a determining role in personality development. A number of overlapping theories have been presented.

[f]

The mechanisms used by adjusted and maladjusted persons differ in degree rather than in kind. Only those adjustments which fail to satisfy individual and social needs are maladjustments.

[g]

The teacher must understand the child if he is to guide his growth. Although convincing evidence of its value has yet to be presented, a systematic program of pupil appraisal should contribute to such an understanding.

[h]

Teachers with their socially oriented middle-class values have difficulty in understanding the lower-class and the delinquent child. Delinquency, underachievement, and dropping out are relatively logical consequences of the school's failure to communicate with and provide suitable learning experiences for a sizable fraction of its student population.

SOURCES OF RELATED MATERIAL

Ball, R. A., et al., "How can we better motivate the underachiever and the indifferent student?" *Bull. Nat. Ass. Sec. Sch. Princ.*, 44: 174–80, 1960.

Bloom, Benjamin, S., et al., *Compensatory Education for Cultural Deprivation.* New York: Holt, Rinehart and Winston, Inc., 1965.

David, M., et al., *Educational Achievement—Its Causes and Effects.* Ann Arbor, Mich.: Survey Research Center, University of Michigan, 1961.

Davitz, Joel R., "Contributions of research with children to a theory of maladjustment," *Child Develpm.*, 29: 3–7, 1958.

Glueck, Sheldon, "The home, the school, and delinquency," *Harv. educ. Rev.*, 23: 17–32, 1953.

Jackson, P. W., and J. W. Getzels, "Psychological health and classroom functioning," *J. educ. Psychol.*, 6: 295–300, 1958.

Kvaraceus, William C., "Forecasting delinquency: A three-year experiment," *Exc. Child.*, 27: 429–35, 1961.

Lichter, Solomon O., et al., *The Drop-Out.* New York: The Free Press of Glencoe, 1962.

Peller, L. E., *Significant Symptoms in the Behavior of Young Children: A Check List for Teachers.* New York: National Association for Mental Health, 1952.

Reisman, Frank, *The Culturally Deprived Child.* New York: Harper & Row, Publishers, 1962.

Schreiber, D. (ed.), *The School Drop-Out.* Washington, D.C.: National Education Association, 1964.

Shertzer, B., and H. J. Peters, *Techniques for Individual Appraisal and Development.* New York: Crowell-Collier and Macmillan, Inc., 1965.

Shoben, Edward J., "Toward a concept of the normal personality," *Amer. Psychol.*, 12: 183–189, 1957.

Smith, M. Brewster, "Mental health reconsidered," *Amer. Psychol.*, 16: 299–306, 1961.

Wilkins, L. T., "Juvenile delinquency: A critical review of research and theory," *Educ. Res.*, 5: 104–119, 1963.

QUESTIONS AND PROJECTS

1

Evaluate the following statements:

[a] The eccentricity of many great people suggests that the concept of normality means nothing more than the encouragement of conformity to mediocrity.

[b] Much of the problem behavior common among boys is nothing more than a healthy nonconformity to impossible standards and demands of adults.

[c] Far too much of the school's efforts has been directed toward the maladjusted, the dull, and the unfit, to the neglect of the adequate and the

gifted, despite its lack of competence and of primary responsibility for dealing with the former.

2

What is the present status of the inherited view of maladjustment? (See Shaffer and Shoben, pp. 360 ff) What "therapeutic" role might we expect tonics, tranquilizers, etc. to play in this connection?

3

The adolescent culture often seems to operate in conflict with that of the broader social context which the school presumably represents. How might the school work for a closer relationship in order to exert a stronger beneficial influence? How can we account for the fact that some of the community's less desirable elements seem to be so successful at times? How might the teaching profession get itself more closely attuned to the ways of children from the lower class? Relate this problem to our relative lack of success in dealing with the underdeveloped nations of the world.

CHAPTER 19

Mental Health
in the Classroom

There is little that the school teaches that is
worth achieving if the price is a maladjusted
youngster. Of what avail is it to give him a rich
array of skills and a wealth of information if
he is too disturbed to be able to use them?
Rivlin, 1955, p. 19

A great deal of attention has been given in recent years to mental health
as an important aspect of the child's total development. Not only has the
school become much more conscious of its responsibility in this connection, but the community has also demonstrated its interest through lay
and professional mental health groups.

EXTENT OF THE PROBLEM

Problems of mental ill health have always been with us. These range from
the mild problems that occasionally bother the most serene to the drastic
disturbances that characterize the psychotic. It is only recently, however,
that mental-health problems have been understood for what they are,
namely, a state of ill health in the mental field comparable to similar

conditions in physical health.[1] Thus, until recently, psychotics were considered possessed of the devil and burned at the stake or hidden at home or pushed out in the street so that neighbors would not know such a person existed in the family. Asylums kept the insane like beasts, often in chains, and floggings were common.

Mental illness is not only our number one health problem but its incidence is on the increase. Whether this implies that people are more maladjusted than they were years ago is a matter of conjecture. It can be argued that the complex age in which we live with its urbanization, its lack of occupational satisfaction resulting from monotonous machine-tending, and other social ills is conducive to mental illness. On the other hand, the higher incidence of mental illnesses may reflect nothing more than a greater awareness of mental-health problems, a greater ability to detect them, and a greater willingness to admit their existence.

Except for cases actually hospitalized as psychotics in state institutions, statistics on the prevalance of mental disorders are difficult to get and interpret. Estimates on the number of persons treated in private clinics or cared for at home vary with the severity of illness used as criterion; undoubtedly some of the institutionalized patients are less disturbed than some who do not become part of the statistics. All we can do is arrive at educated guesses. The National Institute of Mental Health (1962) reports:

> Over a million mental patients are treated annually at hospitals in the United States. In addition, an estimated 502,000 persons receive services in outpatient psychiatric clinics and a substantial number are being treated by private psychiatrists. [p. 2]

In 1961 the nation's 281 public mental hospitals alone reported 144,000 first admissions and over 100,000 readmissions. Approximately one half of the patients in hospitals on any given day are mental patients. The largest single group are the schizophrenics who make up about 20 percent of admissions, and, inasmuch as they are generally younger and have a poorer rate of recovery than other mental patients, they make up a still larger percentage of the total in residence.

It is estimated that 5 percent of the adult population is sufficiently neurotic to be relatively handicapped in social adjustment; the National Association for Mental Health in 1952 estimated that nine million Americans were struggling with severe mental and emotional conflicts. In addi-

[1] The mental health movement was given considerable impetus by the National Mental Health Act passed by Congress in 1945, authorizing the federal government to participate in a comprehensive program for the promotion of positive mental health and the prevention of mental illness. The National Institute of Mental Health, established in 1949 to carry out the provisions of the act, allocates grants to university hospitals, laboratories, and other nonfederal institutions for research projects, for training of personnel, and for the general study of mental health.

tion, many are making a reasonable adjustment in a sheltered environment but would not be able to withstand more severe conditions. It is estimated that half the clientele of the average medical practitioner suffers from illness resulting at least in part from psychogenic factors. It is also estimated that 60 percent of the accidents in which some 350,000 are disabled each year can be traced partly to personality problems. In addition, some three quarters of a million Americans have criminal records; nearly as many are chronic alcoholics; and 50,000 are drug addicts (Bonney, 1960).[2] During World War II, some 900,000 young American men (8 percent of the total draft) were rejected from military service, over a third of them because of personality problems. In addition, nearly half a million were discharged for mental illness (about 36 percent of the total medical discharges) and another quarter of a million were discharged for neuropsychiatric reasons (Ryan, 1952). Many developed hysterical symptoms which not only precluded further military service but also necessitated extended hospitalization.

Thus, as summarized by Griffin et al. (1940), out of 100 elementary school children selected at random, four or five will spend part of their lives in mental hospitals, four or five will develop serious mental illness but will be cared for in special institutions, one or two will commit some major crime and will spend time in a jail or penitentiary, three or four will be so handicapped by retarded or stunted mental development that they will have difficulty in becoming useful and productive citizens. Of the remainder, it is estimated that from 30 to 50 will be prevented from achieving their maximum efficiency and happiness by unwholesome emotional habits and personality traits.

Mental ill health also underlies many of the social problems that confront us daily. The fact that one out of every four marriages ends in divorce—in addition to the legal separations, the dissolution of common-law marriages and other marriages of convenience, as well as the extent of marital infidelity—is a sad reflection on the emotional maturity of many "adults." It is estimated that over two million children under eighteen years of age live with neither parent; twice as many live with only one parent.

Misbehavior ranging from classroom disturbances to juvenile delinquency and adult crime, graft, and corruption is evidence of the same lack of adjustment. It is also true that many people lose their jobs or miss out on promotions not for lack of vocational competence but rather because of inability to get along with others. In fact, what is probably the greatest single weakness of the average person, namely, inability to inspire others to give their best in the attainment of desirable goals— which is quite evident in the failure of many leaders whether in school,

[2] See also David Riesman's *The Lonely Crowd* (1950) and Erich Fromm's *Escape from Freedom* (1941) and *The Sane Society* (1955).

church, business, industry, government, sports, or even club work—is very often due to some personality quirk that antagonizes would-be cooperators and followers. And not least is the distrust that currently characterizes human relations at the personal, national, and international levels.

The cost of these problems to society is high. At any time, there are well over half a million Americans in jails and penitentiaries. The cost of the care and treatment of the mentally ill is reported by the National Institute of Mental Health (1962) at 1.7 billion dollars, exclusive of the loss of earning power of the patients. The cost in human suffering and the disruption of the lives of the patients and their families is, of course, immeasurable.

MENTAL HYGIENE IN THE CLASSROOM

THE NATURE OF MENTAL HYGIENE

These rather sobering statistics suggest the need for constructive action, with the school apparently the agency in the best position to deal with the problem. The extent to which educational institutions should assume responsibility for the mental health of their pupils is a matter of controversy. Some have questioned the wisdom of the school's trying to be all things to all men by assuming responsibility for tasks not within its sphere of function and competence, perhaps even to the neglect of its primary responsibility. On the other hand, the school has an obvious obligation in the matter: Not only is the school itself a major factor in the degree of mental health the child attains, but it also has close contact with him early in life when the damage, if any, is not beyond repair. Furthermore, the school cannot ignore adjustment difficulties since they will interfere with the attainment of academic goals, no matter how narrowly they are conceived.

The home and not the school has primary responsibility for the mental health of the child. Yet, just as in fulfilling their responsibility for their children's physical health, parents have access to doctors, dentists, and other professional personnel, so perhaps they might expect the support and help of other agencies in promoting the maximum development of their children. The school with its more adequately trained personnel and its greater perspective has a definite contribution to make here. While there is a limit to what it can do, the task is not impossible inasmuch as perfection is not required. There is no *right* way of handling a given situation, and generally a certain amount of professional knowledge and technical know-how coupled with good intentions, a wholesome acceptance of children, and a consistency of application tend to produce good results. Children are resilient creatures whose natural desire to grow enables them to adjust to the difference.

The school is in a favorable position to promote the positive aspects of personal development. By working with children day by day, it can help them to develop wholesome attitudes, values, and habits, and to consolidate these in an effective pattern of life. It provides a variety of opportunities for them to learn satisfying ways of working and playing together; it also provides knowledge and skills that enable them to develop into competent, self-dependent individuals, capable of meeting social and vocational demands. It has an even greater effect on personality adjustment through the influence it exerts over the parents of the next generation. The school has a more direct responsibility in saving children from undue frustration and relieving undue pressures so that their natural growth potentialities can take over. Unfortunately, it often heaps its greatest frustration upon those who can stand it least when it applies across the board a curriculum ill-suited to the background and ability of a good percentage of its children.

As an organized program, mental hygiene has three main purposes: [a] the prevention of mental disorders; [b] the preservation and development of mental health; and [c] the removal of maladjustment. As it applies to the classroom, mental hygiene is not a matter of the teacher engaging in a desperate struggle to keep children from going insane or to cure those who are already in difficulty; on the contrary, mental hygiene is a positive program oriented toward adjustment on the part of each and every child. Mental hygiene is not a body of specialized procedures such as might be used in a clinical situation, but rather part-and-parcel of the teaching-learning process; or, as stated by Redl and Wattenberg (1959), the very core of good mental hygiene in school is embodied in the way learning activities are guided. The same point is made by Rivlin (1936):

> Mental hygiene is not a discrete scheme of psychiatric procedures, nor is it a distinct body of facts. It is rather an attitude and a point of view that should influence everything the teacher does professionally: her method of asking questions as well as her manner of accepting answers; the procedures followed in administering tests and that governing the supervision of the playground activities; the appeals by which she stimulates the pupil's desire to participate in classroom activities and the measures to which she resorts to bring the unruly into line, her attitude toward the asocial children, such as the young thief or the bully, and that toward the unsocial pupil whose timidity prevents him from mingling with others. Far from being a distinct group of skills and facts, mental hygiene in the classroom takes on significance only when it is bound so inextricably with all the teacher does that careful analysis alone can reveal its exact influence. [p. 1]

The aim of education and of mental hygiene are one and the same, namely, the promotion of the child's all-round development. Mental hygiene is not an outgrowth of a soft psychology; on the contrary, it is the very essence of modern educational philosophy with its emphasis on self-actualization. Far from being a misguided fad of educationists, mental hygiene deals with the very core of human welfare and pervades all fields of human relations. It is an area that has always received some attention, but it needs special emphasis in these days of mass education and parents-in-a-hurry, where no one has time to consider the child as an individual. Teachers should be clear as to the forces that promote self-actualization and those that impede growth. They need to develop more than a layman's understanding of how development is promoted, how it is distorted from its normal course, and how such distortion can be prevented from accelerating itself.

Teachers and Mental Health

The introduction of mental hygiene in the school has been a slow and reluctant process. This may have been partially caused by the relative lack of orientation of teachers to the clinical aspects of pupil growth and development. It was no doubt also directly related to the older view of the school as a place where teachers taught and pupils learned. In fact, even today, there are rugged individualists who object to babying the child, to having the teacher become a social worker, minister, doctor, nurse, and psychologist, despite the fact that he is qualified only as a teacher. Schools are always pressured into adding new programs and the first impulse is to resist such additions, particularly when they involve extra costs in teacher time and energy. However, as teachers found that concern for the child's mental health was a wise investment from the standpoint of pupil growth as well as teacher satisfaction, mental hygiene became progressively more accepted—although even now many teachers are operating in more or less direct defiance of its principles.

If the school is to be effective in fostering mental health, it is necessary that it define clearly what it can and what it cannot do. The teacher must recognize that his training does not allow him to deal with the therapeutic or corrective aspects of mental hygiene.[3] This is one area where love and good intentions are not enough; in advanced cases the teacher must restrict himself to detection, referral to competent authorities, and cooperation with recommendations for treatment as they apply to the classroom. Actually, the teacher's greatest contribution to mental health lies in providing individual children with meaningful experiences and opportunities for satisfying needs, and in creating an atmosphere of

[3] The classroom situation and the teacher's responsibility for academic growth would not allow him to function as a clinical psychologist even if he were trained. The distinctly different role and situation in which each operates make it impossible for them to exchange roles.

acceptance for all children no matter what they do or who they are, i.e., in being a good teacher rather than in attempting to be a second-rate psychiatrist.

The teacher needs to acquaint himself with the symptoms of maladjustment so that he can recognize its existence early and refer the child to a competent clinician. Unfortunately, teachers are not too well trained in recognizing danger signals; sometimes they consider the quiet retiring child who never causes trouble as a model child and consider the troublemaker as ready to be institutionalized, whereas actually the former is in greater danger from a mental health point of view than is the latter— a fact, Margolin (1953) feels, teachers have been slow to grasp, despite nearly 50 years of exhortation by mental hygienists. He notes that discussing the aggressive child tends to arouse strong feelings in teachers, apparently mirroring their behavior patterns in dealing with such a child. The aggressive child in the classroom *is* a disturbing factor; teachers find it difficult to accept hostility and, instead of channeling it, feel compelled to suppress it. This is rarely successful. Instead it tends to reinforce aggressive behavior and promotes the need for an ever-greater display of authority.

In a similar vein, Meyer and Thompson (1956), found that women teachers were attempting to socialize boys by means of dominative behavior. However, being more aggressive in the first place, boys tend to respond aggressively, which is frequently interpreted by teachers as a challenge to their authority and leads them to counteract at a still higher level of aggressiveness. Women teachers apparently fail to understand that aggressive behavior is simply an aspect of the normal personal and social development of boys. They also tend to encourage the withdrawal behavior of girls—which is also wrong!

The relative inability of teachers to judge the severity of various behavior symptoms as mental health hazards was brought out by Wickman's well-known study (1928) in which he found teachers to rate 50 behavior problems in somewhat the reverse order of the ratings of clinicians. Actually the study contained a number of flaws, and more recent and better studies have shown much closer agreement between teachers and clinicians. Thus, Schrupp and Gjerde (1953), in a repetition of Wickman's study using the same set of directions for both groups, found a correlation of .56 in the ratings of teachers and clinicians (as opposed to Wickman's correlation of .04). Similar results were obtain by Stouffer (1952). Whether one should be disturbed at the discrepancy in outlook that still exists is a matter of opinion. It is possible that, in view of the difference in their function, certain differences in viewpoint are to be expected. On the other hand, there is perhaps a need for a further shift in teacher orientation from a concern over breaches of classroom decorum to a more objective consideration of behavior from the standpoint of the long-term development of the whole child.

Mental Health Factors in the Classroom

Since nearly all the child's experiences during the formative years are connected with first the home and then the school, these two agencies, more than any other, are responsible for his adjustment or maladjustment. Kaplan and O'Dea (1953), for example, found "unsatisfactory home conditions" and "failure of traditional curriculum to meet the needs of many children" to rank first and second among the mental hazards of school children, as reported by teachers.

By its very nature, the classroom incorporates many features which may constitute definite hazards to the mental health of children. The fact that the school has primary responsibility for promoting academic learning may mean frustration, perhaps even continuous and severe frustration, for some children. Americans tend to get entangled in the concept of precocity: we want to do things earlier and better than the person next door. Parents want their children to walk early; teachers want their children to surpass the norms. This can result in unhealthy pressures being applied on certain children for whom pressures can do nothing but harm. On the premise that prevention is a more constructive approach than correction after the harm has been done, the teacher needs to evaluate each and every classroom procedure for its mental health implications.

The following is a partial list of the more obvious factors having a direct bearing on the mental health of the school child:

[a] The wide range of individual differences in the classroom makes it difficult for the teacher to provide meaningful experiences for each child and to have each attain at least minimum satisfaction for his needs.[4] The problem is accentuated by an emphasis on examinations and competition which may result in continuous failure and frustration for some children. The child should welcome examinations as an opportunity to evaluate where he stands as a prelude to planning the next step; but when they take on the flavor of Judgment Day, together with the definite possibility of being found inadequate, the harm examinations can do from the standpoint of the child's total growth far outweighs the good, if any, from the standpoint of academic growth.

[b] Discipline in the sense of setting limits or guidelines is essential for promoting the security necessary for optimal development. When we say the teachers should be permissive, we do not mean he should resign his leadership for a policy of vacillation or abdication; he must remain the leader, not only because of his maturity, experience, and training, but also

---

[4] For every child frustrated because the material is too difficult, there is likely to be another frustrated because the work is obnoxiously easy; and any number who are bored because the material bears no relation to their goals and purposes.

because of his position as representative of the culture to be transmitted to the student. However, he needs to control the class through understanding in an atmosphere of psychological safety in which the child can allow his drive for growth to propel him forward without undue risk. The teacher should also prevent the child from overextending himself into inevitable failure. Discipline especially must be constructive; nothing is to be gained from cataloging in a rigid, moralizing manner the child's failures to meet adult standards.

[c] The most important single factor in the mental health picture is the teacher's ability to generate warm pupil-teacher and pupil-pupil relationships based on understandings, mutual acceptance, and respect. Twenty percent of the children in Tenenbaum's study (1944) greatly disliked their teacher; 28 percent hoped that when they went to work they would not have a boss like their teacher. Six percent disliked all teachers. He concluded: "The evidence indicates that when a student dislikes school, it is largely because of the teacher."

The teacher's role with respect to mental hygiene is crucial, for he is responsible for the emotional tone of the classroom and for translating the principles of mental hygiene into effective group living. This calls for a number of characteristics and abilities, of which none is more important than a sensitivity to the needs and feelings of children which would prevent him from subjecting them to unfair or excessive competition, to an unsuitable curriculum, or to unrealistic demands. The teacher is not qualified to treat severe adjustment problems, but he can show a little friendliness to the child who is left out, to the child who has a trying home situation, and he can make it possible for the slower child to taste occasional success and recognition. He needs to be sympathetic to the child who suffers from headaches and dizziness when faced with a difficult situation. He must understand the child who cheats when this is the only way he can meet expectations and the child who, caught between a meaningless curriculum and impossible demands systematically imposed upon him, decides to go truant. The teacher needs to recognize problem behavior as the result of severe and persistent frustration of needs, and especially to understand that the child who needs his acceptance most desperately is frequently the one who deserves it least. Such an understanding is particularly important inasmuch as not all children can be referred to a clinician and the vast majority will have to rely on the teacher for whatever help he can give.

[d] The academic work of the classroom should be meaningful in terms of the child's abilities, purposes, and interests. When he finds he can satisfy his needs through doing schoolwork, he will not only be content, but he will work as hard as his abilities permit and there will be no need to rely on punishment, or for the teacher to appoint himself

inspector of pupil shortcomings. A meaningful curriculum can do more for the child's mental health and all-around growth than any program of guidance or special help superimposed upon a rigid instructional program supervised by inflexible and authoritarian teachers.

A number of other aspects of the classroom situation can be singled out for similar consideration. Suffice it to say that everything the teacher does as it relates to the child—homework, grouping, grading and reporting, promotion or retention—has implications for better or for worse from the standpoint of his mental health. The teacher needs to be fully aware of the grave responsibility this places on his shoulders.

MENTAL HEALTH AND GUIDANCE

Guidance, mental hygiene, and, in fact, education in the modern sense, all have the same purpose, namely, the promotion of the child's maximum self-realization. They differ in approach and scope. Education tends to be oriented toward promoting his all-round growth with special emphasis on the academic. Guidance and mental hygiene, on the other hand, function largely in the area of personal and social development, although the adjustment they promote certainly has implications for the other phases of his overall development. From the standpoint of promoting personal and social adjustment, mental hygiene is probably more basic than guidance since it permeates everything that goes on in the classroom, and, therefore, tends to have a greater influence on the child than the infrequent contacts he has with the counselor. The distinction is essentially that which distinguishes pupil-personnel work in the elementary school, where mental health activities are integrated with the total program, from that of the high school, whose formal guidance program is often not too closely coordinated with the work of the classroom, where, day after day, teachers continue to put through their academic paces some 150 students they barely know. It would seem that, even at best, counselors can only be a supplement to the teacher and that, at all times, the latter will have to bear the brunt of the guidance of the vast majority of the children in his classes. The guidance program can probably serve its best function in helping the teacher do his job more efficiently.

THE MENTAL HEALTH OF THE TEACHER

IMPORTANCE OF THE MENTAL HEALTH
OF THE TEACHER

Whereas the focus of the modern school should be on the child, the mental health of the teacher is no less important. In fact, when we consider the influence on both the adjustment and achievement of a host of children which the teacher can have, the latter's adjustment assumes even greater importance than that of any other single person in the school. As Cantor (1953) points out:

> The keystone of the entire educational enterprise . . . is the teacher. Without her zeal to teach and her will to learn, the classroom remains the wilderness of wasted logic, however, pretty the words. There can be no substitute for the courageous warmth of the teacher who seeks to understand herself, her pupils, and what happens between them during the teaching-learning process. [p. 347]

Undoubtedly, the teacher is the greatest single determinant of whether the school program will be beneficial to the mental health of wave after wave of children. He needs to be the kind of person with whom children can identify, who respects their dignity, who is sensitive to their needs and capable of orienting the curriculum toward significant goals.

Maladjustment is not unknown among teachers. Whereas research findings vary, depending on the severity of the criteria used, estimates suggest that some 20 percent of teachers in the field are in need of psychiatric help (Fenton, 1943; Hicks, 1943). Altman (1941) found 4 percent of his sample of New York teachers to be mental cases. At more normal levels, research has shown worry, disturbed sleep, shyness, indecision, absent-mindedness, fatigue, and headaches to be (in that order) the most frequent symptoms of nervous instability among teachers. The relative seriousness of maladjustment among teachers in comparison with other occupational groups is difficult to appraise; sampling problems, for example, make it impossible to interpret such studies as that of H. L. Smith and Hightower (1948) showing teachers to have a greater incidence of neurotic symptoms than any other group of patients at the Mayo Clinic. Comparison with other groups, however, is essentially irrelevant; in view of their crucial role, maladjustment among teachers is automatically the cause of greater alarm and apprehension than equal maladjustment in other occupational groups.

The fact remains that there is a substantial incidence of maladjustment among teachers. It may be that the strain and stress of the classroom creates an adjustment problem too severe for all but the most stable, or, perhaps, that teaching attracts individuals with various forms of maladjustment, e.g., those with strong feelings of hostility who see the classroom as a place where they can vent their aggressions against defenseless children. No doubt, it is possible to cite examples of persons who have gone into teaching apparently for the purpose—perhaps among others— of bossing children around or of satisfying a neurotic need to be loved.

A number of teacher personality patterns can be identified. Cronbach (1963), for example, contrasts the impersonal and the supportive teacher. The impersonal teacher may like his pupils but he sees himself as a work director; the classroom is a work laboratory, not a place for social interaction. He may operate a very efficient classroom. Too frequently, however, this atmosphere degenerates into a critical attitude and somewhat of a conflict between teachers and pupils who do not understand each other. The supportive teacher, on the other hand, is interested in children and frequently has a need for loyalty, affection, and trust. He—perhaps more frequently, *she*—often gives children more help than they require. He wants them to learn but he enjoys having them lean on him. Since he rarely disapproves, the pupils may be encouraged to try and perhaps to develop creativity. They are likely to like the teacher and to be liked by him, and he may have a strong influence in their development of attitudes. The classroom atmosphere is likely to be cohesive and warm, and particularly suited to the child with strong affective needs. The achievement-oriented child, on the other hand, may be less happy.

Of major significance is the Ryans study (1960) reviewed in Chapter 1, in which he identified three basic patterns of teacher classroom behavior: [a] friendly, understanding, as opposed to aloof, egocentric and restrictive; [b] responsible, businesslike and systematic, as opposed to evading, unplanned, and slipshod; and [c] stimulating, imaginative, surgent, as opposed to dull and routine. He then related these teacher-behavior patterns to pupil behavior. Teachers with docile classes, for instance, tended to be more systematic and inflexible, more constant and predictable, more responsible but also more autocratic. Greatest pupil initiative was found among teachers who tended to be democratic, understanding of pupils, original, but less responsible and less organized. It seems that the more dominant the part played by the teacher, the less responsibility students accept; perhaps if teachers want to encourage pupil initiative, they need to refrain from exercising excessive leadership in the planning and the execution of classroom activities. Also of interest is the study by Heil et al. (1960), also mentioned in Chapter 1, in which pupil responsibility was again lowest under the orderly teachers and highest under the spontaneous teachers. Pupil achievement was found to be a function of the interaction between teacher and pupil personality; the strivers did about as well under all kinds of teachers, but the conformers did badly under the spontaneous teachers who were less democratic and supportive, while the opposers did best under the firm hand of orderly teachers but badly under the spontaneous and the fearful teachers. Unfortunately, from the standpoint of teacher selection, research so far has yielded little of direct practical value—or at least, the findings have not been commensurate with the needs of American education.

Although the evidence is not conclusive, maladjusted teachers tend to have maladjusted pupils. Boynton and his co-workers (1934), for instance, found that adjusted teachers had more stable pupils than teachers considered maladjusted. Similar results were obtained by Baxter (1950), and, of course, the average person can recall instances of a frustrated teacher who had negative effects upon students, who, in turn, vented their annoyance by making things miserable for him, thereby complicating his adjustment problems. A particularly strong stand against the presence of maladjusted teachers in the classroom was taken by the American Association of School Administrators (1942):

> . . . the emotionally unstable teacher exerts such a detrimental influence on children that she should not be allowed to remain in the classroom . . . . Such teachers need help, but while they are being helped, they should be out of the classroom so their pupils may be freed from the psychic injury, repression, and fear which their presence creates. [p. 139]

On the other hand, the fact that Ash (1944) found no correlation between the teacher's adjustment and the emotional and social behavior of his pupils may suggest that the important thing is not the teacher's adjustment but rather the way it is reflected in his behavior as it affects children. The teacher who is aware of his own problems may be more sympathetic and sensitive to those of his pupils and more capable of channeling their difficulties into constructive outlets. Furthermore, since other factors affect the stability of children, it is not fair to blame the teacher's lack of adjustment for all the problems of children. Nonetheless, it is true that some teachers have their hands so full of their own troubles that they can hardly be expected to work effectively in guiding their pupils' growth. It takes only one or two on any faculty to scuttle, in effect, the mental hygiene program of the school. The harm done by a few teachers who are better suited to be recipients than givers of guidance is often as irreparable as it is inexcusable. Teachers whose maladjustment is reflected in their being bossy, often cross, always fussing, and given to nagging and antagonizing children just cannot inspire them to do their best.

The teacher's mental health is directly related to the work of the classroom. Whereas the plumber can be most maladjusted without it having too much effect on his customers, maladjustment on the part of the teacher is very likely to affect in a vital way the growth of the children in his care. Good mental health on his part therefore generally should be as important a qualification as academic competence or a valid teacher's certificate. This is particularly important in the elementary school where children may be stuck with the same teacher day in and day out for a whole year.

FACTORS AFFECTING THE MENTAL HEALTH
OF THE TEACHER

Much of the material in this text has direct bearing on the teacher's mental health and he should be able to apply the principles we have discussed to his situation as well as to that of his pupils. For example, he must realize that, like any other human being, he must derive certain satisfactions from his job if he is to remain a contented and integrated individual, and that he is not promoting his own adjustment nor that of his pupils when he attempts to satisfy his needs at their expense.

Teaching, like any other occupation incorporates both favorable and unfavorable mental health factors. Among the former are the following:

[a] Teaching presents ample opportunities for satisfying one's needs. The teacher doing a good job has the satisfaction of seeing children grow, feeling their respect and affection, and obtaining the recognition of parents and the community. When the teacher becomes sensitive to the needs of children and makes the classroom a pleasant and profitable place for them, he soon finds that they, in turn, help satisfy his needs so that teaching becomes rewarding. This is probably the greatest satisfaction to be derived from teaching. It tends to be restricted, however, to those who enjoy teaching sufficiently to be good teachers; the poor teacher very often reaps nothing but pupil and parental hostility, if not contempt.

Teaching involves a variety of work and a constant challenge for the teacher interested in children and their growth. Every child is unique and presents unique problems calling for the highest level of professional competence. For the imaginative teacher, each day is a whole new adventure. He will not always be successful in solving all his problems, but there will be no lack of opportunity to use his skills, initiative, and ingenuity for the benefit of children and his own self-fulfillment.

[b] Teaching offers steady employment with reasonable pay, steady increases, a rather short day, and numerous vacations throughout the year. This advantage, is, of course, lost when teachers become straddled with heavy co-curricular responsibilities, when they have to attend university classes, or when they feel compelled to take an extra job to supplement their income.

[c] Among other advantages are association with educated people of like interest, clean work, and contact with youth whose enthusiasm and vitality will never let the teacher grow old—unless he grows sour, in which case, it will be remarkably effective in hastening the process.

There is also an unfavorable side:

[a] For some teachers, the major hazard in teaching is monotony—using the same methods, the same outlines, the same illustrations, the same audiovisual aids; eating the same meals in the same cafeteria; wearing the same style of clothes, etc. They are in a rut! Presenting the same material year after year—and repeating it for the benefit of the slower children for good measure—is bound to get boring. Actually, good teaching can never be routine: it calls for improvement in method, for changes in content depending on the interests, needs, and purposes of the children, and above all it calls for orientation toward children rather than subject matter. On the other hand, teaching is sometimes frustrating because the

results of one's work are not immediately observable. This is especially so in pupil adjustment where a teacher may work for months with no observable results. It is also true that some teachers try too hard and expect too much too soon, and, as a result, end up disappointed and discouraged.

[b] Teaching can involve a great deal of nervous strain. Not only are numerous emotionally charged situations likely to occur in the course of the day, but, even at best, children are full of pep and vinegar and they can be irritating even to the calmest teacher. The teacher also plays a number of roles in and out of the classroom, some of which are conflicting, e.g., friend and guide of youth but also disciplinarian, mental hygienist but also guardian of academic standards, etc.—often with considerable internal conflict. When the teacher is unstable to begin with, the strain on teacher and pupil alike can become unbearable. Such a teacher should probably be guided out of the profession.

The teacher needs time to collect his wits and his energy. A free period when he can take a minute to relax without having children under foot, perhaps time for a cup of coffee, can do wonders in setting the ship back on an even keel. Teaching may actually involve considerable fatigue depending on the size of the classes, the nature of the pupils and of the subject taught, and, of course, the physical stamina of the teacher. Heavy teaching loads, overcrowded classroom, university work, and clerical duties were among the major health hazards of classroom teachers in the Kaplan and O'Dea study (1953). Teachers, especially those in the smaller schools, are often loaded with co-curricular assignments, committee work, unending reports, and clerical—if not janitorial—duties in addition to a full teaching load. Thus, to quote Bowlby (1947):

> . . . the problem of extracurricular duties is really enough to take your time, your health, and your breath away. Every teacher is expected to serve as class advisor as well as sponsor two or more activities, plus a little coaching or dramatic work on the side. Three-in-one oil is modest in its numerical claims when compared to the small high school teacher who is expected to be a seven-in-one paragon—guidance expert, advisor, teacher, clerk, and assistant janitor, plus football and basketball coach. [p. 21]

Yet generally it is the frustration resulting from things undone and problems unsolved as well as from boredom—rather than good hard work— that leads to fatigue. Once the strain starts to accumulate, tension piles up and teachers begin to nag, overemphasize the trivial, and become unable to organize their work on an efficient basis. The result is general annoyance and shortness of temper, which soon leads to animosity on the part of pupils and thus to a vicious circle.

[c] Closely connected with nervous strain as an unfavorable aspect of

teaching are the frequent conflicts that arise during the school day. Maintaining discipline, for example, often poses a problem for the teacher who wants to be loved and appreciated and yet does not know how to be permissive without having students take advantage of him. He may feel he has to choose between bedlam and resulting censure by the principal, and autocratic control and pupil antagonism. Student defiance and hostility are more common in some communities and at certain grade levels than others, but again it seems that some teachers are perpetually running into one conflict after another while other teachers rarely have any trouble. When such conflicts occur too frequently, the teacher might well ask himself whether he is bringing these problems on himself, perhaps by his personal rigidity, his insensitivity, or his incompetence in adjusting the curriculum to pupil needs and purposes. Teachers sometimes run into problems when their need to be loved makes it difficult for them to maintain discipline and insist on a certain amount of work. This often leads them to compromise some of their values, with resulting feelings of guilt and anxiety.

When a relationship of mutual understanding and respect exists between teacher and pupils, such conflicts are likely to be rare and minor, especially when the teacher is proficient in adapting the curriculum to student needs and purposes. He must also give the child a feeling of status and recognition and thus make it unnecessary for the latter to become a behavior problem in order to get attention. He should be sure to provide outlets for draining emotional tension before it reaches explosive proportions.

The teacher needs to understand not only what causes children to behave as they do but he also needs to understand his own behavior. The secure teacher should be able to tolerate irritations without being unduly upset, and certainly a teacher who enjoys children can understand that their buoyancy is bound to get them into trouble once in a while. When he finds himself unduly provoked at a child's behavior, he might well ask himself what in his own background causes him to be so disturbed at this kind of behavior. He needs to stop once in a while and ask himself: "Why is my class getting noisier every day?" "Am I pushing John too hard?" "Was I really helping him or just relieving my own tensions?" It is easy to lose perspective and develop obsessive concern over the routine, mechanical, and often trivial aspects of teaching. It is easy to become hypercritical. The teacher who constantly criticizes students, colleagues, and the system may be revealing insecurity that can be an obstacle to his effectiveness. When tensions become chronic, when he can no longer tolerate horseplay, when he is disturbed over small things, perhaps he should be oriented out of the profession, for the child must be allowed to be a child on his way to becoming an adult.

Some teachers feel the way to handle conflicts with students is to point out in no uncertain terms who is boss. Unfortunately, this often restores order and gives them the illusion that they have solved the problem when, in reality, they have only dealt with superficial behavior and actually aggravated the problem by increasing the inner tension and frustration of which the misbehavior was but a symptom. Tough disciplinarians actually create more problems than they resolve; by increasing pupil resentment and hostility they promote misconduct as well as conflict and maladjustment. Such behavior also precludes building pupil respect and acceptance and denies them the satisfactions they so definitely need. In short order, besieged by pupil and parental hostility, they are forced to depend more and more on autocratic control and punitive measures which inevitably rebound against them.

Yet teachers must be allowed to be different. The compulsive teacher does not necessarily have a detrimental effect on his pupils. Many teachers are pushers; they move students along as rapidly as possible, they tolerate a minimum of nonsense, and yet many are well liked. Many are warm and are appreciated by their students for their effectiveness in getting them to do their best work. There is no tension, no resentment, and the achievement-oriented child may well find in such a teacher a model with whom he can generate strong personal identification.

Conflicts often arise from poor teacher-principal relationships. Just as some teachers are misguided in dealing with pupils, so some administrators consider pupils and teachers as mere cogs in the pedagogical machine. And just as children suffer from repressive controls at the hands of teachers, so do teachers often suffer from the same sort of control at the hands of the administration. Many teachers feel forced to contend with unrealistic standards, rigid requirements, and petty politics. They sometimes feel that they are prevented from doing their best for the child by administrative restrictions, oversize classes, constant interruptions, and endless clerical demands. Some principals insist that teachers engage in outdated practices; many conceive classroom orderliness and quiet as the ultimate criterion of teacher efficiency. And, of course, conflicts also arise from the opposite situation, e.g., when the teacher, exasperated at the behavior of a youngster, sends him to the principal only to be told that perhaps if he were a little more understanding of children, he would have fewer problems.

Communication between teachers and administrator sometimes breaks down to the point that, while each blames and complains about the other, they never get around to dealing constructively with their differences. Teachers often complain about the principal to each other but, in his presence, blame the pupils and their parents. In the meantime, frustration and hostility on the part of the principal and especially of the teachers are directed toward the children as the scapegoat in the situation, while apathy and poor morale bounce from the principal to the teachers and the pupils and back again. The emotional and academic tone of the school revolves around the principal. However, his responsibilities cause him to be concerned with the functioning of the whole school rather than with the work of individual teachers and occasionally a teacher may feel cheated out of deserved recognition, especially when the atmosphere is one of favoritism and petty politics.

Administrators must give teachers freedom to do what their professional judgment tells them is right. Blanket rules affecting all teachers often do more harm than good; teachers, like children, can do their best work when their individuality is respected. The administration has the responsibility to help teachers become better teachers. This implies, among other things, that teachers need security; a teacher is not likely to seek help when doing so entails acknowledging his weaknesses to the very people responsible for judging his effectiveness for purposes of promotion and salary increment. For this reason, the guidance of teachers should be as independent as possible of the element of administrative rating. Undoubtedly no greater service can be given the cause of education than providing for the adequate guidance of teachers through permissive and constructive supervision for, as Edward M. Glaser (1941) points out, if educational practices are ever to be improved, the teacher is the component of the educative process with which we must begin. This is not always easy. Teachers have marked tendencies toward certain behaviors. These are frequently a matter of well-established habits and are quite resistant to change; the authoritarian teacher, for example, cannot give up his authoritarianism without considerable threat.

Conflicts also arise when parents do not see eye to eye with the teacher on such matters as discipline, homework, curriculum, or teaching methods. The poor teacher often finds it difficult to agree simultaneously with the mother of the gifted child who wants rigid grading and a more advanced academic curriculum and with the mother of the duller child who has a different ax to grind, with the parent who wants more homework and the parent who wants less—all of which he is expected to do, while at the same time complying with administrative regulations on the subject. It must be noted in this connection that the parent is generally well-meaning; he simply wants the best for his child, a reaction which is both understandable and perhaps commendable. And he may be right; but his child is only one of 30 or more with whom the teacher has to contend. At any rate, all these demands made upon him to be everything to everybody at once leaves the poor teacher confused and often demoralized.

[d] A fourth source of difficulty (which is fortunately being relaxed in recent years) concerns the isolation of the teacher through unnecessary restrictions on his personal life. The imposition of certain restrictions is psychologically sound: teachers by their own choice have set themselves in a position where they become models to be copied by children. Therefore, they cannot allow themselves to become involved in scandals or

even minor episodes that might go unnoticed in a lesser position. Nevertheless, certain restrictions are unnecessary: the community cannot put restrictions on such things as dating, participation in civic groups, or other activities to which the teacher, as a member of a democratic community, is entitled without in the long run destroying his effectiveness. The solution lies in the teacher convincing himself of his rights as a citizen and his duty as a public servant and leader of youth and insisting on those rights—provided they do not interfere with his responsibility as a teacher. Taking sides in a controversial issue, for example, regardless of the merits of his stand, might easily jeopardize his effectiveness with certain pupils and their parents who have deep-seated convictions favoring the opposite point of view.

[e] Salary is also a point of contention for some teachers, although generally the salary issue comes up only when morale is low and other grievances are present. Some teachers feel they are not understood and appreciated, that effort and competence go unrewarded, that all the administration and the community do is to pile on extra chores with never a word of recognition. Others feel that lack of professional help, e.g., academic consultants and referral services, forces them to struggle with problems they cannot resolve. The question of low salary is usually tied to a general discontent and often to a lack of adjustment to teaching as a career.

Teacher salaries do not compare with those of medicine, law, or engineering, but they are reasonably free from operating expense and risk. Besides, salaries have come up and will maintain this rise as teachers continue to provide competent professional services. Teachers must remember that they are in the profession to provide a service, not to get out of it all the traffic will bear. If a teacher feels underpaid, such a feeling will soon lead to frustration and to a lack of enthusiasm and initiative which can do great harm if transmitted to the children. For that reason, an underpaid teacher is rarely worth what he is getting, and, for the good of all, including himself, he should look for a position elsewhere. Teaching has certain satisfactions and certain annoyances and attracts a particular type of person who is content to operate within such a framework. A teacher who cannot adjust to these conditions owes it to all concerned to get out of the profession.

SUGGESTIONS FOR PROMOTING
THE MENTAL HEALTH OF THE TEACHER

Teaching is not without mental health hazards which take their toll. The fact that not all teachers display signs of maladjustment, however, apparently points to differences either in the stability of teachers entering the profession or in the conditions they encounter after they become teachers. The two sets of factors are closely interrelated: the well-adjusted beginning

teacher is likely to deal with whatever situation he encounters with effectiveness. The unstable teacher, on the other hand, is likely to find himself in a vicious circle, for the unfavorable factors involved in teaching
are magnified in the case of the unfit, with resulting harm to both himself
and the children.

Undoubtedly, the most effective way of improving the mental health
of the teaching profession (and succeeding generations of youngsters) is
to select as prospective teachers emotionally stable individuals who go
into teaching because of a mature interest and liking for children. This
places a great responsibility upon the shoulders of teacher-training institutions, especially since the factors involved in teacher success are not only
relatively unknown but also relatively difficult to measure, particularly in
the setting of the usual lecture-type college class.

The principal has a particular responsibility not only for choosing good
teachers for his school but also for promoting and maintaining high morale
and efficiency, for just as the teacher sets the tone of the classroom, so
in a more general way the principal sets the tone of the school. Implied
are: [a] a democratic organization and operation of the school, including
discussion rather than dictation of policies, constructive supervision, and
group action on school problems; [b] adequate salary, equipment, and
other facilities that befit the dignity of the teaching profession; and [c]
cordial relations among administrators, teachers, pupils, and parents, each
aware of his responsibilities and the need for cooperation.

The teacher himself has the primary responsibility for his own mental
health. Granted a liking for children, he still must acquaint himself with
the principles of psychology so that he can understand children better.
He must be fully sold on teaching as an opportunity for service and convinced that whatever promotes pupil adjustment is also conducive to his
own well-being. He should concentrate on developing positive relationships
with pupils, fellow-teachers, parents, and administrators through developing sensitivity and resourcefulness in dealing with people. He also needs
to understand and accept himself, for only as he accepts his own shortcomings can he accept those of others. Furthermore, inasmuch as nothing
gives the teacher so much of a lift as pride and confidence in his ability
to do the job, he should strive for competence in both his subject area
and teaching methods. It has been found, for example, that teachers are
not only restricted in reading ability but also in reading interests. In a
study by Simpson (1942), 3 percent of high school seniors actually read
better than all the teachers; 75 percent of the twelfth-graders read better
than 15 percent of the administrators and teachers. Even the teachers who
read well made little, if any, more professional use of this ability than
those who read poorly. It would almost seem that the awarding of the
certificate marks the completion of their education—this, on the part of
people who are supposed to instill in children a never-ending desire for

education! Teachers need to recognize that their mental health as well as their effectiveness revolves crucially around their continued professional growth. They should also develop a sense of belonging by taking an active part in the affairs of the profession.

As the teacher grows in ability to consolidate children into a functional and cohesive group bent on the pursuit of common goals, he finds that troubles disappear; as he grows in security he finds it easier to be tolerant, to look upon annoying behavior as something to analyze from the standpoint of causation rather than as a personal affront. Pupil misbehavior then becomes a challenge, just as the principal's criticisms serve as a basis for improvement rather than as a cause for anger and resentment. He can then see things in perspective; he can distinguish the important from the trivial, and he no longer needs to be on the defensive. As he becomes free from having to worry about his security, he finds more time to plan, to organize his working day on an efficient operational basis, and to routinize what should be on a routine schedule; thus, he preserves his energies for devising more meaningful classroom experiences, for developing greater sensitivity to pupils needs, and, in general, for increasing his effectiveness and thus ensuring himself greater satisfaction from teaching.

The teacher should cultivate wide interests and associate with people outside the narrow circle of the classroom so that he does not have to be dependent on his students for the satisfaction of his needs. He can then be more objective in dealing with students and be of greater help to them.[5] He should also remember that "all work and no play makes Jack a dull boy" and he should have time for both. This is particularly true of the woman teacher with a family who may find her attempt to be a wife, a mother, and a teacher results in her being a failure at all three. The teacher must keep in good physical health, and although some teachers, perhaps because of relative freedom from unnecessary tension and ability to put work on an efficient basis, seem full of energy, others definitely need weekends and vacations to recuperate. The teacher should not take pupil assignments home to grade unless he is sure there is no better way and that the time and energy so spent could not be used more constructively. This is not an endorsement of laziness; the author is merely suggesting that teacher effectiveness is probably more closely proportional to the planning and imagination he brings to the classroom than to the number of hours he keeps his nose to the grindstone.[6]

[5] For the clinician to be of maximum service, he must maintain with his clients a relationship which is professional, not personal. To some extent, this also applies to teachers: they should not get so involved with the children that they carry the burden of their pupils' problems on their shoulders.

[6] The teacher needs periodically to appraise the value of what he is doing in terms of pupil growth. Are the hours spent with a red pencil actually helping the child with his English? Is talking in class so bad? Teachers often get too busy to consider whether there might be an easier and more productive way of doing things.

Yet despite all the constructive planning of which the teacher is capable, there will be days when everything will go wrong. If this occurs too frequently, he may well be in the wrong field and despite all the glory that attends the virtue of perseverance, there is even greater virtue in knowing when to quit. Yet he must not waste every ounce of the energy he should be spending in teaching worrying about his effectiveness. Instead he should do the best job he can, and he might do well to remember the words of Wattenberg and Redl (1950):

> There are too few saints to fill all teaching positions, so imperfect human beings must do the bulk of the instruction of youth. What counts is not your virtues or your vices but what you do to children with them.

HIGHLIGHTS OF THE CHAPTER

Although it is receiving increasing attention, mental illness continues to be the United States' number one health problem. Its complexity and magnitude are such as to require the concerted efforts of all social agencies, none of which is in a better position to contribute to its alleviation than the school. Not only does the school have close contact with the child throughout his formative years, but since so much of his life centers on the school, his experiences there are bound to have a profound influence on his mental health.

[a]

Mental hygiene in the classroom is neither a fad nor a body of clinical techniques; on the contrary, it is part-and-parcel of the teaching-learning process through which the child's maximum self-realization is promoted. It is through good teaching that the teacher can make his greatest contribution to the child's mental health.

[b]

Mental hygiene has three main purposes: [1] the prevention of mental illness; [2] the development of mental health; and [3] the correction of mental disorders. Because of the nature of the situation in which he operates and the nature of his competencies, the teacher's efforts in the therapeutic aspects of mental hygiene should be restricted to the early detection of danger signs, referral to a competent clinician, and cooperation with his recommendations.

[c]

Regardless of the availability of clinical and guidance services, the brunt of the guidance of the child and the promotion of his mental health will have to be borne by the classroom teacher.

[d]

A number of factors in the classroom constitute potential mental health hazards. These include the demands of the curriculum, discipline, the emotional climate of the classroom, examinations, and grading and reporting practices.

[e]

The teacher's mental health is of primary importance considering the effect of his personality on a large number of children. Research has uncovered considerable maladjustment among teachers, and, although the same is true of any other occupational group, maladjustment among teachers is potentially more critical.

[f]

Teaching, just like other occupations, has both favorable and unfavorable features and it attracts people who can find happiness in such a framework. For the right person, teaching can be a source of satisfaction and self-fulfillment; for the misfit, the satisfactions are minimized and the drawbacks correspondingly magnified. The latter should be guided out of the teaching profession for the good of all concerned.

[g]

A number of teacher personality patterns have been identified, most of which are probably effective in certain settings; teacher effectiveness is best defined as a function of the interaction between teacher and pupil personality.

[h]

The best way of improving the mental health of the teaching profession is to select as prospective teachers individuals who are well adjusted and who have a mature liking for children.

[i]

Administrators must do all they can to promote teacher adjustment to the job. In the final analysis, however, the teacher must assume responsibility for his own mental health; he needs to understand and accept himself, to develop competence in dealing with children, and to cultivate a sense of perspective that will prevent him from becoming unduly upset at minor irritations.

SOURCES OF RELATED MATERIAL

Association for Supervision and Curriculum Development, *Fostering Mental Health in Our Schools*. 1950 Yearbook. Washington, D.C.: The Association, 1950.

Blos, P., "Aspects of mental health in teaching and learning," *Ment. Hyg.,* 35: 555–569, 1953.

Henry, N. B. (ed.), *Mental Health in Modern Education*. 54th Yearbook, National Society for the Study of Education, Pt. II. Chicago: University of Chicago Press, 1955.

Kline, F. F., "Satisfactions and annoyances in teaching," *J. exp. Educ.*, 18: 77–89, 1949.

Kotinsky, R., and J. V. Coleman, "Mental health as an educational goal," *Teach. Coll. Rec.*, 50: 241–246, 1955.

Laycock, S. R., *Mental Hygiene in the School: A Handbook for the Classroom Teacher.* Toronto: The Copp Clark Publishing Company, 1960.

Louttit, C. M., "The school as a mental hygiene factor," *Ment. Hyg.*, 31: 50–65, 1947.

Rettig, S., and B. Pasaminick, "Status and job satisfaction of public school teachers," *Sch. & Soc.*, 87: 113–116, 1959.

Smith, M. Brewster, "Mental health reconsidered," *Amer. Psychol.*, 16: 299–306, 1961.

Strang, Ruth, and G. Morris, *Guidance in the Classroom.* New York: Crowell-Collier and Macmillan, Inc., 1964.

Szasz, Thomas S., "The myth of mental illness," *Amer. Psychol.*, 15: 113–118, 1960.

Tyson, R., "Current mental hygiene practice: An inventory of basic teachings," *J. clin. Psychol.*, 7: 4–94, 1951.

Watson, G., "Is mental illness mental?" *J. Psychol.*, 41: 323–334, 1956.

QUESTIONS AND PROJECTS

1

Comment: A teacher objects to having to concern himself with the mental health of 150 children whom he barely knows. He contends that it detracts from the primary function of the school, namely, to teach. Anyway, he is trained as a teacher, not as a psychologist.

2

Some parents complain that they sacrificed so much for their children. Analyze the nature of this "sacrifice" from the standpoint of its underlying motivation and its effect upon the children.

3

What are the particular satisfactions you anticipated which caused you to select teaching as a career? Why this particular subject area or level rather than another?

4

Debate: Until such time as the teaching profession implements effective means of eliminating from its ranks the misfit and the maladjusted, it should not be given security of tenure. Is teacher welfare compatible with the best interest of students and community? Should teachers join teacher federations as a means of increasing their bargaining power?

PART V

Synthesis

Serves as a synthesis of the contributions of the previous chapters to a blueprint for effective classroom operation, with discussion based on the premise that understanding the *why* of the child's behavior is the key to the promotion of both pupil self-actualization and classroom effectiveness; presented from the phenomenological standpoint of the fully functioning person in the pursuit of psychologically meaningful goals.

Discusses the relative merits of the pupil-centered and teacher-centered curriculum organization in relation to the psychological principles developed in the previous chapters.

CHAPTER 20

The Modern Classroom: A Psychological Reorientation

> The essentials of education must be located in the dynamics of behavior. They must be in the centers of action. They must operate at the moment when choices are being made, when directions are being selected, when consequences are being weighed. They must permeate the total life of the individual at all times.
>
> *Hopkins, 1945, p. 494*

A course in educational psychology can be justified as part of the teacher-preparation sequence only as it leads to an improvement in the effectiveness with which the teacher carries out the work of promoting pupil growth and development. Throughout the chapters of this text, various psychological principles have been considered against the background of the work of the classroom. This chapter will attempt to pinpoint some of the more important applications and implications of these principles, particularly as they relate to the organization of educational experiences by means of which the maximum self-realization of the whole child is to be promoted. The student must not expect prescriptions and rules of thumb. Furthermore, the present chapter makes no claim to a complete coverage of the implications of psychology for educational practice. The discussion will be restricted to a few of the highlights and the student is urged to review the material covered in the various chapters not as something to learn for the final examination, but rather as a foundation upon which educational practice must be based.

ORGANIZING MEANINGFUL
CLASSROOM EXPERIENCES

INEFFICIENCY IN THE SCHOOL

Education has undergone drastic changes since the turn of the century. Great progress in both educational thought and educational practice has resulted from such influences as: [a] the contribution of educational psychology, especially in the area of a greater understanding of the nature of the learner and of the learning process; and [b] sociological changes leading to a redefinition of the role of the school in modern democratic society. The net results, although not amenable to a succinct synthesis, are probably best reflected in the reorientation of educational practice toward the all-round growth of the child, as opposed to an emphasis on any given aspect at the expense of the others as was characteristic of the school of yesteryear. Moreover, modern schools and modern teachers in various parts of the country not only exemplify the latest philosophical and psychological thinking put into practice, but they also earn recognition and respect through the caliber of the services they provide and the product they turn out.

Yet, alongside this modernism that characterizes certain schools and certain teachers, there also exists throughout the United States, schools and teachers whose Rip Van Winkle procedures are not only woefully ineffective, but, worse, are definitely detrimental to the all-round growth of the unfortunate children who are subjected to their influence. Ironically, much of the harm is caused by teachers and administrators whose sincerity cannot be doubted, who are fully convinced that they are acting in the children's best interest, but whose lack of understanding of the basic principles of psychology makes them nonetheless an undeniable hazard to the self-realization of countless children. Thus, daily, well-meaning teachers force children to participate in exercises in which they have no interest or to do things that are completely beyond their abilities. They scold, nag, and give out failing grades because the children cannot meet their unrealistic standards; they punish them when, in desperation at this constant frustration of their needs, children misbehave. All this, because of a firm belief that, if the children tried hard enough, they could do it. Anyway, the curriculum has to be covered regardless of the cost.

Some teachers are apparently under the impression that unless children are driven like tigers in a circus act, the quality of their performance will be impaired, and that children will neither work nor behave unless kept under the constant threat of failure and punishment. They would never give a compliment for work well done for fear children will immediately

rest on their laurels; but, on the other hand, they never miss an opportunity to criticize (presumably, as a way of building moral fiber and a
striving for perfection). The sad part is that these teachers feel they are
doing their duty. That they might accomplish more by trying to encourage
their pupils to do their best than by trying to crush them and to down-
grade their self-concept, apparently has not occurred to them.[1]

Paralleling these inexcusable violations of the principles of educational
psychology—or perhaps, more correctly, *because* of this failure on the part
of certain teachers to comply with the principles of educational psychology
—our schools have not been overly successful, whatever the criterion of
success one uses: adjustment and mental health, social and emotional
maturity, enlightened self-interest, or academic or intellectual competence.

Our schools are unquestionably superior to those of years ago. To
argue that youngsters of today know less than their counterparts at the
turn of the century is sheer nonsense. Our children have a wider background as a result of a more adequate curriculum as well as television,
travel, and other broadening experiences. Our understanding of children
is more adequate, our methods are better, and the product is also better.
On the other hand, the three R's, or even the usual high school education,
are no longer adequate for an atomic age; we must—we can—do better.
Recent research findings discussed in the previous chapters suggest exciting
new possibilities that need to be incorporated in upgrading educational
practice as well as in redirecting it in more enlightened directions.

Many critics have lambasted our educational institutions for what
they feel is ineptitude, and, whereas these criticisms are not completely
warranted and whereas they are often made to reflect on all schools in
full rather than on the few and in part, they are not entirely without
foundation. Mursell (1952), for example, not only gives instances of
teaching in direct violation of the principles of educational psychology,
but claims that these instances are unfortunately typical of many of our
present educational practices.

Among the many examples of inefficiency and malpractice in the classroom readily obvious to the impartial observer, one might mention the
following:

[a] Classroom activities are too exclusively a matter of verbal behavior
with a heavy reliance on abstract and technical language. The logical outcome in too many cases is verbalism piled on verbalism, frustration, general
disinterest, apathy, and misbehavior. The child's knowledge of grammar
does not lead to an improvement in his oral and written work. The teaching of science is often formalized and systematized into intellectual units
which have no relationship to his daily experiences and interest. Mathematics is often not brought down to the level at which he can under-

---

[1] The strong opposition of some of these same teachers to merit rating, presumably
based on fear of being downgraded, is interesting in this connection.

stand it, let alone use it in living. And social studies is often taught in the abstract so that it is completely foreign to the problems he faces in everyday life. The school's major—and often most "successful"—efforts, it seems, are expended in stifling the child's initiative, creativity, and originality—all in the interest of conformity to stereotyped educational goals defined in narrow and rigid units of the *right* answer.

[b] The curriculum which dominates some of our schools is so unsuitable for a sizable percentage of our children that it interferes with the promotion of their maximum self-realization both directly through the nature of the learning experiences that it contains and indirectly through the shackling of the teacher and the consequent encouragement of ineffective teaching methods. The curriculum in the great majority of our schools is a subject curriculum: in many cases, according to Burton (1962), it is a textbook curriculum "tragically unrelated to life needs" not only for children but also for adults, "for immediate and remote needs of anyone, anywhere, at any time." Under such conditions there can be no good teaching. Page assignments in a single text followed by a verbal quiz and drill aimed at the memorization of facts[2]—with no aim other than covering the text—is used by the "great majority" of secondary school teachers even though, again to quote Burton, "it would be difficult to devise an educational practice so grossly ineffective, so certainly calculated to interfere with learning . . . ." Many of our schools still rely on such potentially damaging measures as coercion, competition, and punishment as a means of pushing meaningless material on defenseless children. As a result, the things that stand out in too many of our schools are apathy, satisfaction with mediocrity and getting by, a great interest in "cinch" courses, and "goofing off."

THE CURRICULUM

Schools exist for the purpose of providing meaningful experiences through which pupil growth can be promoted most effectively. No one denies the fact that the child learns many useful things out of school. However, such out-of-school experiences tend to be too haphazard, uncoordinated, and unconcentrated for society to depend upon them for educating its future citizens. Schools cannot be like life; it is precisely because of the failure of ordinary life experiences to provide a suitable education that schools have been established. Schools exist for the purpose of selecting those experiences that are worthwhile and meaningful to the child, of bringing them into vital relationship with him so that he can integrate them in a functional way, and guiding him in his reactions to these experiences so that they will be educationally profitable.

[2] Many teachers prefer routine, busy work, and the memorization of facts. This calls for little imagination, is easier to enforce through drill, and easier to measure from the standpoint of outcome.

The sequence of experiences through which the school attempts to promote pupil growth is known as the curriculum. Ideally, it should incorporate the best experiences one could devise; and contrariwise, a poor curriculum, in the sense of emphasizing the trivial at the expense of the essentials, of emphasizing the unattainable and the useless, of being unrealistic, would automatically negate the very purpose for which the school exists.

Most, if not all, experiences are educative in the broad sense of the word. Some of these are undoubtedly detrimental to the learner's long-term welfare. More pertinent, however, is the fact that a great many experiences which are educative in the beneficial sense can be found, and if time were unlimited the child could become educated by simply being exposed to them all. But time is not unlimited and the school, if it is to fulfill its responsibility to society, must select among the many experiences to which the child could be subjected those which are likely to result in the maximum growth at the minimum expense in time and effort. Just what these experiences are is, of course, a matter of considerable disagreement.

The experiences incorporated into the curriculum are simply the vehicle through which desirable learning takes place and it is the learning that counts rather than the experiences through which it is achieved. Although it is a psychological fact that children learn only through the medium of subject matter, yet subject matter is incidental to learning and the study of history or algebra is worthwhile only to the extent to which it enables the child to do something which is purposeful to him. The question is not one of teaching the child a given subject but rather of choosing the sequence of experiences that will promote his maximum self-realization.

Although what to include in the curriculum is first of all a problem in educational philosophy, this is an area in which educational psychology can also play a definite role. Whether or not Latin or physical education should be emphasized in our schools, for example, centers on the extent to which the disciplinary and direct values of each in promoting pupil growth are greater than those of other experiences competing for inclusion in the curriculum. Likewise, whether the curriculum should be oriented toward the more formal aspects or those more closely related to the child's experience cannot be considered apart from the effectiveness with which such learnings take place.

Generally speaking, the long-term goals of education, e.g., ability to think clearly, a scientific attitude, tolerance, and social competence, are a matter of educational philosophy. The more immediate goals and the means whereby both short- and long-range goals are attained are more properly the province of educational psychology. Thus, whether the teacher conducts a unit on sanitation, transportation, or city government as a means of promoting learning in the area of number work, reading comprehension, or civic responsibility is probably best decided on the basis of psychological, rather than philosophical, considerations, simply because the extent to which an experience is truly educative depends on such psychological factors as the child's interests and purposes. Likewise, if one has to choose between two equally important goals to be achieved through the curriculum, preference might be given to the one which, according to educational psychology, is relatively more attainable and/or functional.

The school must constantly reevaluate not only its methods but also its curriculum in the light of changing social and philosophical thought, and especially in the light of new discoveries in the area of educational psychology. On the other hand, it must not initiate changes simply for the sake of change. Teachers are not believers in doing things by halves; when convinced that a suggested procedure is better than the current one, they are likely to make a complete shift without realizing that perhaps the solution lies in a middle-of-the-road position. Educational procedures have a long history of pendulumlike swings over the years—from a completely phonetic approach in teaching reading to a total disregard of phonics, from rigid drill procedures to an easy-going curriculum dictated by the whims of immature children, from a rigid teacher-controlled classroom atmosphere to a pupil-dominated state of classroom disorganization.

Some of these changes have come in response to the demands of the public that certain courses be offered in the school or that a greater or lesser emphasis be placed on a certain phase of the curriculum because of its alleged importance or unimportance. Thus, statistics on the physical inadequacies of American youth inducted into service during World War II led to an increased emphasis on physical education, only to have it cede to science and mathematics as a result of the clamor for scientists that accompanied the launching of the Russian *Sputnik*. Generally, Americans consider themselves practical and, in contrast to the European idea of the finishing school and the gentleman scholar, tend to emphasize the practical as opposed to the cultural and the theoretical. Likewise, there tends to be a more or less persistent demand for the specific and the tangible as opposed to the general, a trend which has met with considerable favor among harried teachers eager to meet the demands of still another emphasis in American education, namely, adequate performance on various objective tests of academic achievement.

Some of the demands made upon the school have come from professional educators and psychologists. Thus, the emphasis of the "life adjustment" curriculum on problems closely related to the everyday life of citizens in a democracy, as opposed to the more "classical" curriculum, has roots in the thinking of such educational leaders as Dewey, Thorndike, and others. On the other hand, pressures have also been applied by various groups for a return to a curriculum or to methods which do not make psychological or pedagogical sense. Many seem to have no basis other than the premise that the tougher the subject, the better the training. Corey (1959), in a masterful rebuttal to the Conant report (1959), *The American High School*, points to the absurdity of deliberately taking the harder of two roads leading to the same objective; he hopes that in due course, American educators will return to the basic psychological principle that what is learned is meaningful to the degree that it is relevant to the learner's purposes and not to the degree that it is hard to learn. He also hopes that in due time, educators will once again recognize that the purpose of secondary education is not to teach vast amounts of subject matter but rather to influence behavior.

Unfortunately, rather than attempting to educate the public and to put some of the criticisms of education into proper perspective, educators have at times given way to the pressures of vocal minority groups to the detriment of the child whose welfare should be their only consideration. The fact that teachers still grade children and report their progress on the old-fashioned report card, that they make their primary goal the covering of the subject matter assigned at each grade level is hardly indicative of professional status or professional responsibility. Teachers ought to know what is in the child's best interest and ought to be willing to exercise leadership in school matters rather than relinquish it to the school board, the PTA, or the vocal members of the general public. This is not to imply that all public pressures are misdirected and that the school should not be sensitive to the needs of society as reflected in public opinion. It is simply that educational changes should be based on a conviction of their desirability rather than on expediency.

It must, of course, be recognized that some of the issues involved cannot be resolved on an either-or basis. We also need to define more specifically just what we expect of modern American education. Is the primary criterion of our success in the current decade to be our ability to develop the intellectual powers of the American people, to promote interpersonal goodwill, or perhaps to win the space race? The issue revolves around the question of what constitutes significant learnings. Hopkins in 1945 suggested that the essentials we had set for ourselves were not being achieved and further that they were not the important goals. Psychology shows that knowledge is a necessary but not sufficient condition for effective behavior. Some writers have emphasized that education is best conceived in dimensions of improved attitudes, broadened interests, personal and social adjustment, and other aspects of personality development. According to Combs (1962) and Rogers (1959), the learnings which really make a difference are those which enable the individual to see himself differently and accept himself, as a result of which he becomes more self-confident, more self-directive, more open to his experiences, and more the person he would like to be.

Significant education is more adequately defined in improved problem-solving ability than in memorized solutions, in sharpened and broadened insights and understandings than in the accumulation of isolated facts, in improved behavior and increased significance in the life of the individual than in ability to pass examinations or make the honor roll. Under favorable conditions, for example, group discussion may lead to a more adequate appraisal of a given situation, a more adequate formulation of goals, a more conscientious and constructive attempt at attaining these goals and, what is especially important, a greater likelihood of having any decision effectualized in actual behavior. Overemphasis on the intellectual and the academic, on the other hand, leads to the ability to verbalize material, often without too much understanding of its deeper meaning and especially without having it attain the significance in terms of the learner's purposes necessary for it to result in a change of behavior. Education that does not have personal meaning is no education at all. Children have come to view subject matter as a vehicle for gaining approval, a grade-getting device whose applicability is restricted to the classroom and, more specifically, to the examination—frequently a device designed, not to open new vistas, but rather to funnel all children to a common point. The school's task is to promote excellence but, as Combs points out, it is possible that our preoccupation with excellence will have precisely the opposite effect. High standards are fine—for those for whom they are reasonable levels of expectancy. What produces adequacy however, is accomplishment, not failure; goals that are out of reach can only discourage and disillusion.

PROGRESSIVISM AND TRADITIONALISM

Basic Consideration

The curriculum represents the vehicle through which the school stimulates pupil growth. It is, however, necessary for the curriculum to which the child is subjected to be broken down into units for, obviously, it cannot be assimilated as a whole. A basic issue centers on whether this organization, when presented in the form of a dichotomy for the purpose of accentuating the differences,[3] should be primarily "logical" or "psychological."

The purpose of the logical organization of content is to bring out its interrelationships, e.g., the arrangement of the elements in the periodic table. It is the organization that would be superimposed upon the material by the expert in the field. Such a form is hardly suitable for the beginner; it represents the final organization of one's learnings, the ultimate goal but hardly the starting point since one cannot organize what he does not have. The psychological organization, on the other hand, is

---

[3] It must be recognized, of course, that the two approaches do not form a dichotomy; nor are they incompatible.

a matter of seeing the material in the perspective of the learner's evolving conceptualization, no matter how inadequate it might seem to the expert. Logical organization is desirable but it cannot be attained in a single bound. The only approach suitable for the learner is that which permits the gradual clarification of his cognitive field into evermore "logical" structure as, step by step, he broadens and deepens his insights and integrates his learnings into greater meaningfulness. To the extent that the logical organization of the adult—in all the complexity of its interactions —is beyond the cognitive grasp of the child, the continuity incorporated into the material by the adult will escape the learner, with resulting fragmentation of the material and the accumulation of isolated facts as an excuse for an education.

The logical-psychological issue is best considered in terms of the distinction between: [a] the subject-matter organization in which the learning is arranged around some central topic logically organized and generally selected in advance by the curriculum-maker to fit the school on a local or even state-wide basis; and [b] the experience organization centering on problems related to the desire of students in a class to achieve some purpose. Again, these two approaches are not independent and separate; certainly all curriculum units incorporate both subject-matter and experience. Furthermore, neither is superior except within a certain context and whereas weaknesses can be located with regard to the extremes or abuses of either approach, these are not necessary concomitants of the methods. One needs to guard against the sort of either-or thinking which is quite contrary to fact.

Since in their extreme, these approaches represent opposites in philosophical as well as psychological orientation, however, a study of their major points of contrast will be of interest and value here. They are nicely summarized by Burton (1950) as shown in Table 20-1.

TABLE 20-1

Comparison of Subject-matter and Experience Units*

Subject-matter Units	Experience Units
. . . begin, in the intention of adults to teach approved subject matter to pupils;	. . . begin, in the intention of the learner, to achieve some purpose; to satisfy some need;
. . . are organized logically around a core within the subject matter;	. . . are organized psychologically around a purpose of the learner;
. . . are prepared in advance, by a person or group already familiar with materials and their logic;	. . . are organized as they develop by a group facing a new situation for the first time;

TABLE 20-1 (*Continued*)

Subject-matter Units	Experience Units
. . . are for the purpose of having the pupil acquire the logically arranged subject matter;	. . . are for the immediate purpose of satisfying needs of the learner and with the ultimate purpose of developing desirable understandings, attitudes, skills, etc., in the learner;
. . . are usually organized from simple to complex and within subject fields;	. . . are usually organized functionally and in disregard of subject lines, especially in elementary grades; . . . .
. . . are controlled by the teacher, by adult committee, by course of study;	. . . are controlled by a cooperating group of learners which includes the teacher; the course of study is utilized as needed;
. . . are usually centered in the past, in the "accumulated" not the "accumulating" culture; little reference to present or future; reference to future usually theoretical;	. . . are usually centered in present and future; use accumulated materials from past freely in solving present problems;
. . . rely on formal methods, assignments, distinct lesson types, printed materials as chief sources, learning experiences few and formal;	. . . utilize cooperatively planned procedures suited to situation, sources in great variety, learning experiences numerous and varied;
. . . give all pupils the same contact with the same materials; some provision for individual differences;	. . . give contacts with many materials; individual differences cared for variously and automatically;
. . . have fixed outcomes which are known in advance and required uniformly for all learners;	. . . do not have fixed outcomes which are known in advance and required uniformly for all learners;
. . . at conclusion, evaluate through the use of formal tests of subject-matter acquisition, usually of fact or skill;	. . . evaluate many complex outcomes continually, with constant pupil participation and through the use of many instruments, formal and informal;
. . . close with a backward look, so-called "review," and are done with when finished.	. . . lead to new interests, problems, and purposes.

* abbreviated from Burton (1950, pp. 221–222).

Whereas the differences in the two approaches involve many facets that defy easy synthesis, the major difference lies in their orientation. In fact, in a sense, they are predicated upon relatively incompatible assumptions concerning the nature of the child. The subject-matter approach is teacher-centered. It is predicated on the premise that it is the function of adults to: [a] select and organize the content; [b] present the material; [c] direct the learning; [d] measure the results; and [e] diagnose difficulties and provide remedial help where indicated. There is an implicit assumption that unless teachers organize, teach, prod, test, the child will learn little or nothing. By contrast, the experience classroom is pupil-centered, and the work of the teacher lies in: [a] setting the stage and utilizing the students' purposes in selecting the experiences by means of which they are to learn; [b] giving moral support and whatever help students need to achieve their purposes; and [c] cooperating in evaluation and in the planning of the next step.

A great deal of discussion of the relative advantages and disadvantages of these two approaches can be located in textbooks and professional journals under such headings as *traditional* versus *progressive*, *teacher-centered* versus *pupil-centered*, and even *autocratic* versus *democratic*, all used more or less synonymously. In addition, the progressive method has, at various times, been called the *project* or the *activity* method or the *experience curriculum*. Unfortunately, much of the writing on the subject has simply reflected the biases of writers, each bent on casting his favorite method in the best possible light while, at the same time, emphasizing the shortcomings of the other. Therefore, as we turn to a discussion of the two approaches, the student is cautioned against letting his prejudices on the subject obscure the real issues; it is important to distinguish between what is an inherent strength or weakness in a method and what is more correctly an abuse—or perhaps an abuse to which the method is prone.[4]

PSYCHOLOGICAL EVALUATION

The primary weakness of the teacher-centered approach stems directly from its orientation toward adult goals and reliance on adult direction, a situation which can easily run counter to the principle that an experience is educative to the extent that it is brought into vital relationship with the needs, goals, and purposes of the learner. It is based on the philosophical view of education as a preparation for life, a position which Snygg and Combs (1949) reject since the child cannot solve problems he does

[4] The author makes no claim to impartiality but strongly urges the student to make for himself a critical analysis of the position taken, with a view not so much to note flaws in the arguments presented as to devise effective teaching procedures that will remedy the alleged weaknesses and take full advantage of the strengths. See R. C. Anderson (1959) for a good summary of the issue.

not—and cannot—have. Because he would have to be an adult to have the self-concept of an adult, the only possible outcome of a curriculum based on such a premise is a childish response to an adult problem. According to these authors:

> . . . the process of equipping children with a repertoire of specific facts, skills, and techniques which will enable them to meet specific situations in adult life proves as impractical in theory as many generations of frustrated teachers have found it to be in practice. [pp. 33–34]

With the advance of educational psychology and the consequent clarification of the nature of the learner and of the learning process—out of which the pupil-centered method has evolved—it has become increasingly evident that more effective learning is likely to result from having classroom experiences grow out of the child's purposes than from having them preselected and preplanned in detail by the curriculum-maker. Of course, with a certain degree of psychological insight, the curriculum-maker can make a reasonable attempt at relating the curriculum to the purposes and development of the average child; he would certainly agree, for instance, that the study of the Magna Charta, the Bill of Rights, and other historical events of man's struggle for independence should coincide with the adolescent's need to gain independence from adults. It takes considerable ingenuity, however, for the curriculum-maker to devise a curriculum that will fit all children of a given grade, regardless of ability, interest, and experiential background. It also takes considerable ingenuity for the teacher to promote the readiness and the motivation required for whatever topic comes next in the curriculum sequence. In general, the traditional preplanned curriculum does not lend itself well to taking advantage of the spontaneous interests and purposes of the class and of the opportunities for effective learning that sometimes present themselves.

An obvious question arising out of the discussion of the preceding paragraph concerns the continuity of the experiences from which the child is to learn. In the teacher-centered school, this continuity is provided by the curriculum-maker who plans the whole sequence. The experience school, on the other hand, has no such inbuilt guide toward its ultimate goal and, in extreme instances, can degenerate into the aimless wanderings for which the project method was often ridiculed with the much-repeated: "Teacher, I wish we didn't have to do what we want to do, today." Obviously, placing the planning of the curriculum in the hands of children is likely to result in an education that is fragmentary and incomplete. But proponents of the pupil-centered method do not advocate that the curriculum be left to the whims of children. They are as fully convinced as anyone else of the absolute necessity of having the general curriculum sequence—and particularly the overall goals—planned in advance by experts. The freedom they allow children *under the direction of the teacher* is in the choice of particular experiences by means of which the objectives of the curriculum are to be attained. (Parenthetically, this puts the teacher in a key position, a professional person in a position to do a professional job. And it allows no room for incompetence.)

It is true that the experiences planned by children often lack the tidy organization an adult can give them, and, at times, the teacher may feel a concern for the muddle in which children can get and a compulsion to step in and direct the learning along the lines common to the traditional method. As we have noted, however, the emphasis upon logical organization, often accepted as the greatest strength of the teacher-centered method, needs to be questioned. It rests upon the assumption —obviously false—that the material can be absorbed ready-made from a structural point of view in much the same way as impressions of wet ink are absorbed by a blotter. Organization, continuity, and meaning lie in the learner, not in the material, and it is the learner who must organize his experiences. In fact, the beautiful (adult) organization of the material may have no meaning for the child with his particular background of ability and experience, as many a teacher has realized as he read despairingly the child's garbled rendition of the explanation so clearly outlined in the book or given in class.

The question of motivation has a definite bearing on the relative effectiveness of the two methods. To the extent that the traditional curriculum is selected by adults and oriented toward the attainment of adult goals, it has to rely on the ability of the teacher to sell these goals to children. This, certain teachers are able to do effectively at least a good percentage of the time for a good percentage of the children, especially since certain topics have an inherent appeal to the children for whom they are intended. Teacher approval is an important aspect of the total situation and many good teachers are able to have children gradually develop interest in the subject matter as well as a positive self-concept as it relates to academic work.

The situation is not always so ideal, however. Since the goals are adult goals, often related only remotely to the goals of a fraction of the members of the class, it is not surprising that for some children, their attainment or nonattainment is a matter of relative indifference. As a consequence, a strong emphasis on competition, grades, and other external incentives is a more or less natural adjunct of the traditional school, as a number of pupils, denied the satisfaction which stems from striving for meaningful goals, work to avoid punishment or for a grade as something to salvage out of an otherwise unappealing activity. Very often students have as their primary objective the circumventing of the goals set by the teacher. The latter, on the other hand, uses whatever means his ingenuity enables him to devise—often with a liberal sprinkling of various forms of threatened or actual punishment—in order to force the class toward the prescribed goals, presumably on the assumption that learning is learning, regardless of the means used to promote it. Effective learning actually occurs in many cases. For some children, however, whatever learning does take place is often relatively superficial, but there is nothing superficial about the negative attitudes that occur as by-products.

The pupil-centered classroom, on the contrary, by using the student's purposes as the starting point and by placing on his shoulders a greater share of the responsibility for his education, is more likely to stimulate ego-involvement in the goals toward which he is to strive. Since it is *his* problem, he is more likely not only to work effectively in carrying it out but also to derive a greater degree of satisfaction at its solution. Note, for example, the difference between the student preparing a speech to hand in to his teacher as an assignment and the student preparing a speech in connection with his campaign for election to office in student government. As a result, the need for external incentives with which to goad him is reduced and the likelihood of a virtuous circle of success, interest, and self-actualization is correspondingly increased.

The fact that apathy, misbehavior, and ineffectiveness in learning are more or less direct resultants of the unsuitability of its goals and the unrealistic demands it makes upon children was not fully appreciated by the traditional school. Rather, as pointed out by Beaumont and Macomber (1949), it considered motivation and misbehavior as appendages extraneous to the business of the school to be dealt with through external incentives and, where necessary, through punitive disciplinary measures. Many of the motivational and disciplinary problems to be found in our schools even today, according to Snygg and Combs (1949), are the direct outcomes of their failure to relate their procedures and their curriculum to the needs and purposes of children:

> It is quite likely that much of the conflict between pupils and teachers which still occurs in school is due to the fact that the schools are run by teachers who are chiefly concerned with preparing the student for his function in adult life and are filled with students who want to satisfy their needs here and now. [p. 209]

Thus, whereas the pupil-centered classroom, by adapting the work to the students and, thereby, providing them with the opportunity for the continuous satisfaction of their needs, undercuts their need to misbehave, the traditional school often has to resort to repression. But repression does not make the curriculum any more suitable; it merely increases the students' frustration and often has a detrimental effect on their overall growth.

The significance of the point discussed here cannot be overemphasized.

No matter from which aspect of his self-realization it is viewed—academic growth, personal and social adjustment, attitude and character formation —it is evident that the individual, whether a child in school or an adult at work, must find satisfaction for his needs out of meeting the demands of the classroom or the job, rather than out of having to rely on extrinsic incentives such as grades or salary, or the satisfaction of such side activities as the after-school athletic program, the after-work bowling league, or the coffee-break friendships. As it pertains to the school child, this means that the curriculum must have built-in satisfactions, i.e., it must make it possible for him to derive his major satisfactions, not out of getting a grade or misbehaving, but rather out of solving meaningful and challenging problems. The fact that the student-centered approach tends to have greater possibilities from this standpoint constitutes one of the strongest arguments in its favor. If, on the other hand, it results in aimless wanderings and confusion, where nothing is ever accomplished—as indeed it may —it can have the very opposite effect. Furthermore, it must be recognized that for the children to have enjoyed an experience is no guarantee that they have learned something worthwhile.

The advantages of relating the curriculum to the goals and purposes of the learner are of obvious importance, but one still has to consider what to the layman is the most crucial question, namely, the extent to which experiences so organized lead to effective and desirable learning outcomes. Critics of the progressive school have, at times, expressed concern that giving children a say in the choice of activities will result in their selecting what is easy and pleasurable, and that as they flit from one pleasant activity to another little will be learned. They fear, for example, that children in the progressive schools will be weak in the fundamentals, which are more difficult to integrate into an experience unit.

Two factors prevent the learning in the pupil-centered classroom from being oriented toward the pleasurable but useless. One is the fact, previously stated, that its general curriculum and its overall goals are set by adults and not by children. The second consideration is even more fundamental: children want to grow, to be challenged, to explore new areas. To fear that children will seek easy tasks is to fail to grasp the central theme of the concept of self-actualization. To quote Snygg and Combs (1949):

> Such criticism would fail to take into account the fact that in shifting the major purpose of education from the acquisition of subject matter to the development of an adequate phenomenal self, we have shifted to an activity for which the child does not need to be motivated. Building a satisfactory phenomenal self is the primary motive of his every act. His basic need is for the preservation and enhancement of his phenomenal self. [p. 225]

To postulate that self-direction leads to an easy curriculum is self-contradictory; the absence of challenge would automatically preclude any possibility of self-actualization. The adequate person learns about his strengths and his weaknesses by measuring himself continuously against difficulties. This is done, however, within a framework which has personal significance rather than simply through external imposition. It is only when the child is under threat that he plays it safe; the fact that they do not lead to self-enhancement would normally prevent him from seeking easy goals. Furthermore, new and more mature interests come easily to the child whose curiosity and initiative have not been blunted, so that he will want to forge ahead toward new conquests.

Also related to the question of the effectiveness of the progressive school in promoting desirable learning outcomes is the criticism that time allegedly is wasted by having students select and plan an activity (in contrast with the traditional approach in which the teacher comes fully prepared with the work of the day). There is in any procedure calling for group planning a danger of having endless and pointless discussion; there is the further danger that the final plans and products will not be nearly as perfect as they would have been had the teacher taken a more active part. All of this may be frustrating to the perfectionistic teacher—and even to the brighter members of the class. The highest degree of efficiency and perfection would probably be attained when the teacher did it all by himself or appointed the best students to carry out the project in the name of the class but this would hardly result in much learning on the part of other children. The important thing is not the product but the learning that takes place in the process. Group selection and planning of classroom activities are essential aspects of the pupil-centered approach and they are at the very foundation of its success. Far from being wasted, the time taken results in the selection of an activity which is more realistically related to the goals, capacities, and interests of the group, leading to the ego-involvement of the various members in the cooperative attainment of group goals and to the clarification of the role each is to play. The outcome generally should be not only a more effective contribution on the part of each individual child, but also a greater degree of satisfaction and self-fulfillment. Cooperative selection and planning of units spell the difference between the child going aimlessly and apathetically toward a goal known only to the teacher and one working on an activity which he sees as real and potentially satisfying. As pointed out by Wingo (1950):

> . . . the most fruitful kind of learning experience is one in which a person or group evolves a plan for dealing with a meaningful situation, puts the plan into action, and then evaluates the outcome of the plan in terms of its original purpose. [p. 301]

The fear that student participation in the selection and planning of classroom activities will develop "happy morons" whose learning is meager and fragmentary has not been borne out by research. Comprehensive studies such as the Eight-Year Study (Aiken, 1942; Smith et al., 1942) and many others (See Keliher, 1950) have invariably shown students of progressive schools to be at least up to par on the fundamentals and considerably superior in ability to think critically, to apply what they know, and to integrate their experiences. They also tend to be superior in cooperation, self-confidence, sociability, effectiveness of expression, breadth of interest, and creativity. Perkins (1950), for example, found pupils in teacher-centered classes to have as many facts as those in pupil-centered classes but to be less able to support their views. They also displayed a lack of spontaneity, morale, and cohesion.

It is particularly significant to note that the superiority of the pupil-centered approach is largely from the standpoint of the functionality of the learnings it promotes. The teacher-centered method is relatively effective in promoting the learning of facts and skills (provided it can deal with the motivational problem), but psychology is not interested in knowledge that is not reflected in behavior. When all is said and done, the activities of the school, its curriculum, and its methods must be evaluated in terms of the difference it makes in the life of the learner. This is a fundamental distinction: whereas the traditional school with its subject-matter orientation stresses the acquisition of knowledge as an end in itself, the modern school is interested in knowledge only as it becomes an integral and functional part of the learner's life. Or stated differently, whereas at times the old school seemed oriented toward making the pupil a "cyclopedia of useless information" (Dewey, 1933), the aim of the modern school is not merely to "engender information and skill but to guide his purposes, attitudes, and interests. . . ." (Young, 1950).

Since the activities of the pupil-centered classroom stem from the existing motives of the child and are, therefore, more in line with his background of ability and interest, they are more likely to be functional in guiding his further purposes. A child working on a unit on city government which involves him in interviews with the city commissioners is more likely to appreciate the working of city government—and also more likely to develop civic attitudes, effectiveness of expression, and social graces—as a result of having *lived* the experience rather than having merely studied about it in his civics book. Such an approach is also more likely to be effective in fostering self-reliance, pupil initiative, habits of independent study, or problem-solving techniques. In other words, an experience unit is more likely to promote ego-involvement and to be reflected in changes in the whole child, e.g., understandings, applications, appreciations, etc. which go beyond the confines of subject matter.

Contributing to a considerable extent to the ineffectiveness of the traditional school from the standpoint of the functionality of the learnings it promotes is the fact that, with its compartmentalization of subject matter, it often cuts across real experiences and reduces education to the study of isolated facts along narrow and artificial lines. This is not a necessary accompaniment of the traditional method but perhaps a weakness to which it is prone. Because it is defined in terms of subject matter, it encourages the development and use of a text designed to incorporate said subject matter as decided upon by the curriculum-maker. In the absence of a more meaningful guide, the subject-matter approach often becomes a textbook approach and, in its extreme form, degenerates into a page-at-a-time routine devoid of any purpose beyond that of covering the book before the end of the year. On the contrary, the flexibility of the pupil-centered approach, if nothing else, discourages the exclusive use of a "prescribed" text and encourages the development of resourcefulness and proficiency in locating and integrating information from multiple sources.

Also vitally involved in the relative success of the two methods is the extent of their adaptability to individual differences. Generally speaking, the former with its preplanned curriculum does not permit easy adaptation of the work of the school to differences in ability, interest, and experiential background. This is especially so when it gets tied down to a textbook which is then followed slavishly despite the fact that it frustrates both the duller and the brighter child. For successful operation, without undue departure from its basic procedures and its preplanned curriculum, it has to place considerable emphasis on the development of the required pupil readiness. Equally, if not more, objectionable from the standpoint of effective education is its emphasis on drill oriented toward the attainment of limited objectives, as we have noted in Chapter 10. By the very nature of its curriculum and the apparent assumption that a given lesson is equally educative for all, the traditional subject-matter approach tends to make unrealistic demands on many children. The pupil-centered method is more flexible. Not only is the class likely to select units that are more realistically in line with its interests and resources but it can also make adjustment for individual differences in the allocation of responsibility for the various aspects of the project among members of the group, so that each child can derive the benefit and the satisfaction of making a contribution in keeping with his talents and interests.

Also of major significance is the much more effective use the student-centered approach makes of the fact that the social situation of the classroom constitutes the teacher's best ally in promoting the child's all-round growth. In contrast to the traditional school's emphasis on individual assignments, the student-centered approach encourages each member to contribute to the cooperative attainment of group goals. As a result, not only does it tend to make possible greater academic gains through the interstimulation of members and a greater degree of ego-involvement of the individual child but it also provides practice in the democratic resolution of group problems through group discussion and group planning. The student-centered approach also promotes communication skills. In contrast to the passive and dependent attitudes often characteristic of the traditional approach where the teacher is the center of focus, with the child answering questions when asked or otherwise taking his cue from the teacher, communication under the student-centered approach is more likely to stem from a sense of responsibility relative to the success of the group venture in which each member is ego-involved. The latter is likely, therefore, to be correspondingly more spontaneous and productive, although, as we have noted in Chapter 15, the volume of discussion going on in a classroom is not a particularly good criterion of its quality. The student-centered approach is also generally more effective in promoting wholesome attitudes. The involvement of children in cooperative activities in which each number contributes to the attainment of group goals is conducive not only to the development of cooperation, consideration for others, social and civic responsibility, enlightened self-interest—all of which are of prime importance in a democratic society— but also to the actualization of these attitudes through active participation in worthwhile and meaningful activities.

SYNTHESIS

The previous discussion has pointed to the relative superiority from the standpoint of psychological principles of the pupil-centered over the teacher-centered approach. The evidence also points to its superiority from an empirical point of view, although considerable variation may be expected from situation to situation. The former lends itself more readily to the promotion of the major objectives for which the modern school exists but, as may be expected, the extent to which its potential advantages are realized depends in no small measure upon the capability and the ingenuity of the teacher and the other aspects of the local situation.

The fact is that students can learn under either approach and they might even learn approximately equal amounts, although there is likely to be a difference in the things they learn. The relative effectiveness of the two approaches revolves in a crucial way around a number of variables. The choice of a criterion, for example, is basic; it seems that many of the significant outcomes of the student-centered approach are intangibles (e.g., resourcefulness, intellectual curiosity, citizenship, etc.) which are relatively difficult to measure.[5] To be effective, the student-centered approach requires practice on the part of both students and teachers and

---

[5] This tends to be true of learnings developed along cognitive lines. Learning structured according to associationistic specifications tends to be more directly oriented toward a well-defined goal and more specifically appraised, e.g., through standardized tests.

it is possible that many teachers give up too soon. It is also possible that the method is not suitable for certain people. In general, it seems that a combination of the traditional and progressive methods depending on the suitability of one or the other for a particular unit of the curriculum would result in more effective learning than would complete adherence to either one alone. Not all tasks are amenable to the group project approach, for example. More fundamental is the fact that the teacher-centered and the pupil-centered approaches probably exist only in their extreme and further that each is really an ill-defined conglomeration of methods overlapping in various degrees. As a consequence, any attempt to generalize as to their relative effectiveness—as indeed any attempt to discover *the* best method of teaching—turns out to be relatively futile.

Certain students may find one method more suitable than the other. The traditional method by making fewer demands on the child in terms of self-direction, ingenuity, initiative, and originality may provide a more reassuring atmosphere for the insecure child—and teacher. The child with strong affiliative needs, on the other hand, would probably favor the student-centered approach. Student preferences would also vary with the ability of the student, his personality orientation, and a number of other aspects of the local situation. When college students find that they must pass a traditional examination at the end of the course, they tend to find greater security in the teacher-directed situation, for example (Wispe, 1951). It is also likely that the logical organization of the subject-matter approach is more effective for the bright and mature student and for the college situation and that the activity method is betted suited to the elementary school. Thus, Burton (1950) expresses the following view:

> The education of little children, or beginners . . . is believed to proceed better when experience units are used by competent teachers.
> The education of students who have more *adequate reading ability,* and who have *achieved sufficient maturity* to be able to learn *through verbal abstractions* . . . is believed to proceed better when the assign-study-recite-test procedure as currently employed is used by competent teachers. [p. 226]

Generally, the elementary school is more oriented toward the use of the activity method than the high school. This may stem in part from the fact that teachers choosing the elementary level are perhaps more oriented toward children, whereas those going to the secondary level are more oriented toward subject matter. It may also be that arithmetic is more adaptable for inclusion in a project than is solid geometry, for example. On the other hand, the grade school must be cautioned against exclusive reliance upon projects and activities: the young child needs contact with concrete experiences but experiences are useful only when generalized—

and the subject-matter approach may well be an effective way of synthesizing and integrating these experiences, once he has had them.

The pupil-centered approach is not without its critics. Some of the criticisms are based on a lack of understanding of what the school is trying to do, the psychological principles underlying its techniques and procedures, and the role of the school in modern society. This may perhaps be blamed on the failure of the school to communicate with the public. Criticisms can also be expected inasmuch as some people are against any change and are likely to resent any departure from the "good old days" when they went to school. The fact that those who did graduate from the old school (with the drop-outs and the repeated grades omitted from the discussion) did know how to spell, read, and compute, and that, as a group, they are now successful in the community, only adds strength to their conviction that the progressive school is "off the track." Other criticisms represent valid objections to what may be considered misuse or abuse of the method—or perhaps objections to the price the progressive method may have to pay in order to reap certain other benefits.

The teacher-directed approach is certainly not without merit, particularly as it applies to the promotion of academic growth. Its greatest weakness lies in the area of promoting the all-round growth of the child where, to be effective, it generally has to undergo considerable modification from its usual organization. This is not to say that the traditional method is incapable of dealing with the whole child. Furthermore, there is no denying that many teachers who have used the method with ingenuity and insight into its possibilities have not only made the subject-matter approach highly challenging but also have turned out graduates educated in the best sense of the word.

There is reason to suspect that the superiority of the progressive method stems from the type of teacher it attracts almost as much as it does from any inherent superiority. Many of the teachers in traditional schools upon which criticism of the method has been based are perhaps not as well qualified as those who are willing to experiment with a new method. Important personality difference may also be involved. The teacher who is secure, competent, and resourceful tends to be more willing to experiment even though he realizes that the progressive class, being more loosely organized, might result in bedlam if things go wrong. The insecure teacher, on the other hand, is likely to stick to the safer subject-matter approach, where, if necessary, he can operate on a page-assignment basis. In fact, a definite weakness of the progressive method lies in the demands it makes upon the ingenuity and competence of the teacher. Both methods lead to good results in the hands of competent teachers; the pupil-centered approach tends to allow more freedom for the competent teacher to display his competence.

BLUEPRINT FOR EFFECTIVENESS
IN THE CLASSROOM

The classroom depends for its effectiveness upon its compliance with the principles of psychology. This section will attempt to give a brief overview of the major ideas of this text, an understanding of which is essential to the teacher interested in successful classroom operation.

The author does not wish to minimize in any way the importance of the knowledge of subject matter, of methods, and of other aspects of teaching: a teacher lacking in these areas is simply unqualified. Nevertheless, the text has consistently emphasized the view that an understanding of the *why* of the child's behavior is the key to the guidance of his growth and development. It is the author's contention that the greatest single source of failure in the classroom is the teacher's inability to deal effectively with the motivational and personal aspects of teaching (as indeed it is in any situation involving people as they interact with one another). Many an otherwise beautiful lesson plan has floundered over its failure to provide for an appropriate answer to the question: "Specifically what would make the children interested in the material to be presented?" Accordingly, the following points may bear reconsideration:

[a] The key idea of which any prospective teacher must never lose sight is that behavior is purposive: it always occurs in connection with the satisfaction of the individual's needs.

[b] As a result of his previous experience, the individual learns to satisfy his needs in a specific way, i.e., not only to seek the satisfaction of his needs but to do so through the attainment of specific goals. Thus, motives, rather than needs, determine the individual's behavior. Not only will the individual satisfy his needs but he will satisfy them in ways consistent with his past experiences, his habits, his values, his self-concept.

[c] In the face of the multiplicity of unsatisfied motives with which the individual is invariably confronted (some of them reinforcing, others conflicting, each with a certain vector strength in a given situation), behavior is the net resultant of relevant motives. Thus, behavior is oriented toward the satisfaction of dominant motives. Conversely, the individual can be relied upon to attain the purposes which are important to him. He can do no more and no one can expect him to do more.

[d] Although a certain degree of tension is conducive to learning, anxiety is likely to result in ineffective, if not deviant, behavior. Probably no other developmental concept has greater implication for effective learning as well as effective living than the development on the part of the child of security and openness to experience as the key to self-actualization. Early child-rearing practices are of special importance in determining the kind of person he will become.

[e] Every experience the individual undergoes is potentially satisfying

or frustrating depending on the degree of readiness he brings to bear upon the situation. Recent psychological advances have shed a new light on the concept of readiness and a new emphasis on the importance of early stimulation in the development of the individual.

[f] The concept of the human intellect developed by Guilford has introduced new dimensions in human ability, particularly in the area of creativity; no longer is the concept of ability to be construed in the narrow sense of the traditional IQ.

[g] Maturity implies behavior that is effective in the attainment of goals and constructive from the standpoint of the welfare of others. The educational system must not only orient the child toward the concept of enlightened self-interest, but it must also provide him with practice in making decisions involving the welfare of the group of which he is a member. He must come to recognize that the group provides the best avenue for maximum self-realization.

[h] The school as an agent of society has a major responsibility in helping the child develop sound character based upon a foundation of positive attitudes and ideals of integrity, morality, and consideration for others.

The key to effective educational experiences lies in motivation. The child will exert himself with whatever capacity he can muster when he is working toward goals that are real and meaningful in terms of his motives and purposes, on the one hand, and his background of ability and experience, on the other. His need for self-enhancement will not permit him to do otherwise. Such experiences, in turn, will make for: [a] maximum learning, retention, and functionality from the standpoint of successful living; [b] desirable attitudes and values; and [c] maximum tension-reduction, success, and self-fulfillment. On the contrary, to the extent that the child is forced to participate in experiences that are not related to the attainment of his goals and purposes, aversive effects—apathy, superficial learning, frustration, negative attitudes, misbehavior, maladjustment—are likely to follow.

The implementation of this principle into actual classroom practice is obviously too comprehensive a matter for complete coverage here. This discussion will, therefore, be restricted to a listing of the following as minimal essentials of such a program:

[a] An understanding of children
    1. In general: Teachers need to understand children in terms of the psychological principles that govern their growth and development, e.g., the role of readiness, and especially the forces that promote spontaneity and openness to experience.
    2. Individually: Teachers cannot provide meaningful experiences

for children whose ability, interests, background, values, goals, and purposes they do not know.

[b] A suitable curriculum

    1. Meaningful education calls for a good selection of educational experiences designed to promote to the maximum whatever potentialities exist in the individual child. These experiences must be adapted to provide for all children regardless of the scope and the orientation of their talents.

[c] A social situation conducive to the maximum self-realization of of the child

    1. The children of the class must be integrated into a cohesive group characterized by acceptance of individual members, effective communication among members and between members and teacher, commonness of purpose, and enthusiasm in the attainment of worthwhile goals.

    2. The teacher, as a group leader, must be one who can communicate with and inspire children.

[d] Effective guidance of the process by means of which the child is to achieve his potentialities

    1. The teacher must realize the necessity of having the learner actively involved in the learning process and must provide for ego-involvement through the operation of realistic and clear-cut goals.

    2. Effective learning centers on such concepts as problem solving and meaningfulness, and implies experiences that are real in terms of the child's purposes, interests, abilities, and background. It must, in turn, be reflected in functional behavior and in more mature interests, goals, and purposes.

    3. The school program should capitalize on the child's basic desire to grow and should be synchronized with his natural pattern of development.

    4. Meaningful group participation in the pursuit of realistic and worthwhile goals is one of the best means of (a) promoting the development of personal and social adjustment and of sound attitudes and character, and (b) having them reflected in constructive behavior.

[e] A competent, sensitive, and dedicated teacher

    1. The teacher is the most important cog in the educative machine. As Hullfish and Smith (1961) point out, any attempt to bring about a significant reconstruction of education in a classroom "where mind meets mind" must begin with a reconstruction of the teacher. Although we cannot list all the characteristics and traits it would be desirable for a teacher to have, we may at least mention the following: (a) a thorough grasp of subject-

matter; (b) ingenuity and competence in setting the stage for the maximum growth of the child, in guiding the learning process, and in welding students into a cohesive group working toward common goals; (c) sensitivity to the needs and problems of children, a firm conviction in the inherent dignity of the individual child and a dedication to the cause of promoting his maximum growth; and (d) an awareness of his responsibility as a leader of youth, of the importance of personal integrity, and a sincere interest in the welfare of children.

2. Ability to relate to children and inspire them toward the moral values and democratic ideals of our society.

The education of the child is obviously a complicated task which does not allow for pat solutions or easy prescriptions. Society has a general idea of the type of person a graduate of its schools should be; it can even list tentatively the requirements and perhaps describe the process for educating such a person. And, on the surface, it would seem that these are not only necessary but reasonably sufficient conditions for producing an educated person. Education, however, may be likened to house-building: whether we get an effective and livable house out of the required quantity of cement, lumber and other materials depends to a large extent on the professional caliber of the architect and the builder. So also does the quality of the final product turned out of our schools depend to a large extent on the professional competence of the curriculum-maker who devises the program and the teacher who puts his plan into action. An error on the part of either can negate the best efforts of all concerned.

There is not complete agreement as to what to include in the curriculum and, within limits, perhaps it is not necessary that there should be, since it is the growth that results from a given experience rather than the experience itself that counts. But there should be reasonable agreement as to what constitutes an effective—and an ineffective—teaching method. The technological progress which has put the United States in a position of world leadership has not been achieved through procedures that were "good enough." We should be able to expect from our schools the same degree of efficiency that characterizes other areas of professional endeavor. We need to reevaluate our schools and other procedures, not for the purpose of labeling them "traditional" or "progressive," but rather for the purpose of identifying those that bring about results and those that do not—not with a view toward immediate implementation of a panic-sponsored crash program, but rather with a view toward bringing educational practice in line with sound philosophical and psychological considerations. When this is done, we will no longer have to apologize for our failures, and our students will be as adequate as their potentialities permit.

SOURCES OF RELATED MATERIAL

Alberty, H., "Should the modern secondary-school curriculum be experience centered?" *Bull. Nat. Assn. Sec. Sch. Princ.*, 33: 115–124, 1949.

Benjamin, Harold, *The Sabre-Tooth Curriculum*. New York: McGraw-Hill Publishing Company, Inc., 1939.

Broudy, Harry S. et. al., *Democracy and Excellence in American Secondary Education*. Skokie, Ill.: Rand McNally & Company, 1964.

Bruner, Jerome S., *The Process of Education*. Cambridge, Mass.: Harvard University Press, 1960.

Conant, James B., *The American High School Today*. New York: McGraw-Hill Publishing Company, 1959. (See also Burkett, L. A., "Implications of the Conant Report . . . ," *Bull. Nat. Assn. Sec. Sch. Princ*, 44: 219–29, 1960, and Corey, S. M., "The Conant Report . . . ," *Educ. Forum*, 24: 7–9, 1959)

Highet, Gilbert, *The Art of Teaching*. New York: Alfred A. Knopf, Inc., 1950.

Kelly, Earl C., and M. I. Rasey, *Education and the Nature of Man*. New York: Harper & Row, Publishers, 1952.

Oldin, Philip, "Let's re-examine progressive education," *Phi Delta Kappan*, 38: 309–319, 1957.

Popham, W. J., and S. W. Greenburg, "Teacher education: A decade of criticism," *Phi Delta Kappan*, 40: 118–120, 1958.

Rasmussen, G. R., "An evaluation of a student-centered and instructor-centered method of conducting a graduate course in education," *J. educ. Psychol.*, 47: 449–461, 1956.

Riesman, David, *Constraints and Variety in American Education*. Lincoln, Neb.: University of Nebraska Press, 1956.

Rosenberger, H. T., "What should we expect of education?" *Bull. Nat. Assn. Sec. Sch. Princ.*, 40: 13–348, 1956.

Scott, C. W., et al. (eds.), *The Great Debate: Our Schools in Crisis*. Englewood Cliffs: Prentice Hall, Inc., 1959.

Suppes, Patrick, "Modern learning theory and the elementary school curriculum," *Amer. educ. res. J.*, 1: 79–93, 1964.

QUESTIONS AND PROJECTS

1

What are some of the more significant outcomes of a high school education?

2

[a] The great statesmen of the past have tended to be the products of non-public education. What implications might this have for American public education?

[b] What manner of man might we expect as a product of American public education? How might he differ from the product of nonpublic education? What are some of the attributes of a well-educated person?

3

Spell out in terms of specific measurable outcomes the four major objectives of the Educational Policies Commission of the National Education Association, namely, self-realization, human relationships, economic efficiency, and civic responsibility. Choose as your point of reference the status that might be expected of a high school senior.

4

[a] Evaluate an article critical of modern education. What seems to have been the philosophical or psychological premises on which the criticism was based, e.g., a strong belief in transfer of training.

[b] What might be the implications of the current liberal arts versus education controversy?

[c] How concerned might schools be with their failures, e.g., the relative illiterate, the juvenile delinquent, the educationally apathetic adult, etc.?

APPENDIX

Autoinstructional Devices

By relieving the teacher of much that is routine, the teaching machine and program permit these other opportunities greater play. If much of the science of teaching is taken over by the machine, the art of teaching will again come into its own, residing where it should in the teacher as a person.

Hilgard, 1961, p. 21

The introduction of "teaching machines" into the modern classroom is perhaps the most notable recent innovation in the field of education. Judging from the dramatic growth of programed instruction since the publication of Skinner's first article on the subject (Skinner, 1954), it seems logical that teaching machines will come into progressively greater use as teaching aids in the classroom of the future. Although their advent has been viewed with varying emotions ranging from enthusiasm to apprehension and alarm, they have undoubtedly introduced a new dimension in classroom operation; not only is their invention in itself an event of great import, but of even greater significance is the implications they are bound to have on the entire theory of effective education. It is possible, for example, that their most significant contribution to educational practice will lie in the clarification of the teaching-learning process which they are bound to promote. In the words of Pressey (1964): "Autoinstruction is probably the most publicized, most exploited, possibly the more errant and potentially most valuable of all contributions of American psychology to American education." Actually, teaching "machines" are not new; we have had the abacus for some time, we have had maps and globes, projectors, and other teaching aids. Furthermore, teaching machines do not teach; they are better called autoinstructional devices since they merely permit the learner to learn on his own with a minimum of teacher participation.

ACADEMIC PERSPECTIVE

The recent impetus toward the so-called "teaching machine" stems from the work of Skinner who points out that there are more people in the world to be educated today than ever before. The tremendous challenge cannot be met by building more schools but rather by making education more efficient. This calls for machines to supplement the teacher. Actually, teaching machines date back to the mid-1920s when Pressey (1926) devised a machine for administering multiple-choice tests. Its unique feature was that it provided the student with an immediate feedback as to the accuracy of his answers; it also enabled him to proceed at his own pace, it reduced the need for using class time for routine mass drill, and, especially, it passed the scoring of the responses from the shoulders of the teacher, for whom it is largely a clerical chore, to those of the students, for whom it can be vital learning experience.

Unfortunately, Pressey's brainchild did not seem to generate much enthusiasm; apparently the teaching profession was not ready for such an innovation. The possibilities of autoinstructional devices became more apparent as a result of Skinner's work in the shaping of animal behavior through immediate and systematic reinforcement. As noted in Chapter 2, Skinner's procedure consists of reinforcing at first any response which is in the general direction of the expected behavior, but then reinforcing only behavior which is a progressively closer approximation to the ultimate behavior desired. In other words, he reinforces the components of the eventual behavior he is trying to develop and gradually imposes more and more stringent criteria of adequacy before further reinforcement is given. The teaching machine schedule likewise breaks behavior into subcomponents and provides a gradual progression of selective reinforcement for the subaspects to the point that a relatively complex behavioral repertoire can gradually be shaped. It is Skinner's contention that operant conditioning which has been shown to be so effective in animal training can be equally successful in the classroom.

Skinner is appalled at the inefficiency with which learning takes place in the school; more specifically he claims our classrooms suffer from the following weaknesses:

[a] They are lacking from the standpoint of frequent, immediate, and

consistent reinforcement; according to Skinner, the fact that grades, for example, are delayed anywhere from a couple days to a week or more simply destroys any reinforcement effect which they might otherwise have.[1] In fact, the teacher could not possibly provide each and every child with the thousands of reinforcement contingencies which Skinner postulates are necessary for efficient learning.

[b] They are lacking from the standpoint of providing a skillful sequence of reinforcement contingencies moving forward in a series of progressive approximations to the ultimately desired behavior.

[c] Behavior in the classrooms is dominated by aversive consequences; children typically act to avoid punishment—teacher displeasure, criticism, ridicule, loss of peer status, etc. "In this welter of aversive consequences, getting the right answer is in itself an insignificant event, any effect of which is lost amidst the anxiety, the boredom, the aggressions which are the inevitable by-products of aversive control." (Skinner, 1954).

In other words, our schools fail to capitalize on recognized psychological principles; what is called for is a major reorganization of classroom operations. According to Skinner, the teacher is inadequate as a purely mechanical reinforcing agent. He just cannot meet the competition of the teaching machine with its infinite patience and alertness, always available, always willing to go as fast or as slow as any one child desires, always positively rewarding. There is no danger of the machine ridiculing the student or taking it out on him if he does not succeed. On the other hand, the teaching machine makes the learner responsible for his own learning; it is completely impersonal, and does not get psychologically involved. The student cannot lean on the machine.

This does not mean that the teaching machine will displace teachers, for, as Komoski (1961) points out, "Any teacher who can be replaced by a machine deserves to be replaced." Whereas teaching machines may be a threat to poor teachers, the fact that teachers are outmoded and unable to compete with teaching machines as rewarding devices should be of no great concern. The housewife cannot compete with the washing machine—nor does she care to! Machines are simply capital equipment to which the teacher can assign the mechanizable functions of teaching so as to be able to emerge in his proper role as an indispensable human being and assume his true professional status. It is true that, if abused, teaching machines can dehumanize the learning process but hardly more so than the abuse of textbooks. This does not deny the need to guard against overorientation toward mechanized laboratories manned by electronic controls and designed to convert immature human beings into

[1] It must be noted that with meaningful material the learner provides his own reinforcement; the child who solves a problem in algebra or who bats in a home run does not need to be told he was right.

intellectual machines. We have no need for machines to make more machines!

Many of the teacher's classroom responsibilities constitute a wasteful use of professional talent, occupying his time and energies to the point where he cannot do an effective job on the more meaningful aspects of teaching. Many of the present contacts which children have with their teachers—the latter generally overworked and often demoralized by the overburden of routine and trivia—are not particularly "human" nor educationally profitable. Many are of an aversive nature. Perhaps as much as 75 percent of the activities in which teachers presently engage are of a routine nature which could be delegated to mechanical devices with a corresponding improvement in teacher efficiency. The development of programed learning should free the teacher to play a more productive role in the educational process by attending to the more significant—and often neglected—aspects of teaching. The relief from having to deal with the many routine phases of teaching might permit teachers to play their human relations function more effectively, and, if necessary, teaching machines might even replace some of the dull, bored, listless, lukewarm personalities whose influence on pupils is likely to be more detrimental than that of the coldest machine.

The "Psychology" of Teaching Machines

Generally speaking, teaching machines are predicated upon the psychological principles that: [a] learning proceeds gradually from the less complex to the more complex in an orderly sequence; [b] learning takes place more rapidly when the learner is actively engaged with the subject matter, when immediate knowledge of the results of each response is given, and when frequent and consistent reinforcement is provided; [c] the learning situation must be designed to permit each student to proceed at his own speed; and [d] the teacher's strategy must be consistently reappraised on the basis of an objective analysis of the learner's activities. The basic approach to programed instruction is to arrange the subject matter into a step-by-step hierarchy and to break it down into small units each calling for a response which can be rewarded so that the learning is reinforced each step of the way.[2] Skinner, for example, insists that the program consist of a series of small steps so as to ensure maximum reinforcement and minimum error, and thus promote relatively complete and continuous mastery of content and readiness for the next step. Automatic feedback acting as a guide in orienting the student's effort in the light of the correctness of his previous response further guarantees effectiveness of learning, particularly when the program permits him to skip sections he already

[2] Skinnerian principles are based on associationistic premises; learning is a matter of bringing behavior under the control of relevant stimuli through the relatively mechanical process of differential reinforcement.

knows so that he can devote his energies to the part not yet mastered.

It also appears logical that, by promoting greater mastery of content, teaching machines might also promote greater transfer. On the contrary, it might be argued that, to the extent that they encourage mechanistic learning and dependency on the machine to provide the how, why, and when as the child is led by the hand over a series of minute steps, they might be detrimental to transfer. Teaching machines may promote learning efficiency through requiring active response; when the student knows that what he reads will be followed by a question and that he must commit himself irretrievably to an answer, he is likely to engage in more careful reading and in more thoughtful consideration of the material. On the other hand, critics have argued that the Skinnerian minute-step approach might well lead to guessing of obvious answers leading to no more learning than the old workbooks in which the student simply filled in the blanks by copying from his text; they contend that, to be conducive to learning, activity must be mental rather than simply physical.

Teaching machines are effective means for providing for individual differences. Unlike the usual classroom instruction which is both too fast for some students and too slow for others, teaching machines allow each child to set whatever pace will permit him to grasp the material as he goes along. In a sense, they provide each student with the benefits of a private tutor totally responsive to his individual needs and permitting unlimited repetitions where he needs repetition and for acceleration where he needs acceleration. The bright, for example, are no longer delayed by their less capable schoolmates, nor are the dull pressured by the progress of their more adequate colleagues. In fact, allowing the student's progress to be paced by his own speed, rather than by that of the teacher or the class, is undoubtedly one of the major contributions teaching-machine technology can make to educational practice. Teaching machines also provide a number of practical administrative benefits. They enable the small school to increase its curricular offerings, permitting, for example, the bright student to study a foreign language or to pursue an area of interest. They are especially useful for providing remedial instruction and review material, for dealing with absenteeism, and for training students in the use of equipment.

TEACHING-MACHINE HARDWARE

Strictly speaking, the teaching machine refers to the hardware holding the instructional material through which the student can teach himself; the key to what and how effectively one teaches with the aid of a teaching machine lies in the skill and the wisdom that goes into the construction of the program, an important determinant of which is the adequacy of the machine itself. Unquestionably the major limitation of the flexibility and adaptability of teaching machines must inevitably be factors of cost and operational simplicity. All teaching machines—no matter how elaborate—have to be limited from the standpoint of capacity, a factor which automatically sets the number of alternative responses and the degree of modifiability in teaching techniques somewhat short of unlimited adaptability to student needs. This is a particular limitation of the less expensive models. A more serious weakness of teaching-machine hardware is its lack of standardization so that one program often does not fit another machine, with the result that the particular machine a school has purchased dictates the kind of program it can use—a distinct case of the tail wagging the dog, especially in view of the inferior quality of some of the programs currently available.

Machines must be within the school's financial budget and yet they must be educationally sound. Even though a cheaper machine can conceivably be as adequate for certain purposes as a more expensive model, many schools have allowed the factor of economy to dictate their purchases so that they are now stuck with machines that are not particularly useful. By far the most complex, and generally the most adequate, are the computer models, an installation of which might consist of: [a] a computer which controls the presentation of instructional materials; [b] a slide projector to project the material on a screen; [c] a typewriter on which the student responds; and [d] a control tape telling the computer how to react to each of the student's responses, e.g., skipping items or presenting remedial materials wherever necessary and causing the typewriter to type out the appropriate feedback message. Such a setup probably comes closest to the optimal one-to-one student-tutor relationship. On the other hand, it is expensive.

THE PROGRAM

The subject matter to be taught is composed into a program which may take on a number of forms from a sheet of paper to a tape or even a scrambled textbook. The basic unit of the program is a "frame," i.e., an item presenting an idea to which the student must respond. The first step in programing is to analyze the content to be mastered and translate it into units of behavior: "Specifically what is the student to know?" "What concepts is he to develop?" "What discriminations is he to grasp?" The program then consists of a series of separate frames presented in a carefully controlled sequence. At any time, only one of the frames is visible through a window; the student records his response on a paper exposed through a small opening and, when this is done, moves his answer under a glass while at the same time uncovering the correct answer. In some of the more elaborate machines, there is a device permitting him to punch a hole in the paper when his response agrees with the right answer so that this particular frame will not appear as he goes through the program a second time.

Programs fall into two major types. One is based on Skinnerian principles of operant conditioning and follows a linear design, i.e., a single sequence of frames each providing a specific bit of information and calling for a response to be devised by the student. The other advocated by Crowder (1963) and Pressey (1964) follows a branching design in which the learner selects his answers from a number of alternatives and the specific alternative he chooses determines what frame he will see next. A correct answer leads to the next frame in the sequence; a wrong answer leads to a remedial subsequence from which he returns to the main stream after he has mastered the point involved. Crowder also includes an explanation of why the response is incorrect, thereby taking advantage of the learning opportunity to ensure that the correct response is fully understood. The alternatives are diagnostic, and remedial material is provided for each of the incorrect alternatives. Thus, the branching program is directed specifically to the student's present state of readiness; it takes care of deficiencies as it goes along and avoids putting the student through extra work he does not need.

Programed instruction can also be designed in the form of a textbook which can be either linear or branching. In a linear programed text, e.g., English 3200, the student goes from the first frame on the first page to the first frame on the second page where he finds the answer to the first frame and then on to page 3, frame 1; page 4, frame 1; . . . to the end of the book and back to the second frame of the first page, and so on. In the case of the branching scrambled text, the student goes to different pages or frames depending on the adequacy of his answer. The programed text has advantages and disadvantages over the regular machine program; it allows the student to cheat, for example, although certainly anyone who understands the rationale of the teaching machine would not cheat. A more fundamental weakness of the linear scrambled textbook is that it cannot provide for by-passing items that have been answered correctly.

Basic Issues

A number of issues have been raised concerning the basic premises and uses of teaching machines. These are best considered under the framework of the linear-versus-branching controversy. Actually, according to Crowder, comparing linear and branching programing is relatively difficult inasmuch as they have nothing in common, i.e., inasmuch as historically they have arisen from different contexts, they base their effectiveness on different premises, and make essentially opposite assumptions concerning the nature of the learning process. Critics of linear programing point out, for example, that the characteristic feature of the ideal pupil-teacher relationship is interaction, i.e., a two-way process; just as the learner must align his responses to the demands of the machine, so must the machine be responsive to the needs of the student as reflected by his responses.

[a] A basic point at issue is the size of the steps into which the program is divided. Until recently Skinner insisted that the most effective program is that in which academic content is presented in very small steps so that the probability of error is almost negligible; not only is a given concept repeated from different points of view but, in addition, a number of clues and prompts are provided. Critics of the Skinnerian approach have felt that this emphasis on error-free performance is a carry-over from the learning of animals; Cook (1963), for example, feels that the Skinnerian approach reflects a number of irrelevant features of the Skinner box necessary in the case of animals but hardly for people with their much greater symbol-handling capacity. Crowder suggests that the learner learns very little from making a response which is inevitable, especially because he can frequently get the answer by simply attending to irrelevant cues. He argues that the linear program is too rigid to meet individual needs, that it is not practical, for example, to incorporate into the program designed for everyone all the "remedial" (or foundation) work that might be necessary for the poorest student. He also contends that a strict sequencing of learning frames as in linear programing is hardly necessary; if a student can skip a grade, or different textbooks can introduce material in a different order, certainly students ought to be able to skip a few frames here and there.

Crowder and Pressey argue that a more realistic approach is to provide larger functional units, even though at times errors may occur. They suggest that, whereas no one wants errors for the sake of error, we need to retain errors because they are signals to the most economical pacing of the individual's learning; if errors occur at too high a level of probability, the machine needs to return to simpler material; if the error level is too low, it needs to shift to an accelerated pace. Crowder and Pressey accept errors as the only logical course; the opposite, error-free performance, is patently impractical and undesirable since, in order to ensure success at all times for all students, the program would have to be so obvious as to be inefficient for everyone.

The basic question is whether every student should be made to go through minute steps or whether the program should be oriented toward a relatively brief accelerated basic sequence supplemented by remedial and elaborative subroutines as needed. The issue is accentuated by the fact that, besides requiring everyone to go over every frame (at least in the first run), the linear program tends to be highly repetitive and, of course, time consuming. It would seem logical that the ideal is to keep the program at the level where it will offer no more than the minimum number of cues necessary to guarantee student success. If one must depart from this ideal—and indeed, one must—it is debatable whether the deviation should be in the direction of errorless performance for even the slowest student.

[b] A second issue in the linear-versus-branching controversy is whether the student should devise his own responses or simply select a response from a prearranged set of alternatives, and further, whether the actual writing in of the responses in linear programing (as opposed to a covert mental reaction) serves any purpose. Psychologists agree that active involvement is essential to effective learning. However, active participation in the learning is better interpreted in the sense of mental activity than the physical act of devising and writing one's own answers; writing in obvious answers may result in nothing more than a disruption of the learning process and a delay in reinforcement, for example. Furthermore, writing in responses is time consuming so that less material can be covered in a given unit of time. A number of investigations have suggested that overt response has no major advantage over covert response (Stolurow, 1963; Feldhusen, 1963), but the results are not conclusive (Fry, 1960; Roe et al., 1960; Evans et al., 1960). Apparently the relative effectiveness of overt and covert response depends on the interaction of a number of factors, e.g., the difficulty of the task.

[c] Critics have expressed concern over the failure of programed instruction to promote originality, creativity, and even critical thinking. This criticism is perhaps more pertinent to the linear small-step approach; imagination and creativity are not fostered by a program which precludes everything but the predetermined answer. Skinner would argue that neither is creativity promoted by making the content more difficult through introducing gaps and ambiguity. He suggests that thinking is a lawful process which can be programed just like any other aspect of the educative process; if critical thinking and imagination are important, they should be the goals of a separate program so that they can be made to occur by plan rather than by accident. Skinner would first analyze the skills involved, i.e., defined operationally what is meant by problem solving or creative behavior and then proceed to develop generalized thinking abilities that would transfer to related situations as called for.[3]

Evaluation of Autoinstructional Devices

From the moment of their arrival on the educational scene, teaching machines have been the object of both strong support and violent objections. The reactions of educators have been varied; some have experimented with them while others are waiting for mechanical improvements, greater standardization of material, and more conclusive evidence of their effectiveness. The net worth of teaching machines is indeterminate; yet it now seems clear, as Eigen (1963) suggests, that

[3] Skinner's position is in conflict with the common view that we cannot teach how to think apart from what to think and that thinking should, therefore, be integrated into subject matter rather than developed as in independent ability.

> . . . programed instruction in its present form and state of development is not the panacea that some of its more enthusiastic adherents have predicted it to be; it is equally clear that it is not the tremendous danger to the mental well-being of both the student and the teacher that some of the more hysterical opponents predicted it would be. [p. 242]

Evaluating automated instruction is difficult; the majority of studies have tended to deal with internal problems such as whether to use branching or linear programing, whether the response should be overt or covert, whether the steps should be small or large. Furthermore, the results have been conflicting, and perhaps the question is not whether to use one or the other, or to use them at all, but rather under what circumstances teaching machines should be used and how they are best used. It is essentially impossible to resolve some of the more significant problems such as whether programed instruction is detrimental to the promotion of critical thinking, creativity, and desirable attitudes; these issues can be considered only at the logical level. Many of the claims and the criticisms of autoinstructional devices have logical validity but so far they lack empirical verification. It is difficult to control some of the extraneous factors or to equate gains in one area with losses in another. For example, writing in the response complicates the construction of the machine and increases the time necessary to cover the program. The extent to which these factors can counterbalance extra learning gains which might result from overt response, if any, then becomes a matter of judgment.

Autoinstructional devices have been subjected to a number of criticisms, many of which are relatively unfair. Although there is no point in endorsing inadequacy, many of the critics have blamed teaching machines for failure to do things the conventional classroom cannot do either. Some criticisms revolve around certain assumptions; for example, are the impersonal aspects of the teaching machine necessarily bad? It is only because it is nonhuman and devoid of any feelings that the hot water heater can serve mankind the way it does. Likewise, the thermostat, even though nonhuman, is far more effective in providing for differences in heat requirements than the kindest janitor. Actually, the child may gain a great deal from having to face an impartial and impersonal sequence of demands without being able to alibi or demand special concessions or, on the other hand, being subjected to pressure or abuse.

This does not deny the possibility of abuse: we could be developing robots. Along with Kvaraceus (1961), we might visualize the child of tomorrow stepping off the school bus onto a conveyor belt, past an electronic eye that would record his attendance, on to the first booth where he would perform certain tasks prescribed by the computer, back to the belt, and on to the next booth where the process would be repeated. At the last station he might be handed an inventory of his day's accomplishments together with specifications for tomorrow's schedule and perhaps a condensed report card for his parents. Our schools might then resemble an assembly line with the students going from one vending machine to another, one dispensing mathematics, another literature. Perhaps we might even install a few "chimpomats" dispensing pellets of food for correct answers and thereby harnessing the hunger drive in the cause of education while, at the same time, eliminating the noon lunch.

Some of the critics of programed instruction also express concern over the fact that the child is learning too effortlessly and mechanically. Others fear that the program with its systematic approach, moving students relentlessly on to the ultimate goal, will brainwash them. They argue that, by operating through small, relatively obvious steps, programed instruction might lull students into passivity to the point of dulling their critical powers. Actually, a machine can no more brainwash students than the lecture of an effective teacher; if it is desirable that a teacher be convincing in his teaching, then we cannot blame the machine for being convincing. Autoinstruction can perhaps incorporate a lack of emphasis on the critical evaluation of evidence, but this is not a necessary aspect of programed instruction.

Another concern is that the nationwide standardization of subject matter that will result from the relative availability of certain programs may tend to negate diversity and flexibility of instruction. To the extent that we are more concerned with quality instruction than with diversity for the sake of diversity, this is not necessarily undesirable, especially since the teacher can still make whatever adaptation he thinks necessary. Yet the criticism is not without foundation. It is probably true that whoever controls the program—whether it be a committee of scientists, publishers, or film producers—controls the educational process. This has been somewhat true of textbooks, syllabi, and guides, and there is room for concern that educators might be fitting students to programs rather than programs to students.

Empirical evidence suggests that autoinstructional devices are relatively adequate at least with respect to certain criteria. Galanter (1963), for example, notes that:

> . . . experimental results indicate that the time required for the acquisition of information is materially reduced by . . . programed instruction. Conservative estimates based on existing experimental data suggest that about one-half of the time usually necessary for learning a particular skill can be saved. [p. 588]

He suggests that, assuming the student's ability to grasp and remember, putting all school materials in programed form would permit the coverage of twice as much material in the same amount of time. In the study by

Ferster and Sapon (1958), 47.5 hours of study of German through programed study resulted in as much learning as a first semester course consisting of 48 hours of class time alone.

Unfortunately, the whole issue of comparing programed with conventional instruction or with a textbook revolves around the relative quality of each and is, therefore, a relatively futile enterprise. It can be argued that by comparison with a textbook, teaching machines promote a greater degree of ego-involvement and provide feedback as to the adequacy of the learner's grasp of the content. On the other hand, the repetition and relative discontinuity resulting from the breakdown of material into thousands of subunits may actually be disrupting, particularly to the more capable student. The fact that automated instruction has enabled Skinner to train pigeons to do things not normally in their realm of behavior, and Moore to have preschool children learn to read, does not constitute proof of universal effectiveness. The problem is obviously complicated and dogmatic pronouncements as to its superiority over traditional approaches is clearly out of place.

An important consideration of the relative effectiveness of programed instruction is that it contains within itself the means for self-improvement. Inasmuch as the student supplies an irretrievable record of his responses, the inadequacies of the program become automatically evident; if the student does not profit from the program, presumably the program has failed. Another aspect of the question is the gadget or "pinball" effect; critics have suggested that the effectiveness of programed instruction stems from the novelty of its gadgetry. Skinner argues that, on the contrary, as the novelty effect wears out and overenthusiasm dies down, the student uses the machine more effectively and gives more considered answers.

Like all aspects of education, particularly those which are subject to commercialization, teaching machines need to be carefully and continuously appraised. We need to guard against what might be called the Frankenstein effect; as Broudy (1963) suggests, machines sometimes acquire a career of their own; what sets out as an adjunct to learning frequently ends up as the master whom the teacher must obey. It behooves educators to look at this mechanical or electronic gift horse rather closely before they suffer the fate of the Trojans of old. Unless we are careful, teaching machines may impose on our schools a very narrow conception of education; we cannot consider the goals of educational technology to be merely the mastery of differential calculus in the greatest number of pupils in the shortest possible time, for example. With the present emphasis on teaching machines, there is danger of exploitation of schools and parents by unscrupulous machine makers. We need to know what teaching machines can do and what they cannot do and what constitutes a satisfactory device for the purposes at hand. Stolurow (1963) suggests: "Let's be informed on programed instruction before the rascals take over."[4]

In the meantime, automated instruction will continue to exert considerable influence on American education. The advent of programed instruction has caused educators to reexamine their objectives, the curriculum and pedagogical practice through which they are to be promoted, and the role various instructional media, including the teacher, are to play in the process. It may well be that rigid adherence to the principle of personal pupil-teacher relationships is no longer realistic or even that we have been misguided in our efforts to achieve productive teacher-pupil contacts. Automated instruction is causing teachers and administrators to reconsider what is academically feasible. Keislar and McNeil (1961), for example, have demonstrated that the principles of molecular theory can be taught in the primary grades through programed instruction. The training of teachers in programing techniques is to be recommended on the basis of the valuable insights it provides into teaching procedures and the nature of the learning process. Perhaps its most significant contribution is that it highlights Skinner's conviction (Skinner, 1954) that "a sweeping revision of educational practice is possible and inevitable." As Lumsdaine (1964) suggests:

> . . . it may well be re-emphasized that differences in present conceptions and forms of programing, as well as their current theoretical rationales, are less important than the basic conviction that instruction is amenable to systematic description and improvement through experimental inquiry. [p. 401]

Whereas not all effects will be beneficial, it is inevitable that automated instruction will cause a considerable revolution in educational practice; it is up to educators to capitalize on its potentialities and to safeguard American education against its abuse.

---

[4] Teachers and administrators contemplating the purchase of teaching machines need to be familiar with the standards set by the joint committee of the National Education Association, the American Educational Researchers Association, and the American Psychological Association (A-V Comm., 11, No. 1, 1963).

SOURCES OF RELATED MATERIAL

Crowder, Norman A., "On the differences between linear and intrinsic programing," Phi Delta Kappan, 44: 250–254, 1963.

De Cecco, John P., Educational Technology. New York: Holt, Rinehart and Winston, Inc., 1964.

Dick, Walter, "The development and current status of computer-based instruction," Amer. educ. res. J., 2: 41–53, 1965.

Elam, Stanley (ed.), "Programed instruction," Phi Delta Kappan, 44: 241–302, 1963.

Evans, L. H., and G. E. Arnstein (eds.), *Automation and the Challenge to Education: Symposium on the Educational Implications of Automation.* Washington, D.C.: National Education Association, 1962.

Fry, Edward B., *Teaching Machines and Programmed Instruction.* New York: McGraw-Hill, Inc., 1963.

Galanter, Eugene H. (ed.), *Automatic Teaching: The State of the Art.* New York: John Wiley & Sons, Inc., 1959.

Lambert, Philip (ed.), "The teacher and the machine," *J. educ. Res.*, 55: 405–531, 1962.

Lumsdaine, A. A., and R. Glaser (eds.), *Teaching Machines and Programed Learning: A Source Book.* Washington, D.C.: National Education Association, 1960.

Morrill, Charles S., "Teaching machines: A review," *Psychol. Bull.*, 58: 363–375, 1961.

Schramm, Wilbur, *The Research on Programed Instruction.* Washington, D.C.: U. S. Office of Education, 1964.

Skinner, B. F., "Teaching machines," *Sci. Amer.*, 205: 90–102, 1961.

———, "Why we need teaching machines," *Harv. educ. Rev.*, 31: 377–398, 1961.

Smith, W. I., and J. W. Moore, *Programmed Learning: Theory and Research.* Princeton, N.J.: D. Van Nostrand Company, Inc, 1962.

Wohlwill, J. F., "The teaching machine: Psychology's hobbyhorse," *Teach. Coll. Rec.*, 64: 139–150, 1962.

Bibliography

Adorno, T. W., et al. 1950. *The Authoritarian Personality*. New York: Harper & Row, Publishers, Inc.

Aiken, W. M. 1942. *The Story of the Eight-Year Study*. New York: Harper & Row, Publishers, Inc.

Allport, Gordon W. 1935. "Attitudes," in C. Murchison (ed.), *A Handbook of Social Psychology*. Worcester, Mass.: Clark University Press.

————. 1937. *Personality: A Psychological Interpretation*. New York: Holt, Rinehart and Winston, Inc.

————. 1954. *The Nature of Prejudice*. Reading, Mass.: Addison-Wesley Publishing Company, Inc.

Altman, E. 1941. "Our mentally unbalanced teachers," *Amer. Mercury*, 52: 391–401.

American Association of School Administrators. 1942. *Health in Schools*. 20th Yearbook. Washington, D.C.: The Association.

American Psychological Association. 1966. *Standards for Educational and Psychological Tests and Manuals*. Washington, D.C.: The Association.

Anastasi, Anne. 1953. "Individual differences," *Annu. Rev. Psychol.*, 4: 137–156.

————. 1958. *Differential Psychology*. New York: Crowell-Collier and Macmillan, Inc.

Anderson, C. M. 1950. "The anatomy, physiology, and pathology of the psyche: A new concept of the dynamics of behavior," *Amer. Pract. Dig. Treatmt*, 1: 400–405.

————. 1952. "The self-image: A theory of the dynamics of behavior," *Ment. Hyg.*, 36: 227–244.

Anderson, Harold H. (ed.). 1959. *Creativity and its Cultivation.* New York: Harper & Row, Publishers, Inc.

————, and G. L. Anderson. 1954. "Social development," in L. Carmichael (ed.), *Manual of Child Psychology.* New York: John Wiley & Sons, Inc. Pp. 1162–1215.

Anderson, J. P. 1940. *A Study of the Relationship between Certain Aspects of Parental Behavior and Attitudes and the Behavior of Junior High School Pupils.* New York: Bureau of Publications, Teachers College, Columbia University.

Anderson, Richard C. 1959. "Learning in discussions: A resumé of the authoritarian-democratic studies," *Harv. educ. Rev.*, 29: 201–215.

Andrews, T. G., et al., 1950. "Transfer of training," in W. S. Monroe (ed.), *Encyclopedia of Educational Research.* New York: Crowell-Collier and Macmillan, Pp. 1483–1489.

Arbuckle, Dugald S. 1962. *Personnel Services in American Schools.* Boston: Allyn and Bacon, Inc.

Arny, C. B. 1953. *Evaluation in Home Economics.* New York: Appleton-Century-Crofts.

Asdell, S. A. 1953. "The effect of controlled ovulation upon the fertility of the mammalian egg," in J. E. Wolstenholme (ed.), *Mammalian Germ Cells.* Boston: Little, Brown & Company. Pp. 170–179.

Ash, E. F. 1944. "The effect of teacher adjustment on pupil adjustment," *Diss. Abstr.*, 4: 76–79.

Ashley, W. R., et. al. 1951. "The perceived size of coins in normal and hypnotically induced economic states," *Amer. J. Psychol.*, 64: 564–572.

Atkinson, John W. 1953. "The achievement motive and the recall of interrupted and completed tasks," *J. exp. Psychol.*, 46: 381–390.

———— (ed.). 1958. *Motives in Fantasy, Action, and Society.* Princeton, N. J.: D. Van Nostrand Company, Inc.

Ausubel, David P. 1958. *Theories and Problems of Child Development.* New York: Grune & Stratton, Inc.

————. 1959. "Viewpoints from related disciplines: Human growth and development," *Teach. Coll. Rec.*, 60: 245–254.

————. 1960. "The use of advance organizers in the learning and retention of meaningful verbal material," *J. educ. Psychol.*, 51: 267–272.

————. 1962. "Implications of preadolescent and early adolescent cognitive development for secondary school teaching," *High Sch. J.*, 45: 268–275.

————. 1963. *The Psychology of Meaningful Verbal Learning: An Introduction to School Learning.* New York: Grune & Stratton, Inc.

————, and P. Ausubel. 1966. "Cognitive development in adolescence," *Rev. educ. Res.*, 36: 403–413.

————, et al. 1957. "The influence of intention on the retention of school materials," *J. educ. Psychol.*, 48: 87–92.

Ayres, Leonard P. 1909. *Laggards in Our Schools.* New York: Russell Sage Foundation.

Bagley, W. C. **1922.** *The Educative Process.* New York: Crowell-Collier and Macmillan, Inc.

Baker, H. V. **1942.** "Children's Contributions in Elementary School Discussion," *Child Develpm. Monogr.* No. 29.

Bakwin, H. **1949.** "Emotional deprivation in infants," *J. Pediat.*, 35: 512–521.

Baldwin, Alfred L. **1948.** "Socialization and parent-child relationships," *Child Develpm.*, 19: 127–136.

———, et al. **1945.** "Patterns of parental behavior," *Psychol. Monogr.*, 58, No. 3.

Baldwin, B. T. **1921.** "The physical growth of children from birth to maturity," *University of Iowa Studies in Child Welfare*, 1, No. 1.

Bandura, Albert, and F. J. McDonald. **1963.** "Influence of social reinforcement and the behavior of models in shaping children's moral judgment," *J. abnorm. soc. Psychol.*, 67: 274–281.

Bandura, Albert, and Richard H. Walters. **1959.** *Adolescent Aggression.* New York: The Ronald Press Company.

———. **1963.** *Social Learning and Personality Development.* New York: Holt, Rinehart and Winston, Inc.

Barker, Roger G., et al. (eds.). **1943.** *Child Behavior and Development,* New York: McGraw-Hill, Inc.

Barr, Arvil S. **1961.** "Wisconsin studies of the measurement and prediction of teaching efficiency: A summary of investigations," *J. exp. Educ.*, 30: 1–155.

Bartlett, Edward R., and Dale B. Harris. **1936.** "Personality factors in delinquency," *Sch. Soc.*, 43: 653–656.

Basovitz, Harold, et al. **1955.** *Anxiety and Stress: An Interdisciplinary Study of a Life Situation.* New York: McGraw-Hill, Inc.

Bauer, Raymond A. **1964.** "The obstinate audience: the influence process from the point of view of social communication," *Amer. Psychologist*, 19: 319–328.

Baxter, Bernice. **1950.** *Teacher-Pupil Relationships,* second ed. New York: Crowell-Collier and Macmillan, Inc.

Bayles, Ernest E. **1960.** *Democratic Educational Theory.* New York: Harper & Row, Publishers, Inc.

Bayley, Nancy. **1949.** "Consistency and variability in the growth of intelligence from birth to eighteen years," *J. genet. Psychol.*, 75: 165–196.

———. **1936.** "Table for predicting adult height from skeletal age and present height," *J. Pediat.*, 28: 49–64.

———. **1955.** "On the growth of intelligence," *Amer. Psychologist*, 10: 805–818.

Beach, Leslie R. **1960.** "Sociability and academic achievement in various types of learning situations," *J. educ. Psychol.*, 51: 208–212.

Beaumont, H., and F. G. Macomber. **1949.** *Psychological Factors in Education.* New York: McGraw-Hill, Inc.

Becker, Wesley C. **1960.** "The relationship of factors in parental ratings of self and each other to the behavior of kindergarten children as rated by mothers, fathers, and teachers," *J. consult. Psychol.*, 24: 507–527.

———. **1964.** "Consequences of different kinds of parental disciplines," in

M. L. Hoffman and L. W. Hoffman (eds.), *Review of Child Development Research*. New York: Russell Sage Foundation.

Beilin, Harry. 1959. "Teachers' and clinicians' attitudes toward the behavior problems of children: A reappraisal," *Child Develpm.*, 30: 9–25.

Bender, L., and S. Paster. 1941. "Homosexual trends in children," *Amer. J. Orthopsychiat.*, 11: 730–744.

Berger, E. 1952. "Relation between expressed acceptance of self and expressed acceptance of others," *J. abnorm. soc. Psychol.*, 47: 778–782.

Berlyne, D. E. 1950. "Novelty and curiosity as determinants of exploratory behavior," *Brit. J. Psychol.*, 41: 68–80.

――――. 1957. "Recent developments in Piaget's works," *Brit. J. educ. Psychol.*, 27: 1–12.

Bernard, Harold W. 1961. *Mental Hygiene for Classroom Teachers*, second ed. New York: McGraw-Hill, Inc.

――――. 1965. *Psychology of Learning and Teaching*. New York: McGraw-Hill, Inc.

Bindra, D. 1959. *Motivation: A Systematic Reinterpretation*. New York: The Ronald Press Company.

Binet, Alfred, and T. Simon. 1905. "Methodes nouvelles pour le diagnostic du niveau intellectuel des abnormaux," *Ann. Psychol.*, 11: 191–244.

Birch, H. G., and H. S. Rabinowitz. 1951. "The negative effect of previous experience on productive thinking," *J. exp. Psychol.*, 41: 121–125.

Birney, R. C. 1959. "The reliability of the achievement motive," *J. abnorm. soc. Psych.*, 58: 266–267.

Bischoff, L. J. 1954. *Intelligence: Statistical Conceptions of Its Nature*. New York: Doubleday & Company, Inc.

Bize, P. R., and R. Moricard. 1937. "Psychic changes following injection of testosterone in young boys," *Bull. Soc. Pediat. (Paris)*, 35: 38.

Blair, Glenn M., et al. 1962. *Educational Psychology*. New York: Crowell-Collier and Macmillan, Inc.

Blake, Robert R., and Jane S. Mouton. 1959. "Personality," *Annu. Rev. Psychol.*, 10: 203–232.

Bloom, Benjamin S. (ed.). 1956. *Taxonomy of Educational Objectives: I: Cognitive Domain*. New York: David McKay Company, Inc.

――――. 1964. *Stability and Change in Human Characteristics*. New York: John Wiley & Sons, Inc.

Boehm, Lenore, and Martin L. Nass. 1962. "Social class differences in conscience development," *Child Develpm.*, 33: 565–574.

Bolles, R. C. 1958. "The usefulness of the drive concept," in M. R. Jones (ed.), *Nebraska Symposium on Motivation*. Lincoln, Neb.: University of Nebraska Press. Pp. 1–33.

Boney, C. DeW. 1949. "Shall beginning reading be delayed?" *Childh. Educ.*, 26: 168–172.

Bonney, Merl E. 1947. *Popular and Unpopular Children: A Sociometric Study*. Beacon, N.Y.: Beacon House, Inc.

――――. 1947. "Sociometric study of agreement between teacher judgments and student choices," *Sociometry*, 10: 133–146.

————. 1960. *Mental Health in Education*. Boston: Allyn and Bacon, Inc.

————, and L. Nicholson. 1958. "Comparative social adjustment of elementary school pupils with and without preschool training," *Child Develpm.*, 29: 125–133.

Bowlby, C. L. 1947. "A little 'extra' for those extracurricular duties," *Clearing House*, 22: 20–22.

Bowlby, John. 1953. "Some pathological processes set in train by early mother-child separation," *J. ment. Sci.*, 99: 265–272.

————, et al. 1956. "The effects of mother-child separation: A follow-up study," *Brit. J. med. Psychol.*, 29: 211–247.

Bowman, Paul H. 1963. "Developing potentiality: Creed or pipe dream?" in A. Frazier (ed.), *New Insights and the Curriculum*. Washington, D.C.: Association for Supervision and Curriculum Development. Pp. 38–55.

Boynton, P. L., et al. 1934. "The emotional stability of teachers and pupils," *J. juv. Res.*, 18: 223–232.

Bradley, Beatrice C. 1956. "An experimental study of the readiness approach to reading," *Elem. Sch. J.*, 56: 262–267.

Bradley, W. A. 1943. "Relationship of high and low marks to mental ability for the high school group," *Genet. Psychol. Monogr.*, 28: 99–169.

Braine, Martin D. S. 1959. "The ontogeny of certain logical operations: Piaget's formulation examined by non-verbal methods," *Psychol. Monogr.*, 73, No. 5.

————. 1962. "Piaget on reasoning: A methodological critique and alternative proposals," *Monogr. soc. Res. child Develpm.*, 27: 41–61.

Bridges, Katharine M. B. 1932. "Emotional development in early infancy," *Child Develpm.*, 3: 324–341.

Briggs, T. H. 1913. "Formal English grammar as a discipline," *Teach. Coll. Rec.*, 14: 251–343.

Brookover, W. B. 1945. "The relation of social factors to teaching ability," *J. exp. Educ.*, 13: 191–205.

Broudy, Harry S. 1963. "Socrates and the teaching machine," *Phi Delta Kappan*, 44: 243–246.

Brown, Judson S. 1961. *The Motivation of Behavior*. New York: McGraw-Hill, Inc.

Brownell, S. M. 1947. "A workable plan for recognition of merit," *Nation's Sch.*, 40: 20–22.

Brownell, W. A. 1942. "Problem solving," in N. B. Henry (ed.), *The Psychology of Learning*. 41st Yearbook, National Society for the Study of Education, Pt. II. Chicago: University of Chicago Press. Pp. 415–443.

Broyler, C. R., et al. 1927. "A second study of mental discipline in high school studies," *J. educ. Psychol.*, 18: 377–404.

Bruner, Jerome S. 1960. *The Process of Education*. Cambridge, Mass.: Harvard University Press.

————. 1961. "The act of discovery," *Harv. educ. Rev.*, 31: 21–32.

————, and C. C. Goodman. 1947. "Value and needs as organizing factors in perception," *J. abnorm. soc. Psychol.*, 42: 33–44.

Bugelski, B. R., and T. C. Cadwallader. 1956. "A reappraisal of the transfer and retroaction surface," *J. exp. Psychol.*, 52: 360–370.

Burks, B. S. 1928. "The relative influence of nature and nurture upon mental development: a comparative study of foster-parent, foster-child resemblance and true-parent true-child resemblance," in N. B. Henry (ed.), *Nature and Nurture: Their Influence upon Intelligence.* 27th Yearbook, National Society for the Study of Education, Pt. I. Bloomington, Ill. Public School Publishing Company. Pp. 219–316.

Burt, Cyril. 1955. "The evidence for the concept of intelligence," *Brit. J. educ. Psychol.,* 25: 158–177.

———. 1958. "The inheritance of mental ability," *Amer. Psychologist,* 13: 1–15.

Burton, William H. 1950. "Implications for organization of instruction and instructional adjuncts," in N. B. Henry (ed.), *Learning and Instruction.* 49th Yearbook, National Society for the Study of Education, Pt. I. Chicago: University of Chicago Press. Pp. 217–255.

———. 1958. "Basic principles in a good teaching-learning situation," *Phi Delta Kappan,* 39: 242–248.

———, et al. 1960. *Education for Effective Thinking.* New York: Appleton-Century-Crofts.

———. 1962. *The Guidance of Learning Activities.* New York: Appleton-Century-Crofts.

Butler, Robert A., and Harry F. Harlow. 1957. "Discrimination learning and learning sets to visual exploration incentives," *J. gen. Psychol.,* 57: 257–264.

Cannon, W. B. 1939. *The Wisdom of the Body.* New York: W. W. Norton & Company, Inc.

Cantor, Nathaniel. 1953. *The Teaching-Learning Process.* New York: Holt, Rinehart and Winston, Inc.

Carlson, Earl R. 1956. "Attitude change through modification of attitude structure," *J. abnorm. soc. Psychol.,* 52: 256–261.

Carmichael, L. 1926. "The development of behavior in vertebrates experimentally removed from the influence of external stimulation," *Psychol. Rev.,* 33: 51–58.

——— (ed.). 1954. *Manual of Child Psychology.* New York: John Wiley & Sons, Inc.

———, et al. 1932. "An experimental study of the effect of language on the reproduction of visually perceived form," *J. exp. Psychol.,* 15: 73–86.

Carroll, John B. 1960. "Language development," in C. W. Harris (ed.), *Encyclopedia of Educational Research.* New York: Crowell-Collier and Macmillan, Inc. Pp. 744–752.

Carter, R. S. 1952. "How valid are marks assigned by teachers?" *J. educ. Psychol.,* 43: 218–228.

Cartwright, Dorwin. 1959. "Lewinian theory as a systematic framework," in S. Koch (ed.), *Psychology: A Study of a Science.* Vol. 2. New York: McGraw-Hill, Inc. Pp. 7–91

Casler, Lawrence. 1961. "Maternal deprivation: A critical review of the literature," *Monogr. soc. Res. child Develpm.,* 26, No. 2.

Cassell, R. N., and A. E. Shafer. 1961. "An experiment in leadership training," *J. Psychol.,* 51: 299–305.

Castaneda, Alfred, et al. **1956.** "Complex learning and performance as a function of anxiety in children and task difficulty," *Child Develpm.*, 27: 327–332.

Cattell, Raymond B. **1950.** *Personality.* New York: McGraw-Hill, Inc.

Charles, Don C. **1953.** "Ability and accomplishment of persons earlier judged mentally deficient," *Genet. Psychol. Monogr.*, 47: 3–71.

Chasdi, Eleanor H., and Margaret S. Lawrence. **1951.** "Antecedents of aggression and effects of frustration in doll play," *Personality*, 1: 32–43.

Chauncey, Henry. **1963.** *Annual Report, 1962–1963.* Princeton, N.J.: Educational Testing Service.

Chowdhry, K., and T. M. Newcomb. **1952.** "The relative abilities of leaders and non-leaders to estimate opinions of their own groups," *J. abnorm. soc. Psychol.*, 47: 51–57.

Clark, G., and H. G. Birch. **1945.** "Hormonal modifications of social behavior: I: The effect of sex-hormone administration on the social status of a male castrate chimpanzee," *Psychosomat. Med.*, 7: 321–329.

Clark, P. E. **1938.** "Can college students grade themselves?" *Sch. & Soc.*, 47: 614–616.

Coffield, W. H., and P. Blommers. **1956.** "Effects of non-promotion on educational achievement in the elementary school," *J. educ. Psychol.*, 47: 235–250.

Coghill, G. E. **1929.** *Anatomy and the Problem of Behavior.* New York: Crowell-Collier and Macmillan, Inc.

Cohlan, Sidney Q. **1954.** "Congenital anomalies in the rat produced by excessive intakes of Vitamin A during pregnancy," *Pediatrics*, 13: 556–567.

Coleman, William, and Edward E. Cureton. **1954.** "Intelligence and achievement: The 'jangle fallacy' again," *Educ. psychol. Measmt*, 14: 347–351.

Combs, Arthur W. **1952.** "Intelligence from a perceptual point of view," *J. abnorm. soc. Psychol.*, 47: 662–673.

———. **1957.** "The myth of competition," *Childh. Educ.*, 33: 264–269.

———. (Chmn). **1962.** *Perceiving, Behaving, Becoming.* 1962 Yearbook. Washington, D.C.: Association for Supervision and Curriculum Development.

———, and Donald Snygg. **1959.** *Individual Behavior: A Perceptual Approach to Behavior*, revised ed. New York: Harper & Row, Publishers, Inc.

Commission on Teacher Education. **1944.** *Teachers for Our Times.* Washington, D.C.: American Council on Education.

Conant, James B. **1959.** *The American High School Today.* New York: McGraw-Hill, Inc.

Conradi, Edward. **1905.** "Song and call-notes of English sparrows when reared by canaries," *Amer. J. Psychol.*, 16: 190–199.

Cook, John O. **1963.** "Superstition in the Skinnerian," *Amer. Psychologist*, 18: 516–518.

Cook, Walter W. **1932.** "The measurement of general spelling ability involving controlled comparisons between techniques," *University of Iowa Studies in Education*, 6, No. 6.

———. **1941.** "Some effects of the maintenance of high standards of promotion," *Elem. Sch. J.*, 41: 430–437.

Corey, Stephen M. **1959**. "The Conant Report on the American High School," *Educ. Forum*, 24: 7–9.

Craig, Robert C. **1956**. "Directed versus independent discovery of established relations," *J. educ. Psychol.*, 47: 223–234.

Crandall, Vaughn J., et al. **1960**. "Maternal reactions and the development of independence and achievement behavior in young children," *Child Develpm.*, 31: 243–251.

Cronbach, Lee J. **1960**. *Essentials of Psychological Testing*. New York: Harper & Row, Publishers, Inc.

———. **1963**. *Educational Psychology*. New York: Harcourt, Brace & World, Inc.

Crow, Lester D., and Alice Crow. **1956**. *Human Development and Learning*. New York: American Book Company.

Crowder, Norman A. **1963**. "On the differences between linear and intrinsic programing," *Phi Delta Kappan*, 44: 250–254.

Culbertson, Frances M. **1957**. "Modification of an emotionally held attitude through role playing," *J. abnorm. soc. Psychol.*, 54: 330–333.

Cunningham, Ruth, et al. **1951**. *Understanding Group Behavior of Boys and Girls*. New York: Bureau of Publications, Teachers College, Columbia University.

Cureton, T. K. **1943**. "The unfitness of young men in motor fitness," *J. Amer. med. Ass.*, 123: 69–74.

Darley, John G. **1952**. "Special review: Eells, Kenneth, et al., Intelligence and cultural differences," *J. appl. Psychol.*, 36: 141–143.

Dashiell, J. F. **1949**. *Fundamentals of General Psychology*. Boston: Houghton Mifflin Company.

Davies, D. R. **1945**. "The effect of tuition upon the process of learning a complex motor skill," *J. educ. Psychol.*, 36: 352–365.

Davis, Robert A. **1940**. "The teaching problems of 1075 public school teachers," *J. exp. Educ.*, 9: 41–60.

Davis, W. Allison. **1948**. *Social Class Influence upon Learning*. Cambridge, Mass.: Harvard University Press.

———, and Kenneth Eells. **1952**. *Davis-Eells Games*. New York: Harcourt, Brace & World, Inc.

Davis, W. Allison, and Robert Havighurst. **1946**. "Social class and color differences in child rearing," *Amer. sociol. Rev.*, 11: 698–710.

Dawe, Helen C. **1943**. "A study of the effect of an educational program upon language development and related mental functions in young children," *J. exp. Educ.*, 11: 200–209.

Dearborn, W. F., and J. W. M. Rothney. **1941**. *Predicting the Child's Development*. Cambridge, Mass.: Sci-Art Publishers.

———, et al. **1938**. "Data on the growth of public school children from the materials of the Harvard Growth Studies," *Monogr. soc. Res. child Develpm.*, 3, No. 1.

Deese, James. **1958**. *The Psychology of Learning*. New York: McGraw-Hill, Inc.

Della-Piana, Gabriel, and Nathaniel Gage. **1955**. "Pupils' values and the validity of the MTAI," *J. educ. Psychol.*, 46: 167–178.

Dember, D. N., et al. **1957**. "Response by rats to differential stimulus complexity," *J. comp. physiol. Psychol.*, 50: 514–518.

Dennis, W. **1938**. "Infant development under conditions of restricted practice and of minimum social stimulation," *J. genet. Psychol.*, 53: 149–157.

————. **1960**. "Causes of retardation among institutional children: Iran," *J. genet. Psychol.*, 96: 47–59.

————, and M. G. Dennis. **1940**. "The effect of cradling practices upon the onset of walking in Hopi children," *J. genet. Psychol.*, 56: 77–86.

Dennis, W., and P. Najarian. **1957**. "Infant development under environmental handicap," *Psychol. Monogr.*, 71, No. 7.

Deutsche, J. M. **1943**. "The development of children's grasp of causal relationships," in R. G. Barker, et al. (eds.), *Child Behavior and Development*. New York: McGraw-Hill, Inc. Pp. 129–145.

Dewey, John. **1933**. *How We Think*. Boston: D. C. Heath and Company, Inc.

————. **1938**. *Experience and Education*. New York: Crowell-Collier and Macmillan, Inc.

Dittes, J. E., and H. A. Kelley. **1956**. "Effects of different conditions of acceptance upon conformity to group norms," *J. abnorm. soc. Psychol.*, 53: 100–107.

DiVesta, Francis J. **1961**. "Balance in teaching methods and learning processes," in *Balance in the Curriculum*. Washington, D.C.: Association for Supervision and Curriculum Development. Pp. 66–94.

Dollard, John and Neal E. Miller. **1950**. *Personality and Psychotherapy*. New York: McGraw-Hill, Inc.

————, et al. **1939**. *Frustration and Aggression*. New Haven, Conn.: Yale University Press.

Dominion Bureau of Statistics (Canada). **1942**. *A Height and Weight Survey of Toronto Elementary School Children, 1939*. Ottawa, Ontario, Can.: Department of Trade and Commerce.

Douvan, Elizabeth. **1956**. "Social status and social striving," *J. abnorm. soc. Psychol.*, 52: 219–223.

Dreikurs, Rudolf. **1957**. *Psychology in the Classroom*. New York: Harper & Row, Publishers, Inc.

Drews, Elizabeth M. **1961**. "A critical evaluation of approaches to the identification of gifted students," in A. E. Traxler (ed.), *Measurement and Evaluation in Today's Schools*. Washington, D.C.: American Council on Education.

Duncan, Carl P. **1951**. "The effect of unequal amounts of practice on motor learning before and after rest," *J. exp. Psychol.*, 42: 257–264.

Dunlap, K. **1932**. *Habits: Their Making and Unmaking*. New York: Liveright Publishing Corporation.

Durkin, Dolores. **1959a**. "Children's concepts of justice: A comparison with the Piaget data," *Child Develpm.*, 30: 59–67.

————. **1959b**. "Children's concepts of justice: A further comparison with the Piaget data," *J. educ. Res.*, 52: 252–257.

————. 1961. "The specificity of children's moral judgments," *J. genet. Psychol.*, 98: 3–13.

————. 1966. Children who read early: Two longitudinal studies. New York: Teachers College Press, Columbia University.

Earl, R. W. 1957. "Motivation, performance, and extinction," *J. comp. physiol. Psychol.*, 50. 248–251.

Ebbinghaus, H. 1913 (original, 1885). *Memory: A Contribution to Experimental Psychology.* New York: Bureau of Publications, Teachers College, Columbia University.

Ebbs, J. H., et al. 1942. "The influence of improved prenatal nutrition upon the infant." *Canad. med. Association J.*, 46: 6–8.

Ebel, Robert L. 1963. "The relation of testing programs to educational goals," in Warren G. Findley (ed.), *The Impact and Improvement of School Testing Programs.* 62d Yearbook, National Society for the Study of Education, Pt. II. Chicago: University of Chicago Press.

Edmiston, R. W., and B. Peyton. 1950. "Improving first grade achievement by readiness instruction," *Sch. & Soc.*, 71: 230–232.

Educational Testing Service. 1961. "Judges disagree on qualities that characterize good writing," *ETS Develpm.*, 9, No. 2.

Eells, Kenneth. 1953. "Some implications for school practice of the Chicago studies of cultural bias in intelligence tests," *Harv. educ. Rev.*, 23: 284–297.

————, et al. 1951. *Intelligence and Cultural Differences.* Chicago: University of Chicago Press.

Eichorn, Dorothy H. 1963. "Biological correlates of behavior," in H. W. Stevenson (ed.), *Child Development.* 62d Yearbook, National Society for the Study of Education, Pt. I. Chicago: University of Chicago Press. Pp. 4–61.

Eigen, Lewis D. 1963. "Programming poses problems," *Phi Delta Kappan*, 44: 242.

Elias, L. J. 1949. *High School Youth Look at Their Problems.* Pullman, Wash.: Washington State College.

Engel, Gerald, et al. 1958. "An investigation of anti-semitic feelings in two groups of college students: Jewish and non-Jewish," *J. soc. Psychol.*, 48: 75–82.

Evans, J. L., et al. 1960. "A preliminary investigation of variation in the properties of verbal learning sequences of the teaching machine 'type,'" in A. A. Lumsdaine and R. Glaser (eds.), *Teaching Machines and Programed Learning: A Source Book.* Washington, D.C.: National Education Association. Pp. 446–451.

Faigin, Helen. 1958. "Case report: Social behavior of young children in the kibbutz," *J. abnorm. soc. Psychol.*, 56: 117–129.

Fairbanks, G., and N. Guttman. 1958. "Effects of delayed auditory feedback upon articulation," *J. speech hear. Res.*, 1: 1–11.

Fast, Irene. 1957. "Kindergarten training and grade I reading," *J. educ. Psychol.*, 48: 52–57.

Fawcett, Harold P. **1938.** *The Nature of Proof.* 13th Yearbook. Washington, D.C.: National Council of Teachers of Mathematics.

Feldhusen, John F. **1963.** "Taps for teaching machines," *Phi Delta Kappan*, 44: 265–267.

Fenton, Norman M. **1943.** *Mental Hygiene in School Practice.* Stanford, Calif.: Stanford University Press.

Ferster, Charles B., and S. M. Sapon. **1958.** "Application of recent development in psychology to the teaching of German," *Harv. educ. Rev.*, 28: 58–69.

Festinger, Leon. **1957.** *A Theory of Cognitive Dissonance.* New York: Harper & Row, Publishers, Inc.

———. **1958.** "The motivation effect of cognitive dissonance," in G. Lindzey (ed.), *Assessment of Human Motives.* New York: Holt, Rinehart and Winston, Inc. Pp. 65–86.

———, and J. M. Carlsmith. **1959.** "Cognitive consequences of forced compliance," *J. abnorm. soc. Psychol.*, 58: 203–210.

Fey, William F. **1957.** "Correlates of certain subjective attitudes toward self and others," *J. clin. Psychol.*, 13: 44–49.

Flanagan, John C. **1964.** "Early findings of Project Talent," *NEA J.*, 53: 8–10.

———, et al. **1962.** *The Talent of American Youth.* Boston: Houghton Mifflin Company.

———. **1964.** *The American High-School Student: The Identification and Utilization of Human Talents.* Pittsburgh, Pa.: University of Pittsburgh Press.

Flavell, John H. **1963.** *The Developmental Psychology of Jean Piaget.* Princeton, N.J.: D. Van Nostrand Company, Inc.

Fleishman, Edwin A. **1957.** "A comparative study of aptitude patterns in unskilled and skilled psychomotor performances," *J. appl. Psychol.*, 41: 263–272.

———, and B. Fruchter. **1960.** "Factor structure and predictability of successive stages of learning Morse code," *J. appl. Psychol.*, 44: 97–101.

Flesher, Marie A., and Sidney L. Pressey. **1955.** "Wartime accelerates ten years later," *J. educ. Psychol.*, 46: 228–238.

Forgus, Ronald H. **1956.** "Advantages of early over late perceptual experience in improving form discrimination," *Canad. J. Psychol.*, 10: 147–155.

Forlano. G. **1936.** *School Learning with Various Methods of Practice and Rewards.* Teachers College Contributions to Education No. 688. New York: Bureau of Publications, Teachers College, Columbia University.

Fowler, W. L. **1962.** "Cognitive learning in infancy and early childhood," *Psychol. Bull.*, 59: 116–152.

Fox, James H. **1960.** *Driver Education and Driving Simulators.* Washington, D.C.: National Education Association.

Frank, L. K. **1955.** *Individual Development.* New York: Doubleday & Company, Inc.

Frankel, Edward. **1960.** "A comparative study of achieving and underachieving high school boys of high intellectual ability," *J. educ. Res.*, 53: 172–180.

Franz, S. I., and K. S. Lashley. **1951.** "Studies in the role of the brain in learning," in H. E. Garrett, *Great Experiments in Psychology.* New York: Appleton-Century-Crofts.

Fredericson, Emil. **1951.** "Competition: The effects of infantile experience upon adult behavior," *J. abnorm. soc. Psychol.,* 46: 406–409.

Freeman, Frank N., et al. **1928.** "The influence of environment on the intelligence, school achievement, and conduct of foster children," in G. M. Whipple (ed.), *Nature and Nurture: Their Influence upon Intelligence.* 27th Yearbook, National Society for the Study of Education, Pt. I. Bloomington, Ill.: Public School Publishing Company. Pp. 103–217.

French, Elizabeth G., and F. H. Thomas. **1958.** "The relation of achievement motivation to problem-solving effectiveness," *J. abnorm. soc. Psychol.,* 56: 45–48.

Frenkel-Brunswik, E. **1946.** "Personality and prejudice in women," *Amer. Psychologist,* 1: 239.

Freud, Sigmund. **1935.** *A General Introduction to Psychoanalysis.* New York: Liveright Publishing Corporation.

Friend, Celia M., and John P. Zubek. **1958.** "The effects of age on critical thinking ability," *J. Geront.,* 13: 407–413.

Fromm, Erich. **1941.** *Escape from Freedom.* New York: Holt, Rinehart and Winston, Inc.

———. **1948.** "Individual and social origins of neurosis," *Amer. sociol. Rev.,* 9: 380–384.

———. **1955.** *The Sane Society.* New York: Holt, Rinehart and Winston, Inc.

Fry, Edward B. **1960.** "A study of teaching machine response modes," in A. A. Lumsdaine and R. Glaser (eds.), *Teaching Machines and Programed Learning: A Source Book.* Washington, D.C.: National Education Association. Pp. 469–474.

Fuller, John L., and W. R. Thompson. **1960.** *Behavior Genetics.* New York: John Wiley & Sons, Inc.

Fund for the Advancement of Education. **1957.** *They Went to College Early.* New York: The Fund.

Gage, N. L. **1958.** "Explorations in teachers' perceptions of pupils," *J. teach. Educ.,* 9: 97–101.

———. **1960.** "Perception," in C. W. Harris (ed.), *Encyclopedia of Educational Research.* New York: Crowell-Collier and Macmillan, Inc. Pp. 941–945.

———, (ed.). **1963.** *Handbook of Research on Teaching.* Skokie, Ill.: Rand McNally & Company.

———. **1964.** "Theories of teaching," in E. R. Hilgard (ed.), *Theories of Learning and Instruction.* 63d Yearbook, National Society for the Study of Education, Pt. I. Chicago: University of Chicago Press. Pp. 268–285.

Gagné, Robert M. **1962.** "Simulators," in R. Glaser (ed.), *Training Research and Education.* Pittsburgh, Pa.: University of Pittsburgh Press.

———. **1964.** "Problem solving," in A. W. Melton (ed.), *Categories of Human Learning.* New York: Academic Press, Inc.

———. **1965.** *The Conditions of Learning.* New York: Holt, Rinehart and Winston, Inc.

———, and R. C. Bolles. **1959.** "A review of factors in learning efficiency," in E. H. Galanter (ed.), *Automatic Teaching: The State of the Art.* New York: John Wiley & Sons, Inc. Pp. 13–53.

Gagné, Robert M., and N. E. Paradise. **1961.** "Abilities and learning sets in knowledge acquisition," *Psychol. Monogr.,* 75, No. 14.

Galanter, Eugene H. **1963.** "Recent developments in automated instruction," in F. L. Ruch, *Psychology and Life,* sixth ed. Chicago: Scott, Foresman and Company.

Gardner, John W. **1961.** *Excellence.* New York: Harper & Row, Publishers, Inc.

Gates, Arthur I. **1937.** "The necessary mental age for beginning reading," *Elem. Sch. J.,* 37: 497–508.

———. **1942.** "Connectionism: present concepts and interpretations," in N. B. Henry (ed.), *Psychology of Learning.* 41st Yearbook, National Society for the Study of Education, Pt. II. Chicago: University of Chicago Press. Pp. 141–164.

———, et al. **1948.** *Educational Psychology,* revised ed. New York: Crowell-Collier and Macmillan, Inc.

Gesell, Arnold. **1940.** *The First Five Years of Life.* New York: Harper & Row, Publishers, Inc.

———, and F. L. Ilg. **1946.** *The Child from Five to Ten.* New York: Harper & Row, Publishers, Inc.

———, and H. Thompson. **1929.** "Learning and growth in identical infant twins," *Genet. Psychol. Monogr.,* 6: 5–120.

———, et al. **1956.** *Youth: The Years from Ten to Sixteen.* New York: Harper & Row, Publishers, Inc.

Getzels, Jacob W., and P. W. Jackson. **1962.** *Creativity and Intelligence.* New York: John Wiley & Sons, Inc.

———. **1962.** "The meaning of 'giftedness,' " *Education,* 82: 460–467.

———. **1963.** "The teacher's personality and characteristics," in N. L. Gage (ed.), *Handbook of Research on Teaching.* Skokie, Ill.: Rand McNally & Company. Pp. 506–582.

Glanzer, Murray. **1958.** "Curiosity, exploratory drive, and stimulus satiation," *Psychol. Bull.,* 55: 302–315.

Glaser, Edward M. **1941.** *An Experiment in the Development of Critical Thinking.* Teachers College Contributions to Education, No. 843. New York: Bureau of Publications, Teachers College, Columbia University.

Glaser, Robert (ed.). **1962.** *Training Research and Education.* Pittsburgh: University of Pittsburgh Press.

Gleason, John G. **1949.** "Attitudes vs. information on the Taft-Hartley Law," *Personnel Psychol.,* 2: 293–299.

Glueck, Sheldon. **1952.** *Delinquents in the Making: Paths to Prevention.* New York: Harper & Row, Publishers, Inc.

———. **1953.** "The home, the school, and delinquency," *Harv. educ. Rev.,* 23: 17–32.

——— (ed.). **1959.** *The Problem of Delinquency.* Boston: Houghton Mifflin Company.

Goddard, H. H. **1912.** *The Kallikak Family.* New York: Crowell-Collier and Macmillan, Inc.

Goldfarb, William. 1943. "The effects of early institutional care on adolescent personality," *J. exp. Educ.*, 12: 106–129.

———. 1945. "Psychological privation in infancy and subsequent adjustment," *Amer. J. Orthopsychiat.*, 15: 247–255.

Goldstein, H. 1940. *Reading and Listening Comprehension at Various Controlled Rates.* New York: Bureau of Publications, Teachers College, Columbia University.

Good, Carter V. 1926. "The effect of a single reading versus two readings of a given body of material," *J. educ. Meth.*, 5: 325–329.

Goodenough, Florence L. 1931. *Anger in Young Children.* Minneapolis, Minn.: University of Minnesota Press.

———. 1932. "Expression of the emotions in a blind-deaf child," *J. abnorm. soc. Psychol.*, 27: 428–433.

———. 1940. "Some special problems of nature-nurture research," in G. M. Whipple (ed.), *Intelligence: Its Nature and Nurture.* 39th Yearbook, National Society for the Study of Education, Pt. I. Bloomington, Ill.: Public School Publishing Company. Pp. 367–384.

———. 1941. "Atypical children: 1. Gifted children," in W. S. Monroe (ed.) *Encyclopedia of Educational Research.* New York: Crowell-Collier and Macmillan, Inc. Pp. 75–81.

Goodlad, John I. 1952. "Research and theory regarding promotion and non-promotion," *Elem. Sch. J.*, 53: 150–155.

———. 1954. "Some effects of promotion and non-promotion upon the social and personal adjustment of children," *J. exp. Educ.*, 22: 301–328.

Gordon, Jesse. 1963. *Personality and Behavior.* New York: Crowell-Collier and Macmillan, Inc.

Grant, David A., et al. 1951. "Acquisition and extinction of a verbal conditioned response with different percentages of reinforcement," *J. exp. Psychol.*, 42: 1–5.

Gray, H. A., and J. C. Ayres. 1931. *Growth in Private School Children.* Chicago: University of Chicago Press.

Green, Edward J. 1963. *The Learning Process and Programmed Instruction.* New York: Holt, Rinehart and Winston, Inc.

Green, E. H. 1933. "Friendships and quarrels among preschool children," *Child Develpm.*, 4: 237–252.

Grener, Norma, and Louis Raths. 1945. "Thinking in grade III," *Educ. res. Bull.*, 24: 38–42.

Grice, G. R. 1948. "The relation of secondary reinforcement to delayed reward on visual discrimination learning," *J. exp. Psychol.*, 38: 1-16.

Griffin, J. D., et al. 1940. *Mental Hygiene: A Manual for Teachers.* New York: American Book Company.

Gronlund, Norman E. 1950. "The accuracy of teachers' judgments concerning the sociometric status of sixth-grade pupils," *Sociometry*, 13: 197–225; 329-357.

———. 1959. *Sociometry in the Classroom.* New York: Harper & Row, Publishers, Inc.

———, and L. Anderson. 1957. "Personality characteristics of socially accepted, socially neglected and socially rejected high school pupils," *Educ. Admin. Supervis.*, 43: 329–338.

Gronlund, Norman E., and A. P. Whitney. **1958.** "The relation between teachers' judgments of pupils' sociometric status and intelligence," *Elem. Sch. J.*, 58: 264–268.

Gross, Sr. M. Mynette. **1946.** "The effect of certain types of motivation on the honesty of children," *J. educ. Res.*, 40: 133–140.

Guilford, J. P. **1950.** "Creativity," *Amer. Psychologist*, 5: 444–454.

———. **1956.** "The structure of the intellect," *Psychol. Bull.*, 53: 267–293.

———. **1958.** "A system of the psychomotor abilities," *Amer. J. Psychol.*, 71: 164–174.

———. **1959a.** "Traits of creativity," in H. H. Anderson (ed.), *Creativity and its Cultivation*. New York: Harper & Row, Publishers, Inc. Pp. 142–161.

———. **1959b.** *Personality*. New York: McGraw-Hill, Inc.

———. **1959c.** "Three faces of intellect," *Amer. Psychologist*, 14: 469–479.

———. **1967.** *The Nature of Human Intelligence*. New York: McGraw-Hill, Inc.

Guthrie, Edwin R. **1959.** "Association by contiguity," in S. Koch (ed.), *Psychology: A Study of a Science*. Vol. 2. New York: McGraw-Hill, Inc. Pp. 158–197.

———, and F. F. Powers. **1950.** *Educational Psychology*. New York: The Ronald Press Company.

Haggard, Ernest A. **1955.** "Learning a process of change," *Educ. Leadership*, 12: 149–156.

Haggerty, M. E. **1923.** "The incidence of undesirable behavior in public school children," *J. educ. Res.*, 12: 102–122.

Hagman, E. R. **1932.** "A study of fears of children of preschool age," *J. exp. Educ.*, 1: 110–130.

Hall, C. S. **1938.** "The inheritance of emotionality," *Sigma Xi Quart.*, 26: 17–27.

Hall, Calvin S. **1951.** "The genetics of behavior," in S. S. Stevens (ed.), *Handbook of Experimental Psychology*. New York: John Wiley & Sons, Inc. Pp. 304–329.

———, and Gardner Lindzey. **1957.** *Theories of Personality*. New York: John Wiley & Sons, Inc.

Hall, John F. **1961.** *Psychology of Motivation*. Philadelphia: J. B. Lippincott Company.

Hamblen, A. A. **1925.** "An investigation to determine the extent to which the effect of the study of Latin upon a knowledge of English derivatives can be measured," Ph.D. Thesis. Philadelphia: University of Pennsylvania.

Hand, Harold C. **1948.** *What People Think of Their Schools*. New York: Harcourt, Brace & World, Inc.

Harlow, Harry F. **1949.** "The formation of learning sets," *Psychol. Rev.*, 56: 51–65.

———, **1950.** "Learning and satiation of response in intrinsically motivated complex puzzle performance by monkeys," *J. comp. Psychol.*, 43: 289–294.

————. 1953. "Mice, monkeys, men and motives," *Psychol. Rev.*, 60: 23–32.

————. 1958. "The nature of love," *Amer. Psychologist*, 13: 673–685.

————. 1959. "Learning set and error factor theory," in S. Koch (ed.), *Psychology: A Study of a Science*. Vol. 2. New York: McGraw-Hill, Inc. Pp. 492–537.

————. 1962. "The heterosexual affectional system in monkeys," *Amer. Psychologist*, 17: 1–9.

————, et al. 1956. "Manipulatory motivation in the infant Rhesus monkey," *J. comp. physiol. Psychol.*, 49: 444–448.

Harris, Fred E. 1948. "Do children think critically about classroom procedures?" *J. educ. Psychol.*, 39: 52–59.

Harsh, Charles M., and H. G. Schrickel. 1959. *Personality: Development and Assessment*. New York: The Ronald Press Company.

Hartley, F. L. 1946. *Problems in Prejudice*. New York: King's Crown Press.

Hartmann, George W. 1942. "The field theory of learning and its educational consequences," in N. B. Henry (ed.), *Psychology of Learning*. 41st Yearbook, National Society for the Study of Education, Pt. II. Chicago: University of Chicago Press. Pp. 165–214.

Hartshorne, H., and M. A. May. 1928, 1929, 1930. I: *Studies in Deceit*; II: *Studies in Service and Self-Control*; III: *Studies in the Organization of Character*. New York: Crowell-Collier and Macmillan, Inc.

Harvey, O. J., and J. Rutherford. 1958. "Gradual and absolute approaches to attitude change," *Sociometry*, 21: 61–68.

Havelka, J. 1956. "Problem-solving behavior in rats," *Canad. J. Psychol.*, 10: 91–97.

Havighurst, Robert J. 1952. *Developmental Tasks and Education*. New York: David McKay Company, Inc.

————. 1958. "What to do with the tough hostile boy," *Phi Delta Kappan*, 40: 136–138.

————, and Hilda Taba. 1949. *Adolescent Character and Personality*. New York: John Wiley & Sons, Inc.

Hayes, Keith J. 1962. "Genes, drives, and intellect," *Psychol. Rep.* (Monogr. Suppl. 2), 10: 299–342.

Hebb, Donald O. 1937. "The innate organization of visual activity; 1. Perception of figures by rats reared in total darkness," *J. genet. Psychol.*, 51: 101–126.

————. 1946. "On the nature of fear," *Psychol. Rev.*, 53: 259–276.

————. 1949. *The Organization of Behavior*. New York: John Wiley & Sons, Inc.

————. 1955. "The mammal and his environment," *Amer. J. Psychol.*, 91: 826–831.

————. 1958. "The motivating effects of exteroceptive stimulation," *Amer. Psychologist*, 13: 109–113.

————. 1959. "Neuro-psychological theory," in S. Koch (ed.), *Psychology: A Study of a Science*. Vol. 2. New York: McGraw-Hill, Inc. Pp. 622–643.

Heil, Louis M., et al. 1960. *Characteristics of Teacher Behavior Related to the Achievement of Children in Several Elementary Grades*. Cooperative Research Project. Washington, D.C.: U.S. Office of Education.

Held, Hans. 1929. "Die Lehre von den neuronen," *Forschritte der Naturwissenschaftlichen Forschung n.f.*, 8: 41–44.

Hermanovicz, Henry. 1961. "Problem solving as a teaching method," *Educ. Leadership*, 18: 299–306.

Heron, W. 1957. "The pathology of boredom," *Scientif. Amer.*, 196: 52–56.

Herzog, E. 1960. *Children of Working Mothers*. Publication No. 382. Washington, D.C.: Children's Bureau, U.S. Department of Health, Education, and Welfare.

Hicks, F. R. 1943. *The Mental Health of Teachers*. Nashville, Tenn.: Peabody College.

Hieronymus, A. N. 1951. "A study of social class motivation: Relationships between anxiety for education and certain socio-economic and intellectual variables," *J. educ. Psychol.*, 42: 193–205.

Hilgard, Ernest R. 1956. *Theories of Learning*. New York: Appleton-Century-Crofts. (Hilgard and G. H. Bower. 1966. third ed.)

———. 1959. "Creativity and problem-solving," in H. H. Anderson (ed.), *Creativity and Its Cultivation*. New York: Harper & Row, Publishers, Inc.

———. 1961. "What support from the psychology of learning," *NEA J.*, 50: 20–21.

———. 1962. *Introduction to Psychology*. New York: Harcourt, Brace & World, Inc.

Hill, Winfred F. 1956. "Activity as an autonomous drive," *J. comp. physiol. Psychol.*, 49: 15–19.

Hollingworth, Leta S. 1926. *Gifted Children: Their Nature and Nurture*. New York: Crowell-Collier and Macmillan, Inc.

Holodnak, H. B. 1943. "The effect of positive and negative guidance upon maze learning in children," *J. educ. Psychol.*, 34: 341–354.

Honzik, M. P., et al. 1948. "The stability of mental test performance between two and eighteen years," *J. exp. Educ.*, 17: 309–324.

Hopkins, L. Thomas. 1945. "What are the essentials?" *Teach Coll. Rec.*, 46: 493–500.

Horn, Ernest. 1937. *Methods of Instruction in the Social Studies*. New York: Charles Scribner's Sons.

———. 1942. "Language and meaning," in N. B. Henry (ed.), *Psychology of Learning*. 41st Yearbook, National Society for the Study of Education, Pt. II. Bloomington, Ill.: Public School Publishing Company. Pp. 377–413.

Horney, Karen. 1937. *The Neurotic Personality of Our Times*. New York: W. W. Norton & Company, Inc.

Hovland, Carl I. 1960. "Computer simulation of thinking," *Amer. Psychologist*, 15: 687–693.

———, et al. 1949. *Experiments on Mass Communication*. Vol. 3. *The American Soldier*. Princeton, N.J.: Princeton University Press.

———. 1957. "Assimilation and contrast effects in reactions to communication and attitude change," *J. abnorm. soc. Psychol.*, 55: 244–252.

Hull, Clark L. 1927. "Variability in amount of different traits possessed by the individual," *J. educ. Psychol.*, 18: 97–104.

———. 1943. *Principles of Behavior*. New York: Appleton-Century-Crofts.

Hullfish, H. Gordon, and Philip G. Smith. 1961. *Reflective Thinking: The Method of Education*. New York: Dodd, Mead & Company, Inc.

Hunsicker, P. A. 1958. *Manual, Youth Physical Fitness Test*. Washington, D.C.: National Education Association.

Hunt, J. McV. 1941. "The effects of infant feeding frustrations upon adult hoarding in the albino rat," *J. abnorm. soc. Psychol.*, 36: 338–360.

———. 1960. "Experience and the development of motivation: Some reinterpretations," *Child Develpm.*, 31: 489–504.

———. 1961. *Intelligence and Experience*. New York: The Ronald Press Company.

Hurlock, Elizabeth B. 1925. "An evaluation of certain incentives used in school work," *J. educ. Psychol.*, 16: 145–159.

Hurst, John C., et al. 1961. "An approach to evaluation in educational psychology courses and its instrumentation," *Educ. psychol. Measmt*, 21: 445–456.

Ingalls, T. H. **Dec. 20, 1950.** "Dr. T. H. Ingalls describes tests on mice indicating heredity and environment overlap as determining factors," New York *Times*.

Inhelder, Barbel, and Jean Piaget. 1958. *The Growth of Logical Thinking*. New York: Basic Books, Inc.

Irwin, D. 1960. "Infant speech: Effect of systematic reading of stories," *J. speech hear. Disord.*, 3: 187–190.

Jackson, L. A. 1950. "Emotional attitudes toward the family of normal, neurotic, and delinquent children," *Brit. J. Psychol.*, 41: 35–51; 173–185.

Jacob, Philip E. 1957. *Changing Values in College*. New York: Harper & Row, Publishers, Inc.

Jahoda, Marie. 1958. *Current Concepts of Positive Mental Health*. New York: Basic Books, Inc.

James, William. 1890. *Principles of Psychology*. Vol. I. New York: Holt, Rinehart and Winston, Inc.

———. 1899. *Talks to Teachers on Psychology*. New York: Holt, Rinehart and Winston, Inc.

Janis, Irving L., and Seymour Feshbach. 1953. "Effects of fear-arousing communications," *J. abnorm. soc. Psychol.*, 48: 78–92.

———, and B. T. King. 1954. "The influence of role playing on opinion change," *J abnorm. soc. Psychol.*, 49: 211–218.

Jantzen, J. Marc. 1959. "An opinionnaire on why college students choose to teach," *J. educ. Res.*, 53: 13–17.

Jenkin, Noel. 1957. "Affective processes in perception," *Psychol. Bull.*, 54: 100–127.

Jenkins, William O., and Julian C. Stanley. 1950. "Partial reinforcement: A review and critique," *Psychol. Bull.*, 47: 193–234.

Jensen, M. B., and A. Lemaire. 1937. "Ten experiments on whole and part learning," *J. educ. Psychol.*, 28: 37–54.

Jersild, Arthur T. **1948.** "Child development," Pt. II, in A. I. Gates et al., *Educational Psychology.* New York: Crowell-Collier and Macmillan, Inc.

———. **1951.** "Self-understanding in childhood and adolescent," *Amer. Psychologist,* 6: 122–126.

———. **1952.** *In Search of Self.* New York: Bureau of Publications, Teachers College, Columbia University.

———. **1960.** *Child Psychology.* Englewood Cliffs, N.J.: Prentice-Hall, Inc.

———, and F. V. Markey. **1935.** "Conflict between preschool children," *Child Develpm. Monogr.,* No. 21.

———, et al. **1941.** "Studies of elementary school classes in action. II. Pupil participation and aspects of pupil-teacher relationships," *J. exp. Educ.,* 10: 119–137.

Jones, H. E. **1954.** "The environmental and mental development," in L. Carmichael (ed.), *Manual of Child Psychology.* New York: John Wiley & Sons, Inc. Pp. 631–696.

———, and H. S. Conrad. **1933.** "The growth and decline of intelligence: A study of a homogenous group between the ages of ten and sixty," *Genet. Psychol. Monogr.,* 13: 223–298.

Jones, Mary C. **1957.** "The later careers of boys who were early- or late-maturing," *Child Develpm.,* 28: 113–128.

———, and Paul Mussen. **1958.** "Self-conceptions, motivations, and interpersonal attitudes of early- and late-maturing girls," *Child Develpm.,* 29: 491–501.

Jones, Vernon. **1950.** "Child development, XIII: Moral concepts and conduct," in W. S. Monroe (ed.), *Encyclopedia of Educational Research,* second ed. New York: Crowell-Collier and Macmillan, Inc. Pp. 183–187.

———. **1954.** "Character development in children: An objective approach," in L. Carmichael (ed.), *Manual of Child Psychology.* New York: John Wiley & Sons, Inc. Pp. 781–832.

———. **1960.** "Character education," in C. W. Harris (ed.), *Encyclopedia of Educational Research.* New York: Crowell-Collier and Macmillan, Inc. Pp. 84–91.

Jourard, Sidney M. **1963.** *Personality Adjustment.* New York: Crowell-Collier and Macmillan, Inc.

Judd, C. H. **1908.** "The relation of special training to special intelligence," *Educ. Rev.,* 36: 28–42.

Judson, A. J., and C. N. Cofer. **1956.** "Reasoning as an associative process: 1. Direction in a simple verbal problem," *Psychol. Rep.,* 2: 469–476.

Kagan, Jerome. **1964.** "American longitudinal research on psychological development," *Child Develpm.,* 35: 1–32.

———, and Howard A. Moss. **1960.** "The stability of passive and dependent behavior from childhood through adulthood," *Child Develpm.,* 31: 577–591.

Kallmann, Franz J. **1953.** *Heredity in Health and Mental Disorders.* New York: W. W. Norton & Company, Inc.

Kao, D. L. 1937. "Plateaus and the curve of learning in motor skills," *Psychol. Monogr.*, 49, No. 219.

Kaplan, Louis. 1959. *Mental Health and Human Relations in Education*. New York: Harper & Row, Publishers, Inc.

———, and J. D. O'Dea. 1953. "Mental health hazards in school," *Educ. Leadership*, 10: 351–354.

Karacki, L., and J. Toby. 1962. "The uncommitted adolescent: Candidate for gang socialization," *Sociol. Inquiry*, 32: 203–215.

Karpf, E. 1961. "What's it all about?" *High Points*, 43: 73–77.

Karpinos, Bernard D. 1961. "Current height and weight of youth of military age," *Hum. Biol.*, 33: 335–354.

Katz, B., et al. 1957. "The measurement of ego-defense as related to attitude change," *J. Pers.*, 25: 465–474.

Keislar, Evan R., and John D. McNeil. 1961. "Teaching scientific theory to first grade pupils by auto-instructional devices," *Harv. educ. Rev.*, 31: 73–83.

Keliher, Alice V. 1941. *Life and Growth*. New York: Appleton-Century-Crofts.

———. 1950. "Progressive education," in W. S. Monroe (ed.), *Encyclopedia of Educational Research*. New York: Crowell-Collier and Macmillan, Inc. Pp. 894–897.

Kelley, T. L. 1927. *Interpretation of Educational Measurement*. New York: Harcourt, Brace & World, Inc.

Kendler, Howard H. 1959. "Learning," *Annu. Rev. Psychol.*, 10: 43–88.

———. 1961. "Stimulus-response psychology and audio-visual education," *A-V Communications Rev.*, 9: 33–41.

Kersh, B. Y. 1958. "The adequacy of meaning as an explanation for the superiority of learning by independent discovery," *J. educ. Psychol.*, 49: 282–292.

Kettering, Charles F. 1944. "How can we develop inventors?" *Mech. Engng.*, 66: 231–234.

Keyes, C. H. 1911. *Progress through the Grades of City Schools*. New York: Bureau of Publications, Teachers College, Columbia University.

Keys, A., et al. 1945. *Experimental Starvation in Man*. Minneapolis, Minn.: University of Minnesota Press.

Keys, N. 1940. "Value of group tests IQ's for prediction of progress beyond high school," *J. educ. Psychol.*, 31: 81–93.

Kingsley, H. L., and R. Garry. 1957. *The Nature and Conditioning of Learning*. Englewood Cliffs, N.J.: Prentice-Hall, Inc.

Kinsey, A. C., et al. 1948. *Sexual Behavior in the Human Male*. Philadelphia. W. B. Saunders Company.

———. 1953. *Sexual Behavior in the Human Female*. Philadelphia: W. B. Saunders Company.

Kirk, Samuel A. 1948. "An evaluation of the study by Bernardine G. Schmidt entitled, 'Changes in personal, social, and intellectual behavior of children originally classified as feebleminded,'" *Psychol. Bull.*, 45: 321–333.

———. 1958. *Early Education of the Mentally Retarded*. Urbana, Ill.: University of Illinois Press.

Kirkendall, Lester A. 1939. "Teaching for marks," *Sch. Soc.*, 49: 642–644.

Kirschner, G., and D. Glines. **1957.** "Comparative analysis of Eugene, Oregon, elementary school children in the Kraus-Weber Test of Minimal Muscular Fitness," *Res. Quart.*, 28: 16–25.

Kittell, Jack E. **1957.** "An experimental study of the effects of external direction during learning on transfer and retention of principles," *J. educ. Psychol.*, 48: 391–405.

Klene, V., and E. P. Branson. **1929.** "Trial promotion versus failure," *Educ. Res. Bull. (Los Angeles City Schools)*, 8: 6–11.

Kline, L. W. **1914.** "Some experimental evidence in regard to formal discipline," *J. educ. Psychol.*, 5: 259–266.

Klingberg, G. **1957.** "The distinction between living and not living among 7–10 year-old children," *J. genet. Psychol.*, 90: 227–238.

Knapp, C. G., and W. R. Dixon. **1950.** "Learning to juggle: I. A study to determine the effect of two different distributions of practice on learning efficiency," *Res. Quart.*, 21: 331–336.

Knobloch, H., and B. Pasamanick. **1963.** "Predicting intellectual potential in infancy," *Amer. J. Dis. Child.*, 106: 43–51.

Koch, Helen L. **1955.** "Some personality correlates of sex, sibling position, and sex of siblings among five- and six-year-old children," *Genet. Psychol. Monogr.*, 52: 3–50.

Koenke, Robert H. **1948.** "Arithmetic readiness at the kindergarten level," *J. educ. Res.*, 42: 218–223.

Köhler, W. **1927.** *The Mentality of Apes.* New York: Harcourt, Brace & World, Inc.

———. **1929.** *Gestalt Psychology.* New York: Liveright Publishing Corporation.

Komoski, P. K. **Mar. 24, 1961.** "A teaching machine sampler: Skinner's linear method," *Time*, 77: 38.

Korchin, S. J., and S. Levine. **1957.** "Anxiety and verbal learning," *J. abnorm. soc. Psychol.*, 54: 234–240.

Krathwohl, David R., et al. **1964.** *Taxonomy of Educational Objectives*, II: *Affective Domain.* New York: David McKay Company, Inc.

Krech, D., and R. S. Crutchfield. **1958.** *Elements of Psychology.* New York: Alfred A. Knopf, Inc.

Krueger, William C. F. **1929, 1930.** "The effect of overlearning on retention," *J. exp. Psychol.*, 12: 71–78; 13: 152–163.

Krugman, Arnold D. **1958.** "A comparative study of the effect of induced failure, induced success, and a neutral task upon the retentive process of anxiety and normal subjects," *Diss. Abstr.*, 18: 662.

Kvaraceus, William C. **1948.** "The role of the administrator in relation to juvenile delinquency," in N. B. Henry (ed.), *Juvenile Delinquency and the Schools.* 47th Yearbook, National Society for the Study of Education, Pt. I. Chicago: University of Chicago Press. Pp. 126–144.

———. **1960.** "Behavior problems," in C. W. Harris (ed.) *Encyclopedia of Educational Research.* New York: Crowell-Collier and Macmillan, Inc. Pp. 137–143.

———. **1961.** "Future classroom—an educational automat," *Educ. Leadership*, 18: 288–292.

Labue, Anthony C. 1954. "A study of motivation of 'persistent' vs. 'non-persistent' students in teacher education," *J. teach. Educ.*, 5: 242–243.

Lambert, William W., et al. 1949. "Reinforcement and extinction as factors in size estimation," *J. exp. Psychol.*, 39: 637–641.

Landers, J. 1963. *Higher Horizons: Progress Report*. New York: Board of Education.

Lange, C. J., and W. James. 1922. *The Emotions*. Baltimore: The Williams & Wilkins Company.

Laporte, M. 1946. "Effect of war-imposed dietary limitations on growth of Paris school children," *Amer. J. Dis. Child.* 71: 244–247.

Larson, K. G., and M. R. Karpas. 1963. *Effective Secondary School Discipline*. Englewood Cliffs, N.J.: Prentice Hall, Inc.

Lawrence, D. H., and Leon Festinger. 1962. *Deterrents and Reinforcement: The Psychology of Insufficient Rewards*. Stanford, Calif.: Stanford University Press.

Lawson, P. R. 1960. *Learning and Behavior*. New York: Crowell-Collier and Macmillan, Inc.

Lazarus, R. S., et al. 1952. "The effects of psychological stress upon performance," *Psychol. Bull.*, 49: 293–317.

————. 1957. "Personality and psychological stress," *J. Pers.*, 25: 559–577.

Learned, W. S., and B. D. Wood. 1938. *The Student and His Knowledge*. Bulletin No. 29. New York: Carnegie Foundation for the Advancement of Teaching.

Lecky, P. 1945. *Self-Consistency: A Theory of Personality*. New York: Island Press.

Leuba, C. 1955. "Toward some integration of learning theories: The concept of optimal stimulation," *Psychol. Rev.*, 1: 27–33.

Leuba, O. 1933. "An experimental study of rivalry in young children," *J. comp. Psychol.*, 16: 367–378.

Lewin, Kurt. 1935. *A Dynamic Theory of Personality*. New York: McGraw-Hill, Inc.

————. 1958. "Group decision and social change," in E. E. Maccoby et al. (eds.), *Readings in Social Psychology*, third ed. New York: Holt, Rinehart and Winston, Inc.

————, et al. 1939. "Patterns of aggressive behavior in experimentally created social climates," *J. soc. Psychol.*, 10: 271–299.

Life magazine. Oct. 4, 1963. "DNA's code: Key to all life," *Life*, 55, No. 14: 70–90.

Lilly, J. C. 1956. "Mental effects of reduction of ordinary levels of physical stimulus on intact healthy persons," *Psychiatr. Res. Rep.*, 5: 1–28, (See also *Amer. J. Psychiat.*, Vol. No. 115, December 1958).

Lindgren, Henry C. 1962. *Educational Psychology in the Classroom*. New York: John Wiley & Sons, Inc.

Lindvall, C. M. (ed.). 1964. *Defining Educational Objectives*. Pittsburgh, Pa.: University of Pittsburgh Press.

Ling, Bing-Chung. 1941. "Form discrimination as a learning cue in infants," *Comp. Psychol. Monogr.*, 17, No. 2.

Lobaugh, D. 1942. "Girls, grades, and IQ's," *Nation's Sch.*, 30: 42.

Lodge, William J. 1951. "Classroom cheating—a measure of children's character or teachers' attitudes?" *Calif. J. educ. Res.*, 2: 63–66.

Logan, Frank A. 1959. "The Hull-Spence approach," in S. Koch (ed.), *Psychology: A Study of a Science*. Vol. 2. New York: McGraw-Hill, Inc. Pp. 293–358.

Lorenz, K. 1935. "Der Kumpan in der unwelt des vogels," *J. Ornithologie*, 83: 137–413.

Lorge, Irving, et al. 1958. "A survey of studies contrasting the quality of group performance and individual performance, 1920–1957," *Psychol. Bull.*, 55: 337–372.

Lowell, Edgar L. 1952. "The effect of need for achievement on learning and speed of performance," *J. Psychol.*, 33: 31–40.

Lumsdaine, A. A. 1964. "Educational technology, programed learning, and instructional science," in E. R. Hilgard (ed.), *Theories of Learning and Instruction*. 63d Yearbook, National Society for the Study of Education, Pt. I. Chicago: University of Chicago Press. Pp. 361–401.

————, and Robert Glaser (eds.). 1960. *Teaching Machines and Programmed Learning: A Source Book*. Washington, D.C.: National Education Association.

Lumsdaine, A. A., and I. L. Janis. 1953. "Resistance and counterpropaganda produced by one-sided and two-sided propaganda presentations," *Publ. Opin. Quart.*, 17: 311–318.

Lynn, R., and I. Gordon. 1961. "The relation of neuroticism and extroversion to intelligence and educational attainment," *Brit. J. educ. Psychol.*, 31: 194–203.

McArthur, C. 1956. "Personalities of first and second children," *Psychiatry*, 19: 47–54.

McCandless, Boyd R. 1957. "Should a bright child start to school before he is five?" *Education*, 77: 1–6.

McCarthy, Dorothea. 1954. "Language development in children," in L. Carmichael (ed.), *Manual of Child Psychology*. New York: John Wiley & Sons, Inc. Pp. 492–630.

McClelland, David C. 1942. "Functional autonomy of motives as an extinction phenomenon," *Psychol. Rev.*, 49: 272–283.

————, et al. 1953. *The Achievement Motive*. New York: Appleton-Century-Crofts.

McClelland, W. J. 1956. "Differential handling and weight gain in the albino rat," *Canad. J. Psychol.*, 10: 19–22.

McConnell, T. R. 1942. "Reconciliation of learning theories," in N. B. Henry (ed.), *The Psychology of Learning*. 41st Yearbook, National Society for the Study of Education, Pt. II. Chicago: University of Chicago Press. Pp. 243–286.

————. 1948. "Learning," Pt. III, in A. I. Gates, et al., *Educational Psychology*. New York: Crowell-Collier and Macmillan, Inc.

McCullers, John C., and Walter T. Plant. 1964. "Personality and social development: Cultural influences," *Rev. educ. Res.*, 34: 599–610.

McDougall, William. 1908. *An Introduction to Social Psychology.* London: Methuen & Co., Ltd.

McGehee, W. 1938. "Freshmen grades and the American Council Psychological Examinations," *Sch. & Soc.,* 47: 222–224.

———, and W. D. Lewis. 1942. "The socio-economic status of homes of mentally superior and retarded children and the occupational rank of their parents," *J. genet. Psychol.,* 60: 375–380.

McGraw, Myrtle B. 1935. *Growth: A Study of Johnny and Jimmy.* New York: Appleton-Century-Crofts.

McHugh, G. 1945. "Changes in the Goodenough IQ at the public school kindergarten level," *J. educ. Psychol.,* 36: 17–30.

McKeachie, W. J., and D. Solomon. 1957. "Retention of general psychology," *J. educ. Psychol.,* 48: 110–112.

MacKinnon, D. W. 1962. "The nature and nurture of creative talent," *Amer. Psychologist,* 17: 488–495.

McKinnon, K. 1942. *Consistency and Change in Personality and Behavior Manifestations—as Observed in a Group of 16 Children during a Five-Year Period. Child Develpm. Monogr.,* No. 30. New York: Bureau of Publications, Teachers College, Columbia University.

McLaughlin, K. L. 1950. "Kindergarten education," in W. S. Monroe (ed.), *Encyclopedia of Educational Research.* New York: Crowell-Collier and Macmillan, Inc. Pp. 647–654.

McNeil, John D. 1964. "Programed instruction versus usual classroom procedures in teaching boys to read," *Amer. educ. Res. J.,* 1: 113–119.

McNemar, Quinn. 1940. "A critical examination of the University of Iowa studies of environmental influences upon the IQ," *Psychol. Bull.,* 37: 63–92.

Macomber, F. C., and L. Siegel. 1960. *Final Report on the Experimental Study of Instructional Procedures.* Oxford, Ohio: Miami University.

Maier, Norman R. F. 1931. "Reasoning in humans, 2. The solution of a problem and its appearance in consciousness," *J. comp. Psychol.,* 12: 184–191.

———. 1949. *Frustration: The Study of Behavior Without a Goal.* New York: McGraw-Hill, Inc.

———. 1960. "Maier's Law," *Amer. Psychologist,* 15: 208–212.

———, et al. 1940. "Studies of abnormal behavior in the rat: 3. The development of behavior fixations through frustration," *J. exp. Psychol.,* 26: 521–546.

Maller, J. B. 1929. *Cooperation and Competition.* New York: Bureau of Publications, Teachers College, Columbia University.

Margolin, R. J. 1953. "New perspective for teachers—an evaluation of a mental health institute," *Ment. Hyg.,* 37: 394–424.

Markham, Edwin. 1948. "Outwitted," in C. L. Wallis (ed.), *Selected Poems.* New York: Harper & Row, Publishers, Inc.

Marquart, Dorothy I. 1946. "The pattern of punishment in its relation to abnormal fixation in adult human subjects," Unpublished Doctoral Dissertation. Ann Arbor, Mich.: University of Michigan. (As reported in T. M. Newcomb, *Social Psychology.* New York: Holt, Rinehart and Winston, Inc. 1950.)

Marshall, S. L. A. **1947.** *Men Against Fire.* New York: William Morrow & Company, Inc.

Martire, John G. **1956.** "Relationships between the self-concept and differences in the strength and generality of achievement motivation," *J. Pers.*, 24: 364–375.

Marx, Melvin H. **1960.** "Motivation," in C. W. Harris (ed.), *Encyclopedia of Educational Research.* New York: Crowell-Collier and Macmillan, Inc. Pp. 888–901.

Maslow, Abraham H. **1943.** "A theory of human motivation," *Psychol. Rev.*, 50: 370–396.

———. **1959.** "Cognition of being in the peak experiences," *J. genet. Psychol.*, 94: 43–66.

———. **1959.** "Creativity in self-actualizing people," in H. H. Anderson (ed.), *Creativity and Its Cultivation.* New York: Harper & Row, Publishers, Inc. Pp. 83–95.

———. **1962.** "Some basic propositions of growth and self-actualization," in A. W. Combs (chmn), *Perceiving, Behaving, Becoming.* Washington, D.C.: Association for Supervision and Curriculum Development. Pp. 34–49.

Masserman, J. H. **1943.** *Behavior and Neurosis.* Chicago: University of Chicago Press.

Mayer, B. A. **1935.** "Negativistic reactions of preschool children on the new revision of the Stanford-Binet," *J. genet. Psychol.*, 46: 311–334.

Mead, Margaret. **1935.** *Sex and Temperament in Three Primitive Societies.* New York: William Morrow & Company, Inc.

———. **1937.** *Cooperation and Competition among Primitive Peoples.* New York: McGraw Hill, Inc.

Melton, Arthur W. **1950.** "Learning," in W. S. Monroe (ed.), *Encyclopedia of Educational Research.* New York: Crowell-Collier and Macmillan, Inc. Pp. 668–690.

———. **1956.** "Present accomplishment and future trends in problem solving and learning theory," *Amer. Psychologist*, 11: 278–281.

———. **1959.** "The science of learning and the technology of educational methods," *Harv. educ. Rev.*, 29: 101.

Melzack, Ronald, and T. H. Scott. **1957.** "The effects of early experience on the response to pain," *J. comp. physiol. Psychol.*, 50: 155–161.

———, and W. R. Thompson. **1956.** "Effects of early experience on social behavior," *Canad. J. Psychol.*, 10: 82–90.

Mengert, I. G. **1931.** "A preliminary study of the reactions of two-year-old children to each other when paired in a semi-controlled situation," *J. genet. Psychol.*, 39: 393–398.

Meredith, H. V. **1951.** "Relation between socioeconomic status and body size in boys seven to ten years of age," *Amer. J. Dis. Child.*, 82: 702–709.

Meyer, George. **1936.** "The effect on recall and recognition of the examination set in classroom situations," *J. educ., Psychol.*, 57: 81–99.

Meyer, William J., and George G. Thompson. **1956.** "Sex differences in the distribution of teacher approval and disapproval among sixth-grade children," *J. educ. Psychol.*, 47: 385–396.

Miles, C. C. **1954**. "Gifted children," in L. Carmichael (ed.), *Manual of Child Psychology*. New York: John Wiley & Sons, Inc. Pp. 984–1063.

———. **1960**. "Crucial factors in the life history of talent," in E. P. Torrance (ed.), *Talent and Education*, Minneapolis, Minn.: University of Minnesota Press. Pp. 51–65.

———, and W. R. Miles. **1932**. "The correlation of intelligence scores and chronological age from early to late maturity," *Amer. J. Psychol.*, 44: 44–78.

Mill, J. S. **1873**. *A System of Logic*. New York: Harper & Row, Publishers, Inc.

Miller, Neal E. **1959**. "Liberalization of basic S-R concepts: Extensions to conflict behavior, motivation, and social learning," in S. Koch (ed.), *Psychology: A Study of a Science*. Vol. 2. New York: McGraw-Hill, Inc. Pp. 196–292.

———, and J. Dollard. **1941**. *Social Learning and Imitation*. New Haven, Conn.: Yale University Press.

Milner, Esther A. **1951**. "A study of the relationships between reading readiness in Grade One school children and patterns of parent-child interaction," *Child Develpm.*, 22: 95–112.

Mira E. **1943**. *Psychiatry in War*. New York: W. W. Norton & Company, Inc.

Mitchell, C. **1943**. "Do virtues and vices change?" *Sch. & Soc.*, 57: 111–112.

Mitchell, James V. **1959**. "Goal setting behavior as a function of self-acceptance, over- and under-achievement, and related personality variables," *J. educ. Psychol.*, 50: 93–104.

Moloney, J. C. **1945**. "The psychology of the Okinawan," *Psychiatry*, 8: 391–399.

Montagu, M. F. Ashley. **1950**. "Constitutional and prenatal factors in infant and child health," in M. J. Senn (ed.), *Symposium on the Healthy Personality*. New York: Josiah Macy, Jr., Foundation. Pp. 148–175.

———. **1955**. *The Direction of Human Development*. New York: Harper & Row, Publishers, Inc.

Montgomery, K. C. **1953**. "Exploratory behavior as a function of 'similarity' of stimulus situation," *J. comp. physiol. Psychol.*, 46: 129–133.

———, and M. Segall. **1955**. "Discrimination learning based upon the exploratory drive," *J. comp. physiol. Psychol.*, 48: 225–228.

Moore, J. K. **1947**. "Speech content of selected groups of orphanage and non-orphanage preschool children," *J. exp. Educ.*, 16: 122–133.

Moore, Omar K. **1963**. *Autoelic Responsive Environments and Exceptional Children*. Hamden, Conn.: Responsive Environment Foundation.

———, and A. R. Anderson. **1959**. *Early Reading and Writing: A Film Report*. 1. *Skills*; 2. *Teaching Methods*; 3. *Development*. Guilford, Conn.: Basic Education, Inc. (See also New York *Times*, Dec. 16, 1963.)

Moreno, Jacob L. **1945**. *Psychodrama: Collected Papers*. Beacon, N.Y.: Beacon House.

———. **1953**. *Who Shall Survive?* Beacon, N.Y.: Beacon House.

Morgan, Clifford T. **1961**. *Introduction to Psychology*. New York: McGraw-Hill, Inc.

Morphett, Mabel V., and C. Washburne. **1931**. "When should children begin to read?" *Elem. Sch. J.*, 31: 496–503.

————. 1940. *Postponing Formal Instruction: A Seven-Year Case Study in the Effect of Administrative Practices on the Character of the Education Program.* Washington, D.C.: American Educational Research Association.

Morse, William C., and G. M. Wingo. 1962. *Psychology and Teaching,* revised ed. Chicago: Scott, Foresman and Company.

Mowrer, O. H. 1947. "On the dual nature of learning—a reinterpretation of 'conditioning' and 'problem-solving,'" *Harv. educ. Rev.,* 17: 102–148.

————. 1960. *Learning Theory and Behavior.* New York: John Wiley & Sons, Inc.

Müller, G. E., and A. Pilzecker. 1900. "Experimentelle beitrage zur lehre von gedachtniss," *Ergebnisse,* 1: 1–300.

Murray, Henry A. 1947. *Explorations in Personality,* revised ed. New York: Oxford University Press.

Mursell, James L. 1952. *Psychology for Modern Education.* New York: W. W. Norton & Company, Inc.

Mussen, Paul H. (ed.). 1960. *Handbook of Research Methods in Child Development.* New York: John Wiley & Sons, Inc.

————, et al. 1963. *Child Development and Personality.* New York: Harper & Row, Publishers, Inc.

Myers, A. K., and N. E. Miller. 1954. "Failure to find learned drive based on hunger: Evidence for learning motivated by 'exploration,'" *J. comp. physiol. Psychol.,* 47: 428–436.

National Institute of Mental Health. 1962. *Facts on Mental Health and Mental Illness.* Washington, D.C.: U.S. Department of Health, Education, and Welfare.

Neilon, Patricia. 1948. "Shirley's babies after fifteen years: A personality study," *J. genet. Psychol.,* 73: 175–186.

Nelson, R. H. 1963. "Creativity and intelligence," *Penn. Sch. J.,* 111: 330.

Neugarten, Bernice, and Nelle Wright. 1950. "Encouraging the child's spontaneous interests," in *Fostering Mental Health in Our Schools.* Washington, D. C.: Association for Supervision and Curriculum Development. Pp. 134–145.

Newell, Allen. 1962. "The processes of creative thinking," in H. E. Gruber, et al. (eds.), *Contemporary Approaches to Creative Thinking.* New York: Atherton Press. Pp. 63–119.

————, et al. 1958. "Elements of a theory of human problem solving," *Psychol. Rev.,* 65: 151–166.

Newman, H. H., et al. 1937. *Twins: A Study of Heredity and Environment.* Chicago: University of Chicago Press.

Norris, D. E., and N. I. Noonan. 1941. "Gifted Children," in W. S. Monroe (ed.), *Encyclopedia of Educational Research.* New York: Crowell-Collier and Macmillan, Inc. Pp. 75–81.

Northway, Mary L. 1940. *Appraisal of the Social Development of Children at a Summer Camp.* Psychology Series. Toronto, Ontario, Can.: University of Toronto.

Nye, Ivan. **1952.** "Adolescent-parent adjustment: Age, sex, sibling number, broken homes, and employed mothers as variables," *Marr. Fam. Liv.,* 14: 327–332.

———. **1957.** "Child adjustment in broken and in unhappy unbroken homes," *Marr. Fam. Liv.,* 19: 356–361.

———. **1959.** "Employment status of mothers and adjustment of adolescent children," *Marr. Fam. Liv.,* 21: 240–244.

Oakes, M. E. **1947.** *Children's Explanation of Natural Phenomena.* New York: Bureau of Publications, Teachers College, Columbia University.

Olds, James. **1956.** *The Growth and Structure of Motives.* New York: The Free Press of Glencoe.

Olson, Willard C. **1959.** *Child Development.* Boston: D. C. Heath and Company.

Oppenheimer, J. Robert. **1956.** "Analogy in science," *Amer. Psychologist,* 11: 127–135.

Orgel, S. Z. **1941.** "Personality distortion and early institutional care," *Amer. J. Orthopsychiat.,* 11: 37–73.

Ornstein, J. Feb. **1961.** "New recruits for science," *Parents Magazine,* 36: 42, 101–103.

Osgood, C. E. **1949.** "The similarity paradox in human learning: A resolution," *Psychol. Rev.,* 56: 132–143.

Otto, Henry J., and E. O. Melby. **1935.** "An attempt to evaluate the threat of failure as a factor in achievement," *Elem. Sch. J.,* 35: 588–596.

Overman, J. R. **1930.** "An experimental study of the effect of the method of instruction on transfer in arithmetic," *Elem. Sch. J.,* 31: 183–190.

Padilla, S. G. **1935.** "Further studies on the delayed pecking of chicks," *J. comp. Psychol.,* 20: 412–443.

Palermo, David S., et al. **1956.** "The relationship of anxiety in children to performance in a complex learning task," *Child Develpm.,* 27: 333–337.

Palmer, Carroll E. **1935.** "Height and weight of children of the depression poor," *U.S. Publ. Hlth Serv. Rep.* 50: 1106–1113.

Parten, Mildred L. **1932.** "Social participation among preschool children," *J. abnorm. soc. Psychol.,* 27: 243–269.

Pasamanick, B. et al. **1956.** "Socio-economic status and some precursors of neuropsychiatric disorders," *Amer. J. Orthopsychiat.,* 26: 594–601.

Pavlov, Ivan P. **1927.** *Conditioned Reflexes.* New York: Oxford University Press.

Peck. Robert F., and R. J. Havighurst. **1960.** *The Psychology of Character Development.* New York: John Wiley & Sons, Inc.

———, and J. V. Mitchell. **1962.** *Mental Health.* What Research Says to the Teacher, No. 24. Washington, D.C.: National Education Association.

Penny, R. K., and A. A. Lupton. **1961.** "Children's discrimination learning as a function of reward and punishment," *J. comp. physiol. Psychol.,* 54: 449–451.

Perkins, Hugh V. 1950. "Effects of climate and curriculum on group learning," *J. educ. Res.*, 44: 269–296.

Peters, Sr. Fridiana, and Sr. M. R. Peters. 1936. "Children's attitude toward law as influenced by pupil self-government," *Bull., Purdue University*, 37: 15–26.

Pfaffenberger, C. P., and J. P. Scott. 1959. "The relationship between delayed association and trainability in guide dogs," *J. genet. Psychol.*, 95: 145–155.

Phillips, Beeman N. 1962. "Sex, social class and anxiety as sources of valuation in school achievement," *J. educ. Psychol.*, 53: 316–322.

———, and L. A. D'Amico. 1956. "Effects of cooperation and competition on the cohesiveness of small face-to-face groups," *J. educ. Psychol.*, 47: 65–70.

Piaget, Jean. 1932. *The Moral Judgment of the Child*. New York: Harcourt, Brace & World, Inc.

———. 1948. *Judgment and Reasoning in the Child*. New York: Harcourt, Brace & World, Inc.

———. 1950. *The Psychology of Intelligence*. New York: Harcourt Brace & World, Inc.

———. 1952. *The Child's Conception of Number*. New York: Humanities Press, Inc.

———. 1954. "Language and thought from a genetic point of view," *Acta Psychol.*, 10: 51–60.

Pines, M. May 1963. "How three-year-olds teach themselves to read—and love it," *Harper's Magazine*, 226: 58–64.

Pinneau, Samuel R. 1950. "A critique of the articles by Margaret Ribble," *Child Develpm.*, 21: 203–228.

———. 1955. "The infantile disorders of hospitalism and anaclitic depression," *Psychol. Bull.*, 52: 429–452.

———. 1961. *Changes in Intelligence Quotient: Infancy to Maturity*. Boston: Houghton Mifflin Company.

———, and H. E. Jones. 1959. "A longitudinal study of the consistency of behavior between three and ten years," *Calif. J. educ. Res.*, 10: 119–120 (abstract).

Pistor, F. 1940. "How time concepts are acquired by children," *Educ. Meth.*, 20: 107–112.

Postman, Leo, and J. S. Bruner. 1948. "Perception under stress," *Psychol. Rev.*, 55: 314–323.

Pratt, Edward. 1956. "Experimental evaluation of a program for the improvement of reading," *Elem. Sch. J.*, 56: 315–320.

Pratt, K. C., et al. 1930. *The Behavior of the Newborn Infant*. Columbus, Ohio: Ohio State University.

Prescott, Daniel. 1938. *Emotion and the Educative Process*. Washington, D.C.: American Council on Education.

Pressey, Sidney L. 1926. "A simple apparatus which gives tests and scores—and teaches," *Sch. Soc.*, 23: 373–376. (See also 25: 549–552, 1927; 36: 668–672, 1932.)

———. 1949. *Educational Acceleration: Appraisal and Basic Problems*. Research Monograph, No. 31. Columbus, Ohio: Ohio State University.

———. 1964. "Autoinstruction: Perspectives, problems, potentials," in E. R.

Hilgard (ed.), *Theories of Learning and Instruction.* 63d Yearbook, National Society for the Study of Education, Pt. I. Chicago: University of Chicago Press. Pp. 354–370.

———, et al. **1959.** *Psychology in Education.* New York: Harper & Row, Publishers, Inc.

Rabin, Albert J. **1957.** "Some psychosexual differences between Kibbutz and non-Kibbutz Israeli boys," *J. Proj. Tech.,* 21: 148–153.

Radke, Marion J. **1946.** "The relation of parental authority to children's behavior and attitude," *University of Minnesota Institute of Child Welfare Monographs,* No. 22.

Redl. F., and W. W. Wattenberg. **1959.** *Mental Hygiene in Teaching,* revised ed. New York: Harcourt, Brace & World, Inc.

———, and David Wineman. **1951.** *Children Who Hate.* New York: Free Press of Glencoe.

Reed, Horace B. **1960.** "Anxiety: The ambivalent variable," *Harv. educ. Rev.,* 30: 141–153.

Reimann, M. **1951.** "How children become prejudiced," *Commentary,* 11: 88–94.

Remmers, H. H. (ed.). **1934.** *Studies in Attitudes.* Purdue University Bull. 35, No. 4; Studies in Higher Education, No. 26 Lafayette, Ind.: Purdue University.

Ribble, Margaret. **1943.** *The Rights of Infants.* New York: Columbia University Press.

Riesen, A. H. **1949.** "The development of visual perception in man and chimpanzee," *Science,* 106: 107–108.

Riesen, Anne. **1960.** "Brain and behavior: 4. Effects of stimulus deprivation on the development and atrophy of the visual sensory system," *Amer. J. Orthopsychiat.,* 30: 23–26.

Riesman, David. **1950.** *The Lonely Crowd.* New Haven, Conn.: Yale University Press.

Riessman, Frank. **1962.** *The Culturally Deprived Child.* New York: Harper & Row, Publishers, Inc.

Rivlin, H. N. **1936.** *Educating for Adjustment.* New York: Appleton-Century-Crofts.

———. **1955.** "Role of mental health in education," in H. N. Rivlin (ed.), *Mental Health in Modern Education.* 54th Yearbook, National Society for the Study of Education, Pt. II. Chicago: University of Chicago Press. Pp. 7–28.

Robinson, E. S. **1927.** "The similarity factor in retroaction," *Amer. J. Psychol.,* 38: 297–312.

Rockefeller Brothers Fund. **1958.** *The Pursuit of Excellence: Education and the Future of America.* New York: The Fund.

Roe, Arnold, et al. **1960.** *Automated Teaching Methods Using Linear Programs.* Report No. 60–105. Los Angeles: University of California.

Rogers, Carl R. **1947.** "Some observations on the organization of personality," *Amer. Psychologist,* 2: 359–368.

——. 1948. "Some implications of client-centered counseling for college personnel work," *Educ. psychol. Measmt*, 8: 540–549.

——. 1951. *Client-Centered Therapy*. Boston: Houghton Mifflin Company.

——. 1954. "Toward a theory of creativity," *ETC: A Review of General Semantics*, 11: 249–260.

——. 1956. "Implications of recent advances in prediction and control of behavior," *Teach. Coll. Rec.*, 57: 316–322.

——. 1959. "Some observations on the organization of personality," in A. E. Kuenzli (ed.), *The Phenomenological Problem*. New York: Harper & Row, Publishers, Inc. Pp. 49–75.

——. 1959. "A theory of therapy, personality, and of interpersonal relationships as developed in a client-centered framework," in S. Koch (ed.), *Psychology: A Study of a Science*. Vol. 3. New York: McGraw-Hill, Inc. Pp. 184–256.

——. 1961. *On Becoming a Person*. Boston: Houghton Mifflin Company.

——. 1962. "Toward becoming a fully functioning person," in A. W. Combs (chmn), *Perceiving, Behaving, Becoming*. Washington, D.C.: Association Supervision and Curriculum Development. Pp. 21–33.

Rosenblaum, S., et al. 1955. "Davis-Eells (culture-fair) test performance of lower class retarded children," *J. consult. Psychol.*, 19: 51–54.

Rosenzweig, Saul. 1954. "Babies are taught to cry: A hypothesis," *Ment. Hyg.*, 38: 81–84.

Ruch, Floyd L. 1963. *Psychology and Life*. Chicago: Scott, Foresman and Company.

Rundquist, E. A. 1933. "Inheritance of spontaneous activity in rats," *J. comp. Psychol.*, 16: 415–438.

Russell, Bertrand. 1927. *Philosophy*. New York: W. W. Norton & Company, Inc.

Russell, David H. 1956. *Children's Thinking*. Boston: Ginn & Company.

——. 1960. "Concepts," in C. W. Harris (ed.), *Encyclopedia of Educational Research*. New York: Crowell-Collier and Macmillan, Inc. Pp. 323–333.

Rust, M. R. 1931. The Effect of Resistance on Intelligence Test Scores of Young Children. *Child Develpm. Monogr.* No. 6. New York: Bureau of Publications, Teachers College, Columbia University.

Ryan, W. C. 1952. "Facts and figures in mental health," *Understand. Child.*, 21: 65–66.

Ryans, David G. 1960. *Characteristics of Teachers*. Washington, D.C.: American Council on Education.

Sanford, Fillmore H. 1961. *Psychology: A scientific Study of Man*. Belmont, Calif.: Wadsworth Publishing Co., Inc.

Sarason, Irwin. 1957. "Test anxiety, general anxiety, and intellectual performance," *J. consult. Psychol.*, 21: 485–490.

Sarason, Seymour B., et al. 1960. *Anxiety in Elementary School Children*. New York: John Wiley & Sons, Inc.

Sax, Gilbert, and J. R. Ottina. **1958.** "The arithmetic achievement of pupils differing in school experience," *Calif. J. educ. Res.*, 9: 15–19.

Schmidt, Hermann O. **1941.** "The effects of praise and blame as incentives to learning," *Psychol. Monogr.*, 53, No. 3.

Schreiber, Daniel. **1963.** "Promising practices gleaned from a year of study," *Phi Delta Kappan*, 44: 215–221.

Schrepel, Marie, and H. R. Laslett. **1936.** "On the loss of knowledge by junior high school pupils over the summer vacation," *J. educ. Psychol.*, 27: 299–303.

Schrupp, M. H., and C. M. Gjerde. **1953.** "Teacher growth in attitudes toward behavior problems of children," *J. educ. Psychol.*, 44: 203–214.

Schultz, Raymond, and Merle M. Ohlsen. **1955.** "Interest patterns of best and poorest student teachers," *J. educ. Sociol.*, 29: 108–112.

Scollon, Robert W. **1957.** "A study of some communicator variables related to attitude restructuring through motion picture films," *Diss. Abstr.*, 17: 400.

Scott, William A. **1957.** "Attitude change through reward of verbal behavior," *J. abnorm. soc. Psychol.*, 55: 72–75.

Scott, W. D. **1931.** *Personnel Management.* New York: McGraw-Hill, Inc.

Sears, Pauline S. **1940.** "Levels of aspiration in academically successful and unsuccessful children," *J. abnorm. soc. Psychol.*, 35: 498–536.

————, and E. R. Hilgard. **1964.** "The teacher's role in the motivation of the learner," in E. R. Hilgard (ed.), *Theories of Learning and Instruction.* 63d Yearbook, National Society for the Study of Education, Pt. I. Chicago: University of Chicago Press. Pp. 182–209.

Sears, Robert R. **1936.** "Experimental study of projection: 1. Attribution of traits," *J. soc. Psychol.*, 7: 151–163.

————, et al. **1957.** *Patterns of Child Rearing.* New York: Harper & Row, Publishers, Inc.

Shaffer, L. F., and E. J. Shoben. **1956.** *The Psychology of Adjustment.* Boston: Houghton Mifflin Company.

Shannon, Dan C. **1957.** "What research says about acceleration," *Phi Delta Kappan*, 39: 70–72.

Shaw, Frederick. **1963.** "Educating culturally deprived youth in urban centers," *Phi Delta Kappan*, 45: 91–97.

Shaw, M. C., and James Grubb. **1958.** "Hostility and able high school underachievers," *J. counsel. Psychol.*, 5: 263–266.

Sheffield, Fred D., et al. **1954.** "Drive reduction vs. consummatory behavior as determinants of reinforcement," *J. comp. physiol. Psychol.*, 47: 349–354.

Sheldon, William H., and S. S. Stevens. **1940.** *The Varieties of Human Physiques.* New York: Harper & Row, Publishers, Inc.

Shepard, J. F., and F. S. Breed. **1913.** "Maturation and use in the development of an instinct," *J. Animal Behav.*, 3: 274–285.

Sherman, M. **1927; 1928.** "The differentiation of emotional responses in infants," *J. comp. Psychol.*, 7: 265–284, 335–351; 8: 385, 394.

Sheviakov, G. V., and F. Redl. **1956.** *Discipline for Today's Children and Youth.* Washington, D.C.: National Education Association.

Shirley, M. M. **1931; 1933; 1933.** *The First Two Years of Life: A Study of Twenty-five Babies*, I. *Postural and Locomotor Development*; II. *Intellectual*

Development; III. *Personality Manifestations*. Minneapolis, Minn.: University of Minnesota.

Shoben, Edward J. **1953**. "A theoretical approach to psychotherapy as a personality modification," *Harv. educ. Rev.*, 23: 128–142.

———. **1957**. "Toward a concept of the normal personality," *Amer. Psychologist*, 12: 183–189.

Shuttleworth, F. K. **1939**. "The physical and mental growth of girls and boys age six to nineteen in relation to maximum growth," *Monogr. soc. Res. child Develpm.*, 4, No. 3.

Siegel, A. E., and M. B. Haas. **1963**. "The working mother—a review of research," *Child Develpm.*, 34: 513–542.

Siegel, Laurence, et al. **1959**. "Effectiveness of large group instruction at the university level," *Harv. educ. Rev.*, 29: 216–226.

Silberman, H. F. **1957**. "Effects of praise and reproof on reading growth in a non-laboratory classroom setting," *J. educ. Psychol.*, 48: 199–206.

Simmons, K. **1944**. "The Brush Foundation study of child growth and development, II: physical growth and development," *Monogr. soc. Res. child. Develpm.*, 9, No. 1.

Simon, L. M., and E. A. Levitt. **1950**. "Relation between Wechsler-Bellevue IQ scores and occupations area," *Occupations*, 29: 23–25.

Simpson, Ray H. **1942**. "Reading disabilities among teachers and administrators," *Clearing House*, 17: 11–13.

Sims, V. M. **1928**. "The relative influence of two types of motivation on improvement," *J. educ. Psychol.*, 19: 480–489.

Sisson, E. D. **1939**. "Retroactive inhibition: The temporal position of interpolated activity," *J. exp. Psychol.*, 25: 228–233.

Skaggs, E. B. **1925**. "Further studies in retroactive inhibition," *Psychol. Monogr.*, 34, No. 161.

Skeels, H. M. **1940**. "Some Iowa studies of the mental growth of children in relation to differentials of the environment: A summary," in N. B. Henry (ed.), *Intelligence: Its Nature and Nurture*. 39th Yearbook, National Society for the Study of Education; Pt. II. Bloomington, Ill.: Public School Publishing Company. Pp. 281–308.

Skinner, B. F. **1950**. "Are theories of learning necessary?" *Psychol. Rev.*, 57: 193–217.

———. **1954**. "The science of learning and the art of teaching," *Harv. educ. Rev.*, 24: 86–97.

———. **1958**. "Teaching machines," *Science*, 128: 969–977.

———. **1958**. "Reinforcement today," *Amer. Psychologist*, 13: 94–99.

———. **1959**. "A case history in scientific method," in S. Koch (ed.) *Psychology: A Study of a Science*. Vol. 2. New York: McGraw-Hill, Inc. Pp. 359–379.

———. **1966**. "An operant analysis of problem solving," in B. Kleinmuntz (ed.), *Problem Solving: Research Method and Theory*. New York: John Wiley & Sons, Inc. Pp. 225–257.

Skodak, M., and H. M. Skeels. **1949**. "A final follow-up study of one hundred adopted children," *J. genet. Psychol.*, 75: 85–125, 394–395.

Sleight, W. 1911. "Memory and formal training," *Brit. J. Psychol.*, 4: 386–457.

Smith, E. R., et al. 1942. *Teacher Education: A Reappraisal.* New York: Harper & Row, Publishers, Inc.

Smith, Henry P. 1961. *Psychology in Teaching.* Englewood Cliffs, N.J.: Prentice-Hall, Inc.

Smith, H. L., and N. C. Hightower. 1948. "Incidence of functional disease (neurosis) among patients of various occupations," *Occup. Med.*, 5: 182–185.

Smith, Karl U., and M. F. Smith. 1966. *Cybernetic Principles of Learning and Educational Design.* New York: Holt, Rinehart & Winston, Inc.

Smith, M. Brewster. 1959. "Research strategies toward a conception of mental health," *Amer. Psychologist*, 14: 673–681.

———. 1961. "Mental health reconsidered," *Amer. Psychologist*, 16: 299–306.

Smith, M. E. 1926. "An investigation of the development of the sentence and the extent of vocabulary in young children," *University of Iowa Studies in Child Welfare*, 3, No. 5.

Snygg, Donald, and Arthur W. Combs. 1949. *Individual Behavior: A Perceptual Approach to Behavior.* New York: Harper & Row, Publishers, Inc.

Sontag, Lester W. 1941; 1957. "The significance of fetal environmental differences," *Amer. J. Obst. Gynecol.*, 42: 996–1003.

———. 1958. "Mental growth and personality development: A longitudinal study," *Monogr. soc. Res. child Develpm.*, 23, No. 68.

Spearman, Charles E. 1904. "General intelligence objectively determined and measured," *Amer. J. Psychol.*, 15: 201–293.

———. 1927. *The Abilities of Man: Their Nature and Measurement.* New York: Crowell-Collier and Macmillan, Inc.

Spence, Kenneth W. 1947. "The role of secondary reinforcement in delayed reward learning," *Psychol. Rev.*, 54: 1–8.

———. 1951. "Theoretical interpretations of learning," in S. S. Stevens (ed.), *Handbook of Experimental Psychology.* New York: John Wiley & Sons, Inc. Pp. 690–729.

———. 1954. "Current interpretations of learning data and some recent developments in stimulus-response theory," in *Kentucky Symposium, Learning Theory, Personality Theory, and Clinical Research.* New York: John Wiley & Sons, Inc. Pp. 1–21.

———. 1960. *Behavior Theory and Learning.* Englewood Cliffs, N.J.: Prentice-Hall, Inc.

Spence, Ralph B. 1928. "Lecture and class discussion in teaching educational psychology," *J. educ. Psychol.*, 19: 454–462.

Spitz, René A. 1945. "Hospitalism: An inquiry into the genesis of psychiatric conditions in early childhood," *Psychoanal. Stud. Child*, 1: 53–74.

Spitzer, Herbert F. 1939. "Studies in retention," *J. educ. Psychol.*, 30: 641–656.

Squires, P. C. 1927. "Wolf children in India," *Amer. J. Psychol.*, 38: 313–315.

Staats, Arthur W. 1966. "An integrated-functional learning approach to complex human behavior," in B. Kleinmuntz (ed.), *Problem Solving: Research Method and Theory.* New York: John Wiley & Sons, Inc. Pp. 259–339.

Stacey, C. L., and S. F. DeMartino (eds.). 1958. *Understanding Human Behavior.* Cleveland, Ohio: Howard Allen, Inc.

Stalnaker, John M., and R. C. Stalnaker. 1934. "Reliable reading of essay tests," *Sch. Rev.*, 42: 599–605.

Starch, Daniel, and E. C. Elliott. 1913. "Reliability of grading work in mathematics," *Sch. Rev.*, 21: 254–257.

Steckler, George A. 1957. "Authoritarian ideology in Negro college students," *J. abnorm. soc. Psychol.*, 54: 396–399.

Steier, L. B. 1948. "A comparison of self-evaluation, teacher evaluation, and standardized tests on personality and achievement factors in the fifth and eighth grades," *Unpublished Dissertation.* Berkeley, Calif.: University of California.

Stern, George G. 1963. "Measuring non-cognitive variables in research on teaching," in N. L. Gage (ed.), *Handbook of Research on Teaching.* Skokie, Ill.: Rand McNally & Company. Pp. 398–447.

Stewart, N. 1947. "AGCT scores of Army personnel grouped by occupations," *Occupations*, 26: 5–41.

Stockard, C. R., et al. 1941. *Genetic and Endocrine Basis for Differences in Form and Behavior.* Philadelphia: Wistar Institute of Anatomy and Biology.

Stogdill, R. M. 1948. "Personal factors associated with leadership: A survey of the literature," *J. educ. Psychol.*, 25: 35–71.

Stolurow, L. M. 1963. "Let's be informed on programed instruction," *Phi Delta Kappan*, 44: 255–257.

Stolz, H. R., and L. M. Stolz. 1944. "Adolescent problems related to somatic variations," in N. B. Henry (ed.), *Adolescence* 43d Yearbook, National Society for the Study of Education, Pt. I. Chicago: University of Chicago Press. Pp. 80–99.

Stolz, Lois M. 1960. "Effects of maternal employment on children: Evidence from research," *Child Develpm.*, 31: 749–782.

Stone, Alan A., and Gloria C. Onque. 1959. *Longitudinal Studies of Child Personality: Abstracts with Index.* Cambridge, Mass.: Harvard University Press.

Stouffer, George A. 1952. "Behavior problems of children as viewed by teachers and mental hygienists," *Ment. Hyg.*, 36: 271–285.

Stovall, Thomas F. 1958. "Lecture vs. discussion," *Phi Delta Kappan*, 39: 255–258.

Strodbeck, Fred L. 1958. "Family interaction, values, and achievement," in D. C. McClelland (ed.), *Talent and Society.* Princeton, N.J.: D. Van Nostrand Company, Inc. Pp. 135–194.

Stroud, James B. 1956. *Psychology in Education.* New York: David McKay Company, Inc.

Sumner, F. C. 1932. "Marks as estimated by students," *Education*, 52: 429.

Swenson, Esther J. 1941. *Retroactive Inhibition: A Review of the Literature.* Minneapolis, Minn.: University of Minnesota Studies in Education, No. 1.

Symonds, Percival M. 1936. *The Psychology of Parent-Child Relationships.* New York: Appleton-Century-Crofts.

———, and D. H. Chase. 1929. "Practice vs. motivation," *J. educ. Psychol.*, 20: 19–35.

Tanner, J. M. 1955. *Growth at Adolescence*. New York: Thomas Publishing Company.

Taylor, Calvin W. (ed.). 1959. *The Third University of Utah Research Conference on the Identification of Creative Scientific Talent*. Salt Lake City: University of Utah Press.

———. 1963. "Many-sided intelligence," *Childh. Educ.*, 39: 364–366.

Taylor, Donald W. 1960. "Toward an information processing theory of behavior," in M. R. Jones (ed.), *Nebraska Symposium on Motivation*. Lincoln, Neb.: University of Nebraska Press. Pp. 51–79.

Tenenbaum, Samuel. 1944. "Attitudes of elementary school children to school, teachers, and classmates," *J. appl. Psychol.*, 28: 134–141.

Terman, Lewis M. 1954. "The discovery and encouragement of exceptional talent," *Amer. Psychol.*, 9: 221–230.

———, and M. A. Merrill. 1937. *Measuring Intelligence*. Boston: Houghton Mifflin Company.

———. 1960. *Stanford-Binet Intelligence Scale, Manual for the Third Revision*. Form L-M. Boston: Houghton Mifflin Company.

———, and M. H. Oden. 1951. "The Stanford studies of gifted children," in P. Witty (ed.), *The Gifted Child*. Boston: D. C. Heath and Company.

Terman, Lewis M., et al., *Genetic Studies of Genius*. Stanford, Calif.: Stanford University Press.

1925. Vol. I. *Mental and Physical Traits of a Thousand Gifted Children*.
1926. Vol. II. *The Early Mental Traits of Three Hundred Geniuses*.
1930. Vol. III. *The Promise of Youth*.
1947. Vol. IV. *The Gifted Grows Up*.
1959. Vol. V. *The Gifted at Mid-Life*.

Terrell, G. 1959. "Manipulation motivation in children," *J. comp. physiol. Psychol.*, 52: 705–709.

Thibaut, J. W., and L. H. Strickland. 1955. "Psychological set and social conformity," *J. Pers.*, 25: 115–129.

Thistlethwaite, Donald L. 1958. "The conservation of intellectual talent," *Science*, 128: 822–826.

Thompson, G. G., and C. W. Hunnicutt. 1944. "The effect of repeated praise or blame on the work achievement of 'introverts' and 'extroverts'," *J. educ. Psychol.*, 35: 257–266.

Thompson, William R., and W. Heron. 1954. "The effects of restricting early experience on the problem-solving capacity of dogs," *Canad. J. Psychol.*, 8: 17–31.

———, and R. Melzack. 1956. "Early environment," *Scientif. Amer.*, 194: 38–42.

Thorndike, Edward L. 1913. *Educational Psychology.—I: The Original Nature of Man*; II: *The Psychology of Learning*. New York: Bureau of Publications, Teachers College, Columbia University.

———. 1916. *Educational Psychology: Briefer Course*. New York: Bureau of Publications, Teachers College, Columbia University.

———. 1924. "Mental discipline in high school studies," *J. educ. Psychol.*, 15: 1–22, 83–98.

———. 1931. *Human Learning*. New York: Appleton-Century-Crofts.

———. 1932. *Fundamentals of Learning.* New York: Bureau of Publications, Teachers College, Columbia University.

———. 1935. *The Psychology of Wants, Interests, and Attitudes.* New York: Appleton-Century-Crofts.

———, and Robert S. Woodworth. 1901. "The influence of the improvement in one mental function upon the efficiency of other functions," *Psychol. Rev.,* 8: 247–261, 384–395, 553–564.

———, et al. 1927. *The Measurement of Intelligence.* New York: Bureau of Publications, Teachers College, Columbia University.

Thorndike, Robert L. 1950. "How children learn the principles and techniques of problem-solving," in N. B. Henry (ed.), *Learning and Instruction,* 49th Yearbook, National Society for the Study of Education, Pt. I. Chicago: University of Chicago Press. Pp. 192–216.

———. 1963. "The measurement of creativity," *Teach. Coll. Rec.,* 64: 422–424.

Thurstone, L. L. 1935. *Vectors of the Mind.* Chicago: University of Chicago Press.

Tinbergen, N. 1951. *The Study of Instinct.* New York: Oxford University Press.

Tolman, Edward C. 1932. *Purposive Behavior in Animals and Men.* New York: Appleton-Century-Crofts.

———. 1959. "Principles of purposive behavior," in S. Koch (ed.), *Psychology: A Study of a Science.* Vol. 2. New York: McGraw-Hill, Inc. Pp. 92–157.

———, and C. H. Honzik. 1930. "Introduction and removal of reward in maze performance," *University of California Publications in Psychology,* 4: 257–275.

Torrance, E. Paul. 1953. "Methods of conducting critiques of group problem-solving performance," *J. appl. Psychol.,* 37: 394–398.

———. 1962. *Guiding Creative Talent,* revised ed. Englewood Cliffs, N.J.: Prentice-Hall, Inc.

———. 1963. *Education and the Creative Potential.* Minneapolis, Minn.: University of Minnesota Press.

———, and R. Mason. 1958. "Instructor effort to influence: An experimental evaluation of six approaches," *J. educ. Psychol.,* 49: 211–218.

Travers, Robert M. W. 1963. *Essentials of Learning.* New York: Crowell-Collier and Macmillan, Inc.

Traxler, A. E. 1940. "What is a satisfactory IQ for admission to college?" *Sch. Soc.,* 51: 462–464.

Trivette, Sue E. 1961. "The effect of training in listening for specific purposes," *J. educ. Res.,* 54: 276–277.

Tryon, R. C. 1940. "Genetic differences in maze learning ability in rats," in G. M. Whipple (ed.), *Intelligence: Its Nature and Nurture.* 39th Yearbook, National Society for the Study of Education, Pt. I. Bloomington, Ill.: Public School Publishing Company. Pp. 111–119.

———, and W. E. Henry. 1950. "How children learn personal and social adjustment," in N. B. Henry (ed.), *Learning and Instruction.* 49th Yearbook, National Society for the Study of Education; Pt. I. Chicago: University of Chicago Press. Pp. 156–182.

Tschechtelin, Sr. M. Amatora. 1945. "Self-appraisal of children," *J. educ. Res.*, 39: 25–32. (See also "Validity in self-evaluation," *Educ. psychol., Measmt*, 16: 119–126, 1956.)

Tuddenham, R. D. 1948. "Soldier intelligence in World Wars I and II," *Amer. Psychologist*, 3: 54–56.

Twining, Wilbur. 1949. "Mental practice and physical practice in learning a motor skill," *Res. Quart.*, 20: 432–435.

Tyler, F. T. 1953. "Comments on the correlation analysis reported in intelligence and cultural differences," *J. educ. Psychol.*, 44: 288–295.

———. 1957. "Stability of intra-individual patterning of measures of adjustment during adolescence," *J. educ. Psychol.*, 48: 217–226.

———. 1964. "Issues related to readiness to learn," in E. R. Hilgard (ed.), *Theories of Learning and Instruction*, 63d Yearbook, National Society for the Study of Education, Pt. I. Chicago: University of Chicago Press. Pp. 210–239.

Tyler, Ralph W. 1933. "Permanence of learning," *J. higher Educ.*, 4: 203–204.

Ulmer, Gilbert. 1942. "Some suggestions for teaching geometry to develop clear thinking," *Kansas Studies in Education*, 2, No. 7.

Underwood, Benton. J. 1957. "Interference and forgetting," *Psychol. Rev*, 64: 49–60.

———. 1961. "Ten years of massed practice on distributed practice," *Psychol. Rev.*, 68: 229–247.

———. 1964. "Laboratory studies of verbal learning," in E. R. Hilgard (ed.), *Theories of Learning and Instruction*. 63d Yearbook, National Society for the Study of Education, Pt. I. Chicago: University of Chicago Press. Pp. 133–152.

Uyeno, E. T. 1960. "Hereditary and environmental aspects of dominant behavior in the albino rat," *J. comp. physiol. Psychol.*, 53: 138–141.

Vanuxem, M. 1925. *Education of Feebleminded Women*. New York: Bureau of Publications, Teachers College, Columbia University.

Vinacke, W. E. 1952. *The Psychology of Thinking*. New York: McGraw-Hill, Inc.

Von Senden, M. V. 1932. *Raum-und Gestaltauffassung bei Operierten Blindgeborenen vor Nach Operation*. Leipzig: Barth.

Wagman, M. 1955. "Attitude change and authoritarian personality," *J. Psychol.*, 40: 3–24.

Wallach, Michael A. 1963. "Research on children's thinking," in H. W. Stevenson (ed.), *Child Psychology*. 62d Yearbook, National Society for the Study of Education, Pt. I. Chicago: University of Chicago Press. Pp. 236–276.

————, and N. Kogan. **1965.** *Modes of Thinking in Young Children*. New York: Holt, Rinehart and Winston, Inc.

Watson, B. **1938.** "The similarity factor in transfer and inhibition," *J. educ. Psychol.*, 29: 145–157.

Watson, Goodwin B. **1957.** "Some personality differences in children related to strict or permissive parental discipline," *J. Psychol.*, 44: 227–249.

————, and E. M. Glaser. **1964.** *Watson-Glaser Critical Thinking Appraisal*. New York: Harcourt, Brace & World, Inc.

Watson, John J. B. **1929.** *Psychology from the Standpoint of a Behaviorist*. Philadelphia: J. B. Lippincott Company.

————. **1930.** *Behaviorism*. New York: W. W. Norton & Company, Inc.

————, and R. Rayner. **1920.** "Conditioned emotional reactions," *J. exp. Psychol.*, 3: 1–14.

Wattenberg, W. W., and F. Redl. **1950.** "Mental hygiene," in W. S. Monroe (ed.), *Encyclopedia of Educational Research*, revised ed. New York: Crowell-Collier and Macmillan, Inc. Pp. 733–745.

Webb, L. W. **1936.** "The transfer of training," in C. E. Skinner, *Educational Psychology*. Englewood Cliffs, N.J.: Prentice-Hall, Inc.

Wechsler, D. **1944.** *The Measurement of Adult Intelligence*. Baltimore: The Williams & Wilkins Company.

Wellman, Beth L. **1945.** "IQ changes of preschool and non-school groups during the preschool years: A summary of the literature," *J. Psychol.*, 20: 347–368.

Wertheimer, Max. **1959.** *Productive Thinking*. New York: Harper & Row, Publishers, Inc.

Wesman, A. G. **1945.** "A study of transfer of training from high school subjects to intelligence," *J. educ. Res.*, 39: 254–264.

————. **1956.** "Aptitude, intelligence, and achievement," *Test Service Bull.*, No. 51.

White House Conference on Children and Youth. **1951.** *A Healthy Personality for Every Child*. Raleigh, N.C.: Health Publications Institute. (See also *Golden Anniversary Conference*. New York: Columbia University Press, 1960.)

White, Robert W. **1959.** "Motivation reconsidered: The concept of competence," *Psychol. Rev.*, 66: 297–333.

Wickman, E. K. **1928.** *Children's Behavior and Teachers' Attitudes*. New York: The Commonwealth Fund.

Wingo, G. M. **1950.** "Implications for improving instruction in the upper elementary grades," in N. B. Henry (ed.), *Learning and Instruction*. 49th Yearbook, National Society for the Study of Education, Pt. I. Chicago: University of Chicago Press. Pp. 280–303.

Winterbottom, Marian R. **1953.** *The Relation of Childhood Training in Independence to Achievement Motivation*. Unpublished dissertation. Ann Arbor, Mich.: University of Michigan.

Wispe, Lauren. **1951.** "Evaluating section teaching methods in an introductory course," *J. educ. Res.*, 45: 161–186.

Witty, P. A. **1947.** "An analysis of the personality traits of the effective teacher," *J. educ. Res.*, 40: 662–671.

Wolf, A. **1943**. "The dynamics of the selective inhibition of specific functions in neurotics," *Psychosomat. Med.*, 5: 27–38.

Wolfe, John B. **1936**. "Effectiveness of token rewards for chimpanzees," *Comp. Psychol. Monogr.*, 12. No. 5.

Wolfle, Dael. **1960**. "Diversity of talent," *Amer. Psychologist*, 15: 535–545.

Woodruff, A. D. **1948**. *The Psychology of Teaching*. New York: David McKay Company, Inc.

Woodworth, Robert S. **1941**. *Heredity and Environment: A Critical Survey of Recently Published Material on Twins and Foster Children*. New York: Social Science Research Council.

Worcester, D. A. **1956**. *The Education of Children of Above-Average Mentality*. Lincoln, Neb.: University of Nebraska Press.

Wright, Herbert F. **1948**. "How the psychology of motivation is related to curriculum development," *J. educ. Psychol.*, 39: 149–156.

Wrightstone, J. Wayne, et al. **1964**. *Evaluation of the Higher Horizons Program for Underprivileged Children*. New York: Board of Education.

Wylie, Ruth C. **1961**. *The Self-Concept: A Review of the Literature*. Lincoln, Neb.: University of Nebraska Press.

Yarrow, L. J. **1961**. "Maternal deprivation: Toward an empirical and conceptual re-evaluation," *Psychol. Bull.*, 58: 459–490.

Yarrow, M. R., et al. **1962**. "Child rearing in families of working and nonworking mothers," *Sociometry*, 25: 122–140.

Yeakel, E. N., and R. P. Rhoades. **1941**. "A comparison of the body and endocrine gland weights of emotional and non-emotional rats," *Endocrinology*, 28: 337–340.

Young, Paul T. **1950**. "Motivation," in W. S. Monroe (ed.), *Encyclopedia of Educational Research*. New York: Crowell-Collier and Macmillan, Inc. Pp. 755–761.

Young, W. E. **1936**. "The relation of reading comprehension and retention to hearing comprehension and retention," *J. exp. Educ.*, 5: 30–39.

Zunich, Michael. **1963**. "Development of responsibility perceptions of lower and middle class children," *J. educ. Res.*, 56: 497–499.

Author Index

Subject Index